ActionScript 3.0 Cookbook™

Other resources from O'Reilly

Related titles

ActionScript 3.0 Pocket Reference

ActionScript 3.0 Design Patterns

Flash 8 Cookbook™

Flash Hacks™

Flash 8 Projects for Learning Animation and Interactivity

Flash 8: The Missing Manual

Programming Flex 2

oreilly.com

oreilly.com is more than a complete catalog of O'Reilly books. You'll also find links to news, events, articles, weblogs, sample chapters, and code examples.

oreillynet.com is the essential portal for developers interested in open and emerging technologies, including new platforms, programming languages, and operating systems.

Conferences

O'Reilly brings diverse innovators together to nurture the ideas that spark revolutionary industries. We specialize in documenting the latest tools and systems, translating the innovator's knowledge into useful skills for those in the trenches. Please visit *conferences.oreilly.com* for our upcoming events.

Safari Bookshelf (*safari.oreilly.com*) is the premier online reference library for programmers and IT professionals. Conduct searches across more than 1,000 books. Subscribers can zero in on answers to time-critical questions in a matter of seconds. Read the books on your Bookshelf from cover to cover or simply flip to the page you need. Try it today for free.

ActionScript 3.0 Cookbook™

Joey Lott, Darron Schall, and Keith Peters

O'REILLY®

Beijing · Cambridge · Farnham · Köln · Paris · Sebastopol · Taipei · Tokyo

ActionScript 3.0 Cookbook™
by Joey Lott, Darron Schall, and Keith Peters

Copyright © 2007 O'Reilly Media, Inc. All rights reserved.
Printed in the United States of America.

Published by O'Reilly Media, Inc., 1005 Gravenstein Highway North, Sebastopol, CA 95472.

O'Reilly books may be purchased for educational, business, or sales promotional use. Online editions are also available for most titles (*safari.oreilly.com*). For more information, contact our corporate/institutional sales department: (800) 998-9938 or *corporate@oreilly.com*.

Editor: Chuck Toporek

Production Editor: Laurel R.T. Ruma

Copyeditor: Laurel R.T. Ruma

Proofreader: Ann Atalla

Indexer: Joe Wizda

Cover Designer: Karen Montgomery

Interior Designer: David Futato

Illustrators: Robert Romano and Jessamyn Read

Printing History:

October 2006:   First Edition.

 This book uses RepKover™, a durable and flexible lay-flat binding.

ISBN-10: 0-596-52695-4

ISBN-13: 978-0-596-52695-5

[M]   [9/07]

Adobe Developer Library

Adobe Developer Library, a copublishing partnership between O'Reilly Media Inc. and Adobe Systems, Inc., is the authoritative resource for developers using Adobe technologies. These comprehensive resources offer learning solutions to help developers create cutting-edge interactive web applications that can reach virtually anyone on any platform.

With top-quality books and innovative online resources covering the latest tools for rich-Internet application development, the *Adobe Developer Library* delivers expert training, straight from the source. Topics include ActionScript, Adobe Flex®, Adobe Flash®, and Adobe Acrobat® software.

Get the latest news about books, online resources, and more at *adobedeveloper-library.com*.

Table of Contents

Preface . . . . **xvii**

1. ActionScript Basics **1**
    1.1 Creating an ActionScript Project   2
    1.2 Customizing the Properties of an Application   3
    1.3 Where to Place ActionScript Code   4
    1.4 How to Trace a Message   8
    1.5 Handling Events   10
    1.6 Responding to Mouse and Key Events   12
    1.7 Using Mathematical Operators   14
    1.8 Checking Equality or Comparing Values   16
    1.9 Performing Actions Conditionally   19
    1.10 Performing Complex Conditional Testing   24
    1.11 Repeating an Operation Many Times   26
    1.12 Repeating a Task over Time   30
    1.13 Creating Reusable Code   32
    1.14 Generalizing a Method to Enhance Reusability   34
    1.15 Exiting a Method   36
    1.16 Obtaining the Result of a Method   37
    1.17 Handling Errors   38

2. Custom Classes **43**
    2.1 Creating a Custom Class   43
    2.2 Determining Where to Save a Class   48
    2.3 Creating Properties That Behave As Methods   49
    2.4 Creating Static Methods and Properties   51
    2.5 Creating Subclasses   52

2.6 Implementing Subclass Versions of Superclass Methods   54

2.7 Creating Constants   56

2.8 Dispatching Events   57

3. Runtime Environment **58**

3.1 Detecting the Player Version   58

3.2 Detecting the Operating System   60

3.3 Checking the Player Type   61

3.4 Checking the System Language   61

3.5 Detecting Display Settings   63

3.6 Scaling the Movie   65

3.7 Changing the Alignment   66

3.8 Hiding the Flash Player's Menu Items   67

3.9 Detecting the Device's Audio Capabilities   68

3.10 Detecting the Device's Video Capabilities   69

3.11 Prompting the User to Change Player Settings   70

3.12 Dealing with System Security   71

4. Numbers and Math **74**

4.1 Representing Numbers in Different Bases   74

4.2 Converting Between Different Number Systems   75

4.3 Rounding Numbers   77

4.4 Inserting Leading or Trailing Zeros or Spaces   79

4.5 Formatting Numbers for Display Without a Mask   83

4.6 Formatting Currency Amounts   84

4.7 Generating a Random Number   86

4.8 Simulating a Coin Toss   88

4.9 Simulating Dice   91

4.10 Simulating Playing Cards   93

4.11 Generating a Unique Number   95

4.12 Converting Angle Measurements   96

4.13 Calculating the Distance Between Two Points   97

4.14 Determining Points Along a Circle   98

4.15 Converting Between Units of Measurement   101

5. Arrays **103**

5.1 Adding Elements to the Start or End of an Array   104

5.2 Looping Through an Array   106

5.3 Searching for Matching Elements in an Array   107

5.4 Removing Elements   111

5.5   Inserting Elements in the Middle of an Array   113
5.6   Converting a String to an Array   114
5.7   Converting an Array to a String   115
5.8   Creating a Separate Copy of an Array   116
5.9   Storing Complex or Multidimensional Data   120
5.10   Sorting or Reversing an Array   123
5.11   Implementing a Custom Sort   127
5.12   Randomizing the Elements of an Array   129
5.13   Getting the Minimum or Maximum Element   131
5.14   Comparing Arrays   131
5.15   Creating an Associative Array   133
5.16   Reading Elements of an Associative Array   135

6.   **Display List** **137**
6.1   Adding an Item to the Display List   141
6.2   Removing an Item from the Display List   146
6.3   Moving Objects Forward and Backward   149
6.4   Creating Custom Visual Classes   153
6.5   Creating Simple Buttons   156
6.6   Loading External Images at Runtime   161
6.7   Loading and Interacting with External Movies   165
6.8   Creating Mouse Interactions   168
6.9   Dragging and Dropping Objects with the Mouse   173

7.   **Drawing and Masking** **181**
7.1   Setting a Line Style   182
7.2   Setting Gradient Line Styles   183
7.3   Drawing a Line   184
7.4   Drawing a Curve   186
7.5   Drawing an Arc   187
7.6   Drawing a Rectangle   187
7.7   Drawing a Circle   189
7.8   Drawing an Ellipse   190
7.9   Drawing a Triangle   191
7.10   Drawing Regular Polygons   192
7.11   Drawing a Star   193
7.12   Filling a Shape with a Solid or Translucent Color   194
7.13   Filling a Shape with a Gradient   195
7.14   Filling a Shape with a Bitmap   197
7.15   Scripting Masks   198

8. Bitmaps **200**

    8.1 Creating a BitmapData Object   201

    8.2 Adding a Bitmap to the Display List   202

    8.3 Drawing a Display Object to a Bitmap   203

    8.4 Loading an External Image into a Bitmap   204

    8.5 Manipulating Pixels   205

    8.6 Creating Rectangular Fills   207

    8.7 Creating a Flood Fill   208

    8.8 Copying Pixels   209

    8.9 Copying Channels   211

    8.10 Creating Noise   212

    8.11 Creating Perlin Noise   214

    8.12 Using Threshold   218

    8.13 Applying a Filter to a Bitmap   221

    8.14 Dissolving Between Two Bitmaps   224

    8.15 Scrolling a Bitmap   227

9. Text **229**

    9.1 Creating an Outline Around a Text Field   230

    9.2 Creating a Background for a Text Field   230

    9.3 Making a User Input Field   231

    9.4 Making a Password Input Field   232

    9.5 Filtering Text Input   233

    9.6 Setting a Field's Maximum Length   234

    9.7 Displaying Text   235

    9.8 Displaying HTML-Formatted Text   235

    9.9 Condensing Whitespace   236

    9.10 Sizing Text Fields to Fit Contents   237

    9.11 Scrolling Text Programmatically   238

    9.12 Responding to Scroll Events   241

    9.13 Formatting Text   242

    9.14 Formatting User-Input Text   247

    9.15 Formatting a Portion of Existing Text   248

    9.16 Setting a Text Field's Font   249

    9.17 Embedding Fonts   250

    9.18 Creating Text That Can Be Rotated   252

    9.19 Displaying Unicode Text   252

    9.20 Assigning Focus to a Text Field   253

    9.21 Selecting Text with ActionScript   254

9.22 Setting the Insertion Point in a Text Field 255
9.23 Responding When Text Is Selected or Deselected 256
9.24 Responding to User Text Entry 257
9.25 Adding a Hyperlink to Text 258
9.26 Calling ActionScript from Hyperlinks 260
9.27 Working with Advanced Text Layout 261
9.28 Applying Advanced Anti-Aliasing 264
9.29 Replacing Text 265
9.30 Retrieving a List of System Fonts 265

10. **Filters and Transforms** **266**
10.1 Applying Color Changes 266
10.2 Applying Color Tints 267
10.3 Resetting Color 268
10.4 Shearing 269
10.5 Applying Basic Filters 269
10.6 Applying Advanced Filter Effects (Emboss, etc.) 272
10.7 Embossing 274
10.8 Detecting Edges 275
10.9 Sharpening 276
10.10 Making a Digital Negative 276
10.11 Applying Grayscale 277
10.12 Changing Saturation 278
10.13 Changing Brightness 278
10.14 Changing Contrast 279

11. **Programmatic Animation** **281**
11.1 Moving an Object 282
11.2 Moving an Object in a Specific Direction 283
11.3 Easing 285
11.4 Acceleration 287
11.5 Springs 289
11.6 Using Trigonometry 291
11.7 Applying Animation Techniques to Other Properties 294

12. **Strings** **298**
12.1 Joining Strings 298
12.2 Using Quotes and Apostrophes in Strings 302
12.3 Inserting Special Whitespace Characters 303
12.4 Searching for a Substring 304

12.5	Extracting a Substring	308
12.6	Parsing a String into Words	311
12.7	Removing and Replacing Characters and Words	315
12.8	Retrieving One Character at a Time	317
12.9	Converting Case	319
12.10	Trimming Whitespace	320
12.11	Reversing a String by Word or by Character	322
12.12	Converting Between Strings and Unicode or ASCII	323

13. Regular Expressions **327**

13.1	Understanding Regular Expression Patterns	328
13.2	Testing Regular Expressions	333
13.3	Looking for Pattern Matches	336
13.4	Removing and Replacing Characters and Words Using Patterns	338
13.5	Creating a Nongreedy Pattern	341
13.6	Validating User Input with Common Patterns	343

14. Dates and Times **348**

14.1	Finding the Current Date and Time	348
14.2	Retrieving the Date Values	351
14.3	Retrieving the Day or Month Name	352
14.4	Formatting the Date and Time	353
14.5	Formatting Seconds or Milliseconds as Minutes and Seconds	355
14.6	Converting Between DMYHMSM and Epoch Milliseconds	356
14.7	Using Timers	357
14.8	Calculating Elapsed Time or Intervals Between Dates	358
14.9	Parsing a Date from a String	363

15. Programming Sound **365**

15.1	Creating a Sound Object and Loading a Sound	365
15.2	Starting and Stopping a Sound	367
15.3	Setting the Buffer for a Sound	368
15.4	Offsetting the Start of a Sound	369
15.5	Playing a Sound Multiple Times (Looping)	370
15.6	Getting the Size of a Sound File	371
15.7	Reading the ID3 Tag of a Sound File	373
15.8	Find Out When a Sound Finishes Playing	375
15.9	Tracking the Progress of a Playing Sound	377
15.10	Pausing and Restarting a Sound	379

	15.11 Reading the Level of a Sound	381
	15.12 Stopping All Sounds	382
	15.13 Reading the Sound Spectrum	383
	15.14 Changing the Volume or Pan of a Sound	385
	15.15 Creating a Sound Application	386
16.	**Video**	**392**
	16.1 Loading and Playing Back Video	392
	16.2 Controlling Video Sound	394
	16.3 Reading Playback Time	394
	16.4 Reading Video Duration	395
	16.5 Controlling Playback Time	397
	16.6 Scaling Video	398
	16.7 Managing and Monitoring Buffering and Loading	399
	16.8 Listening for Cue Points	400
	16.9 Applying Filters to Video	401
	16.10 Pausing and Resuming Video	402
	16.11 Stopping Video	402
	16.12 Scrubbing Video	403
	16.13 Clearing the Video Display	405
	16.14 Determining User Bandwidth	405
17.	**Storing Persistent Data**	**409**
	17.1 Creating and Opening a Local Shared Object	409
	17.2 Writing Data to a Shared Object	411
	17.3 Saving a Local Shared Object	411
	17.4 Reading Data from a Shared Object	414
	17.5 Removing Data from a Shared Object	415
	17.6 Serializing Custom Classes	416
	17.7 Sharing Data Between Flash Applications	418
	17.8 Controlling the Size of Local Shared Objects	420
18.	**Communicating with Other Movies**	**422**
	18.1 Creating Local Connections	423
	18.2 Sending Data	427
	18.3 Validating Receipt of Communication over Local Connections	430
	18.4 Accepting Local Communications from Other Domains	432

19. Sending and Loading Data **435**

   19.1 Loading Variables from a Text File   436

   19.2 Loading Variables from a Server-Side Script   440

   19.3 Loading a Block of Text (Including HTML and XML)   442

   19.4 Checking Load Progress   444

   19.5 Accessing Data Being Downloaded   446

   19.6 Sending Data to a Server-Side Script   447

   19.7 Sending Variables and Handling a Returned Result   449

20. XML **452**

   20.1 Understanding XML Structure (Reading and Writing XML)   454

   20.2 Creating an XML Object   456

   20.3 Adding Elements to an XML Object   458

   20.4 Adding Text Nodes to an XML Object   461

   20.5 Adding Attributes to an XML Element   463

   20.6 Reading Elements in an XML Tree   464

   20.7 Finding Elements by Name   465

   20.8 Reading Text Nodes and Their Values   468

   20.9 Reading an Element's Attributes   470

   20.10 Removing Elements, Text Nodes, and Attributes   473

   20.11 Loading XML   474

   20.12 Loading XML from Different Domains   475

   20.13 Sending XML   476

   20.14 Searching XML   482

   20.15 Using HTML and Special Characters in XML   485

21. Web Services and Flash Remoting **487**

   21.1 Calling Web Services Methods   488

   21.2 Handling Web Services Responses   489

   21.3 Handling Web Services Errors   490

   21.4 Calling Flash Remoting Methods   490

   21.5 Handling Flash Remoting Responses   492

22. Building Integrated Applications **494**

   22.1 Calling JavaScript Functions   494

   22.2 Calling ActionScript Functions   495

   22.3 Passing Parameters from HTML   497

23. File Management **499**

23.1 Downloading Files   499

23.2 Detecting When a User Selects a File to Upload   502

23.3 Monitoring Download Progress   503

23.4 Browsing for Files   503

23.5 Filtering Files That Display in the Browser Window   504

23.6 Detecting When the User Has Selected a File to Upload   506

23.7 Uploading Files   506

23.8 Monitoring File Upload Progress   507

24. Socket Programming **509**

24.1 Connecting to a Socket Server   510

24.2 Sending Data   513

24.3 Receiving Data   515

24.4 Handshaking with a Socket Server   519

24.5 Disconnecting from a Socket Server   523

24.6 Handling Socket Errors   524

Appendix. Unicode Escape Sequences for Latin 1 Characters **527**

Index **533**

Preface

The *ActionScript 3.0 Cookbook* is written with all levels of ActionScript developers in mind—people like you who want practical solutions to common problems. Keep this book next to your computer to tackle programming challenges. It is filled with exciting yet accessible and practical examples, solutions, and insights into the situations that Flash and ActionScript developers are sure to encounter.

The book is in the style of the classic O'Reilly Cookbook series format, in which each recipe presents the problem, the solution, and a discussion of the solution. You can quickly locate the recipe that most closely matches your situation and get the solution without having to read the whole book to understand the underlying code. The Discussion sections of each recipe offer a deeper analysis of how the solution works and possible design choices and ramifications. So you get the best of both worlds—quick and easy access to the answers you want and deeper insights into the nature of both the problem and the solution. The *ActionScript 3.0 Cookbook* helps you develop your understanding of concepts by applying them in real situations.

What's Not in This Book

This book contains a lot of information on a wide range of topics. It covers the gamut of client-side ActionScript. Every recipe is presented in the context of an applied solution or example. Although the book discusses some minimal theory, it is not intended as an introduction to any of these subjects. There are many good books, references, and documents that discuss ActionScript in a comprehensive fashion. The *ActionScript 3.0 Cookbook* is not designed to be that sort of book. It is intentionally designed in a particular format to help you with solutions to specific problems.

Compatibility

As the title of the book says, this is the *ActionScript 3.0 Cookbook*. As such, all of the code examples in this book are based on ActionScript 3.0 and only compatible work with products that support ActionScript 3.0. Flex 2.0 and Flash 9 allow you to author ActionScript 3.0 content. Flash Player 9 supports ActionScript 3.0. If you are using a product that does not support ActionScript 3.0, then the code in this book is not likely to work.

Flash Platform Naming Conventions

ActionScript 3.0 is an important part of the Flash Platform. The Flash Platform is inclusive of many related technologies centering on the Flash Player. There are so many Flash Platform technologies these days that it can be difficult to keep track of all of them. To further complicate matters, many of the terminology are used very informally, generically, and even incorrectly by many developers. Although we don't take a harsh view of such informal use of terminology, we do want to be as clear and precise as possible when discussing these technologies throughout this book; therefore, we use terminology in very specific ways. Table P-1 lists the terms we use and their meanings.

Table P-1. Flash naming conventions used in this book

Name	Meaning
Flex framework	The library of ActionScript classes that ship as part of the Flex SDK and Flex Builder.
Flex Builder	The Adobe IDE for authoring Flex applications.
Flex SDK	The compiler and Flex framework used to author Flex applications without Flex Builder.
Flex	A technology used to author SWF files from MXML documents and ActionScript files. Unless a version number follows, all mentions of Flex in this book refer to Flex 2.0.
Flash Player	The deployment platform for SWF files published from Flash or Flex. Unless a version number follows, all mentions of Flash Player in this book refer to Flash Player 9.
Flash	The authoring tool used to author SWF files. Unless a version number follows, all mentions of Flash in this book refer to Flash 9.

The Code

This book contains a lot of ActionScript 3.0 (or more colloquially, code). Many recipes offer suggested custom classes that we have found to be invaluable. We trust you will find them useful as well.

You can download the complete ActionScript 3.0 libraries from *http://www.rightactionscript.com/ascb*. Once you've downloaded the library files, you'll need to add them to the classpath for your projects. Directions for setting your ActionScript 3.0 classpath are also found on that web site.

Audience for This Book

Is this book for you? We surely hope it is. But to be sure, let's review the prerequisites and summary of the goals of this book.

What You'll Need to Know

We assume you are already familiar with the product or products you are using to author Flash Player content. This book won't discuss Flex SDK, Flex Builder, or Flash basics. If you don't yet know how to compile a basic project or how to deploy a project, then you'll probably get the most from this book if you first learn the basics of working with the product or products you're using.

You'll also want to learn programming basics before reading this book. Although we talk about a lot of basic programming concepts in the context of how to solve specific problems (e.g., how to loop through the elements of an array) you won't find a step-by-step tutorial in this book with regard to basic programming skills.

Who This Book Is For

This book is for all ActionScript 3.0 developers. We hope there's something in this book for everyone: from novice to expert. If you want to quickly find a solution, this is the perfect book for you.

Who This Book Isn't For

This book discusses ActionScript 3.0, which is a language that runs within Flash Player. For the most part, this book does not discuss server-side solutions or other client-side languages in detail. For example, although this book does discuss the ActionScript code for working with Flash Remoting (a technology for making remote procedure calls) complete with examples, it does not explain how to write the corresponding server-side code (e.g., a ColdFusion component). Likewise, this book discusses how to use ActionScript to call JavaScript functions, yet we don't explain how to write JavaScript. If you are looking for an ActionScript 3.0 book, then this is it; but if you're looking for a book that discusses non-ActionScript topics in detail, this isn't the book you're looking for.

How This Book Is Organized

This book consists of the following chapters and appendix.

Chapter 1, *ActionScript Basics*
    Basic programming tasks such as looping statements, timers, etc.

Chapter 2, *Custom Classes*
> Writing custom classes for use with ActionScript 3.0.

Chapter 3, *Runtime Environment*
> Getting information about the system, device, and player version in use, as well as security functions.

Chapter 4, *Numbers and Math*
> Working with numbers in ActionScript, including parsing numbers from strings, converting numbers to formatted strings, and using different bases for numbers.

Chapter 5, *Arrays*
> Working with indexed collections of data called arrays: from adding and removing elements to sorting.

Chapter 6, *Display List*
> Using display objects to display visual data on the screen.

Chapter 7, *Drawing and Masking*
> Programmatic drawing and masking using ActionScript.

Chapter 8, *Bitmaps*
> Working with low-level bitmap data.

Chapter 9, *Text*
> Everything text, from displaying text to loading text to formatting text.

Chapter 10, *Filters and Transforms*
> Applying effects to display objects by using transforms (color and geometric) and filters such as drop shadows, bevels, and even emboss and edge detection effects.

Chapter 11, *Programmatic Animation*
> Animating display objects using ActionScript.

Chapter 12, *Strings*
> Working with string data: from finding substrings to working with Unicode.

Chapter 13, *Regular Expressions*
> Using native regular expressions to match patterns in strings.

Chapter 14, *Dates and Times*
> Working with dates and times, including converting between timezones, using timers, and formatting dates.

Chapter 15, *Programming Sound*
> Working with audio, including loading MP3s, reading ID3 tags, and displaying sound waves.

Chapter 16, *Video*
> Programming for Flash video.

Chapter 17, *Storing Persistent Data*
   Using shared objects to store data on the client computer.

Chapter 18, *Communicating with Other Movies*
   Using local connections to communicate between content running in Flash Player instance on the same computer.

Chapter 19, *Sending and Loading Data*
   Enabling two-way communication with a web server and the Flash Player.

Chapter 20, *XML*
   Working with XML using the E4X support in Flash Player.

Chapter 21, *Web Services and Flash Remoting*
   Working with remote procedure calls using web services and Flash Remoting technologies.

Chapter 22, *Building Integrated Applications*
   Using the native Flash Player programming interface for integrating Flash Player content with the host application, such as calling JavaScript functions from ActionScript or calling ActionScript functions from JavaScript.

Chapter 23, *File Management*
   Uploading and downloading files.

Chapter 24, *Socket Programming*
   Working with XML and binary sockets for low-latency applications.

Appendix, *Unicode Escape Sequences for Latin 1 Characters*
   This appendix lists the characters in the Latin 1 character repertoire, with Unicode equivalents in the range of U+0000 to U+00FF (that is, C0 Controls, Basic Latin, C1 Controls, and Latin 1 Supplemental).

How to Use This Book

Think of this book like a friend and a counselor. Don't put it on a shelf. Keep it on your desk where you can consult it often. When you are uncertain as to how something works or how to approach a specific programming issue pick up the book and flip to the relevant recipe(s). We have written this book in a format so that you can get answers to specific questions quickly. And since it's a book you don't ever have to worry that it will laugh at you for asking questions. No question is too big or too small.

Although you can read the book from cover to cover, we encourage you to use this book when you need an answer. Rather than teaching you a bunch of theory, this book intends to help you solve problems and accomplish tasks. This book is meant for field work, not the research lab.

Conventions Used in This Book

The following typographical conventions are used in this book:

Plain text
> Indicates menu titles, menu options, menu buttons, and keyboard accelerators (such as Alt and Ctrl).

Italic
> Indicates new terms, URLs, email addresses, filenames, file extensions, pathnames, directories, and Unix utilities.

`Constant width`
> Indicates commands, options, switches, variables, attributes, keys, functions, types, classes, namespaces, methods, modules, properties, parameters, values, objects, events, event handlers, XML tags, HTML tags, macros, the contents of files, or the output from commands.

`Constant width bold`
> Shows commands or other text that should be typed literally by the user.

`Constant width italic`
> Shows text that should be replaced with user-supplied values.

When referring to properties and methods of objects and classes, the following conventions are used:

- Class-level constants are shown with the both the class name and property in `constant width` because they should both be entered verbatim. For example, `Event.COMPLETE`.

- Instance-level properties are shown with the class or object instance in *`constant width italic`* because they should be replaced by a specific instance. The property itself is shown in `constant width` and should be entered as shown. For example, *`Button`*`.enabled`.

- Method and function names, and the class or object to which they pertain, are always shown in italics and followed by parentheses, as in *BitmapData.clone()*. Refer to the online help to know whether to include the class name literally (i.e., if it is a so-called static method), as in *String.fromCharCode()*, or replace it with an instance name, such as *exampleBitmap.clone()*.

- For brevity, we often omit the class name when discussing a property or method of a class. For example, if discussing the `htmlText` property of the `TextField` class, when we say "set the `htmlText` property," you should infer from context that we mean, "set the *`exampleTextField`*`.htmlText` property, where *`exampleTextField`* is the identifier for your particular text field."

In addition, the following formats are used to grab your attention and relieve the tedium of what could otherwise be monotonous reading:

This icon signifies a tip, suggestion, or general advice.

This icon indicates a warning or caution.

Using Code Examples

ActionScript 3.0 Cookbook is here to help you get your job done. In general, you may use the code in this book in your programs and documentation. You do not need to contact us for permission unless you're reproducing a significant portion of the code. For example, writing a program that uses several chunks of code from this book does not require permission. Selling or distributing a CD-ROM of examples from O'Reilly books *does* require permission. Answering a question by citing this book and quoting example code does not require permission. Incorporating a significant amount of example code from this book into your product's documentation *does* require permission.

We appreciate, but do not require, attribution. An attribution usually includes the title, author, publisher, and ISBN. For example: "*ActionScript 3.0 Cookbook,* by Joey Lott, Darron Schall, and Keith Peters. Copyright 2007 O'Reilly Media, Inc., 978-0-596-52695-5."

If you feel your use of code examples falls outside fair use or the permission given above, feel free to contact us at *permissions@oreilly.com*.

O'Reilly Cookbooks

Looking for the right ingredients to solve a programming problem? Look no further than O'Reilly Cookbooks. Each cookbook contains hundreds of programming recipes, and includes hundreds of scripts, programs, and command sequences you can use to solve specific problems.

The recipes you'll find in an O'Reilly Cookbook follow a simple formula:

Problem
    Each Problem addressed in an O'Reilly Cookbook is clearly stated, specific, and practical.

Solution
    The Solution is easy to understand and implement.

Discussion

The Discussion clarifies and explains the context of the Problem and the Solution. It also contains sample code to show you how to get the job done. Best of all, all of the sample code you see in an O'Reilly Cookbook can be downloaded from the book's web site, at *http://www.oreilly.com/catalog/actscpt3ckbk*.

See Also

The See Also section directs you to additional information related to the topic covered in the recipe. You'll find pointers to other recipes in the book, to other books (including non-O'Reilly titles), web sites, and more.

To learn more about the O'Reilly Cookbook series, or to find other Cookbooks that are up your alley, visit their web site at *http://cookbooks.oreilly.com*.

Safari® Enabled

 When you see a Safari®-enabled icon on the cover of your favorite technology book, that means it's available online through the O'Reilly Network Safari Bookshelf.

Safari offers a solution that's better than e-books. It's a virtual library that lets you easily search thousands of top tech books, cut and paste code samples, download chapters, and find quick answers when you need the most accurate, current information. Try it for free at *http://safari.oreilly.com*.

How to Contact Us

Please address comments and questions concerning this book to the publisher:

O'Reilly Media, Inc.
1005 Gravenstein Highway North
Sebastopol, CA 95472
800-998-9938 (in the United States or Canada)
707-829-0515 (international or local)
707-829-0104 (fax)

There is a web page for this book, where we list errata, examples, and any additional information. You can access this page at:

http://www.oreilly.com/catalog/actscpt3ckbk

The authors maintain a site for the book, located at:

http://www.rightactionscript.com/ascb

To comment or ask technical questions about this book, send email to:

bookquestions@oreilly.com

For more information about our books, conferences, Resource Centers, and the O'Reilly Network, see our web site at:

http://www.oreilly.com

About the Tech Reviewers

Stacey Mulcahy is a Flex and Flash developer who once had a torrid love affair with Macromedia Director. When she's not building Rich Internet Applications that even designers like, she can be found showing others how to do the same thing as a Flash instructor. She rants more than raves on her Flash-centric blog: *http://www. bitchwhocodes.com*.

Sam Robbins has been working with Flash and ActionScript for more than six years and has been experimenting with Flex for almost two. During that time, most of his efforts have been in developing Rich Internet Applications. Sam also started a subgroup of the Boston Flash Platform User Group (BFPUG), which examines design patterns on a monthly basis. In his spare time he tries to update his blog (*http:// pixelconsumption.com*), plays Xbox, and cuts his lawn. He lives in Massachusetts with his fiancée Andrea.

Steven Schelter is a software developer currently employed at Schematic. He's fluent in various front- and backend scripting languages and applications, but his primary concentration is ActionScript development. Steven was pulled into interactive media industry from Flash's appeal as a tool to merge his eye for design with his background in math and logistics. Other interests include 3D modeling, artificial intelligence, and user interactivity.

Roger Braunstein is a developer and designer living in Brooklyn. He is obsessed with beautiful code, motion design, graphics programming, and video games. He also cultivates an interest in cooking, photography, biking, and 8-bit music. One day he hopes to have a real web site at *http://www.partlyhuman.com*.

Muon Thi Van is a software developer at Schematic, a full-service interactive agency with offices in Los Angeles and New York City. She has served as architect, developer, and designer on numerous web and mobile-based Flash applications and games and has spoken at industry conferences such as Flashbelt and Flashforward. Muon holds a BS in computer science from Northwestern University.

Daniel Williams is a software developer at Schematic in New York, where he lives and breathes ActionScript. During those really late nights he dreams it as well. On the side, he has an avid interest in physics, fast two-wheeled vehicles, and the human brain. Occasionally, he'll ramble about his thoughts and experiences on his personal web site, the inappropriately named *http://www.danieldoesdallas.com*.

Acknowledgments

This book is the work of three authors—Joey Lott, Darron Schall, and Keith Peters—whose names are on the cover. However, this book certainly would not be possible without the help of many people whose names don't go on the cover. We'd like to extend our collective thanks and gratitude to the following people.

Thank you Chuck Toporek for your dedication, patience, and fantastic editing.

Likewise, thanks to Steve Weiss for believing in this book and its authors. We thank you for always advocating for what is best for us and the book.

We'd also like to thank Tim O'Reilly for raising the bar in technical publishing and for making this book possible in this format. We are honored to work with such a progressive and forward-thinking company.

Without the many efforts of the entire editorial and support staff at O'Reilly this book would not be where it is today. Thank you to everyone who's time and energy went into this book.

We'd like to thank our agent, Margot Hutchinson at Waterside Productions, for helping coordinate all the necessary details.

The entire Flex, Flash, and Flash Player teams at Adobe are always invaluable and incredibly helpful. They answer our questions so we can answer yours. Thank you to everyone at Adobe.

And we'd also like to thank all the technical reviewers for their assistance in making this book the best it can be.

Joey Lott

Thank you, Keith and Darron, for your help with this book. I am honored to work with two of the foremost experts in this industry.

I'd also like to thank my friends and family for all support and encouragement. And I'd like to thank life for all the support it provides in both expected and unexpected ways.

Darron Schall

Thank you, Joey, for allowing me to help fill in these pages. Keith, thanks for sharing the work as well. You both have been great to write with, and I'm proud to be your co-author. Chuck and Steve, your support was incalculable, and I definitely couldn't have done this without your help.

To my beautiful wife Jen, thank you for your understanding and tireless patience. I love you.

To all of my family—especially my grandfather Edwin—thanks for your encouragement and thanks for believing in me.

Keith Peters

Thank you, Joey, for the opportunity to be part of this project. Thanks also to Steve, Chuck, and Darron for help along the way, and as usual Kazumi and Kristine for putting up with me glued to the monitor all too often.

## CHAPTER 1

ActionScript Basics

1.0   Introduction

Using ActionScript, you can create Flash applications that do just about anything you can imagine. But before launching into the vast possibilities, let's start with the basic foundation. The good news is that ActionScript commands follow a well-defined pattern, sharing similar syntax, structure, and concepts. Mastering the fundamental grammar puts you well on the way to mastering ActionScript.

This chapter addresses the frequent tasks and problems that relate to core Action-Script knowledge. Whether you are a beginner or master—or somewhere in between—these recipes help you handle situations that arise in every ActionScript project.

This book assumes that you have obtained a copy of Flex Builder 2 and have successfully installed it on your computer. It's also helpful if you have some experience using a previous version of ActionScript as well.

When you launch Flex Builder 2, the Eclipse IDE should start up and present you with a welcome screen. You are presented with various options to get started and more information about Flex and ActionScript 3, such as links to documentation, tutorials, and more. You can close that screen by clicking on the small "x" on its tab. Now you are in the Eclipse IDE itself, ready to start coding; but where do you go from here?

Flex Builder 2 allows you to create three kinds of projects: a Flex project, Flex Library project, and an ActionScript project. The difference is that Flex projects have access to the entire Flex Framework, which includes all of the Flex components, layout management, transitions, styles, themes, data binding, and all the other stuff that goes into making a Flex Rich Internet Application. Flex applications are written in MXML (a form of XML), which describes the layout and relationship between components. They use ActionScript for their business logic. Although you can use the

ActionScript knowledge you learn from here in Flex applications you write, this book concentrates on ActionScript projects exclusively.

Now, if you are familiar with Flash 8 or earlier versions of the Flash IDE, you may be a bit baffled the first time you open up Flex Builder 2. There is no timeline, no library, no drawing tools or color pickers. You'll be doing pretty much everything by code alone, which is why it is called an *ActionScript project*, rather than a *Flash project*. So we'll first cover how to create a project and then to get you started with entering your first ActionScript statements.

1.1 Creating an ActionScript Project

Problem

You've launched Flex Builder 2 and want to create an ActionScript project.

Solution

Use the New ActionScript Project Wizard to set up your project.

Discussion

An ActionScript project usually consists of at least one class file and a folder named *bin* that contains the SWF and HTML files output by the compiler. It also consists of a lot of internal settings to let the compiler know where everything is and how to compile it all. Flex Builder 2 takes care of most of this for you when you use the New ActionScript Project Wizard. There are a few ways to start this wizard. You can use the menu File → New → ActionScript Project, or you can click on the New button in the top-right corner and select ActionScript Project from the list of available projects there. You can also click the small arrow next to the New button, which gives you the same list.

Whichever route you take to get there, you should wind up with the New Action-Script Project Wizard. Here you'll be prompted to type in a name for your project, such as *ExampleApplication*. Once you've created the project, you'll notice that the main application file is automatically set to the same name as the project name, with a *.as* extension.

Clicking the Next button gives you the opportunity to set custom class paths, additional libraries, and specify your output folder to something than the default *bin*. For now, you don't need to do anything here, so just press Finish to exit the wizard.

Flex Builder 2 now creates the necessary folders and files and applies all the default compiler settings for your project. In the Navigator view, you should now see a *ExampleApplication* project, which contains an empty *bin* folder and a *ExampleApplication.as* class file. Note that is has created this main class file for you automatically and has opened it up for editing in the code view. Also, in the Outline view, you can see a tree representation of the class, including its methods, properties, and any import statements.

To run your new application, you can press one of two buttons in the toolbar. One has a bug-like icon, which when pressed debugs the application, meaning it includes some extra information for debugging purposes and allows the use of trace statements. The button next to it—a circle with an arrow—runs the application. Both actions will create a *.swf* file and an HTML file, and then launch the HTML file in your default browser.

Of course, at this point, you haven't added anything to the application, so it is the equivalent of testing a blank *.fla* file in the Flash IDE. But go ahead and do so just to verify that everything is set up properly. You should get an empty web page with a blue background.

1.2   Customizing the Properties of an Application

Problem

You want to change the dimensions of the output *.swf*, or its background color, frame rate, etc.

Solution

Specify properties as ActionScript Compiler arguments or metadata in the class file.

Discussion

Unlike earlier versions of Flash, the ActionScript 3.0 compiler is actually a command-line compiler. Technically, you could create all your classes and directories and run the compiler from the command line with a long chain of parameters. However, it's much easier to let Eclipse keep track of all those parameters, add all of them, and run the compiler when you tell it to run.

When you create a new ActionScript project, it sets up default parameters that result in an 500×375 pixel *.swf*, with a frame rate of 24 frames per second (fps) and that blue background color you've seen. You can change any of these settings and many more. As you might expect, there are a few different ways to do this.

The first way to change compiler settings is to set the ActionScript compiler arguments. You do this by right-clicking on the project in the Navigator view and choosing Properties from the menu. Next, choose ActionScript Compiler from the list on the left. This allows you to change several aspects of how the compiler does its job. Look for the text field labeled "Additional compiler arguments." Anything you type in this text field is passed directly to the command-line compiler as an argument.

Here are the most common arguments you will probably be using:

```
-default-size width height

-default-background-color color

-default-frame-rate fps
```

You enter them exactly as presented, with numbers for arguments, like so:

```
-default-size 800 600

-default-background-color 0xffffff

-default-frame-rate 31
```

The first example sets the resulting size of the resulting *.swf* to 800×600 pixels. The second sets its background to white, and the last s4ets its frame rate to 31 fps. Multiple arguments would just be placed one after the other on the same line, like so:

```
-default-size 800 600 -default-frame-rate 31
```

 Check the Flex Builder 2 help files for *mxmlc options* to see the full list of command-line arguments you can enter here.

The second way to change these properties is through metadata in your main class file. Metadata consists of any statements that are not directly interpreted as Action-Script, but which the compiler uses to determine how to compile the final output files. The metadata statement that is equivalent to the previous example looks like this:

```
[SWF(width="800", height="600", backgroundColor="#ffffff", frameRate="31")]
```

This line is placed inside the main package block, but outside any class definitions (usually just before or after any import statements).

1.3   Where to Place ActionScript Code

Problem

You have a new ActionScript project and need to know where to put the code for it to execute properly.

Solution

Place ActionScript code in the constructor and additional methods of the class.

Discussion

In ActionScript 1.0 and 2.0, you had many choices as to where to place your code: on the timeline, on buttons and movie clips, on the timeline of movie clips, in external *.as* files referenced with *#include*, or as external class files. ActionScript 3.0 is completely class-based, so all code must be placed in methods of your project's classes.

When you create a new ActionScript project, the main class is automatically created, and opened in the Code view. It should look something like this:

```
package {
    import flash.display.Sprite;

    public class ExampleApplication extends Sprite
    {
        public function ExampleApplication()
        {

        }
    }
}
```

Even if you are familiar with classes in ActionScript 2.0, there are some new things here. There is a lot more information on this subject in Chapter 2, but let's go through the basics here.

The first thing you'll notice is the word *package* at the top of the code listing. Packages are used to group classes of associated functionality together. In ActionScript 2.0, packages were inferred through the directory structure used to hold the class files. In ActionScript 3.0, however, you must explicitly specify packages. For example, you could have a package of utility classes. This would be declared like so:

```
package com.as3cb.utils {

}
```

If you don't specify a package name, your class is created in the default, top-level package. You should still include the *package* keyword and braces.

Next, place any `import` statements. Importing a class makes that class available to the code in the file and sets up a shortcut so you don't have to type the full package name every time you want to refer to that class. For example, you can use the following `import` statement:

```
import com.as3cb.utils.StringUtils;
```

Thereafter you can refer to the *StringUtils* class directly without typing the rest of the path. As shown in the earlier example, you will need to import the *Sprite* class from the *flash.display* package, as the default class extends the *Sprite* class.

Next up is the main class, `ExampleApplication`. You might notice the keyword *public* in front of the class definition. Although you can't have private classes within a package, you should label the class public. Note that the main class extends *Sprite*. Also, a *.swf* itself is a type of sprite or movie clip, which is why you can load a *.swf* into another *.swf* and largely treat it as if it were just another nested sprite or movie clip.

This main class represents the *.swf* as a whole, so it should extend the *Sprite* class or any class that extends the *Sprite* class (such as *MovieClip*).

Finally, there is a public function (or method, in class terminology) with the same name as the class itself. This makes it a *constructor*. A class's constructor is automatically run as soon as an instance of the class is created. In this case, it is executed as soon as the *.swf* is loaded into the Flash player. So where do you put your code to get it to execute? Generally, you start out by putting some code in the constructor method. Here's a very simple example that just draws a bunch of random lines to the screen:

```
package {
    import flash.display.Sprite;
    public class ExampleApplication extends Sprite {
        public function ExampleApplication( ) {
            graphics.lineStyle(1, 0, 1);
            for(var i:int=0;i<100;i++) {
                graphics.lineTo(Math.random( ) * 400, Math.random( ) * 400);
            }
        }
    }
}
```

Save and run the application. Your browser should open the resulting HTML file and display the *.swf* with 100 random lines in it. As you can see, the constructor was executed as soon as the file was loaded into the player.

In practice, you usually want to keep code in the constructor to a bare minimum. Ideally the constructor would just contain a call to another method that initializes the application. See Recipes 1.13 and 1.14 for more on methods.

For beginners, now that you know where to enter code, here is quick primer on terminology. These definitions are briefly stated and intended to orient people who have never programmed before. For more complete definitions, refer to the Flash help files.

Variables

    Variables are convenient placeholders for data in your code, and you can name them anything you'd like, provided the name isn't already reserved by Action-Script and the name starts with a letter, underscore, or dollar sign (but not a number). The help files installed with Flex Builder 2 contain a list of reserved words. Variables are convenient for holding interim information, such as a sum of numbers, or to refer to something, such as a text field or sprite. Variables are *declared* with the var keyword the first time they are used in a script. You can assign a value to a variable using an equal sign (=), which is also known as the *assignment operator*. If a variable is declared outside a class method, it is a *class variable*. Class variables, or *properties*, can have access modifiers, public, private, protected, or internal. A private variable can only be accessed from within the class itself, whereas public variables can be accessed by objects of another class. Protected variables can be accessed from an instance of the class or an instance of any subclass, and `internal` variables can be accessed by any class within the same package. If no access modifier is specified, it defaults to `internal`.

Functions

Functions are blocks of code that do something. You can *call* or *invoke* a function (that is, execute it) by using its name. When a function is part of a class, it is referred to as a *method* of the class. Methods can use all the same modifiers as properties.

Scope

A variable's *scope* describes when and where the variable can be manipulated by the code in a movie. Scope defines a variable's life span and its accessibility to other blocks of code in a script. Scope determines how long a variable exists and from where in the code you can set or retrieve the variable's value. A function's scope determines where and when the function is accessible to other blocks of code. Recipe 1.13 deals with issues of scope.

Event handler

A *handler* is a function or method that is executed in response to some event such as a mouseclick, a keystroke, or the movement of the playhead in the timeline.

Objects and classes

An *object* is something you can manipulate programmatically in ActionScript, such as a sprite. There are other types of objects, such as those used to manipulate colors, dates, and text fields. Objects are instances of *classes*, which means that a class is a template for creating objects and an object is a particular instance of that class. If you get confused, think of it in biological terms: you can consider yourself an object (instance) that belongs to the general class known as humans.

Methods

A *method* is a function associated with an object that operates on the object. For example, a text field object's *replaceSelectedText( )* method can be used to replace the selected text in the field.

Properties

A *property* is an attribute of an object, which can be read and/or set. For example, a sprite's horizontal location is specified by its x property, which can be both tested and set. On the other hand, a text field's `length` property, which indicates the number of characters in the field, can be tested but cannot be set directly (it can be affected indirectly, however, by adding or removing text from the field).

Statements

ActionScript commands are entered as a series of one or more *statements*. A statement might tell the playhead to jump to a particular frame, or it might change the size of a sprite. Most ActionScript statements are terminated with a semicolon (;). This book uses the terms *statement* and *action* interchangeably.

Comments

> *Comments* are notes within code that are intended for other humans and ignored by Flash. In ActionScript, single-line comments begin with // and terminate automatically at the end of the current line. Multiline comments begin with /* and are terminated with */.

Interpreter

> The *ActionScript interpreter* is that portion of the Flash Player that examines your code and attempts to understand and execute it. Following ActionScript's strict rules of grammar ensures that the interpreter can easily understand your code. If the interpreter encounters an error, it often fails silently, simply refusing to execute the code rather than generating a specific error message.

Don't worry if you don't understand all the specifics. You can use each recipe's solution without understanding the technical details, and this primer should help you understand the terminology.

See Also

Recipes 1.13 and 1.14

1.4   How to Trace a Message

Problem

You need to trace out a message or the value of some data at runtime.

Solution

Use the *trace* function, pass the data to it, run your application, and look for a message in the Console in Eclipse.

Discussion

You can trace out a message, the value of a variable, or just about any other data using *trace*, just as you would in earlier versions of ActionScript. Some examples:

```
trace("Hello, world");

trace(userName);

trace("My name is " + userName + ".");
```

Since the *.swf* is now launched in an external browser, it might seem that there is no way to capture the output of these trace statements. Fortunately, it is possible, and this functionality has been built in to Flex Builder 2 via the Console view. The Console view is the equivalent of the Output panel in the Flash IDE. Although it is not open when you first start Eclipse, it appears when needed.

The only requirement to using *trace* and the Console view is that you use Debug to test your application. Doing so includes extra features in the *.swf* that allows it to communicate back to the Console behind the scenes and pass any messages you trace. The following class creates a variable, assigns a value to it, and then traces it, along with some other string data:

```
package {
    import flash.display.Sprite;

    public class ExampleApplication extends Sprite {
        public function ExampleApplication() {
            var userName:String = "Bill Smith";
            trace("My name is " + userName + ".");
        }
    }
}
```

Now when you debug your application, it launches as usual in your default browser. Close the browser and switch back to Eclipse. You will see that the Console view is now open and has displayed the data you traced out.

When you launch the debug version of an application, you must have the debug version of Flash Player installed. If you don't have the debug version of Flash Player, you'll see an error message notifying you, and you'll have to download and install it from *http://www.adobe.com/support/flashplayer/downloads.html*.

Additionally, the debug version of Flash Player can write trace content to a file. The file that Flash Player uses is determined by *mm.cfg*, a file that is stored in the following locations:

Operating system	Location
Windows XP	C:\Documents and Settings\[*user name*]\mm.cfg
Windows 2000	C:\mm.cfg
Mac OS X	MacHD:Library:Application Support:macromedia:mm.cfg

The *mm.cfg* file allows you to set the following variables:

TraceOutputFileEnable
> The value can be 0 (don't write trace content to a file) or 1 (write to a file).

TraceOutputFileName
> The path to the file to which to write. If a value isn't specified, then the content is written to *flashlog.txt* in the same directory as *mm.cfg*.

ErrorReportingEnable
> The value can be 0 (don't write errors to the logfile) or 1 (write errors to the logfile). The default value is 0.

MaxWarnings

The maximum number of errors to write to the logfile. If this value is set to 0, there is no limit. If a larger value is specified, that limit is imposed and any errors beyond the limit are not written to the log.

At a minimum *mm.cfg* must contain the following enable writing to a file.

```
TraceOutputFileEnable=1
```

If you want to specify more than one variable, you should place each on a new line, as follows

```
TraceOutputFileEnable=1
TraceOutputFileName=C:\flex.log
```

1.5   Handling Events

Problem

You want to have some code repeatedly execute.

Solution

Add a listener to the *enterFrame* event and assign a method as a handler.

Discussion

In ActionScript 2.0 handling the *enterFrame* event was quite simple. You just had to create a timeline function called *onEnterFrame* and it was automatically called each time a new frame began. In ActionScript 3.0, you have much more control over the various events in a *.swf*, but a little more work is required to access them.

If you are familiar with the *EventDispatcher* class from ActionScript 2.0, you should be right at home with ActionScript 3.0's method of handling events. In fact, *EventDispatcher* has graduated from being an externally defined class to being the base class for all interactive objects, such as sprites.

To respond to the *enterFrame* event, you have to tell your application to listen for that event and specify which method you want to be called when the event occurs. This is done with the *addEventListener* method, which is defined as follows:

```
addEventListener(type:String, listener:Function)
```

 There are additional parameters you can look up in the help files, but this is the minimum implementation.

The *type* parameter is the type of event you want to listen to. In this case, it would be the string, "enterFrame". However, using string literals like that opens your code to

errors that the compiler cannot catch. If you accidentally typed "enterFrane", for example, your application would simply listen for an "enterFrane" event. To guard against this, it is recommended that you use the static properties of the *Event* class. You should already have the *Event* class imported, so you can call the *addEventListener* method as follows:

```
addEventListener(Event.ENTER_FRAME, onEnterFrame);
```

Now if you accidentally typed `Event.ENTER_FRANE`, the compiler would complain that such a property did not exist.

The second parameter, `onEnterFrame`, refers to another method in the class. Note, that in ActionScript 3.0, there is no requirement that this method be named `onEnterFrame`. However, naming event handling methods *on* plus the event name is a common convention. This method gets passed an instance of the *Event* class when it is called. Therefore, you'll need to import that class and define the method so it accepts an event object:

```
import flash.events.Event;

private function onEnterFrame(event:Event) {

}
```

The event object contains information regarding the event that may be useful in handling it. Even if you don't use it, you should still set your handler up to accept it. If you are familiar with the ActionScript 2.0 version of *EventDispatcher*, you'll see a difference in implementation here. In the earlier version, there was an issue with the scope of the function used to handle the event, which often required the use of the *Delegate* class to correct. In ActionScript 3.0, the scope of the handling method remains the class of which it is a method, so there is no necessity to use *Delegate* to correct scope issues.

Here is a simple application that draws successive random lines, using all the concepts discussed in this recipe:

```
package {
    import flash.display.Sprite;
    import flash.events.Event;

    public class ExampleApplication extends Sprite {

        public function ExampleApplication() {
            graphics.lineStyle(1, 0, 1);
            addEventListener(Event.ENTER_FRAME, onEnterFrame);
        }

        private function onEnterFrame(event:Event):void {
            graphics.lineTo(Math.random() * 400, Math.random() * 400);
        }
    }
}
```

1.6 Responding to Mouse and Key Events

Problem

You want to do something in response to a mouse or keyboard action.

Solution

Listen for and handle mouse or key events.

Discussion

Handling mouse and key events is very similar to handling the *enterFrame* event, as discussed in the Recipe 1.5, but does require a little work. For mouse events, the main application class will not receive these directly, so it must listen for them on another object in the display list. (For a complete discussion of the display list, see Chapter 5.) The following example creates a sprite, adds it to the display list, and draws a rectangle in it:

```
package {
    import flash.display.Sprite;
    import flash.events.MouseEvent;

    public class ExampleApplication extends Sprite {
        private var _sprite:Sprite;

        public function ExampleApplication() {
            _sprite = new Sprite();
            addChild(_sprite);
            _sprite.graphics.beginFill(0xffffff);
            _sprite.graphics.drawRect(0, 0, 400, 400);
            _sprite.graphics.endFill();
```

Note that the mouse event names are defined in the *MouseEvent* class, and the handler methods get passed an instance of the *MouseEvent* class, so you'll need to import that class. Then you can add mouse listeners to this sprite:

```
            _sprite.addEventListener(MouseEvent.MOUSE_DOWN, onMouseDown);
            _sprite.addEventListener(MouseEvent.MOUSE_UP, onMouseUp);
        }
```

Next, define the two handler methods, onMouseDown and onMouseUp:

```
        private function onMouseDown(event:MouseEvent):void {
            _sprite.graphics.lineStyle(1, 0, 1);
            _sprite.graphics.moveTo(mouseX, mouseY);
            _sprite.addEventListener(MouseEvent.MOUSE_MOVE, onMouseMove);
        }

        private function onMouseUp(event:MouseEvent):void
        {
            _sprite.removeEventListener(MouseEvent.MOUSE_MOVE, onMouseMove);
        }
```

The onMouseDown methods sets a drawing line style on the new sprite and moves the drawing cursor to the mouse position. It then adds yet a third mouse listener for the *MouseMove* event.

The onMouseUp methods removes that listener via the *removeEventListener* method. This has the same syntax as *addEventListener*, but tells the class to stop listening to the specified event.

Finally, define onMouseMove and close up the class and package:

```
private function onMouseMove(event:MouseEvent):void {
    _sprite.graphics.lineTo(mouseX, mouseY);
}
    }
}
```

This creates a simple event-driven drawing program.

Keyboard events are a little easier to handle. The only requirement for listening and responding to keyboard events is that the object that receives the events must have focus. You do this for the main application by adding the line:

```
stage.focus = this;
```

The following example shows a simple class that listens for the *keyDown* event and traces out the character code for that key. This also demonstrates how to use some of the data contained in the event object passed to the handler method. Note that keyboard events use the class *KeyboardEvent*.

```
package {
    import flash.display.Sprite;
    import flash.events.KeyboardEvent;

    public class ExampleApplication extends Sprite {
        public function ExampleApplication( ) {
            stage.focus = this;
            addEventListener(KeyboardEvent.KEY_DOWN, onKeyDown);
        }

        private function onKeyDown(event:KeyboardEvent):void {
            trace("key down: " + event.charCode);
        }
    }
}
```

See Also

Recipe 1.5

1.7   Using Mathematical Operators

Problem

You want to modify something over time, such as the rotation or position of a sprite.

Solution

Use the compound assignment operators to change a variable or property in increments; or, if incrementing or decrementing by one, use the prefix or postfix increment or decrement operators.

Discussion

Often you'll want the new value of a variable or property to depend on the previous value. For example, you might want to move a sprite to a new position that is 10 pixels to the right of its current position.

In an assignment statement—any statement using the assignment operator (an equals sign)—the expression to the right of the equals sign is evaluated and the result is stored in the variable or property on the left side. Therefore, you can modify the value of a variable in an expression on the right side of the equation and assign that new value to the very same variable on the left side of the equation.

Although the following may look strange to those who remember basic algebra, it is very common for a variable to be set equal to itself plus some number:

```
// Add 6 to the current value of quantity, and assign that new
// value back to quantity. For example, if quantity was 4, this
// statement sets it to 10.
quantity = quantity + 6;
```

However, when performing mathematical operations, it is often more convenient to use one of the *compound assignment operators*, which combine a mathematical operator with the assignment operator. The +=, -=, *=, and /= operators are the most prevalent compound assignment operators. When you use one of these compound assignment operators, the value on the right side of the assignment operator is added to, subtracted from, multiplied by, or divided into the value of the variable on the left, and the new value is assigned to the same variable. The following are a few examples of equivalent statements.

These statements both add 6 to the existing value of quantity:

```
quantity = quantity + 6;
quantity += 6;
```

These statements both subtract 6 from the existing value of quantity:

```
quantity = quantity - 6;
quantity -= 6;
```

These statements both multiple quantity by factor:

```
quantity = quantity * factor;
quantity *= factor;
```

These statements both divide quantity by factor:

```
quantity = quantity / factor;
quantity /= factor;
```

There should be no space between the two symbols that make up a compound assignment operator. Additionally, if you are incrementing or decrementing a variable by 1, you can use the increment or decrement operators.

This statement adds 1 to quantity:

```
quantity++;
```

and has the same effect as either of these statements:

```
quantity = quantity + 1;
quantity += 1;
```

This statement subtracts 1 from quantity:

```
quantity --;
```

and has the same effect as either of these statements:

```
quantity = quantity - 1;
quantity -= 1;
```

You can use the increment and decrement operators (-- and ++) either before or after the variable or property they operate upon. If used before the operand, they are called *prefix operators*. If used after the operand, they are called *postfix operators*. The prefix and postfix operators modify the operand in the same way but at different times. In some circumstances, there is no net difference in their operation, but the distinction is still important in many cases. When using prefix operators, the value is modified before the remainder of the statement or expression is evaluated. And if you're using postfix operators, the value is modified after the remainder of the statement has executed. Note how the first example increments quantity after displaying its value, whereas the second example increments quantity before displaying its value:

```
var quantity:Number = 5;
trace(quantity++);  // Displays: 5
trace(quantity);    // Displays: 6

var quantity:Number = 5;
trace(++quantity);  // Displays: 6
trace(quantity);    // Displays: 6
```

Getting back to the original problem, you can use these operators to modify a property over time. This example causes the specified sprite to rotate by five degrees each time the method is called:

```
private function onEnterFrame(event:Event) {
  _sprite.rotation += 5;
}
```

Note that in ActionScript 3.0, you would have to add an event listener to the enterFrame event and set this method as the event handler for this to work properly. See Recipe 1.5 for information on how to handle the enterFrame event.

See Also

Recipe 1.5

1.8   Checking Equality or Comparing Values

Problem

You want to check if two values are equal.

Solution

Use the equality (or inequality) or strict equality (or strict inequality) operator to compare two values. To check whether a value is a valid number, use *isNaN( )*.

Discussion

Equality expressions always return a Boolean value indicating whether the two values are equal. The equality (and inequality) operators come in both regular and strict flavors. The regular equality and inequality operators check whether the two expressions being compared can be resolved to the same value after converting them to the same datatype. For example, note that the string "6" and the number 6 are considered equal because the string "6" is converted to the number 6 before comparison:

```
trace(5 == 6);    // Displays: false
trace(6 == 6);    // Displays: true
trace(6 == "6");  // Displays: true
trace(5 == "6");  // Displays: false
```

Note that in a project with default settings, the previous code example won't even compile. That's because it is compiled with a strict flag, causing the compiler to be more exact in checking datatypes at compile time. It complains that it is being asked to compare an *int* with a *String*. To turn off the strict flag, go to the ActionScript Compiler section of the project's properties, and uncheck the box next to "Enable compile-time type checking (-strict)". It is suggested, however, that you leave this option on for most projects, as it gives you better protection against inadvertent errors.

The logical inequality operator (!=) returns false if two values are equal and true if they aren't. If necessary, the operands are converted to the same datatype before the comparison:

```
trace(5 != 6);      // Displays: true
trace(6 != 6);      // Displays: false
trace(6 != "6");    // Displays: false
trace(5 != "6");    // Displays: true
```

Again, this example only compiles if strict type checking is disabled.

On the other hand, if you have turned off the strict flag, but you want to perform a strict comparison in one section of code, you can use the strict equality and inequality operators, === and !==. These first check whether the values being compared are of the same datatype before performing the comparison. Differences in datatypes causes the strict equality operator to return false and the strict inequality operator to return true:

```
trace(6 === 6);      // Displays: true
trace(6 === "6");    // Displays: false
trace(6 !== 6);      // Displays: false
trace(6 !== "6");    // Displays: true
```

 There is a big difference between the assignment operator (=) and the equality operator (==). If you use the assignment operator instead of the equality operator, the variable's value will change rather than testing its current value.

Using the wrong operator leads to unexpected results. In the following example, quantity equals 5 at first, so you might expect the subsequent *if* statement to always evaluate to false, preventing the *trace()* from being executed:

```
var quantity:int = 5;
// The following code is wrong. It should be if (quantity == 6) instead
if (quantity = 6) {
  trace("Rabbits are bunnies.");
}
trace("quantity is " + quantity);  // Displays: quantity is 6
```

However, the example mistakenly uses the assignment operator (=) instead of the equality operator (==). That is, the expression *quantity = 6* sets quantity to 6 instead of testing whether quantity is 6. When used in an *if* clause, the expression *quantity = 6* is treated as the number 6. Because, any nonzero number used in a test expression converts to the Boolean true, the *trace()* action is called. Replace the test expression with *quantity == 6* instead. Fortunately, the ActionScript 3.0 compiler is smart enough to recognize this common error and although the code still compiles, you aren't given a warning.

You can check an item's datatype using the *is* operator, as follows:

```
var quantity:int = 5;
if (quantity is int) {
  trace("Yippee. It's an integer.");
}
```

 Note that the new ActionScript 3.0 types *int* and *uint* will also test positive as *Number*s.

However, some numeric values are invalid. The following example results in quantity being set equal to NaN (a constant representing invalid numbers, short for not a number) because the calculation cannot be performed in a meaningful way:

```
var quantity:Number = 15 - "rabbits";
```

Despite its name, NaN is a recognized value of the *Number* datatype:

```
trace(typeof quantity);   // Displays: "number"
```

Therefore, to test if something is not just any number, but a valid number, try this:

```
var quantity:Number = 15 - "rabbits";
if (quantity is Number) {

  // Nice try, but this won't work
  if (quantity != NaN) {
    trace("Yippee. It's a number.");
  }
}
```

 However, you can't simply compare a value to the constant NaN to check whether it is a valid number. The ActionScript 3.0 compiler even gives you a warning to this effect. Instead, you must use the special *isNaN( )* function to perform the test.

To determine if a number is invalid, use the special *isNaN( )* function, as follows:

```
var quantity:Number = 15 - "rabbits";
if (isNaN(quantity)) {
  trace("Sorry, that is not a valid number.");
}
```

To test the opposite of a condition (i.e., whether a condition is not true) use the logical *NOT* operator (!). For example, to check whether a variable contains a *valid* number, use *!isNAN( )*, as follows:

```
var quantity:Number = 15 - "rabbits";
if (!isNaN(quantity)) {

  // The number is not invalid, so it must be a valid number
  trace ("That is a valid number.");
}
```

Of course, you can perform comparisons using the well-known comparison operators. For example, you can use the < and > operators to check if one value is less than or greater than another value:

```
trace(5 < 6);    // Displays: true
trace(5 > 5);    // Displays: false
```

Similarly, you can use the <= and >= operators to check if one value is less than or equal to, or greater than or equal to, another value:

```
trace(5 <= 6);    // Displays: true
trace(5 >= 5);    // Displays: true
```

You should also be aware that ActionScript compares datatypes differently. ActionScript datatypes can be categorized either as *primitive* (*string*, *number*, and *Boolean*) or *composite* (*object*, *sprite*, and *array*). When you compare primitive datatypes, ActionScript compares them "by value." In this example, quantity and total are considered equal because they both contain the value 6:

```
var quantity:Number = 6;
var total:Number = 6;
trace (quantity == total);          // Displays: true
```

However, when you compare composite datatypes, ActionScript compares them "by reference." Comparing items by reference means that the two items are considered equal only if both point to exactly the same object, not merely objects with matching contents. For example, two arrays containing exactly the same values are not considered equal:

```
// Create two arrays with the same elements.
var arrayOne:Array = new Array("a", "b", "c");
var arrayTwo:Array = new Array("a", "b", "c");
trace(arrayOne == arrayTwo);        // Displays: false
```

Two composite items are equal only if they both refer to the identical object, array, or sprite. For example:

```
// Create a single array
var arrayOne:Array = new Array("a", "b", "c");
// Create another variable that references the same array.
var arrayTwo:Array = arrayOne;
trace(arrayOne == arrayTwo);        // Displays: true
```

See Also

Recipe 5.8

1.9 Performing Actions Conditionally

Problem

You want to perform some action only when a condition is true.

Solution

Use an *if* or a *switch* statement.

Discussion

You often need your ActionScript code to make decisions, such as whether to execute a particular action or group of actions. To execute some action under certain circumstances, use one of ActionScript's *conditional* statements: *if*, *switch*, or the ternary conditional operator (? :).

Conditional statements allow you to make logical decisions, and you'll learn from experience which is more appropriate for a given situation. For example, the *if* statement is most appropriate when you want to tell a Flash movie to do something only when a certain condition is met (e.g., when the condition is true). When you have several possible conditions to test, you can use the *switch* statement instead. And you can use Flash's ternary conditional operator to perform conditional checking and assignment on a single line.

First let's look at the *if* statement. Of the conditional statements in ActionScript, the *if* statement is the most important to understand. In its most basic form, an *if* statement includes the keyword if followed by the test expression whose truthfulness you want to evaluate to determine which action or actions to execute. The test expression must be in parentheses and the statement(s) to be executed should be within curly braces (the latter is mandatory if there is more than one statement in the statement block).

Here we check whether animalName contains the word "turtle." This might be used to check whether the user answered a quiz question correctly (here, animalName is a variable assumed to contain the user's answer). Note that the double equals sign (==) is used to test whether two items are equal. It should not be confused with the single equals sign (=), which is used to assign a value to an item.

```
if (animalName == "turtle") {
  // This trace( ) statement executes only when animalName is equal
  // to "turtle".
  trace("Yay! 'Turtle' is the correct answer.");
}
```

Additionally, you can add an *else* clause to an *if* statement to perform alternative actions if the condition is false. Note that for the *trace( )* command to have any effect, the *.swf* must be compiled using Debug, and not Run, mode. Make a call to a method named *showMessage()* that displays an appropriate message depending on whether the user got the answer right or wrong:

```
if (animalName == "turtle") {
  // These statements execute only when animalName is equal
  // to "turtle".
  showMessage("Yay! 'Turtle' is the correct answer.");
```

```
}
else {
  // These statements execute only when animalName is not equal
  // to "turtle".
  showMessage("Sorry, you got the question wrong.");
}
```

For testing purposes, you can create a *showMessage()* method that traces out the string sent to it. In a real-world example, you might want to display this message in a text field, or display it to the user some other way, such as in a dialog box.

You can add an *else if* clause to an *if* statement. If the *if* condition is `true`, the *else if* clause is skipped. If the *if* condition is `false`, the ActionScript interpreter checks to see if the *else if* condition is `true`:

```
if (animalName == "turtle") {
  // This trace( ) statement executes only when animalName is equal
  // to "turtle".
  showMessage ("Yay! 'Turtle' is the correct answer.");
}
else if (animalName == "dove") {
  // This trace( ) statement executes only when animalName is not
  // "turtle", but is "dove".
  showMessage ("Sorry, a dove is a bird, not a reptile.");
}
```

What if the preceding example was written as two separate *if* statements (one to check if animalName is "turtle" and another to check if it is "dove")? The example would work as intended, but it would be less efficient. Using the *else if* statement guarantees that if animalName is "turtle"; we don't bother checking if it is also equal to "dove."

If your two conditions are mutually exclusive, use an *else if* clause to check the second condition. If your two conditions are not mutually exclusive, and you want to perform both statement blocks when both conditions are met, use two separate *if* statements.

When you use an *if* statement with both *else if* and *else* clauses, the *else* clause must be the last clause in the statement. The final *else* clause is convenient as a catchall; it's where you can put statements that take the appropriate action if none of the other conditions are met.

```
if (animalName == "turtle") {
  // This trace( ) statement executes only when animalName is equal
  // to "turtle".
  showMessage ("Yay! 'Turtle' is the correct answer.");
}
else if (animalName == "dove") {
```

```
  // This statement executes only when animalName is not
  // "turtle", but is "dove".
  showMessage ("Sorry, a dove is a bird, not a reptile.");
}
else {
  // This statement executes only when animalName is neither
  // "turtle" nor "dove".
  showMessage ("Sorry, try again.");
}
```

You can also include more than one *else if* clause in an *if* statement. However, in that case, you should most likely use a *switch* statement instead; generally, *switch* statements are more legible and succinct than the comparable *if* statement. Where performance is critical, some ActionScripters prefer to use *if* statements, which allow somewhat greater control for optimization purposes.

A *switch* statement is composed of three parts:

The switch *keyword*
> Every *switch* statement must begin with the switch keyword.

Test expression
> An expression, enclosed in parentheses, whose value you want to test to determine which action or actions to execute.

The switch statement body
> The statement body, enclosed in curly braces, is composed of *cases*. Each case is made up of the following parts:

> *The* case *or* default *keyword*
>> A case must begin with a case keyword. The exception is the default case (analogous to an *else* clause in an *if* statement), which uses the default keyword.

> *Case expression*
>> An expression, whose value is to be compared to the *switch* statement's test expression. If the two values are equal, the code in the case body is executed. The default case (the case that uses the default keyword) does not need a case expression.

> *Case body*
>> One or more statements, usually ending in a *break* statement, to be performed if that *case* is true.

The switch keyword is always followed by the test expression in parentheses. Then the *switch* statement body is enclosed in curly braces. There can be one or more *case* statements within the *switch* statement body. Each case (other than the default case) starts with the case keyword followed by the case expression and a colon. The default case (if one is included) starts with the default keyword followed by a colon. Therefore, the general form of a *switch* statement is:

```
switch (testExpression) {
  case caseExpression:
    // case body
```

```
    case caseExpression:
      // case body
    default:
      // case body
  }
```

Note that once a case tests true, all the remaining actions in all subsequent cases within the *switch* statement body also execute. This example is most likely not what the programmer intended.

Here is an example:

```
var animalName:String = "dove";

/* In the following switch statement, the first trace() statement
   does not execute because animalName is not equal to "turtle".
   But both the second and third trace() statements execute,
   because once the "dove" case tests true, all subsequent code
   is executed.
*/
switch (animalName) {
  case "turtle":
    trace("Yay! 'Turtle' is the correct answer.");
  case "dove":
    trace("Sorry, a dove is a bird, not a reptile.");
  default:
    trace("Sorry, try again.");
}
```

Normally, you should use *break* statements at the end of each case body to exit the *switch* statement after executing the actions under the matching case.

The *break* statement terminates the current *switch* statement, preventing statements in subsequent case bodies from being erroneously executed.

You don't need to add a *break* statement to the end of the last *case* or *default* clause, since it is the end of the *switch* statement anyway.

```
var animalName:String = "dove";

// Now, only the second trace() statement executes.
switch (animalName) {
  case "turtle":
    trace("Yay! 'Turtle' is the correct answer.");
    break;
  case "dove":
    trace("Sorry, a dove is a bird, not a reptile.");
    break;
  default:
    trace("Sorry, try again.");
}
```

The *switch* statement is especially useful when you want to perform the same action for one of several matching possibilities. Simply list multiple case expressions one after the other. For example:

```
switch (animalName) {
  case "turtle":
  case "alligator":
  case "iguana":
    trace("Yay! You named a reptile.");
    break;
  case "dove":
  case "pigeon":
  case "cardinal":
    trace("Sorry, you specified a bird, not a reptile.");
    break;
  default:
    trace("Sorry, try again.");
}
```

ActionScript also supports the ternary conditional operator (? :), which allows you to perform a conditional test and an assignment statement on a single line. A *ternary operator* requires three operands, as opposed to the one or two operands required by unary and binary operators. The first operand of the conditional operator is a conditional expression that evaluates to either true or false. The second operand is the value to assign to the variable if the condition is true, and the third operand is the value to assign if the condition is false.

```
varName = (conditional expression) ? valueIfTrue : valueIfFalse;
```

1.10   Performing Complex Conditional Testing

Problem

You want to make a decision based on multiple conditions.

Solution

Use the logical *AND* (&&), *OR* (||), and *NOT* (!) operators to create compound conditional statements.

Discussion

Many statements in ActionScript can involve conditional expressions, including *if*, *while*, and *for* statements, and statements using the ternary conditional operator. To test whether two conditions are both true, use the logical *AND* operator, &&, as follows (see Chapter 14 for details on working with dates):

```
// Check if today is April 17th.
var current:Date = new Date();
if (current.getDate() == 17 && current.getMonth() == 3) {
```

```
    trace ("Happy Birthday, Bruce!");
  }
```

You can add extra parentheses to make the logic more apparent:

```
// Check if today is April 17th.
if ((current.getDate() == 17) && (current.getMonth() == 3)) {
  trace ("Happy Birthday, Bruce!");
}
```

Here we use the logical *OR* operator, ||, to test whether either condition is true:

```
// Check if it is a weekend.
if ((current.getDay() == 0) || (current.getDay() == 6) ) {
  trace ("Why are you working on a weekend?");
}
```

You can also use a logical *NOT* operator, !, to check if a condition is not true:

```
// Check to see if the name is not Bruce.
if (!(userName == "Bruce")) {
  trace ("This application knows only Bruce's birthday.");
}
```

The preceding example could be rewritten using the inequality operator, !=:

```
if (userName != "Bruce") {
  trace ("This application knows only Bruce's birthday.");
}
```

Any Boolean value, or an expression that converts to a Boolean, can be used as the test condition:

```
// Check to see if a sprite is visible. If so, display a
// message. This condition is shorthand for _sprite.visible == true
if (_sprite.visible) {
  trace("The sprite is visible.");
}
```

The logical *NOT* operator is often used to check if something is false instead of true:

```
// Check to see if a sprite is invisible (not visible). If so,
// display a message. This condition is shorthand for
// _sprite.visible != true or _sprite.visible == false.
if (!_sprite.visible) {
  trace("The sprite is invisible. Set it to visible before trying this action.");
}
```

The logical *NOT* operator is often used in compound conditions along with the logical *OR* operator:

```
// Check to see if the name is neither Bruce nor Joey. (This could
// also be rewritten using two inequality operators and a logical
// AND.)
if (!((userName == "Bruce") || (userName == "Joey"))) {
  trace ("Sorry, but only Bruce and Joey have access to this application.");
}
```

ActionScript doesn't bother to evaluate the second half of a logical *AND* statement unless the first half of the expression is true. If the first half is false, the overall expression is always false, so it would be inefficient to bother evaluating the second half. Likewise, ActionScript does not bother to evaluate the second half of a logical *OR* statement unless the first half of the expression is false. If the first half is true, the overall expression is always true.

1.11   Repeating an Operation Many Times

Problem

You want to perform some task multiple times within a single frame.

Solution

Use a looping statement to perform the same task multiple times within a single frame. For example, you can use a *for* statement:

```
for (var i:int = 0; i < 10; i++) {
  // Display the value of i.
  trace(i);
}
```

Discussion

When you want to execute the same action (or slight variations thereof) multiple times within a single frame, use a looping statement to make your code more succinct, easier to read, and easier to update. You can use either a *while* or a *for* statement for this purpose, but generally a *for* statement is a better choice. Both statements achieve the same result, but the *for* statement is more compact and more familiar to most programmers.

The syntax of a *for* statement consists of five basic parts:

The for *keyword*
> Every *for* statement must begin with a for keyword.

Initialization expression
> Loop typically employs an *index variable* (a *loop counter*) that is initialized when the statement is first encountered. The initialization is performed only once regardless of how many times the loop is repeated.

Test expression
> The loop should include a test expression that returns either true or false. The test expression is evaluated once each time through the loop. Generally, the test expression compares the index variable to another value, such as a maximum number of loop iterations. The overall expression must evaluate to true for the *for* statement's body to execute (contrast this with a *do...while* loop, which executes

at least once, even if the test expression is `false`). On the other hand, if the test expression never becomes `false`, you'll create an infinite loop, resulting in a warning that the Flash Player is running slowly.

Update expression

The update expression usually updates the value of the variable used in the test expression so that, at some point, the conditional test becomes `false` and the loop ends. The update expression is executed once each time through the loop. An infinite loop is often caused by failing to update the appropriate variable in the update expression (usually the same variable used in the test expression).

Statement body

The statement body is a block of substatements enclosed within curly braces that is executed each time through the loop. If the test expression is never `true`, the *for* statement's body isn't executed.

The for keyword should come first, and it should be followed by the initialization, test, and update expressions enclosed within parentheses. Semicolons must separate the three expressions from one another (although the initialization, test, and update statements are optional, the semicolons are mandatory). The remainder of the *for* loop is made up of the statement body enclosed in curly braces:

```
for (initialization; test; update) {
    statement body
}
```

Here is an example of a *for* statement that outputs the numbers from 0 to 999:

```
for (var i:int = 0; i < 1000; i++) {
    trace(i);
}
trace ("That's the end.");
```

To understand the *for* statement, you can follow along with the process the Action-Script interpreter uses to process the command. In the preceding example, the for keyword tells the interpreter to perform the statements within the *for* loop as long as the conditional expression is true. The process is as follows:

1. The initialization expression is executed only once, and it sets the variable i to 0.

2. Next, the interpreter checks the test expression (*i < 1000*). Because i is 0, which is less than 1,000, the expression evaluates to true and the *trace()* action within the *for* statement body is executed.

3. The ActionScript interpreter then executes the update statement, in this case i++, which increments i by 1.

4. The interpreter then repeats the process from the top of the loop (but skipping the initialization step). So the interpreter again checks whether the test expression is true and, if so, executes the statement body again. It then executes the update statement again.

This process repeats until the test expression is no longer true. The last value displayed in the Output window is 999 because once i is incremented to 1,000, the test expression no longer evaluates to true and the loop comes to an end. Once the loop terminates, execution continues with whatever commands follow the loop.

Both the initialization and update expressions can include multiple actions separated by commas. You should not, however, use the *var* keyword more than once in the initialization expression. The following example simultaneously increments i, decrements j, and displays their values in the Output window:

```
for (var i:int = 0, j:int = 10; i < 10; i++, j--) {
  trace("i is " + i);
  trace("j is " + j);
}
```

 The preceding example is not the same as two nested for statements (which is shown in the next code block.)

It is also common to use nested *for* statements. When you use a nested *for* statement, use a different index variable than that used in the outer *for* loop. By convention, the outermost *for* loop uses the variable i, and the nested *for* loop uses the variable j. For example:

```
for (var i:int = 1; i <= 3; i++) {
  for (var j:int = 1; j <= 2; j++) {
    trace(i + " X " + j + " = " + (i * j));
  }
}
```

The preceding example displays the following multiplication table in the Output window:

```
1 X 1 = 1
1 X 2 = 2
2 X 1 = 2
2 X 2 = 4
3 X 1 = 3
3 X 2 = 6
```

It is possible to nest multiple levels of *for* statements. By convention, each additional level of nesting uses the next alphabetical character as the index variable. Therefore, the third level of nested *for* statements typically use k as the index variable:

```
for (var i:int = 1; i <= 3; i++) {
  for (var j:int = 1; j <= 3; j++) {
    for (var k:int = 1; k <= 3; k++) {
      trace(i + " X " + j + " X " + k + " = " + (i * j * k));
    }
  }
}
```

Additionally, you can use *for* statements to loop backward or to update the variable in ways other than by simply adding or subtracting one:

```
// Count backward from 10 to 1.
for (var i:int = 10; i > 0; i--) {
  trace(i);
}

// Display a sequence of square roots.
for (var i:Number = 50000; i > 2; i = Math.sqrt(i)) {
  trace(i);
}
```

In this case, the variable i winds up holding values other than integers, so it is best to declare it as a *Number* rather than an *int*.

 You should not use a *for* statement to perform tasks over time.

Many programmers make the mistake of trying to use *for* statements to animate sprites; for example:

```
for (var i:int = 0; i < 20; i++) {
  _sprite.x += 10;
}
```

Whereas the preceding code moves the sprite 200 pixels to the right of its starting point, all the updates take place within the same frame. There are two problems with this. First, the Stage updates only once per frame, so only the last update is shown on the Stage (causing the sprite to jump 200 pixels suddenly rather than moving smoothly in 20 steps). Second, even if the Stage updates often, each iteration through the *for* loop takes only a few milliseconds, so the animation would happen too quickly. For actions that you want to take place over time, use the *enterFrame* event (see Recipe 1.5) or a timer (see Recipe 1.12).

Moreover, tight repeating loops should not be used to perform lengthy processes (anything that takes more than a fraction of a second). The Flash Player displays a warning whenever a single loop executes for more than 15 seconds. Using the other methods (just mentioned) avoids the warning message and allows Flash to perform other actions in addition to the repeated actions that are part of the loop.

See Also

Recipes 1.5 and 1.12. The *for* statement is used in many practical situations, and you can see examples in a great many of the recipes throughout this book. See Recipe 5.2 and Recipe 12.8 for some practical examples. Recipe 5.16 discusses *for...in* loops, which are used to enumerate the properties of an object or array.

1.12 Repeating a Task over Time

Problem

You want to perform some action or actions over time.

Solution

Use the *Timer* class. Alternatively, listen for the *enterFrame* event of a sprite.

Discussion

The *Timer* class is new to ActionScript 3.0, and is recommended over the earlier *setInterval()* and *setTimeout()* functions. When you create an instance of the *Timer* class, it fires *timer* events at regular intervals. You can specify the delay between events and how many times you want the events to fire in the *Timer* constructor:

```
var timer:Timer = new Timer(delay, repeatCount);
```

You use *addEventListener* to set up a method to handle these events. After you create the timer and set up a listener, use its *start()* method to start it and *stop()* to stop it.

The *Timer* class is part of the *flash.utils* package, and there is also a *TimerEvent* class in the *flash.events* package, so those need to be imported:

```
package {
    import flash.display.Sprite;
    import flash.events.TimerEvent;
    import flash.utils.Timer;

    public class ExampleApplication extends Sprite {
        // Declare and initialize a variable to store the value
        // of the previous timer reading.
        private var _PreviousTime:Number = 0;

        public function ExampleApplication() {
            var tTimer:Timer = new Timer(500, 10);
            tTimer.addEventListener(TimerEvent.TIMER, onTimer);
            tTimer.start();
        }

        private function onTimer(event:TimerEvent):void {
            // Output the difference between the current timer value and
            // its value from the last time the function was called.
            trace(flash.utils.getTimer() - _PreviousTime);
            _PreviousTime = flash.utils.getTimer();
        }
    }
}
```

The *getTimer()* function (previously a top-level function), has been moved to the *flash.utils* package as well. This simply returns the number of milliseconds since the application started.

In the preceding example, even though the interval is theoretically 500 milliseconds in practice its accuracy and granularity depend on computer playback performance in relation to other tasks demanded of the processor. There are two implications to this:

- Don't rely on timers to be extremely precise.
- Don't rely on timer intervals to be smaller than approximately 10 milliseconds.

If you want to emulate the functionality of the *setInterval()* function, set the repeat count to zero. This causes the timer event to fire indefinitely. In this case, the *stop()* method is analogous to the *clearInterval()* function, and stops the timer from firing further events.

Similarly, if you want to duplicate the *setTimeout()* function, set the repeat count to one. The timer waits the specified amount of time, fires one event, and ends.

One of the neat things you can do with the *Timer* class is create animations that are independent of the movie's frame rate. With a timer you can call a method at any interval you want. Here is an example in which two timers are set—one for a square sprite (every 50 milliseconds)—and one for a circle sprite (every 100 milliseconds):

```
package {
    import flash.display.Sprite;
    import flash.events.TimerEvent;
    import flash.utils.Timer;

    public class ExampleApplication extends Sprite {
        private var _square:Sprite;
        private var _circle:Sprite;


        public function ExampleApplication( ) {
            // Create the two sprites and draw their shapes
            _square = new Sprite( );
            _square.graphics.beginFill(0xff0000);
            _square.graphics.drawRect(0, 0, 100, 100);
            _square.graphics.endFill( );
            addChild(_square);
            _square.x = 100;
            _square.y = 50;

            _circle = new Sprite( );
            _circle.graphics.beginFill(0x0000ff);
            _circle.graphics.drawCircle(50, 50, 50);
            _circle.graphics.endFill( );
            addChild(_circle);
            _circle.x = 100;
            _circle.y = 200;
```

```
        // Create the two timers and start them
        var squareTimer:Timer = new Timer(50, 0);
        squareTimer.addEventListener(TimerEvent.TIMER, onSquareTimer);
        squareTimer.start( );

        var circleTimer:Timer = new Timer(100, 0);
        circleTimer.addEventListener(TimerEvent.TIMER, onCircleTimer);
        circleTimer.start( );
    }

    // Define the two handler methods
    private function onSquareTimer(event:TimerEvent):void {
        _square.x++;
    }

    private function onCircleTimer(event:TimerEvent):void {
        _circle.x++;
    }
    }
}
```

It is also possible to use the *enterFrame* event of a sprite to have some action (or actions) repeat over time. The *Timer* technique offers some advantages over the *enterFrame* event method, most notably that it allows you to create intervals that differ from the frame rate of the *.swf*. With *enterFrame*, the handling method is called at the frame rate.

With that said, there are still times when using *enterFrame* is appropriate. For example, you may want something to occur at the frame rate of the *.swf*. One such scenario is when you want to reverse the playback of the frames in a movie clip.

1.13 Creating Reusable Code

Problem

You want to perform a series of actions at various times without duplicating code unnecessarily throughout your movie.

Solution

Create a method and then call (i.e., invoke) it by name whenever you need to execute those actions. When a function is a member of a class, it is often called a *method*.

Here is how to create a *method* of a class:

```
accessModifier function functionName ( ):ReturnDataType {
    // Statements go here.
}
```

To *call* (i.e., execute) the named method, refer to it by name, such as:

```
functionName( );
```

Discussion

Grouping statements into a method allows you to define the method once but execute it as many times as you'd like. This is useful when you need to perform similar actions at various times without duplicating the same code in multiple places. Keeping your code centralized in methods makes it easier to understand (because you can write the method once and then ignore the details when using it) and easier to maintain (because you can make changes in one place rather than in multiple places).

Like class variables, methods can be declared with *access modifiers*. These determine which other classes are able to call the methods. The available access modifiers are:

private
: Can only be accessed from within the class itself.

protected
: Can be accessed by the class or any subclass. This is instance-based. In other words, an instance of a class can access its own protected members or those of its superclasses. It cannot access protected members on other instances of the same class.

internal
: Can be accessed by the class or any class within the same package.

public
: Can be accessed by any class.

The definition of private has changed since ActionScript 2.0, where it allowed access by subclasses. If you do not specify an access modifier explicitly, the method takes on the default internal access.

The following class defines a drawLine method and calls it 10 times, rather than repeating the three lines of drawing code for each line:

```
package {
    import flash.display.Sprite;

    public class ExampleApplication extends Sprite
    {
        public function ExampleApplication() {
            for(var i:int=0;i<10;i++) {
                drawLine();
            }
        }

        private function drawLine():void {
            graphics.lineStyle(1, Math.random() * 0xffffff, 1);
            graphics.moveTo(Math.random() * 400, Math.random() * 400);
            graphics.lineTo(Math.random() * 400, Math.random() * 400);
        }
    }
}
```

Another important method type is a *static* method. Static methods aren't available as a member of an instance of that class, but instead are called directly from the class itself. For example, in a class named `ExampleApplication`, you could define a static method as follows:

```
public static function showMessage( ):void {
    trace("Hello world");
}
```

You could then call that method like so:

```
ExampleApplication.showMessage( );
```

Some classes contain nothing but static methods. The *Math* class is an example. Note that you don't have to create a new *Math* object to use its methods; you simply call the methods as properties of the class itself, such as *Math.random()*, *Math.round()*, and so on.

1.14   Generalizing a Method to Enhance Reusability

Problem

You want to perform slight variations of an action without having to duplicate multiple lines of code to accommodate minor differences.

Solution

Add parameters to your method to make it flexible enough to perform slightly different actions when invoked rather than performing exactly the same action or producing the same result each time.

Define the parameters that account for the variability in what you want the method to do:

```
private function average (a:Number, b:Number, c:Number):void {
  trace("The average is " + (c + b + c)/3);
}
```

If you don't know the exact number of parameters the method will receive, use the built-in arguments array to handle a variable number of parameters.

Discussion

A method that doesn't accept parameters generally does exactly the same result each time it is invoked. However, you will often need to perform almost exactly the same actions as an existing method, but with minor variations. Duplicating the entire method and then making minor changes to the second version is a bad idea in most cases. Usually, it makes your code harder to maintain and understand. More importantly, you'll usually find that you need not only two variations but many variations of the method. It can be unnecessarily difficult to maintain five or six variations of what should ideally be wrapped into a single method. The trick is to create a single method that can accept different values to operate on.

For example, let's say you have an *average()* method for averaging a set of numbers. Instead of having it always average the same two numbers, you want to specify arbitrary values to be averaged each time it is invoked. This can be accomplished with parameters.

The most common way to work with parameters is to list them within the parentheses in the method declaration. The parameter names should be separated by commas, and when you invoke the method you should pass it a comma-delimited list of arguments that corresponds to the parameters it expects.

 The terms "parameters" and "arguments" are often used interchangeably to refer to the variables defined in the method declaration or the values that are passed to a method when it is invoked.

The following is a simple example of a method declaration using parameters:

```
// Define the function such that it expects two parameters: a and b.
private function average(a:Number, b:Number):Number {
  return (a + b)/2;
}
```

Now here's a method invocation in which arguments are passed during the method call:

```
// When you invoke the function, pass it two arguments, such as
// 5 and 11, which correspond to the a and b parameters.
var averageValue:Number = average(5, 11);
```

In most situations it is best to declare the parameters that the method should expect. However, there are some scenarios in which the number of parameters is unknown. For example, if you want the *average()* method to average any number of values, you can use the built-in arguments array that is available within any function's body. All the parameters that are passed to a function are automatically placed into that function's arguments array.

```
// There is no need to specify the parameters to accept when using the
// arguments array.
private function average():Number {
  var sum:Number = 0;

  // Loop through each of the elements of the arguments array, and
  // add that value to sum.
  for (var i:int = 0; i < arguments.length; i++) {
    sum += arguments[i];
  }
  // Then divide by the total number of arguments
  return sum/arguments.length;
}
```

```
// You can invoke average( ) with any number of parameters.
var average:Number = average (1, 2, 5, 10, 8, 20);
```

 Technically, arguments is an object with additional properties beyond that of a basic array. However, while arguments is a special kind of array, you can still work with it in the same ways that you would a regular array.

1.15 Exiting a Method

Problem

You want to exit a method.

Solution

Methods terminate automatically after the last statement within the method executes. Use a *return* statement to exit a method before reaching its end.

Discussion

The *return* statement exits the current method and the ActionScript interpreter continues execution of the code that initially invoked the method. Any statements within the method body that follow a *return* statement are ignored.

```
private function sampleFunction ( ):void {
  return;
  trace("Never called");
}
```

```
// Called from within another method:
sampleFunction( );
// Execution continues here after returning from the sampleFuction( ) invocation
```

In the preceding example, the *return* statement causes the method to terminate before performing any actions, so it isn't a very useful method. More commonly, you will use a *return* statement to exit a method under certain conditions. This example exits the method if the password is wrong:

```
private function checkPassword (password:String):void {

  // If password is not "SimonSays", exit the function.
  if (password != "SimonSays") {
    return;
  }

  // Otherwise, perform the rest of the actions.
  showForm ("TreasureMap");
}
```

```
// This method call uses the wrong password, so the
```

```
// function exits.
checkPassword("MotherMayI");

// This method call uses the correct password, so the function
// shows the TreasureMap form.
checkPassword("SimonSays");
```

In the preceding example, you may notice that the method is declared as void, yet it is possible to use a *return* statement within the method without getting a compiler error. When a *return* statement is used simply to exit from a method, it is valid within a method declared as void.

 In ActionScript 2.0, the function was Void. In ActionScript 3.0, it is lowercase void.

However, if you attempt to actually return a value in such a method, the compiler generates an error.

```
private function sampleMethod ():void {
  return "some value";  // This causes the compiler to generate an error.
}
```

1.16   Obtaining the Result of a Method

Problem

You want to perform some method and return the results to the statement that invoked the function.

Solution

Use a *return* statement that specifies the value to return.

Discussion

When used without any parameters, the *return* statement simply terminates a method. However, any value specified after the return keyword is returned to statement that invoked the method. Usually, the returned value is stored in a variable for later use. The datatype of the return value must match the return type of the method:

```
private function average (a:Number, b:Number):Number {
  return (a + b)/2;
}
```

Now we can call the *average( )* method and store the result in a variable and use the result in some way.

```
var playerScore:Number = average(6, 10);
trace("The player's average score is " + playerScore);
```

You can use the return value of a method, without storing it in a variable, by passing it as a parameter to another function, such as:

```
trace("The player's average score is " + average(6, 10));
```

Note, however, that if you do nothing with the return value of the function, the result is effectively lost. For example, this statement has no detectable benefit because the result is never displayed or used in any way:

```
average(6, 10);
```

1.17 Handling Errors

Problem

You want to programmatically detect when certain errors occur and handle them using code.

Solution

Use a *throw* statement to throw an error when it is detected. Place any potentially error-generating code within a *try* block, and then have one or more corresponding *catch* blocks to handle possible errors.

Description

Flash Player 8.5 supports a *try/catch* methodology for handling errors in Action-Script. That means you can write code that can intelligently deal with certain error types should they occur. While you cannot handle syntax errors (the *.swf* won't even compile in that case), you can handle most other error types, such as missing or invalid data. The benefit is that you can attempt to resolve the situation programmatically.

An example may help to illustrate when and how you might use *try/catch* methodology: Consider an application that draws a rectangle based on user-input dimensions. To draw a rectangle within the application, you want to have certain range limitations on the dimensions the user can input. For example, you may want to make sure the values are defined, valid numeric values greater than 1 and less than 200. While there are certainly ways you can work to ensure the quality and validity of the data before even attempting to draw the rectangle, you can also use *try/catch* methodology as a fail-safe. You can have Flash attempt to draw the rectangle, but if the dimension values are detected to be invalid or out of range, you can throw an error that can be handled programmatically. At that point you can do many things, from simply skipping the action, to substituting default data, to alerting the user to enter valid data.

There are two basic parts involved in working with errors in ActionScript: throwing the error and catching the error. There are several errors, which are thrown automatically by the player, such as *IllegalOperationError*, *MemoryError*, and *ScriptTimeoutError*.

These are in the *flash.errors* package. But you can also detect when an error has occurred and throw your own custom error. You can throw an error using the *throw* statement. The *throw* statement uses the *throw* keyword followed by a value or reference that should be thrown. Most frequently you should throw an *Error* object or an instance of an *Error* subclass. For example:

```
throw new Error("A general error occurred.");
```

As you can see, the *Error* constructor accepts one parameter, a message to associate with the error. The parameter is optional, and depending on how you are handling the errors, you may or may not choose to use it. However, in most cases it makes sense to specify an error message. It is possible, then, to log the error messages for debugging purposes.

Once an error has been thrown, Flash halts the current process and looks for a *catch* block to handle the error. This is where the *try* and *catch* blocks come into play. Any code that could potentially throw an error should be enclosed in a *try* block. Then, if an error is thrown, only the code in the *try* block is halted, and the associated *catch* block is called. The following is the simplest scenario:

```
try {
  trace("This code is about to throw an error.");
  throw new Error("A general error occurred.");
  trace("This line won't run");
}
catch (errObject:Error) {
  trace("The catch block has been called.");
  trace("The message is: " + errObject.message);
}
```

The preceding code produces the following in the Output panel:

```
This code is about to throw an error.
The catch block has been called.
The message is: A general error occurred.
```

Of course, the preceding example is overly simplistic, and you wouldn't realistically use code in an actual application, but it does illustrate the basic process. You can see that as soon as the error is thrown, the *try* block is exited, and the *catch* block is run and passed a reference to the *Error* object that was thrown.

Much more frequently, the error is thrown from within a function or method. Then Flash looks to see if the *throw* statement within the function is contained within a *try* block. If so, it calls the associated *catch* block as you've seen already. However, if the *throw* statement in the function is not within a *try* block, Flash exits the function and next looks to see if the function call was made within a *try* block. If so, it halts the code in the *try* block and runs the associated *catch* block. Again, a very simple example:

```
private function displayMessage(message:String):void {
  if(message == undefined) {
    throw new Error("No message was defined.");
  }
```

```
    trace(message);
  }

  try {
    trace("This code is about to throw an error.");
    displayMessage( );
    trace("This line won't run");
  }
  catch (errObject:Error) {
    trace("The catch block has been called.");
    trace("The message is: " + errObject.message);
  }
```

In the preceding example the Output panel would display the following:

```
This code is about to throw an error.
The catch block has been called.
The message is: No message was defined.
```

As you can see from the output, the code works very similarly to the way in which the previous example worked, except the throw statement is hidden within a function instead of being called directly within the *try* block. The advantage is that you can start to then create functions and methods that are intelligent enough to know if and when to throw errors. You can then simply use those functions and methods within *try* blocks, and you can handle any errors should they occur.

The following code illustrates a more realistic example:

```
// Define a function that draws a rectangle within a specified sprite
private function drawRectangle(sprite:Sprite, newWidth:Number, newHeight:Number):void
{

  // Check to see if either of the specified dimensions are not
  // a number. If so, then thrown an error.
  if(isNaN(newWidth) || isNaN(newHeight)) {
    throw new Error("Invalid dimensions specified.");
  }

  // If no error was thrown, then draw the rectangle.
  sprite.graphics.lineStyle(1, 0, 1);
  sprite.graphics.lineTo(nWidth, 0);
  sprite.graphics.lineTo(nWidth, nHeight);
  sprite.graphics.lineTo(0, nHeight);
  sprite.graphics.lineTo(0, 0);
}
```

Now we can call the *drawRectangle()* method using a *try/catch* statement.

```
try {

  // Attempt to draw two rectangles within the current sprite.
  // In this example it is assumed that the variables for the dimensions
  // are retreiving values from user input, a database, an XML file,
  // or some other datasource.
  drawRectangle(this, widthA, heightA);
```

```
    drawRectangle(this, widthB, heightB);
}
catch(errObject:Error) {

    // If an error occurs, clear any rectangles that were drawn from
    // the sprite. Then display a message to the user.
    this.graphics.clear();
    tOutput.text = "An error occurred: " + errObject.message;
}
```

In addition to the *try* and *catch* blocks, you can also specify a *finally* block. The *finally* block contains code that is called regardless of whether an error was thrown. In many cases the *finally* block may not be necessary. For example, the following two examples do the same thing:

```
//Without using finally:
private function displayMessage(message:String):void {
    try {
      if(message == undefined) {
        throw new Error("The message is undefined.");
      }
      trace(message);
    }
    catch (errObject:Error) {
      trace(errObject.message);
    }
    trace("This is the last line displayed.");
}
//With finally:
private function displayMessage(message:String):void {
    try {
      if(message == undefined) {
        throw new Error("The message is undefined.");
      }
      trace(message);
    }
    catch (errObject:Error) {
      trace(errObject.message);
    }
    finally {
      trace("This is the last line displayed.");
    }
}
```

However, the *finally* block runs no matter what occurs within the *try* and *catch* blocks, including a *return* statement. So the following two functions are not the equivalent:

```
//Without using finally:
private function displayMessage(message:String):void {
    try {
      if(message == undefined) {
        throw new Error("The message is undefined.");
      }
```

```
      trace(message);
    }
    catch (errObject:Error) {
      trace(errObject.message);
      return;
    }
    // This line won't run if an error is caught.
    trace("This is the last line displayed.");
  }
  //With finally:
  private function displayMessage(message:String):void {
    try {
      if(message == undefined) {
        throw new Error("The message is undefined.");
      }
      trace(message);
    }
    catch (errObject:Error) {
      trace(errObject.message);
      return;
    }
    finally {
      // This runs, even if an error is caught.
      trace("This is the last line displayed.");
    }
  }
}
```

You can create much more complex error handling systems than what is shown in this recipe. Throughout this book you will find examples of more complex error handling in appropriate contexts.

## CHAPTER 2

Custom Classes

2.0   Introduction

Classes are absolutely essential to ActionScript 3.0. This is truer in ActionScript 3.0 than in any earlier release of the language. ActionScript 1.0 was essentially a procedural language with modest object-oriented features. ActionScript 2.0 formalized the object-oriented features and took a big step in the direction of a truly object-oriented language. However, ActionScript 3.0 shifts the core focus of ActionScript so that the basic building block is that of the class. If you are using ActionScript 3.0 with Flex, and the introduction of the minor exception of code being placed within <mx:Script> tags, all ActionScript code must appear within a class. This chapter discusses the fundamentals of writing custom classes in ActionScript 3.0.

2.1   Creating a Custom Class

Problem

You want to write a custom class.

Solution

Save a new file with the *.as* file extension and the filename matching the name of the class. Then add the class definition to the file with the following structure:

```
package package {
    public class Class {

    }
}
```

Discussion

As noted earlier, the class is the basic building block of all ActionScript 3.0-based applications, so it's essential that you master the basics of writing a class. For starters, all classes must be placed in *.as* files, which are plain text files saved with an *.as* file extension. There can be only one public class definition per *.as* file, and the name of the file must be the same as the name of the class. For example, if you name a class *Example* then the definition must be saved in a file called *Example.as*.

In ActionScript 3.0 all classes must be placed in packages. A package is a way of organizing classes into groups, and in ActionScript 3.0 a package is synonymous with a directory on the filesystem. Packages are relative to the classpath (which is discussed in detail in Recipe 2.2), but for this initial discussion the classpath is defined as a path relative to the project (the *.fla* file, in the case of Flash or the main class or MXML document in the case of Flex). Therefore, the top-level package is synonymous with the project's root. The package declaration is always the first thing that appears in a class file; an example syntax follows:

```
package name {

}
```

When the class is defined as part of the top-level package, the package name doesn't need to be specified. In those cases, the package declaration is as follows:

```
package {

}
```

When the class file is saved within a subdirectory, the package name corresponds to the relative path of the subdirectory using dots (.) between each directory. For example, if a file is saved in a subdirectory (relative to the project root) called *example*, then the package declaration is as follows:

```
package example {

}
```

If the class file is saved in a subdirectory of *example* called *subpackage*, the package declaration is as follows:

```
package example.subpackage {

}
```

Packages are an important part of working with classes because they allow you to ensure that your classes won't conflict with any other classes. For example, it's entirely possible that two developers might write two different classes and name them *MessageManager*. The two classes could have the same name but be responsible for very different tasks. One might manage emails while the other manages binary socket messages. You cannot have two classes with the same name in the same scope. If you did, the compiler wouldn't know which one to use. One option is to always use unique class names.

In this example, you could name the classes *EmailManager* and *BinarySocket-MessageManager*, but there are good reasons why that isn't always possible or preferable. Since a project could use potentially hundreds of classes, it would be very difficult to ensure all the classes have unique names. Furthermore, many projects may rely on preexisting libraries of code, and you may not have written many of the classes. Because many classes in a library might have dependencies on other classes, it would be very difficult to change the names of classes. This is where packages make things much simpler. Even though you cannot have two classes with the same name within the same directory, you can have as many classes with the same name as you want, so long as they are within different directories. Packages allow you to place one *MessageManager* in the *net.messaging.email* package and one in the *net.messaging.binarysocket* package.

Although the preceding package names may initially seem like good choices, it's possible to use better package names to ensure a higher probability of uniqueness. It's generally better to use package names that correspond to the owner and/or relevant project. By convention, package names start with reverse order domain names. For example, if Example Corp (*examplecorp.com*) writes ActionScript 3.0 classes, they would place all classes in the *com.examplecorp* package (or a subpackage of *com.examplecorp*). That way, if another Example Corp from the U.K. (*examplecorp.co.uk*) also writes ActionScript 3.0 classes, they can ensure uniqueness by using the package *uk.co.examplecorp*.

 The exception to this guideline is when the classes are part of a product or library that transcends company/organization boundaries. For example, all the native Flash Player classes are in the Flash package (for example, *flash.net.URLRequest*) and all the classes in the *ActionScript 3.0 Cookbook* library are in the *ascb* package (see *http://www.rightactionscript.com/ascb*).

When classes are part of a common library used by many projects within a company/organization then they can be placed in subpackages directly within the main package. For example, if the aforementioned *MessageManager* classes are part of a common library used by many Example Corp applications then they could be placed in the *com.examplecorp.net.messaging.email* and *com.examplecorp.net.messaging.binarysocket* packages. When a class is part of a specific application, it should be placed within a subpackage specific to that application. For example, Example Corp might have an application called *WidgetStore*. If the *WidgetStore* application uses a class called *ApplicationManager*, then it ought to be placed within *com.examplecorp.widgetstore* or a subpackage of that package.

By convention, package names start with lowercase characters.

The next step is to declare the class itself, as follows:

```
public class Name {

}
```

The name of a class starts with a capital letter by convention. The name of a class must follow the same naming rules as variables and functions (consists of letters, numbers, and underscores, and cannot start with a number). The class declaration appears within the package declaration. The following code defines a class called *Example* within the top-level package:

```
package {
    public class Example {

    }
}
```

The class body appears within the class declaration's curly braces, and it consists of properties and methods. Properties are variables associated with the class, and you declare them much as you would declare variables by using the *var* keyword. However, properties also must be modified by attributes, which determine the scope of the property. The following is a list of the attributes you can use with properties:

private
   Properties are private when they're accessible only within the class.

public
   Properties are public when they're accessible within the class as well as from instances of the class (or directly from the class reference when declared as static).

protected
   Properties are protected when they're accessible only within the class and to subclasses.

internal
   Properties are internal when they're accessible within the package.

The default state of a property is internal unless you specify a different attribute. In most cases, properties should be declared as either private or protected. By convention, it's helpful to start private and protected property names with an underscore (_). The following declares a new private property called _id within the *Example* class:

```
package {
    public class Example {
        private var _id:String;
    }
}
```

Methods are essentially functions associated with a class, and you can declare a method much like you would declare a function using the `function` keyword. However, as with properties, all methods must belong to a namespace defined by one of the attributes from the previous list. The `public`, `private`, `protected`, and `internal` attributes work identically for methods and properties. Methods should be declared `public` only when they need to be called from instances of the class (or from the class itself when declared as static). If the method is designed to be called only from within the class, then it should be declared as `private` or `protected`. A method should be protected only when you want to be able to reference it from a subclass. The following declares a method called *getId( )*:

```
package {
    public class Example {
        private var _id:String;
        public function getId( ):String {
            return _id;
        }
    }
}
```

Method names are subject to the same rules as variables and properties. That means that method names must contain only numbers, letters, underscores, and dollar signs. Additionally, while method names can contain numbers, they cannot begin with numbers. By convention, method names start with lowercase characters. There is one exception to that guideline, however. Every class can have a special method with the same name as the class itself. This special method is called the *constructor*, and as the name implies, you can use the function to construct new instances of the class. In ActionScript 3.0, all constructors must be `public` (this is a change from ActionScript 2.0). Unlike standard methods, constructors cannot return values, and they must not declare a return type. The following declares a constructor method for the *Example* class:

```
package {
    public class Example {
        private var _id:String;
        public function Example( ) {
            _id = "Example Class";
        }
        public function getId( ):String {
            return _id;
        }
    }
}
```

The following illustrates how to construct an instance of the *Example* class:

```
var example:Example = new Example( );
trace(example.getId( )); // Displays: Example Class
```

See Also

Recipe 2.2

2.2 Determining Where to Save a Class

Problem

You want to determine where to save a class file.

Solution

Save the file in a directory path corresponding to the package. Then, if necessary, add the top-level directory to the classpath.

Discussion

Class files must always be saved in a directory path that corresponds to the class package. For example, *com.examplecorp.net.messaging.email.MessageManager* must be saved in *com/examplecorp/net/messaging/email/MessageManager.as*. The compiler knows to look for classes where the path corresponds to the package. However, the compiler also must know where to look for the top-level directory containing the subdirectories. In the example, the compiler needs to know where the *com* directory is on the system. The compiler knows where to look because of something called the *classpath*. The default classpath for any Flex or Flash project includes the project directory. For example, if the *com* directory is saved in the same directory as the *.fla* file (Flash) or the main MXML or ActionScript file (Flex), then the compiler will find the classes. However, you may want to save files in a different directory. For example, if you have a common library used by many projects, you may want to save that library in one location rather than making copies for each project. You can add to and edit the classpath so the compiler knows where to look for all your custom classes.

For Flash, you can edit the classpath either at the project level or globally. At the project level, select File → Publish Settings, and select the ActionScript Settings button in the Flash tab. For the global classpath, select Edit → Preferences, and click the ActionScript Settings button. Both open a similar dialog that allows you to edit the classpath. You can click the + button to add a new directory to the classpath. For example, if the *com* directory for a common library is stored in *C:\libraries,* then you would add *C:\libraries* to the classpath.

For Flex, you can only set the classpath for a project. Using Flex Builder, right-click a project in the project navigator, select Properties, and then select Flex/ActionScript Build Path from the left menu. In the Source Path tab, you can add to and edit the classpath. If you're using the SDK rather than Flex Builder, you have to set the classpath when you're compiling your project. Using *mxmlc* (the command-line compiler included in the Flex SDK), you can add a *-source-path* option, followed by a list of classpath directories, as shown here:

```
mxmlc -source-path . C:\libraries ExampleApplication.as
```

See Also

Recipe 2.1

2.3   Creating Properties That Behave As Methods

Problem

You want to use public properties that behave like methods so you don't break encapsulation.

Solution

Use implicit getters and setters.

Discussion

As mentioned in Recipe 2.1, all properties should be declared as private or protected. public properties are not a good idea because of a principal called *encapsulation*. Good encapsulation is something to strive for. It means that a class doesn't expose its internals in a way that it can be easily broken; public properties can enable developers to easily break a class or an instance of a class. Consider the following simple example that uses a public property:

```
package {
    public class Counter {
        public var count:uint;
        public function Counter() {
            count = 0;
        }
    }
}
```

You can then construct an instance of *Counter*, and you can change the count property value, as shown here:

```
var counter:Counter = new Counter( );
counter.count++;
```

However, what if the business rules of the application state that a *Counter* should never exceed 100? You can see that the *Counter* class with a public count property makes it quite easy to break that rule.

One option is to use explicit getters and setters, as in the following example:

```
package {
    public class Counter {
```

```
        private var _count:uint;
        public function Counter() {
            _count = 0;
        }
        public function getCount():uint {
            return _count;
        }
        public function setCount(value:uint):void {
            if(value < 100) {
                _count = value;
            }
            else {
                throw Error();
            }
        }
    }
}
```

Another option is to use implicit getters and setters. Implicit getters and setters are declared as methods, but they look like properties. The syntax for a getter is as follows:

```
public function get name():Datatype {

}
```

The syntax for a setter is as follows:

```
public function set name(value:Datatype):void {

}
```

The following defines count with implicit getter and setter methods:

```
package {
    public class Counter {
        private var _count:uint;
        public function Counter() {
            _count = 0;
        }
        public function get count():uint {
            return _count;
        }
        public function set count(value:uint):void {
            if(value < 100) {
                _count = value;
            }
            else {
                throw Error();
            }
        }
    }
}
```

You can then treat count as though it were a public property:

```
counter.count = 5;
trace(counter.count);
```

See Also

Recipe 2.1

2.4 Creating Static Methods and Properties

Problem

You want to create methods and properties that are directly accessible from the class rather than from instances of the class.

Solution

Use the `static` attribute when declaring the property or method.

Discussion

By default, properties and methods are instance properties and methods, which means they are defined for each instance of the class. If the *Example* class defines a _id property and a *getId()* method then, by default, each instance of *Example* has its own _id property and *getId()* method. However, there are cases in which you want the property or method to be associated with the class itself rather than with instances of the class. That means that no matter how many instances of the class there may be, there is just one property or method. Such properties and methods are called *static properties and methods*.

There are examples of static properties and methods in several of the intrinsic Flash Player classes. For example, the *Math* class defines a *round()* method. The *round()* method is static and is, therefore, accessible directly from the class:

```
trace(Math.round(1.2345));
```

The *Math* class consists entirely of static methods and constants. However, a class can have both static and instance methods and/or properties. For example, the *String* class consists primarily of instance properties and methods. However, the *fromCharCode()* method is declared as static. The *fromCharCode()* method returns a string based on the character codes passed to the method. Since the method isn't associated with any one *String* instance, it does not make sense to make the method an instance method. However, it does make sense to declare the method as a static method.

You can declare a property or method as static using the static attribute. The static attribute is always used in combination with the `public`, `private`, `protected`, or `internal` attribute.

For example, the following declares a private static property called _example:

```
static private var _example:String;
```

The order in which the attributes appear doesn't matter. For example, `static private` is the equivalent to `private static`.

One common and important use of static properties and methods is the Singleton design pattern, whereby a class has a single managed instance. Singleton classes have a private static property that stores the one instance of the class as well as a public static method that allows access to the one instance.

See Also

Recipe 2.1

2.5   Creating Subclasses

Problem

You want to create a class that inherits from an existing class.

Solution

Write a subclass using the extends keyword.

Discussion

There are cases when a new class is a more specific version of an existing class. The new class may feature much of the same behavior as the existing class. Rather than rewriting all the common functionality you can define the new class so it inherits all the functionality of the existing class. In relation to one another, the new class is then called a *subclass* and the existing class is called a *superclass*.

You can define inheritance between classes in the subclass declaration using the extends keyword, as follows:

```
public class Subclass extends Superclass
```

A subclass can reference any public or protected properties and methods of the superclass. private properties and methods are not accessible outside the class, not even to a subclass.

Inheritance is a powerful technique; however, as with anything else, it is important that you use inheritance correctly. Before writing a subclass you need to determine whether or not the new class actually has a subclass relationship with the existing class. There are two basic types of relationships that classes can have: inheritance and composition. You can usually quickly determine the correct relationship between classes by asking whether it's an "is a" relationship or a "has a" relationship:

- "Is a" relationships are often inheritance relationships. As an example, consider an application that manages a library's collection.

- "Has a" relationships are composition relationships in which a class declares a property. Most classes use composition. Oftentimes composition can be implemented in such a way that it achieves the same results as inheritance with greater flexibility (yet generally requiring more code). For example, a book is not an author, but it has an author (or authors).

The library has different types of items in the collection including books and DVDs. Obviously books and DVDs have different types of data associated with them. Books have page counts and authors, while DVDs might have running times, actors, directors, etc. However, you also want to associate certain common types of data with both books and DVDs. For example, all library items might have Dewey decimal classifications as well as unique identification numbers assigned by the library. And every sort of library item has a title or name. In such a case, it can be advantageous to define a class that generalizes the commonality of all library items:

```
package org.examplelibrary.collection {
    public class LibraryItem {
        protected var _ddc:String;
        protected var _id:String;
        protected var _name:String;

        public function LibraryItem() {}

        public function setDdc(value:String):void {
            _ddc = value;
        }
        public function getDdc():String {
            return _ddc;
        }

        public function setId(value:String):void {
            _id = value;
        }
        public function getId():String {
            return _id;
        }

        public function setName(value:String):void {
            _name = value;
        }
        public function getName():String {
            return _name;
        }
    }
}
```

Then you can say that books and DVDs are both types of *LibraryItem*. It would then be appropriate to define a *Book* class and a *DVD* class that are subclasses of *LibraryItem*. The *Book* class might look like the following:

```
package org.examplelibrary.collection {
    import org.examplelibrary.collection.LibraryItem;
    public class Book extends LibraryItem {
        private var _authors:Array;
        private var _pageCount:uint;
```

```
        public function Book( ) {}

        public function setAuthors(value:Array):void {
            _authors = value;
        }
        public function getAuthors( ):Array {
            return _authors;
        }

        public function setPageCount(value:uint):void {
            _pageCount = value;
        }
        public function getPageCount( ):uint {
            return _pageCount;
        }
    }
}
```

The "Is a" and "Has a" test is helpful, but not always definitive in determining the relationship between classes. Often composition can be used even when inheritance would be acceptable and appropriate. In such cases the developer might opt for composition because it offers an advantage or flexibility not provided by inheritance. Furthermore, there are times when a class may appear to pass the "Is a" test yet inheritance would not be the correct relationship. For example, the library application might allow users to have accounts, and to represent the user, you would define a *User* class. The application might differentiate between types of users; for example, administrator and standard users. You could define *Administrator* and *StandardUser* classes. In such a case, the classes would appear to pass the "Is a" test in relation to *User*. It would seem to make sense that an *Administrator* is a *User*. However, if you consider the context an *Administrator* isn't actually a *User*, but more appropriately an *Administrator* is a role for a *User*. If possible, it would be better to define *User* so it has a role of type *Administrator* or *StandardUser*.

By default it's possible to extend any class. However you may want to ensure that certain classes are never subclassed. For this reason you can add the final attribute to the class declaration, as follows:

```
final public class Example
```

2.6   Implementing Subclass Versions of Superclass Methods

Problem

You want to implement a method in a subclass differently than how it was implemented in the superclass.

Solution

The superclass method must be declared as public or protected. Use the override attribute when declaring the subclass implementation.

Discussion

Often a subclass inherits all superclass methods directly without making any changes to the implementations. In those cases, the method is not redeclared in the subclass. However, there are cases in which a subclass implements a method differently than the superclass. When that occurs, you must override the method. To do that, the method must be declared as public or protected in the superclass. You can then declare the method in the subclass using the override attribute. As an example, you'll first define a class, *Superclass*:

```
package {
    public class Superclass {
        public function Superclass() {}
        public function toString():String {
            return "Superclass.toString()";
        }
    }
}
```

Next, define *Subclass* so it inherits from *Superclass*:

```
package {
    public class Subclass extends Superclass {
        public function Subclass() {}
    }
}
```

By default, *Subclass* inherits the *toString()* method as it's implemented in *Superclass*:

```
var example:Subclass = new Subclass();
trace(example.toString()); // Displays: Superclass.toString()
```

If you want the *toString()* method of *Subclass* to return a different value, you'll need to override it in the subclass, as follows:

```
package {
    public class Subclass extends Superclass {
        public function Subclass() {}
        override public function toString():String {
            return "Subclass.toString()";
        }
    }
}
```

When overriding a method, it must have exactly the same signature as the superclass. That means the number and type of parameters and the return type of the subclass override must be exactly the same as the superclass. If they aren't identical, the compiler throws an error.

Sometimes when you override a method you want the subclass implementation to be entirely different from the superclass implementation. However, sometimes you simply want to add to the superclass implementation. In such cases, you can call the superclass implementation from the subclass implementation using the super keyword to reference the superclass:

```
super.methodName( );
```

See Also

Recipe 2.5

2.7   Creating Constants

Problem

You want to declare a constant.

Solution

Declare it just like you would declare a property, except use the const keyword in place of var.

Discussion

As the name *constant* implies, constant values do not change. Constants are useful when you have complex values that you want to be able to reference by a simple identifier or when you want to be able to use compile-time error checking for values. Math.PI is an example of a constant that contains a complex value (which is the value of pi, or 3.14159). MouseEvent.MOUSE_UP, which contains the value mouseUp, is an example of a constant that allows you to use error-checking. When you add an event listener for the mouse up event, you can use the string value mouseUp. However, if you accidentally have a typo, you won't be notified of an error, and your code won't work as expected:

```
// This is valid code, but because of the typo (mousUp instead of mouseUp) the
// code won't work as expected.
addEventListener("mousUp", onMouseUp);
```

Using a constant helps. If you accidentally misspell the constant, you will receive a compile error that helps you track down the error:

```
// This causes a compile error.
addEventListener(MouseEvent.MOUS_UP, onMouseUp);
```

The syntax for declaring a constant is very similar to that for declaring a standard property. However, rather than using the var keyword you use the const keyword. Although not required, the majority of constants also happen to be public and static.

If you want a constant to be public and static, you must use the correct attributes. Additionally, you must assign a value for a constant when declaring it:

```
static public const EXAMPLE:String = "example";
```

By convention, constant names are all in uppercase. This convention makes it easy to identify and differentiate constants from properties.

See Also

Recipe 2.4

2.8 Dispatching Events

Problem

You want to dispatch events.

Solution

Extend *flash.events.EventDispatcher* and call the *dispatchEvent()* method.

Discussion

Events are an important way for objects to communicate. They are essential for creating flexible systems. Flash Player 9, for example, has a built-in event dispatching mechanism in the *flash.events.EventDispatcher* class. All classes that dispatch events inherit from *EventDispatcher* (e.g., *NetStream* and *Sprite*). If you want to define a class that dispatches events, you can extend *EventDispatcher*, as follows:

```
package {
    import flash.events.EventDispatcher;
    public class Example extends EventDispatcher {

    }
}
```

The *EventDispatcher* class has public methods called *addEventListener()* and *removeEventListener()* that you can call from any instance of an *EventDispatcher* subclass to register event listeners. *EventDispatcher* also defines a protected method called *dispatchEvent()*, which you can call from within a subclass to dispatch an event. The *dispatchEvent()* method requires at least one parameter as a *flash.events. Event* object or a subclass of *Event*.

CHAPTER 3
Runtime Environment

3.0   Introduction

Flash Player 9 offers a relatively large amount of information about and control over the runtime environment. The *flash.system.Capabilities* class has many static methods that return information about the player and the computer on which it is running, such as the operating system, language, audio, and video capabilities. There are other classes such as *flash.display.Stage* and *flash.system.Security* that allow you to control other elements of the Player such as the right-click menu under Windows (Control-click on the Macintosh) and the Settings dialog box. The *flash.display.Stage* class also controls the scaling and alignment of the movie within the Player.

Perhaps one of the most significant updates to Flash Player 7 within this chapter's subject matter is the ability to work with the context menu with more detail and precision than was allowed in previous versions of the player. In Flash Player 7, using the *ContextMenu* class, you can programmatically remove items from the context menu, and perhaps more importantly, you can add items to the menu. And as the name suggests, you can make the context menu so it is actually contextual, so that items in the menu are based on the object on which the menu is being displayed.

3.1   Detecting the Player Version

Problem

You want to ensure that the user has the correct version of the Flash Player.

Solution

Use the Flash Player Detection Kit, available on Adobe's web site to check the version of player and, if necessary, initiate a player upgrade (*http://www.adobe.com/ software/flashplayer/download/detection_kit*).

Discussion

Detecting the currently installed version of the Flash Player in the user's browser has been a problem for years, and there have been many solutions used by various developers. They generally fall into three categories:

- Browser-based script detection
- Server-side detection
- ActionScript detection

The first method uses JavaScript or VBScript to detect the version of the Flash Player the user has installed. Many of these scripts were prone to errors due to differences in platforms and browser types.

Server-side detection can be difficult if you don't have the ability to create server-side scripts.

Most ActionScript-based player detection techniques won't work directly in an ActionScript 3.0-based *.swf*. While ActionScript 1.0 and 2.0 had various object methods, variables, and functions that would return the player version, none of those are now valid in an ActionScript 3.0 class. ActionScript 3.0 has its own way of detecting the player version—the *flash.system.Capabilities.version* property. This, of course, won't work at all with any version of the Flash Player prior to 8.5, so it is rather useless for Flash detection.

Adobe has researched all of these issues thoroughly, and came out with a Flash Player Detection Kit that guides you through the recommended procedures for best detecting the player version.

The kit includes documentation on the various issues and potential solutions, including sample VBScript and JavaScript for browser-based detection; *.flas*, *.as*, and *.swf* files for ActionScript detection; as well as ColdFusion and PHP scripts for server-side detection.

ActionScript-based detection works successfully as long as the user has any version of the Flash Player from Version 4 on up. Basically, it is a Flash 4 *.swf* that executes a script to detect the current player version; all you need to do is set your minimum content version as a variable in the script. If the player version is at least as high as the content version, it loads the specified content. If not, it redirects the browser to an alternate content page. This page can contain a lower version *.swf*, a non-Flash version of the content, or a notice instructing the user to upgrade his Flash Player, with a link to the player install page on Adobe's site.

Furthermore, the kit contains a *.swf* and HTML template that initializes an Express Install of the latest version of the Flash Player. If the user's player is not adequate, the browser is redirected to this *.swf*, which downloads the latest version of the Flash Player from Adobe's site, automatically installs it, and finally redirects the user back to the specified Flash content, all without the user ever leaving your site. This option requires that the user already have Version 6.0.65.0 of the Flash Player installed.

Using a combination of the techniques included in the Flash Player Detection Kit gives you very precise control over the Flash Player version and the content you deliver to your viewers.

For testing purposes, older versions of the Flash Player can be obtained from Macromedia's site (*http://www.adobe.com/cfusion/knowledgebase/index.cfm?id=tn_14266*).

3.2   Detecting the Operating System

Problem

You want to know the operating system under which the Flash movie is being played, perhaps to indicate which operating systems are not supported or to implement a platform-specific feature.

Solution

Use the `flash.system.Capabilities.os` property.

Discussion

In ActionScript 3.0, you can use the `flash.system.Capabilities.os` property, which returns a string indicating the operating system and version name. Possible values include Windows XP, Windows 2000, Windows NT, Windows 98/Me, Windows 95, and Windows CE. On the Macintosh, the string includes the version number, such as Mac OS 9.2.1 or Mac OS X 10.4.4.

You can make design choices based on the operating system. For example, your movie might load different assets depending on the user's operating system. Or, you may simply want to record the operating systems of the users who view your movies for statistical analysis.

If all you care about is the general platform type, instead of the specific version, you can check just the first three letters of the string as follows:

```
var os:String = System.capabilities.os.substr(0, 3);
if (os == "Win") {
    // Windows-specific code goes here
} else if (os == "Mac") {
    // Mac-specific code goes here
} else {
    // Must be Unix or Linux
}
```

3.3   Checking the Player Type

Problem

You want to know what type of Flash Player the *.swf* is being run from.

Solution

Use the `flash.system.Capabilities.playerType` property.

Discussion

The different types of Flash Player include:

- Browser plug-in that runs in web browsers such as Mozilla or Firefox
- ActiveX Control used by Internet Explorer
- Standalone player, which plays *.swfs* outside of the browser
- External player, which is the player integrated in the Flash IDE

There are instances when you need to know which player the *.swf* is currently being run in. For example, if you are doing any type of integration with browser scripts (e.g., JavaScript, VBScript), it may be important to know whether the application is being run in Internet Explorer or some other type of browser, as these browsers can have different behaviors when running scripts. Indeed, it would be vital to know that the *.swf* was being run in a standalone player, since JavaScript, etc., would not be available at all in such a case.

To check the player type, look at the value of `flash.system.Capabilities.playerType`. Possible values are `PlugIn`, `ActiveX`, `StandAlone`, and `External`. You could use this in an *if* statement:

```
if(flash.system.Capabilities.playerType == "Plugin") {
  // do actions for Mozilla, etc. browsers
}
else if(flash.system.Capabilities.playerType == "ActiveX") {
  // do actions for IE
}
else {
  // do actions for no browser
}
```

3.4   Checking the System Language

Problem

You want to know what language is used on the computer viewing the movie and how the user will input text.

Solution

Use the `flash.system.Capabilities.language` property and the `flash.system.IME` class.

Discussion

You can use the `flash.system.Capabilities.language` property to determine the language that is used on the computer on which the movie is being played. The property returns a two-letter ISO-639-1 language code (e.g., "fr" for French). Where applicable, a two-letter country code is appended, separated from the country code with a hyphen (e.g., "zh-CN" for Simplified Chinese and "zh-TW" for Traditional Chinese).

 For a summary of language codes, see *http://lcweb.loc.gov/standards/iso639-2/englangn.html* and *http://www.iso.org/iso/en/prods-services/iso3166ma/02iso-3166-code-lists/list-en1.html*.

Here is an example of how to use the `language` property:

```
// Example output: en-US
trace(flash.system.Capabilities.language);
```

You can use this property to dynamically load content in the appropriate language:

```
// Create an associative array with language codes for the keys
// and greetings for the values.
var greetings:Array = new Array();
greetings["en"] = "Hello";
greetings["es"] = "Hola";
greetings["fr"] = "Bonjour";

// Extract the first two characters from the language code.
var lang:String = flash.system.Capabilities.language.substr(0, 2);

// Use a default language if the language is not in the list
if (greetings[lang] == undefined) {
  lang = "en";
}

// Display the greeting in the appropriate language.
trace(greetings[lang]);
```

When you want to offer multiple language capabilities in your movies, you can choose from several different approaches. One, as shown in the preceding code, is to create associative arrays for all the text that appears in the movie. Another approach is to create static content in multiple movies (one for each language) and to load those movies based on the language code. With this technique, each *.swf* filename should include the language code, such as *myMovie_en.swf*, *myMovie_es.swf*, *myMovie_fr.swf*, etc.

```
// Get the language from the capabilities object.
var lang:String = System.capabilities.language.substr(0, 2);
```

```
// Create an array of the languages you are supporting (i.e.,
// the languages for which you have created movies).
var supportedLanguages:Array = ["en", "es", "fr"];

// Set a default language in case you don't support the user's
// language.
var useLang:String = "en";

// Loop through the supported languages to find a match to the
// user's language. If you find one, set useLang to that value
// and then exit the for statement.
for (var i:int = 0; i < supportedLanguages.length; i++) {
  if (supportedLanguages[i] == lang) {
    useLang = lang;
    break;
  }
}

// Load the corresponding movie.
var movieURL:String =  "myMovie_" + useLang + ".swf");
```

It is also often important to know how a user will be entering text on her system. Languages, such as Chinese, Japanese, and Korean, can have thousands of possible characters. To enter these characters via the keyboard, a special program called an Input Method Editor (IME) is required. This is usually part of the operating system of the particular language.

To detect if the user's system has an IME, check the value of flash.system. Capabilities.hasIME, which will return true or false. Then use the flash.system.IME class to get more information about and interact with the IME. The flash.system. IME.enabled property tells you whether the user is using the IME or entering text straight from the keyboard. This property is actually writable, so you can use it to turn on the IME. On some platforms and OS versions, you can send a string to the IME to be converted into the correct characters, and accept the output of the IME back into a selected text field. Since this does not work on all systems, it is best to check the OS first (see Recipe 3.2).

See Also

Recipe 3.2

3.5   Detecting Display Settings

Problem

You want to know the display settings for the device on which the movie is being played.

Solution

Use the `screenResolutionX` and `screenResolutionY` properties of the `system.capabilities` object.

Discussion

You should use the `flash.system.Capabilities` object to determine the display settings of the device that is playing the movie. The `screenResolutionX` and `screenResolutionY` properties return the display resolution in pixels.

```
// Example output:
// 1024
// 768
trace(flash.system.Capabilities.screenResolutionX);
trace(flash.system.Capabilities.screenResolutionY);
```

You can use these values to determine how to display a movie, or even which movie to load. These decisions are increasingly important as more handheld devices support the Flash Player. For example, the dimensions of a cellphone screen and a typical desktop computer display are different, so you should load different content based on the playback device.

```
var resX:int = flash.system.Capabilities.screenResolutionX;
var resY:int = flash.system.Capabilities.screenResolutionY;

// If the resolution is 240 x 320 or less, then load the PocketPC
// movie version. Otherwise, assume the device is a desktop computer
// and load the regular content.
if ( (resX <= 240) && (resY <= 320) ) {
  var url:String = "main_pocketPC.swf";
}
else {
  var url:String = "main_desktop.swf";
}
loader.load(new URLRequest(url));
```

You can also use the screen resolution values to center a pop-up browser window:

```
var resX:int = flash.system.Capabilities.screenResolutionX;
var resY:int = flash.system.Capabilities.screenResolutionY;

// Set variables for the width and height of the new browser window.
var winW:int = 200;
var winH:int = 200;

// Determine the X and Y values to center the window.
var winX:int = (resX / 2) - (winW / 2);
var winY:int = (resY / 2) - (winH / 2);

// Create the code that, when passed to URLLoader.load( )
// opens the new browser window.
var jsCode:String = "javascript:void(
```

```
newWin=window.open('http://www.person13.com/'," +
"'newWindow', 'width=" + winW +
", height=" +  winH + "," +
"left=" + winX + ",top=" + winY + "'));";

// Call the JavaScript function using a URLLoader object
urlLoader.load(new URLRequest(jsCode));
```

Additionally, it is worth considering using the screen resolution values to determine whether or not to scale a movie. For example, when users have their resolution set to a high value, such as 1600×1200, some fonts may appear too small to read.

3.6   Scaling the Movie

Problem

You want to control the way in which a movie fits in the Player, including the scaling.

Solution

Use the `stage.scaleMode` property.

Discussion

There are several different scale modes that control how a movie is scaled when the player changes size. The modes are defined as the following strings: *exactFit*, *noBorder*, *noScale*, and *showAll*. However, to avoid typographical errors, these strings have also been defined in the `flash.display.StageScaleMode` class as the static properties: `EXACT_FIT`, `NO_BORDER`, `NO_SCALE`, and `SHOW_ALL`.

The Flash Player defaults to a scale mode of *showAll*. In this mode, the Flash movie scales to fit the player's size while maintaining the movie's original aspect ratio. The result is that the movie can potentially have borders on the sides if the Player's aspect ratio does not match the movie's aspect ratio. You can set a movie to *showAll* mode from your main application class as follows (don't forget to import the `flash.display.StageScaleMode` class):

```
stage.scaleMode = StageScaleMode.SHOW_ALL;
```

Note that `stage` is not a global object, but a property of any display object, so this statement only works in a sprite or other class that extends the `DisplayObject` class.

The *noBorder* mode scales a movie to fit the Player while maintaining the original aspect ratio; however, it forces the Player to display no borders around the Stage. If the aspect ratio of the Player does not match that of the movie, some of the movie will be cut off on the sides. You can set a movie to *noBorder* mode as follows:

```
stage.scaleMode = StageScaleMode.NO_BORDER;
```

The *exactFit* mode scales a movie to fit the Player, and it alters the movie's aspect ratio, if necessary, to match that of the Player. The result is that the movie always fills the Player exactly, but the elements of the movie may be distorted. For example:

```
stage.scaleMode = StageScaleMode.EXACT_FIT;
```

In *noScale* mode, the movie is not scaled, and it maintains its original size and aspect ratio regardless of the Stage's size. When you use the *noScale* mode, don't forget to set the movie's alignment (see Recipe 3.7, which includes example code that demonstrates the available alignment options). For example:

```
stage.scaleMode = StageScaleMode.NO_SCALE;
```

The scaleMode property's value does not prevent the user from being able to scale the movie using the right-click/Control-click menu. However, you can disable those options in the menu, as shown in Recipe 3.8.

See Also

Recipes 3.7 and 3.8

3.7   Changing the Alignment

Problem

You want to change the alignment of the movie within the Player.

Solution

Use the stage.align property.

Discussion

Flash movies appear in the center of the Player by default. You can control the alignment of a movie within the Player by setting the stage.align property of any class that extends DisplayObject. The various alignment modes are implemented as strings, such as "T" for "top," "L" for "left," etc. However, to avoid errors in typing, these have also been made properties of the flash.display.StageAlign class, listed in Table 3-1.

Table 3-1. Alignment as controlled by stage.align

Value	Vertical alignment	Horizontal
StageAlign.TOP	Top	Center
StageAlign.BOTTOM	Bottom	Center
StageAlign.LEFT	Center	Left
StageAlign.RIGHT	Center	Right
StageAlign.TOP_LEFT	Top	Left

Table 3-1. Alignment as controlled by stage.align (continued)

Value	Vertical alignment	Horizontal
StageAlign.TOP_RIGHT	Top	Right
StageAlign.BOTTOM_LEFT	Bottom	Left
StageAlign.BOTTOM_RIGHT	Bottom	Right

 There is no "official" value to center the Stage both vertically and horizontally in the Player. Of course, if this is what you want, you don't have to do anything since that is the default mode. But if you have changed to one of the other modes and want to go back to centered alignment, any string that doesn't match one of the other modes will center the Stage. The easiest and safest would be an empty string, "".

The following class demonstrates the effects of both the scale mode and alignment of a movie within the player. Experiment by changing the stage.scaleMode and stage.align properties to their different values and scaling the browser to various sizes.

```
package {
  import flash.display.Sprite;
  import flash.display.StageScaleMode;
  import flash.display.StageAlign;

  public class ExampleApplication extends Sprite {
    public function ExampleApplication( ) {

      stage.scaleMode = StageScaleMode.NO_SCALE;
      stage.align = StageAlign.TOP_RIGHT;

      graphics.beginFill(0xff0000);
      graphics.drawRect(0, 0, stage.stageWidth, stage.stageHeight);
      graphics.endFill( );
    }
  }
}
```

3.8   Hiding the Flash Player's Menu Items

Problem

You want to hide the right-click menu under Windows (Control-click on the Mac).

Solution

You can't disable the Flash Player's pop-up menu entirely, but you can minimize the options shown in the menu by setting the stage.showDefaultContextMenu property to false.

Discussion

By default, the following options appear in the Flash Player's pop-up menu when the user right-clicks in Windows (or Control-clicks on the Mac):

- Zoom In
- Zoom Out
- Show All
- Quality (Low, Medium, or High)
- Settings
- Print
- Show Redraw Regions (if using a debug player)
- Debugger (if using a debug player)
- About Adobe Flash Player 9

You can remove many of the options with the following line of ActionScript code, although the Settings and About and debug player options remain in place:

```
stage.showDefaultContextMenu = false;
```

Unfortunately, Flash does not provide any way to disable the menu entirely. Furthermore, Windows users are accustomed to using right-click to display a pop-up browser menu that allows them to open a link in a new window, for example. Such options are not available due to the Flash pop-up menu's presence.

See Also

See Recipe 3.11 for a way to display Flash's Settings dialog box without requiring the user to right-click (in Windows) or Control-click (on Mac).

3.9   Detecting the Device's Audio Capabilities

Problem

You want to determine the audio capabilities of the device on which the Flash Player is running.

Solution

Use the `hasAudio` and `hasMP3` properties of the *flash.system.Capabilities* class.

Discussion

The `flash.system.Capabilities.hasAudio` property returns `true` if the user's system has audio capabilities and `false` otherwise. This is extremely important for playing movies on multiple devices. If a device has no audio support, you want to avoid forcing users to download something they cannot hear (especially because audio can be quite large).

```
// Load a .swf containing sound only if the Player can play audio
if (flash.system.Capabilities.hasAudio) {
  content = "sound.swf";
} else {
  content = "silent.swf";
}
// code to load the .swf referenced in content
```

Just because a system has audio capabilities, however, does not necessarily mean that it can play back MP3 sounds. Therefore, if publishing MP3 content, you should test for MP3 capabilities using the flash.system.Capabilities.hasMP3 property. MP3 sounds are preferable, if supported, because they offer better sound quality to file size ratios than ADCP sounds.

```
// If the Player can play MP3s, load an MP3 using a Sound object.
// Otherwise, load a .swf containing ADCP sound into a nested
// sprite.
if (flash.system.Capabilities.hasMP3) {
  var url:URLRequest = new URLRequest("sound.mp3");
  sound = new Sound(url);
  sound.play();
} else {
  // code to load an external .swf containing a ADCP sound
}
```

It is important to understand that the hasAudio and hasMP3 property settings are based on the capabilities of the Player and not of the system on which the Player is running. The desktop system players (for Windows, Mac OS, and Linux) always return true for both properties regardless of whether or not the system actually has the hardware (i.e., soundcard and speakers) to play back sounds. However, players for other devices may return false if the device does not support the audio or MP3 features.

3.10   Detecting the Device's Video Capabilities

Problem

You want to determine the video capabilities of the device on which the Flash Player is running.

Solution

Use the hasEmbeddedVideo, hasStreamingVideo, and hasVideoEncoder properties of the flash.system.Capabilities class.

Discussion

Before you attempt to deliver video content to a user, it is important to check whether his system is capable of playing video, and how it should be delivered. The most efficient way to deliver Flash video is to stream it to the player. This allows the user to view the video as it is coming in, rather than waiting until the entire (often quite large) file has downloaded. However, the user's system may not be capable of receiving streaming video. To check this, use the flash.system.Capabilities. hasStreamingVideo property. If this returns false, one option is to have the player load another .swf that contains an embedded video. However, before doing this, you should check the property flash.system.Capabilities.hasEbeddedVideo to ensure that the user can view this content before initiating this download. Your code would look something like this:

```
if(flash.system.Capabilities.hasStreamingVideo) {
  // Code to set up a video stream and start streaming a
  // specific video
}
else if(flash.system.Capabilities.hasEmbeddedVideo) {
  // Code to load an external .swf containing an embedded video
}
else {
  // Alternate content without any video
}
```

Similarly, if your application requires video stream encoding, such as the use of a web cam to transmit live video from the user's system, you want to ensure that the system is capable of doing such encoding. You can test this with the flash.system. Capabilities.hasVideoEncoder property. Like the earlier example, you would probably test this property in an *if* statement and set up the video streaming only if it tested true. Otherwise, you could display a message to the user explaining the situation or redirect him to another page.

3.11 Prompting the User to Change Player Settings

Problem

You want to open the user's Flash Player Settings dialog box to prompt her to allow greater access to her local system.

Solution

Use the *flash.system.Security.showSettings( )* method.

Discussion

The *flash.system.Security.showSettings( )* method opens the Flash Player Settings dialog box, which includes several tabs. You'll pass a string as a parameter to indicate which tab you want it to open. These strings have been made static properties of the *flash.system.SecurityPanel* class, to avoid typographical errors. The possible values are:

SecurityPanel.CAMERA
: Allows the user to select a camera to use.

SecurityPanel.DEFAULT
: Shows whichever tab was opened the last time the Security Panel was open.

SecurityPanel.LOCAL_STORAGE
: Allows the user to specify how local shared objects are stored, including the maximum allowable disk usage.

SecurityPanel.MICROPHONE
: Allows the user to select a microphone and adjust the volume.

SecurityPanel.PRIVACY
: Allows the user to specify whether to allow Flash access to her camera and microphone.

SecurityPanel.SETTINGS_MANAGER
: Opens a new browser window and loads the Settings Manager page, which gives the user several more detailed options and the ability to make global changes, rather than just to the domain of the specific movie that is active.

If you don't pass any parameters to the *showSettings()* method, it uses *SecurityPanel. DEFAULT*. Here, we open the Settings dialog box to the Local Storage tab by explicitly specifying a value of 1.

```
// Open the Settings dialog box to the Local Storage tab.
flash.system.Security.showSettings(SecurityPanel.LOCAL_STORAGE);
```

 Out of courtesy, you should prompt the user to open the Settings dialog with a button rather than simply opening it without warning. Also, you should alert the user beforehand as to which settings she should change.

3.12   Dealing with System Security

Problem

You want to load a *.swf* from another domain into your application and allow it to have access to the ActionScript in the application.

Solution

Use one of the following: *flash.system.Security.allowDomain()*, *flash.system.Security. allowInsecureDomain()*, or a policy file.

Discussion

In many cases, all of the *.swfs* in a multi-*.swf* application would live on the same server (thus the same domain). There may be cases, however, when your application needs to load in an external *.swf* from another domain. In such a case, neither the *.swf* nor the loading application would be able to access the other's code. You can allow such access by using *flash.system.Security.allowDomain()*, *flash.system. Security.allowInsecureDomain()*, or a policy file.

The *.swf* that is going to be accessed must explicitly allow access by *.swfs* in the other domain. It does not matter which *.swf* is loading or being loaded. To clarify, call the *.swf* being accessed, *accessed.swf*, and the *.swf* doing the access, *accessing.swf*. Say *accessing.swf* lives on *mydomain.com* and loads in *accessed.swf* from *otherdomain. com*, into an object named *content* (see Figure 3-1).

Now, *accessing.swf* tries to access a variable called `authorName` from the loaded *accessed.swf*. At this point, *accessed.swf* complains and won't allow access by a *.swf* from another domain.

To overcome this, *accessed.swf* needs the following line:

```
flash.system.Security.allowDomain("http://mydomain.com");
```

This lets it know that it is alright to allow access by any *.swf* from that domain.

> You should note that the permission is one-way. If the loaded *.swf* now needs access to some code in the *.swf* that loaded it, it would not be able to get at that code. In this case, the loading *.swf* would explicitly need to allow access to *otherdomain.com*.

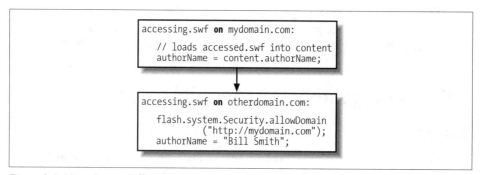

Figure 3-1. Using Security.allowDomain

The domain can be text-based as in the previous examples, or can be a numeric IP address. It also supports wildcards. If, for some reason, you want to grant access to any *.swf*, anywhere, to access it, you can pass in the string "*". However, this effectively cuts out all cross-domain security that has been built into the player, and is not recommended.

If the accessed *.swf* file happens to be on a secure server accessed with *https://*, then by default it won't allow access to any *.swf* being loaded from a non-secure domain (*http://*), even if you have allowed access with *flash.system.Security.allowDomain()*. In this case, use *flash.system.Security.allowInsecureDomain()* to allow access to a non-secure domain.

The method mentioned here requires you to hardcode the domain name or names into your *.swf*. This works fine if you know exactly which domains you will be allowing access from and that these are unlikely to change. However, if you later want to add or change the allowed domains, you have to change the code and recompile and redeploy the *.swf*. In a situation where this is likely to happen often, it is more efficient to create and use a *policy file*.

A *policy file* is an XML file that lists any domains that are allowed access to the code in the *.swf*. The format of the file can be seen here:

```
<?xml version="1.0"?>
<!-- http://www.mydomain.com/crossdomain.xml -->
<cross-domain-policy>
  <allow-access-from domain="www.otherdomain.com" />
  <allow-access-from domain="*.adobe.com" />
  <allow-access-from domain="123.45.67.89" />
</cross-domain-policy>
```

As you can see, it just lists each domain to which you want to allow access. The file should be named *crossdomain.xml*. Prior to Flash 8, the file was required to live in the root directory of the domain of the *.swf* to which it applied. Now you can specify and load a policy file from any other location using *flash.system.Security. loadPolicyFile()*. This takes a string defining the URL of the *crossdomain.xml* file you wish to load. This file should be loaded as an early action in your application, before you attempt to load any content from another domain. With this method, you can add, remove, or change allowed domains by simply rewriting the XML file.

As you can see, this method also supports wildcards. For example, if you wanted to allow access to any and all domains, you could use the following line:

```
<allow-access-from domain="*" />
```

And if you wanted to explicitly deny access to any domain except the current one, you can create an empty policy file:

```
<cross-domain-policy>
</cross-domain-policy>
```

## CHAPTER 4

Numbers and Math

4.0 Introduction

Although numbers aren't always in the spotlight, don't overlook their power and importance in your code. Numbers come in all shapes and sizes—from binary to decimal to hexadecimal. Each type of representation has its own particular niche in which it is most valuable. For example, hexadecimal numbers are often used to represent RGB color values because they make it easy to discern each of the three color components. (See Recipe 4.2 to learn how to convert between different number bases.)

Closely related to numbers is the subject of mathematics. Without mathematical operations, your Flash movies would be rather dull. Simple operations such as addition and subtraction are essential to even the most basic ActionScript applications, and more advanced math, such as random number generation and trigonometric calculations, is equally essential to advanced applications.

ActionScript 3.0 has three basic numeric types: *number*, *int*, and *uint*. *number* is for any floating-point numbers, whereas *int* and *uint* are for integers (whole numbers). The distinction between *int* and *uint* is that *int* is the set of negative and non-negative integers, while *uint* is the set of non-negative integers (unsigned integers).

4.1 Representing Numbers in Different Bases

Problem

You want to specify a value in binary, octal, or hexadecimal.

Solution

Hexadecimal literals start with 0x (where the first character is a zero, not an "oh"), and octal literals start with 0 (again, zero, not "oh"). Binary numbers can't be represented directly, but you can either specify their octal or hexadecimal equivalent or use the *parseInt( )* function to convert a string to a number.

Discussion

You can represent numbers in ActionScript using whichever format is most convenient, such as decimal or hexadecimal notation. For example, if you set the value of the `Sprite.rotation` property, it is most convenient to use a decimal number:

```
rectangleSprite.rotation = 180;
```

On the other hand, hexadecimal numbers are useful for specifying RGB colors. For example, you can set the `rgb` value for a *ColorTransform* object in hexadecimal notation (in this example, `0xF612AB` is a hex number representing a shade of pink):

```
var pink:ColorTransform = new ColorTransform( );
pink.rgb = 0xF612AB;
```

Any numeric literal starting with `0X` or `0x` (where the first character is a zero, not an "oh") is presumed to be a *hexadecimal* number (i.e., *hex* or base-16). Allowable digits in a hexadecimal number are 0 through 9 and A through F (upper- and lowercase letters are equivalent, meaning `0xFF` is the same as `0xff`).

Any numeric literal starting with `0` (again, zero not "oh"), but not `0x` or `0X`, is presumed to be an *octal number* (i.e., base-8). Allowable digits in an octal number are 0 through 7; for example, `0777` is an octal number. Most developers don't ever use octal numbers in ActionScript. For most developers it's simply far more convenient to represent most numbers as decimal numbers (base-10), except color values for which it is generally more convenient to use hexadecimal representation. There aren't many common examples for which octal representation is more convenient than decimal or hexadecimal.

The only digits allowed in *binary numbers* (i.e., base-2) are 0 and 1. Although you can't specify a binary number directly, you can specify its hexadecimal equivalent. Four binary digits (*bits*) are equivalent to a single hex digit. For example, `1111` in binary is equivalent to `F` in hex (15 in decimal). The number `11111111` in binary is equivalent to `FF` in hex (255 in decimal). Binary numbers (or rather their hexadecimal equivalents) are most commonly used with ActionScript's bitwise operators (`&`, `|`, `^`, `>>`, `<<`, and `>>>`).

See Also

Recipe 4.2

4.2   Converting Between Different Number Systems

Problem

You want to convert a number between different bases (such as decimal, binary, hexadecimal, etc.).

Solution

Use the *parseInt()* function with the *radix* parameter (the *radix* is the number's base) to convert a string to a decimal representation. Use the *toString()* method of a *Number*, *uint*, or *int* object with the radix parameter to convert a decimal number to a string representation of the value in another base.

Discussion

No matter how you set a number value in ActionScript, the result is always retrieved as a decimal (base-10) number:

```
// Create a Color object
var pink:ColorTransform = new ColorTransform( );

// Set the RGB value as a hexadecimal
pink.rgb = 0xF612AB;

// This displays the value as decimal: 16126635
trace(pink.rgb);
```

However, if you want to output a value in a different base, you can use *toString(radix)* for a *Number*, *uint*, or *int* object to convert any number value to a string representing that number in the specified base.

These two examples convert numeric literals to *uint* objects and output the string representations in base-2 (binary) and base-16 (hexadecimal) format.

```
// The radix is 2, so output as binary
trace(new uint(51).toString(2));  // Displays: 110011
// The radix is 16, so output as hex
trace(new uint(25).toString(16)); // Displays: 19
```

When using the *toString()* method with a variable that contains a numeric literal value, Flash automatically creates a new *Number*, *uint*, or *int* object before calling the *toString()* method. Although it's not typically the best practice, it is not technically wrong, and in most applications the differences are negligible. This example assigns a primitive number to a variable and calls the *toString()* method to output the value in hexadecimal:

```
var quantity:Number = 164;
trace(quantity.toString(16)); // Displays: a4
```

 The results from these examples are not numeric literals, but rather strings, such as 110011, 19, and A4.

The following example sets the RGB value of a *ColorTransform* object, calls *toString()* on the result to display the value as a hexadecimal (as it had been input, although the alpha digits are converted to lowercase, and the result is a string, not a number):

```
// Create a Color object
var pink:Color = new ColorTransform( );

// Set the RGB value as a hexadecimal
pink.rgb = 0xF612AB;

trace(pink.rgb.toString(16));  // Displays: f612ab
```

The valid range for the *radix* parameter of the *toString()* method is from 2 to 36. If you call *toString()* with no *radix* parameter or an invalid value, decimal format (base-10) is assumed.

You can achieve the inverse of the *toString()* process using the *parseInt()* function with the *radix* parameter. The *parseInt()* function takes a string value and returns a number. This is useful if you want to work with base inputs other than 10.

These examples parse the numbers from the string in base-2 (binary), base-16 (hexadecimal), and base-10, respectively (note that the result is always a decimal):

```
trace(parseInt("110011", 2));  // Displays: 51
trace(parseInt("19", 16));     // Displays: 25
trace(parseInt("17", 10));     // Displays: 17
```

If omitted, the *radix* is assumed to be 10, unless the string starts with 0x, 0X, or 0, in which case hexadecimal or octal is assumed:

```
trace(parseInt("0x12"));    // The radix is implicitly 16. Displays: 18
trace(parseInt("017"));     // The radix is implicitly 8. Displays: 15
```

An explicit *radix* overrides an implicit one. In the next example, the result is 0, not 12. When the number is treated base-10, conversion stops when a non-numeric character—the *x*—is encountered:

```
// The number is treated as a decimal, not a hexadecimal number
trace(parseInt("0x12", 10));    // Displays: 0 (not 12 or 18)
```

Here, although the leading zero doesn't prevent the remainder digits from being interpreted, it is treated as a decimal number, not an octal number:

```
// The number is treated as a decimal, not an octal number
trace(parseInt("017", 10));    // Displays: 17 (not 15)
```

Don't forget to include 0, 0x, or an explicit radix. The following interprets the string as a decimal and returns NaN (not a number) because "A" can't be converted to an integer:

```
trace(parseInt("A9FC9C"));     // NaN
```

4.3   Rounding Numbers

Problem

You want to round a number to the nearest integer, decimal place, or interval (such as to the nearest multiple of five).

Solution

Use *Math.round()* to round a number to the nearest integer. Use *Math.floor()* and *Math.ceil()* to round a number down or up. Use a custom *NumberUtilities.round()* method to round a number to a specified number of decimal places or to a specified multiple.

Discussion

There are numerous reasons to round numbers. For example, when displaying the results of a calculation, you might display only the intended precision. Because all arithmetic in ActionScript is performed with floating-point numbers, some calculations result in unexpected floating-point numbers that must be rounded. For example, the result of a calculation may be 3.9999999 in practice, even though it should be 4.0 in theory.

The *Math.round()* method returns the nearest integer value of any parameter passed to it:

```
trace(Math.round(204.499));  // Displays: 204
trace(Math.round(401.5));    // Displays: 402
```

The *Math.floor()* method rounds down, and the *Math.ceil()* method rounds up:

```
trace(Math.floor(204.99));   // Displays: 204
trace(Math.ceil(401.01));    // Displays: 402
```

To round a number to the nearest decimal place:

1. Decide the number of decimal places to which you want the number rounded. For example, if you want to round 90.337 to 90.34, then you want to round to two decimal places, which means you want to round to the nearest .01.

2. Divide the input value by the number chosen in Step 1 (in this case, .01).

3. Use *Math.round()* to round the calculated value from Step 2 to the nearest integer.

4. Multiple the result of Step 3 by the same value that you used to divide in Step 2.

For example, to round 90.337 to two decimal places, you could use:

```
trace (Math.round(90.337 / .01) * .01);  // Displays: 9.34
```

You can use the identical math to round a number to the nearest multiple of an integer.

For example, this rounds 92.5 to the nearest multiple of 5:

```
trace (Math.round(92.5 / 5)  * 5);   // Displays: 95
```

As another example, this rounds 92.5 to the nearest multiple of 10:

```
trace (Math.round(92.5 / 10) * 10);  // Displays: 90
```

In practice you are likely to find it is much simpler to use a custom *NumberUtilities.round()* method that encapsulates this functionality. The custom method takes two parameters:

number

   The number to round.

roundToInterval

   The interval to which to round the *number*. For example, if you want to round to
   the nearest tenth, use 0.1 as the interval. Or, to round to the nearest multiple of
   six, use 6.

The *NumberUtilities* class is in the *ascb.util* package, so the first thing you'll want to
add to any file that uses the class is an import statement. Here is an example of how
to use the *NumberUtilities.round()* method (the following code assumes that you've
imported *ascb.util.NumberUtilities*):

```
trace(NumberUtilities.round(Math.PI));            // Displays: 3
trace(NumberUtilities.round(Math.PI, .01));       // Displays: 3.14
trace(NumberUtilities.round(Math.PI, .0001));     // Displays: 3.1416
trace(NumberUtilities.round(123.456, 1));         // Displays: 123
trace(NumberUtilities.round(123.456, 6));         // Displays: 126
trace(NumberUtilities.round(123.456, .01));       // Displays: 123.46
```

4.4   Inserting Leading or Trailing Zeros or Spaces

Problem

You want to add leading or trailing zeros or spaces to a number to display it as a
string.

Solution

Use the custom *NumberFormat* class, apply a mask, and then call the *format()*
method.

Discussion

You might need to format numbers with leading or trailing zeros or spaces for display purposes, such as when displaying times or dates. For example, you would want
to format 6 hours and 3 minutes as 6:03 or 06:03, not 6:3. Additionally, sometimes
you'll want to apply leading and/or trailing spaces to align the columns of several
numbers; for example:

```
123456789
  1234567
    12345
```

Although you can certainly work out the algorithms on your own to add leading or
trailing characters, you'll likely find working with a *NumberFormat* object much
faster, simpler, and more flexible. The *NumberFormat* class is a custom class
included with the downloads for this book at *http://www.rightactionscript.com/ascb*.

That class is part of the *ascb.util* package, so the first thing you'll want to do is make sure you have an import statement:

```
import ascb.util.NumberFormat;
```

Next you need to determine the mask that you'll use to format the number. The mask can consist of zeros (0), pound signs (#), dots (.), and commas (,); any other characters are disregarded.

Zeros (0)
> Placeholders that are either filled with the corresponding digit or a zero.

Pound signs (#)
> Placeholders that are either filled with the corresponding digit or a space.

Dots (.)
> Decimal point placeholders; they can be replaced by the localized decimal point symbol.

Commas (,)
> Placeholders for grouping symbols; they are replaced by the localized grouping symbol.

To better understand this, it can be helpful to take a look at some examples; consider the following mask:

```
##,###.0000
```

When the preceding mask is used with the numbers 1.2345, 12.345, 123.45, 1234.5, and 12345, the results are as follows (assuming that the localized settings apply commas as grouping symbols and dots as decimal points):

```
    1.2345
   12.3450
  123.4500
1,234.5000
12,345.0000
```

You can set the mask for a *NumberFormat* object in several ways. You can specify the mask as a parameter when you construct the object, as follows:

```
var styler:NumberFormat = new NumberFormat("##,###.0000");
```

Additionally, you can use the mask property of the object to change the mask at any point:

```
styler.mask = "##.00";
```

> The mask property is a read-write property, so you can also retrieve the current mask string by reading the value from the property.

Once a mask has been applied to a *NumberFormat* object, you can format any number value by calling the *format()* method and passing the number as a parameter:

```
trace(styler.format(12345));
```

The following code is a complete, working example that illustrates the features of the *NumberFormat* class that have been discussed so far:

```
var styler:NumberFormat = new NumberFormat("#,###,###,###");

trace(styler.format(1));
trace(styler.format(12));
trace(styler.format(123));
trace(styler.format(1234));

styler.mask = "#,###,###,###.0000";

trace(styler.format(12345));
trace(styler.format(123456));
trace(styler.format(1234567));
trace(styler.format(12345678));
trace(styler.format(123456789));
```

The output from the preceding example is as follows (assuming U.S.-style localization settings):

```
          1
         12
        123
      1,234
     12,345.0000
    123,456.0000
  1,234,567.0000
 12,345,678.0000
123,456,789.0000
```

By default, *NumberFormat* objects attempt to automatically localize the return values. If the Flash Player is running on a U.S. English operating system, the *NumberFormat* class uses commas as grouping symbols and dots as decimal points. On the other hand, if the computer is running a French operating system, the symbols are reversed; dots for grouping symbols and commas for decimal points. There are several reasons why you may opt to override the automatic localization, including:

- You want the numbers to be formatted in a standard way regardless of the operating system on which the Flash application is run.

- Automatic localization doesn't work properly. This may occur in some situations for at least two reasons:

  — The *Locale* class (the class used by *NumberFormat* to determine the correct localization settings) may not include some languages/countries.

  — The Flash Player does not report very specific settings. It only reports the language code. Because of that, it may be difficult—to nearly impossible—to correctly calculate the locale to use.

There are a variety of ways you can override the automatic localization settings:

- Pass a *Locale* object to the *format()* method as a second parameter. The *format()* method then uses the settings from that *Locale* object instead of the automatic settings. This option works well when you want to apply different custom localization settings each time you call the *format()* method. You can create a *Locale* object by using the constructor. With no parameters, the *Locale* object uses automatic localization detection, so you'll want to pass it one or two parameters. The first parameter is the *language code* (e.g., *en*). The second parameter is the country code (e.g., *US*), also called the *variant*. You should only specify the variant if there are different regions that use the same language, but use different formatting. For example, the language code *es* (Spanish) could potentially apply to many countries, including Mexico (*MX*) and Spain (*ES*)—both of which use different symbols to format numbers.

- Set the *Locale.slanguage* and/or *Locale.svariant* properties to set the localization properties globally. You don't need to specify any additional parameters when calling *format()* with this option. Simply assign values to the static properties, *Locale.slanguage* and/or *Locale.svariant*; those settings affect any subsequent calls to *format()*.

- Use a symbols object as the second parameter when calling *format()*. The symbols object should have two properties: group and decimal. The values for those properties allow you to define the symbols to use when formatting the number. This option is best when the *Locale* object does not have settings for the locale that you want and/or when you want to use custom formatting symbols.

 The *Locale* class is in the *ascb.util* package, so be sure to import that class if you want to use it.

The following example illustrates some of the ways you can override the automatic localization settings:

```
var styler:NumberFormat = new NumberFormat("#,###,###,###.00");

Locale.slanguage = "fr";
trace(styler.format(1234));
trace(styler.format(12345, {group: ",", decimal: "."}));
trace(styler.format(123456));
Locale.slanguage = "en";
trace(styler.format(1234567));
trace(styler.format(12345678, new Locale("es", "ES")));
trace(styler.format(123456789, {group: "|", decimal: ","}));
```

The preceding code displays the following:

```
    1.234,00
   12,345.00
  123.456,00
```

```
    1,234,567.00
   12.345.678,00
  123|456|789,00
```

See Also

Recipes 4.2 and 4.6

4.5   Formatting Numbers for Display Without a Mask

Problem

You want to format a number for display without using a mask.

Solution

Create a *NumberFormat* object with no mask setting, then call the *format()* method.

Discussion

Recipe 4.4 discusses complex ways to format numbers as strings, including using masks and applying leading and trailing zeros and spaces. Sometimes, however, you just want to format a number without those complexities. The *NumberFormat* class provides that simplicity as well. If no mask is applied to a *NumberFormat* object, then the *format()* method applies basic, localized formatting to a number, as shown in the following example:

```
var styler:NumberFormat = new NumberFormat();

trace(styler.format(12.3));
trace(styler.format(123.4));
trace(styler.format(1234.5));
trace(styler.format(12345.6));
```

Notice that a mask wasn't applied to the *NumberFormat* object at any point. Assuming U.S.-style formatting, the preceding code outputs the following:

```
12.3
123.4
1,234.5
12,345.6
```

As with the other use of the *format()* method (discussed in Recipe 4.4), this usage attempts to use automatic localization detection. However, the same issues may be applicable. You may prefer to override the automatic localization settings, and you can accomplish that by using the same techniques discussed in Recipe 4.4, as illustrated with the following example:

```
var styler:NumberFormat = new NumberFormat();

Locale.slanguage = "fr";
```

```
trace(styler.format(1234, new Locale("en")));
trace(styler.format(12345, {group: ":", decimal: "|"}));
trace(styler.format(123456));
```

The output from the preceding code is as follows:

```
1,234
12:345
123.456
```

See Also

Recipes 4.3 and 4.4 can be used to ensure a certain number of digits are displayed past the decimal point. Then aligning numbers is simply a matter of setting the text field's format to right justification using the *TextFormat*.align property. Also refer to Recipe 4.6.

4.6   Formatting Currency Amounts

Problem

You want to format a number as currency, such as dollars.

Solution

Use the *NumberFormat.currencyFormat()* method.

Discussion

Unlike some other languages, such as ColdFusion, ActionScript does not have a built-in function for formatting numbers as currency amounts. However, the custom *NumberFormat* class includes a *currencyFormat()* method that takes care of basic currency formatting for you.

The *currencyFormat()* method requires at least one parameter; the number you want to format as currency. The following example illustrates the simplest use of *currencyFormat()*:

```
var styler:NumberFormat = new NumberFormat();

trace(styler.currencyFormat(123456));
```

Assuming that the preceding code is run on a U.S. English computer, the output is as follows:

```
$123,456.00
```

As with the *format()* method of the *NumberFormat* class discussed in Recipes 4.4 and 4.5, the *currencyFormat()* method uses automatic localization detection settings.

Therefore, if the preceding code is run on a computer in Spain running a Spanish operating system, the output is as follows:

```
123.456,00 €
```

However, the *Locale* class (which is responsible for determining the locale from where the application is being run) may not be able to correctly detect the locale. Furthermore, you may simply want to override automatic localization so you get a consistent value regardless of where the application is run. There are several ways you can override the automatic localization detection; the same ways that you can override the localization settings when using the *format()* method:

- Use a *Locale* object as the second parameter when calling *currencyFormat()*.
- Assign global values to the *Locale.slanguage* and/or *Locale.svariant* properties.
- Use a symbols object as the second parameter when calling *currencyFormat()*.

The symbols object for *currencyFormat()* is slightly more complex than the symbols object for the *format()* object. If you use a symbols object with *currencyFormat()*, you should include the following four properties: group, decimal, currency, and before. The group and decimal properties act just as with the *format()* method. The currency property should have a value of the currency symbol you want to use. The before property is a Boolean value in which true means the currency symbol should appear before the numbers, and false means the symbol should appear after the numbers.

The following is an example of different ways of overriding the localization settings with *currencyFormat()*:

```
var styler:NumberFormat = new NumberFormat( );

trace(styler.currencyFormat(123456));
Locale.slanguage = "nl";
trace(styler.currencyFormat(123456));
trace(styler.currencyFormat(123456, new Locale("sv")));
trace(styler.currencyFormat(123456, {group: ",", decimal: ".", currency: "@", before:
false}));
```

The preceding code outputs the following results:

```
$123,456.00
€123.456,00
123,456.00kr
123,456.00@
```

See Also

Recipes 4.3, 4.5, and Appendix A for creating special characters, including the Euro (€), Yen (¥), and British pound (£) symbols. To align currency amounts in text fields, set the field's format to right justification using the *TextFormat*.align property.

4.7   Generating a Random Number

Problem

You want to use ActionScript to generate a random number.

Solution

Use *Math.random()* to generate a random number between 0 and .999999. Optionally, use the *NumberUtilities.random()* method to generate a random number within a specific range.

Discussion

You can use the *Math.random()* method to generate a random floating-point number from 0 to 0.999999999. In most cases, however, programs call for a random integer, not a random floating-point number. Furthermore, you may want a random value within a specific range. If you do want a random floating-point number, you'll need to specify its precision (the number of decimal places).

The simplest way to generate random numbers within a range and to a specified precision is to use the custom *NumberUtilities.random()* method. This method accepts up to three parameters, described as follows:

minimum
> The smallest value in the range specified as a *Number*.

maximum
> The largest value in the range specified as a *Number*.

roundToInterval
> The optional interval to use for rounding. If omitted, numbers are rounded to the nearest integer. You can specify integer intervals to round to integer multiples. You can also specify numbers smaller than 1 to round to numbers with decimal places.

 The *NumberUtilities* class is in the *ascb.util* package, so be sure to include an import statement.

The following example illustrates some uses of the *round()* method:

```
// Generate a random integer from 0 to 100.
trace(NumberUtilities.random(0, 100));

// Generate a random multiple of 5 from 0 to 100.
trace(NumberUtilities.random(0, 100, 5));

// Generate a random number from -10 to 10, rounded to the
```

```
// nearest tenth.
trace(NumberUtilities.random(-10, 10, .1));

// Generate a random number from -1 to 1, rounded to the
// nearest five-hundredth.
trace(NumberUtilities.random(-1, 1, .05));
```

To test that the random numbers generated by the *NumberUtilities.random()* method are evenly distributed, you can use a script such as the following:

```
package {

  import flash.display.Sprite;
  import ascb.util.NumberUtilities;
  import flash.utils.Timer;
  import flash.events.TimerEvent;

  public class RandomNumberTest extends Sprite {

    private var _total:uint;
    private var _numbers:Object

    public function RandomNumberTest( ) {
      var timer:Timer = new Timer(10);
      timer.addEventListener(TimerEvent.TIMER, randomizer);
      timer.start( );
      _total = 0;
      _numbers = new Object( );
    }

    private function randomizer(event:TimerEvent):void {
      var randomNumber:Number = NumberUtilities.random(1, 10, 1);
      _total++;
      if(_numbers[randomNumber] == undefined) {
        _numbers[randomNumber] = 0;
      }
      _numbers[randomNumber]++;
      trace("random number: " + randomNumber);
      var item:String;
      for(item in _numbers) {
        trace("\t" + item + ": " + Math.round(100 * _numbers[item]/_total));
      }
    }

  }
}
```

See Also

Recipes 4.3 and 4.11

4.8 Simulating a Coin Toss

Problem

You want to simulate tossing a coin or some other Boolean (true/false) event in which you expect a 50 percent chance of either outcome.

Solution

Use the *NumberUtilities.random()* method to generate an integer that is either 0 or 1, and then correlate each possible answer with one of the desired results.

Discussion

You can use the *random()* method from Recipe 4.7 to generate a random integer in the specified range. To relate this result to an event that has two possible states, such as a coin toss (heads or tails) or a Boolean condition (true or false), treat each random integer as representing one of the possible states. By convention, programmers use 0 to represent one state (such as "off") and 1 to represent the opposite state (such as "on"), although you can use 1 and 2 if you prefer. For example, here's how you could simulate a coin toss:

```
package {

    import flash.display.Sprite;
    import flash.text.TextField;
    import flash.events.MouseEvent;
    import ascb.util.NumberUtilities;

    public class CoinExample extends Sprite {

      private var _field:TextField;

    public function CoinExample( ) {
      _field = new TextField( );
      _field.autoSize = "left";
      addChild(_field);
      var circle:Sprite = new Sprite( );
      circle.graphics.beginFill(0, 100);
      circle.graphics.drawCircle(100, 100, 100);
      circle.graphics.endFill( );
        circle.addEventListener(MouseEvent.CLICK, onClick);
        addChild(circle);
    }

    private function onClick(event:MouseEvent):void {
        var randomNumber:Number = NumberUtilities.random(0, 1);
        _field.text = (randomNumber == 0) ? "heads" : "tails";
      }

    }
  }
```

In the following example, a function is used to test the *coinFlip()* routine to see if it is reasonably evenhanded. Do you expect a perfect 50/50 distribution regardless of the number of coin tosses? Test it and see.

```
package {

  import flash.display.Sprite;
  import flash.text.TextField;
  import ascb.util.NumberUtilities;

  public class CoinTest extends Sprite {

    private var _field:TextField;

  public function CoinTest() {
    _field = new TextField();
    _field.autoSize = "left";
    addChild(_field);
    var heads:Number = 0;
    var tails:Number = 0;
    var randomNumber:Number;
    for(var i:Number = 0; i < 10000; i++) {
        randomNumber = NumberUtilities.random(0, 1);
        if(randomNumber == 0) {
          heads++;
        }
        else {
          tails++;
        }
    }
    _field.text = "heads: " + heads + ", tails: " + tails;
  }

  }
}
```

If you are testing the value of your random number, be sure to save the result in a variable (and test that!) rather than generate a new random number each time you perform the test.

The following example is wrong because it generates independent random numbers in the dependent *else if* clauses. In some cases, none of the conditions are true and the method returns an empty string:

```
package {

  import flash.display.Sprite;
  import ascb.util.NumberUtilities;

  public class RandomLetter extends Sprite {

    public function RandomLetter() {
      for(var i:Number = 0; i < 10000; i++) {
```

```
        trace(getRandomLetter( ));
      }
    }

    private function getRandomLetter( ):String {
      if(NumberUtilities.random(0, 2) == 0) {
        return "A";
      }
      else if(NumberUtilities.random(0, 2) == 1) {
        return "B";
      }
      else if(NumberUtilities.random(0, 2) == 2) {
        return "C";
      }
      // It's possible that none of the preceding will evaluate to true,
      // and the method will reach this point without returning a valid
      // string.
      return "";
    }
  }
}
```

This is the correct way to accomplish the goal:

```
package {

  import flash.display.Sprite;
  import ascb.util.NumberUtilities;

  public class RandomLetter extends Sprite {

    public function RandomLetter( ) {
      for(var i:uint = 0; i < 10000; i++) {
        trace(getRandomLetter( ));
      }
    }

    private function getRandomLetter( ):String {
      // Assign the return value from random( ) to a variable
      // before testing the value.
      var randomInteger:uint = NumberUtilities.random(0, 2);
      if(randomInteger == 0) {
        return "A";
      }
      else if(randomInteger == 1) {
        return "B";
      }
      else if(randomInteger == 2) {
        return "C";
      }
      return "";
    }
  }
}
```

Recipe 4.7

4.9 Simulating Dice

Problem

You want to mimic rolling dice.

Solution

Use the *NumberUtilities.random()* method to generate random numbers in the desired range.

Discussion

You can use the *random()* method from Recipe 4.7 to generate random integer values to simulate rolling a die or dice in your Flash movies. Mimicking the rolling of dice is an important feature in many games you might create using ActionScript, and the *random()* method makes your job easy.

 NumberUtilities.random(1, 12) does not correctly simulate a pair of six-sided dice because the results must be between 2 and 12, not 1 and 12. Does *NumberUtilities.random(2, 12)* give the correct result? No, it does not. *NumberUtilities.random(2, 12)* results in a smooth distribution of numbers from 2 to 12, whereas in games played with two dice, 7 is much more common than 2 or 12. Therefore, you must simulate each die separately and then add the result together. Furthermore, in many games, such as backgammon, game play depends on the individual value of each die, not simply the total of both dice, so you'll want to keep them separate.

It is not uncommon to want to generate a random number and then store it for later use. If you want to reuse an existing random number, be sure to save the result rather than generating a new random number. Note the difference in these two scenarios. In the first scenario, dice always is the sum of die1 plus die2:

```
var die1:uint = NumberUtilities.random(1, 6);
var die2:uint = NumberUtilities.random(1, 6);
var dice:uint = die1 + die2;
```

In the following scenario, there is no relation between the value of dice and the earlier random values stored in die1 and die2. In other words, even if die1 and die2 add up to 7, dice stores a completely different value between 2 and 12:

```
var die1:uint = NumberUtilities.random(1, 6);
var die2:uint = NumberUtilities.random(1, 6);
var dice:uint = NumberUtilities.random(1, 6) + NumberUtilities.random(1, 6);
```

You can call *NumberUtilities.random()* with any range to simulate a multisided die. Here it has a range from 1 to 15 and generates a random number as though the user is rolling a 15-sided die, as might be found in a role-playing game:

```
var die1:uint = NumberUtilities.random(1, 15);
```

The following code uses the *NumberUtilities.random()* method in conjunction with programmatic drawing to create a visual representation of a single die:

```
package {

    import flash.display.Sprite;
    import flash.text.TextField;
    import flash.events.MouseEvent;
    import ascb.util.NumberUtilities;

    public class NumbersAndMath extends Sprite {

        var _die:Sprite;
        var _value:uint;

        public function NumbersAndMath( ) {
            _die = new Sprite( );
            addChild(_die);
            _die.addEventListener(MouseEvent.CLICK, rollDie);
            rollDie(null);
        }

        private function rollDie(event:MouseEvent):void {
            _value = NumberUtilities.random(1, 6);
            _die.graphics.clear( );
            _die.graphics.lineStyle( );
            _die.graphics.beginFill(0xFFFFFF);
            _die.graphics.drawRect(0, 0, 50, 50);
            _die.graphics.endFill( );
            _die.graphics.beginFill(0x000000);
            if(_value == 1 || _value == 3 || _value == 5) {
                _die.graphics.drawCircle(25, 25, 4);
            }
            if(_value == 2 || _value == 3 || _value == 4 ||
                _value == 5 || _value == 6)
            {
                _die.graphics.drawCircle(11, 11, 4);
                _die.graphics.drawCircle(39, 39, 4);
            }
            if(_value == 4 || _value == 5 || _value == 6) {
                _die.graphics.drawCircle(11, 39, 4);
                _die.graphics.drawCircle(39, 11, 4);
            }
            if(_value == 6) {
                _die.graphics.drawCircle(11, 25, 4);
                _die.graphics.drawCircle(39, 25, 4);
```

```
      }
    }

  }
}
```

Running the preceding code results in a single, clickable die drawn on the stage. Each time the user clicks the die, the value changes.

See Also

Recipe 4.7

4.10   Simulating Playing Cards

Problem

You want to use ActionScript to deal cards for a card game using a standard 52-card deck (without Jokers).

Solution

Use the custom *Cards* class.

Discussion

Playing cards requires a greater degree of sophistication than, say, rolling a couple dice. Therefore, to work with playing cards within your Flash applications, you should use a custom *Cards* class.

 The *Cards* class is in the *ascb.play* package, and therefore you should be sure to import the class before you try to use it in your code.

```
import ascb.play.Cards;
```

You can create a new *Cards* object using the constructor as follows:

```
var cards:Cards = new Cards( );
```

By default, a *Cards* object creates a standard deck of 52 playing cards. Next you need to deal the cards by using the *deal()* method. The *deal()* method returns an array of *CardHand* objects. You should specify at least one parameter when calling the *deal()* method; the number of hands to deal.

```
// Deal four hands.
var hands:Array = cards.deal(4);
```

By default, the *deal()* method deals every card in the deck (except when 52 is not evenly divisible by the number of hands). Some card games, such as Euchre, require fewer cards in each hand with some cards remaining in the deck. You can, therefore, specify a second, optional parameter that determines the number of cards per hand:

```
// Deal four hands with five cards each.
var hands:Array = cards.deal(4, 5);
```

Each *CardHand* object is an array of *Card* objects. The *CardHand* class also provides an interface to draw and discard cards from the deck from which the hand was originally dealt. You can use the *discard()* method by specifying a list of card indices as parameters. The cards then are removed from the hand and added back to the bottom of the deck:

```
// Discard the cards with indices 0 and 4 from the CardHand object
// stored in the first element of the aHands array.
hands[0].discard(0, 4);
```

Conversely, you can use the *draw()* method to draw cards from the top of the original deck. The *draw()* method draws one card by default if no parameters are specified. If you want to draw more than one card at a time, you can specify the number of cards as a parameter:

```
// Draw one card from the top of the deck, and add it to the
// hand stored in the first element of the hands array.
hands[0].draw( );
```

```
// Draw four cards from the top of the deck, and add them to
// the hand stored in the fourth element of the aHands array.
hands[3].draw(4);
```

You can use the length property of a *CardHand* object to retrieve the number of cards in a hand, and you can use the *getCardAt()* method to retrieve a card at a specified index.

As mentioned, each *CardHand* is composed of *Card* objects. *Card* objects, in turn, have four properties: value, name, suit, and display. The value property returns a numeric value from 0 to 12, where 0 is a two card and 12 is an Ace. The name property returns the name of the card, such as 2, 10, Q, or A. The suit property returns clubs, diamonds, hearts, or spades. The display property returns the name and suit values joined with a space. The following example code illustrates use of the *Cards* class:

```
package {

  import flash.display.Sprite;
  import ascb.play.Cards;
  import flash.util.trace;

  public class CardExample extends Sprite {

    public function CardExample( ) {
      var cards:Cards = new Cards( );
      var hands:Array = cards.deal(4, 10);
      var i:uint;
      var j:uint;
```

```
      for(i = 0; i < hands.length; i++) {
        trace("hand " + i);
        for(j = 0; j < hands[i].length; j++) {
          trace(hands[i].getCardAt(j));
        }
      }
    }

  }
}
```

4.11 Generating a Unique Number

Problem

You want to generate a unique number, such as a number to append to a URL to prevent caching of the URL.

Solution

Use the *NumberUtilities.getUnique()* method.

Discussion

Unique numbers are most commonly used to generate a unique URL (to prevent it from being cached). That is, by appending a unique number to the end of a URL, it is unlike any previous URL; therefore, the browser obtains the data from the remote server instead of the local cache.

The *NumberUtilities.getUnique()* method returns a number based on the current epoch milliseconds. (The following example assumes you've imported *ascb.util. NumberUtilities*.)

```
// Display a unique number.
trace(NumberUtilities.getUnique());
```

In most circumstances the preceding code returns the current epoch in milliseconds. However, it is possible that you may want to generate a set of unique numbers in less than a millisecond of processing time. In that case, you'll find that the *getUnique()* method adds a random number to the epoch milliseconds to ensure a unique number. The following example generates more than one number within the same millisecond:

```
for(var i:Number = 0; i < 100; i++) {
  trace(NumberUtilities.getUnique());
}
```

4.12 Converting Angle Measurements

Problem

You want to work with angle values in ActionScript, but you must convert to the proper units.

Solution

Use the *Unit* and *Converter* classes.

Discussion

The _rotation property of a movie clip object is measured in degrees. Every other angle measurement in ActionScript, however, uses radians, not degrees. This can be a problem in two ways. First, if you want to set the _rotation property based on the output of one of ActionScript's trigonometric methods, you must convert the value from radians to degrees. Second, humans generally prefer to work in degrees, which we must convert to radians before feeding to any of the trigonometric methods. Fortunately, the conversion between radians and degrees is simple. To convert from radians to degrees, you need only to multiply by 180/Math.PI. Likewise, to convert from degrees to radians you need only to multiply by the inverse: Math.PI/180. However, you may find it more convenient to simply use the custom *Unit* and *Converter* classes.

The *Unit* and *Converter* classes are two custom classes found in the *ascb.unit* package that facilitate conversions between various units of measurement, including degrees, radians, and gradians (there are 400 gradians in a complete circle). The first step is to create a *Unit* instance that describes the type of unit from which you want to convert. The *Unit* class provides a large group of constants that make it very convenient. The Unit.DEGREE, Unit.RADIAN, and Unit.GRADIAN constants return new Unit objects that represent degrees, radians, and gradians, respectively. *Unit* objects have a handful of properties, including name, category, label, and labelPlural:

```
var degree:Unit = Unit.DEGREE;
trace(degree.name);        // Displays: degree
trace(degree.category);    // Displays: angle
trace(degree.label);       // Displays: degree
trace(degree.labelPlural); // Displays: degrees
```

Once you've gotten a *Unit* instance that represents the unit from which you want to convert, you can then retrieve a *Converter* instance that can convert to a specific type of unit. Use the *getConverterTo()* method, and pass it a reference to a *Unit* object that represents the type of unit to which you want to convert. For example, the following code creates a *Converter* object that can convert from degrees to radians:

```
var converter:Converter = Unit.DEGREE.getConverterTo(Unit.RADIAN);
```

Once you've created a *Converter* instance, you can run the *convert()* method, specifying a value you want to convert; for example:

```
trace(converter.convert(90));
```

The *convertWithLabel()* method converts the value to a string that includes the appropriate label in the event that you want to display the value:

```
var converterToRadians:Converter = Unit.DEGREE.getConverterTo(Unit.RADIAN);
var converterToDegrees:Converter = Unit.RADIAN.getConverterTo(Unit.DEGREE);
trace(converterToRadians.convertWithLabel(1));
trace(converterToRadians.convertWithLabel(57.2957795130823));
trace(converterToDegrees.convertWithLabel(1));
trace(converterToDegrees.convertWithLabel(0.0174532925199433));

/*
   Displays:
   0.0174532925199433 radians
   1 radian
   57.2957795130823 degrees
   1 degree
*/
```

In the event that you find it more convenient to convert in the opposite direction, you can also use the *getConverterFrom()* method to create a *Converter* instance that converts one unit to another, for example:

```
var converter:Converter = Unit.DEGREE.getConverterFrom(Unit.GRADIAN);
trace(converter.convert(100));
trace(converter.convert(23));
```

4.13 Calculating the Distance Between Two Points

Problem

You want to calculate the distance between two points.

Solution

Use *Math.pow()* and *Math.sqrt()* in conjunction with the Pythagorean theorem.

Discussion

You can calculate the distance (in a straight line) from any two points by using the Pythagorean Theorem. The *Pythagorean Theorem* states that in any right triangle (a triangle in which one of the angles is 90 degrees) the length of the *hypotenuse* (the long side) is equal to the square root of the sum of the squares of the two other sides (referred to as the *legs* of the triangle). The Pythagorean theorem is written as:

$$a^2 + b^2 = c^2$$

You can use this formula to calculate the distance between any two points, where *a* is the difference between the points' X coordinates, *b* is the difference between their Y coordinates, and *c* (the distance to be determined) equals the square root of ($a^2 + b^2$). In ActionScript, this is written as:

```
var c:Number = Math.sqrt(Math.pow(a, 2) + Math.pow(b, 2));
```

How do you calculate the distance between two points using a right triangle? Although it might not seem immediately obvious, you can form an imaginary right triangle using any two points in the Flash coordinate system, as shown in Figure 4-1.

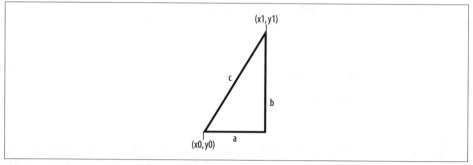

Figure 4-1. The hypotenuse of a right triangle is drawn between two points to calculate the distance between the points

The hypotenuse of the imaginary triangle is formed by the line connecting the two points. The legs of the triangle are formed by lines extending horizontally and vertically from the two points. You can find the lengths of the legs by finding the differences between the X and Y coordinates. The length of leg *a* is determined by the difference in the points' X coordinates, and the length of leg *b* is determined by the difference in the points' Y coordinates. Once you know the lengths of legs *a* and *b*, you can use the Pythagorean Theorem to calculate the length of the hypotenuse, *c*, which represents the distance between the points (our original query).

4.14   Determining Points Along a Circle

Problem

You want to calculate the coordinates of a point along a circle, given the circle's radius and the sweep angle.

Solution

Use the *Math.sin()* and *Math.cos()* methods to calculate the coordinates using basic trigonometric ratios.

Discussion

Finding the coordinates of a point along a circle is easy with some trigonometry. So let's look at the formulas you can use within your ActionScript code and the theory behind them.

Given any point on the Stage—a point we'll call p0, with coordinates (x0, y0)—plus a distance and the angle from the horizontal, you can find the coordinates of another point—which we'll call p1, with coordinates (x1, y1)—using some basic trigonometric ratios. The angle is formed between a conceptual line from p0 to p1 and a line parallel to the X axis, as shown in Figure 4-2. The *opposite side* is the side furthest away from the angle. The *adjacent side* is the side that forms the angle with the help of the hypotenuse.

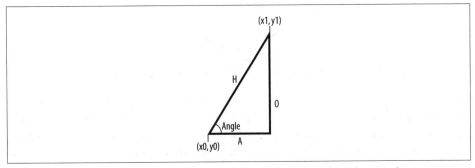

Figure 4-2. The angle, adjacent side, opposite side, and hypotenuse of a right triangle

If you know the distance between two points and the angle to the horizontal, as shown in Figure 4-2, you can calculate the X and Y coordinates of the destination point using trigonometric functions. The trigonometric sine of the angle is equal to the ratio of the opposite side over the hypotenuse, like so:

```
sine(angle) = opposite/hypotenuse
```

Solving for the opposite side's length, this can be written as:

```
opposite = sine(angle) * hypotenuse
```

As you can see in Figure 4-2, the opposite side represents the change in the Y direction.

The trigonometric cosine of the angle is equal to the ratio of the adjacent side over the hypotenuse, like so:

```
cosine(angle) = adjacent/hypotenuse
```

Solving for the adjacent side's length, this can be written as:

```
adjacent = cosine(angle) * hypotenuse
```

You can see from Figure 4-2 that the adjacent side represents the change in the X direction.

Because the lengths of the opposite and adjacent sides yield the changes in the X and Y directions, by adding the original X and Y coordinates to these values, you can calculate the coordinates of the new point.

So how does this help in determining a point along a circle's perimeter? Figure 4-3, which shows the triangle inscribed within a circle emphasizes the equivalency. The triangle's hypotenuse equates to the circle's radius, and the triangle's angle equates to the sweep angle to the point of interest along the circle's perimeter.

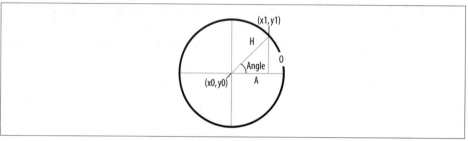

Figure 4-3. Using trigonometry to determine a point along a circle's perimeter

Therefore, the X coordinate of a point along the circle's perimeter is determined by the radius times the cosine of the angle. The Y coordinate is determined by the radius times the sine of the angle. Here is the ActionScript code for finding the coordinates of p1 when the circle's radius and center point (p0) are known:

```
x1 = x0 + (Math.cos(angle) * radius);
y1 = y0 + (Math.sin(angle) * radius);
```

Therefore, these formulas can be used to determine any point along a circle's perimeter, given the circle's center point and radius. By changing the angle over time, you can trace the path of a circle.

The following example uses these trigonometric equations to move a sprite around in a circle:

```
package {

    import flash.display.Sprite;
    import ascb.units.Converter;
    import ascb.units.Unit;
    import flash.events.Event;

    public class NumbersAndMath extends Sprite {

        private var _square:Sprite;
        private var _angle:uint;

        public function NumbersAndMath( ) {
            _square = new Sprite( );
            _square.graphics.lineStyle(0);
            _square.graphics.drawCircle(0, 0, 20);
```

```
    addChild(_square);
    _angle = 0;
    addEventListener(Event.ENTER_FRAME, move);
  }

  private function move(event:Event):void {
    var converter:Converter = Unit.DEGREE.getConverterTo(Unit.RADIAN);
    var angleRadians:Number = converter.convert(_angle);
    _square.x = Math.cos(angleRadians) * 100 + 200;
    _square.y = Math.sin(angleRadians) * 100 + 200;
    _angle++;
  }

  }
}
```

See Also

Recipes 7.7 and 7.8

4.15   Converting Between Units of Measurement

Problem

You want to convert between Fahrenheit and Celsius, pounds and kilograms, or other units of measure.

Solution

Use the *Unit* and *Converter* classes.

Discussion

There are various systems of measurement used throughout the world. For example, temperature is commonly measured in both Fahrenheit and Celsius. Weight is sometimes measured in pounds, but quite frequently, a metric system that uses kilograms is employed instead. And distances are likely to be measured in miles instead of kilometers, or inches instead of centimeters. For these reasons, you may need to convert from one unit of measure to another.

 Technically, pounds are a measurement of weight, while kilograms are a measurement of mass. Weight is a force that changes as the acceleration due to gravitational changes, whereas mass is constant regardless of the effects of gravity. The effect is that an object's weight on the moon and Earth differ since there are different effects, thanks to gravity, but the mass of an object remains the same. However, on the surface of the Earth, mass and weight often are used interchangeably.

Each of these conversions has its own algorithm. For example, to convert from Centigrade to Fahrenheit, you should multiply by 9, divide by 5, and then add 32 (to convert from Fahrenheit to Centigrade, subtract 32, multiply by 5, and then divide by 9). Likewise, you can multiply by 2.2 to convert pounds to kilograms, and you can divide by 2.2 to convert kilograms to pounds. (We also saw in Recipe 4.12 how to convert angles from degrees to radians and vice versa.)

As with converting between different units of measure with angles, you can use the *Unit* and *Converter* classes to convert between other types of units. The *Unit* class has support for quite a range of categories of measurement (angles, temperature, volume, etc.). You can retrieve an array of supported categories using the static *Unit. getCategories()* method:

```
// Display the categories that are supported.
trace(Unit.getCategories());
```

For each category, there are a variety units are supported. For example, in the angle category degrees, radians, and gradians are supported. You can retrieve a list of supported units for a given category using the static *Unit.getUnits()* method. Pass the method a category name to retrieve an array of units supported for that group. If you omit the parameter, then the entire list of supported units is returned:

```
// Display the units supported in the temperature category.
trace(Unit.getUnits("temperature"));
```

You can use the built-in *Unit* constants for any supported unit of measurement, just as in Recipe 4.12. Then you can retrieve a *Converter* object by using the *getConverterTo()* or *getConverterFrom()* methods. The following example creates a *Converter* to calculate the Fahrenheit equivalents of Celcius measurements:

```
var converter:Converter = Unit.CELCIUS.getConverterTo(Unit.FAHRENHEIT);
```

Then, of course, you can use the *convert()* (and/or the *convertWithLabel()*) method to convert values:

```
trace(converter.convert(0));  // Displays: 32
```

See Also

For an example of using a hardcoded function to perform a single type of unit conversion, refer to Recipe 4.12, which includes a function to convert angles from degrees to radians and another function that does the opposite.

CHAPTER 5

Arrays

5.0 Introduction

Arrays are essential to successful ActionScript programming.

An array provides a way of grouping related data together, and then organizing and processing that data. The concept of an array should not be foreign to you. In fact, the concept is used all the time in everyday life. You can view a simple grocery list or to-do list as an array. Your address book is an array containing people's names, addresses, birthdates, and so on. Libraries keep track of books using an indexing system whereby each book becomes, conceptually, an element in a library's array.

In ActionScript, there are two kinds of arrays: integer-indexed and associative. Both array types group related data, but they use different means of accessing the data.

Integer-indexed array
> Uses integers (numbers) as unique identifiers for each element in the array. Such arrays are ordered by *index* (i.e., element number), starting from 0. Each element occupies a numbered slot in the array. Integer-indexed arrays are ideal for sets of data that you want to work with in sequential order.

Associative array
> Uses string *keys* to access each value. You can read more about associative arrays in Recipe 5.15.

 Integer-indexed arrays are the focus of the majority of the recipes in this chapter, and unless otherwise specified, the term "array" refers to an integer-indexed array.

Of course, before you can use an array, you first need to know how to create one. There are two ways to construct a new array in ActionScript: with the constructor function or as an array literal. All arrays are members of the *Array* class. You can use the *Array()* constructor function to instantiate new array objects in one of three ways:

```
// Create an empty array.
var array:Array = new Array();

// Create an array with elements undefined elements.
var array:Array = new Array(elements);

// Create an array with specified elements.
var array:Array = new Array(element0,...elementN);
```

The array literal notation also creates a new array, but without using the constructor function. Literal notation is convenient for specifying elements at the time of creation, such as:

```
var letters:Array = ["a", "b", "c"];
```

Some methods of the *Array* class modify the existing array on which the method is called, and others return a new array (offering an indirect way to create arrays).

You retrieve and set array elements using the array-access operator (square brackets) and the index of the element you wish to get or set, for example:

```
// Set the fifth element of the array called items to "apples"
// (array indexes start at 0).
items[4] = "apples";

// Display the fifth element in the Output window.
trace(items[4]);    // Displays: apples
```

ActionScript doesn't care what kind of values you store in an array. You can store strings, numbers, Booleans, or references to any kind of objects. And, unlike stricter programming languages, you can even store different datatypes in a single array. For example, this array stores a string, an integer, a Boolean, and an object:

```
var data:Array = ["a", 2, true, new Object()];
```

Unlike many languages, ActionScript doesn't force you to specify the number of elements in an array when it is declared.

5.1 Adding Elements to the Start or End of an Array

Problem

You want to add elements to an existing array.

Solution

Use the *push()* method to append elements to the end of an array; use the *unshift()* method to insert elements at the beginning of an array.

Discussion

You append elements to the end of an existing array using the *Array.push()* method, passing it one or more values to be appended:

```
var array:Array = new Array();
array.push("val 1", "val 2");
```

You can also append a single element by using the array's length property as the index. Because ActionScript array indexes are zero-indexed (meaning that the first index is 0, not 1), the last element is at an index of *Array*.length - 1. Therefore, putting an element at index *Array*.length creates a new element right after the current last element; for example:

```
array[array.length] = "val 3";
```

If you set an element with an index that doesn't exist, the array extends itself to include the necessary number of elements automatically. If there are any intervening elements, they are initialized to undefined. For example, letters will contain the elements ["a", "b", "c", undefined, undefined, "f"] after you execute the following statements:

```
var letters:Array = ["a", "b", "c"];
letters[5] = "f";
```

Appending elements onto an array is common when you want to build an array incrementally or when you want to store the history of a user's actions for the purpose of implementing a back button or history feature.

To add elements to the beginning of an array, use the *unshift()* method. This shifts the existing elements up by one index position, and inserts the new element at index 0:

```
// Create an array with four elements:
// "a", "b", "c", and "d".
var letters:Array = new Array();
letters.push("a", "b", "c", "d");

// Add "z" to the beginning of the array. This shifts all
// the other elements so the value of "a" moves from
// index 0 to index 1, etc.
letters.unshift("z");

// Display the results by looping through the elements.
// See Recipe 5.2.
for (var i:int = 0; i < letters.length; i++) {
  trace(letters[i]);
}
```

Should you add elements to the beginning or the end of an array? That generally depends on how you intend to access or remove the elements at a later time. For example, if you want to access items in last in, first out (LIFO) order, you might use *Array.push()* to add elements to an array and *Array.pop()* to remove the elements in reverse order.

See Also

Recipe 5.2

5.2   Looping Through an Array

Problem

You want to access each element of an array in sequential order.

Solution

Use a *for* loop that increments an index variable from 0 until it reaches *Array*.length. Use the index to access each element in turn.

Discussion

To access the values stored in the elements of an array, loop through the array's elements using a *for* loop. Because the first index of an array is 0, the index variable in the *for* statement should start at 0. The last index of an array is always 1 less than the length property of that array. Within the *for* statement, use the loop index variable within square brackets to access array elements. For example:

```
var letters:Array = ["a", "b", "c"];
for (var i:int = 0; i < letters.length; i++) {
  // Display the elements in the Output panel.
  trace("Element " + i + ": " + letters[i]);
}
```

The looping index variable (*i* in the example code) should range from 0 to one less than the value of the length property. Remember that the last index of an array is always one less than its length.

Alternatively, you can use a *for* statement that loops backward from *Array*.length -1 to 0, decrementing by one each time. Looping backward is useful when you want to find the last matching element rather than the first (see Recipe 5.3), for example:

```
var letters:Array = ["a", "b", "c"];
for (var i:int = letters.length - 1; i >= 0; i--){
  // Display the elements in reverse order.
  trace("Element " + i + ": " + letters[i]);
}
```

There are many instances when you might want to loop through all the elements of an array. For example, by looping through an array containing references to sprites, you can perform a particular action on each of the sprites:

```
for (var i:int = 0; i < sprites.length; i++){
  // Move each sprite one pixel to the right.
  sprites[i].x++;
}
```

You can store the array's length in a variable rather than computing it during each loop iteration. For example:

```
var length:int = sprites.length;
for (var i:int = 0; i < length; i++){
  // Move each sprite one pixel to the right.
  sprites[i].x++;
}
```

The effect is that there is a very marginal performance improvement because Flash doesn't have to calculate the length during each iteration. However, it assumes that you are not adding or removing elements during the loop. Adding or removing elements changes the length property. In such a case, it is better to calculate the length of the array with each iteration.

See Also

Recipe 12.8 for ways to loop through characters in a string. Recipe 5.16 for details on enumerating elements of an associative array. See also Recipe 5.3.

5.3   Searching for Matching Elements in an Array

Problem

You want to find the first element in an array that matches a specified value.

Solution

Use a *for* statement to loop through an array and a *break* statement once a match has been found. Optionally, use the *ArrayUtilities.findMatchIndex()*, *ArrayUtilities. findLastMatchIndex()*, and/or *ArrayUtilities.findMatchIndices()* methods.

Discussion

When you search for the first element in an array that matches a specified value, you should use a *for* statement, as shown in Recipe 5.2, and add a *break* statement to exit the loop once the match has been found.

Using a *break* statement within a *for* statement causes the loop to exit once it is encountered. You should place the *break* statement within an *if* statement so it is executed only when a certain condition is met.

When searching for the first matching element, the importance of the *break* statement is twofold. First, you don't need to loop through the remaining elements of an array once the match has been found; that would waste processing time. In the following example, the *break* statement exits the loop after the second iteration, saving six more needless iterations. (Imagine the savings if there were a thousand more elements!)

Furthermore, the *break* statement is vital when searching for the first match because it ensures that only the first element is matched and that subsequent matches are ignored. If the *break* statement is omitted in the following example—all matching elements are displayed, as opposed to the first one only.

```
// Create an array with eight elements.
var letters:Array = ["a", "b", "c", "d", "a", "b", "c", "d"];

// Specify what we want to search for.
var match:String = "b";

// Use a for statement to loop through, potentially,
// all the elements of the array.
for (var i:int = 0; i < letters.length; i++) {

    // Check whether the current element matches
    // the search value.
    if (letters[i] == match) {

        // Do something with the matching element.
        // In this example, display a message
        // for testing purposes.
        trace("Element with index " + i +
            " found to match " + match);

        // Include a break statement to exit the for loop
        // once a match has been found.
        break;
    }
}
```

You can also search for the *last* matching element of an array by reversing the order in which the *for* statement loops through the array. Initialize the index variable to *Array*. length -1 and loop until it reaches 0 by decrementing the index variable, as follows.

```
var letters:Array = ["a", "b", "c", "d", "a", "b", "c", "d"];

var match:String = "b";

// Loop backward through the array. In this example,
// the "b" is at index 5.
for (var i:int = letters.length - 1; i >= 0; i--) {
    if (letters[i] == match) {
        trace("Element with index " + i +
            " found to match " + match);
        break;
    }
}
```

To simplify the process of searching for matching elements, you can use some of the static methods of the custom *ArrayUtilities* class. The class is in the *ascb.util* package, so the first step is to import the class:

```
import ascb.util.ArrayUtilities;
```

The *ArrayUtilities* class has three methods for finding matching elements—*findMatchIndex()*, *findLastMatchIndex()*, and *findMatchIndices()*. The *findMatchIndex()* method requires at least two parameters: a reference to the array you are searching, and the value you want to match. The method then returns either the index of the first matching element or -1 if no matches are found; for example:

```
var letters:Array = ["a", "b", "c", "d"];

trace(ArrayUtilities.findMatchIndex(letters, "b"));
// Displays: 1

trace(ArrayUtilities.findMatchIndex(letters, "r"));
// Displays: -1
```

You can also specify the starting index from which the search begins. That way, you can find matches subsequent to the first match. Specify the starting index as the third parameter; for example:

```
var letters:Array = ["a", "b", "c", "d", "a", "b", "c", "d"];

trace(ArrayUtilities.findMatchIndex(letters, "a", 1));
// Displays: 4
```

You can tell the method to find elements that are partial matches as well. By default, only exact matches are found. However, if you specify a value of true for the third parameter, the method finds any element containing the substring:

```
var words:Array = ["bicycle", "baseball", "mat", "board"];

trace(ArrayUtilities.findMatchIndex(words, "s", true));
// Displays: 1
```

If you want to run a partial match and still specify a starting index, simply pass the starting index as the fourth parameter.

The *findLastMatchIndex()* method works identically to *findMatchIndex()* except that it starts looking from the end of the array.

The *findMatchIndices()* method returns an array of indices for all elements that match the value passed in. The method requires at least two parameters—the array and the element you want to match. For example:

```
var letters:Array = ["a", "b", "c", "d", "a", "b", "c", "d"];

trace(ArrayUtilities.findMatchIndices(letters, "b"));
// Displays: 1,5
```

You can also run partial matches using *findMatchIndices()*. Simply specify a Boolean value of true as the third parameter:

```
var words:Array = ["bicycle", "baseball", "mat", "board"];

trace(ArrayUtilities.findMatchIndices(words, "b", true));
// Displays: 0,1,3
```

Each of the *ArrayUtilities* methods described use the same basic techniques with a for statement. Let's take a look at the code for the methods. The *findMatchIndex()* method is fairly straightforward, and you can see the comments inline. One thing to note, however, is that the method doesn't use any *break* statements within the *for* loop. That's because it uses *return* statements if a match is found. In the context of a function or method, a *return* statement exits the *for* statement, so the *break* statement is not necessary:

```
public static function findMatchIndex(array:Array, element:Object):int {
    // Use a variable to determine the index
    // from which to start. Use a default value of 0.
    var startingIndex:int = 0;

    // By default don't allow a partial match.
    var partialMatch:Boolean = false;

    // If the third parameter is a number,
    // assign it to nStartingIndex.
    // Otherwise, if the fourth parameter is a number,
    // assign it to nStartingIndex instead.
    if(typeof arguments[2] == "number") {
        startingIndex = arguments[2];
    }
    else if(typeof arguments[3] == "number") {
        startingIndex = arguments[3];
    }

    // If the third parameter is a Boolean value,
    // assign it to partialMatch.
    if(typeof arguments[2] == "boolean") {
        partialMatch = arguments[2];
    }

    // Assume no match is found.
    var match:Boolean = false;

    // Loop through each of the elements of the array
    // starting at the specified starting index.
    for(var i:int = startingIndex;
            i < array.length; i++) {

        // Check to see if the element either matches
        // or partially matches.
        if(partialMatch) {
            match = (array[i].indexOf(element) != -1);
        }
        else {
            match = (array[i] == element);
        }
```

```
        // If the element matches, return the index.
        if(match) {
          return i;
        }
      }

      // The following return statement is only reached
      // if no match was found. In that case, return -1.
      return -1;
    }
```

The *findLastMatchIndex()* method is almost identical to the *findMatchIndex()* method, except that it loops in reverse. The *findMatchedIndices()* method loops through the array to find every matching index. It appends each matching index to an array, and then it returns that array. It uses the *findMatchIndex()* method, as shown here:

```
public static function findMatchIndices(array:Array,
element:Object, partialMatch:Boolean = false):Array {
    var indices:Array = new Array();
    var index:int = findMatchIndex(array,
                                   element,
                                   partialMatch);
    while(index != -1) {
        indices.push(index);
        index = findMatchIndex(array,
                               element,
                               partialMatch,
                               index + 1);
    }
    return indices;
}
```

See Also

Recipes 5.2 and 5.10

5.4   Removing Elements

Problem

You want to remove one or more elements from an array and shift any remaining elements to fill the vacant indexes.

Solution

Use the *splice()* method to remove elements from the middle of the array. Use *pop()* to remove the last element or *shift()* to remove the first element.

Discussion

Remove elements from an array by starting at a specified index using the *splice()* method. When using *splice()* to delete elements, you should pass it two parameters:

start

> The index of the array from which to start deleting elements.

deleteCount

> The number of elements to delete. If this value is undefined, all the elements from *start* to the end of the array are deleted:

```
var letters:Array = ["a", "b", "c", "d"];

// Remove one element from letters starting at index 1.
letters.splice(1, 1);

// Display the results. The array now contains three elements:
// "a", "c", and "d".
for (var i:int = 0; i < letters.length; i++) {
    trace(letters [i]);
}
```

The *splice()* method also returns a new array containing the deleted elements; for example:

```
var letters:Array = ["a", "b", "c", "d"];

// Remove two elements from letters starting at index 0.
var deleted:Array = letters.splice(0, 2);

// Display the deleted elements: "a" and "b".
for (var i:int = 0; i < deleted.length; i++) {
    trace(deleted[i]);
}
```

To delete a single element from the beginning or end of the array, you can use the *shift()* and *pop()* methods. The *shift()* method removes the first element of the array and returns its value. The *pop()* method removes the last element of the array and returns its value:

```
var letters:Array = ["a", "b", "c", "d"];

// Remove the first element and display its value.
trace(letters.shift());

// Remove the last element and display its value.
trace(letters.pop());

// Display the remaining elements.
// The array has two elements left: "b" and "c".
for (var i = 0; i < letters.length; i++) {
    trace(letters[i]);
}
```

When you remove elements from an array in a *for* statement, you need to change the value of the index variable accordingly. The following example illustrates what can happen if you don't update the value of the index variable:

```
var numbers:Array = new Array(4, 10);
numbers[4] = 1;
trace(numbers);  // Displays: 4,10,undefined,undefined,1
for(var i:int = 0; i < numbers.length; i++) {
    if(numbers[i] == undefined) {
        numbers.splice(i, 1);
    }
}
trace(numbers);  // Displays: 4,10,undefined,1
```

In the preceding code, you might have expected it to remove both of the undefined elements from the array. However, as shown in the final trace, it removed only one. If you go through the *for* statement step-by-step, you can see why:

1. The first two iterations do nothing because the elements are not undefined.

2. The third iteration sees that the third element is undefined and removes it. At that point, the fourth and fifth elements shift down by one index, becoming the third and fourth elements.

3. The next iteration checks the new fourth element, which is now the last. It skips right over the other undefined element (now third). Instead, you can make sure you decrement the index variable after removing the element. The following code shows how you might do that:

```
var numbers:Array = new Array(4, 10);
numbers[4] = 1;
trace(numbers);  // Displays: 4,10,undefined,undefined,1
for(var i:int = 0; i < numbers.length; i++) {
  if(numbers[i] == undefined) {
    numbers.splice(i, 1);
    i--;
  }
}
trace(numbers);  // Displays: 4,10,1
```

5.5   Inserting Elements in the Middle of an Array

Problem

You want to insert elements in the middle of an array.

Solution

Use the *splice()* method.

Discussion

You can use the *splice()* method to insert elements as well as delete them. Values passed to the *splice()* method after the first and second parameters are inserted into the array at the index specified by the *start* parameter; all existing elements following that index are shifted up to accommodate the inserted values. If 0 is passed to the *splice()* method for the *deleteCount* parameter, no elements are deleted, but the new values are inserted:

```
var letters:Array = ["a", "b", "c", "d"];

// Insert three string values ("one", "two", and "three")
// starting at index 1.
letters.splice(1, 0, "r", "s", "t");

// letters now contains seven elements:
// "a", "r", "s", "t", "b", "c", and "d".
for (var i:int = 0; i < letters.length; i++) {
    trace(letters[i]);
}
```

You can also delete elements and insert new elements at the same time:

```
var letters:Array = ["a", "b", "c", "d"];

// Remove two elements and insert three more
// into letters starting at index 1.
letters.splice(1, 2, "r", "s", "t");

// myArray now contains five elements:
// "a", "r", "s", "t", and "d".
for (var i:int = 0; i < letters.length; i++) {
    trace(letters[i]);
}
```

5.6   Converting a String to an Array

Problem

You have a list of values as a string and you want to parse it into an array of separate elements.

Solution

Use the *String.split()* method.

Discussion

The *split()* method of the *String* class splits a string containing a list of values into an array. The list must be delimited by a uniform substring. For example, the list *Susan,Robert,Paula* is comma-delimited.

The *split()* method takes up to two parameters:

delimiter
> The substring that is used to delimit the elements of the list. If undefined, the entire list is placed into the first element of the new array.

limit
> The maximum number of elements to place into the new array. If undefined, all the elements of the list are placed into the new array.

You can use a space as the delimiter to split a string into an array of words:

```
var list:String = "Peter Piper picked a peck of pickled peppers";
// Split the string using the space as the delimiter. This puts
// each word into an element of the new array, words.
var words:Array = list.split(" ");
```

The *split()* method can be extremely useful when values are loaded into Flash using a *URLLoader* object or another similar technique for loading data. For example, you might retrieve a list of names as a string from the server such as the following:

```
names=Michael,Peter,Linda,Gerome,Catherine
```

You can make it easier to use the names by parsing them into an array using the *split()* method:

```
// Assume _loader is the URLLoader used to load the data.
var namesData:String = _loader.data;
var names:Array = namesData.split(",");
```

See Also

Recipe 5.7

5.7 Converting an Array to a String

Problem

You want to convert an array to a string.

Solution

Use the *join()* method.

Discussion

ActionScript provides you with a built-in way to quickly convert arrays to strings (assuming, of course, that the array elements themselves are either strings or another datatype that ActionScript can automatically cast to a string) using the *join()*

method. You should pass the *join()* method a string that tells Flash which delimiter to use to join the elements:

```
var letters:Array = ["a", "b", "c"];
trace(letters.join("|"));   // Displays: a|b|c
```

If you don't provide a delimiter, Flash uses a comma by default:

```
var letters:Array = ["a", "b", "c"];
trace(letters.join());   // Displays: a,b,c
```

 The *toString()* method does the same thing as the *join()* method either with no parameters or with the comma as the parameter. In fact, if you try to use an array in a situation in which a string is required, Flash automatically calls the *toString()* method, as follows:

```
var letters:Array = ["a", "b", "c"];
trace(letters);  // Displays: a,b,c
```

See Also

Recipe 5.6

5.8   Creating a Separate Copy of an Array

Problem

You want to make an exact copy (a duplicate) of an array—one that contains all of the elements found in the original, but is not just another reference to the original.

Solution

Use the *concat()* method or the *slice()* method. Optionally, you can use the *ArrayUtilities.duplicate()* method. The *duplicate()* method can create recursive duplicates.

Discussion

Because arrays are a composite datatype, they are copied and compared differently from primitive data. A variable that holds an array doesn't truly contain all of the array's data. Instead, the variable simply points to the place in the computer's memory where the array's data resides. This makes sense from an optimization standpoint. Primitive data tends to be small, such as a single number or a short string. But composite data, such as an array, can be very large. It would be inefficient to copy an entire array every time you wanted to perform an operation on it or pass it to a function. Therefore, when you try to copy an array, ActionScript doesn't make a separate copy of the array's data. A simple example illustrates this.

First, let's look at how primitive data is copied from the variable quantity to another variable, newQuantity:

```
// Assign the number 5 to a variable.
var quantity:int = 5;

// Copy quantity's value to another variable, newQuantity.
var newQuantity:int = quantity;

// Change quantity's value.
quantity = 29;

trace(quantity);        // Displays: 29
trace(newQuantity);     // Displays: 5
```

When the copy is made, the contents of quantity are copied to newQuantity. After the copy is made, subsequent changes to quantity have no effect on newQuantity (and vice versa) because primitive data is *copied by value*.

Now let's look at a similar operation with arrays; however, note the difference from the preceding example. The variable letters is assigned to the variable newLetters, but the two variables merely reference the same array in memory. When the value of letters changes, the changes are reflected in newLetters:

```
// Assign elements of an array.
var letters:Array = ["a", "b", "c"];

// Copy letters to another variable, newLetters.
var newLetters:Array = letters;

// Both arrays contain the same values, as expected.
trace(letters);         // Displays: "a,b,c"
trace(newLetters);      // Displays: "a,b,c"

// Change letters's value.
letters = ["d", "e", "f"];

// Surprise! Both arrays contain the new values.
// The old values are lost!
trace(letters);         // Displays: "d,e,f"
trace(newLetters);      // Displays: "d,e,f" (not "a,b,c")
```

Is the relationship between two copies of an array a good thing or a bad thing? The answer depends on what you expect and what you need to accomplish. Let's first understand what is happening, and then learn how to address it.

In the preceding example, the following line does not make a copy of letters' contents, as it would if letters held a primitive datatype:

```
var newLetters:Array = letters;
```

Instead it says to Flash, "Make newLetters point to whatever letters points to, even if the contents change in the future." So the two variables letters and newLetters always point to the same data in memory. If it helps, you can think of this arrangement as being similar to a file *shortcut* on Windows (known as an *alias* on the Macintosh). A shortcut simply points to another file located elsewhere. Whether you open the original file directly or access it via the shortcut, there is only one physical file that contains the content of interest. If the file's contents change, the shortcut still offers access to the current contents of the file. If you wanted two independent files, you'd have to duplicate the original file rather than simply create a shortcut to it.

So, is it a good thing if two variables refer to the same array? As explained earlier, in the normal course of things, it increases efficiency to avoid copying the contents of an array unnecessarily. However, you might want to operate on a copy of an array and not alter the original. You can create a duplicate copy of an array that is separate from the original using *concat()*:

```
// Assign elements of an array.
var letters:Array = ["a", "b", "c"];

// Create an independent copy of letters using concat(),
// which returns a new array.
var newLetters:Array = letters.concat();

// Both arrays contain the same values, as expected.
trace(letters);        // Displays: "a,b,c"
trace(newLetters);     // Displays: "a,b,c"

// Change letters' value.
letters = ["d", "e", "f"];

// Unlike preceding examples, the arrays are independent.
trace(letters);        // Displays: "d,e,f"
trace(newLetters);     // Displays: "a,b,c"
```

In line 6 of the preceding example, you could also use *slice()* instead of *concat()*, as follows:

```
var newLetters:Array = letters.slice(0);
```

The *concat()* or *slice()* methods work fine to duplicate a single-dimensional, integer-indexed array. However, when you have a *multidimensional array* (an array containing other arrays) or an associative array, you cannot use those techniques effectively. (See Recipes 5.9 and 5.15 for more information regarding multidimensional and associative arrays, respectively.) With associative arrays, you won't have a *concat()* or *slice()* method. With multidimensional arrays, however, using *concat()* or *slice()* to duplicate the top level of the array won't duplicate the nested array data. The following code illustrates the effect:

```
var coordinates:Array = new Array();
coordinates.push([0,1,2,3]);
coordinates.push([4,5,6,7]);
coordinates.push([8,9,10,11]);
coordinates.push([12,13,14,15]);
```

```
// Make a duplicate.
var coordinatesDuplicate:Array = coordinates.concat( );

// Replace one of the elements of one of the nested arrays
// in the duplicate.
coordinatesDuplicate[0][0] = 20;
trace(coordinates[0][0]);  // Displays: 20

// Replace one of the top-level elements.
coordinatesDuplicate[1] = [21,22,23,24];
trace(coordinates[1]);  // Displays: 4,5,6,7
```

In the preceding code, coordinates is an array of arrays; this is known as a *two-dimensional array* in ActionScript. coordinatesDuplicate is a duplicate of coordinates. However, even though it is a duplicate, its elements (which are also arrays) are still references to the original elements rather than duplicates. That means that if you assign a new value to one of the elements of one of the nested arrays in coordinatesDuplicate, coordinates is affected similarly. However, just to verify that coordinatesDuplicate does actually duplicate the top-level elements, you can see that in the last two lines of the code, replacing one of those elements does not affect coordinates.

To duplicate an array and ensure that every nested element is also duplicated, you need to use *recursion*. The *ArrayUtilities.duplicate()* method does just that, making it relatively simple for you to duplicate an array recursively. The *duplicate()* method requires just one parameter: a reference to an array or associative array. The method then returns a duplicate of that object. However, by default, *duplicate()* only returns a duplicate of the top-level elements, the same as *concat()* or *slice()*. If you want to duplicate the instance recursively, you need to specify that using a second parameter. Specify a Boolean value of true to recursively duplicate an instance, as shown in the following example:

```
// Create a two-dimensional array.
var coordinates:Array = new Array( );
for(var i:int = 0; i < 4; i++) {
  coordinates[i] = new Array( );
  for(var j:int = 0; j < 4; j++) {
    coordinates[i].push(String(i) + "," + String(j));
  }
}

// Duplicate coordinates. Cast the result as an array.
var newCoordinates:Array = ArrayUtilities.duplicate(coordinates, true) as Array;

// Replace an element in the nested array.
newCoordinates[0][0] = "a";

// Use the toString() method of the ArrayUtilities class
// to quickly output the contents of the arrays.
trace(ArrayUtilities.toString(coordinates));
trace(ArrayUtilities.toString(newCoordinates));
```

The following example illustrates the same *duplicate()* method used with an associative array:

```
var coordinatesMap:Object = new Object();
coordinatesMap.a = [{a: 1},{b: 2}, {c: 3}, {d: 4}];
coordinatesMap.b = [{a: 1},{b: 2}, {c: 3}, {d: 4}];
coordinatesMap.c = [{a: 1},{b: 2}, {c: 3}, {d: 4}];
coordinatesMap.d = [{a: 1},{b: 2}, {c: 3}, {d: 4}];
var newCoordinatesMap:Object = ArrayUtilities.duplicate(coordinatesMap, true);
newCoordinatesMap.a[0] = {r: 5};
trace(ArrayUtilities.toString(coordinatesMap));
trace(ArrayUtilities.toString(newCoordinatesMap));
```

In both examples, you can see that the original array (or associative array) is not affected by changes made to the duplicate.

See Also

Recipes 5.9 and 5.15

5.9   Storing Complex or Multidimensional Data

Problem

You have two or more sets of related data and you want to be able to keep track of the relationships between their elements.

Solution

Use *parallel arrays*, an array of arrays (a *multidimensional array*), or an *array of objects*.

Discussion

You can create two or more parallel arrays in which the elements with the same index in each array are related. For example, the *beginGradientFill()* method, discussed in Chapter 7, uses three parallel arrays for the colors, alphas, and ratios of the values used in the gradient. In each array, the elements with the same index correspond to one another.

To create parallel arrays, populate multiple arrays such that the elements with the same index correspond to one another. When you use parallel arrays, you can easily retrieve related data, since the indexes are the same across the arrays; for example:

```
var colors:Array = ["maroon", "beige",    "blue",     "gray"];
var years:Array  = [1997,    2000,        1985,       1983];
var makes:Array  = ["Honda",  "Chrysler", "Mercedes", "Fiat"];

// Loop through the arrays. Since each array is the same
// length, you can use the length property of any of them
```

```
// in the for statement. Here, we use makes.length.
for (var i:int = 0; i < makes.length; i++) {
    // Displays:
    // A maroon 1997 Honda
    // A beige 2000 Chrysler
    // A blue 1985 Mercedes
    // A gray 1983 Fiat

    // Display the elements with corresponding indexes
    // from the arrays.
    trace("A " + colors[i] + " " +
            years[i] + " " +
            makes[i]);
}
```

 Be careful when manipulating parallel arrays. If you add or remove elements from the arrays, you have to be certain to add or remove related data at the same position in every array. Otherwise the arrays will be out of sync and useless.

Another option for working with multiple sets of data is to create a multidimensional array, which is an array of arrays (i.e., an array in which each element is another array):

```
// Create an array, cars, and populate it with elements that
// are arrays. Each element array represents a car and
// contains three elements (color, year, and make).
var cars:Array = new Array();
cars.push(["maroon", 1997, "Honda"]);
cars.push(["beige", 2000, "Chrysler"]);
cars.push(["blue", 1985, "Mercedes"]);
cars.push(["gray", 1983, "Fiat"]);

// Loop through the elements of the cars array.
for (var i:int = 0; i < cars.length; i++) {
    // The output is the same as in the
    // earlier parallel arrays example:
    // A maroon 1997 Honda
    // A beige 2000 Chrysler
    // A blue 1985 Mercedes
    // A gray 1983 Fiat

    // Output each element of each subarray, cars[i].
    // Note the use of two successive indexes in brackets,
    // such as cars[i][0].
    trace("A " + cars[i][0] + " " +
            cars[i][1] + " " +
            cars[i][2]);
}
```

The following is another way to view the two-dimensional cars arrays' contents. This displays the elements in a long list (the formatting isn't as nice as in the previous example, but it shows the array structure more clearly):

```
// Loop through the elements of the cars array.
for (var i:int = 0; i < cars.length; i++) {
    // Loop through the elements of each subarray, cars[i].
    for (var j:int = 0; j < cars[i].length; j++) {
        // Note the use of two successive indexes in brackets,
        // cars[i][j].
        trace("Element [" + i + "][" + j + "] contains: " +
            cars[i][j]);
    }
}
```

In the preceding example (the array of arrays), it is hard to discern the meaning of something like cars[i][0] or cars[i][j]. Furthermore, if the order of elements in a subarray changes, you would have to modify the code (or it might erroneously display "A Honda maroon 1997" instead of "A maroon 1997 Honda").

One alternative is to work with related data using an array of objects (associative arrays). This technique is similar to working with an array of arrays, but it offers the advantage of named properties. When you use an array of arrays, you must reference each value by its numbered index. However, when you use an array of objects, you can reference the data by property name instead of its index number. You can specify the properties of the object in any order you like because you'll refer to them later by name, not by number:

```
// Create an array, cars, and populate it with objects.
// Each object has a make property, a year property,
// and a color property.
var cars:Array = new Array();

// Here, object literals are used to define three properties
// for each car; the object literals are added to
// the main array.
cars.push({make: "Honda",    year: 1997, color: "maroon"});
cars.push({make: "Chrysler", year: 2000, color: "beige"});
cars.push({make: "Mercedes", year: 1985, color: "blue"});
cars.push({make: "Fiat",     year: 1983, color: "gray"});

// Loop through the cars array.
for (var i:int = 0; i < cars.length; i++) {
    // The output is the same as in the earlier examples,
    // but each value is referenced by its property name,
    // which is more programmer-friendly.
    trace("A " + cars[i].color + " " +
                cars[i].year + " " +
                cars[i].make);
}
```

See Also

Recipe 5.15 covers associative arrays, in which elements are accessed by name instead of number.

5.10 Sorting or Reversing an Array

Problem

You want to sort the elements of an array.

Solution

Use the *sort()* method. For arrays of objects, you can also use the *sortOn()* method.

Discussion

You can perform a simple sort on an array using the *sort()* method. The *sort()* method, without any parameters, sorts the elements of an array in ascending order. Elements are sorted according to the Unicode code points of the characters in the string (roughly alphabetical for Western European languages).

```
var words:Array = ["tricycle", "relative", "aardvark", "jargon"];
words.sort();
trace(words); // Displays: aardvark,jargon,relative,tricycle
```

The *sort()* method, by default, is very useful if you want to sort the elements of an array in ascending, alphabetical order. However, there are some caveats. Namely, the sort is case-sensitive, and it sorts numbers "alphabetically" instead of numerically. Fortunately, ActionScript allows you to pass one of several constants to the *sort()* method in order to sort with different guidelines.

You sort an array in descending order using the *Array.DESCENDING* constant:

```
var words:Array = ["tricycle", "relative", "aardvark", "jargon"];
words.sort(Array.DESCENDING);
trace(words); // Displays: tricycle,relative,jargon,aardvark
```

As mentioned, the *sort()* method runs a case-sensitive sort by default. It places elements starting with uppercase characters before elements starting with lowercase characters. The following illustrates the point:

```
var words:Array = ["Tricycle", "relative", "aardvark", "jargon"];
words.sort();
trace(words); // Displays: Tricycle,aardvark,jargon,relative
```

You can use the *Array.CASEINSENSITIVE* constant to run a case-insensitive sort:

```
var words:Array = ["Tricycle", "relative", "aardvark", "jargon"];
words.sort(Array.CASEINSENSITIVE);
trace(words); // Displays: aardvark,jargon,relative,Tricycle
```

When you sort an array of numbers, the values are sorted according to the ASCII equivalents of the digits rather than in numerical order. The following code illustrates the point:

```
var scores:Array = [10, 2, 14, 5, 8, 20, 19, 6];
scores.sort();
trace(scores);    // Displays: 10,14,19,2,20,5,6,8
```

You can use the *Array.NUMERIC* constant with the *sort()* method to sort an array of numbers numerically:

```
var scores:Array = [10, 2, 14, 5, 8, 20, 19, 6];
scores.sort(Array.NUMERIC);
trace(scores);    // Displays: 2,5,6,8,10,14,19,20
```

There are two other possible constants you can use with the *sort()* method: *Array.UNIQUESORT* and *Array.RETURNINDEXEDARRAY*. In some situations you want to sort the array only if it contains unique elements. In this case, use the *Array.UNIQUESORT* constant; Flash only sorts the array if the elements are unique. Otherwise, the *sort()* method returns 0, and the array is not sorted:

```
var ranking:Array = [2,5,6,3,1,1,4,8,7,10,9];
var sortedRanking:Object = ranking.sort(Array.UNIQUESORT);
trace(sortedRanking);    // Displays: 0
trace(ranking);    // Displays: 2,5,6,3,1,1,4,8,7,10,9
```

Frequently, you may want to get the sorted order of an array's elements, but you don't want to change the original array because other parts of your application may depend on the existing order. For example, if you have parallel arrays, and you sort one array, its relationship with the other arrays is no longer valid. In such scenarios the *Array.RETURNINDEXEDARRAY* constant is very helpful. It allows you to return a new array containing the indices of the elements of the original array in sorted order, as illustrated in the following code:

```
var words:Array = ["tricycle", "relative", "aardvark", "jargon"];
var indices:Array = words.sort(Array.RETURNINDEXEDARRAY);
trace(words);    // Displays: tricycle,relative,aardvark,jargon
trace(indices); // Displays: 2,3,1,0
for(var i:int = 0; i < words.length; i++) {
  /* Displays:
     aardvark
     jargon
     relative
     tricycle
  */
  trace(words[indices[i]]);
}
```

You aren't limited to one sort modifier at a time. You can combine the combine the constants using the bitwise *OR* operator (|). The following code illustrates a case-insensitive, descending sort:

```
var words:Array = ["Tricycle", "relative", "aardvark", "jargon"];
words.sort(Array.CASEINSENSITIVE | Array.DESCENDING);
trace(words);    // Displays: Tricycle,relative,jargon,aardvark
```

Sometimes you want to reverse the order of the elements in an array. The *sort()* method allows you to run ascending, descending, case-sensitive, case-insensitive, and numeric sorts, but it does not allow you to simply reverse the order of the elements. Instead, you can use the *reverse()* method. The *reverse()* method does just what its name suggests; it reverses the order of the elements:

```
var words:Array = ["tricycle", "relative", "aardvark", "jargon"];
words.reverse();
trace(words);    // Displays: jargon,aardvark,relative,tricycle
```

The preceding portion of this recipe described how to sort arrays in which the elements are strings or numbers. You can also sort arrays of objects of any type using the *sortOn()* method. The *sortOn()* method requires a string parameter specifying the name of the property on which to sort the elements:

```
var cars:Array = new Array();
cars.push({make: "Honda",    year: 1997, color: "maroon"});
cars.push({make: "Chrysler", year: 2000, color: "beige"});
cars.push({make: "Mercedes", year: 1985, color: "blue"});
cars.push({make: "Fiat",     year: 1983, color: "gray"});
// Sort the cars array according to the year property
// of each element.cars.sortOn("year");
for (var i:int = 0; i < cars.length; i++) {
  /* Displays:
      gray    1983  Fiat
      blue    1985  Mercedes
      maroon  1997  Honda
      beige   2000  Chrysler
  */
  trace(cars[i].color + "\t" +
        cars[i].year + "\t" +
        cars[i].make);
}
```

The *sortOn()* method also has the ability to sort on more than one field. You can do so by specifying an array of fields on which to sort. The elements are then sorted on those fields in the specified order. To understand how it works, take a look at the following examples:

```
var cars:Array = new Array();
cars.push({make: "Honda",    year: 1997, color: "maroon"});
cars.push({make: "Chrysler", year: 2000, color: "beige"});
cars.push({make: "Mercedes", year: 1985, color: "blue"});
cars.push({make: "Fiat",     year: 1983, color: "gray"});
cars.push({make: "Honda",    year: 1992, color: "silver"});
cars.push({make: "Chrysler", year: 1968, color: "gold"});
cars.push({make: "Mercedes", year: 1975, color: "green"});
cars.push({make: "Fiat",     year: 1983, color: "black"});
cars.push({make: "Honda",    year: 2001, color: "blue"});
cars.push({make: "Chrysler", year: 2004, color: "orange"});
```

```
cars.push({make: "Mercedes", year: 2000, color: "white"});
cars.push({make: "Fiat",     year: 1975, color: "yellow"});

// Sort the cars array according to the year property
// of each element, then by the make.
cars.sortOn(["year", "make"]);

for (var i:int = 0; i < cars.length; i++) {
  /* Displays:
      gold    1968    Chrysler
      yellow  1975    Fiat
      green   1975    Mercedes
      black   1983    Fiat
      gray    1983    Fiat
      blue    1985    Mercedes
      silver  1992    Honda
      maroon  1997    Honda
      beige   2000    Chrysler
      white   2000    Mercedes
      blue    2001    Honda
      orange  2004    Chrysler
  */
  trace(cars[i].color + "\t" +
      cars[i].year + "\t" +
      cars[i].make);
}
```

The next example sorts the same array first by make, then by year—notice what the effect is:

```
cars.sortOn(["make", "year"]);

for (var i:int = 0; i < cars.length; i++) {
  /* Displays:
      gold    1968    Chrysler
      beige   2000    Chrysler
      orange  2004    Chrysler
      yellow  1975    Fiat
      black   1983    Fiat
      gray    1983    Fiat
      silver  1992    Honda
      maroon  1997    Honda
      blue    2001    Honda
      green   1975    Mercedes
      blue    1985    Mercedes
      white   2000    Mercedes
  */
  trace(cars[i].color + "\t" +
      cars[i].year + "\t" +
      cars[i].make);
}
```

As with the *sort()* method, the *sortOn()* method supports sort modifiers. You can use the *Array* constants to sort in descending, case-insensitive, and numeric order.

You can also, as with the *sort()* method, run a unique sort and return an array of sorted indices rather than affecting the original array. The following example sorts cars in descending order:

```
cars.sortOn("year", Array.DESCENDING);

for (var i:int = 0; i < cars.length; i++) {
  /* Displays:
      beige    2000  Chrysler
      maroon   1997  Honda
      blue     1985  Mercedes
      gray     1983  Fiat
  */
  trace(cars[i].color + "\t" +
        cars[i].year + "\t" +
        cars[i].make);
}
```

Sorted arrays can be useful in many scenarios. For example, if you want to display the elements of an array in a UI component or a text field, you often want to list the elements in alphabetical order.

 Unless you use the *Array.RETURNINDEXEDARRAY* constant, the *sort()* and *sortOn()* methods make changes to the order of the original array; they do not return a new array.

See Also

Recipe 5.8 to make a separate copy of an array on which you can perform destructive operations. Recipe 5.11 for details on custom sorting.

5.11   Implementing a Custom Sort

Problem

You want to sort an array using more complex logic than an alphabetical or numeric sort.

Solution

Use the *sort()* method and pass it a reference to a *compare function*.

Discussion

If you want complete control over sorting criteria, use the *sort()* method with a custom *compare function* (also called a *sorter function*). The *sort()* method repeatedly calls the compare function to reorder two elements of an array at a time. It sends the compare function two parameters (let's call them *a* and *b*). The compare function then determines which one should be ordered first by returning a positive number, a negative number, or 0, depending on how the elements are to be sorted. If the function returns a negative number, *a* is ordered before *b*. If the function returns 0, then the current order is preserved. If the function returns a positive number, *a* is ordered after *b*. The *sort()* method calls the compare function with every relevant combination of elements until the entire array has been properly ordered. Using a custom compare function is easier than it sounds. You don't need to concern yourself with the details of sorting the entire array; you simply specify the criteria for comparing any two elements.

One example of when you would want to use a custom sorter is when you need to sort a list of strings, but you need to process the strings somehow before sorting them. Say you are building a music program that needs to display a list of bands. If you just sorted the bands alphabetically, all the bands whose names began with "The" would appear together in the T section, which is probably not what you want. You can define a compare function that strips off "The" from the beginning of the name before comparing the bands. Here is the code to set up the array, perform a simple sort, and display the results:

```
var bands:Array = ["The Clash",
                   "The Who",
                   "Led Zeppelin",
                   "The Beatles",
                   "Aerosmith",
                   "Cream"];
bands.sort();
for(var i:int = 0; i < bands.length; i++) {
    trace(bands[i]);

    /* output:
        Aerosmith
        Cream
        Led Zeppelin
        The Beatles
        The Clash
        The Who
    */
}
```

To handle this, call the *sort()* method passing the *bandNameSort* compare function:

```
var bands:Array = ["The Clash",
                   "The Who",
                   "Led Zeppelin",
                   "The Beatles",
                   "Aerosmith",
                   "Cream"];
bands.sort(bandNameSort);
for(var i:int = 0; i < bands.length; i++) {
    trace(bands[i]);
```

```
    /* output:
        Aerosmith
        The Beatles
        The Clash
        Cream
        Led Zeppelin
        The Who
    */
}

function bandNameSort(band1:String, band2:String):int
{
    band1 = band1.toLowerCase( );
    band2 = band2.toLowerCase( );
    if(band1.substr(0, 4) == "the ") {
        band1 = band1.substr(4);
    }
    if(band2.substr(0, 4) == "the ") {
        band2 = band2.substr(4);
    }
    if(band1 < band2) {
        return -1;
    }
    else {
        return 1;
    }
}
```

The *bandNameSort( )* function first converts both band names to lowercase, ensuring a case-insensitive sort. Then it checks to see if either band name begins with "The ". If so, it grabs the portion of the string from the fourth character to the end, which is everything after the word "The" plus the space.

Finally, it compares the two processed strings, returning -1 if the first string should go first, and 1 if the first string should go second. As you can see, the output is more in line with what you would expect.

There is no limit to how complex the compare function can be. If you are sorting a list of objects, you can build in logic that reads multiple properties of each object, performs calculations on their data, compares them, and returns the results.

 Realize that the compare function may be run hundreds or even thousands of times in a single sort of a large array, so be careful about making it too complex.

5.12 Randomizing the Elements of an Array

Problem

You want to randomize the elements of an array.

Solution

Use the *sort()* method with a compare function that randomly returns a positive or negative number.

Discussion

There are lots of scenarios in which you might plausibly want to randomize the elements of an array. For example, you may have a game in which you want to randomize the letters of a word. Since you already know how to split the letters into elements of an array using the *split()* method, you may need to randomize those elements. Or perhaps you are making a card game where each element in the array is a card, and you want to shuffle the deck.

There is more than one way to accomplish the task. However, one of the simplest ways is to create a compare function that randomly returns a positive or negative number, and use it in the *sort()* method. See Recipe 5.11 for more information on compare functions.

The following is probably the simplest possible compare function for the job:

```
function randomSort(elementA:Object, elementB:Object):Number {
    return Math.random( ) - .5
}
```

Math.random() returns a number between 0.0 and 1.0. If you subtract 0.5 from that number, you'll get a random number between -0.5 and 0.5. Remember that in a compare function, returning a negative number means to order the first element first, and a positive number tells the *sort()* method to put the second element first. Since the odds you'll return are 50/50, the resulting order of the array is completely random.

The following is an example of randomizing an array:

```
var numbers:Array = new Array();
for(var i:int=0;i<20;i++) {
    numbers[i] = i;
}
numbers.sort(randomSort);
for(var i:int=0;i<numbers.length;i++) {
    trace(numbers[i]);
}
```

This creates an array of 20 sequential numbers, and then randomizes and displays them. You can verify that the order is now quite random.

See Also

Recipe 5.11 for more information on compare functions.

5.13   Getting the Minimum or Maximum Element

Problem

You want to retrieve the minimum or maximum element from an array of numbers.

Solution

Sort the array numerically, and then retrieve the first or last element from the sorted array.

Discussion

You can quickly retrieve the minimum or maximum value from an array by sorting it. The following example illustrates how to do just that:

```
var scores:Array = [10, 4, 15, 8];
scores.sort(Array.NUMERIC);
trace("Minimum: " + scores[0]);
trace("Maximum: " + scores[scores.length - 1]);
```

Of course, if the existing order of the array is important, you'll want to make a copy of the array before sorting it. See Recipe 5.8.

You can optionally use the *ArrayUtilities.min()* and *ArrayUtilities.max()* methods.

See Also

Recipe 5.8

5.14   Comparing Arrays

Problem

You want to compare two arrays to see if they are equivalent.

Solution

Loop through each element of both arrays and compare them.

Discussion

Since arrays are reference datatypes, using an equality operator with two array variables only checks to see if they point to the same spot in memory. For example:

```
var letters:Array = ["a", "b", "c", "d"];
var lettersPointer:Array = letters;
trace(letters == lettersPointer);  // Displays: true
```

However, if two arrays are equivalent yet don't point to the same spot in memory, an equality operation returns false:

```
var letters1:Array = ["a", "b", "c", "d"];
var letters2:Array = ["a", "b", "c", "d"];
trace(letters1 == letters2);  // Displays: false
```

Instead, you can loop through each of the elements of the arrays and compare them:

```
var equivalent:Boolean = true;
for(var i:int = 0; i < letters1.length; i++) {
    if(letters1[i] != letters2[i]) {
        equivalent = false;
        break;
    }
}
trace(equivalent);  // Displays: true
```

Optionally, you can use the *ArrayUtilities.equals()* method. This method requires two parameters: the references to the two arrays to compare. The method returns a Boolean value that indicates whether the arrays are equivalent or not:

```
var letters1:Array = ["a", "b", "c", "d"];
var letters2:Array = ["a", "b", "c", "d"];
trace(ArrayUtilities.equals(letters1, letters2));
// Displays: true
```

By default, the order of the elements has to match in the two arrays. If you don't care whether the order of the elements matches, you can specify a third parameter for the *equals()* method; a Boolean value indicating whether or not the order should be disregarded:

```
var letters1:Array = ["a", "b", "c", "d"];
var letters2:Array = ["b", "a", "d", "c"];
trace(ArrayUtilities.equals(letters1, letters2));
// Displays: false
trace(ArrayUtilities.equals(letters1, letters2, true));
// Displays: true
```

The *equals()* method is fairly simple. The code is explained in the comments in the following code block:

```
public static function equals(arrayA:Array,
                              arrayB:Array,
                              bNotOrdered:Boolean):Boolean {

    // If the two arrays don't have the same number of elements,
    // they obviously are not equivalent.
    if(arrayA.length != arrayB.length) {
        return false;
    }

    // Create a copy of each so that anything done to the copies
    // doesn't affect the originals.
    var arrayACopy:Array = arrayA.concat();
```

```
    var arrayBCopy:Array = arrayB.concat();

    // If the order of the elements of the two arrays doesn't
    // matter, sort the two copies so the order of the copies
    // matches when comparing.
    if(bNotOrdered) {
        arrayACopy.sort();
        arrayBCopy.sort();
    }

    // Loop through each element of the arrays, and compare them.
    // If they don't match, delete the copies and return false.
    for(var i:int = 0; i < arrayACopy.length; i++) {
        if(arrayACopy[i] != arrayBCopy[i]) {
            delete arrayACopy;
            delete arrayBCopy;
            return false;
        }
    }

    // Otherwise the arrays are equivalent.
    // So delete the copies and return true.
    delete arrayACopy;
    delete arrayBCopy;
    return true;
}
```

5.15   Creating an Associative Array

Problem

You want to create an array that uses named elements instead of numbered indexes.

Solution

Create an associative array.

Discussion

When working with sets of data in which each element has a specific meaning or importance, a typical, number-indexed array doesn't always suffice.

For example, if you are working with a set of data such as the names of members of a committee, a number-indexed array is sufficient:

```
var aMembers:Array = new Array("Franklin", "Gina", "Sindhu");
```

However, if each member of the committee plays a special role, a standard array offers no way to indicate that. To address the issue, you can use an *associative array*. In some languages, this is called a *hash table*. In ActionScript, it is actually just an instance of the *Object* class. An associative array uses named elements rather than numeric indexes. The names used to refer to elements are often called *keys* or *properties*. The keys can give a meaningful context to the associated element value.

You can create an associative array in ActionScript by using *object literal notation* or adding elements to an object. Despite their name, you don't use the *Array* class to create associative arrays. The *Array* class provides methods and properties that work with number-indexed arrays only—and not with associative arrays. Associative arrays should be instances of the *Object* class. Technically, since the *Object* class is the base class for all ActionScript classes, all ActionScript objects can be used as associative arrays. However, unless you have some specific reason for using another class as an associative array, it is best to simply use the generic *Object* class.

One way you can create an associative array is by using object literal notation. With this technique, use curly braces ({ }) to enclose a comma-delimited list of keys and values, which are separated by a colon (:), as shown in the following example:

```
var memebers:Object = {scribe: "Franklin",
                       chairperson: "Gina",
                       treasurer: "Sindhu"};
```

You can also create an associative array using the following multiline technique with the *Object* constructor. Although the object literal notation is fine for creating small associative arrays in a single step, you should use the *Object* constructor technique for creating larger associative arrays. It improves readability and lets you add properties to an associative array by assigning the properties (keys) on subsequent lines. For example:

```
var members:Object = new Object();
members.scribe = "Franklin";
members.chairperson = "Gina";
members.treasurer = "Sindhu";
```

Although using an *Object* constructor is more common, you can initialize the associative array object by using an empty object literal in place of the *Object* constructor:

```
var members:Object = {};
```

You can retrieve the values from an associative array in two ways. The first way is to access the elements using property notation (with the dot operator):

```
trace(members.scribe); // Displays: Franklin
```

The other option for retrieving values from an associative array is using *array-access notation*. To use array-access notation, reference the associative array followed by the array-access operator ([ ]). Within the array-access operator, you must use the *string* value of the name of the key you wish to access:

```
trace(members["scribe"]); // Displays: Franklin
```

Array-access notation is extremely useful in situations in which there are multiple keys with names in a sequence. This is because you can dynamically generate the key string value, whereas you cannot do this with property notation; for example:

```
var members:Object = new Object();
members.councilperson1 = "Beatrice";
members.councilperson2 = "Danny";
members.councilperson3 = "Vladamir";

for (var i:int = 1; i <= 3; i++) {
    trace(members["councilperson" + i];
}
```

Array access notation is most frequently used when looping through every element in an associative array, as shown in Recipe 5.16.

You can use either the property notation or array-access notation to read or write the values of an associative array:

```
var members:Object = new Object();
members["councilperson"] = "Ruthie";
trace(members.councilperson);          // Displays: Ruthie
members.councilperson = "Rebecca";
trace(members["councilperson"]);       // Displays: Rebecca
```

See Also

Recipe 5.16 contains more details on accessing named elements of an associative array.

5.16   Reading Elements of an Associative Array

Problem

You want to loop through the elements of an associative array.

Solution

Use a *for . . . in* statement.

Discussion

You iterate through the elements of integer-indexed arrays by using a *for* statement. However, named elements in associative arrays cannot be accessed by a numeric index, and the order of associative array elements is not guaranteed, regardless of the order in which the elements are added to the array. For that reason, there are also no methods to sort or reverse an associative array, or otherwise change its order.

Fortunately, you can loop through the enumerable elements of an associative array by using a *for . . . in* statement. This statement iterates through all the readable properties of the specified object. The syntax for a *for . . . in* statement is as follows:

```
for (key in object) {
    // Actions
}
```

The *for . . . in* statement doesn't require an explicit update statement because the number of loop iterations is determined by the number of properties in the object being examined. Note that *key* is a variable name that will be used to store the property name during each iteration, not the name of a specific property or key. On the other hand, *object* is the specific object whose properties you want to read. For example:

```
var members:Object = new Object();
members.scribe = "Franklin";
members.chairperson = "Gina";
members.treasurer = "Sindhu";

// Use a for . . . in statement to loop through all elements.
for (var sRole:String in members) {
    // Displays:
    // treasurer: Sindhu
    // chairperson: Gina
    // scribe: Franklin
    trace(sRole + ": " + members[sRole]);
}
```

When you use a *for . . . in* statement, you must use array-access notation (square brackets) with the associative array. If you try to use property notation (with the dot operator) it won't work properly. This is because the value that is assigned to the key iterator variable is the *string* name of the key, not the key's identifier.

A *for . . . in* loop does not display all built-in properties of an object. For example, it displays custom properties added at runtime, but it does not enumerate methods of built-in objects, even though they are stored in object properties.

See Also

Recipe 5.2

## CHAPTER 6

Display List

6.0   Introduction

The rendering model for ActionScript 3.0 and Flash Player 9 is radically different than in previous versions. Traditionally, the *MovieClip* was the focal point of the renderer. Every *.swf* movie contained a root *MovieClip* (commonly referred to as the *Stage*). The root *MovieClip* could contain child *MovieClips*, which could, in turn, contain more child *MovieClips*. The concept of *depths* was used to control the stacking order in which *MovieClips* were drawn (objects on higher depths appear "on top"). Methods such as *createEmptyMovieClip()*, *attachMovie()*, or *duplicateMovieClip()* were used to create *MovieClips*. Anytime a *MovieClip* was created, it was automatically added into the visual hierarchy and consequently drawn by the renderer. *MovieClips* weren't able to move to different places within the hierarchy; instead, they first had to be destroyed and then recreated before they could be positioned elsewhere in the display.

The new renderer is still hierarchical, but not as rigid, and aims to simplify and optimize the rendering process. The new rendering model centers on the *display list* concept and focuses on the classes available in the *flash.display* package. The display list is a hierarchy that contains all visible objects in the *.swf* movie. Any object not on the display list is not drawn by the renderer. Each *.swf* movie contains exactly one display list, which is comprised of three types of elements:

The stage
> The stage is the root of the display list hierarchy. Every movie has a single stage object that contains the entire object hierarchy of everything displaying on the screen. The stage is a container that typically contains only a single child, the main application class of the *.swf* movie. You can access the stage by referring to the stage property on any display object in the display list.

Display object containers

A display object container is an object that is capable of containing child display objects. The stage is a display object container. Other display object containers include *Sprite*, *MovieClip*, and *Shape*. When a display object container is removed from the display list, all its children are removed as well.

Display objects

A display object is a visual element. Some classes function as both display objects and display object containers, such as *MovieClip*, while other classes are only display objects, such a *TextField*. After a display object is created, it won't appear on-screen until it is added into a display object container.

The hierarchy tree for a display list might look like something in Figure 6-1. The stage is at the very top of the hierarchy, with display object containers as branches and display objects as leaves. The items at the top of the diagram are visually underneath the items at the bottom.

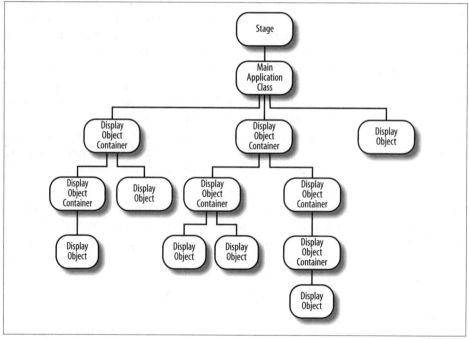

Figure 6-1. An example display list hierarchy

Transitioning to the display list realizes a number of benefits for programmers over working with previous versions of the Flash Player; these include:

Increased performance

The display list contains multiple visual classes besides just *MovieClip*. Classes such as *Sprite* can be used to reduce the memory requirements when a timeline isn't necessary. Additionally, a *Shape* can be used to draw into rather than relying on a full *MovieClip* instance. By having these lighter-weight classes and using them when possible, precious memory and processor resources can be saved, resulting in improved overall performance.

Easier depth management

The hierarchy of the display functions as depth management under the new display list model. In the previous model, methods such as *getNextHighestDepth()* were used to create *MovieClips* on the correct depth, and *swapDepths()* was used to control the visual stacking order. Depth management was cumbersome and tedious before and often required extremely careful programming. It was a fact of life that just had to be dealt with because it was so intertwined with the language. The new display list model handles depth almost automatically now, making depth management almost a thing of the past.

Less rigid structure

The previous model featured a fairly inflexible and rigid hierarchy. To change the hierarchy, *MovieClips* had to be destroyed and recreated at a new location. This was a time-consuming and expensive operation, and often was painfully slow. The new display list model is much more flexible—entire portions of the hierarchy tree can be moved via the new *reparenting* functionality (discussed in Recipe 6.1), without suffering the performance penalties of creating and destroying elements as before.

Easier creation of visual items

The display list rendering model makes creating display objects easier, especially when creating instances of custom visual classes. The previous model required extending *MovieClip*, combined with using special linkage that associated a library item with the ActionScript class. Then *attachMovie()* had to be used to actually create an instance of the custom class. Under the display list model, you extend one of the many display object classes, but you use the new keyword to create instances of custom visual classes, which is much more intuitive, easier, and cleaner. See Recipe 6.4 for details.

As noted earlier, the *flash.display* package contains the core classes for the display list model. The old model focused on the *MovieClip* class, but the display list revolves around the *DisplayObject* class and its various subclasses. Figure 6-2 illustrates the display list class hierarchy.

Each one of the core classes is designed to serve a specific purpose. By having more than just *MovieClip* available, the display list offers more flexibility to programmers than the previous model. The more commonly used display classes are listed in Table 6-1.

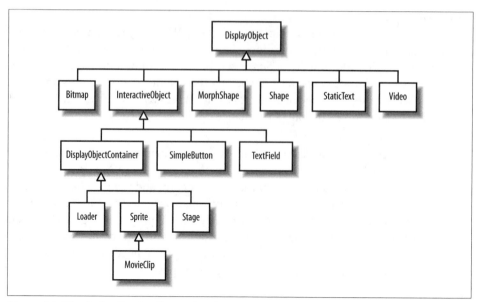

Figure 6-2. The display list class hierarchy

Table 6-1. Commonly used display classes

Display class	Description
DisplayObject	The base class of all display list classes. DisplayObject defines properties and methods common to all display classes. The DisplayObject class is not meant to be instantiated directly.
Bitmap	The Bitmap class allows for the creation and manipulation of images via the BitmapData methods; it is described in Chapter 8.
Shape	The Shape class contains a graphics property that allows for drawing using lines, fills, circles, rectangles, etc. Chapter 7 has more information.
Sprite	Sprites are similar to shapes, but can contain child display objects such as text and video. A Sprite can be thought of as a MovieClip without a timeline.
MovieClip	MovieClip is the familiar class with a timeline and methods for controlling the playhead. Because MovieClip is a subclass of Sprite, you can draw inside of it, and it can contain child display objects as well.
Video	The Video class lives in the *flash.media* package, but is also a subclass of DisplayObject. Video instances are used to play video, as described in Chapter 16.
TextField	The TextField class, found in the *flash.text* package, allows the creation of dynamic and input text fields. See Chapter 9 for more information.
Loader	Loader instances are used to load in external visual assets, such as other *.swf* movies or image files.

If you've worked with Flash in the past, transitioning to the display list model is going to take some time. Old habits are hard to break, and display list programming has a lot of depth. However, once you get into the swing of things you'll see that the time it takes to learn the new model is well worth it. The display list dramatically changes Flash display programming for the better.

6.1   Adding an Item to the Display List

Problem

You want to add a new display object to the display list so it appears on-screen.

Solution

Use the *addChild( )* and *addChildAt( )* methods from the *DisplayObectContainer* class.

Discussion

The Flash Player is composed of two main pieces that function together to form a cohesive unit, the ActionScript Virtual Machine (AVM) and the Rendering Engine. The AVM is responsible for executing ActionScript code, and the Rendering Engine is what draws objects on-screen. Because the Flash Player is composed of these two main pieces, drawing an object on the screen is a two-step process:

1. The display object needs to be created in the ActionScript engine.
2. The display object is then created in the rendering engine and drawn on-screen.

The first step is done by using the new operator to create an instance of the display object. Any object that is going to be added to the display list must be either a direct or indirect subclass of *DisplayObject*, such as *Sprite*, *MovieClip*, *TextField*, or a custom class you create (according to Recipe 6.4). To create a *TextField* instance you would use the following code:

```
var hello:TextField = new TextField( );
```

The preceding line of code creates a *TextField* display object in the AVM, but the object is not drawn on the screen yet because the object doesn't exist in the Rendering Engine. To create the object in the Rendering Engine, the object needs to be added to the display list hierarchy. This can be done by calling the *addChild( )* or *addChildAt( )* method from a *DisplayObjectContainer* instance that is itself already on the display list hierarchy.

The *addChild( )* method takes a single parameter—the display object that the container should add as a child. The following code is a complete example that demonstrates how to create an object in the AVM and then create the object in the Rendering Engine by adding it to the display list:

```
package {
  import flash.display.DisplayObjectContainer;
  import flash.display.Sprite;
  import flash.text.TextField;

  public class DisplayListExample extends Sprite {
    public function DisplayListExample() {
```

```
    // Create a display object in the actionscript engine
    var hello:TextField = new TextField( );
    hello.text = "hello";

    // Create the display object in the rendering engine
    // by adding it to the display list so that the
    // text field is drawn on the screen
    addChild( hello );
  }
 }
}
```

Here the *DisplayListExample* class is the main application class for the *.swf* movie and it extends the *Sprite* class. Because of the class hierarchy described in Figure 6-2, the *DisplayListExample* is therefore an indirect subclass of *DisplayObjectContainer* and is capable of having multiple *DisplayObject* instances as children. This allows for the use of the *addChild()* method to add a display object as a child in the container.

A *TextField* display object is created in the *DisplayListExample* constructor, which creates the object inside the AVM. At this point, the object won't appear on-screen because the Rendering Engine doesn't know about it yet. It is only after the object is added to the display list—via the *addChild()* method call—that the *TextField* is displayed.

The *addChild()* and *addChildAt()* methods only add display objects as children of display object containers. They do not necessarily add display objects to the display list. Children are added to the display list only if the container they are being added to is on the display list as well.

The following code snippet demonstrates how the *addChild()* method doesn't guarantee that a display object is added to the display list. A container is created with some text inside of it, but because the container is not on the display list, the text is not visible:

```
// Create a text field to display some text
var hello:TextField = new TextField( );
hello.text = "hello";

// Create a container to hold the TextField
var container:Sprite = new Sprite( );
// Add the TextField as a child of the container
container.addChild( hello );
```

To make the text display on-screen, the text container needs to be added to the display list. This is accomplished by referencing a display object container already on the display list, such as root or stage, calling *addChild()*, and passing in the text container display object. Both root and stage are properties of the *DisplayObject* class:

```
// Cast the special root reference as a container and add the
// container that holds the text so it appears on-screen
DisplayObjectContainer( root ).addChild( container );
```

Display object containers are capable of holding multiple children. The container keeps a list of children internally, and the order of the children in the list determines the visual stacking order on-screen. Each child has a specific position in the list as specified by an integer index value, much like an array. Position 0 is the very bottom of the list and is drawn underneath the child at position 1, which is, in turn, drawn underneath the child at position 2, etc. This is similar to the depth concept you may be familiar with if you have prior Flash experience, but it's easier to manage. There are no gaps between position numbers. That is, there can never be children at position 0 and position 2 with an opening at position 1.

When a new child display object is added via the *addChild()* method, it is drawn visually on top of all of the other children in the container because *addChild()* places the child at the front of the children list, giving it the next highest position index. To add a child and specify where it belongs in the visual stacking order at the same time, use the *addChildAt()* method.

The *addChildAt()* method takes two parameters: the child display object to add, and the position in the stacking order that the child should use. Specifying a position of 0 causes the child to be added to the very bottom of the list and makes the child appear (visually) underneath all of the other children. If there was previously a child at the position specified, all of the children at and above the position index are shifted forward by one to allow the child to be inserted. Specifying an invalid position value, such as a negative value or a number greater than the number of children in the container, generates a *RangeError* and causes the child to not be added.

The following example creates three different colored circles. The red and blue circles are added with the *addChild()* method, making the blue circle appear on top because it was added after the red circle. After the two calls to *addChild()*, the red circle is at position 0 and the blue circle is at position 1. The green circle is then inserted between the two with the *addChildAt()* method, specifying position 1 as the location in the list. The blue circle, previously at position 1, is shifted to position 2 and the green circle is inserted at position 1 in its place. The final result is the red circle at position 0 being drawn underneath the green circle at position 1, and the green circle being drawn underneath blue circle at position 2.

```
package {
  import flash.display.*;
  public class CircleExample extends Sprite {
    public function CircleExample( ) {
      // Create three different colored circles and
      // change their coordinates so they are staggered
      // and aren't all located at (0,0).
      var red:Shape = createCircle( 0xFF0000, 10 );
      red.x = 10;
      red.y = 20;
      var green:Shape = createCircle( 0x00FF00, 10 );
      green.x = 15;
      green.y = 25;
```

```
      var blue:Shape = createCircle( 0x0000FF, 10 );
      blue.x = 20;
      blue.y = 20;

      // First add the red circle, then add the blue circle (so blue
      // is drawn on top of red)
      addChild( red );
      addChild( blue );

      // Place the green circle between the red and blue circles
      addChildAt( green, 1 );
    }

    // Helper function to create a circle shape with a given color
    // and radius
    public function createCircle( color:uint, radius:Number ):Shape {
      var shape:Shape = new Shape();
      shape.graphics.beginFill( color );
      shape.graphics.drawCircle( 0, 0, radius );
      shape.graphics.endFill();
      return shape;
    }
  }
}
```

So far we've only talked about adding new items to the display list, but what happens when *addChild()* is used on a child that is already on the display list, as a child of another container? This is the concept of *reparenting*. The child is removed from the container that it currently resides in and is placed in the container that it is being added to.

 When you reparent a display object, it is not necessary to remove it first. The *addChild()* method takes care of that for you.

The following example shows reparenting in action. A container is created to display red, green, and blue circles that are all added as children, and the container is added to the display list. Another container is created and added to the display list as well, and then the red circle is moved from the first container to the second. Because the second container is visually above the first container in the display list, all children in the second container appear on top of the children in the first container. This makes the red circle display ontop of the blue and green ones. The red circle was reparented from the first container to the second simply by calling the *addChild()* method.

```
package {
  import flash.display.*;
  public class DisplayListExample extends Sprite {
    public function DisplayListExample() {
      // Create three different colored circles and
```

```
                // change their coordinates so they are staggered
                // and aren't all located at (0,0).
                var red:Shape = createCircle( 0xFF0000, 10 );
                red.x = 10;
                red.y = 20;
                var green:Shape = createCircle( 0x00FF00, 10 );
                green.x = 15;
                green.y = 25;
                var blue:Shape = createCircle( 0x0000FF, 10 );
                blue.x = 20;
                blue.y = 20;

                // Create a container to hold the three circles, and add the
                // circles to the container
                var container1:Sprite = new Sprite();
                container1.addChild( red );
                container1.addChild( green );
                container1.addChild( blue );

                // Add the container to the display list
                addChild( container1 );

                // Create a second container and add it the display list
                var container2:Sprite = new Sprite();
                addChild( container2 );

                // Reparent the red circle from container 1 to container 2,
                // which has the net effect of the red circle being drawn
                // on top of the green and blue ones.
                container2.addChild( red );
            }

            // Helper function to create a circle shape with a given color
            // and radius
            public function createCircle( color:uint, radius:Number ):Shape {
                var shape:Shape = new Shape();
                shape.graphics.beginFill( color );
                shape.graphics.drawCircle( 0, 0, radius );
                shape.graphics.endFill();
                return shape;
            }
        }
    }
```

See Also

Recipes 6.2 and 6.4

6.2 Removing an Item from the Display List

Problem

You want to remove an item from the display list and consequently remove it from the screen.

Solution

Use the *removeChild()* and *removeChildAt()* methods from the *DisplayObectContainer* class.

Discussion

Recipe 6.1 demonstrates how to add display objects to the display list using the *addChild()* and *addChildAt()* methods. To achieve the opposite effect and remove a child via one of these methods, use either the *removeChild()* or *removeChildAt()* method.

The *removeChild()* method takes a single parameter, which is a reference to the display object that should be removed from the container. If an object is supposed to be removed and it isn't a child of the container, an *ArgumentError* is thrown:

```
package {
  import flash.display.Sprite;
  import flash.text.TextField;
  import flash.events.MouseEvent;

  public class RemoveChildExample extends Sprite {

    // Create a local variable to store a reference
    // to the TextField so that we can remove it later
    private var _label:TextField;

    public function RemoveChildExample() {
      _label = new TextField();
      _label.text = "Some Text";

      // Add the hello TextField to the display list
      addChild( _label );

      // When the mouse is clicked anywhere on the stage,
      // remove the label
      stage.addEventListener( MouseEvent.CLICK, removeLabel );
    }

    // Removes the label from this container's display list
    public function removeLabel( event:MouseEvent ):void {
      removeChild( _label );
    }
  }
}
```

The preceding code example creates a local variable label that stores a reference to the *TextField* within the class itself. This is a necessary step because the *removeChild()* method must be passed a reference to the display object to remove, so label is used to store the reference for later. If label were not available, extra work would be required to get a reference to the *TextField* to remove it, or the *removeChildAt()* method could be used instead.

In the case when you do not have a reference to the display object you want to remove, you can use the *removeChildAt()* method. Similar to the *addChildAt()* method, the *removeChildAt()* method takes a single parameter—the index in the container's list of child display objects to remove. The possible values for the index can range from 0 to numChildren -1. If an invalid index is specified, such as a negative value or a value greater than the number of children in the container, a *RangeError* is thrown and no child7 is removed. Adopting the previous code snippet to use *removeChildAt()* instead yields the following:

```
package {
  import flash.display.Sprite;
  import flash.text.TextField;
  import flash.events.MouseEvent;

  public class DisplayListExample extends Sprite {

    public function DisplayListExample() {
      var label:TextField = new TextField();
      label.text = "Some Text";

      // Add the hello TextField to the display list
      addChild( label );

      // When the mouse is clicked anywhere on the stage,
      // remove the label
      stage.addEventListener( MouseEvent.CLICK, removeLabel );
    }

    // Removes the label from this container's display list
    public function removeLabel( event:MouseEvent ):void {
      // Only remove the label if it exists
      if ( numChildren > 0 ) {
        removeChildAt( 0 );
      }
    }
  }
}
```

The biggest change by switching to *removeChildAt()* is that you no longer need to declare label to store a reference to the *TextField* so it can be removed later. Instead, when label is added to the *RemoveChildExample* container, it is added at position 0. To remove the label display object, simply remove the child at position 0.

Removing a child display object does not delete it entirely. Instead, it just removes it from the container and prevents the object from being drawn. To completely delete the display object, set all references to the object to null.

If you want to remove all of a container's children, combine *removeChildAt()* with a *for* loop. Every container has a numChildren property that indicates how many display objects are in the container's display list. By looping one time for each child, you can remove each child based on its position in the container's child list. This is somewhat of a tricky process because of how the position value works.

Whenever a child is removed from a certain position, all of the other children with higher positions shift their position values down by one to eliminate the gap. For example, consider a container with three children at positions 0, 1, and 2. When the child at position 0 is removed, the child at position 1 shifts down to position 0 and the child at position 2 shifts down to position 1. Because the position values change every time a child is removed, there are two ways to handle the removal of all children:

1. Always remove the child at position 0.
2. Remove the children backward, starting from the end.

In the first case, because there will always be a child at position 0 as long as the display object has children, you can continue to remove what is at position 0 because it is a new child display object during each loop iteration.

In the second case, removing the very last child from the container does not cause any children to adjust their positions. Only children with a higher position value than what is removed are shifted down by one. The last child has the highest position value within the container; therefore, no other children need to have their positions adjusted.

The first approach is the one we recommend using, and has been implemented in the *ascb.util.DisplayObjectUtilities* class:

```
package ascb.util {
  import flash.display.*;
  public class DisplayObjectUtilities {
    // Remove all of the children in a container
    public static function removeAllChildren(
                        container:DisplayObjectContainer ):void {

      // Because the numChildren value changes after every time
      // you remove a child, save the original value so you can
      // count correctly
      var count:int = container.numChildren;

      // Loop over the children in the container and remove them
      for ( var i:int = 0; i < count; i++ ) {
        container.removeChildAt( 0 );
```

```
            }
          }
        }
      }
```

Using the *DisplayObjectUtilities.removeAllChildren()* method is relatively straight-forward, as shown here:

```
package {
  import flash.display.*;
  import ascb.util.DisplayObjectUtilities;

  public class DisplayListExample extends Sprite {

    public function DisplayListExample() {

      // Add some empty sprites
      addChild( new Sprite() );
      addChild( new Sprite() );

      // Remove all children from this container
      DisplayObjectUtilities.removeAllChildren( this );

      // Demonstrate that all children have been removed - displays: 0
      trace( numChildren );
    }

  }
}
```

See Also

Recipe 6.1

6.3   Moving Objects Forward and Backward

Problem

You want to change the order in which objects are drawn on-screen, moving them either in front of or behind other display objects.

Solution

Use the *setChildIndex()* method of the *DisplayObectContainer* class to change the position of a particular item. Use the *getChildIndex()* and *getChildAt()* methods to query siblings of the item so the item can be positioned properly relative to them.

Discussion

Recipes 6.1 and 6.2 introduced how the display list model deals with the visual stacking order (depth). Essentially, every *DisplayObjectContainer* instance has a list of children, and the order of the children in this list determines the order in which child display objects are drawn inside of the container. The children are each given a position index, ranging from 0 to numChildren - 1, much like an array. The child at position 0 is drawn on the bottom, underneath the child at position 1, etc. There are no empty position values in the list; if there are three children, the children will always have index values of 0, 1, and 2 (and not, say, 0, 1, and 6).

The *setChildIndex()* method is provided by *DisplayObjectContainer* to reorder the children inside the container. It takes two parameters: a reference to the child to be moved and the child's new position in the container. The index position specified must be a valid value. Negative values or values too large will generate a *RangeError* and the function won't execute properly.

The following example creates three colored circles, with the blue one being drawn on top. The *setChildIndex()* method is used to move the blue circle underneath the two other circles, changing its position from 2 to 0 in the container. The positions of the other children are adjusted accordingly; red is moved to 1 and green is moved to 2:

```
package {
  import flash.display.*;
  public class SetChildIndexExample extends Sprite {
    public function SetChildIndexExample( ) {
      // Create three different colored circles and
      // change their coordinates so they are staggered
      // and aren't all located at (0,0).
      var red:Shape = createCircle( 0xFF0000, 10 );
      red.x = 10;
      red.y = 20;
      var green:Shape = createCircle( 0x00FF00, 10 );
      green.x = 15;
      green.y = 25;
      var blue:Shape = createCircle( 0x0000FF, 10 );
      blue.x = 20;
      blue.y = 20;

      // Add the circles, red has index 0, green 1, and blue 2
      addChild( red );
      addChild( green );
      addChild( blue );

      // Move the blue circle underneath the others by placing
      // it at the very bottom of the list, at index 0
      setChildIndex( blue, 0 );
    }

    // Helper function to create a circle shape with a given color
    // and radius
    public function createCircle( color:uint, radius:Number ):Shape {
      var shape:Shape = new Shape( );
      shape.graphics.beginFill( color );
      shape.graphics.drawCircle( 0, 0, radius );
```

```
        shape.graphics.endFill( );
        return shape;
      }
    }
  }
```

One of the requirements for *setChildIndex()* is that you know the index value you want to give to a specific child. When you're sending a child to the back, you use 0 as the index. When you want to bring a child to the very front, you specify numChildren - 1 as the index. But what if you want to move a child underneath another child?

For example, suppose you have two circles—one green and one blue—and you don't know their positions ahead of time. You want to move the blue circle behind the green one, but *setChildIndex()* requires an integer value for the new position. There are no *setChildAbove* or *setChildBelow* methods, so the solution is to use the *getChildIndex()* method to retrieve the index of a child, and then use that index to change the position of the other child. The *getChildIndex()* method takes a display object as a parameter and returns the index of the display object in the container. If the display object passed in is not a child of the container, an *ArgumentError* is thrown.

The following example creates two circles—one green and one blue—and uses *getChildIndex()* on the green circle so the blue circle can be moved beneath it. By setting the blue circle to the index that the green circle has, the blue circle takes over the position and the green circle moves to the next higher position because blue had a higher position initially:

```
package {
  import flash.display.*;
  public class GetChildIndexExample extends Sprite {
    public function GetChildIndexExample( ) {
      // Create two different sized circles
      var green:Shape = createCircle( 0x00FF00, 10 );
      green.x = 25;
      green.y = 25;
      var blue:Shape = createCircle( 0x0000FF, 20 );
      blue.x = 25;
      blue.y = 25;

      // Add the circles to this container
      addChild( green );
      addChild( blue );

      // Move the blue circle underneath the green circle. First
      // the index of the green circle is retrieved, and then the
      // blue circle is set to that index.
      setChildIndex( blue, getChildIndex( green ) );
    }
```

```
// Helper function to create a circle shape with a given color
// and radius
public function createCircle( color:uint, radius:Number ):Shape {
  var shape:Shape = new Shape();
  shape.graphics.beginFill( color );
  shape.graphics.drawCircle( 0, 0, radius );
  shape.graphics.endFill();
  return shape;
}
}
}
```

When a child is moved to an index lower than the one it currently has, all children from the target index up to the one just before the child index will have their indexes increased by 1 and the child is assigned to the target index. When a child is moved to a higher index, all children from the one just above the child index up to and including the target index are moved down by 1, and the child is assigned the target index value.

In general, if object *a* is above object *b*, the following code to moves *a* directly below *b*:

```
setChildIndex( a, getChildIndex( b ) );
```

Conversely, if object *a* is below object *b*, the preceding code moves *a* directly above *b*.

So far, we've always been moving around children that we've had a reference to. For example, the *blue* variable referenced the display object for the blue circle, and we were able to use this variable to change the index of the blue circle. What happens when you don't have a reference to the object you want to move, and the *blue* variable doesn't exist? The *setChildIndex()* method requires a reference to the object as its first parameter, so you'll need to get the reference somehow if it isn't available with a regular variable. The solution is to use the *getChildAt()* method.

The *getChildAt()* method takes a single argument, an index in the container's children list, and returns a reference to the display object located at that index. If the specified index isn't a valid index in the list, a *RangeError* is thrown.

The following example creates several circles of various colors and sizes and places them at various locations on the screen. Every time the mouse is pressed, the child at the very bottom is placed on top of all the others:

```
package {
  import flash.display.*;
  import flash.events.*;
  public class GetChildAtExample extends Sprite {
    public function GetChildAtExample() {
      // Define a list of colors to use
      var color:Array = [ 0xFF0000, 0x990000, 0x660000, 0x00FF00,
                          0x009900, 0x006600, 0x0000FF, 0x000099,
                          0x000066, 0xCCCCCC ];
      // Create 10 circles and line them up diagonally
      for ( var i:int = 0; i < 10; i++ ) {
        var circle:Shape = createCircle( color[i], 10 );
        circle.x = i;
```

```
      circle.y = i + 10; // the + 10 adds padding from the top

      addChild( circle );
    }

    stage.addEventListener( MouseEvent.CLICK, updateDisplay );
  }

  // Move the circle at the bottom to the very top
  public function updateDisplay( event:MouseEvent ):void {
    // getChildAt(0) returns the display object on the
    // very bottom, which then gets moved to the top
    // by specifying index numChildren - 1 in setChildIndex
    setChildIndex( getChildAt(0), numChildren - 1 );
  }

  // Helper function to create a circle shape with a given color
  // and radius
  public function createCircle( color:uint, radius:Number ):Shape {
    var shape:Shape = new Shape();
    shape.graphics.beginFill( color );
    shape.graphics.drawCircle( 0, 0, radius );
    shape.graphics.endFill();
    return shape;
  }
 }
}
```

See Also

Recipes 6.1 and 6.2

6.4   Creating Custom Visual Classes

Problem

You want to create a new type of *DisplayObject*.

Solution

Create a new class that extends *DisplayObject* or one of its subclasses so it can be added into a display object container via *addChild()* or *addChildAt()*.

Discussion

Among the benefits of moving toward the display list model is the ease of creating new visual classes. In the past, it was possible to extend *MovieClip* to create custom visuals, but there always had to be a *MovieClip* symbol in the library linked to the ActionScript class to create an on-screen instance via *attachMovie()*. Creating a custom visual could never be done entirely in ActionScript. With the display list model, the process has been simplified, allowing you to do everything in pure ActionScript code in a much more intuitive manner.

In the display list model, as discussed in the introduction of this chapter, there are many more display classes available besides just *MovieClip*. Before you create your custom visual, you need to decide which type it is going to be. If you're just creating a custom shape, you'll want to extend the *Shape* class. If you're creating a custom button, you'll probably want to extend *SimpleButton*. If you want to create a container to hold other display objects, *Sprite* is a good choice if you don't require the use of a timeline. If you need a timeline, you'll need to subclass *MovieClip*.

All of the available display object classes are tailored for specific purposes. It's best to decide what purpose your own visual class is going to serve, and then choose the appropriate parent class based on that. By choosing the parent class carefully you optimize size and resource overhead. For example, a simple *Circle* class doesn't need to subclass *MovieClip* because it doesn't need the timeline. The *Shape* class is the better choice in this case because it's the most lightweight option that appropriately fits the concept of a circle.

Once the base class has been decided, all you need to do is write the code for the class. Let's follow through with the circle example and create a new *Circle* class that extends the *Shape* display object. In a new ActionScript file named *Circle.as*, enter the following code:

```
package {
    import flash.display.Shape;

    /* The Circle class is a custom visual class */
    public class Circle extends Shape {

        // Local variables to store the circle properties
        private var _color:uint;
        private var _radius:Number;

        /*
         * Constructor: called when a Circle is created. The default
         * color is black, and the default radius is 10.
         */
        public function Circle( color:uint = 0x000000, radius:Number = 10 ) {
            // Save the color and radius values
            _color = color;
            _radius = radius;

            // When the circle is created, automatically draw it
            draw();
        }

        /*
         * Draws the circle based on the color and radius values
         */
```

```
      private function draw( ):void {
        graphics.beginFill( _color );
        graphics.drawCircle( 0, 0, _radius );
        graphics.endFill( );
      }
    }
  }
}
```

The preceding code defines a new *Circle* display object. When a *Circle* instance is created, you can specify both a color and a radius in the constructor. Methods from the Drawing API (discussed in Recipe 7.3) are used to create the body of the circle with the graphics property, which is inherited from the superclass *Shape*.

 It is always a good idea to separate all drawing code into a separate *draw()* method. The constructor for *Circle* does not draw the circle directly, but it calls the *draw()* method to create the visual elements.

All that is left to do is create new instances of our custom *Circle* class and add them to the display list with *addChild()* or *addChildAt()* so they appear on-screen. To create new instances of the class, use the new keyword. The following code example creates a few *Circle* instances and displays them on the screen:

```
package {
  import flash.display.Sprite;
  public class UsingCircleExample extends Sprite {
    public function UsingCircleExample( ) {
      // Create some circles with the Circle class and
      // change their coordinates so they are staggered
      // and aren't all located at (0,0).
      var red:Circle = new Circle( 0xFF0000, 10 );
      red.x = 10;
      red.y = 20;
      var green:Circle = new Circle( 0x00FF00, 10 );
      green.x = 15;
      green.y = 25;
      var blue:Circle = new Circle( 0x0000FF, 10 );
      blue.x = 20;
      blue.y = 20;

      // Add the circles to the display list
      addChild( red );
      addChild( green );
      addChild( blue );
    }
  }
}
```

See Also

Recipes 6.1 and 7.3

6.5   Creating Simple Buttons

Problem

You want to create an interactive button that enables a user to click and perform an action, such as submitting a form or calculating a total.

Solution

Create an instance of the *SimpleButton* class and create display objects for upState, downState, overState, and hitTestState. Alternatively, create a subclass of *SimpleButton* that describes your desired button behavior.

Use the click event to invoke a method whenever the user presses the button.

Discussion

The display list model provides an easy way to create buttons through the *SimpleButton* class. The *SimpleButton* class allows a user to interact with the display object using their mouse, and makes it easy for you to define that interaction through various button states. The possible button states, listed here, are available as properties of the *SimpleButton* class:

upState

> A display object for the default "up" state of the button. The "up" state is shown whenever the mouse is not over the button.

overState

> A display object that determines what the button looks like when the mouse moves over the button. When the mouse leaves the button area, the button moves back to the "up" state.

downState

> A display object that's shown when the button is pressed (or clicked) "down". When the button is in the "over" state, the "down" state displays when the user presses the left mouse button.

hitTestState

> A display object that defines a button's bounds. When the mouse moves inside of the button's hit area, the button enters the "over" state. The hitTestState is typically set to the same display object as the upState. The hitTestState is never actually displayed on-screen; it is only used for mouse tracking purposes.

A button's state is handled by the *SimpleButton* class, and is based on movement of the user's mouse. You don't have control over setting the internal button state (up, down, or over). Rather, you can only control which display object should appear when the button is in a particular state. By setting the state properties to different display objects, you can provide feedback to the user as they interact with the button using their mouse.

The following example creates a new *SimpleButton* instance and defines button states using the four state properties defined earlier. Because each state property of the button needs to be set to a *DisplayObject* instance, the helper method *createCircle()* is used to create different colored circle shapes to be used for the various button states:

```
package {
  import flash.display.*;
  import flash.events.*;

  public class SimpleButtonDemo extends Sprite {
    public function SimpleButtonDemo( ) {
      // Create a simple button and configure its location
      var button:SimpleButton = new SimpleButton( );
      button.x = 20;
      button.y = 20;

      // Create the different states of the button, using the
      // helper method to create different colors circles
      button.upState = createCircle( 0x00FF00, 15 );
      button.overState = createCircle( 0xFFFFFF, 16 );
      button.downState = createCircle( 0xCCCCCC, 15 );
      button.hitTestState = button.upState;

      // Add an event listener for the click event to be notified
      // when the user clicks the mouse on the button
      button.addEventListener( MouseEvent.CLICK, handleClick );

      // Finally, add the button to the display list
      addChild( button );
    }

    // Helper function to create a circle shape with a given color
    // and radius
    private function createCircle( color:uint, radius:Number ):Shape {
      var circle:Shape = new Shape( );
      circle.graphics.lineStyle( 1, 0x000000 );
      circle.graphics.beginFill( color );
      circle.graphics.drawCircle( 0, 0, radius );
      circle.graphics.endFill( );
      return circle;
    }

    // Event handler invoked whenever the user presses the button
    private function handleClick( event:MouseEvent ):void {
      trace( "Mouse clicked on the button" );
    }
  }
}
```

After running the preceding code block, a green circle appears in the movie. When you move your mouse over the green circle, a slightly bigger white circle appears as a rollover. When you click the white circle, it turns into a slightly smaller gray circle. This visual effect is created by the *SimpleButton* instance changing its state based on the actions of your mouse, switching between the display objects defined in the four state properties.

To listen for events from the button instance, the *addEventListener()* method is used as described in Recipe 1.5. The click event, specified with MouseEvent.CLICK, is handled in the preceding code by the *handleClick()* method. Anytime the user clicks the button instance, the *handleClick()* method is invoked, allowing certain actions to take place. In this simple example, a short message ("Mouse clicked on the button") is displayed to the console.

The hitTestState property is perhaps the most interesting of the button's state properties. You'll notice that the preceding code sets the hitTestState to be the same display object that defines the upState. It is typical to do this because buttons should be activated when the user's mouse is within the bounds of the upState display object.

 Although the hitTestState is never visible, failure to set the hitTestState to a display object results in a button that can't be interacted with. Always remember to set the hitTestState of your *SimpleButton*, even if you simply set it to the same value as upState.

The hitTestState can be set to any display when you'd like to control the active bounds of a button. To create a larger hit area for the button, try modifying the previous code segment to set the hitTestState via this line:

```
button.hitTestState = createCircle( 0x000000, 50 );
```

When running this example, you'll notice that the button displays the white "over" circle before the mouse even enters the area of the green circle, contrary to previous behavior. This is because the hit area was increased to a circle of radius 50, giving a larger target area for the user's mouse. You might also notice that black (0x000000) was specified as the color for the hit area circle. This was done on purpose to reinforce the fact that the hit area display object is never visible.

An alternate approach to creating a *SimpleButton* and setting the four display states for every button is to create a subclass of *SimpleButton* that defines your button's visual style and creates instances of that instead. Recipe 6.4 describes how to create new visual classes. Following this technique, you can create your own version of a *SimpleButton*, making it easier to add multiple buttons to your movie.

The following code creates a new *RectangleButton* class. The *RectangleButton* class defines the behavior for a special type of *SimpleButton* that draws a green rectangle with some text on top of it:

```
package {
  import flash.display.*
  import flash.text.*;
  import flash.filters.DropShadowFilter;

  public class RectangleButton extends SimpleButton {
    // The text to appear on the button
    private var _text:String;
    // Save the width and height of the rectangle
    private var _width:Number;
    private var _height:Number;

    public function RectangleButton( text:String, width:Number, height:Number ) {
      // Save the values to use them to create the button states
      _text = text;
      _width = width;
      _height = height;

      // Create the button states based on width, height, and text value
      upState = createUpState();
      overState = createOverState();
      downState = createDownState();
      hitTestState = upState;
    }

    // Create the display object for the button's up state
    private function createUpState():Sprite {
      var sprite:Sprite = new Sprite();

      var background:Shape = createdColoredRectangle( 0x33FF66 );
      var textField:TextField = createTextField( false );

      sprite.addChild( background );
      sprite.addChild( textField );

      return sprite;
    }

    // Create the display object for the button's up state
    private function createOverState():Sprite {
      var sprite:Sprite = new Sprite();

      var background:Shape = createdColoredRectangle( 0x70FF94 );
      var textField:TextField = createTextField( false );

      sprite.addChild( background );
      sprite.addChild( textField );

      return sprite;
    }

    // Create the display object for the button's down state
    private function createDownState():Sprite {
      var sprite:Sprite = new Sprite();
```

```
    var background:Shape = createdColoredRectangle( 0xCCCCCC );
    var textField:TextField = createTextField( true );

    sprite.addChild( background );
    sprite.addChild( textField );

    return sprite;
}

// Create a rounded rectangle with a specific fill color
private function createdColoredRectangle( color:uint ):Shape {
    var rect:Shape = new Shape();
    rect.graphics.lineStyle( 1, 0x000000 );
    rect.graphics.beginFill( color );
    rect.graphics.drawRoundRect( 0, 0, _width, _height, 15 );
    rect.graphics.endFill();
    rect.filters = [ new DropShadowFilter( 2 ) ];
    return rect;
}

// Create the text field to display the text of the button
private function createTextField( downState:Boolean ):TextField {
    var textField:TextField = new TextField();
    textField.text = _text;
    textField.width = _width;

    // Center the text horizontally
    var format:TextFormat = new TextFormat();
    format.align = TextFormatAlign.CENTER;
    textField.setTextFormat( format );

    // Center the text vertically
    textField.y = ( _height - textField.textHeight ) / 2;
    textField.y -= 2;  // Subtract 2 pixels to adjust for offset

    // The down state places the text down and to the right
    // further than the other states
    if ( downState ) {
        textField.x += 1;
        textField.y += 1;
    }

    return textField;
    }
  }
}
```

Because all of the button drawing is encapsulated into its own reusable class, creating new button instances is much easier. Instead of having to create a *SimpleButton* and define the button states by hand for each instance, you can simply create a new *RectangleButton* instance and add that to the display list.

The following example shows how to create three different rectangular buttons using this new instance:

```
package {
  import flash.display.*;
  public class SimpleButtonDemo extends Sprite {
    public function SimpleButtonDemo( ) {

      // Create three rectangular buttons with different text and
      // different sizes, and place them at various locations within
      // the movie

      var button1:RectangleButton = new RectangleButton( "Button 1", 60, 100 );
      button1.x = 20;
      button1.y = 20;

      var button2:RectangleButton = new RectangleButton( "Button 2", 80, 30 );
      button2.x = 90;
      button2.y = 20;

      var button3:RectangleButton = new RectangleButton( "Button 3", 100, 40 );
      button3.x = 100;
      button3.y = 60;

      // Add the buttons to the display list so they appear on-screen
      addChild( button1 );
      addChild( button2 );
      addChild( button3 );
    }
  }
}
```

See Also

Recipes 1.5, 6.1, 6.4, and 6.8

6.6 Loading External Images at Runtime

Problem

You want to load an external image into a movie while it plays.

Solution

Use the new *Loader* class to load an image (*.jpg*, progressive *.jpg*, *.png*, or *.gif*) and display it on-screen.

Discussion

Recipe 9.17 demonstrates how to embed external assets into a movie at compile time via the [Embed] metadata tag. To load external images or movies at runtime during the playback of a .swf, the *Loader* class needs to be used.

The *flash.display.Loader* class is very similar to the *flash.net.URLLoader* class discussed in Recipe 19.3. One of the key differences is that *Loader* instances are able to load external images and movies and display them on-screen, whereas *URLLoader* instances are useful for transferring data.

There are three fundamental steps for loading external content:

1. Create an instance of the *Loader* class.
2. Add the *Loader* instance to the display list.
3. Call the *load()* method to pull in an external asset.

The *load()* method of the *Loader* class is responsible for downloading the image or .swf file. It takes a single *URLRequest* object as a parameter that specifies the URL of the asset to download and display.

The following is a small example of using a *Loader* instance to download an image named *image.jpg* at runtime. The code in the *LoaderExample* constructor has been commented to coincide with the three basic loading steps previously outlined:

```
package {
  import flash.display.*;
  import flash.net.URLRequest;
  public class LoaderExample extends Sprite {
    public function LoaderExample( ) {
      // 1. Create an instance of the Loader class
      var loader:Loader = new Loader();
      // 2. Add the Loader instance to the display list
      addChild( loader );
      // 3. Call the load( ) method to pull in an external asset
      loader.load( new URLRequest( "image.jpg" ) );
    }
  }
}
```

When running this code, the Flash Player looks for *image.jpg* in the same directory that the .swf movie is being served from because the *URLRequest* object uses a relative URL. Either a relative or absolute URL can be used to point to the location of the target to load, but the actual loading of the asset is governed by Flash Player's security sandbox, as discussed in Recipe 3.12. As soon as the asset has downloaded, it is automatically added as a child of the *Loader* instance.

When loading external assets, it's possible that something could go wrong during the loading process. For instance, perhaps the URL is pointing to the incorrect location due to a spelling mistake, or there's a security sandbox violation that won't allow the asset to be loaded. Or, it's possible that the asset is large and is going to take a long time download. Rather than just having an empty screen while the asset downloads, you'd like to show a preloader to inform the user of the download progress.

In these situations, you should add event listeners to the *contentLoaderInfo* property of the *Loader* instance to be able to respond to the different events as they occur. The *contentLoaderInfo* property is an instance of the *flash.display.LoaderInfo* class, designed to provide information about the target being loaded. The following is a list of useful events dispatched by instances of the *LoaderInfo* class and what those events mean:

open
: Generated when the asset has started downloading.

progress
: Generated when progress has been made while downloading the asset.

complete
: Generated when the asset has finished downloading.

init
: Generated when the properties and methods of a loaded external *.swf* are available.

httpStatus
: Generated when the status code for a failed HTTP request is detected when attempting to load the asset.

ioError
: Generated when a fatal error occurs that results in an aborted download, such as not being able to find the asset.

securityError
: Generated when data you're trying to load resides outside of the security sandbox.

unload
: Generated when either the *unload()* method is called to remove the loaded content or the *load()* method is called again to replace content that already has been loaded.

The following example demonstrates listening for the various download progress related events when loading an image:

```
package {
  import flash.display.*;
  import flash.text.*;
  import flash.net.URLRequest;
  import flash.events.*;

  public class LoaderExample extends Sprite {
    public function LoaderExample() {
      // Create the loader and add it to the display list
      var loader:Loader = new Loader();
      addChild( loader );
```

```
      // Add the event handlers to check for progress
      loader.contentLoaderInfo.addEventListener( Event.OPEN, handleOpen );
      loader.contentLoaderInfo.addEventListener( ProgressEvent.PROGRESS,
handleProgress );
      loader.contentLoaderInfo.addEventListener( Event.COMPLETE, handleComplete );

      // Load in the external image
      loader.load( new URLRequest( "image.jpg" ) );
    }

    private function handleOpen( event:Event ):void {
      trace( "open" );
    }

    private function handleProgress( event:ProgressEvent ):void {
      var percent:Number = event.bytesLoaded / event.bytesTotal * 100;
      trace( "progress, percent = " + percent );
    }

    private function handleComplete( event:Event ):void {
      trace( "complete" );
    }
  }
}
```

When running the preceding code, you'll see the open message appear in the console window followed by one or more progress messages displaying the current percent loaded, followed by the complete message signaling that the download finished successfully.

By placing code in the event handlers for these events, you can show the progress of a download as it's being loaded. For instance, the *handleOpen()* method would be in charge of creating the preloader and adding it to the display list. The *handleProgress()* method would update the percentage value of the preloader, such as setting the text of a *TextField* instance to the percent value. Finally, the *handleComplete()* method would perform "clean up" and remove the preloader, since the asset is fully downloaded. Focusing on those methods, the code might look something like this:

```
    private function handleOpen( event:Event ):void {
      // Create a simple text-based preloader and add it to the
      // display list
      _loaderStatus = new TextField();
      addChild( _loaderStatus );
      _loaderStatus.text = "Loading: 0%";
    }

    private function handleProgress( event:ProgressEvent ):void {
      // Update the loading % to inform the user of progress
      var percent:Number = event.bytesLoaded / event.bytesTotal * 100;
      _loaderStatus.text = "Loading: " + percent + "%";
    }
```

```
private function handleComplete( event:Event ):void {
  // Clean up - preloader is no longer necessary
  removeChild( loaderStatus );
  _loaderStatus = null;
}
```

The preceding code snippet assumes that there is a _loaderStatus variable as part of the class, with type *TextField*:

```
private var _loaderStatus:TextField;
```

Instead of messages appearing via the *trace()* statement as before, modifying the event handlers allows the loading information to be presented inside of the movie itself. This allows users to see the information directly and provides a better experience when loading large external assets.

See Also

Recipes 3.12, 6.7, 9.17, and 19.3

6.7   Loading and Interacting with External Movies

Problem

You want to load, and be able to interact with, an external *.swf* movie into your own movie.

Solution

Use the new *Loader* class to load the *.swf* file, and then access the *.swf* file via the content property of the *Loader* instance.

Discussion

Recipe 6.6 demonstrates how to load external images via the *Loader* class. Loading external *.swf* movies uses the same technique—by calling the *load()* method on a *Loader* instance and passing a URL to a *.swf* instead of an image, the *.swf* is loaded into the movie. If the *Loader* is in the main display hierarchy, the *.swf* also appears on-screen.

This recipe involves creating two separate *.swf* files, *ExternalMovie.swf* and *LoaderExample.swf*. The first movie, *ExternalMovie.swf*, will be loaded at runtime into the second movie, *LoaderExample.swf*. The code for *ExternalMovie.swf* is as follows:

```
package {
  import flash.display.Sprite;
  import flash.display.Shape;
  public class ExternalMovie extends Sprite {
    private var _color:uint = 0x000000;
```

```
    private var _circle:Shape;

    public function ExternalMovie() {
      updateDisplay();
    }

    private function updateDisplay():void {
      // If the circle hasn't been created yet, create it
      // and make it visible by adding it to the display list
      if ( _circle == null ) {
        _circle = new Shape();
        addChild( _circle );
      }

      // Clear any previously drawn content and draw
      // a new circle with the fill color
      _circle.graphics.clear();
      _circle.graphics.beginFill( _color );
      _circle.graphics.drawCircle( 100, 100, 40 );
    }

    // Changes the color of the circle
    public function setColor( color:uint ):void {
      _color = color;
      updateDisplay();
    }

    // Gets the current circle color value
    public function getColor():uint {
      return _color;
    }


  }
}
```

The code for *ExternalMovie.swf* is nothing out of the ordinary—a black circle is created when the movie is executed. The main thing to notice about the code is that there are two public methods for accessing and modifying the color of the circle, *getColor()* and *setColor()*. Whenever the *setColor()* method is invoked, the circle is redrawn with the updated color value.

By declaring these methods as public, the methods are able to be called from a movie that loads the *ExternalMovie.swf* in at runtime. In contrast, the private *updateDisplay()* method won't be available to the loading movie. See Recipe 1.13 for more information about the visibility modifiers for methods.

Now that *ExternalMovie.swf* is created, a new *.swf* needs to be created to load the external movie. This is done with *LoaderExample.swf*, which has the following code:

```
package {
  import flash.display.*;
  import flash.net.URLRequest;
  import flash.events.Event;
```

```
public class LoaderExample extends Sprite {

  private var _loader:Loader;

  public function LoaderExample( ) {
    // Create the Loader and add it to the display list
    _loader = new Loader( );
    addChild( _loader );

    // Add the event handler to interact with the loaded movie
    _loader.contentLoaderInfo.addEventListener( Event.INIT, handleInit );

    // Load the external movie
    _loader.load( new URLRequest( "ExternalMovie.swf" ) );
  }

  // Event handler called when the externally loaded movie is
  // ready to be interacted with
  private function handleInit( event:Event ):void {
    // Typed as * here because the type is not known at compile-time.
    var movie:* = _loader.content;

    // Calls a method in the external movie to get data out
    // Displays: 0
    trace( movie.getColor( ) );

    // Calls a method in the external movie to set data.
    // Sets the color in the external movie, which draws
    // a circle with the new color, in this case red
    movie.setColor( 0xFF0000 );
  }
}
}
```

The code for *LoaderExample.swf* is more interesting in that it communicates with the loaded movie. There are two main aspects in the preceding code:

1. Listening for the init event
2. Accessing the loaded movie via the content property

The init event is fired when the loaded movie has initialized enough that its methods and properties are available to be interacted with. The movie can be controlled only *after* the init event has been fired from the loader. Attempting to interact with a loaded movie before it has initialized will generate runtime errors.

To control the loaded movie, you'll first need to get a reference to it. This is done via the content property of the *Loader* class. In the preceding code, the loader variable refers to the *Loader* that pulled in the external *.swf* file, so you can access the movie via loader.content. If the loader variable weren't available, the event.target.content path could be used instead to get to the contents of the *Loader*. This is because event.target refers to the instance that generated the event, which is the same instance that the loader variable refers to.

The content property is read-only, and returns an object of type *DisplayObject*. In the *LoaderExample.swf* code, you'll notice that instead of typing the movie variable as a *DisplayObject*, the same type as what the content property returns, the * type was used. This is necessary because trying to call the *getColor()* or *setColor()* methods on the movie reference generates compile-time errors if movie is typed as a *DisplayObject*.

The movie being loaded, *ExternalMovie.swf*, has two public methods available for interaction. These methods are not part of the *DisplayObject* class; therefore, trying to call one of the methods from a variable of type *DisplayObject* is an error. The * type allows you to call any method that you'd like on the loaded movie. If the method does not exist in the loaded movie, a *ReferenceError* is thrown during execution.

The *getColor()* method returns the color of the circle in *ExternalMovie.swf* to *LoaderExample.swf*. The *LoaderExample.swf* reports the color as 0, which is the same as 0x000000, or the color black. The *setColor()* method allows *LoaderExample.swf* to change the color of the circle drawn by *ExternalMovie.swf*. In this case, the color of the circle is set to red, and you can see that the *ExternalMovie.swf* updates the display after the new circle color value is set.

 It is only possible to interact with *.swf* files of Version 9 and above using this technique. When loading Version 8 and below *.swf* files, this technique won't work because ActionScript 3.0 code runs independently of ActionScript 1.0 and 2.0. Communication with these *.swf* files is not trivial and involves using *LocalConnection* as a workaround to send and receive messages. See Chapter 19 for details.

See Also

Recipes 1.13 and 6.6

6.8   Creating Mouse Interactions

Problem

You want users to interact with your movie using their mouse.

Solution

Use the various mouse events to listen for mouse interactions on display objects of type *InteractiveObject*. Use the read-only mouseX and mouseY properties from *DisplayObject* to examine the mouse location relative to a display object, or the localX and localY properties from the *MouseEvent* passed to a mouse event handler.

Discussion

Basic mouse interaction can be created with the *SimpleButton* class, as described in Recipe 6.5. The *SimpleButton* class provides an easy way to create a clickable button with different button visual states: up, over, and down.

However, there are times when buttons just don't provide enough interactivity. By listening to the various mouse events, you can create interesting interactive experiences. For instance, consider that you want to track the mouse cursor to create an interactive drawing program, drawing lines on-screen based on the user's mouse movement. Or, consider that you have a maze that a user must navigate their mouse through without colliding with the walls to find the exit. Or, perhaps the user's mouse movement needs to control the direction of a golf club, and the mouse button is used to swing.

These situations require use of the special *InteractiveObject* display object, which provides the ability to respond to the user's mouse. If you go back to the introduction for this chapter, you'll recall that the *InteractiveObject* class is a base class fairly high in the display object class hierarchy. Because of this, the *Sprite*, *Loader*, *TextField*, and *MovieClip* classes are all examples of the *InteractiveObject* class since they fall underneath *InteractiveObject* in the hierarchy, and you may already be familiar with their use.

Instances of the *InteractiveObject* dispatch the necessary events specific to mouse interaction. The following is a list of more useful mouse events:

click
> Generated when the user presses and releases the mouse button over the interactive display object.

doubleClick
> Generated when the user presses and releases the mouse button twice in rapid succession over the interactive display object.

mouseDown
> Generated when the user presses the mouse button over the interactive display object.

mouseUp
> Generated when the user releases the mouse button over the interactive display object.

mouseOver
> Generated when the user moves the mouse pointer from outside of the bounds of interactive display object to inside of them.

mouseMove
> Generated when the user moves the mouse pointer while the pointer is inside the bounds of the interactive display object.

mouseOut

Generated when the user moves the mouse pointer from inside the bounds of an interactive display object to outside of them.

mouseWheel

Generated when the user rotates the mouse wheel while the mouse pointer is over the interactive display object.

Using these events is simply a matter of calling *addEventListener()* on the *InteractiveObject* and defining an event handler to handle the *MouseEvent* passed to it.

The following code snippet creates a *Sprite*, draws a red circle inside of it, and outputs a message to the console whenever the mouse moves over the circle:

```
package {
  import flash.display.Sprite;
  import flash.events.*;
  import flash.geom.Point;

  public class InteractiveMouseDemo extends Sprite {
    public function InteractiveMouseDemo( ) {
      var circle:Sprite = new Sprite( );
      circle.x = 10;
      circle.y = 10;
      circle.graphics.beginFill( 0xFF0000 );
      circle.graphics.drawCircle( 0, 0, 5 );
      circle.graphics.endFill( );

      circle.addEventListener( MouseEvent.MOUSE_MOVE, handleMouseMove );

      addChild( circle );
    }

    // Event handle to capture the move event over the circle
    private function handleMouseMove( event:MouseEvent ):void {
      trace( "mouse move" );
    }
  }
}
```

In this example, notice that the message appears only when the mouse is moved while the pointer is over the circle. The circle defines the bounds for the *Sprite* in this case.

Mouse events are generated from a particular interactive display object only when the pointer is within the bounds of that object.

Another common use of mouse events stems from wanting to inspect the location of the mouse pointer to create mouse interactivity. For example, to draw a line with the mouse, the mouse location needs to be known so the line can be plotted accurately. There are two ways to determine the location of the mouse pointer:

- Using the mouseX and mouseY properties available on any *DisplayObject* instance.
- Using the localX and localY properties available from the *MouseEvent* instance passed to the mouse event handler.

The mouseX and mouseY properties can be inspected to determine the location of the mouse cursor relative to the top-left corner of the *DisplayObject*. Both of the properties are read-only; it is not possible to set the location of the mouse cursor, only to examine the location.

So, imagine that a rectangle is at x location 20 and y location 50 and the user moves the mouse pointer to x location 25 and y location 60. The mouseX property of the rectangle returns 5 and mouseY of the rectangle reports 10 because from the rectangle's perspective, the mouse is 5 pixels in from the left and 10 pixels down from the top.

The localX and localY properties of the *MouseEvent* are also relative. In the *MouseEvent* case, the properties are relative to interactive display object that dispatched the event. Therefore, consider that a rectangle reports mouseX of 10 and dispatches a mouseMove event. The event's localX property is also 10.

To get the global position of the mouse from local coordinates, use the *localToGlobal()* method of the *DisplayObject* class. The *localToGlobal()* method takes *flash.geom.Point* as a parameter that specifies the local coordinates, and returns a new *Point* with the coordinates converted to the global space. The following code snippet focuses on the event handler and demonstrates how to convert localX and localY to global coordinates:

```
// Event handler to respond to a mouseMove event
private function handleMouseMove( event:MouseEvent ):void {
  /* Displays:
  local x: 3.95
  local y: 3.45
  */
  trace( "local x: " + event.localX );
  trace( "local y: " + event.localY );

  // Create the point that localToGlobal should convert
  var localPoint:Point = new Point( event.localX, event.localY );
  // Convert from the local coordinates of the display object that
  // dispatched the event to the global stage coordinates
  var globalPoint:Point = event.target.localToGlobal( localPoint );

  /* Displays:
  global x: 13.95
  global y: 13.45
  */
  trace( "global x: " + globalPoint.x );
  trace( "global y: " + globalPoint.y );
}
```

A complete working example of creating interactivity through handling the various mouse events can be demonstrated by the simple drawing program that follows.

Whenever the mouse is pressed, the drawing starts. As the user moves the mouse around the screen, a line is drawn that follows the movement of the mouse pointer. When the user releases the mouse button, the drawing stops:

```
package {
  import flash.display.Sprite;
  import flash.events.MouseEvent;
  public class DrawingDemo extends Sprite {

    // Flag to indicate whether the mouse is in draw mode
    private var _drawing:Boolean;

    public function DrawingDemo() {
      // Configure the line style
      graphics.lineStyle( 2, 0xFFCC33 );

      // Drawing is false until the user presses the mouse
      _drawing = false;

      // Add the mouse listeners on the stage object to be
      // notfied of any mouse event that happens while the
      // mouse is over the entire movie
      stage.addEventListener( MouseEvent.MOUSE_DOWN, startDrawing );
      stage.addEventListener( MouseEvent.MOUSE_MOVE, draw );
      stage.addEventListener( MouseEvent.MOUSE_UP, stopDrawing );
    }

    public function startDrawing( event:MouseEvent ):void {
      // Move to the current mouse position to be ready for drawing
      graphics.moveTo( mouseX, mouseY );
      _drawing = true;
    }

    public function draw( event:MouseEvent ):void {
      if ( _drawing ) {
        // Draw a line from the last mouse position to the
        // current one
        graphics.lineTo( mouseX, mouseY );
      }
    }

    public function stopDrawing( event:MouseEvent ):void {
      _drawing = false;
    }

  }
}
```

See Also

Recipes 6.5, 6.9, and Chapter 7

6.9   Dragging and Dropping Objects with the Mouse

Problem

You want to provide a drag-and-drop-style interface.

Solution

Use *startDrop()*, *stopDrag()* and `dropTarget` from the *Sprite* class to implement drag-and-drop behavior. Alternatively, extend the *ascb.display.DraggableSprite* class for visually smoother dragging behavior using the *drag()* and *drop()* methods.

Discussion

Creating drag-and-drop behavior is not as difficult as you might think. The *Sprite* class includes methods specifically for the purpose of drag and drop, namely *startDrag()* and *stopDrag()*.

The *startDrag()* method can be called on any *Sprite* instance to have it follow the mouse around the screen, creating the dragging effect. To stop dragging, call the *stopDrag()* method on the *Sprite* instance. After the drag operation is complete, you can examine the `dropTarget` property of the *Sprite* to determine the object that the *Sprite* was dropped on. The value of `dropTarget` is useful for determining if a drop operation is valid (such as dropping a folder icon on a trashcan to delete it).

When calling *startDrag()*, you don't have to specify any parameters; however, the method accepts up to two parameters. The parameters are:

lockCenter
> When `true` the center of the *Sprite* is locked to the mouse position regardless of where the user pressed the mouse. When `false` the *Sprite* follows the mouse from the location where the user first clicked. The default value is `false`.

bounds
> The *Rectangle* region where you want to constrain dragging. The *Sprite* is not capable of being dragged outside of this region. The default value is `null`, meaning there is no area constraint.

The following code example uses these methods to set up a simple drag-and-drop behavior. There are three rectangles on the left capable of being dragged: red, green, and blue. The rectangle on the right is white, and serves as the target area where you drop the color rectangles. Dragging and dropping a colored rectangle onto the white rectangle colorizes the white rectangle the same color of the rectangle that was dropped onto it:

```
package {
  import flash.display.Sprite;
  import flash.display.DisplayObject;
  import flash.events.MouseEvent;
```

```
import flash.geom.Point;
import flash.filters.DropShadowFilter;

public class ColorDrop extends Sprite {

  private var _red:Sprite;
  private var _green:Sprite;
  private var _blue:Sprite;
  private var _white:Sprite;

  // Saves the starting coordinates of a dragging Sprite so
  // it can be placed back
  private var startingLocation:Point;

  // Create the rectangles that comprise the interface
  // and wire the mouse events to make them interactive
  public function ColorDrop() {
    createRectangles();
    addEventListeners();
  }

  private function createRectangles():void {
    _red = new Sprite();
    _red.graphics.beginFill( 0xFF0000 );
    _red.graphics.drawRect( 0, 10, 10, 10 );
    _red.graphics.endFill();

    _green = new Sprite()
    _green.graphics.beginFill( 0x00FF00 );
    _green.graphics.drawRect( 0, 30, 10, 10 );
    _green.graphics.endFill();

    _blue = new Sprite();
    _blue.graphics.beginFill( 0x0000FF );
    _blue.graphics.drawRect( 0, 50, 10, 10 );
    _blue.graphics.endFill();

    _white = new Sprite();
    _white.graphics.beginFill( 0xFFFFFF );
    _white.graphics.drawRect( 20, 10, 50, 50 );
    _white.graphics.endFill();

    addChild( _red );
    addChild( _green );
    addChild( _blue );
    addChild( _white );
  }

  private function addEventListeners():void {
    _red.addEventListener( MouseEvent.MOUSE_DOWN, pickup );
    _red.addEventListener( MouseEvent.MOUSE_UP, place );

    _green.addEventListener( MouseEvent.MOUSE_DOWN, pickup );
    _green.addEventListener( MouseEvent.MOUSE_UP, place );
```

```
    _blue.addEventListener( MouseEvent.MOUSE_DOWN, pickup );
    _blue.addEventListener( MouseEvent.MOUSE_UP, place );
  }

  public function pickup( event:MouseEvent ):void {
    // Save the original location so you can put the target back
    startingLocation = new Point();
    startingLocation.x = event.target.x;
    startingLocation.y = event.target.y;

    // Start dragging the Sprite that was clicked on and apply
    // a drop shadow filter to give it depth
    event.target.startDrag();
    event.target.filters = [ new DropShadowFilter() ];

    // Bring the target to front of the display list so
    // it appears on top of everything else
    setChildIndex( DisplayObject( event.target ), numChildren - 1 );
  }

  public function place( event:MouseEvent ):void {
    // Stop dragging the Sprite around and remove the depth
    // effect (i.e., the drop shadow) from the filter
    event.target.stopDrag();
    event.target.filters = null;

    // Check to see if the Sprite was dropped over the white
    // rectangle, and if so, update the color
    if ( event.target.dropTarget == _white ) {
      // Determine which color was dropped, and apply that color
      // to the white rectangle
      var color:uint;
      switch ( event.target ) {
        case _red: color = 0xFF0000; break;
        case _green: color = 0x00FF00; break;
        case _blue: color = 0x0000FF; break;
      }

      _white.graphics.clear();
      _white.graphics.beginFill( color );
      _white.graphics.drawRect( 20, 10, 50, 50 );
      _white.graphics.endFill();
    }

    // Place the dragging Sprite back to its original location
    event.target.x = startingLocation.x;
    event.target.y = startingLocation.y;
  }

  }
}
```

Breaking down this code a bit, all of the rectangles are added to the display list and then the appropriate mouseDown and mouseUp listeners are defined. Every time a mouseDown is received over one of the colored rectangles, the pickup process starts.

First, the original location of the rectangle is saved. This allows the rectangle's location to be restored after the drop operation. Next, the *startDrag()* method is called on the rectangle to start dragging it around the screen. After that, a *DropShadowFilter* is applied to provide depth during the drag and make it appear as if the rectangle were held above the others in the display list. Finally, the rectangle is moved to the front of the display list via *setChildIndex()* so that it is drawn on top of all of the others as it follows the mouse.

When the mouseUp event is detected, the drop operation commences via the *place()* method. First, the rectangle has *stopDrag()* called on it to stop the mouse follow behavior, and the filters are removed to reverse the depth effect. Next, the rectangle's dropTarget property is examined to determine if it was dropped over the white rectangle. If the white rectangle is indeed the dropTarget, the white rectangle is given the same color as the rectangle that was dropped onto it. Finally, because the rectangle is out of position now from following the mouse around, the original starting location is restored.

The previous code works alright, but there are two small problems with it: the dropTarget property isn't always reliable and the dragging is choppy.

The dropTarget property continually changes during movement after *startDrag()* is issued. This is good because it allows for feedback to be provided as the object is moved over different possible drop targets; you can indicate whether a drop is currently allowed based on whatever dropTarget currently is. However, dropTarget only changes when the pointer passes over a *new* display object, and *not* when the pointer leaves a display object. This presents a problem when you move over an object and then leave that object without moving over a new one. In such a case, the dropTarget property still points to the last object that the mouse moved over, even though the mouse may have moved outside of that object without ever moving over a new object. This means that the mouse is not guaranteed to actually be over the display object that dropTarget refers to.

To see this effect in action:

1. Pick up the red rectangle.
2. Move it over the white rectangle.
3. Move the mouse further to the right so the red rectangle is outside the area of the white rectangle.
4. With the red rectangle *outside* the white rectangle, release it.

You can see that the white rectangle is colored red because the dropTarget is still referring to the white rectangle, even though the red rectangle is dropped outside of the white rectangle bounds.

To fix this behavior, use the *hitTestPoint()* method to determine if the mouse location is within the bounds of the dropTarget display object. The *hitTestPoint()* method takes an *x* and *y* location and returns a true or false value, indicating if the location falls within the bounds of the object. An optional third *Boolean* parameter can be used to specify how the hit test area is calculated. Specifying false as the third parameter will use the bounding box rectangle of the object, whereas true uses the actual shape of the object itself. The default value is false.

Inside of the *place()* method that tests if the colored rectangle was dropped correctly, add a call to *hitTestPoint()* inside the conditional checking the dropTarget. This makes sure the mouse cursor still is within the bounds of the white rectangle before allowing the drop:

```
if ( event.target.dropTarget == _white
    && _white.hitTestPoint( _white.mouseX, _white.mouseY ) ) {
```

Another problem with the code is the choppy screen updating during mouse movement. This is because mouse events happen independently of the rendering process. The movie's frame rate determines how often the screen is updated, so if the mouse changes the display, the updated display won't appear until the screen is normally refreshed (as specified by the frame rate).

To combat this problem, the *MouseEvent* class includes the method *updateAfterEvent()*. Typically called when the mouseMove event is handled, *updateAfterEvent()* notifies the Flash Player that the screen has changed and instructs it to redraw. This avoids the delay that occurs when waiting for the frame rate to update the screen normally after mouse movement.

Unfortunately, *updateAfterEvent()* does not play nice with *startDrag()*. Even if a mouseMove event handler is added for the sole purposes of calling *updateAfterEvent()* to handle the rendering updates, calling *updateAfterEvent()* has no effect. Another problem with *startDrag()* is that you are able to drag only one *Sprite* at a time. Although this isn't necessarily a major problem, it is rather limiting.

To address these issues, a new custom visual class, named *DraggableSprite*, was created as part of the *ActionScript 3.0 Cookbook* Library (found at *http://www.rightactionscript.com/ascb*); it can be found in the *ascb.display* package.

The *DraggableSprite* class inherits from *Sprite*, and adds two aptly named methods: *drag()* and *drop()*. The *drag()* method takes the same parameters and is used the same way as *startDrag()*. The *drop()* method behaves the same as *stopDrag()*.

The primary difference is that the drag-and-drop functionality available in *DraggableSprite* is implemented by custom mouse tracking code, versus having the Flash Player track the mouse internally. Because of this, both negative aspects of *startDrag()* are overcome. Multiple *DraggableSprite* instances are able to move with the mouse at the same time, and the rendering delay issue is eliminated because *updateAfterEvent()* works as expected.

However, when switching to *DraggableSprite*, the dropTarget property is no longer applicable. Instead, you have to use the *getObjectsUnderPoint()* method to return the objects beneath the mouse and determine if a drop is valid based on the information returned.

The *getObjectsUnderPoint()* method returns an array of display objects that are children of the container the method was called on. The item at the end of the array, in position length – 1, is the top-most item (the object directly underneath the mouse). The item at position 0 is the very bottom item underneath the mouse. By testing to see if the white rectangle is in the list of objects under the mouse location at the time of the drop, you can determine if the drop was valid or not.

The following code is the same drag-and-drop behavior as before, but updated to use *DraggableSprite* instead of *Sprite*:

```
package {
  import flash.display.Sprite;
  import flash.display.DisplayObject;
  import flash.events.MouseEvent;
  import flash.geom.Point;
  import flash.filters.DropShadowFilter;

  import ascb.display.DraggableSprite;

  public class ColorDrop extends Sprite {

    private var _red:DraggableSprite;
    private var _green:DraggableSprite;
    private var _blue:DraggableSprite;
    private var _white:Sprite;

    // Saves the starting coordinates of a dragging Sprite so
    // it can be placed back
    private var startingLocation:Point;

    // Create the rectangles that comprise the interface
    // and wire the mouse events to make them interactive
    public function ColorDrop() {
      createRectangles();
      addEventListeners();
    }

    private function createRectangles():void {
      _red = new DraggableSprite();
      _red.graphics.beginFill( 0xFF0000 );
      _red.graphics.drawRect( 0, 10, 10, 10 );
      _red.graphics.endFill();
```

```
  _green = new DraggableSprite( )
  _green.graphics.beginFill( 0x00FF00 );
  _green.graphics.drawRect( 0, 30, 10, 10 );
  _green.graphics.endFill( );

  _blue = new DraggableSprite( );
  _blue.graphics.beginFill( 0x0000FF );
  _blue.graphics.drawRect( 0, 50, 10, 10 );
  _blue.graphics.endFill( );

  _white = new DraggableSprite( );
  _white.graphics.beginFill( 0xFFFFFF );
  _white.graphics.drawRect( 20, 10, 50, 50 );
  _white.graphics.endFill( );

  addChild( _red );
  addChild( _green );
  addChild( _blue );
  addChild( _white );
}

private function addEventListeners( ):void {
  _red.addEventListener( MouseEvent.MOUSE_DOWN, pickup );
  _red.addEventListener( MouseEvent.MOUSE_UP, place );

  _green.addEventListener( MouseEvent.MOUSE_DOWN, pickup );
  _green.addEventListener( MouseEvent.MOUSE_UP, place );

  _blue.addEventListener( MouseEvent.MOUSE_DOWN, pickup );
  _blue.addEventListener( MouseEvent.MOUSE_UP, place );
}

public function pickup( event:MouseEvent ):void {
  // Save the original location so you can put the target back
  startingLocation = new Point( );
  startingLocation.x = event.target.x;
  startingLocation.y = event.target.y;

  // Start dragging the Sprite that was clicked on and apply
  // a drop shadow filter to give it depth
  event.target.drag( );
  event.target.filters = [ new DropShadowFilter( ) ];

  // Bring the target to front of the display list so
  // that it appears on top of everything else
  setChildIndex( DisplayObject( event.target ), numChildren - 1 );
}

public function place( event:MouseEvent ):void {
  // Stop dragging the Sprite around and remove the depth
  // effect from the filter
  event.target.drop( );
  event.target.filters = null;
```

```
// Get a list of objects inside this container that are
// underneath the mouse
var dropTargets:Array = getObjectsUnderPoint( new Point( mouseX, mouseY ) );

// The display object at position length - 1 is the top-most object,
// which is the rectangle that is currently being moved by the mouse.
// If the white rectangle is the one immedialy beneath that, the
// drop is valid
if ( dropTargets[ dropTargets.length - 2 ] == _white ) {
  // Determine which color was dropped, and apply that color
  // to the white rectangle
  var color:uint;
  switch ( event.target ) {
    case _red: color = 0xFF0000; break;
    case _green: color = 0x00FF00; break;
    case _blue: color = 0x0000FF; break;
  }

  _white.graphics.clear();
  _white.graphics.beginFill( color );
  _white.graphics.drawRect( 20, 10, 50, 50 );
  _white.graphics.endFill();
}

// Place the dragging Sprite back to its original location
event.target.x = startingLocation.x;
event.target.y = startingLocation.y;
}

}
}
```

See Also

Recipes 6.4 and 6.8

## CHAPTER 7

Drawing and Masking

7.0 Introduction

With ActionScript, you can programmatically draw many display objects such as *Shape*, *Sprite*, *Button*, and *MovieClip*. Each of these classes has a graphics property that is an instance of the *flash.display.Graphics* class. The *Graphics* class defines an API for drawing content programmatically. Most recipes in this chapter discuss how to use the *Graphics* class API.

Since the *Shape*, *Sprite*, *Button*, and *MovieClip* classes already define graphics properties that are references to *Graphics* instances, it is not necessary to construct new *Graphics* objects. The graphics property for a display object draws within that display object. For example, the following code sets the line style for the *Graphics* object targeting a sprite called sampleSprite:

```
sampleSprite.graphics.lineStyle();
```

The *Graphics* class defines an API for drawing basic lines and simple shapes. However, some common shapes are difficult to draw with the *Graphics* API. For that reason, the AS3CBLibrary (available at *http://www.rightactionscript.com/ascb*) includes an *ascb.drawing.Pen* class. The *Pen* class is a proxy (a wrapper) for the *Graphics* class. You can construct a new *Pen* instance by passing it a reference to the *Graphics* object you want to target:

```
var pen:Pen = new Pen(sampleSprite.graphics);
```

The *Pen* class proxies requests to all the methods of the *Graphics* class. That means you can call any of the *Graphics* methods from the *Pen* class. In addition, the *Pen* class defines an API that allows you to more simply draw arcs, ellipses, polygons, stars, and more. The *Pen* class methods are discussed in the relevant recipes in this chapter.

7.1   Setting a Line Style

Problem

You want to set the line style properties.

Solution

Use the *lineStyle( )* method.

Discussion

Before you can draw programmatically, you must set the line style properties for a *Graphics* object. If you don't set the line style properties, the default line style is undefined and lines and fills won't render. You can set the line style properties by using the *lineStyle( )* method of a *Graphics* object.

The *lineStyle( )* method accepts up to eight parameters, all of which are optional. The parameters are as follows:

thickness
> The thickness (in pixels) for a line. The default value is 1. The valid values range from 0 to 255. 0 is a hairline. Values outside of the valid range are adjusted to the nearest valid value.

color
> The color for the line. The default value is 0x000000.

alpha
> The alpha value for the line. The valid range is from 0 to 1. The default value is 1.

pixelHinting
> A Boolean value indicating whether or not the lines ought to snap to whole pixels. The default is false.

scaleMode
> One of the constants from the *flash.display.LineScaleMode* class. The constants are NORMAL (default), NONE, VERTICAL, and HORIZONTAL. When the value is set to NORMAL, the line thickness scales when the object within which the line is drawn is scaled. For example, if a sprite containing a 1-pixel line is scaled 200 percent, the line thickness scales to 2 pixels. If you set the scale mode to NONE, then the line thickness never scales. If you set the scale mode to VERTICAL, then the line thickness does not scale when the object is scaled only in the vertical direction (though it scales when the object is scaled horizontally). Likewise, if you set the scale mode to HORIZONTAL, the line thickness doesn't scale when the object is scaled only in the horizontal direction.

caps

A string specifying the end caps to use for the line. The value can be one of the *flash.display.CapsStyle* constants. The constants are NONE, ROUND (default), and SQUARE.

joints

A string specifying the type of joints between connecting line segments. The value can be one of the *flash.display.JointStyle* constants. The constants are BEVEL, MITER, and ROUND (default).

miterLimit

When the joint style is set to MITER you can optionally specify a *miter limit*. The default value is 3. The valid range is from 1 to 255. The miter limit determines how far beyond the point at which the line segments join that the miter joint extends. The effect of a miter limit is determined by the value as well as the line thickness and the angle between the line segments.

Since all the parameters are optional, you can minimally call the *lineStyle()* method, as in the following example:

```
sampleSprite.graphics.lineStyle();
```

You can call the *lineStyle()* method at any point to change the line style. For example, you can set the line style to a 20 pixel green line, draw a line segment, set the line style to a 10 pixel blue line, and then draw a second line segment with the new line style.

You must set the line style again after calling the *clear()* method. Calling the *clear()* method effectively resets the line style to the default undefined state.

7.2 Setting Gradient Line Styles

Problem

You want to draw lines using gradient styles.

Solution

Use the *Graphics.lineGradientStyle()* method.

Discussion

The *lineGradientStyle()* method allows you to draw lines with gradient styles. You must still call *lineStyle()* first. However, once you've set the basic line style properties, you can call *lineGradientStyle()* to apply a gradient style to lines. The parameters for the *lineGradientStyle()* method are exactly the same as the parameters for the *beginGradientFill()* method.

See Also

Recipe 7.13 for more about parameters.

7.3 Drawing a Line

Problem

You want to draw a line using ActionScript.

Solution

Use the *Graphics.lineTo()* method to draw a line from the current pen location to a destination point.

Discussion

The most basic type of drawing that you can do with ActionScript is a straight line. Flash uses the current pen location as the starting point, so you need to provide only the coordinates of the destination point. Use the *Grahics.lineTo()* method to create a line from the current pen location to the specified destination point:

```
// Draws a line from the current pen position to (100,100)
// within the coordinate system of sampleSprite.
sampleSprite.graphics.lineTo(100, 100);
```

When ActionScript methods are used to draw, all the lines and fills are drawn within the display object associated with the *Graphics* object from which the methods are invoked. For example, in the preceding code, the line is drawn within sampleSprite.

As mentioned previously, when you use the Drawing API methods such as *lineTo()*, Flash draws the line beginning at the current pen location. If you have not otherwise moved the pen (by calling a *lineTo()*, *curveTo()*, or *moveTo()* method, for example) the pen is positioned at the origin of the display object's coordinate system, point (0,0). You can move the pen without drawing a line by using the *moveTo()* method. The *moveTo()* method simply relocates the pen to the coordinate you specify; it does not draw any lines:

```
// Move the pen in sampleSprite to (200,20)
sampleSprite.graphics.moveTo(200, 20);
```

The *moveTo()* method is important in situations in which you want to either begin drawing from a point other than the display object's center or draw lines or shapes without necessarily connecting all the lines:

```
// Set a 1-pixel, black, completely opaque line style
sampleSprite.graphics.lineStyle();
```

```
// Draw a dashed line using a series of lines and spaces
sampleSprite.graphics.lineTo(10, 0);
sampleSprite.graphics.moveTo(15, 0);
sampleSprite.graphics.lineTo(25, 0);
sampleSprite.graphics.moveTo(30, 0);
sampleSprite.graphics.lineTo(40, 0);
sampleSprite.graphics.moveTo(45, 0);
sampleSprite.graphics.lineTo(55, 0);
```

As noted in Recipe 7.1, you can change the line style between drawing line or curve segments. So while the preceding code draws four black line segments, the following code draws four line segments of different colors:

```
// Set a 1-pixel, black, completely opaque line style
sampleSprite.graphics.lineStyle();

// Draw a dashed line using a series of lines and spaces
sampleSprite.graphics.lineTo(10, 0);
sampleSprite.graphics.moveTo(15, 0);

// Change the color of the line to blue
sampleSprite.graphics.lineStyle(1, 0x0000FF);
sampleSprite.graphics.lineTo(25, 0);
sampleSprite.graphics.moveTo(30, 0);

// Change the color of the line to green
sampleSprite.graphics.lineStyle(1, 0x00FF00);
sampleSprite.graphics.lineTo(40, 0);
sampleSprite.graphics.moveTo(45, 0);

// Change the color of the line to red
sampleSprite.graphics.lineStyle(1, 0xFF0000);
sampleSprite.graphics.lineTo(55, 0);
```

The *Pen.drawLine()* method is useful when you want to draw lines from one specific coordinate to another. For example, an example showed you how to draw a series of line segments to create a dashed line. Using a *Pen* object, that code can be simplified as follows:

```
var pen:Pen = new Pen(sampleSprite.graphics);

// Draw a dashed line using a series of lines segments
pen.drawLine(0, 0, 10, 0);
pen.drawLine(15, 0, 25, 0);
pen.drawLine(30, 0, 40, 0);
pen.drawLine(45, 0, 55, 0);
```

See Also

Recipe 7.1

7.4   Drawing a Curve

Problem

You want to draw a curve using ActionScript.

Solution

Use the *Graphics.curveTo()* method.

Discussion

Once you have set a line style, you can draw a curve using the *curveTo()* method. The *curveTo()* method draws an approximation of a Bezier curve (although optimized for performance), which requires three points: a starting point, a control point, and a destination point:

- The starting point is always determined by the pen's current location.
- The destination point is simply the point on the canvas to which you want to draw.
- The control point is the point that determines the shape of the curve, and it is calculated by determining where the tangents to the curve at the starting and destination points intersect. The control point is not actually on the curve in all cases, except for straight line segments. Figure 7-1 shows the control point for a curve.

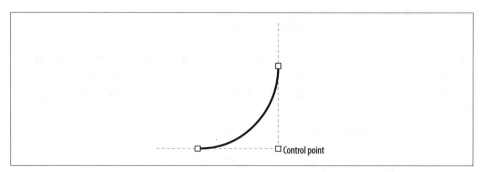

Figure 7-1. The control point of a curve

The *curveTo()* method requires four parameters. The first two parameters specify the X and Y coordinates of the control point; the next two parameters specify the X and Y coordinates of the destination point. The following example draws a curve with a control point at 0,100 and a destination point at 100,100:

```
sampleSprite.graphics.lineStyle( );
sampleSprite.graphics.curveTo(0, 100, 100, 100);
```

7.5 Drawing an Arc

Problem

You want to draw an arc.

Solution

Use the *Pen.drawArc()* method.

Discussion

An arc is a part of the outline from a circle. Drawing an arc with the *curveTo()* method is rather difficult for various reasons. However, by using the *Pen.drawArc()* method, you can quickly draw an arc of any radius and length. The *drawArc()* method accepts the following parameters:

x
> The *x* coordinate of the arc center (the center of the circle).

y
> The *y* coordinate of the arc center.

radius
> The radius of the arc.

arc
> The angle measurement of the arc, specified in degrees.

startingAngle
> The starting angle of the arc. The default value is 0.

radialLines
> A Boolean value that indicates whether to draw the radial lines that connect the arc to the center. The default is false. When set to true, the arc looks like a slice.

The following draws an arc with radial lines; the radius is 50, the arc angle is 80 degrees, and the starting angle is 20 degrees:

```
var pen:Pen = new Pen(graphics);
pen.drawArc(100, 100, 50, 80, 20, true);
```

7.6 Drawing a Rectangle

Problem

You want to draw a rectangle at runtime.

Solution

Draw four connecting line segments at right angles. Use the *Graphics.drawRect()* method. For rectangles with rounded corners, use the *Graphics.drawRoundRect()* or *Graphics.drawRoundRectComplex()* method.

Discussion

To draw a simple rectangle, draw four lines using the *lineTo()* method:

```
// Specify a one-pixel, solid, black line
sampleSprite.graphics.lineStyle(1, 0, 100);

// Draw four lines to form the perimeter of the rectangle
sampleSprite.graphics.lineTo(100, 0);
sampleSprite.graphics.lineTo(100, 50);
sampleSprite.graphics.lineTo(0, 50);
sampleSprite.graphics.lineTo(0, 0);
```

As you can see, drawing a simple rectangle is no huge feat. However, there are several drawbacks to using the preceding technique of calling *lineTo()* four times. The obvious drawback is that it requires at least five lines of code: one to set the line style and four to draw the line segments. Another drawback is that you cannot easily draw the rectangle at an angle or with rounded corners.

You can use the *Graphics.drawRect()* method to simplify drawing a standard rectangle. The method requires four parameters specifying the X and Y coordinates of the upper-left corner and the width and height of the rectangle. The following draws a 100×50 rectangle with the upper-left corner aligned to 0,0:

```
sampleSprite.graphics.lineStyle( );
sampleSprite.graphics.drawRect(0, 0, 100, 50);
```

The *Graphics.drawRoundRect()* method draws a rectangle with rounded corners with equal radii. The method accepts the same parameter list as *drawRect()* with one additional parameter specifying the value for the corner radii. The following draws the same rectangle as in the preceding example, except that it has rounded corners with radii of 20:

```
sampleSprite.graphics.lineStyle( );
sampleSprite.graphics.drawRoundRect(0, 0, 100, 50, 20);
```

The *Graphics.drawRoundRectComplex()* method works just like *drawRoundRect()*, except that you can specify the values for each radius independently. The method accepts the same parameter list as *drawRect()*, with the addition of four parameters for the radii. The addition parameters are in the order of top left, top right, bottom left, and bottom right. The following draws the same rectangle as the preceding example, except that the corners have different radius values:

```
sampleSprite.graphics.lineStyle( );
sampleSprite.graphics.drawRoundRect(0, 0, 100, 50, 0, 20, 5, 25);
```

You can draw filled rectangles by invoking *beginFill()*, *beginGradientFill()*, or *beginBitmapFill()* before calling the method or methods to draw the rectangle. Then call *endFill()* after the method(s):

```
sampleSprite.graphics.lineStyle();
sampleSprite.graphics.beginFill(0xFF0000);
sampleSprite.graphics.drawRectComplex(0, 0, 100, 50);
sampleSprite.graphics.endFill();
```

7.7   Drawing a Circle

Problem

You want to draw a circle at runtime.

Solution

Use the *Grahics.drawCircle()* method.

Discussion

Drawing a circle with the standard drawing methods is not as simple as you might think. Because of Flash's simplified, single control point Bezier calculations, it requires at least eight segments to create a circle that looks convincingly like a circle. Making the calculations in order to draw each segment of the circle requires a fair amount of math and code. However, the Graphics class has a *drawCircle()* method that greatly simplifies drawing a circle. The *drawCircle()* method requires three parameters:

x
: The *x* coordinate of the circle's center point.

y
: The *y* coordinate of the circle's center point.

radius
: The radius of the circle.

The following draws a circle with a radius of 50 and the center point at 100,100:

```
sampleSprite.graphics.lineStyle();
sampleSprite.graphics.drawCircle(100, 100, 50);
```

Drawing concentric circles is simple enough; just specify the same center point for the circles:

```
sampleSprite.graphics.lineStyle();
sampleSprite.graphics.drawCircle(100, 100, 50);
sampleSprite.graphics.drawCircle(100, 100, 100);
```

You can fill a circle by calling *beginFill()*, *beginGradientFill()*, or *beginBitmapFill()* before *drawCircle()*, and calling *endFill()* after *drawCircle()*:

```
sampleSprite.graphics.lineStyle();
sampleSprite.graphics.beginFill(0xFF0000);
sampleSprite.graphics.drawCircle(100, 100, 50);
sampleSprite.graphics.endFill();
```

7.8 Drawing an Ellipse

Problem

You want to draw an ellipse (oval) at runtime.

Solution

Use the *Pen.drawEllipse()* method.

Discussion

An ellipse is a more abstract form of a circle. Rather than having a single, uniform radius, an ellipse is defined by two radii that intersect at right angles. The two radii are called the *major and minor radii*, and also sometimes simply the *x* radius and *y* radius.

Drawing an ellipse is just slightly more complex than drawing a circle. However, unlike circles, the *Graphics* class has no method for drawing ellipses. Therefore, the simplest way to programmatically create an ellipse is to use one of the methods of the *Pen* class. The *drawEllipse()* method allows for the following four parameters:

x
> The *x* coordinate of the center of the ellipse.

y
> The *y* coordinate of the center of the ellipse.

xRadius
> The radius of the ellipse in the *x* direction (major axis).

yRadius
> The radius of the ellipse in the *y* direction (minor axis).

The following code defines a *Pen* object and then draws an ellipse:

```
var pen:Pen = new Pen(sampleSprite.graphics);

pen.drawEllipse(100, 100, 100, 50);
```

7.9   Drawing a Triangle

Problem

You want to draw a triangle at runtime.

Solution

Use the *Pen.drawTriangle()* method.

Discussion

You can determine and plot the vertices of a triangle, given the lengths of two sides and the angle between them. This is a better approach than specifying the lengths of the three sides, because knowing two sides and the angle between them always determines a triangle, whereas three arbitrary sides may not fit together to make a triangle.

The calculations involved in drawing a triangle based on two sides and an angle are slightly complex, so the simplest way to programmatically draw a triangle is to use the *drawTriangle()* method of the *Pen* class. The *drawTriangle()* method accepts up to seven parameters, described as follows:

x
> The X coordinate of the centroid (the center point) of the triangle.

y
> The Y coordinate of the centroid of the triangle.

ab
> The length of the side formed between points *a* and *b*.

ac
> The length of the side formed between points *a* and *c*.

angle
> The angle (in degrees) between sides *ab* and *ac*.

rotation
> The rotation of the triangle in degrees. If 0 or undefined, side *ac* parallels the *x* axis.

Once you've defined a *Pen* instance, you can use the *drawTriangle()* method to quickly draw a triangle, as in the following example:

```
var pen:Pen = new Pen(sampleSprite.graphics);
pen.drawTriangle(100, 100, 100, 200, 40);
```

You can precede *drawTriangle()* with a call to *beginFill()*, *beginGradientFill()*, and *beginBitmapFill()* to apply a fill to the shape. Of course, you'll also want to then call *endFill()* after the call to *drawTriangle()*.

The following code draws a filled triangle aligned to the upper left:

```
var pen:Pen = new Pen(sampleSprite.graphics);
pen.beginFill(0xFF0000);
pen.drawTriangle(100, 100, 100, 200, 40);
pen.endFill();
```

See Also

Recipe 7.10 shows how to draw an isosceles triangle (and specify a shape with three sides) using the *drawRegularPolygon()* method.

7.10 Drawing Regular Polygons

Problem

You want to draw a regular polygon (a polygon where all sides are equal length) at runtime.

Solution

Use the *Pen.drawRegularPolygon()* method.

Discussion

You can create a method to draw a regular polygon using basic trigonometric ratios to determine the necessary angles and coordinates of the segments. Of course, since employing those trigonometric ratios requires quite a lot of code and you actually recall trigonometry, you'll likely find it much easier to simply use the *drawRegularPolygon()* method of the *Pen* class.

The *drawRegularPolygon()* accepts up to five parameters, described as follows:

x
    The *x* coordinate of the center of the polygon.

y
    The *y* coordinate of the center of the polygon.

sides
    The number of sides in the polygon.

length
    The length of each side in pixels.

rotation
    The number of degrees by which the polygon should be rotated.

Once you have defined a *Pen* instance, you can quickly draw regular polygons with any number of sides (with a minimum of three sides, of course, to be a valid polygon):

```
var pen:Pen = new Pen(sampleSprite.graphics);

// Draw a pentagon in which the sides are each 50 pixels
pen.drawRegularPolygon(100, 100, 5, 50);
```

As with the other shape drawing methods in this chapter, you can create a filled polygon by invoking *beginFill()*, *beginGradientFill()*, or *beginBitmapFill()* before *drawRegularPolygon()*, and invoking *endFill()* after *drawRegularPolygon()*:

```
var pen:Pen = new Pen(sampleSprite.graphics);
pen.beginFill(0xFF0000);
pen.drawRegularPolygon(100, 100, 5, 50);
pen.endFill();
```

7.11 Drawing a Star

Problem

You want to draw a star.

Solution

Use the *Pen.drawStar()* method.

Discussion

The *Pen.drawStar()* method enables you to quickly draw a star shape programmatically. The method accepts the following parameters:

x
> The *x* coordinate of the center of the star.

y
> The *y* coordinate of the center of the star.

points
> The number of points on the star.

innerRadius
> The radius of the inner part of the star.

outerRadius
> The radius of the outer part of the star.

rotation
> The default value is 0; you can specify a rotation in degrees.

The following example draws a five-pointed star:

```
var pen:Pen = new Pen(sampleSprite.graphics);
pen.drawStar(100, 100, 5, 50, 100);
```

7.12 Filling a Shape with a Solid or Translucent Color

Problem

You want to draw a shape and fill it with a solid or translucent color at runtime.

Solution

Use the *Graphics.beginFill()* and *Graphics.endFill()* methods to initiate and close a shape drawn at runtime.

Discussion

To draw a filled shape, call *beginFill()* prior to any other drawing methods. Invoke *endFill()* after calling other drawing methods to create the shape.

 You cannot apply a fill to an existing shape drawn at authoring time or runtime. Before drawing the shape you want filled, you must first invoke the *beginFill()* method.

This example creates a solid green square:

```
sampleSprite.graphics.lineStyle();
sampleSprite.graphics.beginFill(0x00FF00);
sampleSprite.graphics.lineTo(100, 0);
sampleSprite.graphics.lineTo(100, 100);
sampleSprite.graphics.lineTo(0, 100);
sampleSprite.graphics.lineTo(0, 0);
sampleSprite.graphics.endFill();
```

The *MovieClip.beginFill()* method accepts two parameters:

fillColor
> The RGB value to use for the fill.

alpha
> The value between 0 (transparent) and 1 (opaque) that controls the opacity. The default is 1.

To create a translucent, filled shape, specify an *alpha* less than 1. If *alpha* is 0, the shape appears unfilled. However, setting the alpha to 0 is often appropriate. For example, you may want to create a draggable movie clip within which parts are transparent. Setting the fill alphas for those parts to 0 can help to accomplish that.

The *endFill()* method does not require any parameters. It simply ends the fill initiated with *beginFill()*, *beginGradientFill()*, or *beginBitmapFill()*. To avoid unexpected results, ensure that the pen returns to the starting point to complete the shape before invoking *endFill()*.

See Also

Recipe 7.13

7.13   Filling a Shape with a Gradient

Problem

You want to draw a shape and fill it with a gradient at runtime.

Solution

Use the *beginGradientFill()* and *endFill()* methods to initiate and close a shape drawn at runtime.

Discussion

A *gradient fill* is one in which there is a graded change in colors. Flash supports linear gradients, in which one color fades into the next from left to right. (If you want the gradient to change vertically then you can simply rotate the gradient using the matrix transform discussed in this recipe.) Flash also supports radial gradients, in which the colors radiate out from a center point. You can initiate a gradient-filled shape by using *beginGradientFill()* in the same way that you can initiate a solid-filled shape with *beginFill()*. The difference is that the call to *beginGradientFill()* requires a more complex set of parameters:

gradientType
> One of the constants from the *flash.display.GradientType* class. The options are LINEAR or RADIAL.

colors
> An array of RGB values for the colors to use in the gradient. They are displayed in the gradient from left to right in a linear gradient, or from the center outward in a radial gradient.

alphas
> An array of alpha values that correspond to the colors in the *colors* parameter array.

ratios
> An array whose elements are numbers corresponding to the *colors* and *alphas* elements. The values in the *ratios* array indicate the point within the gradient at which each color is pure. The range of values for the *ratios* should be from 0 (left-most point in a linear fill, or inner-most point in a radial fill) to 255 (right-most or outer-most).

matrix

A *flash.geom.Matrix* object that defines the transform to apply to the gradient. The default gradient is a unit gradient (1×1) that must be transformed to correctly fill the shape. The Matrix class defines a *createGradientBox()* method that you can use to populate the object. The *createGradientBox()* method accepts the following parameters:

scaleX

The amount by which the object is scaled horizontally. Since the gradient that's being transformed is a unit gradient (1×1) the *scaleX* value is equal to the width of the fill.

scaleY

The amount by which the object is scaled vertically. Since the gradient that's being transformed is a unit gradient (1×1) the *scaleY* value is equal to the height of the fill.

rotation

The amount to rotate the gradient in radians. You can convert from degrees to radians by multiplying by *Math.PI/180*. The default value is 0.

tx

The amount to translate in the *x* direction. The default is 0.

ty

The amount to translate in the *y* direction The default is 0.

spreadMethod

One of the *flash.display.SpreadMethod* constants. The options are PAD, REFLECT, and REPEAT. The default is PAD. When the method is PAD, the gradient is padded on either side with the colors on the sides. For example, if a gradient is defined to be 100 pixels wide with red on the left side and blue on the right side, and if the gradient is applied to a rectangle that is 200 pixels wide, the blue will fill the right-most 100 pixels of the rectangle. If the method is REFLECT, then the gradient continually repeats in a mirror-image fashion. Using the same 100-pixel red to blue gradient example, the gradient will fill a 200-pixel-pixel rectangle with red to blue and blue to red when the *spreadMethod* parameter is set to REFLECT. When the method is set to REPEAT, the gradient repeats end to end.

interpolationMethod

One of the constants of the *flash.display.InterpolationMethod* class. The options are LINEAR_RGB and RGB. The default is RGB. The interpolation method affects how colors gradate.

focalPointRatio

A value from -1 to 1 indicating the focal point for radial gradients (there is no effect for linear gradients). The default value is 0, which places the focal point in the center. A value of -1 places the focal point to the left edge of the gradient, and a value of 1 places the focal point to the right edge of the gradient.

The following example draws a radial gradient that fills a circle:

```
var matrix:Matrix = new Matrix( );
matrix.createGradientBox(100, 100, 0, 50, 50);
var colors:Array = [0xFF0000, 0x0000FF];
var alphas:Array = [100, 100];
var ratios:Array = [0x00, 0xFF];
sampleSprite.graphics.lineStyle( );
sampleSprite.graphics.beginGradientFill(GradientType.GRADIENT, colors, alphas,
ratios, matrix);
sampleSprite.graphics.drawCircle(100, 100, 50);
sampleSprite.graphics.endFill( );
```

7.14   Filling a Shape with a Bitmap

Problem

You want to apply a bitmap fill to a shape.

Solution

Use the *Graphics.beginBitmapFill( )* method.

Discussion

The *Graphics.beginBitmapFill( )* method enables you to apply a bitmap as a fill to a shape. The method accepts the following parameters:

bitmap
> A *BitmapData* object to use as the bitmap fill.

matrix
> By default the bitmap is applied with no transform applied. You can specify a *flash.geom.Matrix* object to transform the bitmap by scaling, rotating, skewing, and translating the image.

repeat
> A Boolean value indicating whether or not the bitmap ought to repeat to tile fill. By default the value is true. When the value is set to false the bitmap edge's pixels are repeated to fill the shape.

smooth
> A Boolean value indicating whether or not to apply smoothing when the bitmap is scaled greater than 100 percent. The default is false.

The following sample class loads a bitmap from a URL, copies it to a *BitmapData* object, and uses that *BitmapData* object as a fill for circles drawn programmatically:

```
package {

  import flash.display.Sprite;
  import flash.geom.Matrix;
```

```
import flash.display.Loader;
import flash.net.URLRequest;
import flash.display.BitmapData;
import flash.events.Event;

public class Drawing extends Sprite {

  private var _loader:Loader;

  public function Drawing( ) {
    _loader = new Loader( );
    _loader.load(new URLRequest("http://www.rightactionscript.com/samplefiles/
image2.jpg"));
    _loader.contentLoaderInfo.addEventListener(Event.COMPELTE, onImageLoad);
  }

  private function onImageLoad(event:Event):void {
    var bitmap:BitmapData = new BitmapData(_loader.width, _loader.height);
    bitmap.draw(_loader, new Matrix( ));
    var matrix:Matrix = new Matrix( );
    matrix.scale(.1, .1);
    var sampleSprite:Sprite = new Sprite( );
    sampleSprite.graphics.lineStyle( );
    sampleSprite.graphics.beginBitmapFill(bitmap, matrix);
    sampleSprite.graphics.drawCircle(100, 100, 100);
    sampleSprite.graphics.endFill( );
    addChild(sampleSprite);

  }

 }
}
```

7.15   Scripting Masks

Problem

You want to create a mask at runtime.

Solution

Use *DisplayObject.mask*.

Discussion

Masks can be used to create unique shapes or visual effects. For example, you can use masks to create wipes and transitions. You can use masks to create interesting animations in which only the masked portion of the artwork is visible at a given time. You can even create masks that shape tween and use them to mask bitmapped graphics (in movie clips).

Any display object can be used as a mask of another display object by using the mask property. The following sets *maskSprite* as the mask for *sampleSprite*:

```
sampleSprite.mask = maskSprite;
```

The following example draws two shapes and uses one as a mask. Note that both display objects are added to the display list via *addChild()*. Although masks will work in most cases, even when the mask object isn't added to the display list, it's recommended that you add the mask object to the display list:

```
var maskSprite:Sprite = new Sprite( );
var pen:Pen = new Pen(maskSprite.graphics);
pen.beginFill(0xFFFFFF);
pen.drawArc(100, 100, 50, 80, 20, true);
pen.endFill( );
var maskedSprite:Sprite = new Sprite( );
maskedSprite.graphics.lineStyle( );
maskedSprite.graphics.beginFill(0xFF0000);
maskedSprite.graphics.drawRect(0, 0, 200, 200);
maskedSprite.graphics.endFill( );
maskedSprite.mask = maskSprite;
addChild(maskedSprite);
addChild(maskSprite);
```

This next example shows a mask being used to follow the mouse. The mask is assigned to a loader containing a loaded image, which makes it so only the users can see the portion of the image over which they have placed the mouse:

```
var loader:Loader = new Loader( );
loader.load(new URLRequest("http://www.rightactionscript.com/samplefiles/image2.
jpg"));
addChild(loader);
var maskSprite:Sprite = new Sprite( );
maskSprite.graphics.lineStyle( );
maskSprite.graphics.beginFill(0xFFFFFF);
maskSprite.graphics.drawCircle(0, 0, 50);
maskSprite.graphics.endFill( );
loader.mask = maskSprite;
addChild(maskSprite);
maskSprite.startDrag(true);
```

## CHAPTER 8

Bitmaps

8.0   Introduction

Flash 8 introduced the *BitmapData* class, one of the most important additions to the program at that time. Since its inception, Flash has been a vector-based tool. Vector graphics consist of mathematical descriptions of each graphical element. For example, a line starts at point *x0*, *y0* and extends to point *x1*, *y1*. A bitmap, on the other hand, describes a graphic as a rectangular grid of values, with one color value assigned to each pixel.

The two main advantages of vector graphics are scaling and file size. When you scale a vector graphic, you are actually moving the points that make up the lines and curves of the graphic further apart or closer together. Thus, you can scale up or down to almost any size and still maintain smooth lines and curves. A bitmap, on the other hand, starts to look "blocky" as soon as you increase its size even slightly, since each pixel is simply made into a larger rectangle.

Since a vector graphic is nothing more than a list of coordinates that make up various lines, curves, and shapes, the file size tends to be quite low when compared to a bitmap graphic. Bitmap graphics, on the other hand, contain value information for each pixel in the image. For a 100×100-pixel image, this is a list of 10,000 individual values. Of course, most bitmap images use some form of compression to reduce the file size. Even so, they can be quite large.

The advantage of vector graphics went a long way to make Flash such a popular media format on the web. However, bitmaps are not without their own advantages. For one, bitmaps are much better at displaying photographic images. The amount of vectors it would take to describe all the shapes and color variations in a photograph would generally result in a larger file size than a bitmap of the same image.

Another benefit of bitmaps is that they are often easier on the processor than vectors are. In a vector image, each point's position must be calculated, and then the formulas for the lines and curves are calculated and drawn. Complex images can take quite a while to render. Bitmaps are relatively easy to render, though, no matter how complex they are. In terms of animation, you usually find very significant gains in speed and efficiency using bitmaps over vectors.

Before Flash 8, support for bitmap images was minimal. Although they could be loaded and displayed, there wasn't much you could do with them at runtime. The *BitmapData* class offers a nice set of tools for creating and manipulating bitmap graphics at runtime in Flash.

8.1 Creating a BitmapData Object

Problem

You want to create a new bitmap in your application.

Solution

Use the *BitmapData* class's constructor to create a new *BitmapData* object.

Discussion

The *BitmapData* class represents the pixels in a bitmap image, and contains many built-in methods for adding content to and manipulating that image. The first step is to create an instance of the class by calling its constructor, as follows:

```
var bitmap:BitmapData = new BitmapData(width, height,
                               transparent, fillColor);
```

This class is part of the *flash.display* package, so make sure you import *flash.display.
BitmapData* at the top of the file. The width and height parameters specify what size bitmap you want to create. The next parameter is a Boolean value, which specifies whether the bitmap is created with an alpha channel (true) or not (false), and the fillColor determines the initial background color of the image.

Although *width* and *height* are mandatory, *transparent* and *fillColor* default to true and 0xFFFFFFFF, respectively if not explicitly passed to the constructor.

The *fillColor* accepts a 32-bit color value, which means that it supports an alpha channel. Of course, the alpha channel of the fill color is only relevant if you create the *BitmapData* specifying transparent as true. Otherwise, all colors are treated as 100 percent opaque.

The following example creates a *BitmapData* that is initially completely transparent, as the alpha channel of the fillColor is set to zero:

```
var bitmap:BitmapData = new BitmapData(100, 100,
                               true, 0x00FFFFFF);
```

After you create a new *BitmapData*, it exists only in memory. Although you can create content in the image and manipulate it, it will not be visible until you add it to the display list.

See Also

Recipe 8.2 for information on how to make a *BitmapData* visible.

8.2   Adding a Bitmap to the Display List

Problem

You have created a *BitmapData* and now want to make it visible.

Solution

Create a *Bitmap* using the *BitmapData* and add that to the display list.

Discussion

To make anything visible in an application in ActionScript 3.0, you must add it to the *display list*. (See Chapter 6 for a full discussion of the display list.) You add objects to the display list by calling the *addChild( )* method from the main application class, or any other object that has already been added to the display list. However, the *addChild( )* method only accepts objects that are subclasses of *flash.display. DisplayObject*. The *BitmapData* class is descended only from *Object*, so you may not add it to the display list directly.

To add it to the display list, use the *flash.display.Bitmap* class, which is a subclass of *DisplayObject*. It is a sort of wrapper for *BitmapData*, allowing a *BitmapData* to be displayed.

When you create a new instance of *Bitmap* by calling its constructor, you pass in a reference to a *BitmapData*. Then you can add the *Bitmap* to the display list using *addChild( )*. The following example creates a *BitmapData* with a red fill, and displays it via a *Bitmap*:

```
var bitmap:BitmapData = new BitmapData(100, 100, true, 0xffff0000);
var image:Bitmap = new Bitmap(bitmap);
addChild(image);
```

See Also

Recipe 8.1 for how to create a bitmap.

8.3   Drawing a Display Object to a Bitmap

Problem

You have some graphical content in a sprite or other display object and want to draw that to a bitmap.

Solution

Use the *BitmapData* class's *draw()* method to draw the content onto the bitmap.

Discussion

When you first create a *BitmapData*, it is simply a blank rectangle of whatever color you specified. You may have some existing graphic content in a movie clip, sprite, or other display object that you would like to draw to the new bitmap. The *draw()* method allows you to do just this. You pass the object you want to draw into the *draw()* method of the *BitmapData* you want to draw it onto. You can also pass an instance of the *flash.geom.Matrix* class to the method. The *Matrix* class allows you to scale, rotate, translate, or skew the object's graphics before they are drawn. This parameter is optional, but if you need to use later parameters and don't want to transform the object, just pass *null*. You can also optionally pass a *ColorTransform* object, which alters the color of the object before it is drawn. See Recipe 10.1 for information on *ColorTransforms*. The following example draws a sprite, named _sprite, into a *BitmapData* named bitmap, with no transformation:

```
bitmap.draw(_sprite);
```

One reason why this becomes important is because the *BitmapData* class has few tools for basic drawing. You can set a pixel to a particular color, create a filled rectangle, or do a flood fill. There are some specialized noise functions, but it lacks basic functions such as line, curve, oval, or outline drawing tools. To overcome this, you can use the drawing API methods to draw content into a movie clip or sprite, and then draw that object into the bitmap. The following example creates a *BitmapData* and a *Sprite*. It then uses the drawing API to draw an oval in the sprite and draws the sprite into the *BitmapData*:

```
var bitmap:BitmapData = new BitmapData(100, 100,
                                       true, 0x00ffffff);
var sprite:Sprite = new Sprite();
sprite.graphics.beginFill(0xff0000, 100);
sprite.graphics.drawEllipse(0, 25, 100, 50);
sprite.graphics.endFill();
bitmap.draw(sprite);
```

Notice that the bitmap's background has been made transparent (0xffffff), so although the bitmap itself is actually a rectangle, all you see is the oval that has been drawn to it.

See Also

Recipe 8.1 for how to create a bitmap, Recipe 8.2 for information on how to make a *BitmapData* visible, and Recipe 10.1.

8.4   Loading an External Image into a Bitmap

Problem

You want to load an external bitmap image and manipulate it as a *BitmapData*.

Solution

Use the *flash.display.Loader* class to load the image. When the image has loaded, access the loader's *content* property, which is a *Bitmap*. Accessing that *Bitmap*'s *bitmapData* property gives you direct access to the *BitmapData* representing the loaded image.

Discussion

You load an external bitmap image via the *Loader* class. This takes a *URLRequest* object with the URL of the image you are loading. Listening for the loader's *complete* event lets you know when the image has loaded. Here is the setup to create the loader—listen for the *complete* event and begin loading an image:

```
package {
    import flash.display.Sprite;
    import flash.display.Loader;
    import flash.events.Event;
    import flash.net.URLRequest;

    public class BitmapLoader extends Sprite {
        private var _loader:Loader = new Loader( );

        public function BitmapLoader( ) {
            _loader.contentLoaderInfo.addEventListener(Event.COMPLETE, onComplete);
            _loader.load(new URLRequest("image.jpg"));
        }
    }
}
```

By itself, this code simply loads and displays the specified image. Next, create the onComplete method that accesses the bitmap information once it has loaded:

```
public function onComplete(event:Event):void {
    var image:Bitmap = Bitmap(_loader.content);
    var bitmap:BitmapData = image.bitmapData;
    addChild(image);
}
```

First, get a reference to the loader's content property. This is a display object representing the content that was loaded. If you have loaded an external *.swf*, it is a *MovieClip* type. In this case, however, you have loaded a bitmap image, so the content contains a *Bitmap*. You should cast it as a *Bitmap* so the compiler doesn't complain when you try to access properties that belong only to *Bitmap*.

Next, you can access the *BitmapData* contained within the *Bitmap* by reading its *BitmapData* property. This gives you the ability to modify and manipulate the newly loaded image. This example draws a white square on the image.

Alternately, you could draw the loaded image into a new *BitmapData* and display that.

```
public function onComplete(event:Event):void {
    var loadedImage:Bitmap = Bitmap(_loader.content);

    // Create a new Bitmap data and draw the
    // loaded image to it.
    var bitmap:BitmapData = new BitmapData(loadedImage.width,
                                           loadedImage.height,
                                           false, 0xffffffff);
    bitmap.draw(loadedImage, new Matrix())

    // Create a new Bitmap using the BitmapData
    // and display it.
    var image:Bitmap = new Bitmap(bitmap);
    addChild(image);

    // Manipulate the pixels as you wish
    bitmap.fillRect(new Rectangle(0, 0, 50, 50), 0xffffffff);
}
```

See Also

Recipe 8.1 for how to create a bitmap and Recipe 8.2 for information on how to make a *BitmapData* visible.

8.5   Manipulating Pixels

Problem

You want to set or read the value of individual pixels in a bitmap.

Solution

Use the *getPixel()*, *setPixel()*, *getPixel32()*, and *setPixel32()* methods of the *BitmapData* class.

Discussion

Setting and reading pixel values of a bitmap is relatively straightforward in Action-Script 3.0. To read the value of a pixel, just pass in the *x*, *y* coordinates of the pixel you want to read to one of the *getPixel* methods. To set a pixel's color, pass in the coordinates and the color value to one of the *setPixel* methods.

The *getPixel()* and *setPixel()* methods are designed for use on opaque *BitmapData* instances, while *getPixel32()* and *setPixel32()* are used on images that support transparency. Opaque images are 24-bit, with 8 bits for each of its red, green, and blue channels. Transparent images add another 8-bit alpha channel for a total of 32 bits. You specify whether the *BitmapData* supports transparency or not in its constructor. See Recipe 8.1.

The following code creates a white, 32-bit *BitmapData*, and then sets 1,000 random pixels to a semi-transparent red color:

```
var bitmap:BitmapData = new BitmapData(100, 100, true, 0xffffffff);
var image:Bitmap = new Bitmap(bitmap);
addChild(image);

for(var i:int = 0; i < 1000; i++) {
    bitmap.setPixel32(Math.round(Math.random( ) * 100),
                    Math.round(Math.random( ) * 100),
                    0x88ff0000);
}
```

If you use *setPixel()* on a transparent *BitmapData*, the alpha channel is set to 100 percent opaque for that pixel, even if you specify something else. Similarly, if you use *setPixel32()* on an opaque image, the alpha channel data is ignored, as such an image does not have an alpha channel. In general, it is best to use the correct pair of methods for the type of bitmap you are working with.

To read the value of a pixel, pass in the *x*, *y* coordinates of the specific pixel to one of the *getPixel* methods, depending on what type of bitmap you are using. The method returns either a 24- or 32-bit number. The following class sets up a rudimentary color picker. It first uses *BitmapData*'s *noise()* method to generate some random colors and adds a text field to the stage. Then it listens for the *enterFrame* event. On each frame, it gets the value of the pixel under the mouse and converts that into a hexadecimal string.

```
package {
    import flash.display.Sprite;
    import flash.display.Bitmap;
    import flash.display.BitmapData;
    import flash.text.TextField;
    import flash.events.Event;

    public class ColorChooser extends Sprite {
        private var _bitmap:BitmapData;
        private var _textfield:TextField;
```

```
public function ColorChooser( ) {
    _bitmap = new BitmapData(100, 100, false, 0xffffffff);
    var image:Bitmap = new Bitmap(_bitmap);
    addChild(image);
    _bitmap.noise(1000, 0, 255, 1|2|4, false);

    _textfield = new TextField( );
    addChild(_textfield);
    _textfield.y = 100;

    addEventListener(Event.ENTER_FRAME, onEnterFrame);
}

public function onEnterFrame(event:Event):void {
    var colorVal:Number = _bitmap.getPixel(mouseX, mouseY)
    _textfield.text = "#" + colorVal.toString(16).toUpperCase( );
}
    }
}
```

See Also

See Recipes 8.1, 8.6, 8.7, 8.8, 8.9, 8.10, and 8.11 for other ways to add graphical content to a bitmap.

8.6   Creating Rectangular Fills

Problem

You want to fill a rectangular area of a bitmap with a color.

Solution

Use the *fillRect( )* method of the *BitmapData* class.

Discussion

The *BitmapData* class does not have the wealth of drawing tools available in the drawing API for movie clips and sprites. It does have a basic rectangle fill tool, though. Using this method is quite simple. Just pass in the rectangle area you want to fill and the color value with which you want to fill it:

```
_bitmap.fillRect(rectangle, color);
```

The rectangle must be an instance of the *flash.geom.Rectangle* class. You can make an instance of the class by calling its constructor with the *x*, *y*, width, and height of the rectangle you want to create, as so:

```
var rect:Rectangle = new Rectangle(0, 0, 50, 100);
```

The following code creates a white bitmap, and then draws a red square in the middle of it:

```
public function RectExample() {
    _bitmap = new BitmapData(100, 100, false, 0xffffffff);
    var image:Bitmap = new Bitmap(_bitmap);
    addChild(image);
    _bitmap.fillRect(new Rectangle(25, 25, 50, 50), 0xffff0000);
}
```

Note that there is only one version of *fillRect()* for both transparent and non-transparent images. If you are using it with an image that does not have an alpha channel, just pass a 24-bit color value, as the extra bits for alpha are ignored anyway. If you are using it with a transparent image, be sure to use a full 32-bit number. If you just pass a 24-bit value, the alpha channel is set at 0 percent alpha.

See Also

Recipes 8.5, 8.7, 8.8, 8.9, 8.10, and 8.11 for other ways to add graphical content to a bitmap.

8.7 Creating a Flood Fill

Problem

You want to fill a large area, possibly irregular, with a color.

Solution

Use the *floodFill()* method of the *BitmapData* class.

Discussion

The *floodFill()* method has the same syntax as the *setPixel()* method. That is, you pass it an *x*, *y* coordinate and a color. The method colors that pixel and any surrounding pixels the same color. This is the same as the bucket tool in most graphics programs, such as Adobe Photoshop.

The following code demonstrates it in action. It first creates a bitmap and a number of random squares and then sets up a mouseDown handler that performs a flood fill on the selected pixel:

```
package {
    import flash.display.Sprite;
    import flash.display.Bitmap;
    import flash.display.BitmapData;
    import flash.events.MouseEvent;
    import flash.geom.Rectangle;

    public class FloodFillDemo extends Sprite {
```

```
private var _bitmap:BitmapData;

public function FloodFillDemo () {
    var sprite:Sprite = new Sprite();
    addChild(sprite);
    _bitmap = new BitmapData(stage.stageWidth,
                            stage.stageHeight,
                            false, 0xffffffff);

    for(var i:int = 0; i < 20; i++) {
        _bitmap.fillRect(new Rectangle(
                    Math.random() * stage.stageWidth,
                    Math.random() * stage.stageHeight,
                    50, 50), Math.random() * 0xffffffff);
    }
    var image:Bitmap = new Bitmap(_bitmap);
    sprite.addChild(image);
    sprite.addEventListener(MouseEvent.MOUSE_DOWN, onMouseDown);
}

public function onMouseDown(event:MouseEvent):void {
    _bitmap.floodFill(mouseX, mouseY, 0xffff0000);
}
    }
}
```

See Also

Recipes 8.5, 8.6, 8.8, 8.9, 8.10, and 8.11 for other ways to add graphical content to a bitmap.

8.8   Copying Pixels

Problem

You want to copy a rectangular area from one *BitmapData* to another.

Solution

Use the *copyPixels()* method of the *BitmapData* class.

Discussion

The theory behind the *copyPixels()* method is quite simple. It takes the pixel data from one bitmap and draws it onto another. In that sense, it is much like the *draw()* method. However, in the case of *copyPixels()*, you get more control over how much of the bitmap is copied and where it is copied to. You do this by specifying a source rectangle and a destination point:

```
bitmap.copyPixels(sourceBmp, srcRect, destPoint);
```

The source rectangle is an instance of the *flash.geom.Rectangle* class. You use this to define a rectangular area of the original *BitmapData*. This is the only portion of that bitmap that is copied.

The destination point is an instance of *flash.geom.Point*. This specifies the *x*, *y* coordinate of the destination bitmap where you want to paste the copied pixels.

The following example shows how to copy several rectangular areas of a loaded bitmap onto another *BitmapData*:

```
package {
    import flash.display.Sprite;
    import flash.display.Bitmap;
    import flash.display.BitmapData;
    import flash.display.Loader;
    import flash.net.URLRequest;
    import flash.events.Event;
    import flash.geom.Point;
    import flash.geom.Rectangle;

    public class AS3CB extends Sprite {
        private var _bitmap:BitmapData;
        private var _loader:Loader;

        public function AS3CB() {
            _loader = new Loader();
            _loader.contentLoaderInfo.addEventListener(Event.COMPLETE, onLoad);
            _loader.load(new URLRequest("myphoto.jpg"));
            _bitmap = new BitmapData(stage.stageWidth,
                            stage.stageHeight,
                            false, 0xffffffff);
            var image:Bitmap = new Bitmap(_bitmap);
            addChild(image);
        }

        public function onLoad(event:Event):void {
            var loaderBmp:Bitmap = Bitmap(_loader.content);
            var w:Number = loaderBmp.width / 10;
            for(var i:int = 0; i < 10; i++) {
                _bitmap.copyPixels(loaderBmp.bitmapData,
                            new Rectangle(i * w, 0,
                                        w, loaderBmp.height),
                            new Point(i * (w + 2), i));
            }
        }
    }
}
```

In the preceding code, the important part is highlighted in **bold**.

The defined rectangle copies progressive vertical strips from the loaded image, and the point places them in the new bitmap, spaced out by a couple of extra pixels.

There are a few more optional parameters. You can specify another *BitmapData* to use as an alpha channel, and you can choose to blend the alpha levels of the existing and new alpha bitmap. The syntax for this is:

```
bitmap.copyPixels(sourceBmp, srcRect, destPoint,
            alphaBmp, alphaDestRect, blend);
```

This is a more advanced use of the metho. We won't cover it here in detail, but you are free to experiment with it on your own.

See Also

Recipes 8.5, 8.6, 8.7, 8.9, 8.10, and 8.11 for other ways to add graphical content to a bitmap.

8.9   Copying Channels

Problem

You want to copy the red, green, blue, or alpha from one *BitmapData* to another.

Solution

Use the *copyChannel( )* method of the *BitmapData* class.

Discussion

The *copyChannel( )* method is yet another method that draws information from one bitmap to another. Actually, the first three arguments are the same as the *copyPixels( )* method. In addition, it has source channel and destination channel parameters:

```
bitmap.copyPixels(sourceBmp, srcRect, destPoint,
            srcChannel, destChannel);
```

The two channel parameters can be one of the integers 1, 2, 4, or 8, which represent the red, green, blue, and alpha channels, respectively. Rather than risking a typographical error, you should use the static properties of the *BitmapDataChannel* class: RED, GREEN, BLUE, and ALPHA.

You simply tell the method which channel you want to take from the original image and which channel you want to copy it into in the destination image. The following code copies the red, green, and blue channels of a loaded image to a new bitmap, slightly offset from one another:

```
var loaderBmp:Bitmap = Bitmap(loader.content);
bitmap.copyChannel(loaderBmp.bitmapData,
            loaderBmp.bitmapData.rect,
            new Point( ),
            BitmapDataChannel.RED,
            BitmapDataChannel.RED);
```

```
bitmap.copyChannel(loaderBmp.bitmapData,
                   loaderBmp.bitmapData.rect,
                   new Point(5, 5),
                   BitmapDataChannel.GREEN,
                   BitmapDataChannel.GREEN);

bitmap.copyChannel(loaderBmp.bitmapData,
                   loaderBmp.bitmapData.rect,
                   new Point(10, 10),
                   BitmapDataChannel.BLUE,
                   BitmapDataChannel.BLUE);
```

See Also

Recipes 8.5, 8.6, 8.7, 8.8, 8.10, and 8.11 for other ways to add graphical content to a bitmap.

8.10   Creating Noise

Problem

You want to create a random noise pattern in a bitmap.

Solution

Use the *noise()* method of the *BitmapData* class.

Discussion

A noise filter or pattern is simply sets each pixel in an affected area to a random value. Although you could loop through each pixel in a bitmap and use *setPixel()* to randomly change its color, there is an easier and more powerful way of doing the same thing in one line: the *noise()* method.

By itself, *noise()* creates a random, speckled image, like what you see when a television is tuned to a channel with no signal. However, by combining noise with other filters, such as the blur filter, you can get some very useful effects.

The *noise()* method is called directly on an instance of *BitmapData*, and its parameters are straightforward:

```
bitmap.noise(seed, low, high, channel, grayscale);
```

Use the *seed* parameter to determine the random pattern; it can be any integer. If you call the method twice with the same *seed*, you get the same noise pattern. To ensure you get a different pattern each time you call it, pass in a random number like so:

```
Math.random( ) * 100000
```

The low and high parameters determine the minimum and maximum values for each pixel. They can range from 0 to 255. Setting them higher gives you a brighter noise pattern; setting them lower makes darker noise.

The channel parameter specifies to which color channel of the bitmap the noise will be applied. You can specify 1, 2, 4, or 8 for red, green, blue, and alpha, respectively; or use the static properties of the *BitmapDataChannel* class: RED, GREEN, BLUE, and ALPHA, to guard against typos.

Finally, grayscale is a Boolean value. true applies the random value to the three color channels equally, resulting in a colorless noise.

Here are some examples. First, create a bitmap, add the noise, and then display it:

```
bitmap = new BitmapData(stage.stageWidth, stage.stageHeight,
                    false, 0xff000000);
bitmap.noise(1000, 0, 255, BitmapDataChannel.RED, false);
var image:Bitmap = new Bitmap(_bitmap);
addChild(image);
```

This creates a random pattern in the red channel. Upping the low value gives you a lighter noise pattern:

```
bitmap.noise(1000, 200, 255, BitmapDataChannel.RED, false);
```

You can easily convert that to a grayscale image by setting the last parameter to true:

```
bitmap.noise(1000, 200, 255, BitmapDataChannel.RED, true);
```

If you have set grayscale to true, it doesn't matter which channel you create the noise on. You can also combine various channels to create multicolored noise, using the | operator:

```
bitmap.noise(1000, 0, 255, BitmapDataChannel.RED |
                    BitmapDataChannel.GREEN |
                    BitmapDataChannel.BLUE,
                    false);
```

Finally, as mentioned earlier, perhaps one of the best uses of noise is when you combine it with other filters or effects. The following code creates some noise in a bitmap, and then applies a horizontal blur filter, producing a passable brushed metal effect:

```
bitmap = new BitmapData(stage.stageWidth, stage.stageHeight,
                    false, 0xff000000);
bitmap.noise(1000, 128, 255, BitmapDataChannel.RED, true);
bitmap.applyFilter(bitmap,
                bitmap.rect,
                new Point( ),
                new BlurFilter(30, 1, 3));
var image:Bitmap = new Bitmap(bitmap);
addChild(image);
```

This is just one example of combining noise with other effects. With some experimenting and practice, you can come up with many more.

See Also

Recipes 8.5, 8.6, 8.7, 8.8, 8.9, and 8.11 for other ways to add graphical content to a bitmap.

8.11 Creating Perlin Noise

Problem

You want to create random organic effects, such as clouds, smoke, or water.

Solution

Use the *perlinNoise( )* method of the *BitmapData* class.

Discussion

Like the *noise( )* method, *perlinNoise( )* creates random patterns on a bitmap. However, Perlin noise uses an algorithm that produces smooth, organic-looking textures. It was created by Ken Perlin for creating textures in the movie *Tron*. These textures are perfect for use as explosions, smoke, water, and many other natural-looking effects, and since they are generated by an algorithm, they require much less memory than bitmap-based textures. The usage is as follows:

```
bitmap.perlinNoise(baseX, baseY, octaves, seed, stitch, fractal,
                   channels, grayscale, offsets);
```

The first six parameters are necessary; the final three are optional. Since there are so many parameters to consider, let's create a simple example and then see what each one does. The following code creates a bitmap, applies Perlin noise to it and then displays it:

```
bitmap = new BitmapData(stage.stageWidth, stage.stageHeight, false, 0xff000000);
bitmap.perlinNoise(100, 100, 1, 1000, false, false, 1, true, null);
var image:Bitmap = new Bitmap(bitmap);
addChild(image);
```

Add this code to a new class, and run it to see a simple Perlin noise pattern. See Figure 8-1 for an example of what you should see. Now you can start changing parameters and see what effect the changes have.

First off, baseX and baseY determine the size of the pattern. Here they are set to 100 each. Try changing baseX to 200 and baseY to 50 and see how that stretches out the noise horizontally. Already you can see that it looks a bit like rippling water, as you can see in Figure 8-2.

The octaves parameter is an integer that determines how many iterations of noise to create. More octaves makes more detailed noise, and of course take longer to produce.

Figure 8-1. Simple Perlin noise

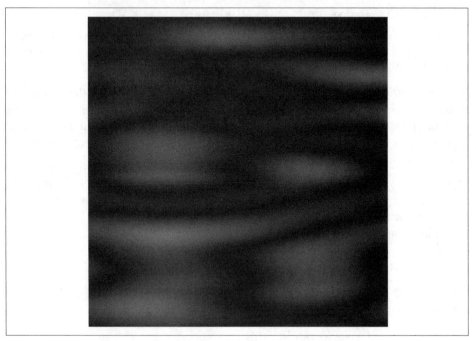

Figure 8-2. Perlin noise stretched on the x axis

The *seed* parameter works exactly like the seed in the *noise()* method. If you specify the same seed each time you run the program, you get the same noise pattern. Setting this to a random number gives you a different pattern each time.

The stitch parameter, when set to true, makes the left and right, and top and bottom sides of the pattern match up. This allows you to make a small bitmap and tile it, such as in a bitmap fill from the drawing API, as shown in the following example:

```
bitmap = new BitmapData(100, 100, false, 0xff000000);
bitmap.perlinNoise(100, 100, 2, 1000, true, false, 1, true);
graphics.beginBitmapFill(bitmap);
graphics.drawRect(0, 0, stage.stageWidth, stage.stageHeight);
graphics.endFill();
```

Here, the bitmap is 100×100, and the stitch parameter is set to true in the *perlinNoise()* call. The bitmap is used as a bitmap fill and tiles seamlessly.

When set to true, the fractal parameter results in the edges of the gradients being smoothed out more. To see it in action, start with this code:

```
bitmap = new BitmapData(stage.stageWidth, stage.stageHeight,
                  false, 0xff000000);
bitmap.perlinNoise(200, 100, 5, 1000, false, false, 1, true, null);
var image:Bitmap = new Bitmap(bitmap);
addChild(image);
```

After you see the image that creates, change fractal to true:

```
bitmap.perlinNoise(200, 100, 5, 1000, false, true, 1, true, null);
```

Notice the difference that made (see Figure 8-3)? This parameter is useful for making things like cloud or fog, as you can see by the example, which is already starting to look like clouds.

The next two parameters, channel and grayscale, work exactly like they do in the *noise()* method. The channel can be any of the following: 1, 2, 4, or 8, representing the red, green, blue, and alpha channels, respectively. 1 has been used in the examples so far, for brevity, but it is recommended that you use the static properties of the *BitmapDataChannel* class: RED, GREEN, BLUE, and ALPHA, to avoid typos.

Of course, if you set grayscale to true, it doesn't matter which color channel you specify, as the resulting image will be grayscale. However, if you set it to false and specify one or more color channels, you can create colored patterns. The next example creates some red clouds:

```
bitmap.perlinNoise(200, 100, 5, 1000, false, true,
            BitmapDataChannel.RED, false, null);
```

The following code produces a multicolor pattern by using all three color channels:

```
bitmap.perlinNoise(200, 100, 5, 1000, false, true,
            BitmapDataChannel.RED |
            BitmapDataChannel.GREEN |
            BitmapDataChannel.BLUE,
            false, null);
```

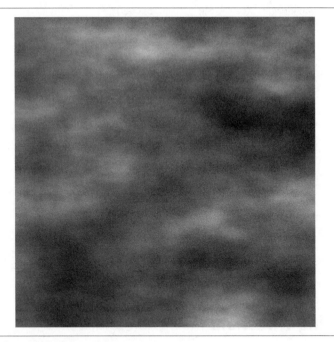

Figure 8-3. Perlin noise with fractal set to true

You can also make Perlin noise on the alpha channel, which is useful for creating transparent cloud effects or fog.

The final parameter is offsets. This is an array of *Point* objects. Each point specifies how much a single octave is offset on the X- and Y-axes. If your Perlin noise has more than one octave, you probably want to make an array of points equal in length to the number of octaves, and include the same point for each element. Otherwise, each octave scrolls differently, or not at all. Of course, you can use this for some interesting parallax effects. The following example shows a two-octave Perlin noise pattern scrolling on the X-axis:

```
package {
    import flash.display.Sprite;
    import flash.display.Bitmap;
    import flash.display.BitmapData;
    import flash.events.Event;
    import flash.geom.Point;

    public class Clouds extends Sprite {
        private var _bitmap:BitmapData;
        private var _xoffset:int = 0;

        public function Clouds() {
            _bitmap = new BitmapData(stage.stageWidth, stage.stageHeight,
                            true, 0xffffffff);
```

```
            var image:Bitmap = new Bitmap(_bitmap);
            addChild(image);
            addEventListener(Event.ENTER_FRAME, onEnterFrame);
        }

        public function onEnterFrame(event:Event):void {
            _xoffset++;
            var point:Point = new Point(_xoffset, 0);

            // use the same point in both elements
            // of the offsets array
            _bitmap.perlinNoise(200, 100, 2, 1000, false, true,
                        1, true, [point, point]);
        }
    }
}
```

See Also

Recipes 8.5, 8.6, 8.7, 8.8, 8.9, and 8.10 for other ways to add graphical content to a bitmap.

8.12   Using Threshold

Problem

You want to change the value of some pixels in a bitmap, based on their current value.

Solution

Use the *threshold()* method of the *BitmapData* class.

Discussion

The *threshold()* method is probably the most complex in the *BitmapData* API, but quite powerful once you understand how it works. The method uses two *BitmapData* objects:

- destBitmap, which is the bitmap that will be altered.
- sourceBitmap, which is the other bitmap that gets passed in as a parameter. The method uses this bitmap's pixel data for its calculations.

The method compares each pixel in sourceBitmap against a specified value, using one of six comparison operators. If the comparison fails, the corresponding pixel in destBitmap is set to a specified color value. If it passes the comparison, the pixel is either not changed, or you have the option of copying over the sourceBitmap's value for that pixel.

Here is the syntax for the method:

```
destBitmap.threshold(sourceBitmap,
                     sourceRect,
                     destPoint,
                     operation,
                     threshold,
                     color,
                     mask,
                     copySource)
```

We've already covered `destBitmap` and `sourceBitmap`. The next parameter, `sourceRect`, is an instance of the *flash.geom.Rectangle* class. It defines what portion of the `sourceBitmap` you want to use for comparison. If you want to use the entire bitmap, you can pass in `sourceBitmap.rect` as a value to this parameter.

The `destPoint` parameter specifies the point in the `destBitmap` at which the pixels start to be affected. Picture the `sourceBitmap` overlaid on `destBitmap`, with its top-left corner on this point. If you want to use 0, 0 as the origin, just pass *new Point()* to this parameter.

The `operation` parameter is one of six strings that are equivalent to the comparison operators in ActionScript. They are `<`, `<=`, `>`, `>=`, `==`, and `!=`. For example, if you specify `<` as an operation, the test passes for a given pixel if its value is less than the threshold value, and it fails if it is greater than that.

Next is `threshold`. Each pixel is compared against this value. You can pass a full 32-bit number in here, and compare each pixel against that, but it may not give you the results you expected. The reason is the way color values work. For example, a pixel of 100 percent red (`0xFFFF0000`) evaluates as "more than" a pixel of 100 percent blue (`0xFF0000FF`) or green (`0xFF00FF00`). So normally what you want to do is use a mask to isolate a specific channel and compare against that.

The `mask` parameter is the hardest for most people to grasp. All it is doing is isolating a particular color channel. Normally you would just pass a hexadecimal value here, with two zeros (`00`) for each color channel that you want to mask out, and `FF` for the channel you want to use. For example, `0x00FF0000` isolates the red channel, and `0xFF000000` isolates the alpha channel. See Figure 8-4 for a breakdown of the channels in a hexadecimal color value.

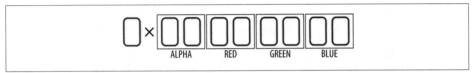

Figure 8-4. The breakdown of a hexadecimal number

The next two parameters determine what happens when a pixel passes or fails a comparison. The color parameter is the color the corresponding pixel is set to in the destBitmap if the comparison passes. The copySource parameter determines what happens if it fails. If this is true, the sourceBitmap's pixel value for that pixel is copied over to the destBitmap. If it is false, nothing happens for that pixel in the destBitmap; it is left as is.

Now let's see a few examples in action. Here's some sample code that creates a source and destination bitmap and creates some Perlin noise in the source. Then it adds the destination bitmap to the display list and applies a threshold using the source bitmap:

```
var srcBmp:BitmapData = new BitmapData(stage.stageWidth,
                                       stage.stageHeight,
                                       true, 0xffffffff);
srcBmp.perlinNoise(200, 100, 2, 1000, false, true, 1, true);

var destBmp:BitmapData = new BitmapData(stage.stageWidth, stage.stageHeight, true,
0xffffffff);
var image:Bitmap = new Bitmap(destBmp);
addChild(image);
destBmp.threshold(srcBmp,            // sourceBitmap
                  srcBmp.rect,       // sourceRectangle
                  new Point(),       // destPoint
                  "<",               // operator
                  0x00880000,        // threshold
                  0x00000000,        // color
                  0x00ff0000,        // mask
                  true);             // copySource
```

Here the method checks to see if a given pixel's red channel (since this is defined in the mask) is less than 0x00880000. If so, it makes that pixel transparent. If not, it copies over the source pixel. Since the Perlin noise was created in grayscale, it doesn't matter which of the three color channels (red, green, or blue) you use. If you are using a full color image as a source, you might want to experiment with different channels to see which gives you the desired effect:

- As you can see if you run this code, it makes all the darker areas of the Perlin noise pattern transparent.

- Changing the operator to ">" has the opposite effect, cutting out all the lighter value pixels.

- Making the threshold value higher or lower, say 0x00330000 or 0x00AA0000, cuts out more or less pixels.

- Try setting a different color value to see what effect this has. Also try changing copySource to false and see that it does not copy over the pixels, but keeps the original values.

One thing to note is that there is no reason why the source and destination bitmaps cannot be the same bitmap. You can use a bitmap's own pixel data as a threshold.

However, realize that you are permanently altering that bitmap, so you won't be able to repeat the operation with the same result, if needed.

As with many of the *BitmapData* methods, they are often most powerful when used in combination. For example, adding one line to the previous example creates a drop shadow, which pops the pattern into 3D:

```
destBmp.applyFilter(destBmp, destBmp.rect,
                    new Point( ), new DropShadowFilter( ));
```

See Also

Recipes 8.13, 8.14, and 8.15 for other ways to manipulate the content in a bitmap.

8.13   Applying a Filter to a Bitmap

Problem

You want to apply a filter to a *BitmapData*.

Solution

Use the *applyFilter()* method of the *BitmapData* class, or add a filter to the filters array of the enclosing *Bitmap*.

Discussion

As mentioned, there are two methods of applying a filter to a bitmap. The first method is to use the *applyFilter()* method directly on the *BitmapData* itself. Like some of the other *BitmapData* methods, this method is applied to one *BitmapData*, which is the destination bitmap, and it can take another *BitmapData* as a source bitmap:

```
destBmp.applyFilter(srcBmp, sourceRect, destPoint, filter);
```

* The srcBmp is the bitmap file you want to apply the filter to.
* The sourceRect is the specific rectangular area from the source bitmap that you want to apply the filter to.
* The destPoint parameter specifies the upper lefthand point from which the pixels will be affected in the destination bitmap.
* The filter, of course, is an instance of the *BitmapFilter* that you want to apply.

 You can, of course, apply a filter using the same bitmap as both source and destination. Doing so is considered "destructive," not because it's a bad thing but because it permanently changes the bitmap.

The values of each pixel are calculated based on the original content and the filter parameters, and these values overwrite the original pixel data. This is useful in a couple of instances:

- If you are sure you will never need to change either the bitmap's content or the filter itself.
- When you have multiple or repeated applications of a filter.

For example, the following code sets 100 random pixels near the mouse position to white and then applies a default blur filter. This is repeated on each frame, so the longer you leave the mouse at one point, the brighter it gets. However, as you move it around, the blur is repeatedly applied to those white pixels, eventually fading them out. The result is a glowing trail.

```
package {
    import flash.display.Sprite;
    import flash.display.Bitmap;
    import flash.display.BitmapData;
    import flash.filters.BlurFilter;
    import flash.events.Event;
    import flash.geom.Point;

    public class FilteredBitmap extends Sprite {
        private var _bitmap:BitmapData;
        private var _image:Bitmap;
        private var _blurFilter:BlurFilter;

        public function FilteredBitmap() {
            _bitmap = new BitmapData(stage.stageWidth, stage.stageHeight,
                            false, 0xff000000);
            _image = new Bitmap(_bitmap);
            addChild(_image);
            _blurFilter = new BlurFilter();
            addEventListener(Event.ENTER_FRAME, onEnterFrame);
        }

        public function onEnterFrame(event:Event):void {
            for(var i:int = 0; i < 100; i++) {
                _bitmap.setPixel(mouseX + Math.random() * 20 - 10,
                            mouseY + Math.random() * 20 - 10,
                            0xffffffff);
            }
            _bitmap.applyFilter(_bitmap, _bitmap.rect, new Point(), _blurFilter);
        }
    }
}
```

As you can see, the destructive method can be quite creative. Contrast that to a nondestructive method that uses two different bitmaps. One is the source bitmap and the other is the destination. The method applies the filter to the bitmap data in the source bitmap, and places the result in the destination bitmap. It is nondestructive because the filter never alters the original pixels in the source bitmap.

```
package {
    import flash.display.Sprite;
    import flash.display.Bitmap;
    import flash.display.BitmapData;
    import flash.filters.BlurFilter;
    import flash.events.Event;
    import flash.geom.Point;

    public class FilteredBitmap2 extends Sprite {
        private var _bitmap:BitmapData;
        private var _bitmap2:BitmapData;
        private var _image:Bitmap;
        private var _blurFilter:BlurFilter;

        public function FilteredBitmap2() {
            _bitmap = new BitmapData(stage.stageWidth, stage.stageHeight,
                            false, 0xff000000);
            _bitmap2 = new BitmapData(stage.stageWidth, stage.stageHeight,
                            false, 0xff000000);
            _image = new Bitmap(_bitmap);
            addChild(_image);
            _blurFilter = new BlurFilter();
            addEventListener(Event.ENTER_FRAME, onEnterFrame);
        }

        public function onEnterFrame(event:Event):void {
            for(var i:int = 0; i < 100; i++) {
            _bitmap2.setPixel(mouseX + Math.random() * 20 - 10,
                        mouseY + Math.random() * 20 - 10,
                        0xffffffff);
            }
            _bitmap.applyFilter(_bitmap2, _bitmap.rect, new Point(), _blurFilter);
        }
    }
}
```

The other method of applying a filter to a bitmap is to add it to the filters property of the *Bitmap* that holds a *BitmapData*. This is another nondestructive method of applying a filter, as the pixel data in the *BitmapData* is not touched. The filter is only applied to the *Bitmap* that wraps the *BitmapData*. The following code shows this method in action.

```
package {
    import flash.display.Sprite;
    import flash.display.Bitmap;
    import flash.display.BitmapData;
    import flash.filters.BlurFilter;
    import flash.events.Event;

    public class FilteredBitmap3 extends Sprite {
```

```
        private var _bitmap:BitmapData;
        private var _image:Bitmap;

        public function FilteredBitmap3() {
            _bitmap = new BitmapData(stage.stageWidth, stage.stageHeight,
                            false, 0xff000000);
            _image = new Bitmap(_bitmap);
            addChild(_image);
            _image.filters = [new BlurFilter()];
            addEventListener(Event.ENTER_FRAME, onEnterFrame);
        }

        public function onEnterFrame(event:Event):void {
            for(var i:int = 0; i < 100; i++) {
                _bitmap.setPixel(mouseX + Math.random() * 20 - 10,
                            mouseY + Math.random() * 20 - 10,
                            0xffffffff);
            }
        }
    }
}
```

Here you can see that the filter is applied only the one time. The drawn pixels are slightly blurred, but they don't continuously blur until they fade out. If at some point you deleted the filter from the *Bitmap*, you would see that the white pixels are still perfectly sharp, as the blur was only applied to the container, not the actual bitmap data.

See Also

Recipes 8.12, 8.14, and 8.15 for other ways to manipulate the content in a bitmap.

8.14   Dissolving Between Two Bitmaps

Problem

You want to fade between one bitmap and another.

Solution

Use the *pixelDissolve()* method of the *BitmapData* class.

Discussion

Like many of the other *BitmapData* methods, *pixelDissolve()* uses a source and destination bitmap. Each time it is called, it copies a specified number of random pixels from the source bitmap to the destination. To complete a full dissolve, call this method repeatedly, either in an *enterFrame* handler or a timer-based function. See Recipe 11.1 for information on timer-based animation.

The first time the *pixelDissolve()* method is called, you pass it a random number to use as a seed for the first round of pixel copying. It returns a number that you should keep track of and use as the seed for the next iteration.

Here is the syntax for the method:

```
seed = srcBmp.pixelDissolve(destBmp, sourceRect, destPoint,
                            seed, numPixels, fillColor);
```

- The *sourceRect* and *destPoint* parameters work the same way they do in other *BitmapData* methods that use two bitmaps. The *seed* is explained more in Recipe 8.10.

- The *numPixels* parameter determines how many pixels are copied each time the method is called.

- The *fillColor* offers an easy way of fading a single bitmap to a specified color. If you use the same *BitmapData* as source and destination, instead of copying identical pixels from one to the other (which would have no visible effect), the chosen pixels are set to the fill color specified in this parameter. You can ignore this when using two different bitmaps.

The first example uses two bitmaps—one white, one black—and dissolves between them at 1,000 pixels per frame:

```
package {
    import flash.display.Sprite;
    import flash.display.Bitmap;
    import flash.display.BitmapData;
    import flash.events.Event;
    import flash.geom.Point;

    public class Dissolve extends Sprite {
        private var _bitmap:BitmapData;
        private var _bitmap2:BitmapData;
        private var _image:Bitmap;
        private var _seed:Number;
        private var _pixelCount:int = 0;

        public function Dissolve( ) {
            _bitmap = new BitmapData(stage.stageWidth,
                            stage.stageHeight,
                            false, 0xffffffff);
            _bitmap2 = new BitmapData(stage.stageWidth,
                            stage.stageHeight,
                            false, 0xff000000);
            _image = new Bitmap(_bitmap);
            addChild(_image);
            _seed = Math.random( ) * 100000;
            addEventListener(Event.ENTER_FRAME, onEnterFrame);
        }

        public function onEnterFrame(event:Event):void {
            _seed = _bitmap.pixelDissolve(_bitmap2,
```

```
                                          _bitmap.rect,
                                          new Point( ),
                                          _seed,
                                          1000);
                    _pixelCount += 1000;
                    if(_pixelCount > _bitmap.width * _bitmap.height) {
                        removeEventListener(Event.ENTER_FRAME,
                                            onEnterFrame);
                    }
                }
            }
        }
    }
```

An important thing to note here is that the *pixelDissolve()* method has no way of knowing when it is done (i.e., when all the pixels have been copied over from one bitmap to the other). It is up to you to keep a count of the number of pixels that have been copied and stop copying when this exceeds the total number of pixels in the image (its width times its height).

In the following example, the same *BitmapData* is used as both source and destination, and a black fill color is applied:

```
package {
    import flash.display.Sprite;
    import flash.display.Bitmap;
    import flash.display.BitmapData;
    import flash.events.Event;
    import flash.geom.Point;

    public class Dissolve2 extends Sprite {
        private var _bitmap:BitmapData;
        private var _image:Bitmap;
        private var _seed:Number;
        private var _pixelCount:int = 0;

        public function Dissolve2( ) {
            _bitmap = new BitmapData(stage.stageWidth,
                                     stage.stageHeight,
                                     false,
                                     0xffffffff);
            _image = new Bitmap(_bitmap);
            addChild(_image);
            _seed = Math.random( ) * 100000;
            addEventListener(Event.ENTER_FRAME, onEnterFrame);
        }

        public function onEnterFrame(event:Event):void {
            _seed = _bitmap.pixelDissolve(_bitmap,
                                          _bitmap.rect,
                                          new Point( ),
                                          _seed,
                                          1000,
                                          0xff000000);
            _pixelCount += 1000;
```

```
            if(_pixelCount > _bitmap.width * _bitmap.height)
            {
                removeEventListener(Event.ENTER_FRAME, onEnterFrame);
            }
        }
    }
}
```

Pixel dissolves are particularly effective when done between two photographic images, at a fast rate. If you don't know what size your images are going to be but you want to keep the speed constant, you can set numPixels to a percentage of the size of the image, like so:

```
var numPixels:Number = _bitmap.width * _bitmap.height / 100;
_seed = _bitmap.pixelDissolve(_bitmap,
                            _bitmap.rect,
                            new Point(),
                            _seed,
                            numPixels,
                            0xff000000);
_pixelCount += numPixels;
```

This copies 1/100th of the total pixels on each iteration. At 30 frames per second, this would be (approximately) a 3-second dissolve, regardless of the size of the images.

See Also

Recipes 8.12, 8.13, and 8.15 for other ways to manipulate the content in a bitmap.

8.15   Scrolling a Bitmap

Problem

You want to scroll the content of a *BitmapData*.

Solution

Use the *scroll()* method of the *BitmapData* class.

Discussion

The operation and syntax is simple and straightforward. You pass the amounts you want to scroll the bitmap's content on the X- and Y-axes:

```
_bitmap.scroll(xAmount, yAmount);
```

The method effectively copies the pixels in the bitmap and pastes them back, offset by the amount specified. Any pixels that aren't overwritten in the operation remain the same as they were originally.

You can call *scroll()* repeatedly in an *enterFrame* handler or timer function to animate the scrolling of the bitmap. The following code demonstrates this by generating a Perlin noise pattern and then scrolling it:

```
public function Scroll( ) {
    _bitmap = new BitmapData(stage.stageWidth, stage.stageHeight,
                        false, 0xffffffff);
    _bitmap.perlinNoise(100, 100, 3, 1000, true, true, 1, true);
    _image = new Bitmap(_bitmap);
    addChild(_image);
    addEventListener(Event.ENTER_FRAME, onEnterFrame);
}

public function onEnterFrame(event:Event):void {
    _bitmap.scroll(-1, -1);
}
```

Note that the edges that are not copied in the scroll are not cleared, but left as they were.

See Also

Recipes 8.12, 8.13, and 8.14 for other ways to manipulate the content in a bitmap.

## CHAPTER 9

Text

9.0 Introduction

The *flash.text.TextField* class is the way in which all text is displayed in Flash Player. Even the text components such as *TextArea* and *TextInput* use the *TextField* class to display text. Flash Player enables a great deal of functionality for text fields from enabling user input to embedding fonts to using Cascading Style Sheets (CSS) to format text. In this chapter, we'll discuss all the many things you can accomplish with text.

As implied in the preceding paragraph, the *TextField* class is packaged in the *flash. display* package. Therefore, you need to either import the class or refer to the class with the fully qualified class name. All examples in this chapter assume you've imported the class with the following line of code:

```
import flash.text.TextField;
```

ActionScript 3.0 uses a display list that is quite different from previous versions of ActionScript. With earlier versions of ActionScript, you construct a text field using the *TextField* constructor as follows:

```
var field:TextField = new TextField( );
```

However, with ActionScript 3.0, the new text field object isn't automatically added to the display list. That means that if you want to make the text field visible, you have to use the *addChild()* method. As discussed in Chapter 6, the *addChild()* method is defined for all container display objects, such as *Sprite*, and it adds the object specified as a parameter to the display list of the object from which it is called. For example, the following line of code adds the field *TextField* object to the display list of the instance of the *TextExample* class:

```
package {

  import flash.display.Sprite;
  import flash.text.TextField;
  public class TextExample extends Sprite {
    public function TextExample( ) {
```

```
        var field:TextField = new TextField();
        addChild(field);
      }
    }
  }
```

When the examples in this chapter reference an object called field, it's frequently assumed that the object is a *TextField* object that was instantiated via the *TextField* constructor and added to the display list with the *addChild()* method.

9.1   Creating an Outline Around a Text Field

Problem

You want to place a border around a text field.

Solution

Set the text field's border property to true. Additionally, you can change the color of the border by setting the object's borderColor property.

Discussion

By default, a text field does not have a visible border, which is assumed to be the most common preferred behavior. For example, you may not want a border around an item label. However, there are many cases in which you will want to apply a border to a text field, such as a field that requires some user input. The border shows the user where to click to input a value. Simply setting a text field's border property to true turns on the border around the object:

```
field.border = true;
```

To turn off the border, simply set the border property to false.

The default border color is black, but that can be changed with the borderColor property, which accepts a hex RGB value corresponding to the desired color:

```
field.borderColor = 0xFF00FF;  // Make the border violet.
```

9.2   Creating a Background for a Text Field

Problem

You want to make a visible background behind the text in a text field.

Solution

Set the text field's background property to true. Additionally, you can change the color of the background by setting the object's backgroundColor property.

Discussion

By default, text fields don't have a visible background. However, you can create a background for a text field by setting the background property for that object to true:

```
field.background = true;
```

By default, the background for a text field is white (if made visible). You can, however, assign the background color by setting the value of the object's backgroundColor property, which accepts a hex RGB value corresponding to the desired color, as shown here:

```
field.backgroundColor = 0x00FFFF; // Set the background to light blue
```

9.3   Making a User Input Field

Problem

You want to create a user input field to allow the user to enter text.

Solution

Set the text field's type property to *TextFieldType.INPUT*.

Discussion

There are two types of text fields: dynamic and input. The default text field type is dynamic. This means that it can be controlled with ActionScript, but the user cannot input text into it. To enable the field for user input, set the type property to the INPUT constant of the *flash.display.TextFieldType* class:

```
field.type = TextFieldType.INPUT;
```

Though it isn't a requirement, input fields generally also have a border and a background. Otherwise, the user might find it difficult to locate and select the field:

```
field.border = true;
field.background = true;
```

For a user to be able to input text, the field's selectable property must be true, which is the default. You don't need to set the selectable property to true, unless you previously set it to false.

If you have previously defined an input text field that you want to make a dynamic text field (so that it does not accept user input) you can set the type property to the DYNAMIC constant of the *flash.display.TextFieldType* class:

```
field.type = TextFieldType.DYNAMIC;
```

9.4 Making a Password Input Field

Problem

You want to create a password-style text field that hides the characters as asterisks. You also want to disable copying from the text field.

Solution

Set the text field's `password` property to `true`.

Discussion

When a user enters a password into a field, you generally want to make it so others aren't able to read the password. This is a basic security precaution. The common convention is to display only asterisks in the field as the user types. This way, the user can see that she is successfully entering a value without anyone else being able to easily read what she's just typed.

To create an input field that is automatically masked with asterisks, you only need to set the *TextField*.`password` property to `true`:

```
field.password = true;
```

When you set the password property to `true`, all text entered into the text field, either programmatically or by user input, displays as asterisks:

```
field.password = true;
field.text = "example text";  // Text field displays: ************
```

Password text fields also disable copying from the text field. That prevents a user from being able to copy passwords or similar data and then paste it into a plain text document.

Password text fields are most commonly also input text fields; however, you can set the password property to `true` for a dynamic text field as well.

 Although password text fields hide the data from the display, they do not encrypt the data or make it more secure for sending over a network. If data security is important to your application, you must use technologies that make data secure as it is transferred over a network. If you send data from Flash using standard HTTP, then the data is sent in an unsecured fashion. Use a technology such as SSL if you must send data in a secure fashion.

9.5   Filtering Text Input

Problem

You want to restrict the characters that a user can type into an input field.

Solution

Set the `restrict` property of the text field.

Discussion

By default, a user can type any character into an input field. However, in many scenarios, you might want to restrict the allowable characters. For example, you might restrict characters to numbers and dashes in the case of an input field for telephone numbers.

The `TextField.restrict` property lets you specify the allowed characters for user input into a field. Specify a string containing the allowable characters, such as:

```
field.restrict = "abcdefg";
```

This example lets the user enter any of the allowable characters: *a*, *b*, *c*, *d*, *e*, *f*, or *g*. Other characters are disallowed. If the user tries to enter *grabs*, only *gab* appears, since the letters *r* and *s* are not in the allowable character set.

 If the restrict string is set to the empty string then *all* characters are allowed. To prevent input entirely, set the type to DYNAMIC.

Also, note that ActionScript distinguishes between upper- and lowercase characters. In other words, there is a difference between *a* and *A*. If the `restrict` property is set to *abcdefg*, the uppercase variants of the allowable characters (such as *A*, *B*, *C*) will be entered as the lowercase (allowable) equivalents (*a*, *b*, *c*). The same is true in reverse, such that if a lowercase character is entered when only the uppercase counterpart is allowed, the character is converted to uppercase.

The restrict property supports certain regular expression-like patterns. Therefore, you can also enter ranges by indicating the first character in the range and the last character in the range separated by a dash (-):

```
field.restrict = "a-zA-Z";    // Allow only upper- and lowercase letters
field.restrict = "a-zA-Z ";   // Allow only letters and spaces
field.restrict = "0-9";       // Allow only numbers
```

In addition to specifying allowable characters, you can also disallow characters with a restrict string by using the caret character (^).

All characters and ranges in a restrict string following the caret are disallowed; for example:

```
field.restrict = "^abcdefg"; // Allows all except lowercase a through g
field.restrict = "^a-z";     // Disallows all lowercase letters (but allows other
                             // characters, including uppercase.)
field.restrict = "0-9^5";    // Allows numbers only, with the exception of 5
```

You can also specify allowable characters by using Unicode escape sequences. For example, if you want to disallow users from entering the → character (Control-Z) into a field, you can specify its Unicode code point in the restrict property, as follows:

```
field.restrict = "^\u001A";
```

To allow a literal character that has a special meaning when used in a restrict string (such as a dash or caret), you must *escape* the character in the restrict string by preceding it with two backslashes (not just one), as shown here:

```
field.restrict = "0-9\\-";        // Allow numbers and dashes
field.restrict = "0-9\\^";        // Allow numbers and caret marks
```

If you want to escape the backslash character, you must precede it with three backslashes, for a total of four backslashes:

```
field.restrict = "0-9\\\\";       // Allow numbers and backslashes
```

The restrict property only affects the characters that the user can input. It does not have any affect on which characters can be displayed programmatically.

9.6   Setting a Field's Maximum Length

Problem

You want to limit the length of the string input into a text field.

Solution

Set the text field's maxChars property.

Discussion

By default, an input text field allows a user to type in as many characters as he desires. However, you may have good reason to want to set a maximum. For example, if an input field prompts a user for his two-character country code, you might want to prevent the user from entering more than two characters. Setting the maxChars property to a number limits the user input to that many characters:

```
field.maxChars = 6;  // maximum of 6 characters can be input
```

Set maxChars to null to allow an entry of unlimited length, if you've previously assigned a non-null value to maxChars.

See Also

Recipe 9.5

9.7 Displaying Text

Problem

You want to display text within a text field.

Solution

Set the text property of a text field.

Discussion

Aside from being used as input fields, text fields are often used to display text to the user. Setting a text field's text property causes the corresponding text to display in the field:

```
field.text = "this will display in the field";
```

Special characters, such as \t for tab and \n for newline, can be used within a text string.

You can append text by using the += operator or the *appendText()* method:

```
field.appendText("new text");
```

See Also

Recipe 9.8 for information on support for HTML-formatted text.

9.8 Displaying HTML-Formatted Text

Problem

You want to display HTML content in a text field.

Solution

Set the text field's htmlText property to the value of the HTML content to display.

Discussion

Text fields can interpret and display basic HTML tags, if properly configured. Using HTML in a text field is a convenient way to add hyperlinks and simple formatting, such as font color and bolded text.

The value of the text field object's `htmlText` property is interpreted as HTML:

```
field.htmlText = "<u>This displays as underlined text.</u>";
```

No matter what, the text property of a text field is rendered as plain text. This means that even if the text property is set to `<u>test</u>`, the object displays `<u>test</u>` instead of test. That means that if you want to display HTML code in its unrendered format assign the HTML value to the text property of the text field, as follows:

```
field.text = "<u>underlined text</u>";

/* text field displays:
<u>underlined text</u>
*/
```

This can be a useful technique if, for example, you want to show both the rendered HTML and the HTML source code in side-by-side text fields:

```
htmlCode = "<i>italicized text</i>";
sourceHTML.text = htmlCode;
renderedHTML.htmlText = htmlCode;
```

You cannot display both rendered and unrendered HTML in the same text field. If you try, you will end up with unreliable results.

The set of HTML tags supported by text fields includes: `<b>`, `<i>`, `<u>`, `<font>` (with face, size, and color attributes), `<p>`, `<br>`, `<a>`, `<li>`, `<img>`, and `<textformat>` (with leftmargin, rightmargin, blockindent, indent, leading, and tabstops attributes corresponding to the *TextFormat* class's properties of the same names).

9.9 Condensing Whitespace

Problem

You want to condense whitespace in an HTML text field display.

Solution

Set the object's `condenseWhite` property to `true`.

Discussion

When you use HTML in a text field, the optional `condenseWhite` setting condenses whitespace, as is done in most HTML browsers. For example, the following text would be rendered in a web browser with only a single space between "hello" and "friend" in spite of the fact that the original source has multiple spaces between the two words.

```
hello          friend
```

In ActionScript text fields, however, all of the spaces are displayed, unless you set the condenseWhite property to true:

```
field.condenseWhite = true;
field.htmlText = "hello          friend";    // Displays: "hello friend"
```

The condenseWhite property works only when the html property is true.

See Also

Recipe 9.8

9.10 Sizing Text Fields to Fit Contents

Problem

You want to size a text field's viewable area to fit the text it contains.

Solution

Use the autoSize property.

Discussion

You can set the autoSize property of a text field so it automatically resizes itself in order to fit its contents. The possible values for autoSize are the RIGHT, LEFT, CENTER, and NONE constants of the *flash.text.TextFieldAutoSize* class. By default, autoSize is set to NONE, meaning that the text field does not automatically resize.

Set the property to LEFT if you want the text field to resize while fixing the upper-left corner's position. In other words, the text field's lower-right corner is the point that moves when it expands and contracts:

```
// These two lines do the same thing
field.autoSize = TextFieldAutoSize.LEFT;
field.autoSize = true;
```

Set the property to CENTER if you want the text field to be anchored at its center point. While the top of the object remains fixed, it expands and contracts downward and equally to the right and left:

```
field.autoSize = TextFieldAutoSize.CENTER;
```

Set the property to RIGHT if you want the upper-right corner of the text field to remain steady while the object expands and contracts in the direction of the lower-left corner:

```
field.autoSize = TextFieldAutoSize.RIGHT;
```

When *wordWrap* is set to false (the default), then the text field expands horizontally to accommodate the text. In such a case, the text field expands vertically only if there are newlines within the text assigned to the text field. The following example illustrates a text field that auto sizes to accommodate all the text on one line:

```
var field:TextField = new TextField( );
field.autoSize = TextFieldAutoSize.LEFT;
field.text = "Lorem ipsum dolor sit amet, consectetuer adipiscing elit. Morbi tortor
purus, aliquet a, ornare ac, suscipit a, est. Nullam hendrerit molestie erat. Nunc
nulla tortor, ullamcorper et, elementum vel, fringilla sed, dui. Praesent fermentum
interdum orci.";
addChild(field);
```

The following adds a newline character to the text assigned to the text field so that it auto sizes to display all the text on two lines:

```
var field:TextField = new TextField( );
field.autoSize = TextFieldAutoSize.LEFT;
field.text = "Lorem ipsum dolor sit amet, consectetuer adipiscing elit. Morbi tortor
purus, aliquet a, ornare ac, suscipit a, est.";
field.text += "\n";
field.text += "Nullam hendrerit molestie erat. Nunc nulla tortor, ullamcorper et,
elementum vel, fringilla sed, dui. Praesent fermentum interdum orci.";
addChild(field);
```

When *wordWrap* is set to true, then the text field never expands beyond the value of the *width* property (100 by default). If necessary, the text automatically wraps to a new line if *autoSize* is set to RIGHT, LEFT, or CENTER:

```
var field:TextField = new TextField( );
field.autoSize = TextFieldAutoSize.LEFT;
field.wordWrap = true;
field.text = "Lorem ipsum dolor sit amet, consectetuer adipiscing elit. Morbi tortor
purus, aliquet a, ornare ac, suscipit a, est. Nullam hendrerit molestie erat. Nunc
nulla tortor, ullamcorper et, elementum vel, fringilla sed, dui. Praesent fermentum
interdum orci.";
addChild(field);
```

See Also

Recipe 9.6

9.11 Scrolling Text Programmatically

Problem

You want to scroll text in a text field via ActionScript.

Solution

Use the scrollV, maxScrollV, bottomScrollV, scrollH, and maxScrollH properties of the text field. Use the mouseWheelEnabled property to enable scrolling of text by way of the mouse wheel.

Discussion

You can control the scrolling of a text field with ActionScript and without the aid of a scrollbar. For example, you may want to scroll the contents of a text field automatically to display a word or selection within the text. You can programmatically control a text field's scrolling in both the vertical and horizontal directions using some built-in properties. You should use the scrollV, maxScrollV, and bottomScrollV properties to control vertical scrolling, and use the scrollH and maxScrollH properties to control horizontal scrolling.

Every text field has a number of lines, whether it is 1 or 100. Each of these lines is identified by a number starting at 1. Some of these lines may be visible, and some may be beyond the border of the text field. Therefore, to view the lines that extend beyond the visible portion of the text field you must scroll to them. Figure 9-1 illustrates this point. It depicts a text field's display where the solid line indicates the object's border (the visible area), and the dotted line surrounds the rest of the text contained within the object but lying outside the its visible area. To the left of the text field are line numbers for each line of text. The three labels—scrollV, bottomScrollV, and maxScrollV—indicate the meaning of the text field properties of the same names.

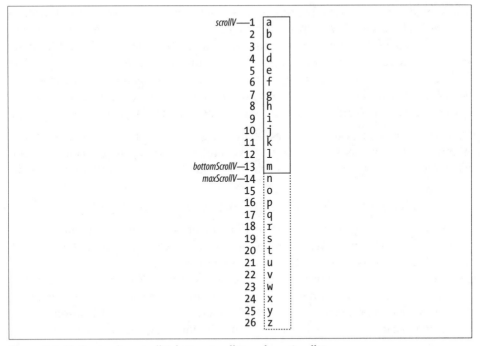

Figure 9-1. Understanding scrollV, bottomScrollV, and maxScrollV

The `scrollV` property is a read-write property that indicates the top line of the text field's visible area. In Figure 9-1, the `scrollV` property's value is 1. To scroll the contents of a text field, assign a newline number to the `scrollV` property. Setting `scrollV` to 6, for example, scrolls the contents of the text field up until line 6 is the top-most line displayed. The value of `scrollV` should always be an integer; Flash cannot scroll to non-integer values:

```
field.scrollV = 1;    // Scroll to the top
field.scrollV += 1;   // Scroll to the next line
field.scrollV = 6;    // Scroll to line 6
```

You can scroll to the next page of a text field's contents by using the `bottomScrollV` property, which indicates the bottom-most visible line in the text field. While you cannot set `bottomScrollV`, you can use it to determine the new value to assign to `scrollV`. In Figure 9-1, `bottomScrollV` is 13. If `scrollV` is set to 6, then `bottomScrollV` is automatically updated to 18:

```
// Scroll to the next page with the previous page's bottom line
// at the top
field.scrollV = field.bottomScrollV;
// Scroll to the next complete page without the bottom line from
// previous page
field.scrollV = field.bottomScrollV + 1;
```

You should use the `maxScrollV` property to scroll to the last page of contents within a text field. The `maxScrollV` property is also a read-only property. This property contains the value of the maximum line number that can be assigned to `scrollV`. Therefore, the `maxScrollV` property changes only when the number of lines in the text field changes (either through user input or ActionScript assignment). In Figure 9-1, `maxScrollV` is 14. This is because with 26 total lines in the text field and 13 visible lines, when `scrollV` is set to 14, the last visible line is 26 (the last line in the text field).

Don't try to set `scrollV` to a value less than 1 or greater than the value of `maxScrollV`. Although this won't cause an error, it won't scroll the text beyond the contents. Add blank lines to the beginning or end of the text field's contents to artificially extend its scrolling range:

```
field.scrollV = field.maxScrollV;    // Scroll to the bottom
```

The vertical scrolling properties are in units of lines, but the horizontal scrolling properties (`scrollH` and `maxScrollH`) are in units of pixels. Other than that, `scrollH` and `maxScrollH` work more or less in the same fashion as `scrollV` and `maxScrollV` (there is no property for horizontal scrolling that corresponds to `bottomScrollV`). The `scrollH` property is a read-write property that allows you to control the value of the leftmost visible pixel starting with 0. The `maxScrollH` property is a read-only property that indicates the pixel value of the maximum value that can be assigned to `scrollH`:

```
field.scrollH = 0;                   // Scroll to the far left
field.scrollH += 1;                  // Scroll to the right 1 pixel
field.scrollH = field.maxScrollH;    // Scroll to the far right
```

Figure 9-2 depicts `maxScrollH` for a dynamic text field (a field whose type is set to `DYNAMIC`). Text shown in gray is outside the visible area of the text field.

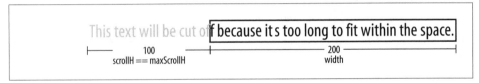

Figure 9-2. The maxScrollH property for a dynamic text field

Figure 9-3 depicts `maxScrollH` for an input text field (a field whose type is set to input).

Flash automatically adds a buffer space to allow room for user input. Again, text shown in gray is outside the visible area of the text field.

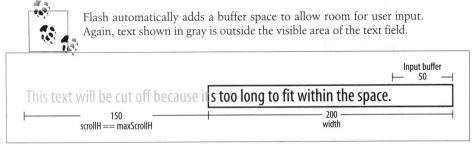

Figure 9-3. The maxScrollH property for an input text field

Use the *mouseWheelEnabled* property to enable text scrolling using a scrollwheel mouse. The property is set to `false` by default; setting the property to `true` enables mouse wheel scrolling, as shown here:

```
field.mouseWheelEnabled = true;
```

9.12   Responding to Scroll Events

Problem

You want to have some actions performed when a text field's contents are scrolled.

Solution

Listen for the scroll event.

Discussion

When a text field is scrolled vertically or horizontally (meaning that the `scrollV` or `scrollH` property has been changed either by your custom ActionScript code or a scrollbar), the text field dispatches a scroll event. The scroll event name is defined by the SCROLL constant of the *flash.events.Event* class, and the event that is dispatched is a *flash.events.Event* object. The following code registers a listener for the scroll event for a text field called `field`:

```
field.addEventListener(Event.SCROLL, onTextScroll);
```

The following defines an example *onTextScroll()* method that listens for the scroll event:

```
private function onTextScroll(event:Event):void {
  trace("scroll");
}
```

See Also

Recipes 9.23 and 9.24

9.13   Formatting Text

Problem

You want to format the text in a text field.

Solution

Use HTML tags, pass a *TextFormat* object to the *TextField.setTextFormat()* method, or use a *StyleSheet* object, and apply it to the text field's `styleSheet` property.

Discussion

Although you can set the color of the entire contents of the text field using the textColor property, for example, the *TextField* class doesn't offer precise control over character formatting. However, there are several ways in which you can apply more exacting formatting to text fields:

- Use HTML tags to apply formatting. For example, you can use <font>, <b>, and <u> tags.
- Use a *TextFormat* object.
- Use CSS.

Each of the three ways in which you can apply formatting to a text field has its own advantages and disadvantages. Applying HTML formatting is relatively simple, but it is the most difficult to manage of the different techniques. Using a *TextFormat* object is the more complex than applying formatting via HTML. However, when you want to apply complex formatting, it is a better option than HTML formatting. Using CSS with a *StyleSheet* object allows the greatest flexibility, and it allows you to load a CSS document, which makes it simple to maintain because you can edit the CSS document without having to re-export the .swf file.

For fast and simple formatting, HTML tags are simplest. For example, the following code displays bolded and underlined text:

```
field.html = true;
field.htmlText = "<b>Bold text</b> <u>Underlined text</u>";
```

You can use *TextFormat* objects to apply more complex formatting to the text displayed in text fields. The first step in formatting text with a *TextFormat* object is to instantiate the object by using the constructor method:

```
var formatter:TextFormat = new TextFormat();
```

Next, assign values to the *TextFormat* object's properties as you want:

```
formatter.bold = true;      // Bold the text
formatter.color = 0xFFFF00; // Make the text yellow
formatter.blockIndent = 5;  // Adjust the margin by 5 points
```

You can apply text formatting to the existing text for an entire text field by passing a *TextFormat* object to the text field's *setTextFormat()* method:

```
field.setTextFormat(formatter);
```

When you invoke the *setTextFormat()* method this way, the formatting from the *TextFormat* object is applied to the text already assigned to the text field. The formatting does not apply to any text assigned to the text field after the *setTextFormat()* method is invoked. If additional text is entered by the user, the original text retains its applied formatting, but the inserted text does not have any special formatting applied to it. All formatting is removed if the text value is modified by appending a value by way of ActionScript:

```
field.text = "this is sample text";
field.setTextFormat(formatter);   // Formatting applied
field.text = "this is new text";  // No formatting applied
field.setTextFormat(formatter);   // Formatting reapplied
field.text += "appended text";    // Formatting removed
```

If you make changes to the *TextFormat* object, you should reapply the formatting to the text field by passing the modified object to the *setTextFormat()* method. Otherwise, the changes are not automatically displayed.

CSS support is available using the *flash.text.StyleSheet* class. The *StyleSheet* constructor does not require any parameters, as shown here:

```
var css:StyleSheet = new StyleSheet();
```

Table 9-1 lists the supported CSS properties and the equivalent ActionScript properties. Use the CSS property names when defining a CSS document or a string to parse as CSS, and use the ActionScript properties when defining style objects (as discussed next).

Table 9-1. CSS properties supported by Flash Player

CSS property	ActionScript property	Description
color	color	The hexadecimal value as a string in the format of #RRGGBB.
display	display	The way in which the text is displayed in the text field. The possible options are inline (no line breaks before or after the text), block (default style with line breaks before and after), or none (hidden).
font-family	fontFamily	A comma-delimited list of font names. In addition to embedded fonts or named device fonts, Flash Player supports the following device font groups: _sans, _serif, _typewriter. You can also use sans-serif, serif, and mono, and they will be interpreted as _sans, _serif, and _typewriter, respectively.
font-size	fontSize	The numeric font size.
font-style	fontStyle	normal or italic.
font-weight	fontWeight	normal or bold.
kerning	kerning	true or false. Kerning only works with embedded fonts that support kerning. Additionally, the .swf must be compiled on Windows for kerning to work.
letter-spacing	letterSpacing	The number of pixels to add between letters.
margin-left	marginLeft	Number of pixels to apply to the left margin.
margin-right	marginRight	Number of pixels to apply to the right margin.
text-align	textAlign	left, center, right, or justify.
text-decoration	textDecoration	none or underline.
text-indent	textIndent	Number of pixels to apply as the indent.

You can construct a new *StyleSheet* object and then populate it in several ways. One way to populate a *StyleSheet* object is to define style objects and assign them by using the *setStyle()* method. A style object is an associative array with properties from the ActionScript properties list of Table 9-1. The following is an example of a style object:

```
var sampleStyle:Object = new Object();
sampleStyle.color = "#FFFFFF";
sampleStyle.textAlign = "center";
```

Note that you can define a style object with object literal notation as well, as shown here:

```
var sampleStyle:Object = {color: "#FFFFFF", textAlign: "center"};
```

Once you've defined one or more style objects, you can add them to the *StyleSheet* object with the *setStyle()* method. The *setStyle()* method requires two parameters: the name of the style and the style object. You can define styles for tags as well as for classes. The following defines a CSS class called sample:

```
css.setStyle(".sample", sampleStyle);
```

Although you can define a stylesheet with style objects and the *setStyle()* method, the most common and practical use of the class is to load and parse an external CSS document. Loading CSS at runtime has the advantage that you can change the styles by editing the CSS document, and you don't have to recompile the *.swf*.

To load a CSS document, use the *flash.net.URLLoader* class. Once data from the document has loaded, you can use that data to populate a *StyleSheet* object by passing the data to the *parseCSS()* method of the object. The next example uses *styles. css*, a CSS document defined as follows and saved in the same directory as the *.swf*:

```
p {
  font-family: _sans;
  color: #FFFFFF;
}
.emphasis {
  font-weight: bold;
  font-style: italic;
}
```

The following example illustrates how to load a CSS document and use that data to populate a *StyleSheet* object:

```
package {

    import flash.display.Sprite;
    import flash.text.TextField;
    import flash.events.Event;
    import flash.text.TextFieldAutoSize;
    import flash.text.StyleSheet;
    import flash.net.URLLoader;
    import flash.net.URLRequest;

    public class CSSText extends Sprite {

        public function CSSText( ) {
            var loader:URLLoader = new URLLoader( );
            loader.addEventListener(Event.COMPLETE, onLoadCSS);
            var request:URLRequest = new URLRequest("styles.css");
            loader.load(request);
        }

        private function onLoadCSS(event:Event):void {
          var css:StyleSheet = new StyleSheet( );
          css.parseCSS(URLLoader(event.target).data);
            var field:TextField = new TextField( );
            field.autoSize = TextFieldAutoSize.LEFT;
            field.wordWrap = true;
            field.width = 200;
            addChild(field);
            field.styleSheet = css;
```

```
        field.htmlText = "<p><span class='emphasis'>Lorem ipsum</span> dolor sit
  amet, consectetuer adipiscing elit. Morbi tortor purus, aliquet a, ornare ac,
  suscipit a, est. Nullam hendrerit molestie erat. Nunc nulla tortor, ullamcorper et,
  elementum vel, fringilla sed, dui. Praesent fermentum interdum orci.</p>";
    }
  }
}
```

There are a few things to watch for when working with CSS in Flash:

- CSS can be applied only to text fields rendering HTML.

- The HTML and CSS must correspond. For example, if the CSS defines a class
  called *someCSSClass*, then it has an effect only if the HTML applies that class to
  some portion of the text (as in the preceding example).

- The HTML text must be applied *after* the CSS is applied.

If you want to allow the user to select from different CSS documents, it may be helpful to store the HTML text in a variable or an associative array. Then you can re-apply
the HTML each time the new CSS is loaded, as in the following example:

```
package {

    import flash.display.Sprite;
    import flash.text.TextField;
    import flash.events.Event;
    import flash.events.MouseEvent;
    import flash.text.TextFieldAutoSize;
    import flash.text.StyleSheet;
    import flash.net.URLLoader;
    import flash.net.URLRequest;

    public class CSSText extends Sprite {

      private var _field:TextField;
      private var _html:String;

      public function CSSText( ) {
        var css1:TextField = new TextField( );
        css1.text = "stylesheet 1";
        css1.selectable = false;
        var css1Container:Sprite = new Sprite( );
        css1Container.addEventListener(MouseEvent.CLICK, onCSS1);
        css1Container.addChild(css1);
        addChild(css1Container);

        var css2:TextField = new TextField( );
        css2.text = "stylesheet 2";
        css2.selectable = false;
        var css2Container:Sprite = new Sprite( );
        css2Container.addEventListener(MouseEvent.CLICK, onCSS2);
        css2Container.addChild(css2);
        addChild(css2Container);
```

```
            css2Container.y = 25;

                _field = new TextField( );
                _field.autoSize = TextFieldAutoSize.LEFT;
                _field.wordWrap = true;
                _field.width = 200;
                addChild(_field);
                _html = "<p><span class='emphasis'>Lorem ipsum</span> dolor sit amet,
consectetuer adipiscing elit. Morbi tortor purus, aliquet a, ornare ac, suscipit a,
est. Nullam hendrerit molestie erat. Nunc nulla tortor, ullamcorper et, elementum
vel, fringilla sed, dui. Praesent fermentum interdum orci.</p>";
                _field.y = 50;
            }

        private function loadCSS(url:String):void {
            var loader:URLLoader = new URLLoader( );
            loader.addEventListener(Event.COMPLETE, onLoadCSS);
            var request:URLRequest = new URLRequest(url);
            loader.load(request);

        }

        private function onCSS1(event:MouseEvent):void {
          loadCSS("styles.css");
        }

        private function onCSS2(event:MouseEvent):void {
          loadCSS("styles2.css");
        }

        private function onLoadCSS(event:Event):void {
          var css:StyleSheet = new StyleSheet( );
          css.parseCSS(URLLoader(event.target).data);
                _field.styleSheet = css;
                _field.htmlText = _html;
        }
      }
    }
```

See Also

Recipe 9.8 explains how to use HTML-formatted text, Recipe 9.14 explains how to apply formatting to new text rather than existing text, and Recipe 9.15 applies formatting to individual characters rather than an entire field.

9.14 Formatting User-Input Text

Problem

You want to apply formatting to text as the user enters it into a text field.

Solution

Apply a *TextFormat* object by using the *defaultTextFormat* property of the text field.

Discussion

You should use the *defaultTextFormat* property of a text field object to apply text formatting to text as it is entered by user input. Create a *TextFormat* object as in Recipe 9.13, and then assign that object to the text field's *defaultTextFormat* property:

```
var formatter:TextFormat = new TextFormat( );
formatter.color = 0x0000FF;      // Make the text blue
field.defaultTextFormat = formatter;
```

When you use *defaultTextFormat*, the formatting is applied to text that the user types into the field.

See Also

Recipes 9.13 and 9.15

9.15   Formatting a Portion of Existing Text

Problem

You want to add formatting to some, but not all, text in a text field, or you want to apply different formatting to various parts of a text field.

Solution

Create a *TextFormat* object and use it to format a substring of the text field by using one of the *setTextFormat()* method variations.

Discussion

You can format an entire text field as shown in Recipe 9.13, or you can use one of the versions of the *setTextFormat()* method to format just a portion of a text field. These variations allow you to apply formatting to the specified character range only.

You can set the formatting for a single character within a text field by invoking the *setTextFormat()* method and passing it two parameters:

index
> The zero-relative index of the character to which the formatting should be applied.

textFormat
> A reference to a *TextFormat* object.

This example applies the formatting to the first character only:

```
field.setTextFormat(0, formatter);
```

Alternatively, if you want to apply the formatting to a range of characters, you can invoke *setTextFormat( )* with three parameters:

startIndex
> The beginning, zero-relative character index.

endIndex
> The index of the character after the last character in the desired range.

textFormat
> A reference to a *TextFormat* object.

This example applies the formatting to the first 10 characters:

```
field.setTextFormat(0, 10, formatter);
```

You may notice that when you try to format portions of a text field, certain formatting options do not get applied under certain circumstances. For example, text alignment is applied only if the formatting is applied to the first character in the line.

See Also

Recipe 9.13

9.16   Setting a Text Field's Font

Problem

You want to use ActionScript to change the font used for some displayed text.

Solution

Use a <font> tag in HTML, set the font property of a *TextFormat* object, or use the font-family property in CSS.

Discussion

You can programmatically specify the font that is used to display text by using one of several different options. You can use a <font> tag if you are applying the formatting using HTML. For example:

```
field.htmlText = "<font face='Arial'>Formatted text</font>";
```

You can also use the font property of a *TextFormat* object. You can assign to this property the string name of the font (or fonts) that should be used:

```
formatter.font = "Arial";
```

And you can also define a font-family property in CSS:

```
p {
  font-family: Arial;
}
```

The font specified must be available on the computer on which the movie is running. Because some computers may not have the preferred font installed, you can specify multiple font names separated by commas, as follows:

```
formatter.font = "Arial, Verdana, Helvetica";
```

 The preceding example uses a *TextFormat* object. However, you can specify a comma-delimited list of fonts by using any of the techniques described.

The first font is used unless it cannot be found, in which case the Flash Player attempts to use the next font in the list.

If none of the specified fonts are found, the default system font is used. You can optionally specify a *font group*. Font groups use the default device font within a category. A font group is often preferable to allowing Flash Player to use the default system font, since at least you'll know what general characteristics the font will have. There are three font groups: *_sans*, *_serif*, and *_typewriter*. The *_sans* group is generally a font such as Arial or Helvetica, the *_serif* group is generally a font such as Times or Times New Roman, and the *_typewriter* group is generally a font such as Courier or Courier New.

See Also

Recipes 9.13, 9.15, and 9.17

9.17 Embedding Fonts

Problem

You want to ensure that text displays properly, even if the intended font isn't installed on the user's computer.

Solution

Embed the font by using the [Embed] metatag. Then set the text field's embedFonts property to true, and apply the font to the text field using a <font> tag, a *TextFormat* object, or CSS.

Discussion

You should embed fonts if you want to ensure that text displays using the intended font, even if the user's computer does not have that font installed. To embed a font, use the [Embed] metatag. The [Embed] metatag should appear in an ActionScript file outside the class declaration. You can embed either TrueType fonts or system fonts. To embed a TrueType font with the [Embed] metatag use the following syntax:

```
[Embed(source="pathToTtfFile", fontName="FontName", mimeType="application/x-font-
truetype")]
```

The path to the TrueType font file can be relative or absolute, such as in the following example:

```
[Embed(source="C:\Windows\Fonts\Example.ttf", fontName="ExampleFont",
mimeType="application/x-font-truetype")]
```

The *fontName* attribute value is how you refer to the font from CSS or ActionScript.

The syntax for embedding system fonts is similar, except that it uses a *systemFont* attribute rather than a source attribute. The *systemFont* attribute value is the name of the system font you want to embed. The following embeds Times New Roman:

```
[Embed(systemFont="Times New Roman", fontName="Times New Roman",
mimeType="application/x-font-truetype")]
```

 The preceding example uses the same name for *fontName* as the actual system font name.

Once you've embedded the font, the next step is to tell the text field to use the embedded font. To do that, simply set the embedFonts property of the text field to true. By default, the property is false, which means that Flash uses device fonts. By setting the embedFonts property to true, the text field can use embedded fonts only. If you try to assign a device font to a text field with embedFonts set to true, nothing is displayed:

```
field.embedFonts = true;
```

Once you've enabled embedded fonts, your next step is to tell the text field which embedded font to use; you do this with a <font> tag, a *TextFormat* object, or with CSS. For example, if the *fontName* value is Times New Roman, your code might look like the following:

```
formatter.font = "Times New Roman";
```

The following example sets the font by using a font tag:

```
field.htmlText = "<font family='Times New Roman'>Example</font>";
```

And the following illustrates how to set the font by using CSS:

```
var css:StyleSheet = new StyleSheet();
css.setStyle("p", {fontFamily: "Times New Roman"});
field.htmlText = "<p>Example</p>";
```

You cannot specify a comma-delimited list of fonts if embedFonts is set to true.

Recipes 9.13 and 9.16

9.18   Creating Text that Can Be Rotated

Problem

You want to make sure that some text continues to display, even when it's rotated.

Solution

Use embedded fonts.

Discussion

Unless you specifically use an embedded font, text fields use device fonts. For most situations, this is perfectly workable. However, in situations in which you want to rotate a text field or its parent container (e.g., you want to place a label next to an object vertically), you must use embedded fonts. Device fonts disappear when rotating a text field.

See Also

Recipe 9.17 explains how to embed fonts.

9.19   Displaying Unicode Text

Problem

You want to display Unicode text in your application, possibly including non-English characters.

Solution

Load the text from an external source. Optionally, use Unicode escape sequences for the characters within the assignment to the text field's text property.

Discussion

If you want to display Unicode text in a text field, there are several ways in which you can accomplish that:

- Load the Unicode text from an external source (e.g., a text file, XML document, database).
- Use the character directly within the ActionScript code as a string value.
- Use a Unicode escape sequence.

If you load the text from an external source, you can load Unicode text and assign it to a text field. For more information regarding loading content from external sources, see Chapter 20.

Assuming you're using an editor that supports Unicode (such as Flex Builder), you can add the character directly within the code. Optionally, if you know the escape sequence for the character, you can assign it to a text field's text property. All Unicode escape sequences in ActionScript begin with \u and are followed by a four-digit hexadecimal number. The escape sequences must be enclosed in quotes. The following example displays a registered mark (®) in both ways:

```
field.text = "Add a registered mark directly (®) or with a Unicode
escape sequence (\u00AE)";
```

 If you want a Unicode character reference online, under Windows, you can open up the Character Map utility using Start → Programs → Accessories → System Tools → Character Map. On Mac OS X, first enable the Input Menu in System Preferences → International → Input Menu, and turn on the checkbox next to Character Palette. To open the Character Palette, go to the menu bar, select the flag for your country (e.g., the Stars and Stripes for the U.S.), and select Show Character Palette.

See Also

Table A-1 in the Appendix lists the Unicode escape sequences.

9.20 Assigning Focus to a Text Field

Problem

You want to use ActionScript to bring focus to a text field.

Solution

Use the *Stage.focus* property.

Discussion

Use the *Stage.focus* property to programmatically assign focus to a specific text field. Every display object has a stage property that references the *Stage* instance. Therefore, from a class that extends a display object class (*Sprite*, *MovieClip*, etc.) the following code assigns focus to a text field called field:

```
stage.focus = field;
```

When an *.swf* first loads in a web browser, it does not have focus. Therefore, you must move focus to the Flash Player before you can programmatically assign focus to an element of the Flash application. The following is a working example that uses a sprite button to assign focus to a text field:

```
package {

  import flash.display.Sprite;
  import flash.text.TextField;
  import flash.text.TextFieldType;
  import flash.events.MouseEvent;

  public class TextExample extends Sprite {

    public function TextExample( ) {
      var field:TextField = new TextField( );
      field.border = true;
      field.background = true;
      field.type = TextFieldType.INPUT;
      addChild(field);
      var button:Sprite = new Sprite( );
      button.graphics.lineStyle( );
      button.graphics.beginFill(0xFFFFFF);
      button.graphics.drawRect(0, 0, 100, 50);
      button.graphics.endFill( );
      button.addEventListener(MouseEvent.CLICK, onClick);
      button.y = 100;
      addChild(button);
    }

    private function onClick(event:MouseEvent):void {
      stage.focus = TextField(getChildAt(0));
    }

  }
}
```

To remove focus from a text field you should assign *Stage.focus* the null value:

```
stage.focus = null;
```

9.21   Selecting Text with ActionScript

Problem

You want to highlight a portion of the text within a text field.

Solution

Use the *TextField.setSelection( )* method.

Discussion

The *TextField.setSelection()* method highlights a portion of the text in the text field. The *setSelection()* method takes two parameters:

startIndex
> The beginning, zero-relative index of the text to highlight.

endIndex
> The index of the character after the text to highlight.

For the selection to work, the text field must have focus, which you can set by using *Stage.focus,* as discussed in Recipe 9.20:

```
stage.focus = field;                      // Set the focus to the text field
field.text = "this is example text";      // Set the text value
field.setSelection(0, 4);                 // Highlight the word "this"
```

Use the read-only selectionBeginIndex and selectionEndIndex properties to retrieve the indices of the selected character range.

See Also

Recipes 9.20 and 9.23

9.22   Setting the Insertion Point in a Text Field

Problem

You want ActionScript to set the insertion point for a text field.

Solution

Use the *TextField.setSelection()* method.

Discussion

You can use *TextField.setSelection()* to set the cursor position in a text field by setting the beginning and ending index parameters to the same value. This example sets the cursor position in the text field, assuming it has focus:

```
// Positions the insertion point before the first character
field.setSelection(0, 0);
```

You can retrieve the index of the cursor position with the read-only *caretIndex* property:

```
trace(field.caretIndex);
```

See Also

Recipe 9.21

9.23 Responding When Text Is Selected or Deselected

Problem

You want to perform a task when a text field is selected or deselected.

Solution

Listen for the *focusIn* and *focusOut* events.

Discussion

Text fields dispatch *focusIn* events when focus is shifted to the field and they dispatch *focusOut* events when focus is shifted away from the field. The events dispatched in both cases are *flash.events.FocusEvent* objects. The *FocusEvent* class defines a *relatedObject* property. In the case of *focusIn* events, the *relatedObject* property is a reference to the object that just had focus. In the case of *focusOut* events, the *relatedObject* property is a reference to the object that just received focus. Use the *flash.events.FocusEvent* constants of FOCUS_IN and FOCUS_OUT when registering listeners:

```
field.addEventListener(FocusEvent.FOCUS_IN, onFocus);
```

The *focusIn* and *focusOut* events both occur after the focus has already changed. They are non-cancelable events. If you want to be able to cancel the events, you must listen for events that occur before *focusIn* and *focusOut* are dispatched. The *keyFocusChange* and *mouseFocusChange* events are cancelable events that occur when the user attempts to move focus from a text field by way of the keyboard or mouse, respectively. You can register listeners by using the *FocusEvent* constants of KEY_FOCUS_CHANGE and MOUSE_FOCUS_CHANGE. Use the *FocusEvent.preventDefault()* method to cancel the default behavior. The following example disallows using the Tab key to move from field1 to field2 if field1 doesn't have any text:

```
package {

  import flash.display.Sprite;
  import flash.text.TextField;
  import flash.text.TextFieldType;
  import flash.events.FocusEvent;

  public class Text extends Sprite {

    private var _field1:TextField;
    private var _field2:TextField;

    public function Text() {
      _field1 = new TextField();
      _field1.border = true;
      _field1.background = true;
      _field1.type = TextFieldType.INPUT;
      addChild(_field1);
```

```
    _field1.addEventListener(FocusEvent.KEY_FOCUS_CHANGE, onKeyFocus);
    _field2 = new TextField();
    _field2.border = true;
    _field2.background = true;
    _field2.type = TextFieldType.INPUT;
    addChild(_field2);
    _field2.y = 100;

  }

  private function onKeyFocus(event:FocusEvent):void {
    if(_field1.text == "") {
        event.preventDefault();
    }
  }

 }
}
```

9.24   Responding to User Text Entry

Problem

You want to perform a task when the content of a text field is modified by user input.

Solution

Listen for the *textInput* event.

Discussion

You can specify actions to be performed each time the content of a text field is changed by user input, whether that change is deleting or cutting characters, typing in a character, or pasting characters. When a user makes any change to the value of an input text field, the text field dispatches a *textInput* event. You can register a listener to listen for the *textInput* event using the *flash.events.TextEvent.TEXT_INPUT* constant:

```
    field.addEventListener(TextEvent.TEXT_INPUT, onTextInput);
```

The *textInput* event is a *TextEvent* object, and it is cancelable. The *TextEvent* class defines a text property, which contains the value of the text entered by the user. The following example ensures that the first character the user types in a text field is not an "a":

```
package {

  import flash.display.Sprite;
  import flash.text.TextField;
  import flash.text.TextFieldType;
```

```
import flash.events.TextEvent;
import flash.events.TextEvent;

public class Text extends Sprite {

  private var _field:TextField;

  public function Text() {
    _field = new TextField();
    _field.border = true;
    _field.background = true;
    _field.type = TextFieldType.INPUT;
    addChild(_field);
    _field.addEventListener(TextEvent.TEXT_INPUT, onTextInput);

  }

  private function onTextInput(event:TextEvent):void {
    if(event.text == "a" && _field.length == 0) {
        event.preventDefault();
    }
  }

}
}
```

See Also

Recipe 9.12

9.25 Adding a Hyperlink to Text

Problem

You want to hyperlink some of the text displayed in a text field.

Solution

Use HTML <a href> tags within the object's htmlText property. Alternatively, use a
TextFormat object with a value assigned to the url property.

Discussion

Both solutions to this problem require that you set the text field's html property to
true:

```
field.html = true;
```

If you want to use HTML to add a hyperlink, add an <a href> tag to the text field's
htmlText property, as follows:

```
field.htmlText = "<a href='http://www.rightactionscript.com'>Website</a>";
```

You can add a target window into which to open the link by adding a target attribute to the `<a href>` HTML tag. For example:

```
field.htmlText = "<a href='http://www.rightactionscript.com'
target='blank'>Website</a>";
```

When text is hyperlinked in Flash, the mouse cursor changes to a hand when it is over the linked text. Flash does not inherently provide any indication that the text is linked, unlike most HTML browsers (which use an underline and color change). For this reason, it is helpful to add HTML markup that underlines and colors the linked text:

```
var htmlLink:String = "<font color='#0000FF'><u>";
htmlLink += "<a href='http://www.rightactionscript.com'>Website</a>";
htmlLink += "</u></font>";
field.htmlText = htmlLink;
```

You can accomplish the same tasks without HTML by using a *TextFormat* object. The *TextFormat* class includes a `url` property for just this purpose. Assigning the URL to the `url` property links the formatted text; for example:

```
field.text = "Website";
var formatter:TextFormat = new TextFormat();
formatter.url = "http://www.rightactionscript.com/";
field.setTextFormat(formatter);
```

If you want to specify a target window into which the link opens, you can set the value of the *TextFormat* object's target property, as follows:

```
field.text = "Website";
var formatter:TextFormat = new TextFormat();
formatter.url = "http://www.rightactionscript.com/";
formatter.target = "_blank";
field.setTextFormat(formatter);
```

As with the HTML technique, when using a *TextFormat* object to create a hyperlink, Flash does not offer any indication as to the link's presence other than the hand cursor when it is moused over. You can add color and/or an underline to the linked text to provide the user with the indication that it is a link. You should use the *TextFormat* object's color and underline properties for this purpose:

```
field.text = "Website";
var formatter:TextFormat = new TextFormat();
formatter.color = 0x0000FF;
formatter.underline = true;
formatter.url = "http://www.rightactionscript.com/";
field.setTextFormat(formatter);
```

You can use either of the techniques in this recipe to add links that point not only to *http* and *https* protocols, as shown in the examples, but also to link to other protocols. For example, you can use the same techniques to open a new email message:

```
field.text = "email";
var formatter:TextFormat = new TextFormat();
formatter.color = 0x0000FF;
```

```
formatter.underline = true;
formatter.url = "mailto:joey@person13.com";
field.setTextFormat(formatter);
```

Be aware, however, that many other types of links (such as *mailto* links) only work when the movie is played in a web browser in which a default client for the protocol has been defined.

Using CSS, you can apply advanced formatting to `<a href>` tags by using the a:
link, a:active, and a:hover styles, as shown in the following example:

```
var css:StyleSheet = new StyleSheet();
css.parseCSS("a {color: #0000FF;} a:hover {text-decoration: underline;}");
field.styleSheet = css;
field.html = true;
field.htmlText = "<a href='http://www.rightactionscript.com'>Website</a>";
```

See Also

Recipes 9.8 and 9.15

9.26 Calling ActionScript from Hyperlinks

Problem

You want to call an ActionScript method when the user clicks a hyperlink.

Solution

Use the *event* protocol and listen for link events.

Discussion

Many applications require calling ActionScript when the user clicks a hyperlink. With ActionScript 3.0, however, it is a very simple task. First, you must define the hyperlink to use the event protocol, as follows:

```
field.htmlText = "<a href='event:http://www.rightactionscript.com'>Website</a>";
```

When you use the *event* protocol, the default behavior does not occur. When the user clicks on a hyperlink, it normally opens the URL in a web browser. However, when you use the *event* protocol, an event is dispatched, which means you have to register a listener to listen for that event. The *event* type is *link*, and you can use the *flash.events.TextEvent.LINK* constant when registering a listener:

```
field.addEventListener(TextEvent.LINK, onClickHyperlink);
```

The *event* that is dispatched is a *flash.events.TextEvent* type. The *text* property of the *event* object contains the value of the href attribute minus the *event* protocol. That means that in the preceding example, the value of the *event* object's *text* property is *http://www.rightactionscript.com*. Since the hyperlink does not attempt to open a URL in a browser window when using the *event* protocol, you don't have to use a valid URL for the href value. You can use any string that would be useful in determining which hyperlink the user clicked.

9.27   Working with Advanced Text Layout

Problem

You want to work with advanced text layout.

Solution

Use the *numLines* property and the *getCharBoundaries()*, *getCharIndexAtPoint()*, *getFirstCharInParagraph()*, *getLineIndexAtPoint()*, *getLineIndexOfChar()*, *getLineLength()*, *getLineMetrics()*, *getLineOffset()*, *getLineText()*, and *getParagraphLength()* methods.

Discussion

In versions of Flash Player up to and including Flash Player 8, it was difficult to control and read text layout with much precision. Starting with Flash Player 8.5, though, the *TextField* class defines an API for more precise reading of text layout.

The *TextField* class defines two methods for retrieving information about characters from text. The *getCharBoundaries()* method returns a *flash.geom.Rectangle* object that defines the boundaries of the character at the index specified by the parameter. The *getCharIndexAtPoint()* method returns the index of a character at the *x* and *y* coordinates specified by the parameters. The following example uses *getCharIndexAtPoint()* and *getCharBoundaries()* to highlight a character when the user clicks on it:

```
package {

  import flash.display.Sprite;
  import flash.text.TextField;
  import flash.events.MouseEvent;
  import flash.geom.Rectangle;

  public class Text extends Sprite {

    private var _field:TextField;
    private var _highlight:Sprite;

    public function Text() {
      _field = new TextField();
      _field.border = true;
      _field.background = true;
      _field.multiline = true;
      _field.wordWrap = true;
      _field.selectable = false;
      _field.width = 400;
      _field.height = 400;
```

```
        addChild(_field);
        _field.text = "Lorem ipsum dolor sit amet, consectetuer adipiscing elit. Morbi
tortor purus, aliquet a, ornare ac, suscipit a, est. Nullam hendrerit molestie erat.
Nunc nulla tortor, ullamcorper et, elementum vel, fringilla sed, dui. Praesent
fermentum interdum orci.";
        _field.addEventListener(MouseEvent.CLICK, onClick);
        _highlight = new Sprite();
        addChild(_highlight);
    }

    private function onClick(event:MouseEvent):void {
        var index:int = _field.getCharIndexAtPoint(mouseX, mouseY);
        var rectangle:Rectangle = _field.getCharBoundaries(index);
        _highlight.graphics.clear();
        _highlight.graphics.lineStyle(0, 0, 0);
        _highlight.graphics.beginFill(0x00FFFF, .25);
        _highlight.graphics.drawRect(rectangle.x, rectangle.y, rectangle.width,
rectangle.height);
        _highlight.graphics.endFill();
    }

    }
}
```

The *TextField* class also defines a property and methods for retrieving information
about lines of text. The *numLines* property tells you how many lines of text a text
field contains. The *getLineIndexAtPoint()* method returns the index of a line at the
coordinates specified as the parameters passed to the method. The *getLine-
IndexOfChar()* returns the line index of the line that contains the character with the
index specified by the parameter passed to the method. The *getLineLength()* method
returns the number of characters in a line specified by its line index. The
getLineText() method returns the text contained within a line at a specified line
index. The *getLineOffset()* method returns the character index the first character of a
line at a specified line index. The *getLineMetrics()* method returns a *flash.text.*
TextLineMetrics object for a line with a specified line index. The *TextLineMetrics*
class defines ascent, descent, height, width, leading, and *x* properties that describe
the line of text.

There are two methods for retrieving information about paragraphs. The
getFirstCharInParagraph() method returns the character index of the first character
in a paragraph that also contains the character at the index specified in the parameter. The *getParagraphLength()* method returns the number of characters in a paragraph that contain the character at the index specified by the parameter.

The following example uses most of the methods discussed in this recipe to highlight a paragraph when the user clicks a character:

```
package {

    import flash.display.Sprite;
    import flash.text.TextField;
    import flash.events.MouseEvent;
```

```
    import flash.geom.Rectangle;
    import flash.text.TextLineMetrics;

    public class Text extends Sprite {

      private var _field:TextField;
      private var _highlight:Sprite;

      public function Text( ) {
        _field = new TextField( );
        _field.border = true;
        _field.background = true;
        _field.multiline = true;
        _field.wordWrap = true;
        _field.selectable = false;
        _field.width = 400;
        _field.height = 400;
        addChild(_field);
        _field.text = "Lorem ipsum dolor sit amet, consectetuer adipiscing elit. Morbi
tortor purus, aliquet a, ornare ac, suscipit a, est. Nullam hendrerit molestie erat.
Nunc nulla tortor, ullamcorper et, elementum vel, fringilla sed, dui. Praesent
fermentum interdum orci.";
        _field.addEventListener(MouseEvent.CLICK, onDoubleClick);
        _highlight = new Sprite( );
        addChild(_highlight);
      }

      private function onDoubleClick(event:MouseEvent):void {
        var index:int = _field.getCharIndexAtPoint(mouseX, mouseY);
        var startIndex:int = _field.getFirstCharInParagraph(index);
        var stopIndex:int = startIndex + _field.getParagraphLength(index);
        var startLine:int = _field.getLineIndexOfChar(startIndex);
        var stopLine:int = _field.getLineIndexOfChar(stopIndex - 1);
        var metrics:TextLineMetrics;
        var lineCharacter:int;
        var rectangle:Rectangle;
        _highlight.graphics.clear( );
        _highlight.graphics.lineStyle(0, 0, 0);
        for(var i:int = startLine; i <= stopLine; i++) {
            lineCharacter = _field.getLineOffset(i);
            rectangle = _field.getCharBoundaries(lineCharacter);
            metrics = _field.getLineMetrics(i);
          _highlight.graphics.beginFill(0x00FFFF, .25);
          _highlight.graphics.drawRect(rectangle.x, rectangle.y, metrics.width,
metrics.height);
          _highlight.graphics.endFill( );
        }
      }

    }
}
```

9.28 Applying Advanced Anti-Aliasing

Problem

You want to have more precise control over anti-aliasing of text.

Solution

Embed the font, set the *antiAliasType* property of the text field to *flash.text. AntiAliasType.ADVANCED*, and set the *gridTypeFit* and sharpness properties.

Discussion

By default, text displays with normal anti-aliasing settings. For most fonts at sizes 10 and higher the normal anti-aliasing settings make for legible text. However, for smaller font sizes and for certain fonts, the normal anti-aliasing settings make the text less than legible. In those cases, you can set the anti-alias type for the text field to advanced and use the *gridFitType* and sharpness properties to more precisely control how the text is rendered.

 To enable advanced anti-alias settings for a text field, you must use embedded fonts. See Recipe 9.17 for more details on how to embed fonts.

The *TextField.antiAliasType* property accepts one of the *flash.text.AntiAliasType* constants of NORMAL (default) or ADVANCED. Set the value of the property to ADVANCED for a text field if you want to enable more precise anti-alias settings:

```
field.antiAliasType = AntiAliasType.ADVANCED;
```

The *gridFitType* property determines how the font outlines snap to whole pixels on the screen. The possible values are the NONE, PIXEL, and SUBPIXEL constants of the *flash.text.GridFitType* class. The default value of NONE means that the text does not snap to whole pixels. That can cause text to appear blurry at smaller font sizes. The PIXEL setting snaps horizontal and vertical lines of the font outlines to whole pixels on the screen. The PIXEL setting works only when text is left-aligned. If you want center- or right-aligned text to snap to pixels, use the SUBPIXEL setting.

```
field.gridFitType = GridTypeFit.PIXEL;
```

The sharpness property ranges from -400 to 400, with a default value of 0; it determines how crisply the edges of the font outlines are rendered. The lower the number, the less sharply the fonts are rendered. The greater the number, the more sharply the fonts are rendered. If the text is not legible because it appears blurry, and you've already set the *gridFitType* to PIXEL or SUBPIXEL, then increase the sharpness value.

See Also

Recipe 9.17

9.29 Replacing Text

Problem

You want to replace text.

Solution

Use the *replaceSelectedText()* method to replace the highlighted text and *replaceText()* to replace a range of text.

Discussion

The *replaceSelectedText()* method enables you to replace the selected text in a text field. Simply pass the method the string to use as the replacement text. For the method to work, the text field must have focus:

```
_field.replaceSelectedText("new text");
```

Use the *replaceText()* method to replace text within a text string given a starting and ending index. The following replaces the text from index 100 to index 150, with the new string specified by the third parameter:

```
_field.replaceText(100, 150, "new text");
```

9.30 Retrieving a List of System Fonts

Problem

You want to retrieve a list of fonts on the user's system.

Solution

Use the static *TextField.fontList* property.

Discussion

When you want to use system fonts (rather than embedding the font or using a font group), first determine which fonts the user has installed. You can retrieve an array of system fonts on the user's computer with the *TextField.fontList* property.

```
trace(TextField.fontList);
```

Retrieving the list of available system fonts simply yields an array of strings. To apply a font to the text, you'll have to use one of the techniques discussed in Recipe 9.16.

CHAPTER 10
Filters and Transforms

10.0   Introduction

ActionScript lets you to apply several different transforms and filters to display objects (and bitmaps) to change their color, shape, rotation, size, and to apply special effects. Transforms are changes in color, shape, rotation, and size. The remainder of special effects discussed in this chapter use filters. Filters are native to Flash Player; they allow you to apply effects ranging from blurs to embossing.

10.1   Applying Color Changes

Problem

You want to apply a color to a display object.

Solution

Assign a *flash.geom.ColorTransform* object to the display object's *transform.colorTransform* property.

Discussion

Every display object has a *transform.colorTransform* property. The *colorTransform* property is a *flash.geom.ColorTransform* object that determines which color transforms are applied to the object. The colorTransform property always returns a copy of the actual *ColorTransform* object applied to the display object. That means that you cannot directly change the properties of the *colorTransform* property. You can, however, retrieve a copy of the actual *ColorTransform* object by assigning the value from the *colorTransform* property to a variable. Then you can change the properties of that copy and reassign it to the *colorTransform* property, as shown in the following example:

```
var color:ColorTransform = sampleSprite.transform.colorTransform;
color.rgb = 0xFFFFFF;
sampleSprite.transform.colorTransform = color;
```

The *ColorTransform* class defines two ways to change the solid color that is applied to a display object. You can set the value of the rgb property, as in the preceding example. The rgb property expects a *uint* value. Generally it's convenient to specify the value in hexadecimal representation (0xRRGGBB), as in the preceding example. You can also set the redOffset, greenOffset, blueOffset, and alphaOffset properties to work with each of the offsets individually. The offset values can range from -255 to 255:

```
var color:ColorTransform = sampleSprite.transform.colorTransform;
color.redOffset = 255;
color.greenOffset = 255;
color.blueOffset = 255;
sampleSprite.transform.colorTransform = color;
```

The preceding code sets each offset for a color transform to 255 to create a white fill effect, and it then applies that transform to sampleSprite. If you changed the alphaOffset value as well, it would affect the transparency of the display object to which the transform is applied. Applying an alphaOffset via a color transform and changing a display object's alpha property has the same effect, except that alphaOffset is on a scale from 0 to 255 and alpha is on a scale from 0 to 100.

See Also

Recipe 10.2

10.2   Applying Color Tints

Problem

You want to apply a tint to a display object rather than a solid color.

Solution

Work with the *transform.colorTransform* property of the display object. However, change the values of the multiplier properties rather than the offset properties.

Discussion

Recipe 10.1 shows how to apply solid colors to display objects. When you apply a solid color to a display object, it causes any contrast within the display object artwork to be indistinguishable. Applying a solid color is essentially the same as applying a fill to the entire shape of the display object. That means that every pixel within the display object is assigned the same color value.

When you apply a tint, each pixel's color is changed relative to the original pixel color value, which means the contrast is maintained. You can apply a tint to a display object in much the same way a solid color is applied. Both use the *transform.colorTransform* property of the object. The difference is that when you apply a tint, you want to set the offset properties to 0 (the default values) and change the values of the multiplier properties.

The multiplier properties (redMultiplier, greenMultiplier, blueMultiplier, and alphaMultiplier) have valid ranges from 0 to 1. The multiplier values determine how much of the red, green, blue, and alpha components of the original pixel color value to display. The default value for the multiplier properties is 1, which means that by default each pixel displays at 100 percent of the red, green, blue, and alpha components of the original pixel value. The following makes a display object appear with a green tint by keeping the greenMultiplier at 1 and setting the redMultiplier and blueMultiplier properties to 0:

```
var color:ColorTransform = sampleSprite.transform.colorTransform;
color.redMultiplier = 0;
color.blueMultiplier = 0;
sampleSprite.transform.colorTransform = color;
```

See Also

Recipe 10.1

10.3   Resetting Color

Problem

You want to reset the color of a display object back to the default.

Solution

Assign a new *ColorTransform* object with default values to the *transform.colorTransform* property of the display object.

Discussion

The default values of a *flash.geom.ColorTransform* object will reset the color of a display object. You can construct a *ColorTransform* object with default values by calling the constructor with no parameters. The following example resets the color settings for sampleSprite:

```
sampleSprite.transform.colorTransform = new ColorTransform( );
```

See Also

Recipes 10.1 and 10.2

10.4 Shearing

Problem

You want to shear (skew) a display object.

Solution

Create a *Matrix* object with default values, without the b and c properties. The b and c properties control the *y* and *x* shearing, respectively. Assign the *Matrix* object to the *transform.matrix* property of the display object.

Discussion

Shearing (or skewing) fixes a point on a plane and translates all the pixels on one side of the point in one direction and all the pixels on the opposite side equally in the opposite direction. The effect is that a rectangle becomes a parallelogram.

The *flash.geom.Matrix* class defines a, b, c, d, tx, and ty properties. The b and c properties determine how much skewing is applied (whereas a and d determine the scale factor and tx and ty determine the x and y translation). The b property determines skewing along the *y* axis, and the c property determines skewing along the *x* axis. The default values for the b and c properties are 0. The greater the values, the greater the skewing is down and to the right. Negative values skew the object up and to the left. The following code draws a square and skews it into a parallelogram along the *y* axis. The *Matrix* object uses the default values for the properties, except for b, which is assigned a non-default value of 1. (The default values are a=1, b=0, c=0, d=1, tx=0, and ty=0.)

```
var box:Sprite = new Sprite( );
box.graphics.lineStyle( );
box.graphics.drawRect(0, 0, 100, 100);
addChild(box);
box.transform.matrix = new Matrix(1, 1, 0, 1, 0, 0);
```

10.5 Applying Basic Filters

Problem

You want to apply basic filters such as drop shadows, blurs, glows, and bevels.

Solution

Construct a new filter object and assign it to the filters array of a display object.

Discussion

The *flash.filters* package contains the following basic filter classes: *DropShadowFilter*, *BlurFilter*, *GlowFilter*, *BevelFilter*, *GradientGlowFilter*, and *GradientBevelFilter*. We distinguish the preceding list as basic filters because they don't require additional display objects to apply as part of surface mapping or matrices to apply for complex transforms. Each of the basic filter classes consist of fairly straightforward properties that have straightforward effects on the display objects to which the filters are applied. For example, the *DropShadowFilter* class allows you to change the drop shadow offset, color, and the amount of blur applied to the shadow by way of properties (and parameters passed to the constructor).

 Since basic filters are discussed in the Flash and Flex documentation, we won't discuss unnecessary details of how to construct and change the basic properties of those classes.

Once you've constructed a filter object, you can apply it to a display object by using the object's *filters* property. The *filters* property is an array of filter objects. The following applies a drop shadow to a display object called `sampleSprite`:

```
sampleSprite.filters = [new DropShadowFilter()];
```

When you assign an array of filters to the *filters* property of a display object, the array is copied rather than referenced. That means that any changes to the array or the filters in the array won't have an effect on the display object until it has been reassigned, as shown in the following example:

```
var dropShadow:DropShadowFilter = new DropShadowFilter();
var sampleFilters:Array = [dropShadow];

// Applies the drop shadow.
sampleSprite.filters = sampleFilters;

// Change the color of the drop shadow to white. However, since the actual filter
// applied to sampleSprite is a copy of dropShadow this doesn't have an effect
// on sampleSprite.
dropShadow.color = 0xFFFFFF;

// Add a glow filter to the array. However, since the array assigned to sampleSprite
// is a copy of sampleFilters there is no effect on sampleSprite.
sampleFilters.push(new GlowFilter());

// Reassign sampleFilters to the filters property of sampleSprite. Now the updates
// to the drop shadow and the array (the addition of the glow filter) affect the
// display object.
sampleSprite.filters = sampleFilters;
```

Likewise, when you read the value of the filters property for a display object, it always returns a copy of the filters array. That means you cannot use methods of the *Array* class directly with the *filters* property to add or remove filters.

```
var dropShadow:DropShadowFilter = new DropShadowFilter( );

// Applies the drop shadow.
sampleSprite.filters = [dropShadow];

// This does not add a glow filter.
sampleSprite.filters.push(new GlowFilter( ));

// Instead, you have to copy the current filters array, append the new filter,
// and reassign the array.
var sampleFilters:Array = sampleSprite.filters;
sampleFilters.push(new GlowFilter( ));
sampleSprite.filters = sampleFilters;
```

The effects of the filters property are cumulative such that each filter in the array is applied in sequence. For example, if the filters array has two elements, a drop shadow, and a glow filter, then the glow (since it is second in the array) is applied to the effect of the object with the drop shadow filter applied to it.

If you want to apply filters non-cumulatively, you have to apply each filter to a new copy of the display object. Consider the following example that applies a drop shadow and a glow filter to the same object. The glow filter is applied to the entire surface, including the drop shadow, which generally is not the intended effect, since in most cases you'd presumably want to apply all filter effects to the original shape rather than having them apply cumulatively.

```
var box:Sprite = new Sprite( );
box.graphics.lineStyle( );
box.graphics.beginFill(0xFFFFFF);
box.graphics.drawRect(0, 0, 100, 100);
box.graphics.endFill( );
addChild(box);
box.filters = [new DropShadowFilter(10), new GlowFilter( )];
```

The following draws two boxes, and applies the glow to one and a drop shadow filter to a copy with the knockout property set to true:

```
var box:Sprite = new Sprite( );
box.graphics.lineStyle( );
box.graphics.beginFill(0xFFFFFF);
box.graphics.drawRect(0, 0, 100, 100);
box.graphics.endFill( );
var boxShadow:Sprite = new Sprite( );
boxShadow.graphics.lineStyle( );
boxShadow.graphics.beginFill(0xFFFFFF);
boxShadow.graphics.drawRect(0, 0, 100, 100);
boxShadow.graphics.endFill( );
addChild(boxShadow);
addChild(box);
box.filters = [new GlowFilter( )];
boxShadow.filters = [new DropShadowFilter(10, 45, 0, 1, 4, 4, 1, 1, false, true)];
```

The *knockout* property is available for the majority of the basic filters, and it applies the filter while hiding the original shape. For example, if you enable the *knockout* property for a drop shadow filter, the result is just the drop shadow without the original shape to which the filter was applied. This is useful in many scenarios, including when you want to composite several filters in a noncumulative manner, as in the preceding example. In the preceding example, the *knockout* property is set to true from the DropShadowFilter constructor. You can consult the documentation for each of the basic filters to learn about the exact parameters for the constructors.

The filters can be cleared from a display object by assigning an empty array or null to the filters property of the object:

```
sampleSprite.filters = [];
```

10.6   Applying Advanced Filter Effects (Emboss, etc.)

Problem

You want to apply an advanced filter effect, such as embossing, edge detection, etc.

Solution

Use a *ConvolutionFilter* object.

Discussion

The *flash.filters.ConvolutionFilter* class allows you to apply many effects ranging from brightness and contrast changes to more dramatic effects such as embossing, blurring, edge detection, and sharpening.

The convolution filters require an array of values that define a matrix to apply, so you can map each pixel to a new bitmap surface by combining adjacent pixel values. (The actual linear mathematics used are beyond the scope of this book.) The *ConvolutionFilter* class simplifies the application of such effects so you don't need to know matrix multiplication or how to apply the pixel mapping. Instead, all you need to know are the basics of the effects of the array of matrix values.

The *ConvolutionFilter* constructor defines all default values for parameters. However, once an effect is applied, you'll need to define nondefault values for at least the first three parameters. The first two parameters define the dimensions of the matrix, and the third parameter is an array of the matrix values.

The first parameter defines the number of columns, and the second parameter defines the number of rows. The following is an example matrix with four columns and two rows:

```
1  2  3  4
5  6  7  8
```

Although you can define matrices with nearly any dimension, all the effects discussed in this book require square matrices (matrices with equal numbers of rows and columns).

The values for the third parameter (the array of matrix values) are specified from left to right and from top to bottom. For example, the preceding matrix example could be described with the following array:

```
[1, 2, 3, 4, 5, 6, 7, 8]
```

A square matrix with a 1 in the center surrounded by zeros has a neutral effect. The following code example applies such a matrix to a display object; the matrix would cause no noticeable effect:

```
sampleSprite.filteres = [ConvolutionFilter(3, 3, [0, 0, 0, 0, 1, 0, 0, 0, 0])];
```

When the sum of matrix values is 1, as with this example, there is no effect on brightness. Higher sums cause an increase in brightness, and lower sums produce less brightness. The following example increases the brightness of the display object without any additional effects:

```
sampleSprite.filteres = [ConvolutionFilter(3, 3, [0, 0, 0, 0, 2, 0, 0, 0, 0])];
```

The following example applies a blur to a display object. However, since the sum of the matrix values is greater than 1, it makes the object brighter. In this case, the brightness effect is so great that it makes it difficult to even distinguish the blur effect:

```
sampleSprite.filters = [new ConvolutionFilter(3, 3, [1, 1, 1, 1, 1, 1, 1, 1, 1])];
```

You can correct unintentional brightness issues by applying a divisor. The divisor does not affect the intended effect (such as a blur or sharpen effect) while correcting unintended brightness. To reset to the default brightness for the object, use a divisor that is equal to the sum of the matrix values. Specify the divisor as the fourth parameter. The following example applies the same blur as in the preceding example, but it uses a divisor to reset the brightness:

```
sampleSprite.filters = [new ConvolutionFilter(3, 3, [1, 1, 1, 1, 1, 1, 1, 1, 1], 9)];
```

For all the effects discussed in this chapter, the effect increases as the center value decreases and decreases as the center value moves increases. For example, the preceding blur effect is lessened if the center value is 2. Note: you'd also have to change the divisor to keep the same brightness.

A more detailed discussion of convolution filters is beyond the scope of this book. If you want to learn more about convolution filter theory and devise your own matrices for directional effects, you can read the technical details at *http://www.cee.hw.ac.uk/hipr/html/convolve.html*.

Also, all examples in this chapter are nondirectional. For example, the blur in the preceding example is nondirectional, which means it does not appear as a motion or radial blur.

See Also

Recipes 10.7, 10.8, and 10.9

10.7 Embossing

Problem

You want to emboss a display object.

Solution

Apply a convolution filter with an emboss matrix.

Discussion

An emboss effect causes the edges of a surface to appear raised or recessed. A emboss matrix has a positive value in the center with values on the left and the opposite values on the right arranged in a symmetrical pattern. They determine the amount of embossing applied. The greater the value, the more embossing is applied. The values on the top and bottom of the center column determine whether the embossing causes a raised or raised effect, and they also need to be symmetrical. The following describes a generic emboss matrix:

```
a    d   -c
b    e   -b
c   -d   -a
```

The following is an example of a basic emboss matrix:

```
-1    1   1
-1    1   1
-1   -1   1
```

The following 3×3 matrix defines a good general purpose emboss effect when applied with a convolution filter:

```
-2   -1   0
-1    1   1
 0    1   2
```

The following example applies the preceding emboss effect to a display object. Note that a divisor isn't necessary, since the values are symmetrical and the center value is 1:

```
sampleSprite.filters = [new ConvolutionFilter(3, 3, [-2, -1, 0, -1, 1, 1, 0, 1, 2])];
```

See Also

Recipe 10.6

10.8   Detecting Edges

Problem

You want to detect the edges of a display object.

Solution

Use an edge detection matrix with a convolution filter.

Discussion

To apply an edge detection effect with a convolution filter, use a matrix with a negative value in the center surrounded by a symmetrical set of positive values, as described in the following generic matrix:

```
a   b   c
d   e   d
c   b   a
```

The following matrix applies a generic edge detection effect:

```
0   1   0
1  -3   1
0   1   0
```

The following applies the preceding edge detection effect to a display object:

```
sampleSprite.filters = [new ConvolutionFilter(3, 3, [0, 1, 0, 1, -3, 1, 0, 1, 0])];
```

The greater the center number, the less edge detection is applied. The following uses a center value of -1 with a divisor:

```
sampleSprite.filters = [new ConvolutionFilter(3, 3, [0, 1, 0, 1, -1, 1, 0, 1, 0],
3)];
```

See Also

Recipe 10.6

10.9 Sharpening

Problem

You want to apply a sharpening effect to a display object.

Solution

Use a sharpening matrix and apply it with a convolution filter.

Discussion

You can sharpen an object by using a matrix very similar to the structure of the matrix that detects edges. The only difference is that with an edge detection matrix the center value is negative surrounded by positive values; the sharpen matrix, instead uses a positive center value surrounded by negative values. The following example sharpens a display object:

```
sampleSprite.filter = [new ConvolutionFilter(3, 3, [0, -1, 0, -1, 5, -1, 0, -1, 0])];
```

You can apply a less dramatic sharpen effect by increasing the center value and using a divisor:

```
sampleSprite.filter = [new ConvolutionFilter(3, 3, [0, -1, 0, -1, 10, -1, 0, -1, 0],
    5)];
```

You can apply a more dramatic sharpen effect by decreasing the center value and either increasing the surrounding values or using a divisor:

```
sampleSprite.filter = [new ConvolutionFilter(3, 3, [0, -1, 0, -1, 1, -1, 0, -1, 0],
    -3)];
```

See Also

Recipe 10.6

10.10 Making a Digital Negative

Problem

You want to make a digital negative from a display object.

Solution

Use a digital negative matrix and apply it with a *ColorMatrixFilter* object.

Discussion

You can use a digital negative matrix in conjunction with a *flash.filters. ColorMatrixFilter* object to apply the matrix. The digital negative matrix is as follows:

```
-1  0  0  0  255
 0 -1  0  0  255
 0  0 -1  0  255
 0  0  0  1  0
```

The following example applies a digital negative effect to a display object:

```
sampleSprite.filters = [new ColorMatrixFilter([-1, 0, 0, 0, 255, 0, -1, 0, 0, 255, 0,
0, -1, 0, 255, 0, 0, 0, 1, 0])];
```

You can also use the ascb.filters.ColorMatrixArrays.DIGITAL_NEGATIVE constant, as shown here:

```
sampleSprite.filters = [new ColorMatrixFilter(ColorMatrixArrays.DIGITAL_NEGATIVE)];
```

10.11 Applying Grayscale

Problem

You want to apply a grayscale effect.

Solution

Use a grayscale matrix, and apply it using a *ColorMatrixFilter* object.

Discussion

You can apply a grayscale effect by converting all colors to their luminance equivalents. A simplified, nontechnical definition of luminance is the measure of brightness. You can convert a color to the equivalent luminance by multiplying the colors by the red, green, and blue luminance constants. The constants used for computer graphics differ from the NTSC standard used for broadcast purposes. The computer graphics luminance constants are 0.3086, 0.694, and 0.0820, respectively, for the RGB values. The following matrix describes a grayscale effect:

```
0.3086  0.6094  0.0820  0  0
0.3086  0.6094  0.0820  0  0
0.3086  0.6094  0.0820  0  0
0       0       0       1  0
```

The following applies a grayscale effect to a display object:

```
sampleSprite.filters = [new ColorMatrixFilter([0.3086, 0.6094, 0.0820, 0, 0, 0.3086,
0.6094, 0.0820, 0, 0, 0.3086, 0.6094, 0.0820, 0, 0, 0, 0, 0, 1, 0])];
```

You can use the ascb.filters.ColorMatrixArrays.GRAYSCALE constant:

```
sampleSprite.filters = [new ColorMatrixFilter(ColorMatrixArrays.GRAYSCALE)];
```

10.12 Changing Saturation

Problem

You want to change the saturation of a display object.

Solution

Use a saturation matrix and apply it with a *ColorMatrixFilter* object.

Discussion

You can affect saturation with the following matrix:

```
a  b  c  0  0
d  e  f  0  0
g  h  i  0  0
0  0  0  1  0
```

In the preceding matrix, you need to determine the values of a through i with the following equations, where red, blue, and green are the luminance constants and value is the saturation value:

```
a = (1 - value) * red + value
b = (1 - value) * green
c = (1 - value) * blue
d = (1 - value) * red
e = (1 - value) * green + value
f = (1 - value) * blue
g = (1 - value) * red
h = (1 - value) * green
i = (1 - value) * blue + value
```

When the saturation value is 0, the matrix is a grayscale matrix.

You can use the *ascb.filters.ColorMatrixArrays.getSaturationArray()* method to construct a saturation matrix array, given just the value.

```
sampleSprite.filters = [new ColorMatrixFilter(ColorMatrixArrays.
getSaturationArray(2))];
```

10.13 Changing Brightness

Problem

You want to change the brightness of a display object.

Solution

Use a matrix, and apply it using a *ColorMatrixFilter* objects. Optionally, you can change brightness using a *ConvolutionFilter* object.

Discussion

You can adjust the brightness using a *ColorMatrixFilter* object by passing it a matrix that scales or offsets the red, green, and blue equally. The following matrix is a general representation of a matrix that scales the red, green, and blue equally:

```
a  0  0  0  0
0  a  0  0  0
0  0  a  0  0
0  0  0  1  0
```

The following matrix offsets the red, green, and blue values equally:

```
1  0  0  0  a
0  1  0  0  a
0  0  1  0  a
0  0  0  1  0
```

The following example increases the brightness of a display object by scaling the colors to twice their original values:

```
sampleSprite.filters = [new ColorMatrixFilter([2, 0, 0, 0, 0, 0, 2, 0, 0, 0, 0, 0, 2,
0, 0, 0, 0, 0, 1, 0])];
```

You can also adjust brightness with a *ConvolutionFilter* object, as mentioned in Recipe 10.6.

See Also

Recipe 10.6

10.14 Changing Contrast

Problem

You want to adjust the contrast of a display object.

Solution

Use a contrast matrix and apply it with a *ColorMatrixFilter* object.

Discussion

As mentioned in Recipe 10.13, you can adjust the brightness by either scaling or offsetting color values. You can change contrast by both scaling *and* offsetting color values at the same time. The following matrix describes a generic contrast matrix:

```
a  0  0  0  b
0  a  0  0  b
0  0  a  0  b
0  0  0  1  0
```

You can calculate the scale and offset values from one contrast value by using the following equations:

```
a = value * 11
b = 63.5 - (value * 698.5)
```

You can use the *ascb.filters.ColorMatrixArrays.getContrastArray()* method to construct a contrast array given the contrast value. The effective range for the contrast value is from 0 to 1:

```
sampleSprite.filters = [new ColorMatrixFilter(ColorMatrixArrays.
getContrastArray(1))];
```

See Also

Recipe 10.13

## CHAPTER 11

Programmatic Animation

11.0 Introduction

Animation can be defined as any visual change over time. If an image does not change over a period of time, it's impossible to tell whether it is a still image or an animation. There are a variety of properties you can manipulate to produce change, and thus animation. The most obvious is changing an object's position to make it move. You can also change its size, shape, rotation, transparency or color, to name a few. As long as something changes visually, the viewer never sees the animation.

In the earliest versions of Flash, most animation was done by using *tweens*. An object was placed on a keyframe, another keyframe was made, and the object was changed in some way. Flash filled in the frames *in between*, hence, the term *tween*. Using ActionScript, you can create much more dynamic and interactive animation.

As for what you can animate, a movie clip or sprite is usually a good answer. These objects can contain graphics, and they can have methods and properties that allow them to be moved, scaled, rotated, and otherwise transformed any way you see fit. A movie clip would normally be used only in the Flash authoring environment, where additional frames are added, as in a tween.

Finally, you need some way of getting the changes to occur over time. Your best bet is either an *enterFrame* handler or a timer. ActionScript statements can be used to make changes to the animated object's properties on each frame, or timer cycle, if you're using a timer. Since motion is the most obvious kind of animation, the examples in this chapter start out by moving objects around. As the chapter progresses, you'll see some examples that apply the same techniques to other properties, such as animating the size of an object or its orientation.

11.1 Moving an Object

Problem

You have a graphic in a sprite and you want to animate it, giving it some motion.

Solution

Decide on a velocity for the *x* or *y*-axis (or both), and add that velocity to the object's position on each frame or animation interval.

Discussion

Velocity is often incorrectly defined as speed. However, velocity also includes a direction factor. For example, "10 miles per hour" is speed, but "10 miles per hour due north" is a velocity. If you are dealing with velocity on the *x* or *y*-axis, the direction is inherent. A positive *x* velocity is to the right; negative to the left. Likewise, a positive *y* velocity is down, and negative is up.

The first example defines the *x* velocity, _vx, and sets it to 3. Since this example uses the *enterFrame* event for animation, the object will move three pixels to the right on each frame:

```
package {
    import flash.display.Sprite;
    import flash.events.Event;

    public class Velocity extends Sprite {
        private var _sprite:Sprite;
        private var _vx:Number = 3;

        public function Velocity() {
            _sprite = new Sprite();
            _sprite.graphics.beginFill(0x0000ff, 100);
            _sprite.graphics.drawCircle(0, 0, 25);
            _sprite.graphics.endFill();
            _sprite.x = 50;
            _sprite.y = 100;
            addChild(_sprite);
            addEventListener(Event.ENTER_FRAME, onEnterFrame);
        }

        public function onEnterFrame(event:Event):void {
            _sprite.x += _vx;
        }
    }
}
```

If you set _vx to -3 instead, you'll see that it goes in the opposite direction. You can also add in some *y* velocity by creating a _vy variable, giving it a value, and changing the onEnterFrame method, as follows:

```
    public function onEnterFrame(event:Event):void {
        _sprite.x += _vx;
        _sprite.y += _vy;
    }
}
```

If you aren't a fan of frame-based animation (as in the previous example), you can use a timer function instead, as shown here in bold:

```
package {
    import flash.display.Sprite;
    import flash.events.Event;
    import flash.events.TimerEvent;
    import flash.utils.Timer;

    public class Velocity extends Sprite {
        private var _sprite:Sprite;
        private var _vx:Number = 3;
        private var _vy:Number = 2;
        private var _timer:Timer;

        public function Velocity() {
            _sprite = new Sprite();
            _sprite.graphics.beginFill(0x0000ff, 100);
            _sprite.graphics.drawCircle(0, 0, 25);
            _sprite.graphics.endFill();
            _sprite.x = 50;
            _sprite.y = 100;
            addChild(_sprite);
            _timer = new Timer(30);
            _timer.addEventListener("timer", onTimer);
            _timer.start();
        }

        public function onTimer(event:TimerEvent):void {
            _sprite.x += _vx;
            _sprite.y += _vy;
        }
    }
}
```

See Also

Recipe 11.2 for information on how to move an object at a given speed and angle.

11.2   Moving an Object in a Specific Direction

Problem

You want to move an object at a certain speed in a specific angular direction.

Solution

Convert the speed and angle to x and y velocities and add these to the object's x and y position on each frame or animation interval.

Discussion

Recipe 11.1 explains how you can move something at specific velocities on the x and y-axes, but what if you just know the angle and speed you want an object to move? For example, you want the object to move at an angle of 135 degrees, with a speed of 4 pixels per frame.

You can use some basic trigonometric functions to convert this angle and speed to component x and y velocities. First, you need to make sure the angle is in radians. If the angle is in degrees, convert it by using the following formula:

```
radians = degrees * Math.PI / 180;
```

If you ever need to convert the opposite way, use:

```
degrees = radians * 180 / Math.PI;
```

Once you have the angle in radians, use the *Math.sin* and *Math.cos* functions, along with the speed, to find the x and y velocities, using the following formulas:

```
vx = Math.cos(angle) * speed;
vy = Math.sin(angle) * speed;
```

Then you can simply move the object as outlined in Recipe 11.1. Here is an example using 135 degrees and a speed of 4 pixels per frame:

```
package {
    import flash.display.Sprite;
    import flash.events.Event;
    import flash.events.TimerEvent;
    import flash.utils.Timer;

    public class AngularVelocity extends Sprite {
        private var _sprite:Sprite;
        private var _angle:Number = 135;
        private var _speed:Number = 4;
        private var _timer:Timer;

        public function AngularVelocity () {
            _sprite = new Sprite();
            _sprite.graphics.beginFill(0x0000ff, 100);
            _sprite.graphics.drawCircle(0, 0, 25);
            _sprite.graphics.endFill();
            _sprite.x = 200;
            _sprite.y = 100;
            addChild(_sprite);
            _timer = new Timer(30);
            _timer.addEventListener("timer", onTimer);
            _timer.start();
        }
```

```
public function onTimer(event:TimerEvent):void {
    var radians:Number = _angle * Math.PI / 180;
    var vx:Number = Math.cos(radians) * _speed;
    var vy:Number = Math.sin(radians) * _speed;
    _sprite.x += vx;
    _sprite.y += vy;
}
    }
}
```

Of course, in such a simple example, it wouldn't make sense to recalculate the *x* and *y* velocities on each interval, as they never change. Instead, just calculate it one time, save the result, and use it on each frame. In many cases, however, the speed and direction will be constantly changing, and therefore need to be computed new for each frame.

See Also

Recipe 11.1

11.3 Easing

Problem

You want an object to smoothly move to a specific location, slow down, and stop as it reaches that spot.

Solution

Use an easing formula.

Discussion

First, we'll look at the concept of simple *easing*. You have an object at a certain position and you want it to ease to another position. Take the distance between the two points and move the object a fraction of that distance—maybe one-half, one-third, or less. On the next iteration, find the new distance and move the object a fraction of that. Continue this way until the object is so close to the target that you can consider it there.

You'll see that the first couple of jumps are quite big, but successive jumps get smaller and smaller until the object appears not to be moving at all. Viewed in terms of velocity, the velocity starts out high and approaches zero. Another way of looking at it is that velocity is dependent on distance. A large distance makes for a high velocity.

The following example shows a simple example of easing. The target position is specified by _targetX and _targetY. The fraction that the object moves each time is set in _easingSpeed. Here it is set to 0.1, which means the object moves one-tenth of the distance to the target on each animation interval:

```
package {
    import flash.display.Sprite;
    import flash.events.Event;
    import flash.events.TimerEvent;
    import flash.utils.Timer;

    public class Easing extends Sprite {
        private var _sprite:Sprite;
        private var _easingSpeed:Number = 0.1;
        private var _targetX:Number = 400;
        private var _targetY:Number = 200;
        private var _timer:Timer;

        public function Easing() {
            _sprite = new Sprite();
            _sprite.graphics.beginFill(0x0000ff, 100);
            _sprite.graphics.drawCircle(0, 0, 25);
            _sprite.graphics.endFill();
            _sprite.x = 50;
            _sprite.y = 50;
            addChild(_sprite);
            _timer = new Timer(30);
            _timer.addEventListener("timer", onTimer);
            _timer.start();
        }

        public function onTimer(event:TimerEvent):void {
            var vx:Number = (_targetX - _sprite.x) * _easingSpeed;
            var vy:Number = (_targetY - _sprite.y) * _easingSpeed;
            _sprite.x += vx;
            _sprite.y += vy;
        }
    }
}
```

One problem with this setup is that the timer continues to run, even after the object has gotten as close as it's going to get to the target. To handle that, find the distance to the target and if it is less than a certain value, just turn off the timer, as illustrated by the bolded code in the following example:

```
public function onTimer(event:TimerEvent):void {
    var dx:Number = _targetX - _sprite.x;
    var dy:Number = _targetY - _sprite.y;
    var dist:Number = Math.sqrt(dx * dx + dy * dy);
    if(dist < 1)
    {
        _sprite.x = _targetX;
        _sprite.y = _targetY;
        _timer.stop();
    }
    else
```

```
    {
        var vx:Number = dx * _easingSpeed;
        var vy:Number = dy * _easingSpeed;
        _sprite.x += vx;
        _sprite.y += vy;
    }
}
```

This example first finds the distance on the two axes and the total distance. If the distance is less than 1, it places the object at the target point and kills the timer. Otherwise, it continues as normal.

Sometimes though, you may not want the easing to stop; for example, in a moving target. The following example has the object easing toward the mouse. In other words, it simply replaces mouseX and mouseY for _targetX and _targetY:

```
public function onTimer(event:TimerEvent):void {
    var vx:Number = (mouseX - _sprite.x) * _easingSpeed;
    var vy:Number = (mouseY - _sprite.y) * _easingSpeed;
    _sprite.x += vx;
    _sprite.y += vy;
}
```

This is the simplest form of easing, and will suffice in a good many cases. Robert Penner (*http://www.robertpenner.com*), a well-known and highly respected Flash programmer, has developed a set of much more complex easing formulas that have become a sort of standard for easing applications. They even have been incorporated into the standard ActionScript classes that come with both Flash and Flex. At this writing, the equations are written for ActionScript 1.0 and 2.0 only, but they could easily be adapted for ActionScript 3.0. These equations do such things as easing in, easing out, easing in *and* out, or easing based on a specific time interval or number of frames, with many different formulas.

See Also

Recipes 11.1 and 11.2 for the basics on velocity.

11.4   Acceleration

Problem

You want an object to start moving slowly and then speed up over time.

Solution

Apply acceleration.

Discussion

Many people think of acceleration as simply speeding up. After all, when you want to go faster in your car, you step on the accelerator. A more scientific definition would be a change in velocity. Although this certainly encompasses increasing an object's speed, it also applies to slowing it down or changing its direction.

Acceleration requires an understanding of velocity as covered in Recipes 11.1 and 11.2. Acceleration also has a *magnitude* and *direction*, which can be represented as acceleration on the *x* and *y*-axes. With each frame or animation interval, the acceleration of each axis is added to the velocity on that axis, and then the velocity is added to the position, as in Recipe 11.1.

The following example uses the variables _ax and _ay for acceleration and _vx and _vy for velocity:

```
package {
    import flash.display.Sprite;
    import flash.events.Event;

    public class Accel extends Sprite {
        private var _sprite:Sprite;
        private var _ax:Number = .3;
        private var _ay:Number = .2;
        private var _vx:Number = 0;
        private var _vy:Number = 0;

        public function Accel() {
            _sprite = new Sprite();
            _sprite.graphics.beginFill(0x0000ff, 100);
            _sprite.graphics.drawCircle(0, 0, 25);
            _sprite.graphics.endFill();
            _sprite.x = 50;
            _sprite.y = 100;
            addChild(_sprite);
            addEventListener(Event.ENTER_FRAME, onEnterFrame);
        }

        public function onEnterFrame(event:Event):void {
            _vx += _ax;
            _vy += _ay;
            _sprite.x += _vx;
            _sprite.y += _vy;
        }
    }
}
```

As you can see, the sprite starts out motionless and gradually picks up speed as it goes across the stage. Generally, since acceleration is additive, the acceleration values should start out small; velocity builds up quickly over time.

Also, similar to Recipe 11.2, you can start with a direction and magnitude for the acceleration force:

```
var angle:Number = 45;
var accel:Number = .5;
```

Then convert this to acceleration on each axis:

```
var radians:Number = angle * Math.PI / 180;
_ax = Math.cos(radians) * accel;
_ay = Math.sin(radians) * accel;
```

Now you have values that you can add to the velocity.

It's worth noting that gravity is simply acceleration on the y-axis. You can create a gravity variable and set it to a constant value. Then add it to the y velocity on each frame, and you will have realistic gravity.

See Also

Recipes 11.1 and 11.2 for information on velocity.

11.5   Springs

Problem

You want an object to jump to and settle at a specific point, as if it were attached by a spring or rubber band.

Solution

Use *Hooke's Law*, the formula for a spring.

Discussion

Hooke's Law describes the forces at work in a spring. In simple terms, it says that the force applied by the spring (acceleration) is proportional to how far it is stretched. This makes total sense. For example, if you barely pull on a rubber band, it snaps back lightly. But if you pull it back as far as you can, it snaps back with enough force to be painful.

Obviously, springs have different amounts of "springiness" or tension. Some are easy to stretch and won't snap back too strongly. Others require a lot more force to pull, and will spring back with an equally strong force. A number can be used to represent each spring's strength. The variable _k represents this constant, and it is generally a small fraction of 1. A value such as 0.1 or 0.2 works well.

When a spring is modeled with ActionScript, you also need to specify a target point that the spring will pull the object to. Finally, you need to apply some damping or friction. In the real world, as an object springs back and forth, it loses a bit of energy and eventually comes to rest somewhere. If you don't add dampening to your code, the object just springs back and forth forever. To apply damping, multiply the velocity values by a fraction, such as 0.95. This removes 5 percent of its speed on each frame, eventually slowing it down to a stop. Here is an example, with all these principles in place:

```
package {
    import flash.display.Sprite;
    import flash.events.Event;

    public class Spring extends Sprite {
        private var _sprite:Sprite;
        private var _vx:Number = 20;
        private var _vy:Number = 0;
        private var _k:Number = .1;
        private var _damp:Number = .94;
        private var _targetX:Number = 200;
        private var _targetY:Number = 200;

        public function Spring() {
            _sprite = new Sprite();
            _sprite.graphics.beginFill(0x0000ff, 100);
            _sprite.graphics.drawCircle(0, 0, 25);
            _sprite.graphics.endFill();
            _sprite.x = 0;
            _sprite.y = 0;
            addChild(_sprite);
            addEventListener(Event.ENTER_FRAME, onEnterFrame);
        }

        public function onEnterFrame(event:Event):void {
            var ax:Number = (_targetX - _sprite.x) * _k;
            var ay:Number = (_targetY - _sprite.y) * _k;
            _vx += ax;
            _vy += ay;
            _sprite.x += _vx;
            _sprite.y += _vy;
            _vx *= _damp;
            _vy *= _damp;
        }
    }
}
```

In this example, the spring's force, represented by the variable _k, is set to 0.1. The variable _damp is set to 0.94; this variable controls the damping or friction. The target point 200, 200 is stored in the variables _targetX and _targetY.

In the onEnterFrame method, get the distance from the target to the object's current position. This tells you how far the spring is stretched. Multiply this by _k, the spring's strength. This gives you the force (or acceleration) to apply. Add this to the velocity and add the velocity to the position.

Finally, apply the damping by multiplying the velocity by the damp variable.

When you test this, you should see the sprite spring quickly to the target point, go past it, and spring back. Eventually it settles down and comes to rest.

The target point does not have to be stationary. You can easily alter the previous example to use the mouse coordinates as a target by changing the two lines that determine the acceleration:

```
var ax:Number = (mouseX - _sprite.x) * _k;
var ay:Number = (mouseY - _sprite.y) * _k;
```

This gives you a very smooth, interactive spring.

Try using different values for _k and _damp to see how you can alter the spring's properties.

See Also

Recipes 11.1, 11.2, and 11.4 for information velocity and acceleration.

11.6   Using Trigonometry

Problem

You want to do some advanced animation, involving rotation, circular motion, or oscillation.

Solution

Use the built-in math functions *Math.sin()*, *Math.cos()*, and *Math.atan2()*.

Discussion

Recipes 11.2 and 11.4 touched on the use of the sine and cosine functions, but they can be used for many other useful effects, such as moving objects in circular or oval paths, smoothly back and forth around a position, or rotating to a particular angle. Both *Math.sin()* and *Math.cos()* are based on the properties of a right triangle (a triangle that has one 90-degree angle). Without getting into a trigonometry lesson, if you feed either function a series of increasing numbers, they will return values that go smoothly back and forth from -1 to 0, 1, 0, and back to -1, continuously. The following code snippet demonstrates this:

```
for(var i:Number = 0; i < 10; i += 0.1) {
    trace(Math.sin(i));
}
```

This traces a long list of numbers. If you examine those numbers, you'll see that they start at 0, go up to 0.999, back down to -0.999, back up, and so on. You can now multiply that by another number, say 40, and get a list of values from -40 to 40. If you use this in an *enterFrame* handler, or timer-based method, and apply the result to an object's position, you can get it to oscillate back and forth, or up and down, as the following example shows:

```
package {
    import flash.display.Sprite;
    import flash.events.Event;

    public class Oscillation extends Sprite {
        private var _sprite:Sprite;
        private var _angle:Number = 0;
        private var _radius:Number = 100;

        public function AS3CB( ) {
            _sprite = new Sprite( );
            _sprite.graphics.beginFill(0x0000ff, 100);
            _sprite.graphics.drawCircle(0, 0, 25);
            _sprite.graphics.endFill( );
            _sprite.x = 0;
            _sprite.y = 100;
            addChild(_sprite);
            addEventListener(Event.ENTER_FRAME, onEnterFrame);
        }

        public function onEnterFrame(event:Event):void {
            _sprite.x = 200 + Math.sin(_angle) * _radius;
            _angle += .05;
        }
    }
}
```

Here, _angle is the variable holding the increasing value fed to *Math.sin()*. The result is multiplied by the _radius variable, which is set at 100. This causes the sprite to go back and forth 100 pixels.

If you use *Math.cos()* and do the same thing with the sprite's *y* position, you have circular motion:

```
public function onEnterFrame(event:Event):void {
    _sprite.x = 200 + Math.sin(_angle) * _radius;
    _sprite.y = 200 + Math.cos(_angle) * _radius;
    _angle += .05;
}
```

To make more of an oval shaped path, just use a different radius value on each axis. For example, set _xRadius to 100, _yRadius to 50, and do the following:

```
public function onEnterFrame(event:Event):void {
    _sprite.x = 200 + Math.sin(_angle) * _xRadius;
    _sprite.y = 200 + Math.cos(_angle) * _yRadius;
    _angle += .05;
}
```

Now, if you create separate angles and amounts to add to each angle, you can get a very random-looking motion. First, create separate variables for each axes' factors:

```
private var _xAngle:Number = 0;
private var _yAngle:Number = 0;
private var _xSpeed:Number = .13;
private var _ySpeed:Number = .09;
private var _xRadius:Number = 100;
private var _yRadius:Number = 50;
```

Then apply those to the motion code:

```
public function onEnterFrame(event:Event):void {
    _sprite.x = 200 + Math.sin(_xAngle) * _xRadius;
    _sprite.y = 200 + Math.cos(_yAngle) * _yRadius;
    _xAngle += _xSpeed;
    _yAngle += _ySpeed;
}
```

One possible use for this example is to simulate a fly, randomly buzzing around a room.

Another very useful trig function is *Math.atan2()*. The main use for this is in finding the angle between two points. It takes two parameters: the distance between the two points on the y-axis, and the distance between them on the x-axis. It then returns the angle, in radians, between the points.

A common scenario for using *Math.atan2()* is in making an object (a sprite, for example) point at the mouse. The y distance is mouseY – _sprite.y, and the x distance is mouseX – _sprite.x. *Math.atan2()* returns an angle. Convert that to degrees and use it to set _sprite.rotation. Of course, you'll need some sort of sprite graphic that shows which direction it is rotating. The next example creates the classic "following eyes," a little desktop toy that follows the mouse around the screen and has been created for just about every graphical operating system out there (actually, this example creates only a single eye, but it demonstrates the principle):

```
package {
    import flash.display.Sprite;
    import flash.events.Event;

    public class FollowingEye extends Sprite {
        private var _sprite:Sprite;

        public function AS3CB() {
            _sprite = new Sprite();
            _sprite.graphics.beginFill(0xffffff, 100);
            _sprite.graphics.drawCircle(0, 0, 25);
            _sprite.graphics.endFill();
            _sprite.graphics.beginFill(0x000000, 100);
            _sprite.graphics.drawCircle(20, 0, 5);
            _sprite.graphics.endFill();
            _sprite.x = 100;
            _sprite.y = 100;
            addChild(_sprite);
            addEventListener(Event.ENTER_FRAME, onEnterFrame);
        }
```

```
        public function onEnterFrame(event:Event):void {
            var dx:Number = mouseX - _sprite.x;
            var dy:Number = mouseY - _sprite.y;
            var radians:Number = Math.atan2(dy, dx);
            _sprite.rotation = radians * 180 / Math.PI;
        }
    }
}
```

The setup code draws an extra circle on the right edge of the first. When you are
doing this kind of rotation, align your graphics so that "zero degrees" is facing to the
right like this. The *enterFrame* handler calculates the two distances and the resulting
angle, converts to degrees and assigns it to the eye's rotation.

11.7   Applying Animation Techniques to Other Properties

Problem

You want to apply the techniques in this chapter's recipes to something other than
an object's motion.

Solution

Apply the techniques as given, but assign the results to a property other than the
object's *x* and *y* position.

Discussion

Although changing an object's position is the most obvious method of animation, all
of the techniques in this chapter can be applied to almost any property of a movie
clip or sprite. This recipe provides several examples to get you started, but the possibilities are so numerous that it would be impossible to list them all.

First, try applying some velocity to the rotation property; this variable is called _vr
for rotational velocity:

```
package {
    import flash.display.Sprite;
    import flash.events.Event;

    public class AnimatingRotation extends Sprite {
        private var _sprite:Sprite;
        private var _vr:Number = 4;

        public function AS3CB() {
            _sprite = new Sprite();
            _sprite.graphics.beginFill(0xffffff, 100);
            _sprite.graphics.drawRect(-50, -20, 100, 40);
            _sprite.graphics.endFill();
```

```
            _sprite.x = 100;
            _sprite.y = 100;
            addChild(_sprite);
            addEventListener(Event.ENTER_FRAME, onEnterFrame);
        }

        public function onEnterFrame(event:Event):void {
            _sprite.rotation += _vr;
        }
    }
}
```

This example uses a rectangle instead of a circle, so you can see the rotation in action. It sets _vr to 4, and then adds that to the sprite's rotation on each frame.

The next example applies a spring formula to the scale of the sprite. A click handler sets a random target scale, and the *enterFrame* handler applies the spring action. When you click on the sprite, it bounces to a new size:

```
package {
    import flash.display.Sprite;
    import flash.events.Event;
    import flash.events.MouseEvent;

    public class AnimatingProperties extends Sprite {
        private var _sprite:Sprite;
        private var _k:Number = 0.1;
        private var _damp:Number = 0.9;
        private var _scaleVel:Number = 0;
        private var _targetScale:Number = 1;

        public function AS3CB() {
            _sprite = new Sprite();
            _sprite.graphics.beginFill(0xffffff, 100);
            _sprite.graphics.drawRect(-50, -50, 100, 100);
            _sprite.graphics.endFill();
            _sprite.x = 100;
            _sprite.y = 100;
            addChild(_sprite);
            addEventListener(Event.ENTER_FRAME, onEnterFrame);
            _sprite.addEventListener(MouseEvent.CLICK, onClick)
        }

        public function onEnterFrame(event:Event):void {
            _scaleVel += (_targetScale - _sprite.scaleX) * _k
            _sprite.scaleX += _scaleVel;
            _sprite.scaleY = _sprite.scaleX;
            _scaleVel *= _damp;
        }

        public function onClick(event:MouseEvent):void {
            _targetScale = Math.random() * 2 - .5;
        }
    }
}
```

You could create similar functionality using easing (see Recipe 11.3) instead of springs. Photo gallery applications often use this technique for displaying differently sized photos. The photo content area eases to the new size, and then the photo fades in.

A more complex application of motion code is to use the techniques to color transforms to smoothly go from one color to another. This is probably best done with easing. Start out with one color and gradually ease into another color.

The following example sets up two sets of color values: _red1, _green1, _blue1, and _red2, _green2, _blue2. Each value is a number from 0.0 to 1.0. In the *enterFrame* handler, these values are fed to the red, green, and blue multiplier values of a *color transform* object that is applied to the sprite. All of the values ease from the first to the second value, so they smoothly transition from one to the other. There is also a click handler on the sprite, which randomly sets three new multiplier values; each time you click on the square, it eases to a new color:

```
package {
    import flash.display.Sprite;
    import flash.events.Event;
    import flash.events.MouseEvent;
    import flash.geom.ColorTransform;

    public class AnimatingColor extends Sprite {
        private var _sprite:Sprite;

        private var _red1:Number = 1;
        private var _green1:Number = 0;
        private var _blue1:Number = 0;

        private var _red2:Number = 0;
        private var _green2:Number = .5;
        private var _blue2:Number = 1;

        private var _easingSpeed:Number = 0.05;

        public function AS3CB() {
            _sprite = new Sprite();
            _sprite.graphics.beginFill(0xffffff, 100);
            _sprite.graphics.drawRect(-50, -50, 100, 100);
            _sprite.graphics.endFill();
            _sprite.x = 100;
            _sprite.y = 100;
            addChild(_sprite);
            addEventListener(Event.ENTER_FRAME, onEnterFrame);
            addEventListener(MouseEvent.CLICK, onClick);
        }
```

```
public function onEnterFrame(event:Event):void {
    _red1 += (_red2 - _red1) * _easingSpeed;
    _green1 += (_green2 - _green1) * _easingSpeed;
    _blue1 += (_blue2 - _blue1) * _easingSpeed;
    _sprite.transform.colorTransform =
            new ColorTransform(_red1, _green1, _blue1);
}

public function onClick(event:MouseEvent):void {
    _red2 = Math.random();
    _green2 = Math.random();
    _blue2 = Math.random();
}
        }
    }
}
```

See Also

Recipe 11.3

CHAPTER 12

Strings

12.0 Introduction

Strings are the fundamental textual element of the ActionScript language. A string is a series of zero or more characters enclosed in single or double quotes. Unlike some other languages, ActionScript does not differentiate between single characters and strings. Both characters and strings are grouped into the *String* datatype. For example:

```
var exampleA:String = "this is a string";
var exampleB:String = 'this is also a string';
var exampleC:String = "strings can contain characters such as -(*+5~";
var exampleD:String = ""; // Empty string
var exampleE:String = "x"; // Single character
var exampleF:String; // Defaults to null when no value is assigned
```

String values must always be enclosed within quotes. You can use either single or double quotes, but the starting and ending quotes enclosing a string must be of the same type.

```
// Both of these strings cause errors because of mismatched quotes.
var exampleA:String = "an incorrect string';       // Ending quote should be double
var exampleB:String = 'another incorrect string"; // Ending quote should be single
```

ActionScript provides functionality that allows you to work with strings and characters in many ways. A new feature of ActionScript 3.0 relating to strings is the built-in support for regular expressions (pattern matching), which is covered in Chapter 13.

12.1 Joining Strings

Problem

You want to concatenate (join) together two or more strings into a single value.

Solution

Use the string concatenation operator +, the combination concatenation-assignment operator +=, or the *String.concat()* method.

Discussion

Multiple strings can be joined in a single expression using the concatenation operator, +, between two string operands:

```
// This results in a single value of "Thisworks" (no space)
var example:String = "This" + "works";
```

If you want to join more than two strings, use additional concatenation operators and string value operands in the appropriate order:

```
// Results in a single value of "This works" (with a space)
var example:String = "This" + " " + "works";
```

In the preceding examples, there is little reason why you would need to join the string literals instead of assigning a single string value ("This works" instead of "This" + " " + "works"). However, this demonstrates the technique you'll use when working with dynamic values. You can use the concatenation operator to join not only string literals, but also variables containing string values (or values that can be converted to strings). For example:

```
var attendance:int = 24;
// Results in a single value of "There are 24 people"
var output:String = "There are " + attendance + " people";
```

The concatenation operator automatically converts any nonstring values to strings, as long as at least one of the operands in the statement is a string. In the preceding example, the numerical value 24 is converted to the string value 24 automatically before being joined with the other strings. However, if all the operands are numbers, the ActionScript interpreter treats the + operator as the addition operator instead of the concatenation operator:

```
var first:int = 24;
var second:int = 42;
// Results in the compiler error, "Implicit coercion of a value
// type 'Number' to an unrelated type 'String'"
var result:String = first + second;
```

You can concatenate, rather than add, two or more numbers in several ways. One way is to concatenate an empty string to the beginning of the statement:

```
var first:int = 24;
var second:int = 42;
// Results in a string value of "2442"
var result:String = "" + first + second;
```

The empty string must be placed first in the expression because if the two numbers appear first, they are added rather than concatenated, even though the final value is still converted to a string:

```
var first:int = 24;
var second:int = 42;
// Results in a string value of "66"
var result:String = first + second + "";
```

Another option is to use the *String()* conversion function to ensure that at least one of the numbers is cast to a string before performing the concatenation:

```
var first:int = 24;
var second:int = 42;
// Results in a string value of "2442"
var result:String = String( first ) + second;
```

When you use this technique for only two numbers, it does not matter which one you convert to a string (or you can convert both). But if you are joining more than two numbers, you should convert the first or second number to a string. Otherwise, the numbers preceding the value that is converted to a string will be added rather than concatenated:

```
var first:int = 24;
var second:int = 42;
var third:int = 21;
// Results in a string value of "6621"
var result:String = first + second + String( third );
```

Yet another option is to use the *toString()* method available on most built-in objects. Both *Number* and *int* data types have a *toString()* method available:

```
var first:int = 24;
var second:int = 42;
var third:int = 21;
// Results in a string value of "244221"
var result:String = first.toString() + second + third;
```

If you want to add, rather than concatenate, two number values in the middle of a string concatenation statement, you should enclose that expression in parentheses. This changes the order of operation and evaluates the inner expression first, treating it as an addition operation rather than a concatenation operation:

```
var first:int = 24;
var second:int = 42;
// Results in "There are 66 people"
var result:String = "There are " + ( first + second ) + " people";
```

You can also append text to existing strings by using the concatenation assignment += operator:

```
var attendance:int = 24;
var example:String = "There are ";
example += attendance;
// Results in a string value of "There are 24 people"
example += " people";
```

This technique can be useful for several reasons. First of all, sometimes you want to join long string values and your code remains more readable when you break it up into multiple lines:

```
var example:String = "This is the first sentence in a long paragraph of text.";
example += "By adding line by line to the string variable you make ";
example += "your code more readable.";
```

However, instead of using three separate statements the preceding code can be expressed more efficiently by using clever spacing and line breaking with the regular + operator. Note that there is only one ; making the entire assignment statement expand over three lines:

```
var example:String = "This is the first sentence in a long paragraph of text. "
    + "By splitting the long string into smaller, more manageable pieces "
    + "and using the + operator, you can make your code more readable.";
```

The most practical use of concatenation assignment is when you need to append more text to a string over time rather than all at once. For example, you may have a chat history window that updates whenever someone contributes text to the conversation. You can append the new text to an existing string by using the combination concatenation assignment operator. For example:

```
// A method that will append the username and message to
// a chat history string variable
private function updateChatHistory( message:String, username:String ):void {
    // Assume history is a string variable that contains past conversation history.
    // Append the username and message with a new line to the existing string.
    _history += username + ":" + message + '\n';
};
```

You can also use the *String.concat()* method to append new values to the end of an existing string. The *concat()* method does not affect the original string. Instead, it returns a new string containing the result of the concatenation:

```
var original:String = "original string value.";

// Set modified to "original string value.now modified."
// The value of original remains unchanged.
var modified:String = original.concat( "now modified." );
```

> Flash 4 used the & operator for string concatenation. Flash converts the & operator to the *add* operator when updating Flash 4 files to Flash 5 or Flash 6 format. The + operator is the preferred string concatenation operator in Flash 5 and later.

See Also

Recipe 12.6

12.2   Using Quotes and Apostrophes in Strings

Problem

You want to use quotes or apostrophes within a string value.

Solution

Use a backslash to escape the quotes or apostrophes contained within the string. Alternatively, use single quotes within double quotes, or vice versa.

Discussion

The ActionScript compiler tries to match up quotes of the same kind (single quotes with single quotes and double quotes with double quotes) when processing string literals. Therefore, if you enclose a string literal within quotes of one type and also try to include the same kinds of quotes in the string value, the code fails to compile as you intended.

This string assignment causes an error because of mismatched quotes. In the following example, the string starts with a double quote ("Yes), therefore, the double quote character before the Y signals the end of the string to the compiler. As such, it does not understand what to do with the remaining characters:

```
var error:String = "He said, "Yes.""; // Incorrect.
```

One possible solution is to use single quotes to enclose a string literal that contains double quotes, or double quotes to enclose a string literal that contains single quotes, as follows:

```
// This assignment works. The result is a string: He said, "Yes."
var exampleA:String = 'He said, "Yes."';

// This assignment also works. The result is a string: He said, 'Yes.'
var exampleB:String = "He said, 'Yes.'";
```

However, if the string value contains both single and double quotes, this technique does not work. Furthermore, you have to pay close attention to what type of quotes are used when creating the strings, and you lose consistency in your program with constant quote switching. An alternative solution, which works all the time, is to use the backslash character (\) to escape any quotes used within the string value (i.e., escape the quote by preceding it by a backslash):

```
// This assignment works. The result is a string: He said, "Yes."
var sExample:String = "He said, \"Yes.\"";
```

The backslash tells the compiler to interpret the next character literally, and not with any special meaning it might normally have. Therefore, when you precede a quotation mark within a string value with the backslash character, you tell the compiler that the quote does not signal the boundary of the string value, but rather it is to be interpreted as just another character in the string.

12.3   Inserting Special Whitespace Characters

Problem

You want to add whitespace characters, such as tabs or newline characters, to your string.

Solution

Use the escape sequences for the special characters.

Discussion

There are five special whitespace characters with escape sequences, as shown in Table 12-1.

Table 12-1. Whitespace escape sequences

Whitespace character	Escape sequence
Newline	\n
Tab	\t
Backspace	\b
Form feed	\f
Carriage return	\r

You can use these escape sequences within a string; they are most useful when displaying a string value in a text field:

```
// Results in a string value: these    words    are    separated    by    tabs
var example:String = "these\twords\tare\tseparated\tby\ttabs";

/* Results in a string value:
these
words
are
separated
by
newlines
*/
var example:String = "these\nwords\nare\nseparated\nby\nnewlines";
```

Unlike previous versions of ActionScript, ActionScript 3.0 no longer includes support for the newline constant. If you have code that uses newline anywhere, you will need to replace it with the \n escape sequence.

The result is the same.

```
// Generates a compile error - replace newline with "\n" to compile
var error:String = "two" + newline + "lines"; // Compile error: "Access of
                                               // undefined property 'newline'"
```

Within Flash, the newline, form feed, and carriage return characters all result in the same display. However, when you load content into Flash from external sources, some values will have newline characters, some will have form feeds, and some will have carriage returns.

12.4   Searching for a Substring

Problem

You want to find a string value inside of a string.

Solution

Use the *indexOf()* or *lastIndexOf()* methods from the *String* class.

Discussion

You can use the *indexOf()* and *lastIndexOf()* methods to determine whether a string contains a specified substring value. Each method returns the starting index of the substring found. The *indexOf()* method searches from left to right, whereas the *lastIndexOf()* methods searches from right to left in the string. If the substring is not found, the value -1 is returned.

The *indexOf()* method takes two parameters:

substring
    The substring value for which you want to search.

startIndex
    The optional zero-based starting position from which to search within the string. Zero-based means the first character in the string is at position 0, not 1. If omitted, the method begins the search from the beginning of the string (at index 0).

If you want to test whether a string contains another string, you can use the *indexOf()* method with only one parameter. For example:

```
var example:String = "This string contains the word cool twice. Very cool.";

// Get the index of the first occurrence of the substring "cool" within example.
var index:int = example.indexOf( "cool" );

// If the indexOf() method returns -1, no occurrences of "cool" were found.
if ( index != -1 ) {
```

```
  // Displays: "String contains word cool at index 30" because the first
  // occurrence of the substring appears starting at index 30 within example.
  trace( "String contains word cool at index " + index );
}
```

You can get the indices of subsequent occurrences of a substring by specifying the second, optional parameter of the *indexOf()* method. A simple and effective way to search for the next occurrence of a substring is to pass the method a starting index parameter value of one more than what was returned by the previous search.

```
var example:String = "This string contains the word cool twice. Very cool.";

// Get the index of the first occurrence of the substring "cool" within example.
var index:int = example.indexOf( "cool" );

if ( index != -1 ) {
  // Displays: "String contains word cool at index 30"
  trace( "String contains word cool at index " + index );
}

// Get the index of the second occurrence of the substring "cool" within example.
// Pass the method the previous value of index + 1. This starts the
// search past the starting index of the previous occurrence, thus finding
// the next occurrence. If you do not add 1 to index when passing it to
// indexOf( ), the method returns the location of the first occurrence again.
index = example.indexOf( "cool", index + 1 );

if ( index != -1 ) {
  // Displays: "String contains word cool at index 47" because the next
  // occurrence of the substring appears starting at index 47 within example.
  trace( "String contains word cool at index " + index );
}
```

You can use *indexOf()* in a *while* statement to get the indices of every occurrence of a substring. For example:

```
var example:String = "This string contains the word cool. Very cool. Yes, cool.";

// Initialize index to -1 so that the while statement searches
// the string from the beginning (index 0, at index + 1)
var index:int =  -1;

// Loop until indexOf( ) returns -1.
while ( ( index = example.indexOf( "cool", index + 1 ) ) != -1 ) {

  /* Displays:
     String contains word cool at index 30
     String contains word cool at index 41
     String contains word cool at index 52
  */
  trace( "String contains word cool at index " + index );
}
```

The *while* conditional in the preceding code looks more complicated than it really is. If you take it apart, you can see that it is composed of manageable and understandable parts. The first part assigns to index the value returned by the *indexOf()* method:

```
index = example.indexOf( "cool", index + 1 );
```

The first time this statement is encountered, the initial value of index is -1 because it was set to -1 prior to the *while* statement. It is absolutely essential that this be done for the process to work properly, since 1 is added to the index each loop iteration. If index is not given a value, a default value of 0 is used; adding 1 to 0 causes the search to start at the second character of the string, at index 1. Each subsequent time the *while* condition is evaluated, the value of index has the value of the starting index of the previously found match. If we fail to add 1 to index in the loop, the index never moves past the first match and loops infinitely. That is, if the *indexOf()* method returns 30 and it starts looking from 30 on the next iteration, 30 is returned again by *indexOf()* and the cycle repeats.

The second part of the *while* conditional tests to make sure that the result of the *indexOf()* method is not -1 before executing the loop body again. This is important because without it the *while* loop would continue infinitely since any non-zero numerical value, positive or negative, in a conditional is interpreted as true. When *indexOf()* returns -1, it means that no more matches exist, so the *while* loop terminates.

The *lastIndexOf()* method works much like *indexOf()*, except that it searches from right to left in the string, effectively searching the string backward. The *lastIndexOf()* method returns the starting index of the last occurrence of the substring. The starting index returned is the position of the beginning of the found substring, not its end, even though the search is performed backward.

Like *indexOf()*, the *lastIndexOf()* method takes two parameters:

substring
> The substring value for which you want to search.

startIndex
> The optional zero-based starting position from which to search within the string. Zero-based means the first character in the string is at position 0, not 1. If omitted the method begins the search from the end of the string (at index string. length - 1).

When the substring cannot be found in the string, *lastIndexOf()* returns -1:

```
var example:String = "This string contains the word cool twice. Very cool.";

// Get the index of the last occurrence of the substring "cool" within example.
var index:int =  example.lastIndexOf( "cool" );

if ( index != -1 ) {
  // Displays: "String contains word cool at index 47" because the last
  // occurrence of the substring appears starting at index 47 within example.
```

```
    trace( "String contains word cool at index " + index );
}
// Get the index of the next to last occurrence of "cool" within example.
// Pass the method the previous value of index - 1. This starts the
// search one to the left original occurrence, thus finding an earlier occurrence
// from right to left. If you  do not subtract 1 to index when passing it to
// lastIndexOf( ), the method returns the location of the last occurrence again.
index = example.lastIndexOf( "cool", index - 1 );

if ( index != -1 ) {
    // Displays: "String contains word cool at index 30" because the next to last
    // occurrence of the substring appears starting at index 30 within example.
    trace( "String contains word cool at index " + index );
}
```

If you want to retrieve the indices of every occurrence of a substring, you can use the same technique we previously used for *indexOf()*, a combination of a *while* loop and *lastIndexOf()* with a starting index value.

```
var example:String = "This string contains the word cool. Very cool. Yes, cool.";

// Initialize index to example.length so that the while statement starts searching
// at the very last index. The last index is actually example.length - 1, but we
// subtract 1 from the index in the loop so we initialize index carefully here.
var index:int =  example.length;

// Loop until lastIndexOf( ) returns -1.
while ( ( index = example.lastIndexOf( "cool", index - 1 ) ) != -1 ) {

    /* Displays:
       String contains word cool at index 52
       String contains word cool at index 41
       String contains word cool at index 30
    */
    trace( "String contains word cool at index " + index );
}
```

This code block is very similar to the one used for *indexOf()* but there are two subtle differences. The first difference is that we initialize index to example.length instead of -1 as before because *lastIndexOf()* searches from right to left instead of left to right and we need to start our search at the end of the example string. The second difference is that instead of adding 1 to the index for the search, we subtract 1 so that *lastIndexOf()* will search to the left of a previously found occurrence to find all occurrences.

Both the *indexOf()* and *lastIndexOf()* methods are case-sensitive in their searches. For example, the substring "cool" would not be found in the string "Cool" because the cases are not the same. To perform a case-insensitive search, use the *toLowerCase()* method in conjunction with the *indexOf()* or *lastIndexOf()* method.

```
// Create a string that spells "cool" as both "cool" and "Cool".
var example:String = "Cool. This is a string with the word cool. It spells"
                   + " cool as both cool (lowercase) and Cool (capitalized).";
```

```
var search:String = "cool";

// Output the index of the first occurrence of "cool". The result is 37,
// because it does not find "Cool" due to the case-sensitive search.
trace( example.indexOf( search ) );

// Output the index of the first occurrence of "cool" after lowercasing the
// string with toLowerCase(). The result is 0 because it now finds "Cool"
// (which has been converted to cool) at the beginning of the string.
trace( example.toLowerCase().indexOf( search ) );

// Output the index of the last occurrence of "cool". The result is 66,
// because it does not find the last "Cool" due to the case-sensitivity.
trace( example.lastIndexOf( search ) );

// Output the index of the last occurrence of cool after lowercasing the
// string. The result is 87, because it finds the last "Cool".
trace( example.toLowerCase().lastIndexOf( search ) );

// Now, change the search string to "Cool" (capitalized).
search = "Cool";

// Output the index of the first occurrence of "Cool" after lowercasing the
// string. The result is -1, because "Cool" doesn't exist in the lowercase string.
trace( example.toLowerCase().indexOf( search ) );

// This is similar to the preceding line of code, but the search string is also
// converted to lowercase. Therefore, the result is 0, because the starting index
// of the first occurrence of "cool" (regardless of case) is 0. Lowercasing both
// the string being searched and the substring for which you are searching
// ensures that a completely case-insensitive search is performed.
trace( example.toLowerCase().indexOf( search.toLowerCase() ) );
```

In this code snippet, you can freely substitute *toUpperCase()* for *toLowerCase()* for case-insensitive searching. The key is that you force the original string and the substring to the same case (either upper or lower) before starting the search.

See Also

Recipe 13.3

12.5   Extracting a Substring

Problem

You want to extract a substring from a string.

Solution

Use the *substring()*, *substr()*, or *slice()* methods.

Discussion

The *substring()*, *substr()*, and *slice()* methods all return the value of a substring without affecting the original string. The only difference between the three methods is in the parameters they accept.

The *substr()* method takes up to two parameters.

startIndex

> The position of the first character of the substring. The value can be negative, in which case the index is calculated from the end of the string, where -1 is the last character, -2 is the second-to-last character, and so on.

length

> The number of characters in the substring to extract. If this parameter is omitted, all the characters from the start index to the end are used.

```
var example:String = "Bunnies";
trace( example.substr( 0 ) );      // Displays: Bunnies
trace( example.substr( 0, 3 ) );   // Displays: Bun
trace( example.substr( 3, 3 ) );   // Displays: nie
trace( example.substr( -1 ) );     // Displays: s
trace( example.substr( -2, 5 ) );  // Displays: es
```

The *substring()* and *slice()* method both take the same parameters.

startIndex

> The position of the first character of the substring to extract.

endIndex

> The position of one character after the last character in the substring to extract. That is, the substring will include from start index up to, but not including, the character at endIndex. If this parameter is omitted, all the characters from the start index to the end of the string are used.

The *substring()* and *slice()* methods differ in that *substring()* accepts positive index values only; it interprets negative values as 0. Also, if *endIndex* is less than *startIndex*, the *substring()* method automatically reverses them before executing, always using the smaller of the two parameters as the starting index. The *slice()* method, on the other hand, accepts negative values for both *startIndex* and *endIndex*; it interprets negative values as counting back from the end of the string, where -1 is the last character in the string. The *slice()* method returns an empty string if you specify an *endIndex* that is less than *startIndex*.

```
var example:String = "Rabbits";

// Both of these output the entire string, beginning at index 0 and
// going to the last index (the value of which is example.length - 1).
trace( example.substring( 0 ) );   // Displays: Rabbits
trace( example.slice( 0 ) );       // Displays: Rabbits
```

```
// The substring() method outputs nothing because it converts the negative
// indices to 0. The slice() method outputs "it", which is the substring from
// the third-to-last character (index -3) to next-to-last character (index -1).
trace( example.substring( -3, -1 ) );  // Displays nothing (an empty string)
trace( example.slice( -3, -1 ) );      // Displays: it

// Both of these output the substring "ab".
trace( example.substring( 1, 3 ) );    // Displays: ab
trace( example.slice( 1, 3 ) );        // Displays: ab

// The substring() method outputs the substring "ab" because it reverses the
// order of the parameters automatically. The slice() method outputs nothing
// because the slice() method does not reverse the order of the parameters.
trace( example.substring( 3, 1 ) );    // Displays: ab
trace( example.slice( 3, 1 ) );        // Displays nothing (an empty string)
```

You commonly use the substring extraction methods in conjunction with the *indexOf()* and *lastIndexOf()* methods. You can use *indexOf()* and *lastIndexOf()* methods to search for the substring within a string, and then use the substring extraction methods to get the substrings.

This example extracts a file's extension and its filename (without the extension), presumed to be separated from each other by a period:

```
var filename:String = "document.jpg";
// Find the location of the period.
var extensionIndex:Number = filename.lastIndexOf( '.' );

// The extension-less filename ("mydocument") is everything before the period.
var extensionless:String = filename.substr( 0, extensionIndex );
trace( "The filename is " + extensionless );

// The extension ("jpg") is everything after the period.
var extension:String = filename.substr( extensionIndex + 1, filename.length );
trace( "The file extension is " + extension );
```

You can also use the *split()* method, assuming there is only one period in the filename:

```
var filename:String = "document.jpg";
// Split the string wherever the period occurs.
var nameParts:Array = filename.split(".");

// The first element is "document" (everything before the first period).
var extensionless:String = nameParts[0];
trace ("The filename is " + extensionless);

// The next element is "jpg" (anything after the first
// period and before the next one).
var extension:String = nameParts[1];
trace ("The file extension is " + extension);
```

Compare and contrast the two preceding examples. What if the filename doesn't contain a period, e.g., *document*? (Hint: The first example produces invalid results.) What if the filename contains more than one period, such as *ascb_fig8.1.bmp*? (Hint: The second example produces invalid results.)

Here is a general solution:

```
// This method returns everything before the last period, if any.
private function removeExtension( filename:String ):String {
  // Find the location of the period.
  var extensionIndex:Number = filename.lastIndexOf( '.' );
  if ( extensionIndex == -1 ) {
    // Oops, there is no period. Just return the filename.
    return filename;
  } else {
    return filename.substr( 0, extensionIndex );
  }
}

// This method returns everything after the last period, if any.
private function extractExtension( filename:String ):String {
  // Find the location of the period.
  var extensionIndex:Number = filename.lastIndexOf( '.' );
  if ( extensionIndex == -1 ) {
    // Oops, there is no period, so return the empty string.
    return "";
  } else {
    return filename.substr( extensionIndex + 1, filename.length );
  }
}
```

Here's example usage:

```
trace( removeExtension( "document.jpg" ) );      // Displays: document
trace( removeExtension( "document" ) );          // Displays: document
trace( removeExtension( "document.1.jpg" ) );    // Displays: document.1
trace( extractExtension( "document.jpg" ) );     // Displays: .jpg
trace( extractExtension( "document" ) );         // Displays nothing
trace( extractExtension( "document.1.jpg" ) );   // Displays: .jpg
```

See Also

Recipe 12.6

12.6   Parsing a String into Words

Problem

You want to process the individual words in a string.

Solution

Use the *split()* method.

Discussion

The *split()* method, Recipe 5.6, splits a string into an array using the specified delimiter. To split a string into words, use the *split()* method with a space as the delimiter.

```
// Create a string with multiple words.
var example:String = "This is a string of words";

// Split the string into an array of words using a space as the delimiter.
var words:Array = example.split( " " );

// Loop through the array and do something with each word.
// In this example, just output the values.
for ( var i:int = 0; i < words.length; i++ ) {
  /* Displays:
     this
     is
     a
     string
     of
     words
  */
  trace( words[i] );
}
```

You can process the individual words in many ways. The following is a complete example that uses this technique to split a string into words and then creates sprites containing those words. The user can then drag the words around on stage to form various sentences or statements similar to the popular magnetic poetry kits:

```
package {

  import flash.display.Sprite;
  import flash.events.MouseEvent;
  import flash.text.TextField;
  import flash.text.TextFieldAutoSize;
  import flash.display.StageAlign;
  import flash.display.StageScaleMode;

  public class ActionScriptPoetry extends Sprite {

    public function ActionScriptPoetry( ) {

      stage.align = StageAlign.TOP_LEFT;
      stage.scaleMode = StageScaleMode.NO_SCALE;

      // Create a string, and split the string into an array of words.
      var example:String = "This is a string of ActionScript poetry words";
      var words:Array = example.split(" ");
      var word:Sprite;
      var wordText:TextField;
```

```
  // Loop through all the words in the array.
  for ( var i:int = 0; i < words.length; i++ ) {

    // Create a new sprite for each word and add it to the
    // display list so the sprite is drawn on-screen
    word = new Sprite( );
    addChild( word );

    // Create a text field within the sprite by creating a new
    // TextField instance and adding it as a child
    wordText = new TextField( );
    word.addChild( wordText );

    // The text field should autosize to fit its contents. It should also have
    // a border and background so that it mimics the look of poetry magnets,
    // and the text should not be selectable since we want to drag it around.
    wordText.autoSize   = TextFieldAutoSize.LEFT; // Left-justify the text
    wordText.border     = true;
    wordText.background = true;
    wordText.selectable = false;

    // Set each text fields's text value to one of the words from the array.
    wordText.text = words[i];

    // The sprite is draggable when clicked, and it stops being
    // draggable when released.
    word.addEventListener( MouseEvent.MOUSE_DOWN, handleDrag );
    word.addEventListener( MouseEvent.MOUSE_UP, handleDrop );

    // Randomize the position of the sprites containing words
    var rx:Number = Math.random( ) * stage.stageWidth  - word.width;
    var ry:Number = Math.random( ) * stage.stageHeight - word.height;
    word.x = rx;
    word.y = ry;
    trace(word);
  }
}

// This function is called when the uses presses a word with the mouse
private function handleDrag( event:MouseEvent ):void {
  // The event target will be the TextField, so to get the
  // word we work up to the parent
  var word:Sprite = event.target.parent;

  // Make the clicked on word draw on top of everything else
  setChildIndex( word, numChildren - 1 );

  // Drag the word around to coincide with mouse movement
  word.startDrag( );
}

// This function is called when the user releases the mouse
private function handleDrop( event:MouseEvent ):void {
```

```
    // The event target will be the TextField, the parent is the Sprite
    var word:Sprite = event.target.parent;

    // Stop moving the word around with the mouse
    word.stopDrag();
  }
 }
}
```

The preceding use of *split()* by itself is all you need when the original string value contains words and spaces but no punctuation. If the string has punctuation or other miscellaneous characters, you should use a regular expression as the parameter to *split()* to remove them. The regular expression to match punctuation around words should be constructed using the value /[^a-zA-Z0-9]+/.

```
// Create a string that uses punctuation.
var example:String = "Here are some words. Also, here is some punctuation!";

// Create an array of words from the string without first removing punctuation.
var words:Array = example.split( ' ' );

// Display the elements of the array. Some of the elements also contain the
// punctuation. This is likely undesirable.
for ( var i:int = 0; i < words.length; i++ ) {
  /* Outputs:
     Here
     are
     some
     words.
     Also,
     here
     is
     some
     punctuation!
  */
  trace( words[i] );
}

// Use a regular expression for punctuation and splits around that to produce
// a cleaned array of words from the string
words = example.split( /[^a-zA-Z0-9]+/ );

// Output all the elements of the words array. This time each element is a word,
// and none of the elements include punctuation.
for ( i = 0; i < words.length; i++ ) {
  /* Outputs:
     Here
     are
     some
     words
     Also
     here
     is
     some
```

```
          punctuation
    */
    trace( words[i] );
  }
```

Regular expressions, covered in Chapter 13, are a powerful new feature of Action-Script 3.0.

See Also

Chapter 13; Recipes 5.6 and 12.5

12.7   Removing and Replacing Characters and Words

Problem

You want to remove characters from a string or replace one substring with another.

Solution

Use the *replace()* method or *split()* and *join()* combination.

Discussion

ActionScript 3.0 includes a new method *String.replace()*, not found in previous versions, that allows you to replace substrings within a string. This method accepts two parameters:

pattern
> The substring or regular expression you want to find and replace.

replace
> The value with which to replace each pattern match. This value is typically a string but can also be a function that returns a string. It is useful when pattern is a regular expression.

There are two uses of this method based on the parameters provided. This recipe focuses on using a string for the pattern. A regular expression pattern also can be used, as covered in Recipe 13.4.

Here is a simple example of replacing a substring in a sentence. The *replace()* method returns a new string with pattern replaced by replace, leaving the original string unmodified.

```
var example:String = "This is a cool sentence."

// Replace " is " with " is not " in example.
// Displays: This is not a cool sentence.
trace( example.replace( " is ", " is not " ) );
```

In this example, the word "is" is surrounded by spaces when used as the pattern. This is important because failing to do so matches the "is" in "This" and the sentence starts with "This not is," which is not the desired effect.

When a string is used for the pattern in the *replace()* method, the method lacks functionality compared to using a regular expression. The two biggest problems are that only the first occurrence of pattern is replaced and you have to roll your own solution for case-insensitive replacement.

To replace all occurrences, you have to use a combination of a loop and the replace method:

```
// Create a string with contractions, and another string to store the replacements
var example:String = "It's a bird, it's a plane, it's ActionScript Man!";
var replaced:String = example; // Initialize replaced with the original text

// As long as the pattern substring is found in replaced, we need to replace again
while ( replaced.indexOf( "it's" ) != -1 ) {
  // Replace the first instance of "it's" with "it is".
  replaced = replaced.replace( "it's", "it is" );
}

// To get around the case-sensitivity problem, we need to change the pattern and
// go through the replace process again. This fixes the uppercase "It's"
replaced = replaced.replace( "It's", "It is" );

// Outputs: It is a bird, it is a plane, it is ActionScript Man!
trace( replaced );
```

The *split()* method also can be used to replace and remove characters and words in a string. Unlike using *replace()* with a string pattern, *split* replaces all occurrences of a word. However, both methods share the same case-sensitivity problem. The following is an example of replacing the HTML <br> tag with the \n character to properly break a sentence into multiple lines:

```
var example:String = "This is<br>a sentence<br>on 3 lines";

// Remove the <br> tags and replace them with newline characters ('\n')
/* Display:
  This is
  a sentence
  on 3 lines
*/
trace( example.split( "<br>" ).join( '\n' ) );
```

When a string is split, an array of strings is returned. The *Array.join()* method can then be used to build a new string out of the individual array elements. Splitting removes the delimiter, allowing us to join the string again with a new delimiter passed to the *join()* method. This technique replaces all occurrences of the delimiter passed to split.

To remove characters or words instead of replacing them simply use the empty string as the replacement string:

```
var example:String = "This is a cool sentence.";
// Remove the word "cool" and it's trailing space from example
// Displays: This is a sentence.
trace( example.replace( "cool ", "" ) );
```

See Also

Recipes 12.4 and 12.7

12.8   Retrieving One Character at a Time

Problem

You want to retrieve one character at a time from a string.

Solution

Use a *for* statement and the *String.charAt()* method. Alternatively, use *String.split()* with the empty string as the delimiter to split the string into an array of all the characters, and then use a *for* statement to loop through the array.

Discussion

The simplest way to extract each character of a string is to use a *for* statement that loops over all of the character positions in the string from index zero to string. length - 1, incrementing by one on each iteration. Within the *for* statement body, you can use the *charAt()* method to extract the character for processing.

```
var example:String = "a string";

// Loop over all of the chatacters of the string.
for ( var i:int = 0; i < example.length; i++ ) {
  /* Output each character, one at a time. This displays:
    a

    s
    t
    r
    i
    n
    g
  */
  trace( example.charAt( i ) );
}
```

You can achieve the same effect by using the *split()* method to first split the string into an array of characters, and then looping through the array to process each character. Use the empty string as the delimiter parameter for the *split()* method to break between each character.

```
var example:String = "a string";

// Split the string into an array of characters (one-character strings).
var characters:Array = example.split( "" );

// Loop through all the elements of the characters array.
for ( var i:int = 0; i < characters.length; i++ ) {
  /* Output each character element. This displays:
    a

    s
    t
    r
    i
    n
    g
  */
  trace( characters[i] );
}
```

Both techniques are generally interchangeable, though the second one offers some advantages if you want to work with the characters by using common array methods. For example, if you first split a string into an array of characters, you can sort that array. This is not as easily done when you use the *charAt()* technique:

```
var example:String = "a string";

var characters:Array = example.split( "" );

// Alphabetically sort the array of characters.
characters.sort( );

for ( var i:int = 0; i < characters.length; i++) {
  /* Displays:

    a
    g
    i
    n
    r
    s
    t
  */
  trace( characters[i] );
}
```

Also, if you want to use this process to remove every instance of a particular character, it is easier with an array than with the *charAt()* technique:

```
var example:String = "a string";

var characters:Array = example.split( "" );

for ( var i:Number = 0; i < characters.length; i++ ) {
  // Remove all "r" elements from the array. Be sure to decrement i if an
  // element is removed; otherwise, the next element is improperly skipped.
  if ( characters[i] == "r") {
    characters.splice( i, 1 );
    i--;
  }
}

// Displays: a sting
trace( characters.join( "" ) );
```

Although the preceding technique for replacing characters works for simple cases, you should see Recipe 12.7 for more capable alternatives.

See Also

Recipe 12.7

12.9   Converting Case

Problem

You want to change the case of a string or perform a case-insensitive comparison.

Solution

Use the *toUpperCase()* and *toLowerCase()* methods.

Discussion

The *toUpperCase()* and *toLowerCase()* methods return new strings in which all the characters are uppercase or lowercase, respectively, without modifying the original string. This is useful in situations in which you want to ensure uniformity of case. For example, you can use *toLowerCase()* or *toUpperCase()* to perform case-insensitive searches within strings, as is shown in Recipe 12.4. Both methods affect alphabetical characters only, leaving non-alphabetic characters unchanged:

```
var example:String = "What case?";

// Displays: what case?
trace( example.toLowerCase() );

// Displays: WHAT CASE?
trace( example.toUpperCase() );

// The original string value is unchanged: What case?
trace( example );
```

Both methods return a new string. To alter the original string, reassign the return value to it, as follows:

```
var example:String = example.toLowerCase( );
```

You can use *toLowerCase( )* and *toUpperCase( )* in concert to capitalize the first letter of a word. The custom *ascb.util.StringUtilities.toInitialCap( )* method does just that. The following is the code in the *StringUtilities* class in which the *toInitialCap( )* method is defined:

```
public static function toInitialCap( original:String ):String {
    return original.charAt( 0 ).toUpperCase( ) + original.substr( 1 ).toLowerCase( );
}
```

The following is an example usage of the method:

```
var example:String = "bRuCE";
trace( StringUtilities.toInitialCap( example ) );    // Displays: Bruce
```

The *toTitleCase( )* method converts a string to so-called title case (initial letters capitalized). The following is the definition of the method:

```
public static function toTitleCase( original:String ):String {
    var words:Array = original.split( " " );
    for (var i:int = 0; i < words.length; i++) {
        words[i] = toInitialCap( words[i] );
    }
    return ( words.join( " " ) );
}
```

And the following is a sample usage of the method:

```
var example:String = "the actionScript cookbook";

// Displays: The ActionScript Cookbook
trace( StringUtilities.toTitleCase( example ) );
```

See Also

Recipe 12.4

12.10 Trimming Whitespace

Problem

You want to trim the whitespace from the beginning and end of a string.

Solution

Use the custom *ascb.util.StringUtilities.trim( )* method. Alternatively, if you are using the Flex 2 framework, you can use the *mx.utils.StringUtil.trim( )* static method.

Discussion

Extra whitespace at the beginning and end of a string is a common enough annoyance that you should have a way of dealing with it. ActionScript does not provide a native *trim()* implementation, so you have to either write your own or use a precoded solution.

The basic steps involved are as follows.

1. Split the string into an array of characters.
2. Remove whitespace elements at the beginning of the array until there is not a whitespace character (tab, form feed, carriage return, newline, or space).
3. Remove whitespace elements at the end of the array.
4. Use *join()* to form the array characters into a single string and return that value.

The *ascb.util.StringUtilities.trim()* method works as described in the preceding steps. The following is the actual definition of the method, along with the *isWhitespace()* helper method:

```
// Returns true if the character is a whitespace character
public static function isWhitespace( ch:String ):Boolean {
  return ch == '\r' ||
         ch == '\n' ||
         ch == '\f' ||
         ch == '\t' ||
         ch == ' ';
}

public static function trim( original:String ):String {

  // Split the string into an array of characters.
  var characters:Array = original.split( "" );

  // Remove any whitespace elements from the beginning of the array using
  // splice(). Use a break statement to exit the loop when you reach a
  // non-whitespace character to prevent it from removing whitespace
  // in the middle of the string.
  for ( var i:int = 0; i < characters.length; i++ ) {
    if ( isWhitespace( characters[i] ) ) {
      characters.splice( i, 1 );
      i--;
    } else {
      break;
    }
  }

  // Loop backward through the array removing whitespace elements until a
  // non-whitespace character is encountered. Then break out of the loop.
  for ( i = characters.length - 1; i >= 0; i-- ) {
    if ( isWhitespace( characters[i] ) ) {
      characters.splice( i, 1 );
```

```
    } else {
      break;
    }
  }

  // Recreate the string with the join() method and return the result.
  return characters.join("");
}
```

The following illustrates how you can use the *trim()* method.

```
// Create a string with beginning and ending whitespace.
var example:String = "\n\r\f\ta string\t\t\n\n";

/* Display the value before calling the trim() method. Displays:
this string value is:


    a string

<end>
*/
trace( "this string value is: " + example + "<end>" );

// Set example to the value returned by the trim() method.
example = StringUtilities.trim( example );

// Now, display the value again using the same trace() statement.
//Displays: this string value is: a string<end>
trace( "this string value is: " + example + "<end>" );
```

The Flex 2 framework implementation of trim is almost exactly the same. Here is some example code for that:

```
// Displays: a string<end>
trace( StringUtil.trim( "\n  \r\ta string\t\t\n\n" ) + "<end>" );
```

12.11 Reversing a String by Word or by Character

Problem

You want to reverse a string either by word or by character.

Solution

Use the *split()* method to create an array of the words/characters and use the *reverse()* and *join()* methods on that array.

Discussion

You can reverse a string by word or character by using the same process. The only difference is in the delimiter you use in the *split()* method and the joiner you use in the *join()* method. In either case, the basic algorithm is:

1. Split the string into an array, using a space as the delimiter for words or the empty string as the delimiter for characters.
2. Call the *reverse()* method of the array, which reverses the order of the elements.
3. Use the *join()* method to reconstruct the string. When you are reversing by word, use a space as the joiner; when reversing by character, use the empty string as the joiner:

The following code illustrates the process:

```
var example:String = "hello dear reader";

// Split the string into an array of words.
var words:Array = example.split( " " );

// Reverse the array.
words.reverse( );

// Join the elements of the array into a string using spaces.
var exampleRevByWord:String = words.join( " " );

// Displays: reader dear hello
trace( exampleRevByWord );

// Split the string into an array of characters.
var characters:Array = example.split( "" );

// Reverse the array elements.
characters.reverse( );

// Join the array elements into a string using the empty string.
var exampleRevByChar:String = characters.join( "" );

// Displays: redaer raed olleh
trace( exampleRevByChar );
```

12.12 Converting Between Strings and Unicode or ASCII

Problem

You want to convert between characters and their corresponding Unicode code point (a.k.a. character code). Or you want to convert strings to and from ASCII codes.

Solution

Use the *String.charCodeAt()* and *String.fromCharCode()* methods.

Discussion

You can use *fromCharCode()* to display characters you cannot directly enter into your Flash document. The method is a static method, which means that it is invoked from the top-level *String* object instead of from a string instance. It takes an integer or a series of integers and coverts the character codes to their string equivalents. When values less than 128 are used, *fromCharCode()* essentially converts a numeric ASCII code to its equivalent character:

```
/* Displays:
   New paragraph: &#182;
   Cents: &#162;
   Name: Darron
*/
trace( "New paragraph: " + String.fromCharCode( 182 ) );
trace( "Cents: " + String.fromCharCode( 162 ) );
trace( "Name: " + String.fromCharCode( 68, 97, 114, 114, 111, 110 ) );
```

The *charCodeAt()* method can be used to retrieve the code point of the character at a particular index of a string. For characters whose Unicode code point is less than 128, *charCodeAt()* converts a character to its equivalent ASCII code:

```
var example:String = "abcd";

// Outputs the code point, 97, of the first character, a.
trace( example.charCodeAt( 0 ) );
```

The *fromCharCode()* method is an alternative to using Unicode escape sequences to display special characters. However, you can also use *fromCharCode()* in concert with *charCodeAt()* to test for the existence of special characters:

```
var example:String = String.fromCharCode( 191 ) + "D"
            + String.fromCharCode( 243 ) + "nde est"
            + String.fromCharCode( 225 ) + " el ba"
            + String.fromCharCode( 241 )  + "o?";

// Test whether the first character of the string has the code point of
// 191. Use the unicode escape sequence instead of fromCharCode( 191 ) to
// produce the speical character. If so displays: The string "&#191;D&#243;nde
est&#225;
// el ba&#241;o?" has a &#191; at the beginning.
if ( example.charCodeAt( 0 ) == 191 ) {
  trace( "The string \"" + example + "\" has a \u00BF at the beginning." );
}
```

You can use the *charCodeAt()* and *fromCharCode()* methods in concert to encode and decode a string.

The following methods are useful for creating cryptographic word games, but they are not secure and should not be used for sensitive data.

```
public static function encode( original:String ):String {

  // The codeMap property is assigned to the StringUtilities class when the encode( )
  // method is first run. Therefore, if no codeMap is yet defined, it needs
  // to be created.
  if ( codeMap == null ) {

    // The codeMap property is an associative array that maps each original code
    // point to another code point.
    codeMap = new Object( );

    // Create an array of all the code points from 0 to 255.
    var originalMap:Array = new Array( );
    for ( var i:int = 0; i < 256 ; i++ ) {
      originalMap.push( i );
    }

    // Create a temporary array that is a copy of the originalMap array.
    var tempChars:Array = originalMap.concat( );

    // Loop through all the character code points in originalMap.
    for ( var i:int = 0; i < originalMap.length; i++ ) {

      // Create a random number that is between 0 and the last index of tempChars.
      var randomIndex:int = Math.floor( Math.random( ) * ( tempChars.length - 1 ) );

      // Assign to codeMap values such that the keys are the original code points,
      // and the values are the code points to which they should be mapped.
      codeMap[ originalMap[i] ] = tempChars[ randomIndex ];

      // Remove the elements from tempChars that was just assigned to codeMap.
      // This prevents duplicates.
      tempChars.splice( randomIndex, 1 );
    }
  }

  // Split the string into an array of characters.
  var characters:Array = original.split("");

  // Replace each character in the array with the corresponding value from codeMap.
  for ( i = 0; i < characters.length; i++ ) {
    characters[i] = String.fromCharCode( codeMap[ characters[i].charCodeAt( 0 ) ] );
  }

  // Return the encoded string.
  return characters.join( "" );
}
```

```
public static function decode( encoded:String ):String {

  // Split the encoded string into an array of characters.
  var characters:Array = encoded.split( "" );

  // The reverseCodeMap property is assigned the first time the decode( ) method is
  // first run. Therefore, if no reverseCodeMap is yet defined, it needs to be
  // created.
  if ( reverseCodeMap == null ) {

    // Create an associative array that reverses the keys and values of codeMap.
    // This allows you to do a reverse lookup based on the encoded character
    // rather than the original character.
    reverseCodeMap = new Object();
    for ( var key in codeMap ) {
      reverseCodesMap[ codeMap[key] ] = key;
    }
  }

  // Loop through all the characters in the array, and replace them
  // with the corresponding value from reverseCodeMap, thus recovering
  // the original character values.
  for ( var i:int = 0; i < characters.length; i++ ) {
    characters[i] = String.fromCharCode( reverseCodeMap[ characters[i].charCodeAt( 0
) ] );
  }

  // Return the decoded string.
  return characters.join( "" );
}
```

The following is a simple usage example:

```
var example:String = "Peter Piper picked a peck of pickled peppers.";

// Create the encoded version of example using the encode( ) method.
var encoded:String = StringUtilities.encode( example );

// Output the value of the encoded string. This will be randomly generated
// each time you run the movie. It might look something like this:
//
æT#Tm&#239;æ~*Tm&#239;*~NcT&#173;&#239;?&#239;*TNc&#239;?2&#239;*~Nc?T&#173;&#239;*T*
*Tm:V
trace( encoded );

// Output the value returned by the decode( ) method:
// Displays: Peter Piper picked a peck of pickled peppers.
trace( StringUtilities.decode( encoded ) );
```

Regular Expressions

13.0 Introduction

One of the most powerful features added to ActionScript 3.0 is *regular expressions* (more commonly known as *regexes* or *regexps*). Regular expressions are, put simply, patterns that can be matched against strings. You may be familiar with other types of patterns, such as wildcards (e.g., * and ?), which can be used to match patterns while searching for files. Patterns are also used in Recipe 9.5. Regular expressions support this type of pattern matching, but they are also much more sophisticated.

Regular expressions can be useful in many situations. For instance, the patterns can be applied against strings to perform a variety of tasks, including:

- Finding substrings beginning with a vowel (a, e, i, o, or u)
- Extracting specific values within a string, such as the year value from a full date
- Validating user input to ensure an email address is formatted correctly
- Stripping out HTML tags from a block of text to remove the markup

The patterns used for regular expressions are built by combining characters that have special meaning and can range from being very simple:

```
[a-zA-Z]
```

to being extremely complex and cryptic, such as this regex for matching a valid IP address:

```
^([01]?\d\d?|2[0-4]\d|25[0-5])\.([01]?\d\d?|2[0-4]\d|25[0-5])\.([01]?\d\d?|2[0-4]\d|25[0-5])\.([01]?\d\d?|2[0-4]\d|25[0-5])$
```

Simple patterns, such as .*, are easy to understand, but more complex patterns are difficult to learn and are even harder to implement. Thankfully, every regular expression can be broken down into a plain English description. For example, the simple regular expression .* means "any character repeated any number of times." More complex patterns, such as (A|a)ction(S|s)cript, are no different because they are built by combining simple patterns in various ways. The pattern (A|a)ction(S|s)cript means "either a capital or lowercase 'a', followed by the string 'ction', followed by either a capital or lowercase 's', followed by the string 'cript'," and can be used to find occurrences of "ActionScript" (and subtle variations, such as "actionScript") in a string.

 Mastering the syntax of regular expressions is not trivial. As with anything else, a little effort to learn the basic principles can go a long way, and knowing and understanding regular expressions is a powerful tool to have at your fingertips.

To learn more about regular expressions, you should get a copy of *Mastering Regular Expressions*, by Jeffrey E.F. Friedl (O'Reilly), or *Regular Expressions Pocket Reference*, by Tony Stubblebine (O'Reilly). Both books teach you everything you need to know about regexes.

Despite how complex regular expression patterns can be, it's fairly easy to use regular expressions in ActionScript, as you'll soon discover. This chapter focuses on the more common uses of regular expressions within the context of Flash and Action-Script, and by no means is an exhaustive or comprehensive guide.

13.1 Understanding Regular Expression Patterns

Problem

You want to understand the basic building blocks of regular expressions.

Solution

Regular expressions are built by combining characters with special meaning. First start by learning the basic patterns, and then use this knowledge to put together more complex patterns.

Discussion

A regular expression is a *pattern* constructed using the regular expression syntax and is typically used during text processing and pattern matching. The syntax consists of characters, *metacharacters*, and *metasequences*. Characters are interpreted literally, whereas metacharacters and metasequences have special meaning in the regular expression context. For example, the regular expression built from the characters hello matches the string "hello," whereas the regular expression consisting only of the . metacharacter means "any character" and matches "a", "b", "1", etc. Additionally, the regular expression built from using the \d metasequence matches any digit, such as "1" or "9".

Before getting too in-depth with the regular expression syntax, let's start by discussing how regular expressions are created in ActionScript 3.0. Regular expressions are built with the *RegExp* class and can be constructed from either a string describing the pattern or from a *regular expression literal*. A regular expression literal is a forward slash, followed by the regular expression pattern, followed by another forward slash, such as */pattern/*. The follow code demonstrates how to create a regular expression for the pattern hello by using both a string and the *RegExp* constructor, as well as a regular expression literal:

```
// Create a pattern for hello using the RegExp class constructor
// passing in a string describing the pattern
var example1:RegExp = new RegExp( "hello" );

// Create the same hello pattern using a regular expression literal
var example2:RegExp = /hello/;
```

Both the example1 and example2 regular expressions match the same pattern, namely the string "hello." In general, the pattern is the same regardless of which method you use to create the regular expression. However, when a backslash (\) is part of the regular expression pattern, using a string and the *RegExp* constructor gets tricky.

Because the *RegExp* object is created by passing a string to the constructor, all references to \ within the string must be escaped as \\. Since \ is also a special character in *RegExp* patterns, to search for backslash in a regular expression, you must escape it like this: \\\\.

Backslashes mark the beginning of an escape sequence inside a string (see Recipe 12.3) and lose their meaning in the regular expression context. That is, the backslash is interpreted as a special string character before being interpreted in the regex. Therefore, if you want to match a pattern with a backslash, you have to use a double backslash in the string approach. The regular expression literal does not have the same problem:

```
// Create a regular expression to match a digit (note the double
// backslash)
var example1:RegExp = new RegExp( "\\d" );

// Create a regular expression to match a digit
var example2:RegExp = /\d/;

// Create a regular expression that matches a backslash.
var example3:RegExp = new RegExp("\\\\");

// Create a regular expression to match a backslash
Var example4:RegExp = /\\/;
```

The preferred way to create regular expressions is by using regular expression literals, and this convention is used throughout the rest of this chapter.

By now you know that characters in a regular expression pattern are interpreted literally. By combining metacharacters and metasequences with regular characters, you can create powerful combinations useful for matching many pattern types. Let's take a look at the metacharacters, what they mean, and how they might be used.

Table 13-1 summarizes the regular expression metacharacters. Any time you want to use one of these metacharacters literally, it must be preceded by a backslash. For example, to match an open curly brace, use the regular expression \{.

Table 13-1. Regular expression metacharacters

Expression	Meaning	Example
?	Matches the preceding character zero or one time (i.e., preceding character is optional)	ta?k matches *tak* or *tk* but not *tik* or *taak*
*	Matches the preceding character zero or more times	wo*k matches *wok*, *wk*, or *woook*, but not *wak*
+	Matches the preceding character one or more times	craw+l matches *crawl* or *crawwwl* but not *cral*
. (period)	Matches any one character except newline (unless the *dotall* flag is set)	c.ow matches *crow* or *clow* but not *cow*
^	Matches the start of the string (also matches the start of a line when the *multiline* flag is set)	^wap matches *wap* but not *swap*
$	Matches the end of the string (also matches the position before a newline "\n" when the *multiline* flag is set)	ow$ matches *ow* but not *owl*
|	Matches either the left or right side of the pipe	one|two matches *one* or *two* but not *ten*
\	Escapes the special meaning of the metacharacter following the backslash	\. matches a period, instead of "any one character" like the metacharacter . would
(and)	Creates groups within the regular expression to: • Define the scope of | • Define the scope of { and } • Use back references, where \1 refers to whatever is matched in the first group, etc.	l(o|a)g matches *log* or *lag* but not *lug* a(b){1,2} matches *ab* or *abb* but not *a* (a|b)\1 matches *aa* or *bb* but not *ab* or *ba*
[and]	Defines character classes that represent matches for a single character. • Presence of a - indicates a range of characters • A caret (^) at the beginning negates the character class (everything except what is defined by the class matches) • Metacharacters do not need to be escaped with a backslash (but a dash and beginning caret do)	l[oa]g matches *log* or *lag* but not *lug* [a-z] matches any lowercase character such as *a* or *h* but not *1*, *2*, or *F* l[^oa]g matches *lug* but not *lag* or *log* [+\-] matches + or -

Similar to metacharacters, the metasequences are described in Table 13-2 listing what the expression matches along with an example.

Table 13-2. Regular expression metasequences

Expression	Matches	Example
{*n*}	Exactly *n* occurrences of the preceding character or group	Cre{2}l matches *creel* but not *crel* or *creel*
{*n*,}	At least *n* occurrences of the preceding character or group	Cre{2,}l matches *creel* or *creeeel* but not *crel*
{*n*,*m*}	At least *n* but no more than *m* instances of preceding character or group	Cre{2,3}l matches *creel* or *creeel* but not *crel* or *creel*
\A	At the start of the string; similar to (^)	\Awap matches *wap* but not *swap*
\b	Word boundary	\b7\b matches *7* but not *71* or *573*
\B	Non-word boundary	\B7\B matches *573* but not *71* or *7* or *37*
\d	Any numeric digit; same as [0-9]	a\d matches *a1* and *a8* but not *ab* or *ad*
\D	Any non-digit character; same as [^0-9]	a\D matches *aB* and *ak*, but not *a8* or *a1*
\n	The newline character	a\nb matches "a\nb"
\r	The return character	a\rb matches "a\rb"
\s	Single whitespace character (space, tab, line feed, or form feed)	King\sTut matches *King Tut* and *King\tTut*
\S	Single nonwhitespace character	\STut matches *gTut* but not *Tut*
\t	The tab character	a\tb matches "a\tb"
\u*nnnn*	The Unicode character specified by the hex digits *nnnn*	\u000a matches "\n"
\w	Any word character; same as [A-Za-z0-9_]	a\wm matches *arm* and *a8m*, but not *a m* or *aém*
\W	Any non-word character; same as [^A-Za-z0-9_]	a\Wm matches *a m* or *aém*, but not *a7m* or *aim*
\x*nn*	The ASCII character specified by the hex digits *nn*	\x0a matches "\n"
\Z	The end of the string; matches *before* the line break if the string ends in one	ab\Z matches "ab\n" and ab, but not "ab\nc"
\z	The end of the string; matches *after* the line break if the string ends in one	ab\z matches ab, but not "ab\n" or "ab\nc"

Table 13-1 and Table 13-2 describe the basic syntax rules that make up regular expressions. By combining characters, metacharacters, and metasequences, you can match a wide variety of patterns. There is more to the story, however.

Regular expressions can also include certain flags that indicate if any special processing should be done with the pattern. There are five flags that can be accessed as properties of a *RegExp* object: global, ignoreCase, multiline, dotall, and extended.

The flags must be set when the expression is created; trying to modify a flag on a *RegExp* instance results in a compile-time error:

```
// Generates a compile-time error in strict mode:
// Property is read-only
example.global = true;
```

There are two ways to set flags, depending on which method is used to create the regex. When using the *RegExp* constructor, you can pass a second string parameter that lists the flags for the regex. When using a regular expression literal, the flags should follow the trailing forward slash that ends the expression:

```
// Create a regular expression with the global and ignoreCase flags
var example1:RegExp = new RegExp( "hello", "gi" );

// Create a regular expression with the global and ignoreCase flags
var example2:RegExp = /hello/gi;
```

By default, all the flags are set to `false` unless they are explicitly declared when the regex is created. Table 13-3 lists the various flags and their meaning.

Table 13-3. Regular expression flags

Flag	Meaning	Example
g (global)	Matches more than one match	/the/g matches *the* multiple times
i (ignoreCase)	Performs a case-insensitive match for [a-z] and [A-Z] (and not special characters like é)	/a/i matches *a* and *A*
m (multiline)	Allows ^ to match the end of a line; allows $ to match the beginning of a line	/^a/m matches both \n*a* and *a*
s (dotall)	Allows . to match the newline character \n	/a./s matches both *a*\n and *ab*
x (extended)	Allows spaces in the regex that are ignored by the pattern, allowing regex to be written more clearly	/a \d/x matches *a2* but not *a 2* (with a space between the characters)

The most commonly used flags are `ignoreCase` and `global`, but specifying the extended flag can help in understanding regexes. With the extended flag set, you can insert extra whitespace to highlight the different parts that make up the expression; for example:

```
var example1:RegExp = /(a(b)*){2,}/
```

```
// Use the extended flag for slightly more readability
var example2:RegExp = /(a (b)* ){2,}/x;
```

The preceding code creates a regular expression for "a, followed by b any number of times, with the whole expression repeated at least 2 times" and matches "abba" and "abbbabbbbbbb," but not "abbb."

A key point to remember is that every regex can be reduced to these fundamental building blocks. Understanding this and learning how to break down complex regex patterns will help avoid some of the frustration associated with learning regular expressions. It's worth your time to learn regular expressions, and once you've got them down, they'll prove to be a valuable tool to have on your belt.

See Also

Recipes 9.5 and 12.3. A good reference for regular expressions can be found at *http://www.regular-expressions.info*. See *Mastering Regular Expressions*, by Jeffrey Friedl (O'Reilly) for extensive practice with regular expressions and *Regular Expressions Pocket Reference*, by Tony Stubblebine (O'Reilly) for a quick lookup guide.

13.2 Testing Regular Expressions

Problem

You want to test a regex against a string to determine if a match can be made.

Solution

Use the *RegExp.test()* and *RexExp.exec()* methods.

Discussion

Recipe 13.1 discusses the building blocks of regular expressions. Once you have created a regular expression that describes the pattern of what you want to find in a string, there are two methods from the *RegExp* class that can perform the search, *test()* and *exec()*.

To determine whether a pattern can be matched against a string, use the *test()* method on a *RegExp* instance. The *test()* method takes the string being tested against as the parameter and returns a Boolean value of true if the pattern can be matched, and false otherwise:

```
// Create a pattern to match against a string
var example:RegExp = /abc/;

// Displays: true
trace( example.test( "A string with abc in it" ) );

// Displays: true
trace( example.test( "abc" ) );

// Displays: false
trace( example.test( "Another string to test against..." ) );
```

The *test()* method returns true if the regular expression can be matched anywhere in the string, but it won't allow you to extract the match or determine where in the string the match was found. To retrieve this information, use the *exec()* method.

The *exec()* method works in much the same way that *test()* does, except that instead of returning a Boolean value, an array is returned containing the substring that matched the pattern. If no match is found, *exec()* returns null.

```
// Create a pattern to match against a string
var example:RegExp = /abc/;

// Save the result of a string with a substring that matches
// the pattern
var result:Array = example.exec( "A string with abc in it" );

// Displays: abc
trace( result );
// Displays: 14
trace( result.index );

// Save the result of a string that doesn't contain a match for
// the pattern
result = example.exec( "A string with no match" );

// Displays null
trace( result );
```

By default, the *exec()* starts searching from the beginning of the string and returns an array containing the first match that it finds, or null if no match is found. The array returned contains two properties when a match is found:

- index, which points to the starting location in which the matching substring was found.
- input, which is the string that the regex was executed against.

In most cases, the array returned from *exec()* contains a single element—the substring that matched the regex. However, when parentheses are used in the pattern to group certain elements together, each substring that matches a group is another element in the returned result:

```
var example:RegExp = /(\d)abc(\d*)/;

var result:Array = example.exec( "7abc" );

// Displays: 3
trace( result.length );
// Displays: 7abc
trace( result[0] );
// Displays: 7
trace( result[1] );
// Displays:
trace( result[2] );
```

The pattern used for example contains two groups—one for "a digit" and another for "a digit repeated any number of times, including 0." After the *exec()* method is invoked, the result is an array containing three elements instead of just one.

- The first element, at position 0, is the actual substring that matched the regular expression, in this case "7abc."
- The second element, at position 1, is the string that matched the first parenthetical group \d, which in this case is "7" because the group calls for a digit.
- The third element, at position 2, is the empty string because the second group \d*, which means "a digit repeated any number of times, including 0," was matched against the empty string.

As noted earlier, *exec()* always starts searching from the beginning of the target string, at position 0, to find a match. However, when a regex is flagged as global, the lastIndex property of the regex determines the starting position to look for a pattern match. Every time the *exec()* method is called on a global regex, the lastIndex property is automatically set to the position that immediately follows the last character in the matching substring. To match all occurrences of a pattern in a string, *exec()* needs to be called multiple times on a global regex—one time for each match. Additionally, the lastIndex property can be set by hand to find a match after a specific position in the string.

 The *exec()* method continues to cycle through the string with each call when a regex is flagged as global. After the method returns null, the regex returns to the beginning of the string for the next search.

```
// Create a global regex to match multiple times in a string
var example:RegExp = /abc/g;

// Search for the first match
var result:Array = example.exec( "abc abc" );

// Displays 0
trace( result.index );
// Displays 3
trace( example.lastIndex );

// Search for the second match
result = example.exec( "abc abc" );

// Displays 4
trace( result.index );
// Displays 7
trace( example.lastIndex );

// Search for a match again, but none is found so null is returned
result = example.exec( "abc abc" );

// Displays: null
trace( result );
// Displays: 0
trace( example.lastIndex );
```

After the first call to *exec( )* in the preceding example, a match is found at index 0 and the lastIndex property is automatically set to 3. When *exec( )* is called the second time, the regex starts looking for a match at position 3 and finds the second match at index 4 (automatically setting lastIndex to position 7). When *exec( )* is called the final time, no match can be found and result is null. In this case, the lastIndex is set to 0 so that the next call to *exec( )* starts at the beginning of the string.

You can use a *while* statement with the *exec( )* method to find all the matches, like so:

```
// Create a regular expression that matches three-letter words
var example:RegExp = /\b[a-z]{3}\b/g;
var target:String = "This string has two three letter words";

/* Loop until the exec( ) method returns null. This while loop outputs:
   has
   two
*/
var result:Array;
while ( ( result = example.exec( target ) ) != null ) {
  trace( result );
}
```

See Also

Recipes 13.1 and 13.3

13.3   Looking for Pattern Matches

Problem

You want to search a string with a regex to find matches to the pattern.

Solution

Use the *String.search( )* and *String.match( )* methods.

Discussion

The *String.search( )* and *RegExp.test( )* methods behave similarly, as discussed in Recipe 13.2. The *search( )* method works on a string object and takes a regular expression as a parameter. If the regex can be matched in the string, the starting position for the matching substring is returned. If the regex cannot be matched, -1 is returned:

```
var example:String = "ActionScript 3 Cookbook";

// Displays: 6
trace( example.search( /script/i ) );

// Displays: -1
trace( example.search( /script/ ) );
```

In the preceding code block, the *search()* method is first invoked by using a regex that matches the substring `script` in a case-insensitive manner. The matching substring `Script` is found at position 6. In the second call to *search()*, the same regex is used, but this time without the `ignoreCase` flag being set. Because the verbatim substring `script` does not appear in the *example* string, -1 is returned.

 The *search()* method does not respect the global flag or `lastIndex` property of the regex passed to it. It always begins its search from the beginning of the string.

```
// Create a global regular expression that matches three-letter words
var regex:RegExp = /\b[a-z]{3}\b/g;
var sentence:String = "This string has two three letter words.";

/* Displays:
   12
   0
   12
*/
trace( sentence.search( regex ) );
trace( regex.lastIndex );
trace( sentence.search( regex ) );
```

When looking for a match with *search()*, it is only ever possible to find the position of the first match, even if the regex is flagged as `global`. The `lastIndex` property is not automatically adjusted like it is with *RegExp.exec()* (see Recipe 13.2). Additionally, even if you set the `lastIndex` property by hand, it is not respected by the *search()* method:

```
// Force the last index to be past the first matching position
regex.lastIndex = 13;

/* Displays:
   12
   13
*/
trace( sentence.search( regex ) );
trace( regex.lastIndex );
```

Because the *search()* method doesn't respect global regexes, it's only possible to determine if the string can match a given regex—not how many times a match can be made (just like the *RegExp.test()* method). For situations when you want to extract all of the substring matches to a regex pattern, use the *String.match()* method, which behaves similarly to the *RegExp.exec()* method (again, discussed in Recipe 13.2).

The *match()* method works on a string object and takes a regular expression as a parameter. It returns an array containing the substrings that were matched to the pattern. If the regex is not flagged as `global`, the array contains only one element—the first matching substring found. If the regex is `global`, the array starts looking for matches at the beginning of the string and returns an array containing every match found in the string. If no match can be made, *match()* returns null.

```
// Create a global regular expression that matches three-letter words
var regex:RegExp = /\b[a-z]{3}\b/g;
var sentence:String = "This string has two three letter words.";

var matches:Array = sentence.match( regex );

/* Displays:
  has,two
  2
*/
trace( matches );
trace( matches.length );
```

See Also

Recipes 13.1 and 13.2

13.4   Removing and Replacing Characters and Words Using Patterns

Problem

You want to remove characters from a string that matches a regex, or you want to replace pattern matches with a different substring.

Solution

Use the *String.replace()* method.

Discussion

The *String.replace()* method (see Recipe 12.7) allows you to use a string pattern to replace characters and words. Instead of using a string to define the pattern to replace, a more powerful approach is to use a regular expression.

You'll recall from Recipe 12.7 that the *replace()* method takes two parameters:

pattern
  The substring or regular expression you want to find and replace.

replace
  The value with which to replace each *pattern* match. This value is typically a string, but can also be a function that returns a string; this is particularly useful when *pattern* is a regular expression.

Using the *replace()* method is the same as what you're already familiar with, except instead of using a string pattern, you use a regex. Remember that *replace()* does not modify the original string, so make sure you use the string returned by *replace()* to work with the result:

```
var example:String = "<p>A string with <b>HTML</b> in it</p>";

// Replace the HTML by using a non-greedy global regex, using the empty
// string as the replacement substring for every match to the pattern.
example = example.replace( /<.*?>/g, "" );

// Displays: A string with HTML in it
trace( example );
```

The preceding code demonstrates how to remove HTML tags within a string. The use of a nongreedy regex is required, as discussed in Recipe 13.5. By using the empty string as the replacement string for all pattern matches, the result is the pattern matches being removed from the original string.

The *RegExp*'s global flag determines how the *replace()* method behaves. When the flag is set, all instances of the pattern are replaced. When the flag is not set, only the first occurrence of the pattern is replaced.

Using a regular expression as the pattern parameter makes the replace parameter more powerful as well. When the replace parameter is a string, there are special *replacement codes* that exist to allow parts of the pattern to be used as the replacement. Table 13-4 lists the replacement codes that can appear in the replace string, as well as what the code is replaced by.

Table 13-4. Replacement codes

Code	Is replaced by
$$	The $ character.
$&	The matched substring.
$`	The text in the string that precedes the matched substring. Note that the character after the $ is an accent grave, usually found just to the left of the 1 key and above the tab key.
$'	The text in the string that follows the matched substring.
$n	The nth group match when n ranges from 1–9.
$nn	The nnth group match where nn is a two-digit number from 10-99.

The replacement codes give you a powerful way to replace text. Say you have a plain text string and you want to replace every link starting with *http://* with its HTML equivalent, surrounding the link with anchor tags and setting the *href* attribute correctly. This task is virtually impossible when using a string as the pattern, but with a regex pattern and the replacement codes that replace accepts, the desired effect is achieved much more easily:

```
var example:String = "Visit me at http://www.darronschall.com, or Adobe at "
                   + "http://www.adobe.com.";
```

```
// Replace links starting with http:// and ending in .com, .net,
// or .org with the matched substring wrapped inside of an anchor
// tag, using the match as both the href attribute and the link text
example = example.replace( /http:\/\/.*?\.(com|net|org)/g, "<a href=\"$&\">$&</a>" );

/* Displays:
Visit me at <a href="http://www.darronschall.com">http://www.darronschall.com</a>, or
Adobe at <a href="http://www.adobe.com">http://www.adobe.com</a>.
*/
trace( example );
```

Although replacement codes are valuable—and let you do creative and useful things—perhaps a more powerful method to replace text is to use a replacement function as the replace parameter. The replacement function is invoked every time a match to the pattern is found and the string value returned by the function is used as the replacement value. The replacement function is passed a varying number of arguments that can be used to generate the appropriate string replacement for the match. The parameters passed to the function, in order, are:

- The matched substring
- The matched groups, dependant upon the number of groups that appear in the pattern, one parameter for each group; use arguments.length - 3 to determine the number of matching group substrings passed into the function
- The starting index of the matched substring within the string
- The string *replace()* was called on

Because the number of groups in the regex could vary, there isn't a strongly typed method header to use. Instead, you have to declare the replacement function as taking no arguments and rely on the arguments array to get the information you need:

```
var example:String = "Visit me at http://www.darronschall.com, or Adobe at "
                     + "http://www.adobe.com.";

// Replace all links according to the replaceLinks function, which
// determines what the text for the anchor tag should say
example = example.replace( /http:\/\/.*?\.(com|net|org)/g, replaceLinks );

/* Displays:
Visit me at <a href="http://www.darronschall.com">my website</a>,
or Adobe at <a href="http://www.adobe.com">their website</a>.
*/
trace( example );
```

You can then define replaceLinks() as follows.

```
public function replaceLinks():String {
  var linkText:String;
  // Whenever the link being replaced is darronschall.com, use
  // "my website" as the text value for the anchor tag, otherwise
  // use "their website"
  if ( arguments[0] == "http://www.darronschall.com" ) {
    linkText = "my website";
```

```
    } else {
      linkText = "their website";
    }
    // Construct an HTML link from the matched text using the
    // appropriate link text
    return "<a href=\"" + arguments[0] + "\">" + linkText + "</a>";
  }
```

By using a replacement function, the preceding code conditionally changed the text in the anchor tag based on the value of the matched substring. This type of functionality goes above and beyond what replacement codes are able to accomplish.

See Also

Recipes 12.7 and 13.5

13.5 Creating a Nongreedy Pattern

Problem

You're using a regular expression but not seeing the correct results. The pattern is acting greedy, matching more characters than you want it to.

Solution

Replace the regex with a nongreedy version to match the smallest amount of characters possible.

Discussion

Whenever you create a pattern that includes matches for character repetition using the * and + metacharacters or the {n,m} metasequence, the pattern is *greedy*. A greedy pattern is one that tries to consume as much text as possible, matching the largest substring it can. Patterns are greedy because of the underlying code in the regular expression engine, and understanding how that engine works allows you to create more precise regexes.

Consider that you want to remove HTML tags in a string, as described in Recipe 13.4. Every HTML tag starts with an opening < and ends in a closing >. In between the angle brackets, there could be a wide variety of characters, such a numbers, letters, quotes, the equal sign, etc. For the sake of simplicity, instead of creating a character class for everything that could appear between the < and >, a .* will match "any character, any number of times." So, you construct the regular expression /<.*>/g and try running it against a string that contains HTML tags:

```
var example:String = "<b>hello</b>, world!";

// Displays: <b>hello</b>
trace( example.match( /<.*>/g ) );
```

You might have expected that the regular expression would produce two matches, one for <b> and another for </b>. From the preceding code block, you can see that only one match was produced, the entire string <b>hello</b>. This is an example of a greedy pattern in action.

The first character in the expression is a <, which is taken literally. It matches in the string at the very first position so the engine moves on in the pattern and keeps processing. The next character in the pattern is a ., which matches everything except a newline, followed by the *, which repeats the . zero or more times. This is where the pattern becomes greedy.

The . matches the b because it falls under the "any character" umbrella. After the b in the string is a >, which again falls under "any character" and—as you guessed it— is matched by the .. The engine keeps repeating the ., matching hello</b>, world! up until the end of the string. At the end of the string, the . fails because there is nothing left; however, the pattern still needs to match a closing >. Because the engine knows that the * repetition has been fulfilled in matching the ., the engine *backtracks* and starts looking for a match to the > to complete the pattern. Moving backward in the string from the end, the ! is not a match to the > required by the pattern, so the engine moves backward yet again knowing that the .* has been fulfilled. It keeps moving backward through the d, l, r, o, etc. until it meets the > character just before the comma. The angle bracket at this location matches the closing angle bracket in the pattern, and the engine considers the pattern to have been matched successfully, returning a match of <b>hello</b>.

The *RegExp* engine wants to match a pattern as quickly as possible. Because a match has been made at this point, there is no need to continue to backtrack and try to find a smaller match. Therefore, greedy patterns always return the longest match.

There are two possible solutions to greedy patterns. The first is to make a pattern nongreedy, sometimes called a *lazy pattern*. The second is to creatively use a character class.

You make a pattern lazy by removing greedy repetition. Lazy patterns match the smallest possible substring. Creating a lazy pattern is as simple as adding the ? metacharacter to the end of the repetition expression, as described in Table 13-5.

Table 13-5. Lazy patterns

Expression	Lazily matches the preceding character or group
??	Zero or one time
*?	Zero or more times
+?	One or more times
$\{n,\}?$	At least n times
$\{n,m\}?$	At least n but no more than m times

The greedy /<.*>/g pattern used earlier to match HTML tags can be replaced with the lazy pattern of /<.*?>/g, giving the desired effect of matching all of the HTML tags:

```
var example:String = "<b>hello</b>, world!";

// Displays: <b>,</b>
trace( example.match( /<.*?>/g ) );
```

By making the pattern lazy, the underlying *RegExp* engine treats the pattern differently than it would a greedy pattern. The < is matched just like before, but this time the . is followed by a lazy * (as signified by the ?), and the engine knows to match as few characters as possible. At this point, the requirement of "any character, zero or more times" has already been met since zero characters have been consumed and the engine starts looking for the closing >. The b in the string is encountered, which doesn't match >. The engine backtracks just like before, but in doing so forces the lazy * to consume more text. The .* is expanded to match the b, and the engine again looks to match the >. The next character in the string is >, which matches successfully and completes the pattern. The engine therefore returns <b> as a match, which is exactly the desired result.

Instead of making a lazy pattern, you can replace the . with a character class that includes every character except the >, resulting in the /<[^>]*>/g pattern:

```
var example:String = "<b>hello</b>, world!";

// Displays: <b>,</b>
trace( example.match( /<[^>]*>/g ) );
```

In this case, a character class might be the better option because it eliminates the backtracking done by the engine. The engine processes the < as normal, and then matches characters up until the > in the string since it's not a part of the character class. It then moves on to the > in the pattern and reports a successful match because > is found in the string.

See Also

Recipes 13.1, 13.3, and 13.4

13.6   Validating User Input with Common Patterns

Problem

You want to make sure that a user correctly entered information, such as an email address, social security number, telephone number, or Zip/Postal Code.

Solution

Use one of the common patterns included in this recipe.

Discussion

Regular expressions are extremely useful for validating a wide range user input. For example, you might have a form that allows a user to enter an email address to sign up for your latest online game and you need to ensure the email address is valid. Or, you might possibly want to make sure that a birth date was entered correctly. Or, you might want to verify that a credit card number was input properly. The following list of regular expressions will help:

- Match a date in the format ##/##/####, where both the day and month value can be 1 or 2 digits, and the year can be either 2 digits or 4 digits when starting with 19 or 20:

      ^\d{1,2}\/\d{1,2}\/(\d{2}|(19|20)\d{2})$

- Match a social security number in the format ###-##-####, where the dashes are optional and the three groups can have optional spacing between them:

      ^\d{3}\s*-?\s*\d{2}\s*-?\s*\d{4}$

- Match a five-digit U.S. Zip Code with an optional dash and four-digit extension:

      ^\d{5}(-\d{4})?$

- Match a Canadian Postal Code in the format L#L #L# (where L is a letter). There is a restriction placed on the first letter in the Postal Code to ensure that a valid province, territory, or region is specified:

      ^[ABCEGHJKLMNPRSTVXY]\d[A-Z] \d[A-Z]\d$

- Match a U.S. telephone number in the format (###) ###-####, where the area code is optional, the parentheses around the area code are optional and could be replaced with a dash, and there is optional spacing between the number groups:

      ^(\(\s*\d{3}\s*\)|(\d{3}\s*-?))?\s*\d{3}\s*-?\s*\d{4}$

- Match a U.S. telephone number, like the previous expression, except allow for an optional one- to five-digit extension specified with an "x", "ext", or "ext." and optional spacing:

      ^(\(\s*\d{3}\s*\)|(\d{3}\s*-?))?\s*\d{3}\s*-?\s*\d{4}\s*((x|ext|ext\.)\s*\d{1,5})?$

- Match a credit card number with four group of four digits separated by optional dashes and optional spacing between the groups:

      ^(\d{4}\s*-?\s*){3}\d{4}$

- Match U.S. currency starting with a $ and followed by any number with at most two optional decimal digits:

      ^\$\d(\.\d{1,2})?$

- Match an email address where the domain is not an IP address and may contain any number of optional subdomains. When creating this regex, it's a good idea to set the ignoreCare flag to true:

      ^[a-z0-9][-._a-z0-9]*@([a-z0-9][-_a-z0-9]*\.)+[a-z]{2,6}$

- Match an IP address when you are only concerned that the address is formatted correctly with four groups of one to three digits separated by periods:

  ```
  ^(\d{1,3}\.){3}\d{1,3}$
  ```

 The preceding regex matches 999.999.999.999, which technically is not a valid IP address, but it has the correct IP address formatting.

- Match an IP address when you are concerned that the address is formatted correctly and that each number group only ranges from 0-255:

  ```
  ^((25[0-5]|2[0-4]\d|[01]?\d\d?)\.){3}(25[0-5]|2[0-4]\d|[01]?\d\d?)$
  ```

- Match an email address when the domain is either a domain name consisting of any number of optional subdomains or an IP address:

  ```
  ^[a-z0-9][-._a-z0-9]*@(([a-z0-9][-_a-z0-9]*\.)+[a-z]{2,6}|((25[0-5]|2[0-4]\d|[01]?\d\d?)\.
  ){3}(25[0-5]|2[0-4]\d|[01]?\d\d?))$
  ```

To use one of the preceding regular expressions in the context of validating user input, use the *RegExp.test()* method described in Recipe 13.2:

```
// Create a regular expression to test for a valid Zip Code
var zipCode:RegExp = /^\d{5}(-\d{4})?$/;

// Check to see if the user input is a valid Zip Code
if ( !zipCode.test( "12384-1231" ) ) {
  // Zip Code is not valid, alert the user of an error here
} else {
  // Zip Code is valid, probably don't need to do anything here
}
```

When creating regular expressions, there is usually a tradeoff between accuracy and complexity. Consider the two IP address regexes provided in the preceding list. The first IP address regex is fairly easy to understand; it matches one to three digits followed by a period three times, and then matches another group of one to three digits. Although this regex is simple, it's not entirely accurate. IP addresses limit each number group in the range of 0 to 255, whereas this regex accepts any number between 0 and 999. Therefore, the first regex is only good at determining if the IP address is formatted correctly and not reliable for determining if the IP address is actually valid.

The second IP address regex is much more complex, but also more accurate. It limits the number groups to values from 0 to 255, and also ensures that four number groups exist and are separated by periods. It's up to you to determine which regex is best for your situation.

Complex regexes are hard to understand and create, but tend to offer the most accuracy. Simple regexes are much easier to understand and create, but may either match more than what you really want them to (false positives), or may not match something that that you want them to (false negatives).

Another example of the complexity and accuracy tradeoff is the regex for matching a date. The regex provided to match a date in the format ##/##/#### allows for false positives. For instance, 01/99/2006 is accepted by the pattern, but January does not have 99 days in it.

Unfortunately, trying to create a regex to match a date in a specific format that accepts only valid month, day, and year combinations is virtually impossible because of the conditional dependencies. In these situations, use a combination of regex grouping and ActionScript code. You can inspect the groups matched in the regex and perform logic to ensure that the group values make sense:

```
// Verify a date based on a string input from the user
var inputDate:Date = extractDate( theInputString );

// Test to see if the date was valid or not
if ( inputDate == null ) {
  // Could not parse the date correctly, invalid
} else {
  // Valid date
}
```

The following is the definition for *extractDate()*:

```
// Attempts to extract a date value from a string in the
// format of ##/##/#### or ##/##/##. Returns a Date object
// described by the string value if successful, or null
// otherwise.
public function extractDate( possibleDate:String ):Date {
  var datePattern:RegExp = /^(\d{1,2})\/(\d{1,2})\/(\d{2}|(19|20)\d{2})$/;

  // Use the regex to filter out badly formatted dates right away
  var result:Array = datePattern.exec( possibleDate );

  // A null result means the format was invalid
  if ( result == null ) {
    return null;
  }

  // At this point, the date is formatted corrected and the result
  // array contains the matched substring as well as all of the matched
  // groups. If the possibleDate is "02/08/2006", then the result array
  // contains: 02/08/2006,02,08,2006,20

  // Convert the string values to ints
```

```
var month:int = parseInt( result[1] );
var day:int = parseInt( result[2] );
var year:int = parseInt( result[3] );

// Perform additional logic to make sure month, day, and year all make sense
if ( month > 12 || day > 31 || month == 0 || day == 0 ) {
  // Month or day value is too high or too low - not valid
  return null;
} else if ( day == 31 && ( month == 9 || month == 4 || month == 6
                          || month == 11 || month == 2 ) ) {
  // 31 days for September, April, June, November, or February - not valid
  return null;
} else if ( day == 30 && month == 2 ) {
  // 30 days for February - not valid
  return null;
} else if ( day == 29 && month == 2
            && !( year % 4 == 0 && ( year % 100 != 0 || year % 400 == 0 ) ) ) {
  // 29 days in February, but not a leap year - not valid
  return null;
} else {
  // Handling two digit years is tricky.  The year 99 should be 1999, but 06
  // should be 2006.  Using 06 in the Date constructor will yield 1906 as the
  // year, so pick an arbitrary year, say, 15, and everything less than that
  // will be converted to 20xx. Everything after that will be 19xx by default.
  if ( year <= 15 ) {
    year += 2000;
  }
  // Logically, month, day, and year all make sense, so return the
  // proper Date object. Subtract 1 from the month because months
  // are zero indexed in ActionScript.
  return new Date( year, month - 1, day );
}
}
```

See Also

Recipes 13.1 and 13.2

CHAPTER 14
Dates and Times

14.0 Introduction

Dates and times are important to many ActionScript applications, particularly when more robust applications are developed to offer services to users. For example, date and time values are important for determining the amount of time that has elapsed for timed operations, for determining whether a user's trial membership is active or about to expire, and for storing transaction dates.

ActionScript stores dates and times internally as *epoch milliseconds*, the number of milliseconds that have elapsed since the Epoch—midnight, January 1, 1970 Coordinated Universal Time (UTC). For our purposes, UTC is essentially equivalent to the more familiar Greenwich Mean Time (GMT). See the U.S. Naval Observatory's site (*http://aa.usno.navy.mil/faq/docs/UT.html*) regarding the subtle distinctions. Many programming languages store dates in terms of the epoch (often in seconds instead of milliseconds); therefore, you can readily work with date and time values that have been imported from other sources (and vice versa).

In addition, the *Date* class allows you to set and get date and time values in terms of years, months, days, and so on by using properties such as `fullYear`, `month`, etc. These properties are for your convenience, but the values are stored internally as epoch milliseconds.

14.1 Finding the Current Date and Time

Problem

You want to know the current date and time.

Solution

Create a new date by using the *Date()* constructor with no parameters. Alternatively, use a CGI script or any other server-side program to return the server time and create a new *Date* object from that value.

Discussion

The date and time that ActionScript calculates on its own is based on the client computer's date and time settings. Therefore, if the user's computer has the incorrect time, so will the *Date* object. With that caveat in mind, you can retrieve the current client-side date and time by creating a new *Date* object by using a constructor without parameters, as follows:

```
// Create a new Date object.
var current:Date = new Date( );

// Displays client-side date and time.
trace(current);
```

If you have an Internet connection, the Flash movie attempts to retrieve the date and time from a server. This technique can ensure more accurate dates and times. Although the server's time settings might be inaccurate, at least the time will be consistent for all clients.

The basic process when reading the time from a server is as follows:

1. Create a CGI script on the web server that outputs the number of seconds since midnight of January 1, 1970 (the epoch).

2. Use a *flash.net.URLLoader* object from ActionScript to load the epoch seconds.

3. Convert the loaded seconds from a string to a number, multiply by 1,000, and construct a new *Date* object by passing the value to the constructor.

PHP is a scripting language that can be found on a large number of web hosts. It is quite simple to create a PHP page to output the current time and date as the number of seconds since the epoch. All you need to do is create a PHP document with the following content and upload it to the server:

```
<?php echo time( );?>
```

If you don't have PHP on your server, or if you are simply more comfortable with Perl (another language that is almost universally available on web servers), then here is a Perl script that outputs the number of seconds since the epoch:

```
#!/usr/local/bin/perl
print "Content-type:text/plain\n\n";
print time;
```

There are a few tips to keep in mind when setting up this script on your server:

- The first line indicates where the Perl interpreter can be found. The value given in the example is fairly universal. However, contact your web server administrator if you encounter problems.

- Many servers disable remote script execution without particular file extensions; however, the *.cgi* extension is commonly allowed. Try renaming the script *getDate.cgi*.

- Most web servers limit CGI access to specific directories. These directories are normally found in the account's root directory (or within the web root of the account), and are named either *cgi* or *cgi-bin*. Make sure you save the script in the correct directory.
- On Unix servers, your CGI script must have its permissions set to 755. Most FTP programs allow you to change permissions. If you are working from a shell script, use the following command:

```
chmod 755 filename
```

Regardless of what server-side language you use, you need to load the time value from the server using ActionScript. You can accomplish that by using a *flash.net. URLLoader* object.

If you pass the *Date* constructor a single value, ActionScript interprets it as the number of milliseconds since the epoch and creates a new *Date* object that corresponds to that value. Therefore, you must multiply the value returned by the script (which is in seconds) by 1,000; for example:

```
package {

    import flash.net.URLLoader;
    import flash.net.URLRequest;
    import flash.events.Event;

    public class ServerDateTimeExample {

        public function ServerDateTimeExample( ) {
            // The following code constructs a URLLoader object, adds
            // an event listener so that the onDateTimeLoad( ) method is
            // called when the data loads, and then it makes the request
            // to the server script.
            var loader:URLLoader = new URLLoader( );
            loader.addEventListener(Event.COMPLETE, onDateTimeLoad);
            loader.load(new URLRequest("script.cgi"));
        }

        private function onDateTimeLoad(event:Event):void {
            var loader:URLLoader = URLLoader(event.target);
            var data:int = parseInt(loader.data);
            var current:Date = new Date(data * 1000);
            trace(current);
        }

    }
```

The date is always stored in ActionScript as the milliseconds since the epoch, and it is always displayed with proper offsets, based on the user's local time zone setting (unless you specifically use the UTC methods). So, if the user's computer has the incorrect time zone setting, the display might be incorrect. However, the actual date (as stored in epoch milliseconds) is still correct.

See Also

Recipe 14.9; if your server's time is not reliable or accurate enough for your needs, there are many existing date and time servers on the Internet from which you can retrieve reasonably accurate date and time information. See, for example, *http://tycho. usno.navy.mil*. For details on synchronizing time via the Network Time Protocol, see *http://www.ntp.org*.

14.2   Retrieving the Date Values

Problem

You want to retrieve the year, month, day of month, day of week, hour, minute, second, or millisecond value from a *Date* object.

Solution

Use the *fullYear*, *date*, *month*, *day*, *hours*, *minutes*, *seconds*, or *milliseconds* properties.

Discussion

The *fullYear*, *date*, *month*, *day*, *hours*, *minutes*, *seconds*, and *milliseconds* properties return the values from a *Date* object:

- The *fullYear* property specifies the year as a four-digit value, such as 2010.
- The *date* property specifies the day of the month as a value from 1 to 31.
- The *month* property specifies the month as an integer from 0 (January) to 11 (December).
- The *day* property specifies the day of the week as an integer from 0 (Sunday) to 6 (Saturday).
- The *hours* property returns the hours value as an integer from 0 (midnight) to 23 (11 p.m.).
- The *minutes* and *seconds* properties return values from 0 to 59.
- The *milliseconds* property returns a value from 0 to 999.

Each of these properties has a UTC (Coordinated Universal Time, also known as Greenwich Mean Time) correspondent. For example, although the *hours* property returns the current hours value based on the client computer's clock, the *hoursUTC* property returns the current hours value in UTC time.

14.3   Retrieving the Day or Month Name

Problem

You want to retrieve the name of the day or month.

Solution

Create arrays that contain the string values for the names of the days of the week and the names of the months of the year. Use the numeric day and month to extract the string values from the arrays.

Discussion

The ActionScript *Date* class provides the *day* and *month* properties, which return integer values representing the day of the week (from 0 to 6) and the month of the year (from 0 to 11). However, you may want the name of the day or month instead of its zero-relative number. To address this, create arrays containing the names of the days and months. Or, more conveniently, you can use constants of the custom *ascb. util.DateFormat* class. The constants DAYS, DAYS_ABBREVIATED, MONTHS, and MONTHS_ABBREVIATED are each arrays that contain strings that correspond to the numeric values returned by *day* and *month*. The actual definitions of those constants are as follows:

```
public static const DAYS:Array = ["Sunday", "Monday", "Tuesday", "Wednesday",
"Thursday", "Friday", "Saturday"];
public static const DAYSABBREVIATED:Array = ["Sun", "Mon", "Tues", "Wed", "Thurs",
"Fri", "Sat"];
public static const MONTHS:Array = ["January", "February", "March", "April", "May",
"June", "July", "August", "September", "October", "November", "December"];
public static const MONTHSABBREVIATED:Array = ["Jan", "Feb", "Mar", "Apr", "May",
"Jun", "Jul", "Aug", "Sep", "Oct", "Nov", "Dec"];
```

You can then use those constants as shown in the following example:

```
var example:Date = new Date(2010, 3, 10);

trace(DateFormat.DAYS[example.day]);  // Displays: Saturday
trace(DateFormat.DAYSABBREVIATED[example.day]);  // Displays: Sat
trace(DateFormat.MONTHS[example.month]);  // Displays: April
trace(DateFormat.MONTHSABBREVIATED[example.month]);  // Displays: Apr
```

See Also

Recipe 14.4

14.4   Formatting the Date and Time

Problem

You want to display a formatted date and/or time value.

Solution

Use *Date.toString()*, or use the custom *DateFormat.format()* method that returns the date and time as a string in the requested format.

Discussion

The *Date.toString()* method returns a user-friendly string version of the target *Date* object; for example:

```
// Displays (something like): Tue Jan 5 14:25:20 GMT-0800 2010
trace((new Date()).toString());
```

Because ActionScript automatically invokes the *toString()* method on any object used in a string context, you can obtain the same result even if you omit *toString()*, as in the following example:

```
// Also displays: Tue Jan 5 14:25:20 GMT-0800 2010
trace(new Date());
```

The *Date* class doesn't have any other built-in functionality for formatting a date or time in a customized way. You can, of course, compose a string value, as in the following example:

```
var example:Date = new Date(2010, 0, 5, 10, 25);
var formatted:String = (example.month + 1) + "/" + example.fullYear;
trace(formatted);  // Displays: 1/2010
```

However, you may have to write a lot of custom code each time you want to display the date and/or time. Instead, you can use the *format()* method of an *ascb.util. DateFormat* instance. The *DateFormat* class is a custom class that is specifically designed to assist with formatting dates and times when given a mask. The mask can be composed of any characters, but some characters act like variables. Table 14-1 shows the characters you can use as variables when creating the mask.

Table 14-1. Date and time symbols

Symbol	Meaning	Example
a	Lowercase a.m. or p.m.	a.m.
A	Uppercase A.M. or P.M.	P.M.
d	Day of month (leading 0)	01
D	Abbreviated day of week	Sun
F	Month	January

Table 14-1. Date and time symbols (continued)

Symbol	Meaning	Example
g	12-hour	1
G	24-hour	1
h	12-hour (leading 0)	01
H	24-hour (leading 0)	01
i	Minutes (leading 0)	01
j	Day of month	1
l	Day of week	Sunday
m	Numeric month (leading 0)	01
M	Abbreviated month	Jan
n	Numeric month	1
s	Seconds (leading 0)	01
t	Days in month	31
w	Numeric day of week	0
y	2-digit year	06
Y	4-digit year	2006

When you create a *DateFormat* object, you should pass it a mask string as a parameter to the constructor. Most characters that aren't used as variables in the mask context are interpreted literally. For example, the following creates a *DateFormat* object that outputs the date in standard U.S. format with forward slashes between the month, date, and year:

```
var formatter:DateFormat = new DateFormat("m/d/Y");
```

Once you've created a *DateFormat* object, you can call the *format()* method to format any *Date* instance as a string using the mask you specified:

```
var example:Date = new Date(2010, 0, 5, 10, 25);
var formatter:DateFormat = new DateFormat("m/d/Y");
trace(formatter.format(example));  // Displays: 01/05/2010
```

You can use the mask property to get and set the mask string. That means you can change the mask for an existing *DateFormat* object:

```
var example:Date = new Date(2010, 0, 5, 10, 25);
var formatter:DateFormat = new DateFormat("m/d/Y");
trace(formatter.format(example));  // Displays: 01/05/2010
formatter.mask = "m/d/Y h:i a";
trace(formatter.format(example));  // Displays: 01/05/2010 10:25 am
```

You can also use single quotes around any portion of the mask that you want to have interpreted literally.

That's important if you want to display any of the characters that would otherwise be interpreted as variables within the mask:

```
var example:Date = new Date(2010, 0, 5, 10, 25);
var formatter:DateFormat = new DateFormat("m/d/Y at h:i a");
trace(formatter.format(example));  // Displays: 01/05/2010 am31 10:25 am
formatter.mask = "m/d/Y 'at' h:i a";
trace(formatter.format(example));  // Displays: 01/05/2010 at 10:25 am
```

See Also

Recipe 14.5; the variable characters used in the mask are the same as those used by PHP. You may find the information at *http://www.php.net/manual/en/function.date. php* useful for reference.

14.5 Formatting Seconds or Milliseconds as Minutes and Seconds

Problem

You want to display seconds or milliseconds in minutes and seconds (*mm:ss*) format.

Solution

Use either the custom *ascb.util.DateFormat.formatSeconds()* or *ascb.util.DateFormat. formatMilliseconds()* methods.

Discussion

Many values in ActionScript are given in milliseconds or seconds. For example, sound lengths are given in milliseconds. However, in most cases, you want to format the value as minutes and seconds when displaying it to the user. You can accomplish this with a short amount of code. To further simplify things, that code has already been made into static methods of the *DateFormat* class.

The *ascb.utils.DateFormat* class has two methods that convert a number to the format *mm:ss*. The *formatSeconds()* method converts seconds to that format, while the *formatMilliseconds()* method converts milliseconds to that format.

See Also

Recipe 14.4

14.6 Converting Between DMYHMSM and Epoch Milliseconds

Problem

You want to convert between DMYHMSM format (days, months, years, hours, minutes, seconds, milliseconds) and epoch milliseconds.

Solution

Use the *time* property.

Discussion

Most of us are more comfortable thinking of dates and times in terms of their components such as hours, days, and years than working with epoch milliseconds or seconds. For example, it's much easier to give the time and date as 10:25 a.m., Tuesday, January 5, 2010 than to discuss the corresponding epoch value of 1,262,715,900,000 milliseconds. However, languages such as ActionScript store times in the epoch milliseconds (or epoch seconds) format. Therefore, it's important to be able to convert between different formats when displaying dates and times to users, or when sharing dates between applications that use different formats.

When constructing a date in ActionScript, you can use the DMYHMSM approach, as follows:

```
// Construct a date for 10:25 AM, Tuesday, January 5, 2010
var example:Date = new Date(2010, 0, 5, 10, 25);
```

ActionScript automatically performs the conversion and stores the date as the corresponding epoch milliseconds value. To retrieve that value, all you need to do is call the *time* property from the *Date* object, as follows:

```
// For Pacific Standard Time, displays: 1262715900000
// The output may vary depending on your time zone.
trace(example.time);
```

You can pass the epoch seconds value returned by *time* to another application (such as a CGI script) or use it for performing date mathematics (see Recipe 14.1).

On the other hand, you may want to set a date using the epoch milliseconds. For example, in Recipe 14.1 the CGI script returns the current server time to Flash in epoch seconds (which needs to be converted to milliseconds by multiplying by 1,000). Also, when performing date mathematics you may want to set a date according to epoch milliseconds. You have two options for setting a date according to the epoch milliseconds. One choice is to pass the milliseconds value to the *Date* constructor as the only parameter, and the other is to assign the milliseconds value to the *time* property of an existing date. Both techniques are effectively the same.

```
// Construct a new Date object for 310:25 AM, Tuesday, January 5,
// 2010. Here, we use the value displayed in the Output window from
// the preceding example.
var example:Date = new Date(1262715900000);

// Displays: Tue Jan 5 10:25:00 GMT-0800 2010 (timezone offset
// may vary)
trace(example);
```

See Also

Recipe 14.1

14.7 Using Timers

Problem

You want to poll a method at a specific interval or add a delay.

Solution

Use the *flash.util.Timer* class.

Discussion

The *flash.util.Timer* class allows you to add timed events or a delay to method calls.
You can construct a *Timer* instance with the constructor. Pass the constructor a
number of milliseconds to use as the interval between timer events. The following
example instantiates a *Timer* object that dispatches events every 1,000 milliseconds
(1 second):

```
var timer:Timer = new Timer(1000);
```

Once you've constructed the *Timer*, you next need to add an event listener to handle
the events it dispatches. *Timer* objects dispatch *flash.event.TimerEvent* events. The
timer event is dispatched at the interval specified when constructing the *Timer* object
(or as set by the delay property). The following example code defines an event listener for the timer event (using the *TimerEvent.TIMER* constant), which calls a
method named *onTimer()*:

```
timer.addEventListener(TimerEvent.TIMER, onTimer);
```

The event handler method is passed a *TimerEvent* object:

```
function onTimer(event:TimerEvent):void {
  trace("on timer");
}
```

Timer objects do not start automatically; you must call the *start()* method first:

```
timer.start();
```

By default, timers run until stopped by the *stop()* method. However, you can also specify a number of intervals by passing a second parameter to the constructor. The default value of 0 causes the timer to repeat indefinitely, while non-zero values specify a finite number of intervals. The following constructs a timer that has just five intervals:

```
var timer:Timer = new Timer(1000, 5);
```

You can use a timer with just one interval to add a delay. The following timer code defers the call to the *deferredMethod()* method for five seconds:

```
var timer:Timer = new Timer(5000, 1);
timer.addEventListener(TimerEvent.TIMER, deferredMethod);
timer.start();
```

14.8 Calculating Elapsed Time or Intervals Between Dates

Problem

You want to calculate an elapsed time, elapsed date, or relative time.

Solution

For simple elapsed time, you can add and subtract from the epoch milliseconds, or use the value returned by *getTimer()*. For more complex conversions, use the methods of the custom *DateUtilities* class.

Discussion

For simple conversions such as adding or subtracting an hour, day, or week to or from a date, simply add or subtract from the date's epoch milliseconds value. For this purpose, note that a second is 1,000 milliseconds, a minute is 60,000 milliseconds, an hour is 3,600,000 milliseconds, a week is 604,800,000 milliseconds, and so on. Unless you have a knack for remembering these conversion values, storing them as constants is a convenient option. The constants have already been defined in the custom *ascb.util.DateUtilities* class as follows:

```
public static const MILLISECOND:Number = 1;
public static const SECOND:Number = MILLISECOND * 1000;
public static const MINUTE:Number = SECOND * 60;
public static const HOUR:Number = MINUTE * 60;
public static const DAY:Number = HOUR * 24;
public static const WEEK:Number = DAY * 7;
```

You can use the *Date.time* property to retrieve a date's current value in epoch milliseconds, and then assign a new value to the *time* property relative to the current value. The following example adds one day to a given *Date* object:

```
var example:Date = new Date(2010, 0, 5, 10, 25);

// Displays: Tue Jan 5 10:25:00 GMT-0800 2010
trace(example);

// Add one day to the previous date by setting the new date/time
// to the original date/time plus DateUtilities.DAY (the number
// of milliseconds in a day).
example.time += DateUtilities.DAY;

// Displays: Wed Jan 6 10:25:00 GMT-0800 2010
trace(example);
```

You'll often want to calculate an elapsed time to create a timer for a game or other
activity. Calculating the elapsed time is simply a matter of recording the time during
initialization and then comparing it to the current time later during execution. You
can use a *Date* object to make those calculations; however, it is much more efficient
to use the *flash.util.getTimer()* function. The *getTimer()* function returns the number of milliseconds since the Player started running. By checking its value at successive times, the *getTimer()* function can also be used to determine the elapsed time.
The following example uses the *getTimer()* function to repeatedly update the displayed text:

```
package {

    import flash.display.Sprite;
    import flash.display.TextField;
    import flash.util.Timer;
    import flash.events.TimerEvent;
    import flash.util.getTimer;

    public class Example extends Sprite {

        private var _text:TextField;
        private var _start:uint;

        public function Example() {
            _start = getTimer();
            _text = new TextField();
            addChild(_text);
            var timer:Timer = new Timer(1000);
            timer.addEventListener(TimerEvent.TIMER, onTimer);
            timer.start();
        }

        private function onTimer(event:TimerEvent):void {
            _text.text = (getTimer() - _start) + " milliseconds";
        }

    }
}
```

Here, the previous example is tweaked to create a countdown timer:

```
package {

    import flash.display.Sprite;
    import flash.display.TextField;
    import flash.util.Timer;
    import flash.events.TimerEvent;
    import flash.util.getTimer;

    public class Example extends Sprite {

      private var _text:TextField;
      private var _timer:Timer;
      private var _start:uint;
      private var _count:uint = 20;

      public function Example() {
        _start = getTimer();
        _text = new TextField();
        addChild(_text);
        _timer = new Timer(500);
        _timer.addEventListener(TimerEvent.TIMER, onTimer);
        _timer.start();
      }

      private function onTimer(event:TimerEvent):void {
        var elapsed:int = Math.round(_count - (getTimer() - _start) / 1000);
        _text.text = ellapsed + " seconds";
        if(elapsed < 0) {
          _text.text = "---------";
          _timer.stop();
        }
      }

    }
}
```

The earlier example calculated elapsed times using *Date* objects. When it comes to adding and subtracting years and months from dates, you cannot rely on constants. This is because the number of milliseconds in a month varies with the number of days in the month, and leap years have more milliseconds than other years. However, the *Date* class handles wraparound calculations transparently when using the *getter* and *setter* methods. The most effective way to handle date math is to use the custom *DateUtilities.addTo()* method and have it perform the calculations for you. The method takes up to eight parameters, seven of which are defined in Table 14-2. The first is required, and it is the *Date* object to which you want to add (or subtract as the case may be). The parameters defined in Table 14-2 are optional numeric parameters, each of which can be positive or negative.

Table 14-2. Parameters for the addTo() method

Parameter	Description
years	A number of years to add to the date.
months	A number of months to add to the date.
days	A number of days to add to the date.
hours	A number of hours to add to the date.
minutes	A number of minutes to add to the date.
seconds	A number of seconds to add to the date.
milliseconds	A number of milliseconds to add to the date.

The following shows how you might use the *addTo()* method to add (and subtract) years, months, and days to a date:

```
var example:Date = new Date(2010, 0, 5, 10, 25);

trace(DateUtilities.addTo(example, 10));
trace(DateUtilities.addTo(example, -4));
trace(DateUtilities.addTo(example, 0, 1, 1));
trace(DateUtilities.addTo(example, 0, -1, -1));

/* Displays:
Sun Jan 5 10:25:00 GMT-0800 2020
Thu Jan 5 10:25:00 GMT-0800 2006
Sat Feb 6 10:25:00 GMT-0800 2010
Fri Dec 4 10:25:00 GMT-0800 2009
*/
```

This example demonstrates how to create a new *Date* object based on an elapsed time from an existing *Date* object. However, you may want to calculate the elapsed time between two existing *Date* objects, which is not as trivial as you might think. You might try subtracting the return value of the *time* property of one *Date* object from another. However, this doesn't offer a general solution for calculating the elapsed time between two *Date* objects. Although the operation yields the number of milliseconds between the two dates, the result isn't easy to manipulate when the times are not within the same day. Manually converting the number of milliseconds to a number of years, months, and days is difficult due to the varying number of days per month, leap year, etc. Furthermore, handling negative elapsed times can be cumbersome.

One convenient solution is to create a *Date* object representing an elapsed time. This lets you use the *Date* class's built-in methods to calculate the number of years, months, and days between two *Date* objects. You can use the UTC *get* methods to retrieve most of the offsets, as illustrated in the following example:

```
var one:Date = new Date();

var two:Date = DateUtilities.addTo(one, 4, 1, 3, 10);

var elapsed:Date = new Date(two.time - one.time);
```

```
trace(elapsed);   // Displays: Sun Feb 3 16:00:00 GMT-0800 1974
trace(elapsed.hoursUTC);  // Displays: 10
trace(elapsed.monthUTC); // Displays: 1
```

There are several caveats, however. Although ActionScript internally stores dates relative to the epoch time, most *Date* class methods return absolute values, not values relative to the Epoch. For example, the year for a date in 1971 is returned as 1971, not 1. For the *elapsed* time object to be useful, you need to subtract constants from the *year* and *day* values. (The *month*, *hour*, *minute*, *second*, and *millisecond* of the epoch time are all 0, so there is no need for custom methods to return relative values for these values.) Subtract 1970 from the year, and then subtract 1 from the day:

```
trace(elapsed.dateUTC);   // Displays: 4 (incorrect)
trace(elapsed.dateUTC - 1);  // Displays: 3 (correct)
trace(elapsed.dateUTC);   // Displays: 1974 (incorrect);
trace(elapsed.dateUTC - 1970); // Displays: 4 (correct);
```

To work with elapsed times more efficiently, you might want to use some of the methods of the custom *DateUtilities* class. The class has a static method called *elapsed()* that returns an object with the amount of elapsed time between two dates, as illustrated in the following example:

```
var one:Date = new Date();

var two:Date = DateUtilities.addTo(one, 4, 1, 3);

var elapsed:Object = DateUtilities.elapsed(two);
for(var item:String in elapsed) {
  trace(item + ": " + elapsed[item]);
}

/* Displays:
milliseconds: 0
seconds: 0
minutes: 0
hours: 0
days: 3
months: 1
years: 4
*/
```

If you pass only one parameter to the *elapsed()* method, it assumes that you want to find the amount of time that has elapsed between the specified date and the current date.

The *DateUtilities* class also has several additional static methods that return elapsed times between two dates in specific intervals (*years*, *months*, *days*, etc.). By default, each of those methods calculates the total number of specified intervals between the two dates, as shown here:

```
var one:Date = new Date();

var two:Date = DateUtilities.addTo(one, 4, 1, 3);
```

```
trace(DateUtilities.elapsedYears(two, one));        // Displays: 4
trace(DateUtilities.elapsedMonths(two, one));       // Displays: 49
trace(DateUtilities.elapsedDays(two, one));         // Displays: 1495
trace(DateUtilities.elapsedHours(two, one));        // Displays: 35880
trace(DateUtilities.elapsedMinutes(two, one));      // Displays: 2152800
trace(DateUtilities.elapsedSeconds(two, one));      // Displays: 129168000
trace(DateUtilities.elapsedMilliseconds(two, one)); // Displays: 129168000000
```

Optionally, you can pass a Boolean value as a third parameter to any of the methods. A value of true causes the methods to return the relative values instead. The *elapsedYears()* method is the exception, since it returns the same value either way, as shown in the following example:

```
var one:Date = new Date( );

var two:Date = DateUtilities.addTo(one, 4, 1, 3);

trace(DateUtilities.elapsedMonths(two, one, true));       // Displays: 1
trace(DateUtilities.elapsedDays(two, one, true));         // Displays: 3
trace(DateUtilities.elapsedHours(two, one, true));        // Displays: 0
trace(DateUtilities.elapsedMinutes(two, one, true));      // Displays: 0
trace(DateUtilities.elapsedSeconds(two, one, true));      // Displays: 0
trace(DateUtilities.elapsedMilliseconds(two, one, true)); // Displays: 0
```

14.9   Parsing a Date from a String

Problem

You want to create a *Date* object from a string.

Solution

Use the *parse()* method of a *DateFormat* object.

Discussion

ActionScript does not provide native methods for parsing a string into a *Date* object, and in many cases, that doesn't pose any difficulty. For example, Flash Remoting allows you to return native *Date* objects from other applications. Even if you are not working with Flash Remoting, you can pass values between Flash and other applications using epoch seconds/milliseconds. However, if you need to parse a string into a date, you should use the parse method of the custom *ascb.util.DateFormat* class. The method takes the string value as a parameter, parses out each of the date's parts (the year, hour, etc.), and then returns a new *Date* object.

To use the *DateFormat* class, you need to create an instance with the constructor. When you create the instance, you should pass a mask string to the constructor as a parameter. Recipe 14.4 has more details on creating a mask string:

```
var formatter:DateFormat = new DateFormat("m/d/Y");
```

Once you've created a *DateFormat* instance, you can next call the *parse()* method. Pass it a string in the format specified by the mask, and it parses the date, returning a new *Date* instance:

```
// Displays: Sat May 1 00:00:00 GMT-0700 2010 (timezone offset may vary)
trace(formatter.parse("05/01/2010"));

formatter.mask = "m/d/Y 'at' h:i a";

// Displays: Sat May 1 22:25:00 GMT-0700 2010 (timezone offset may vary)
trace(formatter.parse("05/01/2010 at 10:25 PM"));
```

See Also

Recipe 14.4

## CHAPTER 15

Programming Sound

15.0 Introduction

Proper use of sound in an application, game, or web site can greatly enhance the user's experience. In the Flash IDE, you can import sound into the library, put sound on timeline frames, attach sounds to movie clips, and so on. This chapter covers programming sound with ActionScript 3.0, using the *Sound* class and its related classes.

The *Sound* class is set up to load and stream external MP3 sound files. Since the files aren't embedded in the *.swf* and are being loaded from an external URL, the domain security restrictions outlined in Chapter 3 apply.

Classes covered in this chapter include:

- *Sound*
- *SoundChannel*
- *SoundLoaderContext*
- *SoundMixer*
- *SoundTransform*

These are all part of the *flash.media* package, so as your first order of business, make sure that you import flash.media.Sound in each example as well as any of the other classes the example uses.

15.1 Creating a Sound Object and Loading a Sound

Problem

You want to load into your *.swf* and have it available to the application.

Solution

Create a *Sound* object and load an external sound file into it.

Discussion

Creating a *Sound* object is as easy as making an instance of any class. First, though, make sure the *Sound* class is imported:

```
import flash.media.Sound;
```

and then just create an instance of the *Sound* class:

```
_sound = new Sound( );
```

Now of course, you need to give it a sound file to play. As mentioned earlier, this will be an external MP3 file, such as a song. For all of the examples in this chapter, it's assumed that you have an MP3 file named *song.mp3*, and that this is stored in the same directory as the *.swf* on your server or hard drive.

To load a sound file into your *Sound* object, first create a *URLRequest* object (you'll need to import *flash.net.URLRequest*), passing in the string containing the path to the MP3 file:

```
soundFile = new URLRequest("song.mp3");
```

You can then pass this to the load method of your *Sound* object:

```
_sound.load(soundFile);
```

You can even shortcut these last two steps, as seen in the following class example:

```
package {
    import flash.display.Sprite;
    import flash.media.Sound;
    import flash.net.URLRequest;

    public class LoadSoundExample extends Sprite {
        private var _sound:Sound;

        public function LoadSoundExample ( ) {
            _sound = new Sound( );
            _sound.load(new URLRequest("song.mp3"));
        }
    }
}
```

The class now has a property, _sound, which you can use any time you need to play that sound. Note that the sound does not actually start playing yet. You have merely set it up and started the sound information coming in. See Recipe 15.2 for information on how to control a sound's playing.

An even quicker way is to pass the *URLRequest* right into the constructor when you create the sound, like so:

```
public function LoadSoundExample( ) {
    _sound = new Sound(new URLRequest("song.mp3"));
}
```

When you pass in the request in the constructor like this, the sound automatically calls its own *load( )* method right away and starts to load that sound data. This is especially useful if you are only loading a single sound file into the *Sound* object.

Otherwise, it may be better to create the *Sound* object beforehand and call the *load( )* method when you know which sound file you want to load. An example of this is a music player application in which users can select a song from a play list. When the song is selected, the application sends its path to the sound's *load( )* method, and it is ready to play.

15.2   Starting and Stopping a Sound

Problem

You've created a *Sound* object and started streaming a sound file into it. Now you want to play it and eventually stop it.

Solution

Use the *play( )* method to start the sound playing. Use the *close( )* method to stop the sound from streaming.

Discussion

Playing a sound which has been loaded into a *Sound* object is very easy. Simply call the *play( )* method of that *Sound* object, like so:

```
_sound = new Sound(new URLRequest("song.mp3"));
_sound.play();
```

It is that simple. There are some additional optional parameters to the *play( )* method, which are covered in Recipes 15.1 and 15.10.

The *close( )* method of the *Sound* object not only stops the sound from playing, but also stops the streaming of the sound file. To play that sound again, call the *load( )* method to restart loading the sound data. The *close( )* method should be called only when you are sure you are finished with that particular sound. Recipe 15.1 discusses a way to stop the sound from playing without stopping the stream, using the *SoundChannel* class.

See Also

Recipe 15.1 for information on how to load external sound files and Recipe 15.10.

15.3 Setting the Buffer for a Sound

Problem

You want to ensure that a streaming sound plays smoothly.

Solution

Set a buffer time by using the *SoundLoaderContext* class.

Discussion

The *Sound* class streams audio as it plays, which means that a sound starts playing before it is fully downloaded. This is especially useful for larger sound files, such as full songs, which can be several megabytes in size.

Depending on how your sound is encoded and the available bandwidth, a sound may be playing faster than it is downloading. In this case, the sound may pause while it waits for more sound data to load in. To safeguard against this, you can set a buffer. This causes the *Sound* object to pre-load a certain amount of sound data before it starts playing. Then, if there is a momentary slowdown in bandwidth, the sound can keep playing the buffered data without pausing.

By default, a *Sound* object creates a one-second buffer when you tell it to load a sound file. In other words, even if you tell it to play immediately, the *Sound* object waits until at least one second's worth of sound data has come in. Additionally, if that buffer is used up and the sound needs to stop to wait for more data, it refills that one-second buffer before it resumes playing again.

If you are unsure of network conditions or have sound files that were encoded at a high bitrate (requiring more bits of information per second of playing time), then you may want to increase the size of this buffer to ensure smoother playback. You do this by creating a *SoundLoaderContext* object, passing in the size of the buffer, in milliseconds, to the constructor. For example, if you wanted to create a five-second buffer, you would do the following:

```
buffer = new SoundLoaderContext(5000);
```

You can use this object for either method of loading a sound—in the constructor of the *Sound* object, or in the *load()* method (see Recipe 15.1). Just pass it in as the second parameter after the *URLRequest* parameter, as shown here:

```
var request:URLRequest = new URLRequest("song.mp3");
var buffer:SoundLoaderContext = new SoundLoaderContext(5000);
_sound = new Sound(request, buffer);
_sound.play();
```

or:

```
var request:URLRequest = new URLRequest("song.mp3");
var buffer:SoundLoaderContext = new SoundLoaderContext(5000);
```

```
_sound = new Sound( );
_sound.load(request, buffer);
_sound.play( );
```

See Also

Recipe 15.1 for information on how to load external sound files.

15.4   Offsetting the Start of a Sound

Problem

You want a sound to start playing, not from the start of the sound, but at a position some ways into it.

Solution

Pass a start time to the *play( )* method.

Discussion

There may be instances when you want to start playing a sound file, but not from the very beginning of the sound. In other words, you want to cut off some amount from the start of the sound and play it from that offset point. The *Sound* object gives you very precise control so you can pinpoint the exact place where a sound will start playing, right down to the millisecond.

If you call a *Sound* object's *play( )* method without any parameters, it starts playing from the very beginning. But you can pass it an optional parameter that is the number of milliseconds into the sound at which you want it to start. For example, the following causes the sound to start playing at exactly 5.5 seconds after its beginning point:

```
_sound.play(5500);
```

This particularly comes in handy when you have a sound file that has some introductory material at the beginning that you want to skip over. If you can't edit the sound file to cut that part out, all you need to do is set the start time and skip over the initial portion.

Another example would be to create a system of cue points in the sound. Say you had a recording of a speech and you wanted to allow users to listen to any of several portions of that speech. Taking note of the points at which each portion begins, you can set these up as cue point values in an array. Now, by specifying which cue point to start playing the sound from, you can get the start time from the array and pass that to the *play( )* method. The following class demonstrates a simple example of this:

```
package {
    import flash.display.Sprite;
    import flash.media.Sound;
```

```
import flash.net.URLRequest;

public class CuePoints extends Sprite {
    private var _sound:Sound;
    private var _cuePoints:Array;

    public function CuePoints() {
        _cuePoints = [0, 10000, 30000, 68000, 120000];
        _sound = new Sound(new URLRequest("song.mp3"));

        // Play from the third cuepoint (30 seconds in)
        playCuePoint(2);
    }

    public function playCuePoint(index:int):void {
        _sound.play(_cuePoints[index]);
    }

}
}
```

Of course, in a full application you would have buttons or some other user interface element allowing the user to choose a cue point, which would then pass the index to the playCuePoint( ) method.

Recipe 15.1 explains the functionality to create a pause/restart function in a sound player.

See Also

Recipes 15.1 and 15.2

15.5   Playing a Sound Multiple Times (Looping)

Problem

You want to play a sound file more than once, or have it play over and over in a continuous loop.

Solution

Set a looping value in the *play()* method.

Discussion

When you play a sound, it only plays once—from beginning to end—by default. There may be cases when you want to have the sound play more than once, or even play continuously. For example, you may have a short music loop for the background to a game or for a web site. You can set this loop to play continuously so it sounds like one long song.

The way to set the number of loops (or times) to play is by passing in a value as the second parameter of the *play()* method. Of course, if you do this, you'll also have to set a value for the optional first parameter of the start offset (see Recipe 15.1). If you don't want to offset the start of the sound, but want to use the loop parameter, just pass zero as the first parameter, like so:

```
_sound.play(0, 3);
```

This plays the sound file from the very beginning (zero offset) and loops it three times.

The minimum sensible value you can set for a loop is one, which causes the sound to play only once. If you pass in zero (or even a negative number), the sound still plays only one time.

There is no automatic way to cause the sound to loop forever; however, you can pass a very high value. An easy solution is to pass in int.MAX_VALUE, which is the highest value that an integer variable can hold, and is equal to 2,147,483,647. Even if your sound was only one second long, this would cause it to play for almost 70 years, which is pretty safe to call "continuously."

See Also

Recipes 15.1 and 15.2

15.6   Getting the Size of a Sound File

Problem

You want to know the total size of the MP3 audio file you are loading, as well as the amount that has downloaded so far (so you can create a visual streaming indicator).

Solution

Access the *bytesTotal* and *bytesLoaded* properties of the *Sound* object.

Discussion

When streaming an audio file, it's often a good idea to let the user know how much data has been loaded. The Flash Player loads the sound as fast as it can, and plays the sound at its encoded rate. Ideally, the sound data will load faster than the sound is playing so there won't be a point at which the audio stops playing to load more data. However, in cases of poor connectivity or low bandwidth, and when sounds have been encoded with a high bitrate, the Flash Player may be struggling to keep enough sound data buffered so the sound doesn't stop.

Therefore, it's a good idea to give the user some sort of visual representation for the amount of buffered sound data, alongside the progress of the sound as it plays.

You've probably seen this in many types of streaming media players, such as Windows Media Player or QuickTime Player. Usually there's a progress bar tracking the song as it plays. The background of the bar might be white. On top of that would be a growing black bar representing the progress of the song. Additionally, you might have a gray bar that indicates the buffered amount. As long as the gray bar (buffer) stays ahead of the black one (play position), you know you'll have smooth playback. When it catches up, the media stops playing while the gray bar moves ahead, buffering more data. When it has enough, the media starts again, and the black bar starts moving again, and hopefully the gray has enough of a head start this time.

This recipe covers how to create that gray bar, using two properties of a Sound object: *bytesTotal* and *bytesLoaded*. (Recipe 15.9 shows how to create the black bar.) These properties are pretty self-explanatory; *bytesTotal* contains the total size of the MP3 file you're streaming, and *bytesLoaded* contains how much of it has actually downloaded. If you divide these two values, you'll have the percentage of the sound that has loaded.

The following example sets up an *enterFrame* handler. On each frame it draws a white rectangle on the stage, and then calculates the percent of the sound that has loaded. It uses this to draw another bar (gray, of course) that represents that percent.

```
package {
    import flash.display.Sprite;
    import flash.media.Sound;
    import flash.net.URLRequest;
    import flash.events.Event;

    public class ProgressBar extends Sprite {
        private var _sound:Sound;

        public function ProgressBar() {
            addEventListener(Event.ENTER_FRAME, onEnterFrame);
            _sound = new Sound(new URLRequest("song.mp3"));
            _sound.play();
        }

        public function onEnterFrame(event:Event):void
        {
            var barWidth:int = 200;
            var barHeight:int = 5;
            var loaded:int = _sound.bytesLoaded;
            var total:int = _sound.bytesTotal;
            if(total > 0) {
                // Draw a background bar
                graphics.clear();
                graphics.beginFill(0xFFFFFF);
                graphics.drawRect(10, 10, barWidth, barHeight);
                graphics.endFill();
```

```
                    // The percent of the sound that has loaded
                    var percent:Number = loaded / total;

                    // Draw a bar that represents the percent of
                    // the sound that has loaded
                    graphics.beginFill(0xCCCCCC);
                    graphics.drawRect(10, 10,
                                barWidth * percent, barHeight);
                    graphics.endFill( );
                }
            }
        }
    }
```

If you are playing a sound from your hard disk or local server, you'll barely be able to see the progress bar move; the sound loads almost instantly and the bar will quickly jump to 100 percent. If possible, try to put the MP3 file on an external web server somewhere and access it over the Internet. This gives you a more accurate view of what your end users will see. Also, the browser tends to cache the sound file as it plays, so try clearing your browser's cache before testing this file to give a more realistic view of the buffering.

See Also

Recipe 15.1 for information on how to load external sound files and Recipe 15.7.

15.7   Reading the ID3 Tag of a Sound File

Problem

You want to access information about the MP3 file you are playing, such as the name of the song, artist, album, genre, etc.

Solution

Read the *id3* property of the *Sound* object.

Discussion

MP3 audio files are able to contain an abundance of metadata about the sound. This is most often used in music files to record the name of the song, the artist, album, genre, year of release, composer, etc. How much information is actually included in these tags depends on who encoded or tagged the file. In most cases though, you'll at least be able to get at the *songname* and *artist* tag.

This data is available to you in ActionScript through the *id3* property of a *Sound* object.

This property is an instance of the *flash.media.ID3Info* class, which contains the following properties:

- album
- artist
- comment
- genre
- songName
- track
- year

So, to read the song's name, you would access it as follows:

```
_sound.id3.songName
```

There is just one catch to all of this, though: you can't access these *id3* tags until they have actually downloaded into your *.swf*. If you try to read a tag immediately after you create your *Sound* object or call *play()*, it won't be defined. Factually, the request for the sound file has probably not even reached the server at that point, so of course there will be no tag data available.

So, how do you know when this *id3* data is available? Fortunately, the *Sound* object has an *ID3* event that you can listen for. When this event fires, it is safe to read the *id3* tags. The *Sound* class extends the *EventDispatcher* class, so you can use *addEventDispatcher* to listen for this event, which is defined as *flash.events.Event.ID3*, and assign a handler method to it; this is the method to use for reading the *id3* tags.

The following example creates a text field and lists all available *id3* tags:

```
package {
    import flash.display.Sprite;
    import flash.media.Sound;
    import flash.net.URLRequest;
    import flash.events.Event;
    import flash.text.TextField;

    public class ID3Reader extends Sprite {
        private var _sound:Sound;

        public function ID3Reader () {
            _sound = new Sound(new URLRequest("song.mp3"));
            _sound.addEventListener(Event.ID3, onID3);
            _sound.play();
        }

        public function onID3(event:Event):void {
            // Create a text field and display it
            var id3Display:TextField = new TextField();
            addChild(id3Display);
            id3Display.x = 10;
```

```
            id3Display.y = 20;
            id3Display.width = 200;
            id3Display.height = 200;
            id3Display.background = true;
            id3Display.multiline = true;
            id3Display.wordWrap = true;

            // Add some info about the song to the text field
            id3Display.text += _sound.id3.songName + "\n";
            id3Display.text += _sound.id3.artist + "\n";
            id3Display.text += _sound.id3.album + "\n";
            id3Display.text += _sound.id3.year + "\n";            }
        }
    }
}
```

See Also

Recipe 15.1 for information on how to load external sound files and Recipe 15.6.

15.8 Find Out When a Sound Finishes Playing

Problem

You've started playing a sound file and need to know when it has finished playing.

Solution

Listen for the *soundComplete* event.

Discussion

There are many cases when you might need to know when a sound is finished playing. For example, if have an audio introduction that you want to play before a user moves onto the next section of a site, you will want to know when it is safe to go to the next section. Or perhaps you have a music player with a playlist of songs. You'll want to know when each song is complete so you can start the next one.

For this recipe, and the next few, you'll be working with another class in the *flash. media* package, *SoundChannel*. When you call a *Sound* object's *play()* method, it returns a *SoundChannel* object. Thus, each sound playing in a *.swf* is represented by a single *SoundChannel* object. These channels are mixed together to produce the final audio output.

When a sound file has finished playing, its corresponding *SoundChannel* object fires a *soundComplete* event. This is defined as *flash.events.Event.SOUND_COMPLETE*. You can add a listener to the *SoundChannel* object and supply a handler method, which is called when the sound has finished playing.

The following example sets up a simple playlist:

```
package {
    import flash.display.Sprite;
    import flash.media.Sound;
    import flash.net.URLRequest;
    import flash.events.Event;
    import flash.media.SoundChannel;

    public class PlayList extends Sprite {
        private var _sound:Sound;
        private var _channel:SoundChannel;
        private var _playList:Array;      // the list of songs
        private var _index:int = 0;       // the current song

        public function PlayList() {
            // Create the playlist and start playing
            _playList = ["song1.mp3",
                         "song2.mp3",
                         "song3.mp3"];
            playNextSong();
        }

        private function playNextSong():void
        {
            // If there are still songs in the playlist
            if(_index < _playList.length) {
                // Create a new Sound object, load and play it
                // _playList[_index] contains the name and path of
                // the next song
                _sound = new Sound();
                _sound.load(new URLRequest(_playList[_index]));
                _channel = _sound.play();

                // Add the listener to the channel

                _channel.addEventListener(Event.SOUND_COMPLETE,
                                          onComplete);

                // Increase the counter
                _index++;
            }
        }

        public function onComplete(event:Event):void
        {
            playNextSong();
        }
    }
}
```

Here, the index variable starts out as zero. This causes _playList[index] to be evaluated as "song.mp3", which gets loaded first. Then index is incremented. When

the *soundComplete* event fires, the *playNextSong( )* method loads the next song in
_playList, until the index is greater than the number of songs in the playlist.

See Also

Recipe 15.1 for information on how to load external sound files.

15.9   Tracking the Progress of a Playing Sound

Problem

You want to know where the playhead is in the current song so you can see how
much of the song has played, in relation to the full song.

Solution

Use *Sound.length* to determine how long a song is, and *SoundChannel.position* to
determine how much of it has played.

Discussion

Recipe 15.6 discussed how to add a progress bar that not only shows the playing
position of a sound file, but also how much of that file has been loaded into the
player. That recipe created the part of the bar that showed how much of the song has
loaded.

This recipe covers the other part, showing you how to track a sound's progress as it
plays. To do this, you'll need to know two things: the length of the sound and its
current playing position. Although it may seem counterintuitive, these two properties are found in two different classes. The length of the sound is a property of the
Sound object, and the playing position is part of the *SoundChannel*. Similar to how
the buffering progress bar was created, these two values can be compared against
each other to get the percentage of the sound that has played.

Unfortunately, it gets just a bit more complex than the buffering bar. The problem is
that the *length* property isn't accurate until the sound file is fully loaded. It actually
just shows the length of the loaded data. So, for example, if 10 percent of a 10-
minute audio file has loaded so far, then *length* would report that the file was 1
minute long. (Actually, both *length* and *position* report the time in milliseconds, but
you can convert that to minutes and seconds if you needed to display the numbers.)

Fortunately, you can do some simple math to get an estimate of the sound file's
actual length. Since *length* reports a fraction of the actual length, if you divide it by
that fraction, the result is very close to the true time of the sound. Taking the example just mentioned, *length* shows a time of one minute. However, that's based on just
1/10th of the file being loaded. If you divide 1 by 1/10 (the same as multiplying by
10), you get 10 minutes as the length of the sound.

The fraction in this case is *bytesLoaded/bytesTotal*, which has already been calculated and stored in a variable to draw the buffering bar. So all it really takes is one more line of code to correct the length:

```
length /= percentBuffered;
```

 As in Recipe 15.2, you'll get a more accurate picture of how this works if you access the MP3 file over the web and clear your browser's cache each time.

The following example shows both progress bars together:

```
package {
    import flash.display.Sprite;
    import flash.media.Sound;
    import flash.media.SoundChannel;
    import flash.net.URLRequest;
    import flash.events.Event;

    public class ProgressBar2 extends Sprite {
        private var _sound:Sound;
        private var _channel:SoundChannel;

        public function ProgressBar2( ) {
            addEventListener(Event.ENTER_FRAME, onEnterFrame);
            _sound = new Sound(new URLRequest("song.mp3"));
            _channel = _sound.play( );
        }

        public function onEnterFrame(event:Event):void
        {
            var barWidth:int = 200;
            var barHeight:int = 5;

            var loaded:int = _sound.bytesLoaded;
            var total:int = _sound.bytesTotal;

            var length:int = _sound.length;
            var position:int = _channel.position;

            // Draw a background bar
            graphics.clear( );
            graphics.beginFill(0xFFFFFF);
            graphics.drawRect(10, 10, barWidth, barHeight);
            graphics.endFill( );

            if(total > 0) {
                // The percent of the sound that has loaded
                var percentBuffered:Number = loaded / total;

                // Draw a bar that represents the percent of
                // the sound that has loaded
```

```
graphics.beginFill(0xCCCCCC);
graphics.drawRect(10, 10,
                      barWidth * percentBuffered,
                      barHeight);
graphics.endFill();

// Correct the sound length calculation
length /= percentBuffered;

  // The percent of the sound that has played
  var percentPlayed:Number = position / length;

// Draw a bar that represents the percent of
// the sound that has played
graphics.beginFill(0x666666);
graphics.drawRect(10, 10,
                      barWidth * percentPlayed,
                      barHeight);
graphics.endFill();
        }
      }
    }
  }
```

See Also

Recipe 15.1 for information on how to load external sound files and Recipe 15.2.

15.10 Pausing and Restarting a Sound

Problem

You want to pause a sound and restart it later from where it stopped playing.

Solution

Take note of the *position* property of the sound's *SoundChannel*. When you restart the sound, use that value as an offset.

Discussion

As noted in Recipe 15.2, you can call the *close()* method of a *Sound* object to make it stop playing. However, this also stops the sound from streaming, so to replay it, you'll need to re-call the *load()* method.

Fortunately, the *SoundChannel* class offers a *stop()* method, which causes the sound to stop playing without affecting the loading. To restart the sound, just call the *play()* method again.

You should note, however, that the *play()* method causes the sound to start from the beginning. This is the expected behavior for a "stop" button, as seen on many media players. Creating a "pause" button takes a bit more work. The strategy is to set up a handler method that's called when a pause button is pressed. In this function, read and store the current *position* of the *SoundChannel*, which gives you the time in milliseconds from the sound's beginning. Store this in a class variable so it can be accessed later. At this point, the pause button becomes a play button. When pressed again, call the *play()* method of the *Sound* object, passing in the saved position. This causes the sound to play from that point, which is the exact point at which it stopped. The following example demonstrates this strategy:

```
package {
    import flash.display.Sprite;
    import flash.media.Sound;
    import flash.media.SoundChannel;
    import flash.net.URLRequest;
    import flash.events.Event;
    import flash.display.Sprite;
    import flash.events.MouseEvent;

    public class PlayPause extends Sprite {
        private var _sound:Sound;
        private var _channel:SoundChannel;
        private var _playPauseButton:Sprite;
        private var _playing:Boolean = false;
        private var _position:int;

        public function PlayPause() {
            // Create sound and start it
            _sound = new Sound(new URLRequest("song.mp3"));
            _channel = _sound.play();
            _playing = true;

            // A sprite to use as a Play/Pause button
            _playPauseButton = new Sprite();
            addChild(_playPauseButton);
            _playPauseButton.x = 10;
            _playPauseButton.y = 20;
            _playPauseButton.graphics.beginFill(0xcccccc);
            _playPauseButton.graphics.drawRect(0, 0, 20, 20);
            _playPauseButton.addEventListener(MouseEvent.MOUSE_UP,
                                              onPlayPause);
        }

        public function onPlayPause(event:MouseEvent):void {
            // If playing, stop. Take note of position
            if(_playing) {
                _position = _channel.position;
                _channel.stop();
            }
            else {
                // If not playing, re-start it at
                // last known position
                _channel = _sound.play(_position);
```

```
            }
                _playing = !_playing;
            }
        }
    }
```

The code creates a sprite to serve as a button. In the mouse up handler, the sound is stopped if it is playing, and its position is noted. The next time the button is pressed, the sound starts playing at the position where it left off.

See Also

Recipe 15.2

15.11 Reading the Level of a Sound

Problem

You want to know how loud a currently playing sound is.

Solution

Access the *SoundChannel.leftPeak* and *SoundChannel.rightPeak* properties.

Discussion

Any sound, as it is playing, goes through various levels of loudness and softness. This is known as its *amplitude*. ActionScript 3.0 lets you access the amplitude for the left and right channels of a stereo sound separately. These are the *leftPeak* and *rightPeak* properties of the *SoundChannel* object that is created when you start playing a sound.

These values are in a range from 0.0 to 1.0, with 1.0 being the maximum amplitude. Don't confuse this with volume, which can be an overall setting for a sound, and is controlled via the *SoundTransorm* object (see Recipe 15.14). This is the level of sound volume at a particular instance, and it varies constantly as the sound plays.

The following example reads these values and creates two bars, the lengths of which are based on the current amplitude of each channel on each frame:

```
package {
    import flash.display.Sprite;
    import flash.media.Sound;
    import flash.media.SoundChannel;
    import flash.net.URLRequest;
    import flash.events.Event;

    public class SoundLevels extends Sprite {
        private var _sound:Sound;
        private var _channel:SoundChannel;

        public function SoundLevels() {
```

```
        addEventListener(Event.ENTER_FRAME, onEnterFrame);
        _sound = new Sound(new URLRequest("song.mp3"));
        _channel = _sound.play( );
    }

    public function onEnterFrame(event:Event):void
    {
        var leftLevel:Number = _channel.leftPeak * 100;
        var rightLevel:Number = _channel.rightPeak * 100;
        graphics.clear( );
        graphics.beginFill(0xcccccc);
        graphics.drawRect(10, 10, leftLevel, 10);
        graphics.endFill( );
        graphics.beginFill(0xcccccc);
        graphics.drawRect(10, 25, rightLevel, 10);
        graphics.endFill( );

    }
  }
}
```

See Also

Recipe 15.1 for information on how to load external sound files and Recipe 15.14.

15.12 Stopping All Sounds

Problem

You want to stop all currently playing sounds.

Solution

Use the *stopAll( )* method of the *SoundMixer* object.

Discussion

As mentioned earlier, whenever you start playing a sound, it creates a *SoundChannel* object. You can play multiple sounds in a *.swf*, and each one will be assigned to a separate sound channel. Some aspects of a sound are controlled via the *Sound* object itself, some from the sound channel. In the end, all of the currently playing channels are mixed together to create the final sound coming from the speakers. The object responsible for this is the *SoundMixer* object. Its properties and methods apply to all the sounds in the movie as they are mixed together.

One of these methods is the *stopAll( )* method. As expected, this stops every currently playing sound in the *.swf*.

Although sound can greatly enhance the experience of a web site, game, etc., you should always give the user the option to turn off the sound. The *stopAll( )* method is the simplest way to do this. It is a static method of the *SoundMixer* class, so you can call it directly from there. Usually this would be done in an event handler attached to a button or sprite, like so:

```
public function stopSounds(event:Event):void {
    SoundMixer.stopAll( );
}
```

See Also

Recipe 15.2

15.13 Reading the Sound Spectrum

Problem

You want to visually represent the sound wave of the sounds playing in your *.swf*.

Solution

Use *SoundMixer.computeSpectrum( )* to fill a byte array with the spectrum data of the sound playing in the *.swf*. Read the values of this array to create a visualization of that data.

Discussion

One of the most exciting additions to the sound capabilities in ActionScript 3.0 is the ability to access sound spectrum data. Throughout the years and versions of Flash, developers have yearned to get at this data. Some third-party tools read this data in and created a separate text file containing the values of the sound spectrum data. This file could be read in and synchronized to the sound. However, these solutions were complex to work with and not very efficient. Now that this feature is built into the *SoundMixer* class, and with the addition of the new *ByteArray* class, you can easily display this data with just a few lines of code.

First, let's cover the *ByteArray* class. This new special class in ActionScript 3.0 is used to handle blocks of binary data in a highly compact, efficient, and optimized way. It is part of the *flash.utils* package. Essentially, it is what it sounds like: an array of bytes. But its methods allow for fast manipulation and access of its data—much faster than a traditional ActionScript array.

For use in computing the sound spectrum, you first need to create an empty *ByteArray*, as shown in the following example:

```
var spectrum:ByteArray = new ByteArray( );
```

This *ByteArray* is then passed into *SoundMixer.computeSpectrum( )*. This method takes a snapshot of the sound as it's playing and calculates the current sound wave on both the left and right channels. It breaks this into 256 values on each channel, each from -1.0 to 1.0. It stores these values in the empty *ByteArray* you just passed in.

This data is now available for you to use however you want. You just need to loop through the *ByteArray* 512 times, calling *getFloat()*. The first 256 calls give you the values for the left channel; the next 256 are for the right channel.

The following example uses these values, along with a *BitmapData* object and *setPixel32()* to create a visual representation of both channels' sound waves:

```
package {
    import flash.display.Bitmap;
    import flash.display.BitmapData;
    import flash.display.Sprite;
    import flash.events.Event;
    import flash.media.Sound;
    import flash.media.SoundChannel;
    import flash.net.URLRequest;
    import flash.utils.ByteArray;


    public class Spectrum extends Sprite {
        private var _sound:Sound;
        private var _channel:SoundChannel;
        private var _spectrumGraph:BitmapData;

        public function Spectrum( ) {
            // Create bitmap for spectrum display
            _spectrumGraph = new BitmapData(256, 60,
                                            true,
                                            0x00000000);
            var bitmap:Bitmap = new Bitmap(_spectrumGraph);
            addChild(bitmap);
            bitmap.x = 10;
            bitmap.y = 10;

            addEventListener(Event.ENTER_FRAME, onEnterFrame);
            _sound = new Sound(new URLRequest("song.mp3"));
            _channel = _sound.play( );
        }

        public function onEnterFrame(event:Event):void
        {
            // Create the byte array and fill it with data
            var spectrum:ByteArray = new ByteArray( );
            SoundMixer.computeSpectrum(spectrum);

            // Clear the bitmap
            _spectrumGraph.fillRect(_spectrumGraph.rect,
                                    0x00000000);

            // Create the left channel visualization
            for(var i:int=0;i<256;i++) {
                _spectrumGraph.setPixel32(i,
                            20 + spectrum.readFloat( ) * 20,
                            0xffffffff);
            }
```

```
        // Create the right channel visualization
        for(var i:int=0;i<256;i++) {
            _spectrumGraph.setPixel32(i,
                            40 + spectrum.readFloat( ) * 20,
                            0xffffffff);
        }
    }
  }
 }
}
```

See Also

Recipe 15.14

15.14 Changing the Volume or Pan of a Sound

Problem

You want to change the volume of a sound, making it softer or louder, or set the pan (amount of left/right balance) of a sound.

Solution

Create a new *SoundTransform* object, specifying the volume at which you want the sound to play, or the amount and direction of panning you want to apply. Pass this to the *soundTransform* property of the *SoundChannel* object associated with the sound you want to control.

Discussion

In previous versions of ActionScript, you could set the volume and panning of a sound directly on the *Sound* object itself. Now these aspects of the sound playback are abstracted into the *SoundTransform* class.

A *SoundChannel* object has a *soundTransform* property, which is an instance of the *SoundTransform* class. To change a sound's volume or panning, create a new *SoundTransform* object and set the desired values. Next, set the *SoundChannel's* *soundTransform* property to this new object. For example, the following sets the sound volume to 50 percent:

```
var _sound:Sound = new Sound(new URLRequest("song.mp3"));
var channel:SoundChannel = _sound.play( );
var transform:SoundTransform = new SoundTransform( );
transform.volume = .5;
channel.soundTransform = transform;
```

As you can gather, the volume can range from 0.0 (silent) to 1.0 (full volume). Similarly, you can set the panning of a sound:

```
var channel:SoundChannel = _sound.play();
var transform:SoundTransform = new SoundTransform();
transform.pan = -1.0;
channel.soundTransform = transform;
```

This sets the sound to play only in the left speaker, as the values here can range from -1.0 (full left) to 1.0 (full right).

You can also pass the volume and pan amounts straight to the *SoundTransform*'s constructor, like so:

```
var channel:SoundChannel = _sound.play();
var transform:SoundTransform = new SoundTransform(.5, -1.0);
channel.soundTransform = transform;
```

The first parameter is volume, and the second is pan.

See Also

Recipe 15.13

15.15 Creating a Sound Application

Problem

You want to create a full-featured sound application, such as a streaming MP3 player.

Solution

Apply the other recipes in this chapter to play a streaming sound and add as many features as you want.

Discussion

This recipe combines many of the techniques shown throughout this chapter, integrated into a single application. There is much more that could be done with this, but it should give you a start at seeing how to use all these features together.

```
package {
    import flash.display.Sprite;
    import flash.display.Stage;
    import flash.display.StageAlign;
    import flash.display.StageScaleMode;
    import flash.text.TextField;
    import flash.events.Event;
    import flash.events.MouseEvent;
    import flash.events.TimerEvent;
    import flash.media.Sound;
    import flash.media.SoundChannel;
```

```
import flash.media.SoundTransform;
import flash.net.URLRequest;
import flash.text.TextFormat;
import flash.utils.Timer;

public class CookBookPlayer extends Sprite {
    private var _channel:SoundChannel;
    private var _displayText:TextField;
    private var _sound:Sound;
    private var _panControl:PanControl;
    private var _playing:Boolean = false;
    private var _playPauseButton:Sprite;
    private var _position:int = 0;
    private var _spectrumGraph:SpectrumGraph;
    private var _volumeControl:VolumeControl;

    public function CookBookPlayer( ) {
        // Stage alignment
        stage.scaleMode =
                    flash.display.StageScaleMode.NO_SCALE;
        stage.align = flash.display.StageAlign.TOP_LEFT;

        // Enter frame listener
        var timer:Timer = new Timer(20);
        timer.addEventListener(TimerEvent.TIMER, onTimer);
        timer.start( );
        _playing = true;

        // Display a text field
        _displayText = new TextField( );
        addChild(_displayText);
        _displayText.x = 10;
        _displayText.y = 17;
        _displayText.width = 256;
        _displayText.height = 14;

        // Create a sound object
        _sound = new Sound(new URLRequest(""http://www.rightactionscript.com
        samplefiles/sample.mp3""));
        _sound.addEventListener(Event.ID3, onID3);
        _channel = _sound.play( );

        // Create a bitmap for spectrum display
        _spectrumGraph = new SpectrumGraph( );
        _spectrumGraph.x = 10;
        _spectrumGraph.y = 33;
        addChild(_spectrumGraph);

        // Create the Play and Pause buttons
        _playPauseButton = new PlayButton( );
        _playPauseButton.x = 10;
        _playPauseButton.y = 68;
        addChild(_playPauseButton);
        _playPauseButton.addEventListener(MouseEvent.MOUSE_UP,
```

```
                                    onPlayPause);

    // Create volume and pan controls
    _volumeControl = new VolumeControl();
    _volumeControl.x = 45;
    _volumeControl.y = 68;
    addChild(_volumeControl);
    _volumeControl.addEventListener(Event.CHANGE,
                                    onTransform);

    _panControl = new PanControl();
    _panControl.x = 164;
    _panControl.y = 68;
    addChild(_panControl);
    _panControl.addEventListener(Event.CHANGE,
                                 onTransform);
}

public function onTransform(event:Event):void
{
    // Get volume and pan data from controls
    // and apply to a new SoundTransform object
    _channel.soundTransform = new SoundTransform(
                              _volumeControl.volume,
                              _panControl.pan);
}

public function onPlayPause(event:MouseEvent):void
{
    // If playing, stop and record that position
    if(_playing) {
        _position = _channel.position;
        _channel.stop();
    }
    else {
        // Else, restart at the saved position
        _channel = _sound.play(_position);
    }
    _playing = !_playing;
}

public function onID3(event:Event):void {
    // Display selected id3 tags in the text field
    _displayText.text = _sound.id3.artist + " : " +
                        _sound.id3.songName;
    _displayText.setTextFormat(
            new TextFormat("_typewriter", 8, 0));
}

public function onTimer(event:TimerEvent):void {
    var barWidth:int = 256;
    var barHeight:int = 5;

    var loaded:int = _sound.bytesLoaded;
    var total:int = _sound.bytesTotal;
```

```
            var length:int = _sound.length;
            var position:int = _channel.position;

            // Draw a background bar
            graphics.clear();
            graphics.beginFill(0xFFFFFF);
            graphics.drawRect(10, 10, barWidth, barHeight);
            graphics.endFill();

            if(total > 0) {
                // The percent of the sound that has loaded
                var percentBuffered:Number = loaded / total;

                // Draw a bar that represents the percent of
                // the sound that has loaded
                graphics.beginFill(0xCCCCCC);
                graphics.drawRect(10, 10,
                                  barWidth * percentBuffered,
                                  barHeight);
                graphics.endFill();

                // Correct the sound length calculation
                length /= percentBuffered;

                // The percent of the sound that has played
                var percentPlayed:Number = position / length;
                // Draw a bar that represents the percent of
                // the sound that has played
                graphics.beginFill(0x666666);
                graphics.drawRect(10, 10,
                                  barWidth * percentPlayed,
                                  barHeight);
                graphics.endFill();

                _spectrumGraph.update();
            }


        }
    }
}


// "helper classes"
// (This is an outside package, but it's available to classes
// in the same file)
import flash.display.Bitmap;
import flash.display.BitmapData;
import flash.display.Sprite;
import flash.events.Event;
import flash.events.MouseEvent;
import flash.filters.DropShadowFilter;
import flash.geom.Rectangle;
import flash.media.SoundMixer;
import flash.utils.ByteArray;
```

```
class PlayButton extends Sprite {
    public function PlayButton() {
        // Draw the Play/Pause graphic
        graphics.beginFill(0xcccccc);
        graphics.drawRoundRect(0, 0, 20, 16, 4, 4);
        graphics.endFill();
        graphics.beginFill(0x333333);
        graphics.moveTo(4, 4);
        graphics.lineTo(8, 8);
        graphics.lineTo(4, 12);
        graphics.lineTo(4, 4);
        graphics.drawRect(10, 4, 2, 8);
        graphics.drawRect(14, 4, 2, 8);
        graphics.endFill();

    }
}
class SpectrumGraph extends Sprite {
    private var _spectrumBMP:BitmapData;

    public function SpectrumGraph()
    {
        // Bitmap to draw spectrum data in
        _spectrumBMP = new BitmapData(256, 30,
                                      true, 0x00000000);
        var bitmap:Bitmap = new Bitmap(_spectrumBMP);
        bitmap.filters = [new DropShadowFilter(3, 45, 0, 1,
                                               3, 2, .3, 3)];
        addChild(bitmap);
    }

    public function update():void
    {
        // Get spectrum data
        var spectrum:ByteArray = new ByteArray();
        SoundMixer.computeSpectrum(spectrum);

        // Draw to bitmap
        _spectrumBMP.fillRect(_spectrumBMP.rect, 0xff666666);
        _spectrumBMP.fillRect(new Rectangle(1, 1, 254, 28),
                    0x00000000);
        for(var i:int=0;i<256;i++) {
            _spectrumBMP.setPixel32(i,
                               10 + spectrum.readFloat() * 10,
                               0xff000000);
        }
        for(var i:int=0;i<256;i++) {
            _spectrumBMP.setPixel32(i,
                               20 + spectrum.readFloat() * 10,
                               0xff000000);
        }
    }
}

class VolumeControl extends Sprite {
```

```
    public var volume:Number = 1.0;

    public function VolumeControl( )
    {
        addEventListener(MouseEvent.CLICK, onClick);
        draw( );
    }

    public function onClick(event:MouseEvent):void
    {
        // When user clicks the bar, set the volume
        volume = event.localX / 100;
        draw( );
        dispatchEvent(new Event(Event.CHANGE));
    }

    private function draw( ):void {
        // Draw a bar and the current volume position
        graphics.beginFill(0xcccccc);
        graphics.drawRect(0, 0, 102, 16);
        graphics.endFill( );

        graphics.beginFill(0x000000);
        graphics.drawRect(volume * 100, 0, 2, 16);
    }
}

class PanControl extends Sprite {
    public var pan:Number = 0;

    public function PanControl( )
    {
        addEventListener(MouseEvent.CLICK, onClick);
        draw( );
    }

    public function onClick(event:MouseEvent):void
    {
        // When the user clicks bar, set pan
        pan = event.localX / 50 - 1;
        draw( );
        dispatchEvent(new Event(Event.CHANGE));
    }

    private function draw( ):void {
        // Draw the bar and current pan position
        graphics.beginFill(0xcccccc);
        graphics.drawRect(0, 0, 102, 16);
        graphics.endFill( );

        graphics.beginFill(0x000000);
        graphics.drawRect(50 + pan * 50, 0, 2, 16);
    }
}
```

## CHAPTER 16

Video

16.0 Introduction

The Flash Player is capable of playing back video. Although it's possible to embed video content within an *.swf* file, most Flash video content is stored in Flash video files (*.flv* files) and loaded into the Flash Player at runtime using ActionScript. By loading *.flv* files at runtime, you have smaller *.swf* files, more flexible content management, and greater control over the loading and playback of the video content.

Flash video loaded from *.flv* files has two faces: progressive download and streaming. Streaming *.flv* video requires a streaming server, such as Flash Media Server. In contrast, progressive download doesn't require any additional software. However, for the most part, the ActionScript required to work with streaming and progressive download video is identical. The recipes in this chapter discuss how to work with progressive download video and focus exclusively on working with *.flv* files.

16.1 Loading and Playing Back Video

Problem

You want to load and playback progressive download Flash video.

Solution

Use a *NetStream* object to load and playback the video and use a *Video* object to display the video.

Discussion

ActionScript 3.0 requires several classes working together to load and playback Flash video. You must use a *NetStream* object to load the video and control the playback; however, the *NetStream* class is only concerned with moving data, it doesn't know how to render the data as a video. For that you have to use a *Video* object. The *Video* object allows you to pass it a *NetStream* object, which then uses the *NetStream* data to render the video to the screen.

The *NetStream* constructor requires that you pass it a *NetConnection* object. The *NetConnection* object determines the origin of the data that the *NetStream* object handles. When the Flash video streams from a Flash Communication Server or Flash Media Server, the *NetConnection* object points to the server. However, for progressive download video content the *NetConnection* object uses a *null* connection string. The following code constructs a *NetConnection* object and initializes it for use with progressive download video. Note that the code assumes you've imported the *flash. net.NetConnection* class:

```
var videoConnection:NetConnection = new NetConnection( );
videoConnection.connect(null);
```

Once you've constructed a *NetConnection* object and called the *connect()* method with a null value, construct the *NetStream* object, and then pass the *NetStream* constructor a reference to the *NetConnection* object. The following code constructs a *NetStream* object (assuming you've imported *flash.net.NetStream*):

```
var videoStream:NetStream = new NetStream(videoConnection);
```

Once you've constructed the *NetStream* object, add a *Video* object, and associate the *NetStream* with the *Video*.

The *flash.media.Video* class is a display object, which means that you have to add it to the display list once constructed. The following code constructs a new *Video* object and then adds it to the display list:

```
var video:Video = new Video( );
addChild(video);
```

You can associate a *NetStream* object with a *Video* object by using the *Video* object's *attachNetStream()* method, passing a reference to the *NetStream* object as a parameter to the method:

```
video.attachNetStream(videoStream);
```

After you attached the *NetStream* object to the *Video* object, any video data controlled by the *NetStream* object gets rendered by the *Video* object.

Everything discussed up to this point is necessary to initialize all the requisite objects and associations. However, nothing so far actually tells the Flash Player to load the video and start playback—both of which are accomplished with one simple method call. The *NetStream* class defines a *play()* method that loads and starts the Flash video playback as specified by the parameter passed to it. The parameter can be a relative or absolute URL. The following tells the Flash Player to load and start the playback of a Flash video called *example.flv* that's in the same directory as the calling *.swf*:

```
videoStream.play("example.flv");
```

If the *.flv* file is in the same domain as the calling *.swf*, then the *play()* call isn't subject to Flash Player security. However, if the FLV is in a different domain, then a security policy file is required to allow the calling SWF to load and playback the FLV.

Flash video playback starts automatically as soon as enough has buffered. You can control buffering and monitor loading, both of which are discussed in Recipe 16.7.

If the FLV file has metadata embedded within it (and most encoders do embed metadata) you'll also have to handle the metadata event as described in Recipe 16.4. Additionally, if the FLV contains cue points, you'll have to handle the cue point events as described in Recipe 16.8. If the FLV contains metadata and/or cue points and you don't handle the events, Flash Player throws errors.

See Also

Recipes 16.4, 16.7, and 16.8

16.2   Controlling Video Sound

Problem

You want to control the volume and pan transform of the sound portion of the video.

Solution

Use the soundTransform property of the *NetStream* object.

Discussion

If a Flash video has an audio track, the audio plays back automatically along with the video. If you want to manage the volume or pan transform of the sound you can use the soundTransform property of the *NetStream* object to retrieve a reference to the *SoundTransform* object associated with the audio. For more details on working with *SoundTransform* objects, see Recipe 15.14.

See Also

Recipe 15.14

16.3   Reading Playback Time

Problem

You want to read the current playback time of a video.

Solution

Use the time property of the *NetStream* object.

Discussion

The time property of the *NetStream* class is a read-only property that reports the playback time of the video. The value is in seconds from the start of the video. The following displays the playback time of a video in a text field:

```
textField.text = videoStream.time + " seconds";
```

Note that the value is not rounded to the nearest whole number. That means you can have values such as 1 as well as values such as 5.235. If you need whole numbers, you can use *Math.round()*, *Math.floor()*, or *Math.ceil()*.

Since the time property is read-only, you cannot use it to control playback. If you want to control playback, use the *seek()* method as described in Recipe 16.5.

See Also

Recipes 4.3 and 16.5.

16.4   Reading Video Duration

Problem

You want to read the total length (duration) of a video.

Solution

Use an *onMetaData()* callback and read the duration metadata value.

Discussion

The *NetStream* class does *not* define a property that reports the total length of a Flash video. However, in most cases, it is possible to read that value from the FLV file itself. FLV files can contain metadata, and almost all video encoders include a duration metadata value, which stores the length of the video in seconds (which can be fractions of seconds). Assuming the FLV has a duration metadata value, you can read that value with ActionScript.

When a *NetStream* object is loading an FLV file, it automatically calls an *onMetaData()* callback method when the metadata has loaded. The callback model differs from the standard event model used by most of the ActionScript 3.0 APIs. In most cases in which you work with events you add a listener using *addEventListener()*. However, in the case of metadata events you must define an *onMetaData()* method for an object and then assign that object to the client property of the *NetStream* object. The method is automatically passed an associative array parameter typed as *Object* that contains properties and values corresponding to each of the metadata properties that have been read from the FLV. The following example uses *trace()* to display the duration metadata value of a video clip:

```
var client:Object = new Object();
client.onMetaData = function(metadata:Object):void {
    trace(metadata.duration);
};
videoStream.client = client;
```

In practice, the preceding example isn't all that useful. Rather, you're more likely to assign a function reference to the onMetaData property of the *NetStream* object. When the function is called, it is called with the correct scope. The following example class loads, plays back a video, and displays the playback time and duration:

```
package {

    import flash.display.TextField;
    import flash.media.Video;
    import flash.net.NetConnection;
    import flash.net.NetStream;
    import flash.events.NetStatusEvent;
    import flash.display.TextFieldAutoSize;
    import flash.display.Sprite;
    import flash.events.Event;

    public class Example extends Sprite {

        private var _stream:NetStream;
        private var _video:Video;
        private var _playbackTime:TextField;
        private var _duration:uint;

        public function Example() {
            _video = new Video(160, 120);
            _playbackTime = new TextField();
            _playbackTime.autoSize = TextFieldAutoSize.LEFT;
            _playbackTime.y = 120;
            _playbackTime.text = "test";
            _duration = 0;
            var connection:NetConnection = new NetConnection();
            connection.connect(null);
            _stream = new NetStream(connection);
            _stream.play("video.flv");
            var client:Object = new Object();
            client.onMetaData = onMetaData;
            _stream.client = client;
            _video.attachNetStream(_stream);
            addChild(_video);
            addChild(_playbackTime);
            addEventListener(Event.ENTER_FRAME, onEnterFrame);
        }
```

```
private function onMetaData(data:Object):void {
    _duration = data.duration;
}

private function onEnterFrame(event:Event):void {
    if(_duration > 0 && _stream.time > 0) {
        _playbackTime.text = Math.round(_stream.time) + " / " +
        Math.round(_duration);
    }
}

}
}
```

See Also

Recipe 16.8

16.5   Controlling Playback Time

Problem

You want to control the playback of a video.

Solution

Use the *seek()* method of the *NetStream* object.

Discussion

Although you may assume you can set the playback time by assigning a value to the time property of the *NetStream* object that controls the video, that won't work. As mentioned in Recipe 16.3, the time property is read-only. Rather, you must use the *seek()* method. The *seek()* method requires one parameter to specify the number of seconds from the start of the video to which you want to move the playback. The following example seeks five seconds from the start of the video before starting the playback:

```
videoStream.seek(5);
```

When using *seek()* with progressive download video, you can seek to only a part of the video that has downloaded. For example, if half of a 60-second video has downloaded, you can seek to 10 seconds, but you cannot seek to 50 seconds.

When you use *seek()*, Flash Player jumps to the nearest video keyframe to the value you specify. Videos are encoded with different keyframe rates. Higher keyframe rates have larger bandwidth requirements than lower keyframe rates. However, higher keyframe rates enables greater granularity when seeking.

See Also

Recipe 16.12

16.6 Scaling Video

Problem

You want to change the dimensions of the video display.

Solution

Set the width and height properties of the *Video* object. If you want the video to play-back at the dimensions at which it was encoded, use the videoWidth and videoHeight values.

Discussion

The dimensions at which a video plays back are determined by the width and height of the *Video* object. When you construct a *Video* object, you can specify the display's initial width and height; for example, the following constructs a *Video* object that is 160×120 pixels:

```
var video:Video = new Video(160, 120);
```

However, you can still change the dimensions after the object is constructed by using the width and height properties. The following doubles the dimensions of the *Video* object constructed in the preceding example:

```
video.width = 320;
video.height = 240;
```

The *Video* class also defines two read-only properties, videoWidth and videoHeight, which return the width and height at which the video was encoded. You can use the videoWidth and videoHeight properties to set the width and height of the *Video* object, as follows:

```
video.width = video.videoWidth;
video.height = video.videoHeight;
```

However, note that the videoWidth and videoHeight properties are not correctly defined until the FLV has started to download. Therefore, if you want to set the width and height of the *Video* object based on the encoded dimensions, you must wait until the videoWidth and videoHeight properties are correctly defined. You can use a netStatus event listener for that purpose:

```
videoStream.addEventListener(NetStatusEvent.NET_STATUS, onStatus);
```

Then define the listener with an if statement that tests for videoWidth and videoHeight greater than 0, as well as width and height values not equal to videoWidth and `videoHeight`. Since the `videoWidth` and `videoHeight` are set at the same time, you only need to test for one of them:

```
private function onStatus(event:NetStatusEvent):void {
    if(_video.videoWidth > 0 && _video.width != _video.videoWidth) {
        _video.width = _video.videoWidth;
        _video.height = _video.videoHeight;
    }
}
```

16.7 Managing and Monitoring Buffering and Loading

Problem

You want to manage video buffering and monitor the progress of a video as it downloads.

Solution

Use the `bufferTime` property to set the number of seconds that must buffer before playback starts, and then use `bytesLoaded` and `bytesTotal` to monitor the download's progress.

Discussion

By default, video starts to playback as soon as 0.1 (one-tenth) seconds of the video has buffered. Larger buffers can ensure a smoother playback. At 0.1 seconds, it is possible that users with slower connections or connections with spikes in network usage could experience choppy playback or frequent rebuffering. If you increase the buffer size, users will most likely experience a smoother playback. You can set the buffer using the `bufferTime` property; the following sets the buffer time to 10 seconds:

```
videoStream.bufferTime = 10;
```

Generally a one-buffer-fits-all approach is not the optimal solution. Although it may work in most cases, you cannot ensure the best user experience with that approach. Guaranteeing the best playback experience for all users requires slightly more work. The first step is to detect each user's bandwidth. Once you've detected a user's bandwidth (see Recipe 16.14), you have two basic options:

- If it's acceptable that users with slower connections view lower quality encodings of the video, you can encode many versions of the video at different bit rates and select the appropriate one for the user based on the detected bandwidth.

- If you want all users to view the same video (encoded at the same bit rate), then you can set the buffer based on the detected bandwidth. That means users with slower connections will have much higher buffer values and will have to wait longer before the video starts to playback.

If you want to display progress to the user while video is buffering, you can use the `bufferLength` property in conjunction with the `bufferTime` property. The `bufferLength` property is a read-only property that returns the number of seconds currently in the buffer. You can use `bufferLength/bufferTime` to return a ratio for the buffer progress.

The `bufferLength` property tells you how many seconds have loaded into the buffer, but it doesn't tell you how much of the entire video has downloaded. You can use the `bytesLoaded` and `bytesTotal` properties to determine how much of the entire video has downloaded.

See Also

Recipe 16.1 and 16.14

16.8   Listening for Cue Points

Problem

You want to listen for cue points encoded in the FLV.

Solution

Use an *onCuePoint( )* callback.

Discussion

The FLV format allows you to embed cue points within the file. You can use cue points for many purposes, such as:

- Captions
- Synchronizing animations with video
- Logging video playback statistics

You have to embed the cue points in the FLV file using one of the FLV encoders such as the Flash Video Exporter (which ships with Flash Professional), On2 Flix (*http://www.on2.com*), or Sorenson Squeeze (*http://www.sorensonmedia.com*). When playing back the video, the Flash Player receives a notification when a cue point is reached. As with metadata, cue points don't use the standard event model used by most of ActionScript 3.0. Rather, when a cue point is reached Flash Player calls a callback method called *onCuePoint( )*. As with *onMetaData( )* the *onCuePoint( )* method must be defined for an object that is assigned to the client property of the *NetStream* object. The *onCuePoint( )* method accepts one parameter, which is an object with the following properties:

name
    The name assigned to the cue point when encoding.

time

> The time at which the cue point occurs (in seconds)

type

> Either "event" or "navigation," depending on which type was selected when encoding

parameters

> An associative array with string key/value pairs assigned when encoding the FLV

The following illustrates one way in which you can create a client object, assign the *onCuePoint* reference, and assign the client object to the *NetStream* object:

```
var client:Object = new Object( );
client.onCuePoint = onCuePoint;
videoStream.client = client;
```

Then define the method appropriately:

```
private function onCuePoint(cuePoint:Object):void {
    trace(cuePoint.name + " " + cuePoint.time);
}
```

See Also

Recipe 16.4

16.9   Applying Filters to Video

Problem

You want to apply filter effects (blur, color, displacement map, etc.) to a video.

Solution

Assign an array of all the filters you want to apply to the *Video* object's `filters` property.

Discussion

The *Video* class inherits the `filters` property from the *DisplayObject* class. That means you can apply filters to *Video* objects just as you would any display object (see Recipe 10.5).

See Also

Recipe 10.5

16.10 Pausing and Resuming Video

Problem

You want to pause or resume video playback.

Solution

Use the *pause()* method of the *NetStream* class.

Discussion

The *pause()* method of the *NetStream* class allows you to pause and resume play-back of a video. When you call the method without parameters, it toggles the pause state of the video (pauses if it's playing and resumes if it's already paused):

```
videoStream.pause( );
```

If you pass the method a `true` value, the video pauses if it's currently playing, and nothing occurs if the video is already paused:

```
videoStream.pause(true);
```

Likewise, if you call the method with a `false` value, it resumes if the video is paused, and nothing occurs if the video is already playing:

```
videoStream.pause(false);
```

Although it's a common mistake, you should not use the *play()* method to resume playback of a paused video. The *play()* method is only used to load and start the initial playback of a video.

16.11 Stopping Video

Problem

You want to stop a video from playing and downloading.

Solution

Use the *close()* method of the *NetStream* class.

Discussion

When you want to stop a video from playing back, use the *close()* method of the *NetStream* object that controls the video. When you use the *pause()* method, the video simply pauses and starts playing again (typically when a UI button is pressed by the user), but even when paused, the FLV data continues to download. If you want to completely stop a video from downloading, use the *close()* method, as follows:

```
videoStream.close( );
```

When you call the *close()* method, Flash Player deletes the FLV data from the player. If you request the video again, it needs to start the download all over again. It is possible, however, that a web browser might cache the FLV, and subsequent requests to the same FLV might retrieve the cached version. In such instances, subsequent requests for the same FLV would be faster to playback. However, if an FLV is cached, it's possible that a user might see a cached version rather than an updated version. To ensure that the user always sees the latest version of the FLV, append a unique query string to the FLV request URL, as shown in the following example:

```
videoStream.play("video.flv?uniqueIndex=" + (new Date( )).getTime( ));
```

If you don't want a video to be cached for digital rights purposes, you cannot use progressive download video. In such cases, you need to stream the video by using a technology such as Flash Media Server, which is outside of the scope of this book.

16.12 Scrubbing Video

Problem

You want to scrub the playback of video (move the playhead forward or backward while the video plays).

Solution

Use a slider controller in conjunction with the *seek()* method.

Discussion

A common way to control video playback is to "scrub" the video using a slider controller. You can implement a scrub controller by building a slider that uses the *seek()* method to control a *NetStream* object.

The following sample code illustrates one way to write such a controller:

```
package com.oreilly.as3cb.components {

    import flash.display.Sprite;
    import flash.net.NetStream;
    import flash.events.Event;
    import flash.events.MouseEvent;
    import flash.geom.Rectangle;

    public class VideoScrubber extends Sprite {

        private var _thumb:Sprite;
        private var _track:Sprite;
        private var _stream:NetStream;
        private var _duration:Number;
        private var _scrubbing:Boolean;
```

```
public function VideoScrubber(stream:NetStream, duration:Number) {
    _stream = stream;
    _duration = duration;
    _track = new Sprite();
    _track.graphics.lineStyle();
    _track.graphics.drawRect(0, -2.5, 100, 5);
    addChild(_track);
    _thumb = new Sprite();
    _thumb.graphics.lineStyle();
    _thumb.graphics.beginFill(0xFFFFFF);
    _thumb.graphics.drawRect(-5, -5, 10, 10);
    _thumb.graphics.endFill();
    addChild(_thumb);
    addEventListener(Event.ENTER_FRAME, onEnterFrame);
    _thumb.addEventListener(MouseEvent.MOUSE_DOWN, onMouseDown);
    _thumb.addEventListener(MouseEvent.MOUSE_UP, onMouseUp);
}

private function onMouseDown(event:MouseEvent):void {
    _scrubbing = true;
    var rectangle:Rectangle = new Rectangle(0, 0, _track.width, 0);
    _thumb.startDrag(false, rectangle);
}

private function onMouseUp(event:MouseEvent):void {
    _scrubbing = false;
    _thumb.stopDrag();
}

private function onEnterFrame(event:Event):void {
    if(_duration > 0) {
        if(_scrubbing) {
            _stream.seek(_duration * _thumb.x / _track.width);
        }
        else {
            _thumb.x = _stream.time / _duration * _track.width;
        }
    }
}


}
}
```

In the preceding code example, the constructor accepts a *NetStream* parameter and a parameter specifying the duration of the video. The constructor then creates the elements for a slider control. When the user clicks on the slider, the code calls the *startDrag()* method and sets _scrubbing to true. While _scrubbing is true, the code calls the *seek()* method of the stream, passing it the playback time value corresponding to the placement of the slider control.

Note that the preceding example does not detect *mouseUp* events because it's possible that the mouse could be outside the slider control when the user releases the button. The solution to this issue is rather complex (hence the reason it's not discussed in this recipe). The solution is detailed in Recipe 6.9.

See Also

Recipe 6.9

16.13 Clearing the Video Display

Problem

You want to clear a video display.

Solution

Call the *clear()* method of the *Video* object.

Discussion

When you close a *NetStream* object, it doesn't automatically clear the video display. The last frame of the video remains visible in the *Video* object until you either remove the *Video* object or call the *clear()* method. The following example clears a *Video* object by calling the *clear()* method.

```
video.clear();
```

You can remove a Video object from the display list by way of *removeChild()*.

```
removeChild(video);
```

16.14 Determining User Bandwidth

Problem

You want to optimize a user's video playback by determining her network bandwidth.

Solution

Download an image file and time the download to calculate the speed of the user's network connection.

Discussion

Unfortunately, the Flash Player doesn't have a built-in bandwidth detection system. And because actual bandwidth varies based on many factors (such as network usage, interference in wireless networks, applications running on the same system competing for bandwidth, etc.), there is no way to accurately predict what a user's bandwidth will be for the next 10 minutes, hour, or any amount of time. However, you can measure a user's actual bandwidth over a period of time and use that to determine what her bandwidth *could be* in the near future.

To measure a user's bandwidth, you need to download a (noncompressed) file, such as a JPEG file using Flash Player. Using ActionScript, you can measure both the total bytes downloaded and the amount of time it took to download those bytes. Using those two values, you can calculate an average amount of data downloaded per unit of time. For the purposes of video, bandwidth is usually measured as bit rate in units of kilobits per second. There are 8 bits in a byte and 1,000 bytes per kilobyte. That means you can use the following to convert from bytes to kilobits:

```
kilobits = bytes / 1000 * 8;
```

 The ratio of bytes/kilobytes and bits/kilobits is different if you are talking about data communication or disk storage. For disk storage, the ratio is 1/1024, while for data communications it is 1/1000.

The larger the file that the user has to download, the more accurate the measurement is likely to be. For example, if the user downloads a 10 kilobyte file, it may be that the request hits a network lag and the measurement can be significantly lower than the actual average bandwidth. On the other hand, you don't want to force the user to download too large a file, since that would cause the user to have to wait too long while testing bandwidth.

One option is to use a moderately sized file (something in the 50–100 kilobytes range) and run the test several times. That way, if the first two tests are within a certain range of each other you can assume subsequent tests would also be relatively close, and you don't need to run further tests. If the first two tests have a wide margin, then you can run additional tests. If the same file is downloaded several times, you need to make sure that you use a unique URL each time so the Flash Player doesn't retrieve the file from a browser's cache. The following class illustrates how this sort of bandwidth test works:

```
package com.oreilly.as3cb.util {

    import flash.events.EventDispatcher;
    import flash.net.URLLoader;
    import flash.net.URLRequest;
    import flash.events.Event;
    import flash.util.getTimer;
```

```
public class BandwidthTest extends EventDispatcher {

    private var _downloadCount:uint;
    private var _bandwidthTests:Array;
    private var _detectedBandwidth:Number;
    private var _startTime:uint;

    public function get detectedBandwidth( ):Number {
        return _detectedBandwidth;
    }

    public function BandwidthTest( ) {
        _downloadCount = 0;
        _bandwidthTests = new Array( );
    }

    // Run the bandwidth test.
    public function test( ):void {

        // Use a URLLoader to load the data.
        var loader:URLLoader = new URLLoader( );

        // Use a URL with a unique query string to ensure the data is
        // loaded from the server and not from browser cache.
        var request:URLRequest = new URLRequest("bandwidthtestimage.jpg?unique="
        + (new Date( )).getTime( ));
        loader.load(request);
        loader.addEventListener(Event.OPEN, onStart);
        loader.addEventListener(Event.COMPLETE, onLoad);
    }

    // When the file starts to download get the current timer value.
    private function onStart(event:Event):void {
        _startTime = getTimer( );
    }

    private function onLoad(event:Event):void {

        // The download time is the timer value when the file has downloaded
        // minus the timer value when the value started downloading. Then
        // divide by 1000 to convert from milliseconds to seconds.
        var downloadTime:Number = (getTimer( ) - _startTime) / 1000;
        _downloadCount++;

        // Convert from bytes to kilobits.
        var kilobits:Number = event.target.bytesTotal / 1000 * 8;

        // Divide the kilobits by the download time.
        var kbps:Number = kilobits / downloadTime;

        // Add the test value to the array.
        _bandwidthTests.push(kbps);

        if(_downloadCount == 1) {
```

```
            // If it's only run one test then run the second.
            test();
        }
        else if(_downloadCount == 2) {

            // If it's run two tests then determine the margin between the
            // first two tests.
            // If the margin is small (in this example, less than 50 kbps)
            // then dispatch a complete event. If not run a test.
            if(Math.abs(_bandwidthTests[0] - _bandwidthTests[1]) < 50) {
                dispatchCompleteEvent();
            }
            else {
                test();
            }
        }
        else {
            // Following the third test dispatch a complete event.
            dispatchCompleteEvent();
        }

    }
    private function dispatchCompleteEvent():void {
        // Determine the avarage bandwidth detection value.
        _detectedBandwidth = 0;
        var i:uint;
        for(i = 0; i < _bandwidthTests.length; i++) {
            _detectedBandwidth += _bandwidthTests[i];
        }
        _detectedBandwidth /= _downloadCount;
        // Dispatch a complete event.
        dispatchEvent(new Event(Event.COMPLETE));
    }

    }
}
```

You can use instances of the preceding class to run a bandwidth test. To do so, create a new instance, add a listener, and run the *test()* method.

```
var bandwidthTester:BandwidthTest = new BandwidthTest();
bandwidthTester.addEventListener(Event.COMPLETE, onBandwidthTest);
bandwidthTester.test();
```

When the complete event occurs, you can retrieve the detected bandwidth using the detectedBandwidth property.

```
private function onBandwidthTest(event:Event):void {
  trace(event.target.detectedBandwidth);
}
```

See Also

Recipes 19.1 (the APIs that load binary data, such as image files, can be used) and 19.4

## CHAPTER 17

Storing Persistent Data

17.0 Introduction

Much of the data you work with in ActionScript is stored in memory while the movie is executing. When the movie is closed, the memory is released and the data is no longer available. What if you want to be able to store data between different visits to the movie? Or what if you want to be able to share data between movies running on the same client? To accomplish these feats, you'll need to look at how you can store data outside of the Flash Player.

In ActionScript, the *SharedObject* class lets you to implement persistence on the client machine. There are two types of *shared objects* that can be created: local and remote. This chapter focuses solely on *local shared objects* (LSOs).

Local shared objects are similar to browser cookies in that they are stored on the client's machine. LSOs are useful for storing the same kind of information for which cookies have traditionally been used, such as the ability for a web site to remember a user so that the user does not have to manually login during each visit. However, LSOs are more powerful than cookies because, by default, they never expire, they can store more data than cookies, they aren't transmitted between the client and server, and they can store native ActionScript datatypes. In contrast to *remote shared objects* (RSOs), LSOs are available to use without any additional software involved on either the client or server.

17.1 Creating and Opening a Local Shared Object

Problem

You want to store information that persists between visits to a *.swf* file.

Solution

Use a LSO.

Discussion

As mentioned in the introduction to this chapter, LSOs are to Flash what cookies are to web browsers—but more so. They are called "super cookies" by some developers because they allow you to store large amounts of data and store and retrieve many intrinsic ActionScript datatypes (as well as objects created from custom classes). In general, LSOs are referred to as *Flash cookies*.

The default maximum size that LSOs can grow to is 100 KB. However, counting on the use of this much storage space for a movie could lead to potential problems because users have full control over the size of LSOs through the Flash Player's Settings Manager and can restrict growth as they see fit. LSO files are saved to the client computer in a binary file ending with a *.sol* extension. Flash movies within the same domain can write to and read from the *.sol* files by means of ActionScript's *flash.net. SharedObject* class.

When a *.sol* file is created, it is placed in an application data directory for the Flash Player. For users using Microsoft Windows, it will be in a directory something like this: *C:\Documents and Settings\[username]\Application Data\Macromedia\Flash Player\#SharedObjects\[random character directory name]*. On Mac OS X, the directory will be something like */Users/[username]/Library/Preferences/Macromedia/Flash Player/#SharedObject/[random character directory name]*. The *random character directory name* is essential for security purposes. A rogue *.swf* movie might try guessing the name and location of a shared object from a particular web site so that it can load the LSO from the filesystem to gain access to data it normally doesn't have access to. After all, *.sol* files are stored in a standard location. By augmenting the path with randomness, guessing the path to the *.sol* files is virtually impossible.

The static *getLocal()* method is the mechanism by which LSOs are both created and opened for reading. The method requires at least one parameter; a string that specifies the name of the shared object to create or open:

```
var example:SharedObject = SharedObject.getLocal( "example" );
```

The *getLocal()* method attempts to first locate an existing LSO by the specified name with a *.sol* extension stored on the client computer. If none is found, the Flash Player creates a new LSO with that name. In either case, the existing or new LSO is opened. The *getLocal()* method returns a *SharedObject* instance. It is used instead of the *new* operator to instantiate a new local shared object.

See Also

Recipe 17.2 has important information on how to store data in a local shared object. Recipe 17.3 has details on how to retrieve data from a local shared object. Recipe 17.4 has information on the *SharedObject.flush()* method, which is used to manually save data to a shared object. Recipe 17.5 discusses sharing data between movies. Recipe 17.6 has details on opening the Flash Player Settings dialog box to the Local Storage tab to configure disk space usage.

17.2 Writing Data to a Shared Object

Problem

You want to add data to an LSO.

Solution

Add the values as properties of the shared object's data object.

Discussion

Shared objects have a special built-in property named data. The data property is an object to which you should add any information that you want stored in the shared object:

```
// Store a username value to the example shared object.
example.data.username = "Darron";
```

Unlike previous versions of ActionScript, properties can no longer be attached directly to the shared object. A compile-time error is generated when trying to store data on the *SharedObject* instance itself instead of in the data property. This prevents potential erroneous attempts to save data:

```
example.variable = "This will cause a compile-time error.";
```

Additionally, trying to assign a value to the data property directly is incorrect:

```
example.data = "This will cause another compile-time error.";
```

The correct approach is to attach the value to a new property under the data property, as follows:

```
example.data.variable = "This is the correct way to store data.";
```

You can store several native ActionScript datatypes to the shared object's data property, as follows.

```
example.data.exampleArray = new Array( "a", "b", "c" );
example.data.exampleDate = new Date();
example.data.exampleObject = { key1: "example", key2: -12, key3: null };
```

However, you cannot store visual elements (such as movie clips, sprites, buttons, or text fields) or shared objects themselves to a shared object's data property so that the data persists correctly between sessions.

17.3 Saving a Local Shared Object

Problem

You want to save data in an LSO to the client computer.

Solution

Use the *SharedObject.flush()* method.

Discussion

Flash automatically attempts to save LSO data to disk when either the movie is unloaded from the Player (such as when the Player closes), when the *SharedObject* instance is garbage collected (which occurs when there are no longer any references to the instance) or when the *SharedObject.clear()* method is invoked. However, it isn't a good practice to rely on the automatic save function, as there are several reasons why the data might be written to disk successfully. Instead, you should explicitly instruct the LSO to write the data to disk using the *SharedObject.flush()* method:

```
var flushResult:String = example.flush( );
```

The *flush()* method takes an optional parameter specifying the minimum amount of disk space, in bytes, that should be used when writing the shared object. The value specified defaults to 0, meaning that only the minimum required space should be used to write the local shared object to disk.

When the *flush()* method is invoked, it attempts to write the data to the client computer. The result of a *flush()* invocation can be one of three possibilities:

- If the user denies LSO storage for the domain, or if the Flash Player fails to save the data for some reason, the data is not saved and the method throws an *Error*.

- If the amount of disk space required to save the LSO's data is less than the local storage setting for the domain, the data is written to disk and the method returns *SharedObjectFlushStatus.FLUSHED*, indicating a successful call. When the optional minimum disk space is passed to *flush()*, the amount of space allotted must be greater than or equal to that value for the data to be flushed successfully.

- If the user has not allotted as much space as the shared object data requires, she is prompted to allow enough space or to deny access to save the data. When this happens, the method returns *SharedObjectFlushStatus.PENDING*. If the user chooses to grant access, the extra space is automatically allotted and the data is saved.

In the third case, in which the *flush()* method returns the *SharedObjectFlushStatus.PENDING* constant, there is an additional step you can take to determine whether the user grants or denies access to save the data. When the user makes a selection from the automatic prompt, the netStatus event is raised. It is up to you to define an event handler to handle the results in the way that is appropriate for your application. When the event handler is invoked, it is passed a parameter of type *flash.events.NetStatusEvent*. Examine the info.code string property to determine if the user granted access (when code is set to *SharedObject.Flush.Success*) or if the user denied access (when code is set to *SharedObject.Flush.Failed*).

Here is an example that invokes *flush()* to save the data explicitly. It then handles the possible responses:

```
var example:SharedObject = SharedObject.getLocal( "example" );
example.data.someData = "a value";
try {
  var flushResult:String = example.flush();
  // If the flush operation is pending, add an event handler for
  // netStatus to determine if the user grants or denies access.
  // Otherwise, just check the result.
  if ( flushResult == SharedObjectFlushStatus.PENDING ) {
    // Add an event handler for netStatus so we can check if the user
    // granted enough disk space to save the shared object. Invoke
    // the onStatus method when the netStatus event is raised.
    example.addEventListener( NetStatusEvent.NET_STATUS, onStatus );

  } else if ( flushResult == SharedObjectFlushStatus.FLUSHED ) {
    // Saved successfully. Place any code here that you want to
    // execute after the data was successfully saved.
  }
} catch ( e:Error ) {
  // This means the user has the local storage settings to 'Never.'
  // If it is important to save your data, you may want to alert the
  // user here. Also, if you want to make it easy for the user to change
  // his settings, you can open the local storage tab of the Player
  // Settings dialog box with the following code:
  // Security.showSettings( SecurityPanel.LOCAL_STORAGE );.
}

// Define the onStatus() function to handle the shared object's
// status event that is raised after the user makes a selection from
// the prompt that occurs when flush() returns "pending."
function onStatus( event:NetStatusEvent ):void {
  if ( event.info.code == "SharedObject.Flush.Success" ) {
    // If the event.info.code property is "SharedObject.Flush.Success",
    // it means the user granted access. Place any code here that
    // you want to execute when the user grants access.
  } else if ( event.info.code == "SharedObject.Flush.Failed" ) {
    // If the event.info.code property is "SharedObject.Flush.Failed", it
    // means the user denied access. Place any code here that you
    // want to execute when the user denies access.
  }

  // Remove the event listener now since we only needed to listen once
  example.removeEventListener( NetStatusEvent.NET_STATUS, onStatus );
};
```

If you know in advance that a shared object is likely to continue to increase in size with each session, it is prudent to request a larger amount of local storage space when the shared object is created. Otherwise, each time the current allotted space is exceeded, the user is prompted again to accept or deny the storage request. Setting aside extra space avoids repeatedly asking the user for permission to store incrementally more data. In this situation, the minimum disk space parameter should be passed to the *flush( )* method to specify a certain number of bytes to set aside for the shared object:

```
// Request 500 KB of space for the shared object.
var flashResult:String = example.flush( 500 * 1024 );
```

See Also

Recipe 17.8

17.4   Reading Data from a Shared Object

Problem

You want to read values that have been previously written to a LSO.

Solution

Read the values from the properties stored in the shared object's data property.

Discussion

There is nothing difficult about reading the values from a client-side shared object. All persistent values are stored in the shared object's data property, so you simply read the values from the data property, as follows:

```
// Read the value of exampleProperty from the shared object,
// example, and display it in the Output window.
trace( example.data.exampleProperty );
```

By using a combination of reading and writing data, you can determine if this is the first time a user is viewing a *.swf* file.

```
// Create a shared object and store some data in it
var example:SharedObject = SharedObject.getLocal( "example" );

if ( example.data.previouslyViewed ) {
  // The user has already viewed the .swf file before, perhaps
  // we skip an introductory help screen here.
} else {
  // This is the first time the user is viewing the .swf file
  // because previouslyViewed has not yet been set to true.
  // Set previouslyViewed to true so that the next time this
  // code is run we know the user has been here before.
  example.data.previouslyViewed = true;
  example.flush( );
}
```

17.5   Removing Data from a Shared Object

Problem

You want to remove properties from a shared object, or you want to remove the entire shared object from the disk.

Solution

Use *delete* to delete a property from the shared object's data property, or use the *clear()* method to remove the shared object.

Discussion

Removing data from a shared object is a straightforward process, but it has to be done the correct way. In ActionScript you will commonly find that people set complex variables such as objects or arrays to null or undefined to remove them. Doing this with a shared object, however, is the wrong approach.

```
// Attempt to delete someVariable from the example shared object.
// This statement will compile but does not do as we intend it to.
example.data.someVariable = null;
```

A shared object is capable of storing both null and undefined as valid values. Therefore, the preceding code does not remove someVariable from the data property, but rather someVariable is given the value of null in the assignment statement instead of being removed from the shared object. The correct way to completely remove something from a shared object is to *delete* it, like this.

```
// Remove someVariable from the example shared object.
delete example.data.someVariable;
```

You can also remove an entire shared object by invoking the *clear()* method on it. After the *clear()* method is called, the physical *.sol* file that stores the shared object is removed form the disk. The following code is an example of removing a shared object.

```
// Create a shared object and store some data in it
var example:SharedObject = SharedObject.getLocal( "example" );
example.data.someData = "a value";

// Displays: a value
trace( example.data.someData );

// Remove the shared object from the disk
example.clear();

// Displays: undefined
trace( example.data.someData );
```

After a shared object has been cleared, the shared object reference is still valid. This means that you can use the shared object as if it were newly created. Adding values to the data property makes them persistent, as you would expect with normal shared object behavior. In effect, the *clear()* method empties the shared object entirely, making it ready to be used again if needed.

17.6 Serializing Custom Classes

Problem

You want to store an instance of a custom class in an LSO.

Solution

Use the *flash.net.registerClassAlias()* method to preserve type information and add the class instance to the shared object's data property.

Discussion

LSOs use a special binary format, *Action Message Format* (AMF), for encoding information. When you store a class instance in an LSO, the instance is encoded as a generic object that contains properties. Thus, when you try to read the instance back from the shared object, it cannot be read as a class instance because it was not encoded with type information.

To get around this limitation, the *registerClassAlias()* method from the *flash.net* package is used. This method is very similar to the *Object.registerClass()* method used in ActionScript 1.0 and 2.0; however, *Object.registerClass()* has been removed from ActionScript 3.0 and replaced with *flash.net.registerClassAlias()*.

The *registerClassAlias()* method takes two parameters. The first parameter is a *string alias* that is used to represent a class. You can use an arbitrary string value that you want as the alias, but the best practice is to use the fully qualified class name. If you have a Person class in a model package, the string alias you should use is model.Person to provide clarity and avoid ambiguity. This approach also avoids accidentally using a string alias multiple times, since it is impossible to have two classes with the same fully qualified class name. The second parameter is the *reference* to the class you want to map the class alias to.

```
registerClassAlias( "somePackage.ExampleClass", ExampleClass );
```

This code tricks the LSO into storing information about the class that created it. Therefore, when the data is retrieved from the shared object, the Flash Player knows what kind of object it is.

The custom class must have an alias registered in any movie that retrieves the custom object data from a shared object.

The following code example is a complete implementation of saving an instance of a class to an LSO. First, create a custom class to serialize.

```
// Create a Person class in the model package
package model {

  public class Person {

    private var _firstName:String;
    private var _age:int;

    public function Person(firstName:String, age:int) {
      _firstName = firstName;
      _age = age;
    }

    public function toString():String {
      return _firstName + " is " + _age + " years old";
    }

  }

}
```

Next, create a main class to read and write the data.

```
package {
  import flash.net.registerClassAlias;
  import flash.net.SharedObject;
  import model.Person;

  public class Example {

    public function Example() {
      // Map "model.Person" to the Person class
      registerClassAlias( "model.Person", Person );

      // Create a shared object and store a Person instance in it
      var example:SharedObject = SharedObject.getLocal( "example" );

      // Test to see if the person instance has been saved already
      if ( example.data.person == undefined ) {
        trace( "first time, saving person instance" );
        var person:Person = new Person("Darron", 24);

        // Write the class instance to the local shared object
        example.data.person = person;

      } else {
```

```
        trace( "person instance already saved, using stored values" );
    }

    /* Every time this code is executed, the following is displayed:
    Darron is 24 years old
    */
    trace( example.data.person.toString() );
}
```

There is an important piece to point out about the preceding code. The call to *registerClassAlias( )* must happen *before* the *SharedObject.getLocal( )* method call. For the shared object to be read correctly, the class alias has to be created *before* the shared object is decoded. Creating the shared object without first creating the alias results in the Person instance not being read; instead, it is decoded as a generic object instead of a class instance.

17.7   Sharing Data Between Flash Applications

Problem

You want two movies within the same domain to have access to the same LSO.

Solution

Specify a local path parameter when creating and opening the LSO.

Discussion

By default, LSOs are saved to a path on the client computer that is unique to the domain, path, and name of the *.swf* file calling the *getLocal( )* method. This prevents name conflicts between LSOs from different domains, or even different movies on the same domain. For example, on a system running Windows XP, if a movie named *movie.swf* served from *http://www.person13.com/ascb* writes an LSO named example, the data is saved in a location such as the following:

```
    C:\Documents and Settings\[user name]\Application Data\Macromedia\Flash Player\
    #SharedObjects\[random directory name]\person13.com\ascb\movie.swf\example.sol
```

The name of the *.swf* file is included in the path to which the LSO is saved so it won't conflict with an LSO named example created by another movie served from the same domain and path. However, in some cases, you want two movies on the same domain to have access to the same LSO. In these cases, you should use the optional *local path parameter* when creating and opening the LSO using *getLocal( )*.

The local path parameter (the second parameter passed to *getLocal( )*) must be a string that specifies the full or partial path to the *.swf* file that created the LSO; for example:

```
    var example:SharedObject = SharedObject.getLocal( "example", "/" );
```

If the preceding code exists in *movie.swf*, which is served from *http://www.person13. com/ascb*, the LSO is stored at a location such as the following:

```
C:\Documents and Settings\[user name]\Application Data\Macromedia\Flash Player\
#SharedObjects\[random directory name]\person13.com\example.sol
```

The difference in this directory versus the one presented earlier is that it lacks the movie and path information. An LSO created this way can be opened by any other Flash movie in the same domain with the following line of ActionScript:

```
var example:SharedObject = SharedObject.getLocal( "example", "/" );
```

It is important to understand that a movie can only create and/or open an LSO within the same full or partial path. To understand this, consider an example with two Flash movies: *movieOne.swf* and *movieTwo.swf*. Both movies are served from the same domain (*http://www.person13.com*) but at different paths. *movieOne.swf* is served from *http://www.person13.com/ascb/firstGroup*, and *movieTwo.swf* is served from *http://www.person13.com/ascb/secondGroup*. In this scenario, *movieOne.swf* can create and read LSOs with any of the following local path values:

```
/
/ascb
/ascb/firstGroup
```

and *movieTwo.swf* can create and read LSOs with any of the following local path values:

```
/
/ascb
/ascb/secondGroup
```

Therefore, if you want both movies to be able to access a common LSO, you must specify one of the two local paths that the movies share (/ or /ascb) when you invoke the *getLocal()* method.

To illustrate how you can share data between two (or more) Flash movies within the same domain, take a look at the following example. If the movies don't exist within the same directory, you must first specify a common local path to both of them in the directory hierarchies. Start by looking at what happens if you fail to specify a common local path:

1. Create a new *.swf* movie that contains the following code, and name it *movieA.swf*:

   ```
   var count:SharedObject = SharedObject.getLocal( "count" );

   // The first time the shared object is read, default the value to 0
   if ( count.data.value == undefined ) {
     count.data.value = 0;
   } else {
     // Every time the shared object is read, increment the count value
     count.data.value++;
   }
   ```

```
// Create a text field to display the count value
var output:TextField = new TextField();
output.text = "count value: " + count.data.value;
addChild( output );
```

2. Create a new directory somewhere on your computer. Name this directory *LSOTest*.

3. Create two subdirectories within *LSOTest*. Name these subdirectories *movieAPath* and *movieBPath*.

4. Copy the *movieA.swf* file to both of the subdirectories that were just created.

5. Rename the movie as *movieA.swf* to *movieB.swf* in the *LSOTest/movieBPath* directory.

6. Open and close the *movieA.swf* file multiple times. Each time the file is loaded, the count value should increment by one.

7. Open and close the *movieB.swf* file multiple times. Each time the file is loaded, the count value should increment by one. However, notice that the number starts at 0. This is because, as it stands, *movieA.swf* and *movieB.swf* use different shared objects. Even though the shared objects have the same name, they have different paths, which created different *.sol* shared object files.

8. To cause both movies to use the same shared object, you must tell them to look in the same path. Modify the line of code that opens the shared object so that it reads as follows:

```
var count:SharedObject = SharedObject.getLocal( "count", "/" );
```

This causes both movies to look to a common path for the shared object, and hence use the same file.

9. Copy and rename the *.swf* file with the updated code to the appropriate directories to match previous steps, placing *movieA.swf* in the *movieAPath* directory and *movieB.swf* in the *movieBPath* directory.

10. Repeat Steps 5 and 6. This time, notice that each update to one movie also increments the value used by the other movie. This is because they are now using the same shared object.

17.8   Controlling the Size of Local Shared Objects

Problem

You want to control the amount of disk space used by a shared object.

Solution

Use the *Security.showSettings()* method or visit the web site for the Flash Player Settings Manager.

Discussion

As mentioned in Recipe 17.8, the default size for an LSO is 100 KB. Recipe 17.3 explained that the *flush()* method can be used to request a certain amount of disk space for an LSO. If the disk space requested exceeds the maximum allowed value, the user is prompted to either allow or deny the request. Through the use of the *flash.system.Security.showSettings()* method, it is possible to bring up a dialog that allows the user to set the maximum amount of data allowed to be stored in an LSO. The following code opens the Settings UI to the local disk storage section.

```
// Show the settings for local storage
Security.showSettings( SecurityPanel.LOCAL_STORAGE );
```

To coincide with the Settings UI for a specific domain, there is a more comprehensive Settings Manager that allows a user to change to global settings. Athough the Settings UI and Settings Manager provide similar functionality, they are completely different items. The Settings UI is a special form inside the Flash Player that is displayed via the *showSettings()* method, allowing the user to control the settings for a specific domain. The Settings UI can be opened through ActionScript as the preceding code block shows. It can also be opened manually by right/Control-clicking inside the Flash Player, and then selecting Settings from the contextual menu. In contrast, the Settings Manager is accessed via the *macromedia.com* web site. To open the Settings Manager to the Website Storage form, go to *http://www.macromedia.com/support/documentation/en/flashplayer/help/settings_manager07.html*.

This URL may look like just a simple a web page or screenshot, but it's actually a functional Flash application that modifies the global settings of the Flash Player. Updating a value via the Settings Manager URL affects how the Flash Player behaves. For instance, if you want to change the default size of an LSO (for LSOs that have not been initially created yet), navigate to the Global Storage Settings page (*http://www.macromedia.com/support/documentation/en/flashplayer/help/settings_manager03.html*).

Adjust the slider until it displays an acceptable value to you. After the slider value has been changed, the default maximum size for LSOs has been modified.

Remember, as a developer you have no control over LSO disk space on a client's computer. The best you can do is request a certain amount of space, explain why you might need that space, and hope that the user grants it to you. It is not recommended, however, to rely on LSOs for functionality critical to your application because the client has the final say of the LSO size—if the LSO is even allowed at all.

CHAPTER 18
Communicating with Other Movies

18.0 Introduction

When discussing Flash movies interacting with one another, there are two possible scenarios to consider. First, two movies running on the same client computer may have the ability to communicate with each other. Second, there is communication between movies running on different computers.

Prior to Version 6 of the Flash Player, the only way to communicate between movies on the same computer (without using server-side functionality) was to use the *fscommand()* function to execute JavaScript methods and use that JavaScript to bridge the communication gap between the movies. Unfortunately, these methods were both cumbersome to use and not always reliable (due to lack of support in various browsers). Also, these methods worked only with Flash movies running in web browsers in which the browser windows had references to one another. However, Flash Player 6 introduced *local connections*, a means by which any Flash movie can broadcast to and listen for broadcasts from any other movie on the same computer. The advantages of local connections are:

- They are relatively simple to use.
- They are implemented entirely in ActionScript and they work for movies running in Flash Player 6 or later.

To communicate between movies on separate client computers, the use of a server-side technology is required. There are three possible approaches to use in this scenario:

- Remote shared objects can be used in conjunction with Flash Media Server (formerly Flash Communication Server) to allow separate movies to send and receive data between themselves.
- A socket connection can be made to a server that can handle a message passing between all connected clients.

- For communication that is not considered real-time, it is possible to use a polling methodology coupled with a server-side technology to send and receive new information from the server at certain intervals.

This chapter focuses on inter-movie communication through the use of *LocalConnection*, allowing multiple movies on the same client computer to interact with each other.

See Also

Chapter 24 has more information about communicating between clients on different computers through the use of socket connections. Chapter 19 has information about sending and receiving data, which may be useful in situations where real-time communication is not a requirement.

18.1 Creating Local Connections

Problem

You want to communicate from one or more Flash movie(s) to another Flash movie playing on the same client computer.

Solution

Use the *LocalConnection* class in the *flash.net* package to invoke a function in the receiving movie from the sending movie. Use *LocalConnection.connect( )* to listen for messages in the receiving movie and define the function that will be invoked. Use *LocalConnection.send( )* from the sending movie(s) to invoke a function in the remote movie. Both the sending and receiving movies must specify the same named channel for communication.

Discussion

When two or more Flash movies are playing on the same client computer, they can communicate with one another via a local connection created with the *flash.net. LocalConnection* class. As long as the movies are playing on the same computer, a connection can be made regardless of the domains from which the movies are being served.

 By default, movies accept communications from movies on the same domain only. However, you can configure them to receive from other domains as well. See Recipe 18.4.

To successfully communicate between multiple movies on the same computer, you must do three things:

1. Configure the receiving movie to listen for communications.
2. Tell the receiving movie what to do when messages are received.
3. Send messages to the receiving movie from the sending movie(s).

A receiving movie must listen for messages over a specific, named local connection. To establish this communication channel, you should create a local connection object in the receiving movie and tell it to listen to a named connection using the *connect()* method:

```
import flash.net.LocalConnection;

// Create the local connection object in the receiving movie.
var receiver:LocalConnection = new LocalConnection( );

// Instruct the local connection instance to listen for messages
// sent over the "_exampleChannel" channel.
receiver.connect( "_exampleChannel" );
```

As shown in the preceding example, the best practice is to name your communication channel (not the local connection object) with an initial underscore (_). Naming your connections in this way also simplifies communicating across domains. By starting the connection name with an underscore, the Flash Player does not augment the connection name with domain-specific information behind the scenes. When an underscore is not the first character in the connection name, the connection name string is converted into *domain:connectionName* automatically, where domain is either the domain name that served up the *.swf* file or local host when the *.swf* file is run locally.

All communications over the local connection are mapped by the receiving local connection instance. By default, the receiving local connection object looks for methods defined on the instance with the same name as the method sent in the request. For example, if the sending movie sends a communication that looks for a method named *example()*, the receiving local connection object looks for an *example()* method that it defines. In previous versions of ActionScript, this was simply a matter of creating a function and attaching it to the instance through a name of example.

```
// Previous to ActionScript 3.0, this would create an example function
// that could be invoked through a local connection.
receiver.example = function ( ) {
  output.text = "communication received";
};
```

However, in ActionScript 3.0, this will not work. By default, the *LocalConnection* class does not allow properties and methods to be created on class instances at runtime. That means there are three basic solutions:

- Create a dynamic *LocalConnection* subclass, and use instances of that for all receiving local connections.
- Create a *LocalConnection* subclass that defines the methods you intend to call from the sending *.swf*.
- Redirect requests to a client object.

We'll next look at each of these solutions.

To allow runtime modification of a class to then attach functions to an instance, the class has to be declared *dynamic*. The easiest way to do this in ActionScript 3.0 is to *extend* the *LocalConnection* class with a *dynamic* class, and use the newly created class as the receiver to attach methods to. That class would look like this:

```
package {

  import flash.net.LocalConnection;

  // Create a dynamic Location Connection class that we can
  // attach functions to.
  dynamic public class DynamicLocalConnection extends LocalConnection {
    // Empty - all we need is the dynamic keyword
  }
}
```

Now use the *DynamicLocalConnection* in place of the regular *LocalConnection* class and create a receiving function as in previous versions of ActionScript:

```
// Create the local connection object in the receiving movie.
var receiver:DynamicLocalConnection = new DynamicLocalConnection();

// Instruct the local connection instance to listen for messages
// sent over the "_exampleChannel" channel.
receiver.connect( "_exampleChannel" );

// Because the DynamicLocalConnection class is dynamic, we can
// create a new function on the instance to respond to local
// conection messages.
receiver.example = function():void {
  trace( "communication received" );
};
```

This first solution has the advantage of being very flexible. You can use the *DynamicLocalConnection* class for all receiving local connections in all projects. The problem is that it is so flexible that it doesn't lend itself to well-defined interfaces, which is something you typically strive for in object-oriented design.

The second solution requires you use a well-defined API. You can create a *LocalConnection* subclass that defines the specific method or methods you want to handle. For example, the following class defines an *example()* method.

```
package {
  import flash.net.LocalConnection;
```

```
    public class ExampleLocalConnection extends LocalConnection {
      public function ExampleLocalConnection() {}
      public function example():void {
        trace("communication received");
      }
    }
  }
}
```

The next solution uses a *LocalConnection* property called client to redirect requests to a different object other than the receiving local connection instance. The client object must define the requested methods as public methods. The following example illustrates this:

```
package {
  import flash.net.LocalConnection;
  public class Example {
    private var _localConnection:LocalConnection;
    public function Example() {
      _localConnection = new LocalConnection();
      _localConnection.connect( "_exampleChannel" );
      _localConnection.client = this;
    }
    public function example():void {
      trace("communication received");
    }
  }
}
```

If you want to define the requested methods as private, then you have the option if you use a generic object as a proxy, as shown in the following example:

```
package {
  import flash.net.LocalConnection;
  public class Example {
    private var _localConnection:LocalConnection;
    public function Example() {
      _localConnection = new LocalConnection();
      _localConnection.connect( "_exampleChannel" );
      _localConnection.client = {example: example};
    }
    private function example():void {
      trace("communication received");
    }
  }
}
```

Now that we've configured the receiving *.swf*, we next need to build the sending *.swf*. The sending *.swf* uses the *LocalConnection.send()* method to send a communication. The first parameter of the *send()* method is a string that specifies the name of a connection over which to send the communication, enabling you to create multiple discrete connections. The second parameter of the *send()* method is a string specifying the name of the method to call in the receiving movie. When a movie receives a message, it invokes the method of the same name on the receiving local connection object.

The following example invokes a remote method named example:

```
// Send a communication across the "_exampleChannel" channel that
// invokes a method named example( ) in the receiving movie.
var sender:LocalConnection = new LocalConnection( );
sender.send( "_exampleChannel", "example" );
```

When using the *LocalConnection* class, communication is many-to-one. That is, there can be multiple senders for a specific channel but only a single receiver. If a receiver tries to connect to a channel that another receiver has already opened, the *connect()* method throws an error and won't allow the connection to be made. You can use a *try...catch* block to test for a receiver being able to successfully create a listening connection on a channel, like this:

```
var receiver:LocalConnection = new LocalConnection( );
try {
  receiver.connect( "_exampleChannel" );
} catch( e:Error ) {
  // Error - could not listen on _exampleChannel because another
  // receiver has already claimed it.
}
```

For *LocalConnection* to work properly, note that both the sending and receiving movies have to be playing on the same computer at the same time. To communicate between movies that play on the same computer at different times, use an LSO. See Recipe 17.1 and Recipe 17.7 for information on using LSOs.

See Also

Recipes 17.1, 17.7, and 18.2

18.2   Sending Data

Problem

You want to send data to one or more movies playing on the same computer.

Solution

Pass the data as additional parameters to the *send()* method of the sending local connection object.

Discussion

You can send data to another movie using a local connection by passing the data as additional parameters to the *send()* method of the sending local connection object. The *send()* method requires at least two parameters: the name of the connection and the name of the method to invoke on the receiving movie. Any additional parameters passed to the *send()* method are automatically passed as parameters to the receiving movie's method. Note that the name of the method you are invoking on the receiving movie cannot be one of the built-in method or properties of the *LocalConnection* class, or the *send()* call will fail. The built-in method and property names that cannot be used as the method name parameter are *send*, *connect*, *close*, *allowDomain*, *allowInsecureDomain*, *client*, and *domain*.

You should define the receiving method so it accepts the parameters sent to it. In this example, a local connection receiver class is created that contains a method named *example()*. The method expects three parameters: str, num, and bool; for example:

```
package {

    import flash.net.LocalConnection;

    public class ExampleReceiver {

        private var _receiver:LocalConnection;

        public function ExampleReceiver( ) {
            // Instantiate the local connection receiver and listen on the
            // "_exampleChannel" channel for other movies calling the example
            // method.
            _receiver = new LocalConnection( );
            _receiver.connect( "_exampleChannel" );
            _receiver.client = this;
        }

        public function example( str:String, num:Number, bool:Boolean):void {
            trace( "The parameters are: " + str + "\n" + num + "\n" + bool );
        }
    }
}
```

The following code snippet sends a message that calls *example()* in the receiving movie and passes it parameters, similar to invoking it like: *example("a string", 6.5, true)*:

```
// Send three parameters to a receiving movie's local connection
// method named example( ). The parameters happen to be a String, a
// Number, and a Boolean.
var sender:LocalConnection = new LocalConnection( );
sender.send( "_exampleChannel", "example", "a string", 6.5, true);
```

You are not limited to sending just primitive datatypes. Specifically, you can send data of the following complex types: *Object*, *Array*, *Date*, *TextFormat*, and *XML*.

Additionally, you can send objects of custom types. The process for doing so involves many of the same steps as storing and retrieving custom object types from a shared object. You can find more details about the theory behind this in Recipe 17.6, but the required steps are:

1. Define the custom class, and if necessary, import it in both the sending and receiving movies.

2. Register the class in the sending and receiving movies by using the *flash.net. registerClass()* method, making sure to use the same alias in all movies.

3. Send a class instance over a local connection with the *send()* method.

The following is an example of the code in a sending movie and a receiving movie that passes data of a custom object type from one to the other.

First, let's define the custom class called `Person`:

```
// Create a Person class in the model package
package model {

  public class Person {

    private var _firstName:String;
    private var _age:int;

    public function Person(firstName:String, age:int) {
      _firstName = firstName;
      _age = age;
    }

    public function toString():String {
      return _firstName + " is " + _age + " years old";
    }

  }

}
```

Here's the receiving *.swf* code:

```
import flash.net.registerClassAlias;
import model.Person;

registerClassAlias( "model.Person", model.Person );

package {
  import flash.net.LocalConnection;
  public class ExampleReceiver {

    private var _localConnection:LocalConnection;

    public function ExampleReceiver() {
      _localConnection = new LocalConnection();
      _localConnection.connect("_exampleChannel");
      _localConnection.client = this;
    }

    public function example( person:Person ):void {
      trace( person.toString() );
    }

  }
}
```

And here's the sending *.swf* code:

```
package {
  import flash.net.registerClassAlias;
  import model.Person;
  public class ExampleSender {

    public function ExampleSender( ) {
      registerClassAlias( "model.Person", Person );

      // Create a Person instance to send across
      var person:Person = new Person("Darron", 24);

      // Create the local connection and send a Person instance
      // to the receiving movie.
      var sender:LocalConnection = new LocalConnection( );
      sender.send( "_exampleChannel", "example", person );
    }
  }
}
```

Regardless of what type of data is being sent, the same rules apply to any type of local connection communication. Both movies must be running on the same computer at the same time, and the receiving movie must be listening on the same channel that the sending movie uses to send. Also, it's worth noting that once you have defined a custom datatype in both the sending and receiving movies, you can send that type of data in both directions (although you should use two separate channels for bidirectional communication, as discussed in Recipe 18.3).

See Also

Recipes 17.6 and 18.3.

18.3 Validating Receipt of Communication over Local Connections

Problem

You want a sending movie to receive confirmation that the communication was successfully received.

Solution

Configure the receiving movie to return a receipt to the sending movie.

Discussion

To confirm that a communication was received, you can have the receiving movie send a message back to the original sending movie. Due to the nature of local connections, a single channel cannot be used for two-way communication. For this reason, we have to create a local connection channel for each direction of communication. Use the following steps to confirm receipt of a message:

1. Set up the sending and receiving movies, as described in Recipe 18.1.

2. In addition to whatever code you include in the method that is invoked on the receiving movie, write code to send a receipt over a new channel (for example, "_exampleChannelReceipt"). You can use *this.send()* within the local connection's method to send a receipt back to the original sender.

3. In the sending movie, call the *connect()* method, passing it the name of the channel over which the receiving movie sends the receipt ("_exampleChannelReceipt").

4. In the sending movie, create a method on the local connection object to handle the receipt communication. Make sure this method name matches the name of the method that the receiving movie invokes when sending the receipt.

The following is an example of some code from a sending movie and a receiving movie.

First, the receiving movie code, using the *DynamicLocalConnection* class:

```
// Create the receiving code to listen on the "_exampleChannel"
// channel.
var receiver:DynamicLocalConnection = new DynamicLocalConnection( );
receiver.connect( "_exampleChannel" );
receiver.example = function( ):void {
  // In addition to whatever other code goes in the
  // receiving method, add this code to issue a receipt
  // back to the sending movie over the "_exampleChannelReceipt"
  // channel. The this keyword refers to the current local
  // connection object.
  this.send( "_exampleChannelReceipt", "receipt" );
};
```

Then, the sending movie code:

```
// Create the local connection object for sending over the
// "_exampleChannel" channel.
var sender:DynamicLocalConnection = new DynamicLocalConnection( );
seder.send( "_exampleChannel", "example" );

// Tell the local connection to listen on the
// "_exampleChannelReceipt" channel for the receipt broadcast
// by the receiving movie.
sender.connect( "_exampleChannelReceipt" );

// Define the receipt( ) method that gets called from the
// receiving movie.
sender.receipt = function( ):void {
  output.text = "Receiver has delivered sent receipt";
};
```

The key is that the name of the channel on which a local connection object listens (using *connect()*) must be the same as the name of the channel over which another movie's local connection object sends a message (using *send()*).

To take this one step further, you can tell the receiving local connection the name of the channel to send a receipt to. This is useful when multiple movies are sending data to the same movie and the receiving movie does not necessarily know which movie delivered the data. To achieve this effect, pass the channel name to the receiver by using code like this:

```
sender.send( "_exampleChannel", "example", "_exampleChannelReceipt1" );
```

The sender movie would send the name of the channel it's listening for a receipt on. The receiving movie then sends the receipt over that channel name:

```
receiver.example = function( receiptChannelName:String ):void {
  this.send( receiptChannelName, "receipt" );
}
```

By passing around the receipt channel name, the receipt channel is never hardcoded into the receiving movie, making the approach more flexible.

See Also

Recipe 18.1

18.4 Accepting Local Communications from Other Domains

Problem

You want a movie to accept local connection communications from movies served from other domains.

Solution

Use the *allowDomain()* method of the receiving local connection object.

Discussion

By default, receiving movies accept communications from sending movies on the same domain only. However, you can use the *allowDomain()* method of a local connection object to allow or disallow communications from any domain. You need to call the *allowDomain()* method for each receiving local connection object for which you wish to define a custom list of domains to accept or deny.

The behavior of *allowDomain()* has changed from previous versions of ActionScript. Before, the method acted as a callback. It would automatically invoke when a local connection object received a communication. Based on the return value of the method, the communication was either accepted or denied.

In ActionScript 3.0, the *allowDomain()* method needs to be explicitly called on a *LocalConnection* instance. The method takes one or more strings, specifying the domains that are allowed to send messages to the local connection instance that *allowDomain()* is called from. In this example, we specifically allow movies from *darronschall.com* to send messages to the current movie.

```
var receiver:LocalConnection = new LocalConnection();
receiver.connect( "_exampleChannel" );

// Allow movies from darronschall.com to send data over
// "_exampleChannel" to execute code within this movie.
receiver.allowDomain( "darronschall.com" );
```

To allow more than one domain to be able to send data to a movie, pass additional parameters to the *allowDomain()* method with one string for each domain to allow:

```
receiver.allowDomain( "macromedia.com", "adobe.com", "google.com" );
```

There are two special domain strings that can be used in *allowDomain()*. To allow any domain, use ~ as the domain string. It is generally not a good practice to allow communications from all domains, because doing so allows any other movie to invoke an arbitrary method on your movie. It is better to specify trusted domains from which to accept connections. To allow any locally instantiated movie to send data, use *localhost* as the domain string.

Local connection objects also provide a convenient means of determining the domain of the receiving movie. The *domain* property can be accessed from any local connection instance to reveal the domain from which the movie is being served. It is a read-only property, meaning you can only inspect it. Trying to set *domain* results in a compiler error. You can pass the *domain* to the *allowDomain()* method to allow communications from the same domain; for example:

```
receiver.allowDomain( receiver.domain );
```

The preceding example accomplishes exactly the same thing as though you had not called the *allowDomain()* method at all; it allows communications from the same domain only. Normally, therefore, you use the *allowDomain()* method and *domain* property to allow communications from the same domain as well as communications from other domains:

```
receiver.allowDomain( "darronschall.com", receiver.domain );
```

The preceding code allows local connection messages to be sent from *darronschall. com*, and also from the same domain that the movie is served from.

Similar to the *allowDomain()* method is the *allowInsecureDomain()* method. For the most part, the methods are the same. The difference lies in the use of HTTPS. When a movie is served over HTTPS, the local connection instances inside won't accept data and communication from movies that are delivered via HTTP. Unless the Flash Player is instructed otherwise via *allowInsecureDomain()*, by default communication from an HTTP movie to an HTTPS movie is denied, even if the movies are served from the same domain.

It is generally not good practice to use *allowInsecureDomain()* because it can comprise the security benefits offered by HTTPS. You can't trust the integrity of local connection communication received from movies delivered over HTTP, as it may be possible for the movie to be altered during delivery. Nevertheless, if you must use *allowInsecureDomain()*, call it just like you would *allowDomain()*.

```
receiver.allowInsecureDomain( "adobe.com" );
```

See Also

Recipe 3.12

## CHAPTER 19

Sending and Loading Data

19.0 Introduction

There are many reasons why you may want to send and load values from and to your Flash movies, including to:

- Send form values to a server-side script to store in a database.
- Send values from an email form to a server-side script to send the email.
- Load values from a text file (appropriate when the values are subject to change, such as for the current weather or for a links page).
- Load values from a server-side script where the values are drawn from a database, such as categories in an e-commerce application.
- Send values to a server-side script for processing, and return a value to the Flash movie, such as for a login process.

When loading data from a URL, the Flash Player interprets the data in one of three possible ways: as text, raw binary data, or URL-encoded variables. URL-encoded variables follow these rules:

- Each variable name is associated with a value using an equals sign, without spaces on either side of the equals sign.
- Variable values loaded into Flash movies are always treated as strings; therefore, you should not enclose any values in quotes, as you would within ActionScript. A proper example of this is `artist=Picasso`.
- When there is more than one name/value pair, each pair is separated by an ampersand—for example, `artist=Picasso&type=painting`.
- Spaces within the values should be replaced by plus signs (+), not %20, as in: `title=The+Old+Guitarist`. (Spaces and %20 may also work, but stick with plus signs for the greatest compatibility.)

- Any character that is not a digit, a Latin 1 letter (non-accented), or a space should be converted to the hexadecimal escape sequence. For example, the value "L'Atelier" should be encoded as `L%27Atelier` (%27 is the escape sequence for an apostrophe). See Table 19-1 for a list of common escape sequences.

Table 19-1. Common URL-encoded escape sequences

Character	Escape sequence	Character	Escape sequence
<space>	%20 or +	.	%2E
!	%21	/	%2F
"	%22	:	%3A
#	%23	;	%3B
$	%24	<	%3C
%	%25	=	%3D
&	%26	>	%3E
'	%27	?	%3F
(	%28	@	%40
)	%29	|	%7C
*	%2A	~	%7E
+	%2B	\	%5C
,	%2C	^	%5E
-	%2D	_	%5F

Here is an example of variables in URL-encoded format:

```
artist=Picasso&type=painting&title=Guernica&room=L%27Atelier
```

Sending and loading data has changed dramatically in ActionScript 3.0. The *LoadVars* class has been removed and replaced with a more robust *URLLoader* class in the *flash.net* package. *URLLoader* is supported by a new cast of characters, namely *URLRequest*, *URLVariables*, and *URLStream* (and a few others). These classes combine to form a rich API that offers more functionality and flexibility than what was available in previous versions.

Something that has not changed, however, is that loading data into the Flash Player is still subject to the standard security sandbox. That is, you can load from a file or script only if it is within the same domain that the movie is served from. For ways around the domain security limitation, see Recipe 3.12.

19.1 Loading Variables from a Text File

Problem

You want to load variables from an external text file into your Flash movie.

Solution

Use the *URLLoader.load()* method in conjunction with `DataFormat.VARIABLES` as the `dataFormat` to read URL-encoded data into a Flash movie.

Discussion

You should use the *URLLoader.load()* method whenever you want to load URL-encoded data into your Flash movie from a text file. This technique allows your Flash movie to access values that frequently change without modifying the Flash movie itself.

The *load()* method requires a *URLRequest* instance as a parameter that points to the URL of the text file. The URL can be an absolute or relative address. Additionally, the *URLLoader* needs to be configured to interpret the text as URL-encoded variables instead of plain text. Setting the `dataFormat` property of the *URLLoader* instance to the `DataFormat.VARIABLES` constant accomplishes this. Here is code to illustrate loading data from a text file:

```
import flash.net.*;

// You must first create the URLLoader object.
var example:URLLoader = new URLLoader();

// Configure the instance to interpret data as URL-encoded variables
example.dataFormat = DataFormat.VARIABLES;

// This example loads values from a text file at an absolute URL.
example.load( new URLRequest( "http://www.darronschall.com/example.txt" ) );

// This example loads values from a text file located at a relative
// URL, in this case, in the same directory as the .swf file.
example.load( new URLRequest( "example.txt" ) );
```

Here is an example of what the text file might contain:

```
someText=testing&someNumber=123
```

Once you invoke the *load()* method of a *URLLoader* instance, the Flash Player attempts to load the values from a URL into the data property of the same *URLLoader* instance. After the data loads, Flash attempts to decode the values and dispatches a `complete` event when done, signaling that the data is now available in the movie. It is up to you to add an event handler so you can do something useful once the data is loaded and decoded.

In the event that the load fails, the *URLLoader* dispatches a different type of event based on the type of failure. Therefore, you should not only listen for the `complete` event on success, but also for any of the failure events.

The failure events that a *load()* call can generate include:

httpStatus

> Generated when the Flash Player can detect the status code for a failed HTTP request when attempting to load data.

ioError

> Generated when the Flash Player encounters a fatal error that results in an aborted download.

securityError

> Generated when data is attempted to be loaded from a domain that resides outside of the security sandbox.

Here is an example of listening for the various events:

```
package {
  import flash.events.*;
  import flash.net.*;
  import flash.util.trace;

  public class Example {

    public function Example( ) {
      // Create the URLLoader instance to be able to load data
      var loader:URLLoader = new URLLoader( );

      // Define the event handlers to listen for success and failure
      loader.addEventListener( IOErrorEvent.IO_ERROR, handleIOError );
      loader.addEventListener( HTTPStatusEvent.HTTP_STATUS, handleHttpStatus );
      loader.addEventListener( SecurityErrorEvent.SECURITY_ERROR,
                               handleSecurityError );
      loader.addEventListener( Event.COMPLETE, handleComplete );

      // Configure the loader to load URL-encoded variables
      loader.dataFormat = DataFormat.VARIABLES;

      // Attempt to load some data
      loader.load( new URLRequest( "example.txt" ) );
    }

    function handleIOError( event:IOErrorEvent ):void {
      trace( "Load failed: IO error: " + event.text );
    }

    function handleHttpStatus( event:HTTPStatusEvent ):void {
      trace( "Load failed: HTTP Status = " + event.status );
    }

    function handleSecurityError( event:SecurityErrorEvent ):void {
      trace( "Load failed: Security Error: " + event.text );
    }
```

```
    function handleComplete( event:Event ):Void {
      trace( "The data has successfully loaded" );
    }
  }
```

If loading is successful, the Flash Player stores the loaded variables as properties of the data property of the *URLLoader* instance and dispatches the complete event. The following example is an event handler for the complete event that accesses known properties loaded from a file. It assumes that there are variables named *someText* and *someNumber* in the text file from which the data was loaded:

```
function handleComplete( event:Event ):void {
  // Cast the event target as a URLLoader instance because that is
  // what generated the event.
  var loader:URLLoader = URLLoader( event.target );

  // Access the variable(s) that were loaded by referencing the
  // variable name off of the data property of the URLLoader
  // instance.
  trace( "someText = " + data.someText );
  trace( "someNumber = " + data.someNumber );
}
```

Here is what the text file might look like:

```
someText=ActionScript+3.0+Cookbook&someNumber=3
```

In most cases, you already know the names of the variables that are loaded from the external file or script. For example, you might use a *URLLoader* instance to load a daily article from a server-side script or file, and regardless of the article's content, you expect three variables (title, author, and articleBody) to be loaded. You know which variables to expect because you wrote the server-side script, work with the person who wrote the script, or have access to documentation on the script. However, there are some situations in which you might not know all the variables that are being loaded. As such, you can use a *for . . . in* statement to enumerate all the variables that have loaded; for example:

```
function handleComplete( event:Event ):void {
  var loader:URLLoader = URLLoader( event.target );

  // Use a for . . . in loop to loop over all of the variables that
  // were loaded
  for ( var property:String in loader.data ) {
    // The property name is stored in the property variable,
    // and the value is retrieved by lookig up the property
    // off of data.
    trace( property + " = " + loader.data[property] );
  }
}
```

In previous versions of ActionScript, the loaded variables were added directly to an instance of the *LoadVars* class. This presented a problem with the loop defined in the preceding code block because property was not always a loaded variable. It was sometimes a regular property of the *LoadVars* instance, giving false positives for variable names loaded. In ActionScript 3.0, all of the loaded variables are stored in a vanilla data object off of the instance. This makes the preceding loop safe, since property is always the name of a variable that was loaded and never a property of the *URLLoader* instance itself.

19.2 Loading Variables from a Server-Side Script

Problem

You want to load variables into a Flash movie from a server-side script (ColdFusion, Perl, PHP, etc.).

Solution

Use the *URLLoader.load()* method in conjunction with `DataFormat.VARIABLES` as the `dataFormat` to read URL-encoded data generated by a server-side script into a Flash movie.

Discussion

The ActionScript to load variables from a server-side script is exactly the same as that used to load variables from a text file. When you call the *load()* method, you should pass it the URL of the script from which you want to load the variables, and then handle the results by listening for the `complete` event as shown in Recipe 19.1.

When the values for variables are generated from a database or another resource accessible only to the server, use server-side scripts as the source for variables loaded into the Flash Player. The script that you use must output URL-encoded data only, beginning from the first character. If you are writing a CGI script in Perl, the result is URL-encoded, so you won't need to make any special adjustments; for example:

```
#!/usr/bin/perl

# In a more practical example this value would be retrieved
# from a database or other server-side resource.
$someText = "test";

# Define the Content-Type header.
print "Content-Type: text/plain\n\n";

# Output the name-value pair.
print "someText=$someText";
```

However, when you use a ColdFusion page to generate variables to load into your movie, you need to take steps to ensure that it outputs URL-encoded data and that the output begins from the first character. Otherwise, extra whitespace characters may precede the output of the URL-encoded data, causing improperly decoded values. Here is what you should do:

1. Include the `<cfsetting enablecfoutputonly="yes">` tag at the beginning of the document.

2. Make sure to enclose any values you want to output within a `<cfoutput>` element.

3. Place the whole document in a `<cfprocessingdirective suppresswhitespace="yes">` tag. This ensures that no extra whitespace characters are output.

For example:

```
<cfsetting enablecfoutputonly="yes">
<cfprocessingdirective suppresswhitespace="yes">
  <cfset someText = "test">
  <cfoutput>someText=#someText#</cfoutput>
</cfprocessingdirective>
```

If you use PHP, perform output using echo or print from within a processing directive, such as:

```
<?php
$someText = "test";
echo "someText=$someText";
?>
```

Other preprocessor markup languages may or may not require additional steps to ensure proper output. JSP and ASP (.NET and classic) do not require any special considerations. One trick that seems to work in most cases is to simply surround each name/value pair with ampersands. This ensures that the variable delimiter is present so the variables can be correctly decoded by the Flash Player. This solution should work regardless of the language/platform you are using (ASP, JSP, CFML, etc.). For example, if you don't want to use the `<cfprocessingdirective>` and `<cfsetting>` tags in your ColdFusion page, you should be able to rewrite the preceding ColdFusion example as follows (note the ampersands in bold):

```
<cfset someText="test">
<cfoutput>&someText=#someText#&</cfoutput>
```

In each of the preceding examples, the server-side script returns a single variable, someText, to the Flash Player. The following example uses ActionScript code to load the variable from a script and display it in the movie:

```
package {

  import flash.events.*;
  import flash.net.*;
  import flash.util.trace;

  public class Example( ) {

    public function Example( ) {
      // Create the URLLoader instance to be able to load data
      var loader:URLLoader = new URLLoader( );

      // Define the event handler to be invoked when the load completes
      loader.addEventListener( Event.COMPLETE, handleComplete );
```

```
                // Configure the loader to load URL-encoded variables
                loader.dataFormat = DataFormat.VARIABLES;

                // Attempt to load some data
                loader.load( new URLRequest( "getSomeText.cfm" ) );
            }

            private function handleComplete( event:Event ):void {
                // Cast the event target as a URLLoader instance because that is
                // what generated the event.
                var loader:URLLoader = URLLoader( event.target );

                // Access the variable(s) that were loaded by referencing the
                // variable name off the data property of the URLLoader instance.
                trace( "someText = " + loader.data.someText );
            }

        }
    }
```

Of course, many of the same things apply to loading variables from a script as when loading from a file. For example, if you don't know all the variable names, you can use a *for…in* statement to list them and their values, as shown in Recipe 19.1.

See Also

Recipe 19.1

19.3   Loading a Block of Text (Including HTML and XML)

Problem

You want to load a block of text, possibly some HTML or XML.

Solution

Use the *URLLoader.load()* method in conjunction with `DataFormat.TEXT` as the dataFormat to read the text from a file or output from a server-side script.

Discussion

ActionScript 3.0 handles loading text differently than ActionScript 1.0 and 2.0. In previous versions, there were two different callback methods that you could define on a *LoadVars* instance to interpret data loaded from a URL. The *onLoad()* callback method was invoked when URL-encoded data was processed. The *onData()* method fired when the data was finished downloading, but before it was processed (before *onLoad()*). By using *onData()* instead of *onLoad()*, you were able to access the text that was downloaded before it was processed as URL-encoded data and lost.

The *flash.net.URLLoader* class behaves differently than *LoadVars*, its predecessor. The *URLLoader* does not distinguish between data that has finished downloading and data that has been processed and decoded. Rather, there is only a complete event broadcast when data finishes download, and the dataFormat property determines how the downloaded data is interpreted. Setting the dataFormat property to DataFormat.TEXT instructs the *URLLoader* instance to interpret the data as plain text. In Recipes 19.1 and 19.2, the dataFormat property is set to DataFormat.VARIABLES to interpret the data as URL-encoded variables. By default, a *URLLoader* instance processes the data downloaded as text.

Consider that you want to load the following HTML text from an external file called *example.html*, and then display it in an HTML-enabled text field:

```
<b>Title:</b> ActionScript 3.0 Cookbook<br />
<b>Authors:</b> Joey Lott, Darron Schall, Keith Peters<br />
<b>Publisher URL:</b> <a href="http://www.oreilly.com">www.oreilly.com</a>
```

The following ActionScript class works to load text from the file, and then displays the text in an HTML-enabled text field:

```
package {
  import flash.display.*;
  import flash.text.*;
  import flash.events.*
  import flash.net.*;

  public class HTMLLoadingExample extends Sprite {
    private var _output:TextField;

    public function HTMLLoadingExample() {
      initializeOutput();

      loadData();
    }

    private function initializeOutput():void {
      _output = new TextField( );
      _output.width = stage.stageWidth;
      _output.height = stage.stageHeight;
      _output.html = true; // Enable HTML for the text field

      addChild( _output );
    }

    private function loadData():void {
      var loader:URLLoader = new URLLoader();

      // Instruct the loader to read the file as plain text - This line is not
      // necessary because the dataFormat is DataFormat.TEXT by default.
      loader.dataFormat = DataFormat.TEXT;
```

```
        // Register an event handler for when the data is finished downloading
        loader.addEventListener( Event.COMPLETE, handleComplete );

        // Load the HTML text from the example.html file
        loader.load( new URLRequest( "example.html" ) );
    }

    private function handleComplete( event:Event ):void {
        var loader:URLLoader = URLLoader( event.target );

        // Assign the htmlText of the text field to the HTML text that was contained
        // in example.html. The data property of the URLLoader is the file contents.
        _output.htmlText = loader.data;
    }
  }
}
```

The data property takes on different characteristics based on what dataFormat is set to. When the dataFormat is DataFormat.TEXT, the data property of the *URLLoader* instance is a *String* containing the text that was inside of the file that was loaded. When the dataFormat is set to DataFormat.VARIABLES, the data property is an *Object* that maps variable names with their values. When the dataFormat is set to DataFormat.BINARY, the data property becomes a *flash.util.ByteArray* instance.

See Also

Recipes 19.1 and 19.2

19.4   Checking Load Progress

Problem

You want to know how much of the data has loaded.

Solution

Subscribe to the progress event of the *URLLoader*.

Discussion

The *URLLoader* class has a progress event that is dispatched whenever progress is made in downloading data. The Flash Player passes a *flash.events.ProgressEvent* instance to the event handler, allowing you to inspect the bytesLoaded and bytesTotal properties of the event. The bytesLoaded property contains the number of bytes that have been received so far. The bytesTotal property contains the total number of bytes in the file being loaded, or zero if the information is unknown.

The data is fully loaded when the bytesLoaded property of the *ProgressEvent* is the same as the bytesTotal property. However, this is usually not something you check

---

in your progress event handler. Instead, listen for the complete event, which is dispatched when the data is fully loaded. See Recipes 19.1, 19.2, and 19.3 for examples of handling the complete event.

To check on the loading progress, use code like the following:

```
package {
    import flash.display.*;
    import flash.text.*;
    import flash.events.*
    import flash.net.*;

    public class CheckProgressExample extends Sprite {
        private var _output:TextField;

        public function CheckProgressExample() {
            initializeOutput();
            loadData();
        }

        private function initializeOutput():void {
            _output = new TextField( );
            _output.width = stage.stageWidth;
            _output.height = stage.stageHeight;

            addChild( _output );
        }

        private function loadData():void {
            var loader:URLLoader = new URLLoader();

            // Listen for the progress event to check download progress
            loader.addEventListener( ProgressEvent.PROGRESS, handleProgress );

            loader.load( new URLRequest( "example.txt" ) );
        }

        private function handleProgress( event:ProgressEvent ):void {
            // Calculate the percentage by multiplying the loaded-to-total
            // ratio by 100
            var percent:Number = Math.round( event.bytesLoaded
                                    / event.bytesTotal * 100 );

            _output.text = " Loaded: " + event.bytesLoaded + "\n"
                            + " Total: " + event.bytesTotal + "\n"
                            + "Percent: " + percent;
        }
    }
}
```

In practice, it's fairly unlikely that you'll need to actually monitor the loading of data via the progress event. It is only plausibly necessary in cases of very large amounts of data being downloaded.

When using *URLLoader*, you cannot read the data while the download is in progress. The progress event is simply a notification of download progress because of this behavior. To access the data as it downloads, use *URLStream*, as discussed in Recipe 19.5.

See Also

Recipes 19.1, 19.2, 19.3, and 19.5

19.5 Accessing Data Being Downloaded

Problem

You want to access data as it downloads.

Solution

Use a *flash.net.URLStream* instance to load binary data that you can read as the data loads into your movie.

Discussion

Recipe 19.4 outlines how to check on the progress of data as it is downloaded. However, due to the nature of the *URLLoader* class, the data cannot be read until the download is complete. To read data as it arrives, you must use the *URLStream* class instead.

The *URLStream* class allows you to read data in a binary format as it loads into the Flash Player, similar to using a *URLLoader* with its `dataFormat` property set to `DataFormat.BINARY`. The interface of *URLStream* is very similar to *URLLoader*. You use the same events described in Recipe 19.1 to check for loading success and failure in both *URLStream* and *URLLoader*. The key difference is how the progress event is handled.

In the case of *URLLoader*, the progress event is only useful to indicate the amount of data that has been received and perhaps display the percentage loaded somewhere onscreen. In the case of *URLStream*, the progress event allows you to inspect the data by using the `bytesAvailable` property and one of the various read methods, such as *readInt()*, *readByte()*, *readBoolean()*, etc.

 Using *URLStream* is an advanced feature and is recommended only if *URLLoader* is not sufficient and if you have a good understanding of data on a byte level.

The following is some example code that uses a *URLStream* to load a *.txt* file, accessing the bytes of the file as it downloads into the Flash Player:

```
package {
  import flash.display.*;
  import flash.events.*
  import flash.net.*;

  public class CheckProgressExample extends Sprite {

    public function CheckProgressExample( ) {
      var streamer:URLStream = new URLStream( );

      // Listen for the progress event to act on data
      // as it is received
      streamer.addEventListener( ProgressEvent.PROGRESS, handleProgress );

      streamer.load( new URLRequest( "example.txt" ) );
    }

    private function handleProgress( event:ProgressEvent ):void {
      // Cast the target of the vent as a URLStream
      var streamer:URLStream = URLStream( event.target );

      // Loop over all of the bytes that are available
      while ( streamer.bytesAvailable > 0 ) {
        // Read a byte value and output it to the console window
        trace( "Read byte: " + streamer.readByte( ) );
      }
    }
  }
}
```

 In the preceding code example, it is important to look at how many bytes are available via the bytesAvailable property before attempting a read operation. Trying to read more bytes than what is available in the input buffer results in an *EOFError* exception being thrown.

See Also

Recipes 19.1 and 19.4

19.6   Sending Data to a Server-Side Script

Problem

You want to send data from a Flash movie to a server-side script.

Solution

Create a *URLRequest* instance that contains the data and pass it to the script with the *flash.net.sendToURL()* method. If you want to open the results of the script in a specific browser window, use the *flash.net.navigateToURL()* method. If you expect a response, use the *URLLoader.load()* method instead, as described in Recipes 3.12 and 19.7.

Discussion

Use the *sendToUrl()* method from the *flash.net* package to send data to a server-side script if you do not need to process the result. For example, you might want to submit a web form's data to a server-side script without displaying any result from the server-side processing. However, the *sendToURL()* method does not return any confirmation that the data was received, so it isn't practical in most cases. Even if you just want to display a static message, such as "Thank you for submitting the form," you need confirmation that the variables were successfully received on the server. Therefore, if you want confirmation of receipt, use the *URLLoader.load()* method, as described in Recipes 3.12 and 19.7.

The *URLRequest* instance passed to *sendToUrl* determines what (and how) data is sent to a server-side script. Typically, the data property of the request is set to a *URLVariables* instance to send name-value pairs to the server. It can also be set to a *flash.util.ByteArray* to HTTP POST binary data to a server, or data can be set to a *String* to send text, perhaps an XML-RPC request (see *http://www.xmlrpc.com*), to a server. The following code snippet shows how to create a *URLRequest* by using a *URLVariables* instance to send name-value pairs to a server-side script:

```
function sendData( ):void {
  // Create a request that sends data to the process.cfm page
  var request:URLRequest = new URLRequest( "process.cfm" );

  // Create some variables to send, someText and someNumber.
  var variables:URLVariables = new URLVariables( );
  variables.someText = "Some text to send";
  variables.someNumber = 26.2;

  // Set the data to be sent to the variables, created earlier
  request.data = variables;

  // Send the data to the script for processing
  sendToURL( request );
}
```

The URL passed during the *URLRequest* creation can be absolute or relative, and is governed by the Flash Player security sandbox. For more information about security, see Recipe 3.12.

```
// Set the url property to a CGI script with an absolute URL
request.url = "http://www.darronschall.com/cgi-bin/submitVars.cgi";

// Set the url property to a script relative to the location
// of the .swf file
request.url = "cgi-bin/submitVars.cgi";
```

The server's response to a *sendToURL()* method is disregarded by the Flash movie and data is sent transparently behind the scenes. To send data to a script and open the results in a specific browser window, use the *navigateToURL()* method instead. This method is almost exactly the same as *sendToURL()* except it takes an additional parameter—the name of the window to send the results to. Use the window name of _blank to display the response in a new browser window, or you can display the result in another, named window or frame that is already open if you know the correct target name for it. Neither of these two options have any effect on the browser window containing the Flash movie. However, specifying the target as _self or _parent replaces the page contained the Flash movie.

```
// Send variables containted in a URLRequest instance to a script
// and display the output in a new browser
navigateToURL( request, "_blank" );
```

If you want the response to be returned to the Flash movie, use the *URLLoader.load()* method, as discussed in Recipes 3.12 and 19.7.

By default, data is sent to the specified script via the HTTP POST method when you use *sendToURL()* or *navigateToURL()*. Set the method property of the *URLRequest* instance containing the data to change this behavior. Use URLRequestMethod.GET for HTTP GET and use URLRequestMethod.POST for HTTP POST.

```
var request:URLRequest = new URLRequest( "cgi-bin/submit.cgi" );

// Create some variables to send
var variables:URLVariables = new URLVariables( );
variables.someText = "Post me!";
request.data = variables;

// Configure the variables to be sent via HTTP POST
request.method = URLRequestMethod.POST;

// Send the request and open the response in a new window
navigateToURL( request, "_blank" );
```

See Also

Recipes 3.12 and 19.7

19.7   Sending Variables and Handling a Returned Result

Problem

You want to send variables to a server-side script and handle the results of the server-side processing.

Solution

Use the *URLLoader.load()* method coupled with a *URLRequest* instance that has its data property set.

Discussion

You should use the *URLLoader.load()* method when you want to send variables to a server-side script and have the results returned to Flash. An example of such a scenario is a Flash storefront for a product catalog whose data is stored in a database. Typically, items are categorized. When a user selects a category, the Flash movie might send the selected category ID to a server-side script and expect the script to return all the items in the category.

The *URLLoader.load()* method sends variables to a server-side script in the same way that the *sendToURL()* and *navigateToURL()* methods do. The data set in the *URLRequest* instance passed to the *load()* method is sent to the script at the specified URL. Handling results is exactly the same as discussed in Recipe 19.2. When the complete event is handled, the data property of the *URLLoader* that dispatched the event contains the result of the script processing.

Here is a complete example that sends data to a script that returns URL-encoded values and places the result in a text field on the screen:

```
package {
  import flash.display.*;
  import flash.text.*;
  import flash.events.*
  import flash.net.*;

  public class SendAndLoadExample extends Sprite {
    private var _output:TextField;

    public function SendAndLoadExample( ) {
      initializeOutput( );
      sendData( );
    }

    private function initializeOutput( ):void {
      _output = new TextField();
      _output.width = stage.stageWidth;
      _output.height = stage.stageHeight;

      addChild( output );
    }

    private function sendData( ):Void {
      // Create a URLRequest to contain the data to send
      // to process.cfm
      var request:URLRequest = new URLRequest( "process.cfm" );
```

```
      // Create name-value pairs to send to the server
      var variables:URLVariables = new URLVariables();
      variables.method = "getProductDetail"
      variables.productId = 2;
      request.data = variables;

      // Create a URLLoader to send the data and receive a
      // response
      var loader:URLLoader = new URLLoader();

      // Expect the script to return URL-encoded variables
      loader.dataFormat = DataFormat.VARIABLES;

      // Listen for the complete event to read the server response
      loader.addEventListener( Event.COMPLETE, handleComplete );

      // Send the data in the URLRequest off to the script
      loader.load( request );
   }

   private function handleComplete( event:Event ):void {
      var loader:URLLoader = URLLoader( event.target );

      // Expect the script to return name and description variables.
      // Display these values in a text field on the screen.
      _output.text = "Name: " + loader.data.name + "\n"
                     + "Description: " + loader.data.description;
   }
  }
}
```

See Also

Recipes 19.1, 19.2, 19.3, 19.4, and 19.6

CHAPTER 20

XML

20.0 Introduction

XML is a structured, text-based way of formatting and describing data. It was originally designed to be to both simple and flexible and has rapidly grown into an industry standard because of its portability, especially for data exchange and interoperability between applications.

When working in ActionScript, XML will probably cross your path. Chapter 19 explains how to send and load data in a URL-encoded format. URL-encoding is fine for passing simple data between the Flash Player and server-side scripts, but for complex data or Unicode characters, XML generally works much better because of its structured format. For example, if you want to load data from a text file that represents a simple datatype such as a string, URL-encoded data, such as the following, can be loaded using a *URLLoader* instance:

```
myString=a+string+value
```

However, when you want to load data from an external source and use that data to create an ActionScript object, you are presented with the problem of how to represent that data as a URL-encoded string. You might try something like the following, in which each property value pair is separated by an asterisk (*), and each property is separated from its corresponding value by a vertical pipe (|):

```
myObject=prop0|val0*prop1|val1*prop2|val2
```

Once the string value is returned for myObject, you could use *String.split()* to recreate the elements that make up the object. Although you can get by with this approach, it is often much easier to represent complex values in XML. For example, the same object can be represented by the following XML snippet:

```
<myObject>
  <prop0>val0</prop0>
  <prop1>val1</prop1>
  <prop2>val2</prop2>
</myObject>
```

XML data offers several advantages over URL-encoded data, including:

- When creating XML manually (for a static XML document) or programmatically (from a ColdFusion script, PHP script, etc.), it is much easier to represent complex data.

- Most server-side scripting languages offer built-in functionality for reading and generating XML data.

- XML is a standard used for the transfer and storage of data across all kinds of applications and platforms.

Of course, XML isn't the only way of transferring data in and out of the Flash Player. Chapters 19, 21, and 24 discuss ways to communicate outside of the Flash Player as well. However, this chapter focuses solely on XML, an industry standard technique for exchanging data that doesn't require the use of additional server-side software (as Flash Remoting and Sockets do). XML has become an important part of Action-Script 3.0 and has been given special treatment this time around.

ActionScript 3.0 boasts a revolutionary new syntax for working with XML. *ECMAScript for XML*, otherwise known as *E4X*, is a language extension that gives you a simpler, easier to read approach for working with XML objects than the traditional Document Object Model (DOM), an interface of the past. Using E4X, you'll find that you can work with XML much easier than before. Additionally, if this is your first time working with XML, E4X dramatically lowers the learning curve of using XML.

In this chapter, the following terminology is used:

XML document

A file that contains XML. This term may also refer to XML data that is being loaded or sent. An XML document is not to be confused with the *XMLDocument* class.

XML packet

An XML packet can be any snippet of XML—from an entire XML document to just a single node—as long as it is represents a complete, well-formed piece of information in XML.

XML node

The basic building block for XML. Nodes can be elements, text nodes, attributes, and so on. We refer to elements and text nodes collectively as "nodes" when talking in general terms.

XML element

The term "element" is often used interchangeably with the term "tag." More accurately, however, an element contains tags. Elements must have an opening and closing tag (`<element></element>`), or the opening and closing tags can be combined into one when the element has no nested elements (`<element />`).

Root node
> An element that is at the top of the XML hierarchy of elements.

Text node
> A node containing text. Text nodes are generally nested within elements.

Attribute
> Is part of an element. Attributes are placed within the tags of elements in name/value pair format, such as `<element name="value">`.

XML declaration
> The declaration typically looks like this: `<?xml version="1.0" ?>`. This is a special tag that the XML parser recognizes as containing information about the XML document, and it is not parsed as an element.

XML tree
> Also sometimes called the "data tree," an XML tree is the hierarchy of nodes in XML data.

20.1 Understanding XML Structure (Reading and Writing XML)

Problem

You want to understand how to read or write XML.

Solution

XML is tag-based and hierarchical. If you are familiar with HTML, learning the basics of XML should not be very difficult.

Discussion

Although reading and writing good XML is not a skill that is specific to Action-Script, it is, nonetheless, a skill from which your ActionScript can benefit. If you are not yet familiar with XML, don't worry. This is going to be painless.

XML is a way of representing structured data. This means that you explicitly define the context for the data. For example, without XML you might have a string of data such as:

```
Jerry,Carolyn,Laura
```

You can use XML to tell us *who* these people are:

```
<family>
  <father>Jerry</father>
  <mother>Carolyn</mother>
  <sister>Laura</sister>
</family>
```

Now, as you can see, the XML tells us a lot more about the data. Here are a few other points to notice about XML:

- XML is composed mainly of nodes. A node is a general term that can refer to many parts within the XML. For example, `<family>` is a node in the preceding XML snippet; these nodes are called *elements*. Also, the values Jerry, Carolyn, and Laura are nodes; these nodes are called *text nodes*.

- Every XML element must have a matching opening and closing tag. The opening tag might look like `<family>`, and the closing tag is identical, except that it uses a forward slash to indicate it is closing the element, as in `</family>`. The opening and closing tags can be combined if the element does not contain any nested nodes. For example, `<emptyElement />` is an element that combines the opening and closing tags. Notice that there is a space between the element name, `emptyElement`, and the forward slash. The space isn't necessary; it's just a matter of personal style.

- Elements can contain nested nodes (be they other elements or text nodes). There are several examples of this in the `<family>` XML document shown earlier. The `<family>` element, which is the *root node* in this example, contains three nested elements: `<father>`, `<mother>`, and `<sister>`; these nested nodes are also called *child nodes*. Each of these child nodes also contains a nested node. However, their nested nodes are text nodes, not elements. Regardless, they are still treated as child nodes.

There is one other type of node that we want to look at here. An *attribute* is a special kind of node that can be assigned to an element, and in many cases it can even be used as an alternative to a nested node. If you've ever worked with HTML, you are already familiar with attributes. Some common attributes in HTML include the `href` attribute of the `<a>` element and the `colspan` attribute of the `<td>` element. Here is how we can rewrite the same XML document we examined previously using attributes instead of nested nodes:

```
<family father="Jerry" mother="Carolyn" sister="Laura" />
```

Notice that we were able to eliminate the nested elements and write the same data all in one element. Also notice that since `<family>` no longer contains any nested nodes, we can combine the opening and closing tags into one.

You may be wondering when and why to use attributes versus nested nodes. This is often a matter of preference. Sometimes it may appear easier or clearer to you to write the XML data by using attributes. Generally, attributes are a good idea when you want to represent a fairly small number of values and when those values are relatively short. Also, the attributes' names need to be unique within the element. When you want to represent a larger amount of data, such as when the data is long (more than a few words) or when the attribute names would not be unique within the element, use nested elements instead.

Also, you can use a combination of both attributes and nested nodes. Here is an example of an `<article>` element that includes attributes for the `title` and `author`, but uses a nested text node to represent the article text. This is a good example of when one of the values (the article text) is simply too long to reasonably be an attribute.

```
<article title="XML: It's Not Just for Geeks" author="Samuel R.
Shimowitz">
My friends couldn't believe it when I started working with XML.
I became an outcast, confined to my dark office illuminated only
by the glow of my trusty CRT.
</article>
```

You can create XML strings right in Flash for cases in which you are constructing XML data to send to an external script. For example:

```
var dataToSend:String = "<feedback name='Anon' comments='nice'>";
```

To construct a static XML document outside of Flash, use a simple text editor and save it as plain text. To create an XML document dynamically by using a server-side script, consult the appropriate reference for the language you are using.

See Also

The preceding examples are very simple cases. XML can get much more complex, including namespaces, document type declarations, etc. Most of these details are well beyond the scope of this book and beyond what you need to know to work with XML and ActionScript. For more information on XML in general, see *http://www.xml.com*. Also, for a general overview of XML, you might consider *XML in a Nutshell* by Elliotte Rusty Harold and W. Scott Means (O'Reilly) and/or the *XML Pocket Reference* by Simon St.Laurent and Michael Fitzgerald (O'Reilly).

20.2   Creating an XML Object

Problem

You want to create an XML object complete with a tree structure and data.

Solution

A *populated* XML object contains data, just as a populated city contains people.

Use one of the following to create a populated XML object:

- Create an XML object and populate it by assigning to it an XML literal.
- Populate an XML object tree by passing an XML string to the *XML* constructor.
- Create an empty XML object and use E4X to populate the XML tree one node at a time.
- Create a blank object, and load the XML data from an external source.

Discussion

There are many possibilities for creating a populated XML object in ActionScript. Each technique offers its own advantages, and you should base your decision on the needs of your project.

The simplest way to create a populated XML object is create a new XML object and assign an XML literal to it:

```
var example:XML = <abc><a>eh</a><b>bee</b><c>see</c></abc>;
```

This is an example of E4X in action. Notice that directly inside the code file, an XML packet is used on the right-hand side of an equals sign. If the XML had been contained in quotation marks, this would be interpreted as a string, but ActionScript 3.0 provides native support for XML datatypes. The ActionScript compiler understands that the expression on the right is XML, and it populates the example XML instance with the XML packet provided.

This first technique is appropriate when you already know the XML structure before you want to create the object. It is even applicable if you want to use dynamic data inside of the XML literal. Place a variable name inside of curly braces ({and }) to use its value inside the XML literal. For example, if you want to create a simple XML object to send a user's name and score to the server, you would construct the XML literal as follows:

```
// Assume two variables exist, username and score
var username:String = "Darron";
var score:int = 1000;

// Use curly braces around the variable name to use its value when
// assigning XML via an XML literal
var example:XML = <gamescore>
                    <username>{username}</username>
                    <score>{score}</score>
                  </gamescore>;
```

You can also create a string and pass it as a parameter to the XML constructor. The preceding example can also be written as follows:

```
// Create the XML structure with a string so use the value of both
// username and score inside of the XML packet.
var str:String = "<gamescore><username>" + username + "</username>"
                + "<score>" + score + "</score></gamescore>";

// Pass the string to the constructor to create an XML object
var example:XML = new XML( str );
```

The example XML objects created in the two previous code blocks are identical in structure. In general, use the curly brace approach to create XML objects when you know what the structure is going to be at compile time but need data at runtime (like a score that's generated after the game has been played).

There are other cases in which you don't necessarily know all the data at one time. You might want to build the XML object's tree over time. For example, if you use an XML object to store a user's shopping cart information, you need to modify the object's data each time the user modifies his shopping cart. In such cases, you should construct a new XML object at the start and use E4X to manipulate it by adding and removing nodes, as described in Recipes 20.3 and 20.10.

And let's not forget about populating XML objects with data retrieved from an external source, such as a static XML document or a script that generates dynamic XML. Up to this point, we've looked only at constructing XML objects to send data to a server or to use throughout our programs, but you can load data from the server for all kinds of reasons: retrieving user data, catalog information, or movie initialization information, just to name a few. For these scenarios, see Recipe 20.11 for how to load an XML document from a server.

See Also

Recipes 20.3, 20.4, 20.5, and 20.10 for more information on constructing an XML tree using E4X. For more information on loading information from external sources, see Recipe 20.11.

20.3   Adding Elements to an XML Object

Problem

You want to construct an *XML* object and add elements to it.

Solution

Use E4X syntax to create child elements and add them to an XML tree. Additionally, use the *insertChildBefore()* and *insertChildAfter()* methods for more control over how new elements are added.

Discussion

You might want to add elements to an XML object to construct an XML data structure to pass to another application. There are several ways to accomplish this, as discussed in Recipe 20.2.

Adding elements to an existing XML object is simple with E4X syntax. Use the dot operator (.) on the XML instance and add the element much the same way a generic property is added to a regular Object:

```
// Create an XML instance to add elements to
var example:XML = <example />;

// Create a new XML node named newElement and add it to the
// example instance
example.newElement = <newElement />;
```

```
/* Displays:
  <example>
    <newElement/>
  </example>
*/
trace( example );
```

In the preceding example, an XML literal is created for an empty `newElement` node. This is then added to the `example` instance by using the dot operator and assigning a `newElement` property to the `newElement` node. In this situation, the property name and the element name do not need to be the same. However, it would be confusing if they were not. The element name overrides the property name when adding an XML node to an existing XML object.

You can also create a new element by creating a property on the XML instance and assigning it a value, as follows:

```
// Create an XML instance to work with
var example:XML = <example />;

// Create a new property emptyElement and assign it an empty
// string value
example.emptyElement = "";

/* Displays:
  <example>
    <emptyElement/>
  </example>
*/
trace( example );
```

The preceding example demonstrates that you can create child elements on an XML object without actually adding XML nodes, like in the first example. Assigning an empty string value to a new `emptyElement` property creates an empty element node named `emptyElement`.

If you don't know the name of the element you'd like to add, or if you want it based off of the value of a variable, you can use the alternative bracket notation. Instead of using the dot operator, place a string inside of brackets ([and]). The string is evaluated and the value is used as the property name. This allows you to build a property name and, consequently, an element name, dynamically:

```
// Create an XML instance to work with
var example:XML = <example />;

var id:int = 10;

// Create a string to incorporate the value of id in the node name
example[ "user" + id ] = "";

/* Displays:
  <example>
    <user10/>
```

```
    </example>
*/
trace( example );
```

There are some cases when using the bracket syntax is required. For example, it is perfectly legal XML to have an element node name with a hyphen in it. Trying to create an element name with a hyphen by using the dot operator gives a compiler error:

```
example.some-element = ""; // Generates a compiler error
```

The hyphen has a special meaning to the compiler; it is used to for subtraction. The preceding code snippet is interpreted as a subtraction statement, attempting to subtract the variable *element* from *example.some*, and then assigning the empty string to that value. This subtraction statement is not syntactically valid, which explains the compiler error. Furthermore, even if the statement above would compile as valid use of subtraction, it is not the intended behavior of creating an element node. Using bracket notation fixes this:

```
example[ "some-element" ] = "";
```

One problem with the simplicity of E4X is that any time a new element is added, it is always added at the end of the XML tree. To solve this, use the *insertChildBefore()* and *insertChildAfter()* methods to have more control over how new element nodes are added. The *insertChildBefore()* method inserts a new element before an existing element in the XML tree, while *insertChildAfter()* inserts a new element after an existing element. Each method takes the same two parameters: the node marking the inserting point and the data to insert. The following code snippet shows how to use both of these methods to modify an XML tree:

```
// Create an XML instance to work with
var example:XML = <example/>;

// Create an empty two element node
example.two = "";

// Before the two element node, add a one element node
example = example.insertChildBefore( example.two, <one /> );

// After the two element node, add a three element node
example = example.insertChildAfter( example.two, <three /> );

/* Displays:
<example>
  <one/>
  <two/>
  <three/>
</example>
*/
trace( example );
```

In the preceding example, note that the *insertChildBefore()* and *insertChildAfter()* methods do not modify the XML instance in which they are called. Instead, they return a new instance containing the modifications. To capture the modifications, assign the result of the method call to the XML instance again, as the previous example shows.

See Also

Recipes 20.2 and 20.4

20.4   Adding Text Nodes to an XML Object

Problem

You want to add text nodes to an *XML* object.

Solution

Use E4X syntax to create text nodes and add them to an XML tree. Use the *appendChild()*, *prependChild()*, *insertChildAfter()*, and *insertChildBefore()* methods for more control over how the text nodes are added.

Discussion

Creating text nodes with E4X is, you guessed it, simple. The process is very similar to the method described in Recipe 20.3. As with elements, creating text nodes is just a matter of using the dot operator (.) to set a property on an XML instance to any value that can be converted to a string. Here is an example:

```
// Create an XML instance to work with
var example:XML = <example/>;

// Create a text node from a string
example.firstname = "Darron";

// Create a text node from a number
example.number = 24.9;

// Create a text node from a boolean
example.boolean = true;

// Create a text node from an array
example.abc = ["a", undefined, "b", "c", null, 7, false];

/* Displays:
<example>
  <firstname>Darron</firstname>
  <number>24.9</number>
  <boolean>true</boolean>
  <abc>a,,b,c,,7,false</abc>
</example>
*/
trace( example );
```

This example adds both text and element nodes to the example XML instance. The value on the righthand side of the assignment statement is converted into a string and becomes the text node. Then the property name is converted into an element node with the text node as a child, and the entire element node is appended to the XML instance.

For more control over where the text nodes are placed inside of element nodes, use either *appendChild()*, *prependChild()*, *insertChildBefore()*, or *insertChildAfter()*. These methods allow you to control precisely where the text node is inserted into the XML tree:

```
// Create an XML instance to work with
var example:XML = <example/>;

// Append a two element node containing a text node child
// with value 2
example.appendChild( <two>2</two> );

// Prepend a one element node containing a text node child
// with value "number 1"
example.prependChild( <one>"number 1"</one> );

// After the one element node, insert a text node with
// value 1.5
example.insertChildAfter( example.one[0], 1.5 );

// Before the two element node, insert a part element node
// containing a text node child with value 1.75
example.insertChildBefore( example.two[0], <part>1.75</part> );

/* Displays:
<example>
  <one>"number 1"</one>
  1.5
  <part>1.75</part>
  <two>2</two>
</example>
*/
trace( example );
```

In the preceding code example, a *mixed element* was created. A mixed element is one that contains not only a child text node or child elements, but both. The example element is mixed because it contains not only child elements (<one>, <part>, and <two>) but also a nested text node (with the value of 1.5). This is perfectly valid XML, and it demonstrates that an element can have more children than just a single text node.

See Also

Recipe 20.3

20.5   Adding Attributes to an XML Element

Problem

You want to add attributes to an XML element.

Solution

Use the @ operator in E4X syntax to assign attributes to element nodes.

Discussion

Use the @ operator to assign attributes to an element with E4X; the basic syntax looks like this:

```
elementNode.@attributeName = "value";
```

Use the dot operator (.) after an element node variable, followed by the @ operator. Immediately after the @ symbol, specify the name of the attribute, and use a regular assignment statement to give the attribute a value. The value to the right of the equals sign is converted to a string before being assigned:

```
// Create an XML instance to work with
var example:XML = <example><someElement/></example>;

// Add some attributes to the someElement element node
example.someElement.@number = 12.1;
example.someElement.@string = "example";
example.someElement.@boolean = true;
example.someElement.@array = ["a", null, 7, undefined, "c"];

/* Displays:
<example>
  <someElement number="12.1" string="example" boolean="true"
  array="a,,7,,c"/>
</example>
*/
trace( example );
```

When using this syntax, the attribute name must be a valid variable name. This means that the attributes must have names consisting of numbers, letters, and under-scores, and the first character cannot be a number. However, XML attribute names can sometimes contain other characters that, when used with the @ operator, gener-ate compile errors. In these situations, you can use bracket notation to create attributes whose names contain invalid variable name characters. For example:

```
example.someElement.@["bad-variable-name"] = "yes";
```

You can also use bracket notation to create attributes dynamically, building the attribute name with variable values. For example:

```
example.someElement.@["color" + num] = "red";
```

See Also

Recipe 20.9

20.6 Reading Elements in an XML Tree

Problem

You want to extract the child elements of an *XML* object.

Solution

Use the *elements()* method to return all of the elements as an *XMLList* and a *for each* loop to iterate over the list.

Discussion

You'll often want to "walk" (traverse) an XML tree to extract or examine one or more elements. This is convenient for searching for a given element or processing elements in which you don't know (or don't care about) their precise order.

E4X provides a convenient *elements()* method that returns all of the element child nodes of an XML object. By using this method inside a *for each* loop, you can walk through the XML tree:

```
var menu:XML = <menu>
                  <menuitem label="File">
                    <menuitem label="New"/>
                  </menuitem>
                  <menuitem label="Help">
                    <menuitem label="About"/>
                  </menuitem>
                  This is a text node
                </menu>;

for each ( var element:XML in menu.elements() ) {
  /* Displays:
  File
  Help
  */
  trace( element.@label );
}
```

The preceding example demonstrates that the *elements()* method only returns the child nodes of an XML object that are of type *element* (ignoring the other node types like text). It also only returns the immediate children of the XML object. The New and

About menuitems are not returned by the *menu.elements()* call in the previous code snippet because they are not immediate children of the menu element. To walk the entire tree, you'll need to create a recursive function, as follows:

```
var menu:XML = <menu>
                  <menuitem label="File">
                    <menuitem label="New"/>
                  </menuitem>
                  <menuitem label="Help">
                    <menuitem label="About"/>
                  </menuitem>
                  This is a text node
               </menu>;

/* Displays:
File
New
Help
About
*/
walk( menu );

// A recursive function that reaches every element in an XML tree
function walk( node:XML ):void {
  // Loop over all of the child elements of the node
  for each ( var element:XML in node.elements() ) {
    // Output the label attribute
    trace( element.@label );
    // Recursively walk the child element to reach its children
    walk( element );
  }
}
```

See Also

Recipe 20.7, 20.8, and 20.9

20.7   Finding Elements by Name

Problem

You want to find an element by its node name rather than by its position in the XML hierarchy.

Solution

Use E4X syntax to "dot down" to a particular element.

Discussion

E4X makes working with XML objects as simple as working with regular objects. For each element node, you access that element in the same way you access the property of an object; for example:

```
var fruit:XML = <fruit><name>Apple</name></fruit>;

// Displays: Apple
trace( fruit.name );
```

As you can see here, to access the name element in the XML packet, use the dot operator (.) and reference name directly of the fruit XML instance. For elements nested deeper in the XML tree, use a series of dots and element names to reach the element, as follows:

```
var author:XML = <author><name><firstName>Darron</firstName></name></author>;

// Displays: Darron
trace( author.name.firstName );
```

One shortcut to consider for accessing deeply nested element nodes without knowing the path to get to the node is to use the double-dot operator. For example, you can omit the path and extract the firstName node directly, like this:

```
var author:XML = <author><name><firstName>Darron</firstName></name></author>;

// Displays: Darron
trace( author..firstName );
```

The double-dot operator works for any level of nesting; it doesn't matter if the target node is two or ten levels deep.

When there are multiple element nodes that share the same name, accessing the element name from an XML instance becomes indexable, much like an *Array*. Use bracket notation, coupled with an integer, to access a particular element node; for example:

```
var items:XML = <items>
                    <item>
                      <name>Apple</name>
                      <color>red</color>
                    </item>
                    <item>
                      <name>Orange</name>
                      <color>orange</color>
                    </item>
                </items>;

// Displays: Apple
trace( items.item[0].name );
// Displays: Orange
trace( items.item[1].name );
```

Using items.item returns an *XMLList* with two elements, each representing one of the item element nodes in the XML literal. The first item element node can be accessed by examining index 0, and the second item element node is accessed with index 1. The first element index is always 0, and the last element index is always one less than the total number of elements. Use the *length()* method to count the number of elements found:

```
// Displays: 2
trace( items.item.length( ) );
```

If you want to examine every element node with a particular node name and you don't know how many there are, use a *for each* loop, like this:

```
var items:XML = <items>
                    <item>
                      <name>Apple</name>
                      <color>red</color>
                    </item>
                    <item>
                      <name>Orange</name>
                      <color>orange</color>
                    </item>
                </items>;

// Use the double dot syntax so we can omit the path
for each ( var name:XML in items..name ) {
  /* Displays:
  Apple
  Orange
  */
  trace( name );
}
```

As with other applications of the dot operator, you can use bracket notation instead of the dot operator. This is useful for situations in which you want to use a variable's value as the element name to find:

```
var nodeName:String = "color";

var fruit:XML = <fruit><color>red</color></fruit>;

// Displays: red
trace( fruit[nodeName] );
```

Bracket notation cannot be used with the double-dot operator. For example, the following code generates an error:

```
trace( fruit..[nodeName] ); // Generates a compile error
```

See Also

Recipe 20.14

20.8 Reading Text Nodes and Their Values

Problem

You want to extract the value from a text node.

Solution

Use E4X syntax, or, alternatively, use the *text()* method to return an *XMLList* of text nodes for an element. Then use the *toString()* method to convert the text node's value to a string, use a conversion function such as *int()* or *Number()* to convert the value to another datatype, or let the Flash Player automatically convert the value to a specific type.

Discussion

Recipe 20.4 looks at text nodes and how to create them in XML objects. This recipe explains how to extract the value from a text node. You can get a reference to the text node in much the same as you reference element nodes, discussed in Recipes 20.6 and 20.7. Once you have a reference to the text node, you can extract its value by using *toString()* or a conversion method on the node. For example, consider the following XML packet:

```
<book>
  <title>ActionScript 3.0 Cookbook</title>
</book>
```

The root node of this XML packet is `<book>`, which contains `<title>` as its child element. The `<title>` element, in turn, contains a nested node; a text node with a value of `ActionScript 3.0 Cookbook`.

If this XML packet is assigned to an *XML* object, you can "dot down" with E4X syntax to get to the `title` element node by name, and then use the *toString()* method to access the text node child of `title`:

```
var book:XML = <book>
                 <title>ActionScript 3.0 Cookbook</title>
               </book>;

// Use E4X syntax to access the title element, and assign
// it to the title variable.
var title:String = book.title.toString();

// Displays: ActionScript 3.0 Cookbook
trace( title );
```

In this example, converting the `title` element node to a *String* is done by explicitly invoking the *toString()* method. In truth, you can omit the call to *toString()* because the Flash Player does this for us automatically. However, it is generally a good idea to explicitly use *toString()* so your code communicates its intent.

Similarly, you can convert a text node to other types besides *String*. The following example demonstrates converting text nodes to various types by using both conversion functions *Boolean()* and *int()*, and letting the Flash Player automatically do the conversion for the *Number* type (instead of explicitly using *Number()*):

```
var example:XML = <example>
                    <bool>true</bool>
                    <integer>12</integer>
                    <number>.9</number>
                  </example>;

// Convert a text node of "true" to boolean true
var bool:Boolean = Boolean( example.bool );

// Convert a text node of "12" to an integer
var integer:int = int( example.integer );

// Convert a text node of ".9" to a number
var number:Number = example.number;

/* Displays:
true
12
.9
*/
trace( bool );
trace( integer );
trace( number );
```

The preceding example is slightly misleading. The *Boolean()* conversion function may not work exactly the way you think it does. Changing the text node value in the <bool> element from true to false results in the bool variable being set to true, and not false like you might think. This behavior is by design, frustrating as it may be. A simple technique to convert the string false to a Boolean false is to use the *toLowerCase()* method and compare the value with the string true:

```
var bool:Boolean = example.bool.toLowerCase( ) == "true";
```

Until now we've examined element nodes with a single text node as a child. What about mixed elements? Trying to convert a mixed element into a string results in a formatted XML string as output:

```
var fruit:XML = <fruit>
                    <name>Apple</name>
                    An apple a day...
                  </fruit>;

// Explicity using toString( ) here is required
var value:String = fruit.toString( );

/* Displays:
<fruit>
```

```
    <name>Apple</name>
    An apple a day...
  </fruit>
*/
trace( value );
```

In these situations, the *text()* method should be used to return only the text nodes of an element. As demonstrated in Recipe 20.6, use a *for each* loop to iterate over the nodes:

```
var fruit:XML = <fruit>
                    <name>Apple</name>
                    An apple a day...
                </fruit>;

for each ( var textNode:XML in fruit.text() ) {
  // Displays: An apple a day...
  trace( textNode );
}
```

See Also

Recipes 20.4, 20.6, and 20.7

20.9   Reading an Element's Attributes

Problem

You want to extract the attributes of an element.

Solution

Use the *attributes()* method to return a list of attributes for an element. Alternatively, use the @ operator in E4X syntax or *attribute()* method to access an attribute by name.

Discussion

You should use the *attributes()* method to return an *XMLList* of attributes for a particular element node. The *XMLList* returned is indexable, just like an *Array* instance. Examining a particular index returns the value for the attribute at that index:

```
var fruit:XML = <fruit name="Apple" color="red" />;

// Use the attributes() method and save the results as an XMLList
var attributes:XMLList = fruit.attributes();

// Displays: Apple
trace( attributes[0] );
// Displays: red
trace( attributes[1] );
```

In this example, only the values of the attributes are retrieved. Use the *name()* method on the attribute reference to retrieve its name. In the following example, the second attribute (located at index 1) is examined for its name:

```
var fruit:XML = <fruit name="Apple" color="red" />;

// Displays: color
trace( fruit.attributes()[1].name() );
```

To loop over all of the attributes of an element, use a *for each* loop. Use a combination of the *name()* method to retrieve the attribute's name and the attribute reference itself for its value. In the following example, *toString()* is explicitly called on the attribute reference to convert its value to a string, like in Recipe 20.8:

```
var fruit:XML = <fruit name="Apple" color="red" />;

for each ( var attribute:XML in fruit.attributes() ) {
  /* Displays:
  name = Apple
  color = red
  */
  trace( attribute.name() + " = " + attribute.toString() );
}
```

If you are interested in a particular attribute and know its name, the E4X syntax makes accessing the element trivial. Use E4X to dot down to the particular element node, and then use the @ operator followed by the attribute's name to access its value:

```
var fruit:XML = <fruit name="Apple" color="red" />;

// Displays: red
trace( fruit.@color );
```

Additionally, you can use the *attribute()* method and pass in the name of the attribute to access its value:

```
var fruit:XML = <fruit name="Apple" color="red" />;

// Displays: red
trace( fruit.attribute("color") );
```

You can also use a wildcard (*) with the @ operator to access all attributes of an element, similar to using the *attributes()* method:

```
var fruit:XML = <fruit name="Apple" color="red" />;

// Displays: Apple
trace( fruit.@*[0] );

// Displays: red
trace( fruit.@*[1] );

// Displays: 2
trace( fruit.@*.length() );
```

Because the attributes are always returned as an *XMLList*, the attributes are indexable, making them easy to access.

E4X syntax is extremely powerful. Consider having an XML packet that contains multiple elements, with certain elements having an attribute named price. The following code snippet shows how you might use E4X to total the prices of all of the elements with a price attribute:

```
// Create a fictitious shopping cart
var cart:XML = <cart>
                  <item price=".98">crayons</item>
                  <item price="3.29">pencils</item>
                  <group>
                     <item price=".48">blue pen</item>
                     <item price=".48">black pen</item>
                  </group>
               </cart>;

// Create a total variable to represent represent the cart total
var total:Number = 0;

// Find every price attribute, and add its value to the running total
for each ( var price:XML in cart..@price ) {
  total += price;
}

// Displays: 5.23
trace( total );
```

By using the double-dot operator before the @ operator in E4X syntax, the search for price attributes looks at the entire XML tree underneath the cart element node.

As shown in Recipe 20.5, you can also use bracket syntax to access an attribute by name in a dynamic manner, or when the attribute name contains characters not allowed in variable names:

```
var example:XML = <example bad-variable-name="yes" color12="blue" />;
var num:Number = 12;

// Displays: yes
trace( example.@["bad-variable-name"] );

// Displays: blue
trace( example.@["color" + num] );
```

See Also

Recipes 20.5 and 20.8

20.10 Removing Elements, Text Nodes, and Attributes

Problem

You want to remove an element node, text node, or attribute from an *XML* object.

Solution

Use the delete keyword.

Discussion

In previous recipes you have learned how to add element and text nodes, and attributes to *XML* objects. You've also learned how to read them back in and loop over them. But what if you want to delete a particular element or attribute? The secret is to use the delete keyword, followed by what you want to delete:

```
var example:XML = <example>
                    <fruit color="Red">Apple</fruit>
                    <vegetable color="Green">Broccoli</vegetable>
                    <dairy color="White">Milk</dairy>
                  </example>;

// Remove the color attribute from the fruit element
delete example.fruit.@color;

// Remove the dairy element entirely
delete example.dairy;

// Remove the text node from the vegetable element node
delete example.vegetable.text()[0];

/* Displays:
<example>
  <fruit>Apple</fruit>
  <vegetable color="Green"/>
</example>
*/
trace( example );
```

Of particular interest in the preceding example is how the text node was deleted. Using certain methods like *text()* and *elements()* on an *XML* object, or, in certain situations, using E4X syntax, returns an *XMLList* with multiple items. The delete keyword only works in conjunction with a single item, and as such, you must use bracket notation to reference a particular item in the *XMLList* that you want to delete. To delete all the items in the *XMLList*, use a *for* loop and iterate over the items in reverse order:

```
var example:XML = <example>
                    <fruit color="red" name="Apple" />
                  </example>;
```

```
// Get an XMLList of the attributes for fruit
var attributes:XMLList = example.fruit.@*;

// Loop over the items backwards to delete every attribute.
// By removing items from the end of the array we avoid problems
// with the array indices changing while trying to loop over them.
for ( var i:int = attributes.length() - 1; i >= 0; i-- ) {
    delete attributes[i];
}

/* Displays:
<example>
  <fruit/>
</example>
*/
trace( example );
```

20.11 Loading XML

Problem

You want to load XML data from an XML document or a server-side script that generates XML.

Solution

Use the *URLLoader.load()* method with its dataFormat property set to DataFormat.TEXT to load the data as plain text. Use an event handler for the complete event and convert the text into an *XML* instance.

Discussion

In previous versions of ActionScript, loading an XML file was done by invoking the *load()* method directly on an *XML* object. In ActionScript 3.0, sending and loading of data has been consolidated into the new *URLLoader* class and its related classes. There are no special considerations given to loading XML in ActionScript 3.0, leaving it up to you to implement your own solution.

The process of loading an XML file, while multistep, is relatively painless. First, a *URLLoader* instance must be made to load the data from the URL. To instruct the *URLLoader* to load the data as plain text, its dataFormat property must be set to DataFormat.Text. An event listener for the complete event needs to be added so you receive notification when the data has finished downloading. In the complete event handler, one of the techniques outlined in Recipe 20.2 should be used to convert the loaded data into an *XML* object. Finally, the *URLLoader.load()* method must be invoked to kick off the loading process, being passed a *URLRequest* instance that points to the URL of the XML file. A complete example looks like this:

```
package {
  import flash.display.*;
  import flash.events.*;
  import flash.net.*;
  import flash.util.*;

  public class LoadXMLExample extends Sprite {

    public function LoadXMLExample() {
      var loader:URLLoader = new URLLoader();
      loader.dataFormat = DataFormat.TEXT;
      loader.addEventListener( Event.COMPLETE, handleComplete );
      loader.load( new URLRequest( "example.xml" ) );
    }

    private function handleComplete( event:Event ):void {
      try {
        // Convert the downlaoded text into an XML instance
        var example:XML = new XML( event.target.data );
        // At this point, example is ready to be used with E4X
        trace( example );

      } catch ( e:TypeError ) {
        // If we get here, that means the downloaded text could
        // not be converted into an XML instance, probably because
        // it is not formatted correctly.
        trace( "Could not parse text into XML" );
        trace( e.message );
      }
    }
  }
}
```

In the preceding example, note the use of the *try...catch* block in the handleComplete method. In the event that the XML file did not contain valid XML markup, a *TypeError* is generated when the downloaded data is converted into an *XML* instance. The error is caught by the catch block, allowing you to handle the parsing failure gracefully.

For more information about using *URLLoader*, refer to Chapter 19.

See Also

Recipe 20.2 and Chapter 19, specifically Recipe 19.3.

20.12 Loading XML from Different Domains

Problem

You want to be able to load XML from domains other than the domain that the *.swf* is served from.

Solution

Use a *crossdomain.xml policy file* on the remote domain with an entry to allow access from the domain the *.swf* is served from.

Discussion

See Recipe 3.12 for information about using a *crossdomain.xml policy file*.

See Also

Recipe 3.12

20.13 Sending XML

Problem

You want to send XML data to a server-side script.

Solution

Create a *URLRequest* instance containing the XML data to send. Use *flash.net. sendToURL()* to send the data and ignore the server response, use *flash.net. navigateToURL()* to send the data and open the server response in a specific browser window, or use *URLLoader.load()* to both send the data and download the response into the *.swf* file.

Discussion

XML is normally used to transfer data to and from applications, and in this case, Flash movies. Therefore, it is quite unusual that you would want to create XML objects in your Flash movies for use within Flash alone. Instead, you generally load XML data from another source, create XML data in Flash for the purpose of sending to another application, or both.

This recipe examines sending XML data from Flash to another application, and there are lots of reasons to do this. For example, in a Flash game you might want to use XML to send the user's name and score to the server. At other times, you might want to send XML packets to a server-side script to invoke server-side functionality. This is a process that is sometimes called a *remote procedure call* (RPC), and it can use XML to send the function invocation information (function name, parameters, etc.) to the server. There is a formal specification for using XML in this manner called XML-RPC (see *http://www.xmlrpc.com*). So, as you can see, the possibilities for sending XML to the server are quite diverse.

As discussed in Recipe 20.11 and Chapter 19, ActionScript 3.0 consolidates sending and loading data into the methods of the *flash.net* package. Previously, the *XML* class contained both *send()* and *sendAndLoad()* methods to send XML to a server, but in ActionScript 3.0 you must use *URLRequest* instead. Recipes 19.6 and 19.7 cover the basic techniques using a *URLReuest* instance to send and receive data.

Let's take a look at a complete working example. In what follows, you'll first create the necessary client-side ActionScript code, and then you should choose from one of the server-side solutions. Choose one that's supported by your server (or your personal computer, if you use that as your server). There are server-side scripts in Perl, PHP, and ColdFusion.

The first thing you should do is create a new ActionScript 3.0 class with the following code:

```
package {
  import flash.display.*;
  import flash.text.*;
  import flash.filters.*;
  import flash.events.*;
  import flash.net.*;

  public class XMLSendLoadExample extends Sprite {

    private var _message:TextField;
    private var _username:TextField;
    private var _save:SimpleButton;

    public function XMLSendLoadExample() {
      initializeDispaly();
    }

    private function initializeDispaly():void {
      _message = new TextField();
      _message.autoSize = TextFieldAutoSize.LEFT;
      _message.x = 10;
      _message.y = 10;
      _message.text = "Enter a user name";

      _username = new TextField();
      _username.width = 100;
      _username.height = 18;
      _username.x = 10;
      _username.y = 30;
      _username.type = TextFieldType.INPUT;
      _username.border = true;
      _username.background = true;

      _save = new SimpleButton();
      _save.upState = createSaveButtonState( 0xFFCC33 );
      _save.overState = createSaveButtonState( 0xFFFFFF );
      _save.downState = createSaveButtonState( 0xCCCCCC );
      _save.hitTestState = save.upState;
      _save.x = 10;
      _save.y = 50;
```

```
    // When the save button is clicked, call the handleSave method
    _save.addEventListener( MouseEvent.CLICK, handleSave );

    addChild( _message );
    addChild( _username );
    addChild( _save );
}

// Creates a button state with a specific background color
private function createSaveButtonState( color:uint ):Sprite {
    var state:Sprite = new Sprite();

    var label:TextField = new TextField();
    label.text = "Save";
    label.x = 2;
    label.height = 18;
    label.width = 30;
    var background:Shape = new Shape();
    background.graphics.beginFill( color );
    background.graphics.lineStyle( 1, 0x000000 );
    background.graphics.drawRoundRect( 0, 0, 32, 18, 9 );
    background.filters = [ new DropShadowFilter( 1 ) ];

    state.addChild( background );
    state.addChild( label );
    return state;
}

private function handleSave( event:MouseEvent ):void {
    // Generate a random score to save with the username
    var score:int = Math.floor( Math.random() * 10 );

    // Create a new XML instance containing the data to be saved
    var dataToSave:XML = <gamescore>
                            <username>{username.text}</username>
                            <score>{score}</score>
                         </gamescore>;

    // Point the request to the script that will handle the XML
    var request:URLRequest = new URLRequest( "/gamescores.cfm" );
    // Set the data property to the dataToSave XML instance to send the XML
    // data to the server
    request.data = dataToSave;
    // Set the contentType to signal XML data being sent
    request.contentType = "text/xml";
    // Use the post method to send the data
    request.method = URLRequestMethod.POST;

    // Create a URLLoader to handle sending and loading of the XML data
    var loader:URLLoader = new URLLoader();
    // When the server response is finished downloading, invoke handleResponse
    loader.addEventListener( Event.COMPLETE, handleResponse );
    // Finally, send off the XML data to the URL
    loader.load( request );
```

```
    }

    private function handleResponse( event:Event ):void {
      try {
        // Attempt to convert the server's response into XML
        var success:XML = new XML( event.target.data );

        // Inspect the value of the success element node
        if ( success.toString() == "1" ) {
          _message.text = "Saved successfully.";
        } else {
          _message.text = "Error encountered while saving.";
        }

      } catch ( e:TypeError ) {
        // Display an error message since the server response was not understood
        _message.text = "Could not parse XML response from server.";
      }
    }
  }
}
```

The contentType property of a *URLRequest* instance is set to application/x-www-form-urlencoded by default, so it's important to set contentType to text/xml whenever you want to send XML data. Additionally, you'll want to set the method of the request to *URLRequestMethod.POST* to send the XML data to the server via HTTP POST.

 Obviously, in a real-world example, the user's score would be generated by her performance in a game. In this example, we just want to demonstrate sending and receiving XML, so we generate the score randomly.

The next step is to create the server-side script. First, here's the Perl option. If you use this option, place the following code in a text file named *gamescores.cgi* (or *gamescores.pl*) in a directory on your web server that has CGI access enabled (usually *cgi* or *cgi-bin*).

```perl
#!/usr/bin/perl

# Flash/Perl+CGI XML interaction demo
# Arun Bhalla (arun@groogroo.com)

use strict;
use XML::Simple;
use CGI;

my $ScoreFile = "scores.txt";

# Here we assume that this CGI script is receiving XML in text/xml
# form via POST. Because of this, the XML appears to the script
```

```
# via STDIN.
my $input = XMLin(join('',<STDIN>));

# Write out the HTTP header
print CGI::header('text/xml');

# Try to open score file for writing, or return an error message.
open(SCORES, ">> $ScoreFile") || (printMessage(0) &&
                    die "Error opening $ScoreFile");

# Save the score in a pipe-delimited text file.
print SCORES join('|', $input->{username}, $input->{score}), "\n";

# Return the result in XML.
printMessage(1);

# Subroutine to output the result in XML.
sub printMessage {
  my $value = shift;
  my $message = {};
  $message->{success} = $value;
  print XMLout($message, keeproot => 1, rootname => 'success');
}
```

If you are using ColdFusion, a sample ColdFusion script is provided in the following code block. Place this code in a ColdFusion page named *gamescores.cfm* within a directory on your web server that can run ColdFusion pages:

```
<cfsilent>
<cfsetting enablecfoutputonly="Yes">
<cfset success = 0>
<cftry>
  <!--- XML packet sent by Flash. --->
  <cfset scores_xml = XmlParse( getHTTPRequestData(  ).content ) >

  <!--- Parse out the XML packet sent from Flash. --->

  <!--- Grab the username and score from the XML document and save as
        local variables so they are easier to work with. // --->
  <cfset username = scores_xml.gamescore.username.XmlText >
  <cfset score = scores_xml.gamescore.score.XmlText >

  <!--- Append the latest score to our scores file. This could also be
        stored in the database or another XML document. // --->
  <cffile action="APPEND" file="#ExpandPath( 'scores.txt' )#"
  output="#username#|#score#|#getHTTPRequestData(  ).content#" addnewline="Yes">
  <cfset success = 1 >
  <cfcatch type="Any">
    <cfset success = 0 >
    <cffile action="APPEND" file="#ExpandPath( 'attempts.txt' )#" output="ERROR"
    addnewline="Yes">
  </cfcatch>
</cftry>
</cfsilent>
```

```
<cfcontent type="text/xml">
<cfoutput><?xml version="1.0" ?><success>#success#</success></cfoutput>
<cfsetting showdebugoutput="no" enablecfoutputonly="No">
```

If you are using PHP on your server, place the following code in a PHP page named *gamescores.php* on your web server in a directory that allows PHP access:

```php
<?php

// Read In XML from Raw Post Data.
$xml = $GLOBALS['HTTP_RAW_POST_DATA'];

// Process XML using DOM PHP extension.
$document = xmldoc($xml);

// Read root element <gameinfo>.
$rootElement = $document->root( );

// Read child nodes <username> and <score>.
$childNodes = $rootElement->children( );

$data = "";

// Loop through child nodes and place in array.
foreach($childNodes as $childNode){
  // Add data to array;
  $name = $childNode->tagName( );
  $value = $childNode->get_content( );
  $data[$name] = $value;
}

// Append data to scores.txt ( format: username|score )
$fp = fopen("scores.txt","a+");
$dataString = $data['username'] . "|" . $data['score'] . "\n";
fputs($fp,$dataString,strlen($dataString));
fclose($fp);

// Return success code to Flash
echo "<success>1</success>";
?>
```

All three scripts have one thing in common: they all output an XML response with <success> as the root node, containing a text node value of 1 for successful save and 0, which indicates some type of error.

To test the Flash movie once you have it and the server-side script in place, you need only to run the movie and click on the button. The movie should get a successful response, and if you check in the directory on the server in which the script has been created, you should find a *scores.txt* file containing the data that was entered via the Flash movie.

See Also

Chapter 19—specifically Recipes 19.6 and 19.7, and Recipe 20.11.

20.14 Searching XML

Problem

You want to search an *XML* object for nodes or attributes that meet certain criteria.

Solution

Use the E4X syntax along with *predicate filtering* on an *XML* object to pick out certain values from an XML tree.

Discussion

This chapter examines how E4X syntax with *XML* objects simplifies reading and writing values in an XML tree. As simple as E4X is to use, it is also extremely powerful. E4X syntax is similar to using *XPath* for searching XML documents. If you are familiar with *XPath* concepts, using the advanced features of E4X (such as its predicate filtering) should come naturally. Predicate filtering allows you to pick out element nodes that meet a certain Boolean expression condition using the syntax .(condition), as you'll see later in this recipe.

Let's start by creating an *XML* object from an XML literal:

```
var foodgroup:XML = <foodgroup>
                    <fruits>
                      <fruit color="red">Apple</fruit>
                      <fruit color="orange">Orange</fruit>
                      <fruit color="green">Pear</fruit>
                      <fruit color="red">Watermelon</fruit>
                      <servings>3</servings>
                    </fruits>
                    <vegetables>
                      <vegetable color="red">Tomato</vegetable>
                      <vegetable color="brown">Potato</vegetable>
                      <vegetable color="green">Broccoli</vegetable>
                      <servings>2</servings>
                    </vegetables>
                  </foodgroup>;
```

When you know the name of element nodes, you simply dot down to reach them. For example, to return a list of all of the <fruit> element nodes, use the following E4X expression:

```
var fruitList:XMLList = foodgroup.fruits.fruit;
```

If you're interested in a particular <fruit> element node, you can access the node by specifying an index value using bracket notation:

```
var theApple:XML = foodgroup.fruits.fruit[0];
```

If you don't know (or care) about the full path from the root node to the node (or nodes) for which you are searching, use the double-dot operator to indicate that you want to locate all matching nodes at any level in the XML tree. For example, the following returns all <vegetable> nodes regardless of where they are in the hierarchy:

```
var vegetableList:XMLList = foodgroup..vegetable;
```

An asterisk (*) is a wildcard for "any node." For example, the following E4X expression returns assigns to *servings* an *XMLList* containing all <servings> element nodes that are children of any nodes that are, in turn, children of the <foodgroup> node:

```
var servings:XMLList = foodgroup.*.servings;
```

The @ sign is used to signify an attribute. The following example generates an *XMLList* containing the values of the color attributes for the <fruit> nodes:

```
var colorValues:XMLList = foodgroup.fruits.fruit.@color;
```

Now let's look at predicate filtering. Predicate filtering uses the syntax .(*condition*) to pick out element nodes that meet the condition specified. The condition is specified via a Boolean expression. The filtering acts on the *XML* or *XMLList* object that precedes the predicate filter expression.

For example, let's say you want to pick out all of the <fruit> element nodes where the color attribute is red. This can be accomplished by first generating an *XMLList* of all of the <fruit> element nodes using E4X dot-down syntax, and then filtering with the Boolean expression @color == "red":

```
/* Displays:
<fruit color="red">Apple</fruit>
<fruit color="red">Watermelon</fruit>
*/
trace( foodgroup..fruit.( @color == "red" ) );
```

In this example, two things are happening in the expression passed to the trace statement:

- The foodgroups..fruit portion returns an *XMLList* of all of the <fruit> element nodes that appear in the XML tree.

- Predicate filtering is applied on the *XMLList* of <fruit> nodes and a new *XMLList* is created that contains only those <fruit> elements matching the filtering expression, in this case, the elements with color attributes equal to red. You can see that both of the fruit element nodes with red as the value of the color attribute appear in the trace output.

The preceding example selected the red <fruit> element nodes, but what if we wanted to select any node that had red as the value for the color attribute? Use the asterisk to look for any node, along with a predicate filter that looks for the existence of a color attribute, and if the color attribute exists, checks to make sure its value is red:

```
/* Displays:
<fruit color="red">Apple</fruit>
<fruit color="red">Watermelon</fruit>
```

```
<vegetable color="red">Tomato</vegetable>
*/
trace( foodgroup..*.( hasOwnProperty( "@color" ) && @color == "red" )  );
```

The Boolean expression used as the condition can be any expression that results in a Boolean true or false value. In the preceding example, hasOwnProperty checks to make sure the element has an attribute for color, and if so tests the value of the color attribute to see if its value is red. Only when the condition evaluates to true is the element added to the *XMLList* that the E4X expression returns.

So far, predicate filtering has only been done with attributes; however, it can also be used to specify that a certain element node needs to have a particular text node as a value. This is particularly useful when you have an XML document that has repeated element nodes that contain child nodes. For example, here is how to display the value of the color attribute for whichever <fruit> element node has a <name> element node with a text node value of Apple:

```
var fruits:XML = <fruits>
                   <fruit color="red">
                     <name>Apple</name>
                   </fruit>
                   <fruit color="orange">
                     <name>Orange</name>
                   </fruit>
                   <fruit color="green">
                     <name>Pear</name>
                   </fruit>
                   <fruit color="red">
                     <name>Watermelon</name>
                   </fruit>
                 </fruits>;

// Displays: red
trace( fruits.fruit.(name == "Apple").@color );
```

As you can see, predicate filtering is quite powerful, and it gets even more powerful when combined with regular expressions. The following example uses a regular expression to find all of the <fruit> element nodes that have a <name> child node containing a text node starting with a vowel:

```
var fruits:XML = <fruits>
                   <fruit color="red">
                     <name>Apple</name>
                   </fruit>
                   <fruit color="orange">
                     <name>Orange</name>
                   </fruit>
                   <fruit color="green">
                     <name>Pear</name>
                   </fruit>
                   <fruit color="red">
                     <name>Watermelon</name>
                   </fruit>
                 </fruits>;
```

```
/* Displays:
<fruit color="red">
  <name>Apple</name>
</fruit>
<fruit color="orange">
  <name>Orange</name>
</fruit>
*/
trace( fruits.fruit.( /^[aeiouAEIOU].*/.test( name ) ) );
```

The preceding code snippet creates a regular expression (between the / and /) that in plain English reads as "start with a vowel, upper- or lowercase, and be followed by any character any number of times." The *test()* method is invoked on the regular expression to test it against the parameter passed in—in this case, the <name> element node, which is converted to its text node value for the particular <fruit> element being evaluated. Because the *test()* method returns a Boolean value, it's safe to use as part of predicate filter Boolean condition.

Regular expressions are covered in detail in Chapter 13.

See Also

Recipes 20.7, 20.8, 20.9, and Chapter 13

20.15 Using HTML and Special Characters in XML

Problem

You want to use HTML or other text that uses characters with specific meaning in the context of XML.

Solution

Use a CDATA tag to enclose the text.

Discussion

While this recipe doesn't deal with anything specific to ActionScript per se, it is relevant in that it addresses something you'll likely encounter when working with XML with respect to Flash or otherwise. In XML, certain characters are interpreted in specific ways. For example, the greater-than and less-than characters are interpreted as the delimiters of XML tags. If you try to use one of those characters as part of some group of text within the XML document, it causes parser errors when you try to use the document; for example:

```
<example>a < b</example>
```

As you can see, the preceding encloses the text a < b in a text node. However, because the less-than character is interpreted in a specific way in the context of an

XML document, the example causes a parser error. Another common example is one in which you want to store some HTML within an XML document; for example:

```
<htmlExample><a href="http://www.darronschall.com">Darron</a></htmlExample>
```

In such a case the HTML is interpreted as XML, not as a string. The preceding XML packet contains <htmlExample> as the root node, with a child <a> node that contains a text node with the string value of Darron.

In any case, you can enclose text in a CDATA (Character Data) tag, which won't be interpreted by the XML parser. Instead, the parser simply treats the enclosed data as a string.

A CDATA tag begins with <![CDATA[and it ends with]]>. Therefore, the first example can be written as follows:

```
<example><![CDATA[a < b]]></example>
```

The second example can be rewritten as follows:

```
<htmlExample><![CDATA[<a href="http://www.darronschall.com">Darron</a>]]></
htmlExample>
```

When the XML is parsed, the character data inside the CDATA tag is treated as a single string, but the CDATA tag itself is discarded. So, for example, the text node in the first example would be retrieved as a < b, not <![CDATA[a < b]]>. In the second example, the XML packet is interpreted as a root node of <htmlExample>, with a single text node containing the entire HTML link as a string. Because of the CDATA tag, the <a> is not interpreted as a child node as it was previously, and instead is just part of the string value of the text node.

## CHAPTER 21

Web Services and Flash Remoting

21.0 Introduction

Remote procedure calls (RPCs) are a powerful way to build distributed and robust applications. RPC is essential for most Flash platform applications. For example, you can use RPC to send data to the server from Flash Player or retrieve data from the server to display to the user. There are many ways for making remote procedure calls from Flash Player; however, there are two ways that stand out: web services and Flash Remoting.

When referring to web services in this book, the focus is on Simple Object Access Protocol (SOAP). Web services of this type use SOAP for communication between the server and client. SOAP can serialize complex datatypes, which means you can call server-side methods from a client and pass it parameters of both simple (numbers, strings, and Boolean values) and complex types (objects.) The server-side method can even return complex data to the client, such as arrays, Date objects, and even custom datatypes. SOAP web services are supported by nearly every platform, including Java, ColdFusion, PHP, .NET, and Perl to name a few. Flash Player, however, does not have built-in web services support, and it doesn't natively understand SOAP either.

However, Flash Player can communicate over HTTP, and it can parse XML data. Since SOAP web services communicate over HTTP and SOAP is an XML-based protocol, it is possible to use ActionScript to call web services methods.

Flash Remoting is very similar to web services, but with a few significant advantages:

- Flash Remoting uses HTTP as well, but rather than using SOAP, it uses a binary protocol called Active Messaging Format (AMF). Since AMF packets are binary, you can send much more data across the wire at much less expense. The result is that Flash Remoting is faster than other web services.

- Flash Remoting is natively supported by Flash Player.

- Flash Remoting is also available for Java, ColdFusion, .NET, and Perl, though it is quite likely that there are many less prominent platforms that support web services that don't currently support Flash Remoting.

Flash Remoting and Web services both make asynchronous requests to service methods, and both can be used to create sophisticated client-server applications. The recipes in this chapter look at how to work with these technologies.

21.1   Calling Web Services Methods

Problem

You want to call a web service method.

Solution

Use an *mx.rpc.soap.WebService* object, and call the method from the *WebService* object.

Discussion

As mentioned earlier, Flash Player has no built-in web services capabilities, but the Flex framework does include a solution. This recipe discusses how to use the Flex 2 solution for working with web services. For a Flash solution, see additional notes at *http://www.rightactionscript.com/ascb*.

The Flex framework includes *mx.rpc.soap.WebService*, a class that simplifies calling web services methods by using ActionScript. The first step is to construct a new *WebService* object, as follows:

```
var webService.WebService = new WebService();
```

Every web service must have a Web Service Description Language (WSDL) resource that describes the service. You can tell the *WebService* object where to locate the WSDL using the wsdl property:

```
webService.wsdl = "http://www.rightactionscript.com/webservices/FlashSurvey.
php?wsdl";
```

Before you can call methods, you must load the WSDL data from the specified URL by using the *loadWSDL()* method:

```
webService.loadWSDL();
```

The *loadWSDL()* method makes a request for the WSDL data asynchronously. That means you have to listen for an event to know when the WSDL data has loaded. When the data has loaded, the *WebService* object dispatches a load event of type *mx.rpc.soap.LoadEvent*, as shown here:

```
webService.addEventListener(LoadEvent.LOAD, onWSDL);
```

Once the WSDL data has correctly loaded, call the web services methods directly from the *WebService* object. For example, the WSDL URL used in this example points to a real web service, which has a method called *getAverages()* that can be called from the *WebService* object, as follows:

```
webService.getAverages();
```

If the method happens to expect parameters, pass them to the method as you would any normal ActionScript method. For example, the same web service also has a method called *takeSurvey()*, which expects two integer values; the following calls the method and passes it values of 10 and 15:

```
webService.takeSurvey(10, 15);
```

Web services method calls occur asynchronously, which means a response is not returned immediately. See Recipe 21.2 for more details on how to retrieve the return value from a web services method.

See Also

Recipe 21.2

21.2   Handling Web Services Responses

Problem

You want to retrieve the return value from a web services method.

Solution

Add a result event listener to the web services method object.

Discussion

Web services methods are complex objects of type *mx.rpc.soap.Operation*, to which you can assign event listeners. When a web services method returns a value, the method object dispatches a result event of type *mx.rpc.events.ResultEvent*. If you want to handle the event, you can add a listener to the method object. For example, if webService is a *WebService* object that maps to a web service that defines a method called *getAverages()*, you can add a listener as follows:

```
webService.getAverages.addEventListener(ResultEvent.RESULT, onGetAverages);
```

You then call the method normally:

```
webService.getAverages();
```

When the listener is called, it is passed a *ResultEvent* parameter. The *ResultEvent* class defines a property called result that contains the return value. Assuming the *getAverages()* web services method returns an associative array with two properties called flash and actionscript, the following displays those values in a text area called textArea:

```
private function onGetAverages(event:ResultEvent):void {
    textArea.text = "The averages for Flash and ActionScript are " +
event.result.flash + " and " + event.result.actionscript;
}
```

21.3   Handling Web Services Errors

Problem

You want to handle errors from a web service.

Solution

Listen for a fault event.

Discussion

When a web services error occurs, the operation dispatches a fault event of type *mx.rpc.events.FaultEvent*. You can add a listener to the *Operation* object directly. However, it's generally advisable to handle fault events at the *WebService* object level. Operation fault events bubble up to the *WebService* object if they aren't handled at the *Operation* level. The following adds a fault event listener to a *WebService* object:

```
webService.addEventListener(FaultEvent.FAULT, onWebServiceFault);
```

The *FaultEvent* class defines a fault property of type *mx.rpc.Fault*. *Fault* objects return details about the error using the faultCode, faultDetail, faultString, and rootCause properties. The following displays an *Alert* when an error occurs:

```
private onWebServiceFault(event:FaultEvent):void {
    var fault:Fault = FaultEvent.fault;
    var message:String = "An error occurred. The details are as follows\ncode: " +
fault.faultCode;
    message += "\ndetail: " + faul.faultDetail;
    Alert.show("Web Service Error", message);
}
```

21.4   Calling Flash Remoting Methods

Problem

You want to call a Flash Remoting method.

Solution

Use a *NetConnection* object, connect to the Flash Remoting gateway and use the *call()* method to call the method.

Discussion

Flex and Flash have ActionScript-based APIs that are designed to simplify Flash Remoting method calls. However, this recipe discusses the low-level solution that relies only on the intrinsic (native to Flash Player) solution.

All Flash Remoting operations rely on the *flash.net.NetConnection* class. The first step when making Flash Remoting method calls is to construct a new *NetConnection* object. You should use one *NetConnection* object per Flash Remoting service (a service generally being a class):

```
var connection:NetConnection = new NetConnection();
```

Next, call the *connect()* method, passing it the URL to the Flash Remoting gateway. For example, if you are using ColdFusion running locally as a standalone product, then try the following:

```
connection.connect("http://localhost:8500/flashservices/gateway/");
```

The following connects to a working example AMFPHP Flash Remoting gateway:

```
connection.connect("http://www.rightactionscript.com/flashremoting/gateway.php");
```

 If you don't know which gateway URL to use, consult either the documentation for the Flash Remoting server product or your network administrator responsible for managing the server portion of Flash Remoting.

The *connect()* method does not immediately attempt to connect to the gateway URL. If the URL is invalid, or if there is a server-side error, you won't receive an error until you actually call a method.

The next step is to call a Flash Remoting method using the *call()* method of the *NetConnection* object. The *call()* method requires two parameters. The first parameter specifies the name and path of the service and method. The second parameter tells the *NetConnection* object how to handle the response from the method call. For a discussion of how to handle responses from Flash Remoting, see Recipe 21.2. In this initial discussion, it's assumed that the application doesn't need to handle a response; as such, a null value is passed for the second parameter.

The first parameter for the *call()* method specifies the method using a dot-delimited path in the following format:

```
package.ServiceObject.method
```

For example, if you are using a ColdFusion component (CFC) accessible at *http://localhost:8500/com/oreilly/as3cb/Example.cfc*, and the CFC defines a method called *test()*, the following code calls the method:

```
connection.call("com.oreilly.as3cb.Example.test", null);
```

You can pass parameters to the method by adding them to the parameter list of the *call()* method. For example, if the *test()* method accepts a number and a string parameter, you can use the following code to pass those values:

```
connection.call("com.oreilly.as3cb.Example.test", null, 15, "abcd");
```

See Also

Recipes 21.2 and 21.5

21.5   Handling Flash Remoting Responses

Problem

You want to retrieve a return value from a Flash Remoting method.

Solution

Use a *Responder* object with *call()*.

Discussion

Recipe 21.1 discusses how to use the *call()* method of a *NetConnection* object to call a Flash Remoting method. The second parameter of that method is designed for specifying how Flash Player should handle responses. If you pass a value of null (as in the examples in that recipe), then no responses are handled. If you want to handle the responses, use a *flash.net.Responder* object.

The *Responder* constructor lets you pass it two function references, which handle return values and errors:

```
var responder:Responder = new Responder(onResult, onError);
```

When the result function gets called, it's passed one parameter with the value returned by the Flash Remoting method:

```
private function onResult(returnValue:Datatype):void {
}
```

The error handler method is passed an object with properties that describe the error in greater detail.

The following example makes a call to a Flash Remoting method called *getAverages()* and uses *trace()* to display the values. The *getAverages()* method returns an associative array with two properties called flash and actionscript:

```
package {
    import flash.net.NetConnection;
    import flash.net.Responder;

    public class Example {
        private var _connection:NetConnection;
        public function Example() {
            _connection = new NetConnection();
            _connection.connect("http://www.rightactionscript.com/flashremoting/
                gateway.php");
            var responder:Responder = new Responder(onResult, onError);
            _connection.call("FlashSurvey.getAverages", responder);
        }

        private function onResult(result:Object):void {
            trace(result.flash + " " + result.actionscript);
        }

        private function onError(error:Object):void {
            trace(error.description);
        }
    }
}
```

When returning values from Flash Remoting methods, you should always return types that serialize well; do not return record sets. Instead, you should always convert record sets to arrays of associative arrays. That ensures the greatest interoperability.

See Also

Recipe 21.4

CHAPTER 22
Building Integrated Applications

22.0 Introduction

The *ExternalInterface* class allows the Flash Player to communicate in a synchronous manner with the application within which it is embedded. In many cases that host application is a web browser. As such, this chapter focuses exclusively on how to build applications that integrate ActionScript and JavaScript when Flash Player is embedded in a browser.

22.1 Calling JavaScript Functions

Problem

You want to call a JavaScript function from ActionScript.

Solution

Use *ExternalInterface.call()*.

Discussion

Use the *ExternalInterface.call()* method to make synchronous calls to JavaScript functions from ActionScript. The *call()* method requires at least one parameter as a string specifying the name of the function to call:

```
ExternalInterface.call("changeTitle");
```

The function must be defined in the HTML page with the same name:

```
<script language="JavaScript">
    function changeTitle(title) {
        if(title == undefined) {
            title = "New Title";
        }
        window.title = title;
    }
</script>
```

If the JavaScript function accepts parameters, you can pass values to it by adding additional parameters when calling the *call()* method. For example, the following passes a value to the *changeTitle()* function:

```
ExternalInterface.call("changeTitle", "ActionScript 3.0 Cookbook");
```

Since *call()* is synchronous, any values returned by the JavaScript function are immediately returned to ActionScript. That means you can assign the return value from a call to a variable. The following ActionScript illustrates how that can work:

```
var title:String = ExternalInterface.call("getTitle");
```

The JavaScript function for the preceding ActionScript call might look like:

```
<script language="JavaScript">
    function getTitle( ) {
        return window.title;
    }
</script>
```

ExternalInterface works for the following browsers:

- Internet Explorer 5.0+ (Windows)
- Netscape 8.0+ (Windows and Mac OS X)
- Mozilla 1.7.5+ (Windows and Mac OS X)
- Firefox 1.0+ (Windows and Mac OS X)
- Safari 1.3+ (Mac OS X)

If you need to support a browser that *ExternalInterface* does not work with, you can still make calls to JavaScript functions. However, you must then use the *flash.net. navigateToURL()* function.

The *navigateToURL()* function is asynchronous, meaning it does not return a value. To call a JavaScript function using *navigateToURL()* you must use a *flash.net URLRequest* object that has a value using the javascript protocol. The following is an example that calls the JavaScript *alert()* function:

```
var request:URLRequest = new URLRequest("javascript:alert('example');");
navigateToURL(request);
```

See Also

Recipe 22.2

22.2 Calling ActionScript Functions

Problem

You want to call an ActionScript function from JavaScript.

Solution

Use *ExternalInterface.addCallback()* to register the ActionScript function, and then call the function from the JavaScript reference to the Flash Player object.

Discussion

The *ExternalInterface* API allows you to register ActionScript functions, which makes them accessible to JavaScript. Use the static *addCallback()* method to register the ActionScript functions. The *addCallback()* method requires two parameters: the name by which you want to be able to reference the function from JavaScript and a reference to the function. The following example registers a function called displayMessage using an identifier (the name by which the function can be called from JavaScript) of showMessage:

```
ExternalInterface.addCallback("showMessage", displayMessage);
```

From JavaScript, you need to get a reference to the Flash Player object. There are two basic Flash Player versions that run in the browser: ActiveX and the plug-in version. The ActiveX version runs natively in Internet Explorer, while the plug-in version is used by the rest of the browsers.

The ActiveX player is controlled by the <object> tag in an HTML page, and you can retrieve a JavaScript reference using window.*objectId* where *objectId* is the value of the id attribute of the <object> tag. For example, if the <object> tag's id attribute is example, then the reference to the ActiveX player would be window.example.

The plug-in player is controlled by the <embed> tag in an HTML page, and you can retrieve a JavaScript reference by using window.document.*embedName*, where *embedName* is the value of the name attribute of the <embed> tag. For example, if the <embed> tag's name attribute is example, then the reference to the plug-in player would be window. document.example.

In most cases, you probably won't know which Flash Player version the user will have. You can use navigator.appName in JavaScript to determine which browser the user has:

- If navigator.appName contains the string Microsoft, then the user is running Internet Explorer, which means they have the ActiveX player.
- If navigator.appName doesn't contain the string Microsoft, then the user is using the plug-in version of the player.

Use the following JavaScript to detect which version of the player the user has and retrieve the correct reference:

```
<script language="JavaScript">
var flashPlayer;
function detectFlashPlayer( ) {
    if(navigator.appName.indexOf("Microsoft") != -1) {
        flashPlayer = window.objectId;
```

```
        }
        else {
            flashPlayer = window.document.embedName;
        }
    }
</script>
```

Next, use the `onLoad` attribute in the `<body>` tag to call *detectFlashPlayer()* when the page loads, for example:

```
<body onLoad="detectFlashPlayer">
```

The `flashPlayer` variable contains the correct reference to the Flash Player the user has on his system.

You can call any registered ActionScript function directly from the Flash Player reference. For example, if a function has been registered with the identifier `showMessage`, the following calls that function from JavaScript (assuming `flashPlayer` is a variable referencing the Flash Player):

```
flashPlayer.showMessage();
```

You can pass parameters to the functions, as well. If the ActionScript function with the *ExternalInterface* identifier of `showMessage` accepts a string parameter, then you can call it from JavaScript as follows:

```
flashPlayer.showMessage("example message");
```

See Also

Recipe 22.1

22.3   Passing Parameters from HTML

Problem

You want to pass parameters from HTML to an SWF.

Solution

Use `FlashVars`.

Discussion

`FlashVars` provides a solution by which you can pass parameters to an SWF from HTML. This can be very useful when you want to pass simple data to an SWF and the data is likely to change, depending on where the application is deployed. For example, you might want to pass web services URLs to an SWF when the URLs change, depending on the server on which the SWF is deployed. That enables you to redeploy the SWF with new values without having to recompile the SWF.

The FlashVars solution requires two parts: one part is implemented in HTML, and the other is implemented in ActionScript.

The HTML portion of the FlashVars solution requires adding a `<param name="FlashVars">` tag to the `<object>` tag, and a FlashVars attribute to the `<embed>` tag. The value for the tag and attribute is a URL-encoded sequence of name-value pairs. For example, the following constitutes a valid FlashVars value that defines two name-value pairs, url1 and url2:

```
url1=http://www.example.com&url2=http://www.sample.com
```

Within ActionScript, you can reference the variables and values passed via FlashVars using the root.loaderInfo.parameters property of any display object. The root.loaderInfo.parameters property is an associative array, the keys of which are the names of the variables passed to the SWF via FlashVars. For example, using the preceding example value, the root.loaderInfo.parameters property would have two keys: url1 and url2.

Using FlashVars with JavaScript, you can pass a query string from the HTML page to an SWF. The following JavaScript illustrates how to write the `<object>` and `<embed>` tags with JavaScript so they pass the query string data from the HTML page to the SWF using FlashVars:

```
// Retrieve the query string, and assign it to a variable.
var parameters = window.location.search.substr(1);
var objectEmbed = '<object classid="clsid:D27CDB6E-AE6D-11cf-96B8-444553540000"
id="Example" width="100%" height="100%" codebase="http://download.macromedia.com/pub/
shockwave/cabs/flash/swflash.cab">';
objectEmbed += '<param name="movie" value="Example.swf" />';
objectEmbed += '<param name="quality" value="high" />';
objectEmbed += '<param name="bgcolor" value="#869ca7" />';
objectEmbed += '<param name="allowScriptAccess" value="sameDomain" />';
objectEmbed += '<param name="FlashVars" value="' + parameters + '" />';
objectEmbed += '<embed src="Example.swf" quality="high" bgcolor="#869ca7"
width="100%" height="100%" name="Example" align="middle" play="true" loop="false"
quality="high" allowScriptAccess="sameDomain" type="application/x-shockwave-flash"
pluginspage="http://www.macromedia.com/go/getflashplayer" FlashVars="' + parameters +
'"></embed>';
objectEmbed += '</object>';
document.write(objectEmbed);
```

FlashVars is an important feature of Flash Player. However, it's important to use FlashVars correctly. FlashVars is not designed to be a universal mechanism for passing data to an SWF. FlashVars is only for simple data that is likely to change, depending on where the SWF is deployed. For more complex initialization data loading, use a *URLLoader* object to load data at runtime.

## CHAPTER 23

File Management

23.0 Introduction

Prior to Version 8, the Flash Player did not support any mechanism for allowing the user to browse her computer for files. Furthermore, Flash Player didn't have a mechanism for uploading or downloading files, either. As such, most web applications used HTML-based solutions for uploading and downloading files. Flash-based applications not deployed on the Web often had to use customized solutions for uploading and downloading files. Flash Player 8 and higher now supports the new APIs, which greatly simplify file I/O by allowing Flash Player to browse a user's system for files to upload and download.

Flash Player allows users to browse to files on their local disks and upload and download files using the *FileReference* and *FileReferenceList* classes. This chapter discusses the details of working with those APIs.

23.1 Downloading Files

Problem

You want to let users download files to their computer.

Solution

Use the *download()* method of a *FileReference* object.

Discussion

The *flash.net.FileReference* class defines a *download()* method that allows users to download a file from a URL to their computers. When Flash Player calls the *download()* method, it attempts to open a dialog box, titled "Select location for download." This dialog box allows users to use a standard operating system dialog to browse their local disks for a location to which they want to save files.

The first step before calling the *download()* method is to construct a *FileReference* object, as follows:

```
var fileReference:FileReference = new FileReference( );
```

The *download()* method requires at least one parameter as a *URLRequest* object, specifying the URL from which you want to download the file. In the simplest case, the URL points to a static file that the user can download. The following example opens a save dialog box that allows users to select a location to which they can save a copy of *example.txt* from the same directory on the server where the SWF resides:

```
var urlRequest:URLRequest = new URLRequest("example.txt");
fileReference.download(urlRequest);
```

Specifying a full path to a file is as simple as specifying the URL when constructing the *URLRequest* object, as the following example illustrates:

```
var urlRequest:URLRequest = new URLRequest("http://www.myexamplesite.com/example.
txt");
fileReference.download(urlRequest);
```

The save dialog box also allows users to change the name of the file they're downloading. By default, the filename field displays the name of the file as it exists on the server. In the preceding example, the filename field in the save dialog box displays *example.txt*. In many cases, though, you may want to use a different default name than the name of the file specified in the URL. For example, if a static file was created by a server-side script, it may have a unique identifier name as its filename (e.g., *R7AS82892KHWI014.jpg*) that you may not want to display to users by default. Additionally, there are cases when the file is created dynamically at request time by a script, and the *URLRequest* object points to that script. In those cases, the default value for the filename field in the save dialog box is the name of the script (e.g., *script.cgi*), which not only isn't user-friendly, but it can cause the file to be misread by Windows computers if it has the incorrect file extension.

The *download()* method accepts a second, optional parameter by which you can specify a different default value for the filename field in the save dialog box. The second parameter is a string, the value of which is displayed in the filename field. The following example prompts the user to download a file that is created dynamically at request time by a script (*script.cgi*). In this example, the script outputs a JPEG image file. Rather than using the default filename value (*script.cgi*), the code specifies a filename value of *example.jpg*:

```
var urlRequest:URLRequest = new URLRequest("script.cgi");
fileReference.download(urlRequest, "example.jpg");
```

When working with the *download()* method, it's important to use a `try...catch` statement because the method can throw errors. If an error isn't handled properly, it can cause things to malfunction (if the code assumes the operation was successful) and can display a default error message to the user. It's almost never a good idea to allow Flash Player to throw an unhandled event that would display a default error message to the user, as that would likely cause the user to feel as though something has broken. Handling the error with ActionScript code allows the application to respond to the error much more gracefully than it would if the error were unhandled. The two most common errors are *IllegalOperationError* and *SecurityError*. The *IllegalOperationError* occurs when you call *download( )* and a save dialog box is already open; only one such dialog box can be open at a time. The *SecurityError* occurs when the SWF doesn't have permission to download the file because the SWF is an untrusted file:

```
try {
    fileReference.download(urlRequest, fileName);
}
catch (illegalOperation:IllegalOperationError) {
    // code to handle an illegal operation error
}
catch (security:SecurityError) {
    // code to handle a security error
}
```

Although less common, the *download( )* method can also throw errors of type *ArgumentError* and *MemoryError*. *ArgumentError* errors occur when the *URLRequest* parameter has a data property that isn't of type *URLVariables* or *String*. Although your *URLRequest* allows you to assign a byte array to the data property, the *download( )* method works only when the data property is of type *URLVariables* of *String*. The memory error is fairly obscure, and it can occur when one of two conditions is present. If the *URLRequest* is set to make a GET request and System. useCodePage is true, Flash Player may not be able to convert characters from Unicode to multibyte character format as required. Alternatively, Flash Player may not be able to allocate the necessary memory to open the save dialog box.

In addition to the errors that the *download( )* method throws, it also dispatches error events. The *download( )* method dispatches a security error event of type *SecurityErrorEvent* when Flash Player was unable to download the file for security reasons. Security error events occur when Flash Player's sandbox security doesn't grant the SWF permission to download a file from the specified URL. The *download( )* method can dispatch an I/O error event of type *IOErrorEvent* when there is an error downloading the file due to one of the following reasons:

- A network error
- The server requires authentication and Flash Player isn't running in a browser
- An invalid protocol (only HTTP, HTTPS, and FTP work)

You must add an event listener to handle error events such as *SecurityErrorEvent* and *IOErrorEvent*. You can add an event listener for an error event just as you would for a standard event. The following example adds a listener for an *IOErrorEvent* type.

```
fileReference.addEventListener(IOErrorEvent.IO_ERROR, onIOError);
```

See Also

Recipe 23.2

23.2 Detecting When a User Selects a File to Upload

Problem

You want to detect when a user selects a file in order to start a download.

Solution

Listen for the select event. Listen for the cancel event to detect when the user has clicked the cancel button.

Discussion

The *download()* method does not pause the execution of ActionScript code. As soon as the *download()* method is called, Flash Player attempts to open the save dialog box. Once it either successfully opens the save dialog box or throws an error, the Flash Player continues to the next line of ActionScript code. That means you cannot expect the user to have selected a file and clicked the Save button immediately following the *download()* method call. Rather, you must listen for a select event to tell you when the user has pressed the Save button. The select event is of type *Event*, and you can use the Event.SELECT constant to add the listener, as follows:

```
fileReference.addEventListener(Event.SELECT, onSelectFile);
```

As soon as the select event occurs, you can retrieve the filename the user has selected by reading the name property of the *FileReference* object:

```
private function onSelectFile(event:Event):void {
    trace(event.target.name);
}
```

The user also has the option of clicking the Cancel button from the save dialog box. If the user clicks the Cancel button, the file is not downloaded, and the dialog closes. When the user clicks the Cancel button, the *FileReference* object dispatches a cancel event of type *Event*. You can use the Event.CANCEL constant to add a listener, as follows:

```
fileReference.addEventListener(Event.CANCEL, onCancelDialog);
```

See Also

Recipe 23.1

23.3   Monitoring Download Progress

Problem

You want to monitor download progress.

Solution

Listen for the progress event.

Discussion

You can monitor the progress of a file(s) as it downloads by using the progress event. Every time part of the file downloads to the user's computer, the *FileReference* object dispatches a progress event of type *ProgressEvent*. You can use the ProgressEvent. PROGRESS constant to add a listener, as follows:

```
fileReference.addEventListener(ProgressEvent.PROGRESS, onFileProgress);
```

The progress event object has two properties, bytesLoaded and bytesTotal, which return the bytes that have downloaded and the total bytes, respectively. The following example method uses the values of those properties to display the download progress in a text field called fileProgressField:

```
private function onFileProgress(event:ProgressEvent):void {
    fileProgressField.text = event.bytesLoaded + " of " + event.bytesTotal + "
bytes";
}
```

When the file has completed downloading, the *FileReference* object dispatches a complete event of type *Event*. Use the Event.COMPLETE constant to add a listener:

```
fileReference.addEventListener(Event.COMPLETE, onFileComplete);
```

See Also

Recipe 23.1

23.4   Browsing for Files

Problem

You want to let the user browse his local disk(s) for a file (s) to upload.

Solution

Use the *browse()* method of either a *FileReference* or *FileReferenceList* object.

Discussion

Using the *browse()* method of a *FileReference* of *FileReferenceList* object, you can open a dialog box that allows the user to browse his local disks for a file or files. The difference between the *browse()* methods of the *FileReference* and *FileReferenceList* classes is that the former allows the user to select just one file, while the latter allows the user to select more than one file by holding the Control or Shift key (or the Command key on a Macintosh):

```
fileReference.browse();
```

As with the *download()* method, the *browse()* method can throw errors, and it's best to handle the errors using try/catch. An illegal operation error can occur in one of two scenarios:

- Only one browse dialog box can be open at a time. If a dialog box is already open and you call *browse()*, it throws an error of type *IllegalOperationError*.
- If the user has configured his global Flash Player settings to disallow file browsing, calling the *browse()* method will throw an error.

This block of code illustrates how to use a try/catch block to handle an *IllegalOperationError* thrown when calling *browse()*.

```
try {
    fileReference.browse();
}
catch (illegalOperation:IllegalOperationError) {
    // code to handle error
}
```

Handling the error ensures that Flash Player will not display a default error message to the user (which could be disconcerting to the user).

See Also

Recipe 23.5

23.5 Filtering Files That Display in the Browser Window

Problem

You want to filter the type of files that display in the browse dialog box so the user only sees the types of files you want to allow her to upload.

Solution

Pass an array of *FileFilter* objects to the *browse()* method.

Discussion

By default the *browse()* method displays a dialog box that displays all files on the user's filesystem. However, you also have the option of filtering the types of files that are displayed. For example, you may want to display only image files or only text files. You can accomplish this by passing an array of *flash.net.FileFilter* objects to the *browse()* method.

The *FileFilter* constructor requires at least two parameters:

- The first parameter determines what displays in the "Files of type" drop-down menu in the browse dialog box.
- The second parameter determines which file extensions are filtered.

File extensions must be semicolon-delimited, each prepended with an asterisk and a dot. The following constructs a *FileFilter* object that filters for files with file extensions of *.png*, *.gif*, and *.jpg*:

```
var fileFilter:FileFilter = new FileFilter("Images", "*.png;*.gif;*.jpg");
```

Additionally, you may opt to specify a third parameter of Macintosh file types. As with file extensions, file types are semicolon delimited. When the Macintosh file types parameter is omitted, the file extensions are used as a filter for both Windows and Macintosh files. When the Macintosh file types parameter is specified, the file extensions are used as a filter for Windows files, while they are ignored for Macintosh files in preference of the Macintosh file types. Macintosh operating systems now support file extensions as a way of determining the file type, yet they also continue to support type codes assigned to the files.

You can specify which filter (or filters) to use by passing them as elements of an array to the *browse()* method, as follows:

```
fileReference.browse([fileFilter]);
```

In the preceding example, only one filter is passed to the *browse()* method. Each filter that's passed to the *browse()* method adds a new option to the "Files of type" drop-down menu in the browse dialog box. For example, the following code allows four options in the Files of type menu—Images, Documents, Archives, and All.

```
var fileFilter1:FileFilter = new FileFilter("Images", "*.png;*.gif;*.jpg");
var fileFilter2:FileFilter = new FileFilter("Documents", "*.txt;*.doc;*.pdf;*.rtf");
var fileFilter3:FileFilter = new FileFilter("Archives", "*.zip;*.tar;*.hqx");
var fileFilter4:FileFilter = new FileFilter("All", "*.*");
_fileReference.browse([fileFilter1, fileFilter2, fileFilter3, fileFilter4]);
```

When you pass an array of *FileFilter* objects to the *browse()* method, there is a possibility that the *browse()* method can throw an argument error of type *ArgumentError*. Argument errors occur if any of the *FileFilter* objects have incorrectly formatted values.

The file filter parameter also works with the *browse()* method of *FileReferenceList*.

See Also

Recipe 23.4

23.6 Detecting When the User Has Selected a File to Upload

Problem

You want to detect when the user has selected a file from the browse dialog box.

Solution

Listen for a select event. Listen for a cancel event to determine if and when the user clicks the Cancel button.

Discussion

When the user selects a file and clicks the Open button from a browse dialog box, the *FileReference* object dispatches a select event of type *Event*. You can use the Event.SELECT constant to add a listener, as follows:

```
fileReference.addEventListener(Event.SELECT, onSelectFile);
```

When the user has selected a file, the details of that file are immediately available (name, size, createdDate, etc.). For example, as soon as a *FileReference* object dispatches a *SELECT* event you can retrieve the filename, as in the following example:

```
selectedFileTextField.text = fileReference.name;
```

When the user clicks the Cancel button from a browse dialog box, the *FileReference* object dispatches a cancel event of type *Event*. You can use the Event.CANCEL constant to add a listener, as follows:

```
fileReference.addEventListener(Event.CANCEL, onCancelBrowse);
```

The select and cancel events also work for *FileReferenceList* objects.

See Also

Recipe 23.7

23.7 Uploading Files

Problem

You want to allow users to upload files.

Solution

Use the *upload( )* method of the *FileReference* object.

Discussion

The *upload( )* method of a *FileReference* object allows you to upload a file to a server by using a server-side script that is configured to accept uploads using HTTP(S). At a minimum, the *upload( )* method requires one parameter as a *URLRequest* object specifying the URL of the script to which you want to send the file data:

```
var urlRequest:URLRequest = new URLRequest("uploadScript.cgi");
fileReference.upload(urlRequest);
```

All uploads use POST with a Content-Type of multipart/form-data. By default, the Content-Disposition is set to Filedata. The script needs to know the Content-Disposition value so it can read the file data. If the script needs to use a Content-Disposition other than the default, you can specify a value as the second, optional parameter you pass to the *upload( )* method, as follows:

```
fileReference.upload(urlRequest, "UploadFile");
```

You can only upload a file if the user has selected the file using *browse( )*. If the user selects a file using a *FileReference* object's *browse( )* method, then you can call *upload( )* after the select event occurs. If the user selects files using *FileReferenceList*, then you must call the *upload( )* method for each file in the object's fileList property. The fileList property of a *FileReferenceList* object is an array of *FileReference* objects corresponding to each of the files selected by the user.

The *upload( )* method can throw errors. The possible errors thrown by *upload( )* are identical to those thrown by *download( )*. Additionally, like *download( )*, the *upload( )* method can dispatch security error events and IO error events. See Recipe 23.1 for more details on handling these errors and error events.

See Also

Recipe 23.1

23.8   Monitoring File Upload Progress

Problem

You want to monitor the progress of a file as it uploads to your server.

Solution

Listen for a progress event.

Discussion

You can monitor file upload progress, much as you can monitor a file download progress. A *FileReference* object dispatches progress events when the file is uploading. When the file has completed uploading, it dispatches a complete event. See Recipe 23.3 for details.

See Also

Recipe 23.3

## CHAPTER 24

Socket Programming

24.0 Introduction

Socket connections allow the Flash Player to send and load data from a server over a specified network port. The main difference between socket and server connections in Chapter 20 is that socket connections don't automatically close after data transfer is complete.

When a socket connection is made, the connection stays open until the client (the Flash Player) or the server explicitly closes it. Because of this, sockets enable a special type of communication called data push, which means that the server sends information to the Flash Player at any time without a request coming from the Player itself.

Socket connections are typically used to create multiuser applications. An example of one such application would be an online chat room. The chat program might consist of a central chat server with various connected Flash Player clients. Each time a client *.swf* sends a message to the server, the server determines which client should receive the message and pushes the message to that specific client over the open connection. In this case, the receiving client didn't ask for the message, but rather the message was simply pushed out to it by the server. When a client closes a connection, the server notifies the other clients that someone has logged off of the system.

Two types of socket connections can be made from the Flash Player to a socket server. They are very similar in behavior and operation, but have a few subtle differences. The first is an XML socket connection that is similar to the *XMLSocket* in previous versions of the Flash Player. New for Flash Player 9 is a binary socket connection.

To create an XML socket connection, use the *flash.net.XMLSocket* class. To create a binary socket connection, use the *flash.net.Socket* class.

XML socket connections are focused around text. The client and server communicate by exchanging XML packets containing data. Actions are carried out by analyzing the contents of the XML packets.

Binary socket connections are new in ActionScript 3.0 and enable raw connections that allow for transfer of binary information. Binary sockets are slightly more advanced than XML sockets because they require a low-level knowledge of binary datatypes, but they are also more powerful because you can connect to a wider range of socket servers and generally do more with them. For example, binary sockets allow you to connect to mail servers (via POP3, SMTP, and IMAP), news servers (via NNTP), chat servers, or even implement screen sharing and remote desktop applications by connection to a VNC server (via RFB).

Regardless of which socket connection type you use, the connection behaves in an asynchronous manner. This means that you can't read data from the socket connection until you have been notified that data is available via an event handler. All data reading must be done in an event handler that executes automatically when data is available. Synchronous socket connections, when attempting to read data from the socket causes your program to wait until data becomes available in the socket, are easier to program but not as efficient. You'll learn more about how to deal with the asynchronous nature of the Flash Players socket connections as you go through this chapter.

24.1   Connecting to a Socket Server

Problem

You want to establish a connection with a socket server.

Solution

Use either the *Socket.connect()* or *XMLSocket.connect()* method and listen for the connect event to be notified when a connection is made.

Discussion

To connect to a socket server, there are two critical pieces of information that you need to know before attempting to make a connection. The first is the domain name or IP address of the server to which the connection will be made, and the second is the port over which the connection should take place.

Whether you are using a *Socket* or an *XMLSocket* instance, the connection process is exactly the same; both classes define a *connect()* method that takes two parameters:

host

> A string value specifying the host to connect to, either with a domain name such as www.example.com, or with an IP address such as 192.168.1.101. To connect to the web server the Flash movie is being served from, pass null instead of a string hostname.

port

An *int* value specifying the port number that should be used to connect to the host. The port value must be at least 1024, unless the server has a policy file specifically allowing ports less than 1024.

Because of the asynchronous nature of socket programming in Flash, the *connect()* method does not wait for a connection to happen before continuing to the next line of ActionScript code. If you try to interact with a socket before a connection has been fully established, you'll encounter unexpected results and your code won't work correctly.

The proper way to connect to a socket is to first add an event listener for the connect event before attempting to call *connect()*. The connect event is dispatched by both *Socket* and *XMLSocket* objects when a successful connection has been made, letting you know that the socket is ready to be interacted with.

The code for connecting a *Socket* instance to a socket server running on localhost over port 2900 looks like this:

```
package {
  import flash.display.Sprite;
  import flash.events.*;
  import flash.net.Socket;

  public class SocketExample extends Sprite {

    private var socket:Socket;

    public function SocketExample() {
      socket = new Socket();

      // Add an event listener to be notified when the connection
      // is made
      socket.addEventListener( Event.CONNECT, onConnect );

      // Connect to the server
      socket.connect( "localhost", 2900 );
    }

    private function onConnect( event:Event ):void {
      trace( "The socket is now connected..." );
    }

  }
}
```

If you want to connect via *XMLSocket* instead, the code is almost exactly the same. First, you create the event listener for the connect event, and then you invoke the *connect()* method. The only difference is that all *Socket* references should be replaced with *XMLSocket*:

```
package {
  import flash.display.Sprite;
  import flash.events.*;
  import flash.net.XMLSocket;

  public class SocketExample extends Sprite {

    private var socket:XMLSocket;

    public function SocketExample( ) {
      socket = new XMLSocket( );

      // Add an event listener to be notified when the connection is made
      socket.addEventListener( Event.CONNECT, onConnect );

      // Connect to the server
      socket.connect( "localhost", 2900 );
    }

    private function onConnect( event:Event ):void {
      trace( "The xml socket is now connected..." );
    }

  }
}
```

If the connection fails, one of two things can happen: either the connection fails right away and a runtime error is generated, or an `ioError` or `securityError` event is raised to indicate that the connection could not be completed successfully. For more information about handling the error events, see Recipe 24.6.

Remember, when connecting to a host with a socket connection, the following Flash Player security sandbox rules apply:

1. The *.swf* and host must be in the exact same domain in order for a successful connection to be made.

2. A *.swf* delivered over a network cannot connect to a local server.

3. A local untrusted *.swf* cannot access any network resources.

4. To allow cross-domain access or connections to a port lower than 1024, a cross-domain policy file can be used.

Violating the security sandbox by attempting to connect to an untrusted domain or on a low port raises a `securityError` event. These issues can both be worked around by using a cross-domain policy file, discussed in Recipe 3.12. To use a cross-domain policy file with either a *Socket* or *XMLSocket* object, you need to load the policy file by using *flash.system.Security.loadPolicyFile()*, as shown here:

```
Security.loadPolicyFile("http://www.rightactionscript.com/crossdomain.xml");
```

When assembling the cross-domain policy file, you should specify not only the allowed domains, but also the allowed ports. If you do not specify allowed ports, Flash Player assumes that port 80 (standard HTTP port) is the only allowed port. You can specify a comma-delimited list using the port attribute of the <allow-access-from> tag. The following policy file allows all domains to connect to ports 80 and 110 (standard HTTP and POP mail ports):

```
<?xml version="1.0"?>

<!DOCTYPE cross-domain-policy SYSTEM "http://www.macromedia.com/xml/dtds/cross-domain-policy.dtd">
<cross-domain-policy>
    <allow-access-from domain="*" to-ports="80,110" />
</cross-domain-policy>
```

See Also

Recipes 3.12, 24.5, and 24.6

24.2 Sending Data

Problem

You want to send data to a socket server.

Solution

For *Socket* objects, use the write methods (*writeByte()*, *writeUTFBytes()*, etc.) to write the data to the buffer and call *flush()* to send the data. For *XMLSocket* objects, use the *send()* method.

Discussion

The *Socket* and *XMLSocket* classes define different APIs for sending data to the socket server. Let's look at the *Socket* API first.

When you want to send data to a socket server using a *Socket* object, you first must write the data to the buffer. The *Socket* class defines a slew of methods for writing data. Each of the methods writes a different type of data (or writes the data differently). The methods are *writeBoolean()*, *writeByte()*, *writeBytes()*, *writeDouble()*, *writeFloat()*, *writeInt()*, *writeMultiByte()*, *writeObject()*, *writeShort()*, *writeUnsignedInt()*, *writeUTF()*, and *writeUTFBytes()*. Most of the methods accept one parameter of the type implied by the name of the method. For example, *writeBoolean()* accepts a Boolean parameter and *writeByte()*, *writeDouble()*, *writeFloat()*, *writeInt()*, *writeShort()*, and *writeUnsignedInt()* accept numeric parameters. The *writeObject()* method accepts an object parameter that must be serializable to AMF format. The *writeBytes()* method allows you to pass it a *ByteArray* parameter along with *offset* and *length* parameters. For example, the following calls *writeBytes()* passing, it a reference to a *ByteArray* object and specifying that it should write all the bytes (starting at offset 0 with length equal to the length of the *ByteArray*):

```
socket.writeBytes(byteArray, 0, byteArray.length);
```

The *writeUTF()* and *writeUTFBytes()* methods allow you to write strings. Each method accepts a *string* parameter. The *writeUTFBytes()* method simply writes the string as bytes. The *writeUTF()* method first writes the number of bytes before writing the actual byte data.

The *writeMultiByte()* method also writes string data, but using a nondefault character set. The method requires two parameters: the string to write and the name of the character set to use. The help documentation for Flash and Flex list the supported character sets along with the labels and aliases for each. Use the label value as a string when specifying the character set for *writeMultiByte()*. The following example writes a string example using Unicode:

```
socket.writeMultiByte("example", "unicode");
```

Which method or methods you use to write data to a *Socket* object is entirely dependent on what sort of data you want to write and what sort of data the server expects. Using a *Socket* object, you can write a Telnet or POP mail client entirely by using ActionScript. Both protocols expect ASCII text commands. For example, after connecting to a POP server, you can specify a user with the USER command. The following writes such a command to a *Socket* object:

```
// POP servers expect a newline (\n) to execute the preceding command.
socket.writeUTFBytes("USER exampleUsername\n");
```

Writing the data to the *Socket* object does not actually send the data to the socket server. Each call to a *write* method appends the data to the *Socket* object. For example, the following writes four bytes to a *Socket* object, but none of them are sent:

```
socket.writeByte(1);
socket.writeByte(5);
socket.writeByte(4);
socket.writeByte(8);
```

When you want to send the accumulated data to the socket server, use the *flush()* method. The *flush()* method simply sends all the written data and clears the buffer:

```
socket.flush();
```

The *XMLSocket* class has a much simpler API for sending data. Writing and sending data occur with one method aptly named *send()*. The *send()* method accepts parameter of any datatype. It converts the parameter to a string and sends it to the server. Traditionally the parameter is an XML object or a string containing data structured as XML:

```
xmlSocket.send(xml);
```

However, the exact format of the data is entirely dependent on the format the server expects. If the server expects XML-formatted data, then you'll need to send XML-formatted data. If the server expects URL-encoded data, then you'll need to send URL-encoded data.

See Also

Recipes 24.1 and 24.3

24.3 Receiving Data

Problem

You want to read data from a socket server.

Solution

For *Socket* instances, subscribe to the socketData event and invoke one of the *read* methods, such as *readByte()* or *readInt()*, in the event handler, making sure not to read past bytesAvailable.

For *XMLSocket* instances, subscribe to the data event and interpret the XML data received inside of the event handler.

Discussion

Receiving data from a socket connection depends on the type of socket you use. Both *Socket* and *XMLSocket* are capable of receiving data from a server, but they do so using slightly different techniques. Let's focus on how the *Socket* class works first before discussing *XMLSocket*.

As you've learned in the introduction to this chapter, sockets in Flash behave asynchronously. Therefore, it's not possible to simply create a socket connection and attempt to read data from the socket right away. The *read* methods don't wait for data to be transferred from the server before returning. Instead, you can only read data from a socket after the client has already downloaded the data from the host server. It is an error to try and read data from a *Socket* before any data is available.

To know when data is available to be read, the socketData event is broadcasted from *Socket* instances. By adding an event listener for the socketData event, your event handler is invoked anytime there is new data received from the socket server. Inside the event handler is where you write code to read and interpret the received data.

To read the data sent from the server, the *Socket* class provides a number of different *read* methods, depending on the type of data you want to read. For instance, you can read a byte with the *readByte()* method, or read an unsigned integer with the *readUnsignedInt()* method. See Table 24-1 for a list of the different datatypes that can be read from the socket server, what the return value is, and how many bytes the *read* method consumes.

Table 24-1. Socket read methods for various datatypes

Method : Return type	Description	Bytes read
readBoolean( ):Boolean	Reads a Boolean value from the socket	1
readByte( ):int	Reads a signed byte from the socket	1
readDouble( ):Number	Reads an IEEE 754 double-precision floating-point number from the socket	8
readFloat( ):Number	Reads an IEEE 754 single-precision floating-point number from the socket	4
readInt( ):int	Reads a signed 32-bit integer from the socket	4
readObject( ):*	Reads an AMF-encoded object from the socket	n
readShort( ):int	Reads a signed 16-bit integer from the socket	2
readUnsignedByte( ):uint	Reads an unsigned byte from the socket	1
readUnsignedInt( ):uint	Reads an unsigned 32-bit integer from the socket	4
readUnsignedShort( ):uint	Reads an unsigned 16-bit integer from the socket	2
readUTF( ):String	Reads a UTF-8 string from the socket	n

There are also two additional read methods not covered in Table 24-1. They are *readBytes()* and *readUTFBytes()*. The *readBytes()* method is the only *Socket* read method to not return a value, and it takes the following three parameters:

bytes
   A *flash.util.ByteArray* instance to read the data from the socket into.

offset
   A *uint* value specifying the offset into bytes where read data from the socket should start being placed. The default value is 0.

length
   A *uint* value for the number of bytes to read. The default is 0, meaning all available data will be read from the socket into the bytes *ByteArray*.

The *readUTFBytes()* method, on the other handle, takes a single *length* parameter specifying the number of UTF-8 bytes to read, and it returns the *String* corresponding to the read bytes.

 Before reading data from a *Socket*, it is important to check the socket's bytesAvailable property first. Attempting to read more data than what is available will result in a *flash.errors.EOFError*.

The following code example connects to a socket server, and reads and displays the data sent from the server one byte at a time:

```
package {
  import flash.display.Sprite;
  import flash.events.ProgressEvent;
  import flash.net.Socket;

  public class SocketExample extends Sprite {

    private var socket:Socket;

    public function SocketExample() {
      socket = new Socket();

      // Listen for when data is received from the socket server
      socket.addEventListener( ProgressEvent.SOCKET_DATA, onSocketData );

      // Connect to the server
      socket.connect( "localhost", 2900 );
    }

    private function onSocketData( event:ProgressEvent ):void {
      trace( "Socket received " + socket.bytesAvailable + " byte(s) of data:" );

      // Loop over all of the received data, and only read a byte if there
      // is one available
      while ( socket.bytesAvailable ) {
        // Read a byte from the socket and display it
        var data:int = socket.readByte();
        trace( data );
      }
    }
  }
}
```

In the preceding example, if the socket server sends back a message (such as "Hello"), the output of the code would look like this when a client connects:

```
Socket received 5 byte(s) of data:
72
101
108
108
111
```

 Once data is read from the *Socket*, it cannot be read again. For example, after reading a byte, that byte cannot be "put back" and read as part of an *int* later.

When the data received by a *Socket* object is ASCII text, you can reconstruct a string by using the *readUTFBytes()* method. The *readUTFBytes()* method requires that you tell it how many bytes to read and convert to a string. You can use `bytesAvailable` to read all the bytes:

```
var string:String = socket.readUTFBytes(socket.bytesAvailable);
```

The *XMLSocket* class behaves in a similar manner to the *Socket* class in regard to how it receives data from the server. In both cases, an event listener must be used to be notified that data is available due to Flash's asynchronous socket implementation. However, the process used to actually read the data is very different.

An *XMLSocket* instance dispatches a data event when data has finished downloading from the server. The data event, defined by the *flash.events.DataEvent.DATA* constant, contains a *String* data property that contains the information received from the server.

> When using *XMLSocket*, the data returned from the server is always interpreted as a *String*. There are no specific read methods for various datatypes.

The data returned from the server is the raw server response. Because of this, you're not limited to just using *XML* with *XMLSocket* connections, but rather you can send and receive plain *String* information as well. If you're expecting *XML* back from the server, however, you must first convert the data into an *XML* instance before working with it.

The following code example initiates a connection over *XMLSocket* to a server running on port 2900 on the local computer. After the connection is successfully made, a *<test>* message is sent to the server. The *onData* event listener handles the response from the server, which in this case is the string `<response><test success='true'/></response>`. You can see that the data property of the event passed to *onData* is just a *String*, and that the *XML* constructor is used to convert the *String* into an *XML* instance. Finally, *E4X* syntax is used to output a portion of the converted *XML* (for more information about working with *XML* and using *E4X*, see Chapter 21):

```
package {
  import flash.display.Sprite;
  import flash.events.Event;
  import flash.events.DataEvent;
  import flash.net.XMLSocket;

  public class SocketExample extends Sprite {

    private var xmlSocket:XMLSocket;

    public function SocketExample() {
      xmlSocket = new XMLSocket();
```

```
      // Connect listener to send a message to the server
      // after we make a successful connection
      xmlSocket.addEventListener( Event.CONNECT, onConnect );

      // Listen for when data is received from the socket server
      xmlSocket.addEventListener( DataEvent.DATA, onData );

      // Connect to the server
      xmlSocket.connect( "localhost", 2900 );
    }

    private function onConnect( event:Event ):void {
      xmlSocket.send( "<test/>" );
    }

    private function onData( event:DataEvent ):void {
      // The raw string returned from the server.
      // It might look something like this:
      // <response><test success='true'/></response>
      trace( event.data );

      // Convert the string into XML
      var response:XML = new XML( event.data );

      // Using E4X, access the success attribute of the "test"
      // element node in the response.
      // Output: true
      trace( response.test.@success );
    }
  }
}
```

 Before the data event can be dispatched, the *XMLSocket* instance must detect the null byte ('\0') from the server. That is, sending a string from the server is not enough for the client to receive it. Instead, the string must be terminated by the null byte.

See Also

Recipes 18.2, 24.1, and 24.4

24.4   Handshaking with a Socket Server

Problem

You want to do handshaking with a socket server and need to know what the received data's context is to know how to process it.

Solution

Create different constant variables to represent states of the protocol. Use the constants to map particular processing functions with the corresponding state. In a socketData event handler, call the appropriate function by invoking it through the state map.

Discussion

A common scenario when connecting to a socket is going through a handshake process. Typically, the server initially sends data to the client. The client then responds to the data in a particular manner, and the server responds again accordingly. This entire process repeats until the handshaking is complete and a "normal" connection is established.

It gets difficult to process the response from the server because the socketData event handler does not keep track of context. That is, there is no "why" sent along with the server response, or no "this data is in response to" processing directive. Knowing how to process the response from the server is not usually something that can be gathered through the response itself, especially when the response varies. Perhaps one response returns two bytes and another returns an integer followed by a double. You can begin to see how this presents itself as a problem.

The solution is to create various state constants to represent the different contexts in which the server sends data to the client. By associating each of these constants with a particular function to handle the data, you can easily call the correct processing function based on the current state of the protocol.

Consider the following handshaking scenario that happens when you connect to a socket server:

1. The server responds immediately when it connects with an integer representing the highest version of the protocol that the server supports.

2. The client responds with an integer to indicate the actual version of the protocol that should be used for communication.

3. The server sends back an 8-byte authentication challenge.

4. The client sends the authentication challenge back to the server.

5. The server closes the connection if the client response was not what the server was expecting, or, at this point, the protocol moves into a normal operating mode and the handshaking is complete.

In reality, Step 4 involves a more secure response to an authentication challenge. Instead of just sending back the challenge verbatim, you would really want to use some sort of encryption with a user-supplied key. Perhaps the client asks the user for a password, and then the password entered is used as the encryption key for the 8-byte challenge. The encrypted challenge is then sent back to the server. If this challenge response matches what the server expected, then the client knew the right password and the connection should be allowed.

To implement the handshaking processed outlined, you first want to create constants to represent the different kinds of data returned from the server. First, there is determining the version from Step 1. Second, there is receiving the challenge from Step 3. Finally, there is the normal operating mode from Step 5. These can be represented by the following constants:

```
public const DETERMINE_VERSION:int = 0;
public const RECEIVE_CHALLENGE:int = 1;
public const NORMAL:int = 2;
```

It doesn't matter what values are given to the constants. Rather, the only important part is that all the values are different so no two constants represent the same *int* value.

The next step is to create different functions to process the data. The three functions created will be named *readVersion()*, *readChallenge()*, and *readNormalProtocol()*. After the functions have been defined, a map must be created to associate one of the previous state constants with the function used to process the data received during that state. The code for that looks like this:

```
stateMap = new Object();
stateMap[ DETERMINE_VERSION ] = readVersion;
stateMap[ RECEIVE_CHALLENGE ] = readChallenge;
stateMap[ NORMAL           ] = readNormalProtocol;
```

The final step is to code the socketData event handler in such a way that the correct processing function is invoked based on the current state of the protocol. To do this, a currentState *int* variable is created. Then, using the stateMap, the processing function is invoked by looking up the function associated with currentState:

```
var processFunc:Function = stateMap[ currentState ];
processFunc(); // Invoke the appropriate processing function
```

There is a little bit of bookkeeping involved in this process. Be sure to update currentState in your code to accurately reflect the current state of the protocol.

The entire code example to process the handshaking scenario previously described looks like the following:

```
package {
  import flash.display.Sprite;
  import flash.events.ProgressEvent;
  import flash.net.Socket;
  import flash.utils.ByteArray;

  public class SocketExample extends Sprite {

    // The state constants to describe the protocol
    public const DETERMINE_VERSION:int = 0;
    public const RECEIVE_CHALLENGE:int = 1;
    public const NORMAL:int = 2;
```

```
// Maps a state to a processing function
private var stateMap:Object;

// Keeps track of the current protocol state
private var currentState:int;

private var socket:Socket;

public function SocketExample() {
  // Initialzes the states map
  stateMap = new Object();
  stateMap[ DETERMINE_VERSION ] = readVersion;
  stateMap[ RECEIVE_CHALLENGE ] = readChallenge;
  stateMap[ NORMAL            ] = readNormalProtocol;

  // Initialze the current state
  currentState = DETERMINE_VERSION;

  // Create and connect the socket
  socket = new Socket();
  socket.addEventListener( ProgressEvent.SOCKET_DATA, onSocketData );
  socket.connect( "localhost", 2900 );
}

private function onSocketData( event:ProgressEvent ):void {
  // Look up the processing function based on the current state
  var processFunc:Function = stateMap[ currentState ];
  processFunc();
}

private function readVersion():void {
  // Step 1 - read the version from the server
  var version:int = socket.readInt();

  // Once the version is read, the next state is receiving
  // the challenge from the server
  currentState = RECEIVE_CHALLENGE;

  // Step 2 - write the version back to the server
  socket.writeInt( version );
  socket.flush();
}

private function readChallenge():void {
  // Step 3 - read the 8 byte challenge into a byte array
  var bytes:ByteArray = new ByteArray();
  socket.readBytes( bytes, 0, 8 );

  // After the challenge is received, the next state is
  // the normal protocol operation
  currentState = NORMAL;

  // Step 4 - write the bytes back to the server
```

```
            socket.writeBytes( bytes );
            socket.flush( );
        }

        private function readNormalProtocol( ):void {
            // Step 5 - process the normal socket messages here now that
            // that handshaking process is complete
        }
    }
}
```

See Also

Recipes 18.2, 24.1, and 24.3

24.5   Disconnecting from a Socket Server

Problem

You want to disconnect from a socket server, or be notified when the server disconnects you.

Solution

Invoke the *Socket.close()* or *XMLSocket.close()* method to explicitly close the connection, or listen for the close event to be notified when the server closes the connection for you.

Discussion

A general rule to follow when programming is to clean up after yourself. That is, if you create an object, you should also delete it when it is no longer necessary. In this case, whenever you connect to a socket server, you should explicitly close the connection when you're done. Leaving an unused socket connection open is a waste of resources and should be avoided if at all possible. If you don't close a connection, then the server may continue to keep an open socket connection that is not being used, which can quickly cause a server to overrun its allotment of allowed socket connections.

Closing a socket connection is the same for both *Socket* and *XMLSocket* instances. All you need to do is invoke the *close()* method on the socket instance:

```
// Assume socket is a connected Socket instance
socket.close( );  // Disconnect from the server
```

Using an *XMLSocket* is exactly the same:

```
// Assume xmlSocket is a connected XMLSocket instance
xmlSocket.close( );  // Disconnect from the server
```

The *close()* method is useful for letting the server know that the client wants to disconnect. To be notified when the server closes the connection on its own, you should listen for the `close` event by calling *addEventListener()* on the *Socket* or *XMLSocket* instance with `Event.CLOSE` as the event type; for example:

```
var socket:Socket = new Socket( );

// Add an event listener to be notified when the server disconnects
// the client
socket.addEventListener( Event.CLOSE, onClose );
```

 Invoking the *close()* method does not raise the `close` event. Instead, the `close` event is raised only when the server initiates the disconnection.

Once a socket is closed, it is no longer capable of reading or writing data. If you'd like to reuse the socket, you have to establish a connection again as described in Recipe 24.1.

See Also

Recipe 24.1

24.6 Handling Socket Errors

Problem

You want to handle errors that might occur when using sockets.

Solution

Use `try`/`catch` to handle I/O and end of file (EOF) errors.

Discussion

Both the *Socket* and *XMLSocket* classes behave similarly in regard to errors and error events. When calling the *connect()* method, *Socket* and *XMLSocket* objects can throw an error of type *SecurityError* when either of the following conditions is true:

- The *.swf* is classified as local untrusted.
- The port number is higher than 655535.

When calling *send()* (*XMLSocket*) or *flush()* (*Socket*), the method can throw an error of type *IOError* if the socket isn't connected. Although you can (and likely should) place the *send()* or *flush()* method calls within try/catch blocks, you should not rely on try/catch blocks as part of your application logic. Rather, use an if statement to test whether or not the socket object's connected property is true before calling *send()* of *flush()* if you want such a test to be part of the application logic. For example, the following uses an if statement as part of the application logic to call a *connectToSocketServer()* method if the *Socket* object isn't currently connected. It also uses a try/catch block to write to a log if the *flush()* method throws an error:

```
if ( socket.connected ) {
    try {
        socket.flush( );
    }
    catch( error:IOError ) {
        logInstance.write( "socket.flush error\n" + error );
    }
}
else {
    connectToSocketServer( );
}
```

All of the *Socket* read methods can throw errors of type *EOFError* and *IOError*. EOF errors occur when you try to read data, but nothing is available. I/O errors occur when you try to read from a socket that is closed.

In addition to the errors thrown by methods of the *Socket* and *XMLSocket* classes, objects of those classes also dispatch error events. There are two basic types of error events that occur with sockets—*IOError* and *securityError*. The *IOError* event is of type *IOErrorEvent*, and it occurs when data fails to send or load. The *securityError* event is of type *SecurityErrorEvent*, and it occurs when a socket attempts to connect to a server but fails because the server is either outside of the sandbox or because the port number is lower than 1024.

 Both security error event scenarios are correctable by way of a cross-domain policy file.

Unicode Escape Sequences for Latin 1 Characters

Table A-1 lists the characters in the Latin 1 character repertoire, with Unicode equivalents in the range of U+0000 to U+00FF (that is, C0 Controls, Basic Latin, C1 Controls, and Latin 1 Supplemental). It is reproduced from Appendix B of *ActionScript for Flash MX: The Definitive Guide* with the permission of the author, Colin Moock.

The table's first column (labeled *Dec*) lists each character's code point in decimal (the standard ASCII or Latin 1 value), the second column provides the Unicode escape sequence for the character, and the third column describes or shows the character itself.

Table A-1. ISO 8859-1 (Latin 1) characters and Unicode mappings

Dec	Unicode	Description	Dec	Unicode	Description
0	\u0000	[null]	15	\u000f	[shift in]
1	\u0001	[start of heading]	16	\u0010	[data link escape]
2	\u0002	[start of text]	17	\u0011	[device control one]
3	\u0003	[end of text]	18	\u0012	[device control two]
4	\u0004	[end of transmission]	19	\u0013	[device control three]
5	\u0005	[enquiry]	20	\u0014	[device control four]
6	\u0006	[acknowledge]	21	\u0015	[negative acknowledge]
7	\u0007	[bell]	22	\u0016	[synchronous idle]
8	\u0008	[backspace]	23	\u0017	[end of transmission block]
9	\u0009	[horizontal tabulation]	24	\u0018	[cancel]
10	\u000a	[line feed]	25	\u0019	[end of medium]
11	\u000b	[vertical tabulation]	26	\u001a	[substitute]
12	\u000c	[form feed]	27	\u001b	[escape]
13	\u000d	[carriage feed]	28	\u001c	[file separator]
14	\u000e	[shift out]	29	\u001d	[group separator]
30	\u001e	[record separator]	66	\u0042	B

Table A-1. ISO 8859-1 (Latin 1) characters and Unicode mappings (continued)

Dec	Unicode	Description	Dec	Unicode	Description
31	\u001f	[unit separator]	67	\u0043	C
32	\u0020	[space]	68	\u0044	D
33	\u0021	!	69	\u0045	E
34	\u0022	" (straight quotes)	70	\u0046	F
35	\u0023	#	71	\u0047	G
36	\u0024	$	72	\u0048	H
37	\u0025	%	73	\u0049	I
38	\u0026	&	74	\u004a	J
39	\u0027	' (straight apostrophe)	75	\u004b	K
40	\u0028	(	76	\u004c	L
41	\u0029	)	77	\u004d	M
42	\u002a	*	78	\u004e	N
43	\u002b	+	79	\u004f	O
44	\u002c	, (comma)	80	\u0050	P
45	\u002d	– (minus)	81	\u0051	Q
46	\u002e	. (period)	82	\u0052	R
47	\u002f	/	83	\u0053	S
48	\u0030	0	84	\u0054	T
49	\u0031	1	85	\u0055	U
50	\u0032	2	86	\u0056	V
51	\u0033	3	87	\u0057	W
52	\u0034	4	88	\u0058	X
53	\u0035	5	89	\u0059	Y
54	\u0036	6	90	\u005a	Z
55	\u0037	7	91	\u005b	[
56	\u0038	8	92	\u005c	\
57	\u0039	9	93	\u005d	]
58	\u003a	:	94	\u005e	^
59	\u003b	;	95	\u005f	_ (underscore)
60	\u003c	<	96	\u0060	` (accent grave)
61	\u003d	=	97	\u0061	a
62	\u003e	>	98	\u0062	b
63	\u003f	?	99	\u0063	c
64	\u0040	@	100	\u0064	d
65	\u0041	A	101	\u0065	e
102	\u0066	f	138	\u008a	control chr

Table A-1. ISO 8859-1 (Latin 1) characters and Unicode mappings (continued)

Dec	Unicode	Description	Dec	Unicode	Description
103	\u0067	g	139	\u008b	control chr
104	\u0068	h	140	\u008c	control chr
105	\u0069	i	141	\u008d	control chr
106	\u006a	j	142	\u008e	control chr
107	\u006b	k	143	\u008f	control chr
108	\u006c	l	144	\u0090	control chr
109	\u006d	m	145	\u0091	control chr
110	\u006e	n	146	\u0092	control chr
111	\u006f	o	147	\u0093	control chr
112	\u0070	p	148	\u0094	control chr
113	\u0071	q	149	\u0095	control chr
114	\u0072	r	150	\u0096	control chr
115	\u0073	s	151	\u0097	control chr
116	\u0074	t	152	\u0098	control chr
117	\u0075	u	153	\u0099	control chr
118	\u0076	v	154	\u009a	control chr
119	\u0077	w	155	\u009b	control chr
120	\u0078	x	156	\u009c	control chr
121	\u0079	y	157	\u009d	control chr
122	\u007a	z	158	\u009e	control chr
123	\u007b	{	159	\u009f	control chr
124	\u007c	|	160	\u00a0	[no break space]
125	\u007d	}	161	\u00a1	¡
126	\u007e	~	162	\u00a2	¢
127	\u007f	[delete]	163	\u00a3	£
128	\u0080	control chr	164	\u00a4	¤
129	\u0081	control chr	165	\u00a5	¥
130	\u0082	control chr	166	\u00a6	¦
131	\u0083	control chr	167	\u00a7	§
132	\u0084	control chr	168	\u00a8	¨
133	\u0085	control chr	169	\u00a9	©
134	\u0086	control chr	170	\u00aa	ª
135	\u0087	control chr	171	\u00ab	«
136	\u0088	control chr	172	\u00ac	¬
137	\u0089	control chr	173	\u00ad	-
174	\u00ae	®	210	\u00d2	Ò

Table A-1. ISO 8859-1 (Latin 1) characters and Unicode mappings (continued)

Dec	Unicode	Description	Dec	Unicode	Description
175	\u00af	¯	211	\u00d3	Ó
176	\u00b0	°	212	\u00d4	Ô
177	\u00b1	±	213	\u00d5	Õ
178	\u00b2	²	214	\u00d6	…
179	\u00b3	³	215	\u00d7	×
180	\u00b4	´	216	\u00d8	Ø
181	\u00b5	µ	217	\u00d9	Ù
182	\u00b6	¶	218	\u00da	Ú
183	\u00b7	·	210	\u00d2	Ò
184	\u00b8	¸	219	\u00db	Û
185	\u00b9	¹	220	\u00dc	Ü
186	\u00ba	º	221	\u00dd	Ý
187	\u00bb	»	222	\u00de	Þ
188	\u00bc	¼	223	\u00df	ß
189	\u00bd	½	224	\u00e0	à
190	\u00be	¾	225	\u00e1	á
191	\u00bf	¿	226	\u00e2	â
192	\u00c0	À	227	\u00e3	ã
193	\u00c1	Á	228	\u00e4	ä
194	\u00c2	Â	229	\u00e5	å
195	\u00c3	Ã	230	\u00e6	æ
196	\u00c4	Ä	231	\u00e7	ç
197	\u00c5	Å	232	\u00e8	è
198	\u00c6	Æ	233	\u00e9	é
199	\u00c7	Ç	234	\u00ea	ê
200	\u00c8	È	235	\u00eb	ë
201	\u00c9	É	236	\u00ec	ì
202	\u00ca	Ê	237	\u00ed	í
203	\u00cb	Ë	238	\u00ee	î
204	\u00cc	Ì	239	\u00ef	ï
205	\u00cd	Í	240	\u00f0	ð
206	\u00ce	Î	241	\u00f1	ñ
207	\u00cf	Ï	242	\u00f2	ò
208	\u00d0	Ð	243	\u00f3	ó
209	\u00d1	Ñ	244	\u00f4	ô
245	\u00f5	õ	250	\u00fa	ú

Table A-1. ISO 8859-1 (Latin 1) characters and Unicode mappings (continued)

Dec	Unicode	Description	Dec	Unicode	Description
246	\u00f6	ö	251	\u00fb	û
247	\u00f7	÷	252	\u00fc	ü
248	\u00f8	ø	253	\u00fd	ý
249	\u00f9	ù	254	\u00fe	þ

Index

Symbols

- (dash)
    pattern matching, 233
    URL-encoded escape sequence for, 436
-- decrement operator, 15
! (exclamation point), escape sequence
    for, 436
! logical NOT, 24–26
!= (logical inequality operator), 17, 25
!== (inequality operator), 17
" (double quotes), escape sequence for, 436
(pound sign), 80
    escape sequence for, 436
$ (dollar sign)
    escape sequence for, 436
    regular expression metacharacter, 330
$$ replacement code, 339
$& replacement code, 339
$' replacement code, 339
$` replacement code, 339
$n replacement code, 339
$nn replacement code, 339
% (percent sign), escape sequence for, 436
& (ampersand)
    concatenating strings and, 301
    escape sequence for, 436
& bitwise operator, 75
&& logical AND, 24–26
' (quotes), 302
    URL-encoded escape sequence for, 436
( ) (parentheses)
    conditional operators and, 25
    regular expression metacharacters, 330
    URL-encoded escape sequence for, 436

* (asterisks)
    in password input fields, 232
    loading data from external sources
        and, 452
    regular expression metacharacters, 330
        nongreedy patterns, 341
    URL-encoded escape sequence for, 436
*= (compound assignment operator), 14
*? expression, 342
+ (plus sign)
    as a regular expression
        metacharacter, 330
        nongreedy patterns and, 341
    concatenation operator, 299
    URL-encoded escape sequence for, 436
++ increment operator, 15
+=
    compound assignment operator, 14
    concatenation-assignment operator, 299
+= operator, appending text, 235
+? expression, 342
, (comma), 80
    URL-encoded escape sequence for, 436
. (dot), 80
    regular expression metacharacter, 330
    saving class files, 44
    XML objects, adding elements, 458, 463
.cfm files
    gamescores.cfm, 480
/ (forward slash), storing data and, 419
/* */ comments, 8
// (comments), 8
/= (compound assignment operator), 14
; (semicolon), 7
    concatenating strings and, 301

We'd like to hear your suggestions for improving our indexes. Send email to *index@oreilly.com*.

< (less than)
    equality operators and, 19
<< bitwise operator, 75
<= operator, 19
-= (compound assignment operator), 14
= (equal sign)
    assignment statements and, 14
        differences with == and, 17
    variables, assigning, 6
=== equality operator, 17
> (greater than)
    equality operators and, 19
    threshold( ) method, as a parameter, 220
>= operator, 19
>> bitwise operator, 75
>>> bitwise operator, 75
? (question mark), as a regular expression
        metacharacter, 330
? : (ternary conditional operator), 20
?? expression, 342
@ (at sign)
    adding attributes to XML elements, 463
    reading XML attributes, 470
[ ] (square brackets), 104
    regular expression metacharacters, 330
\ (backslash)
    escaping quotes and apostrophes, 302
    pattern matching, 234
    regular expressions, 329
^ (caret)
    bitwise operator, 75
    pattern matching, 233, 330
_ (underscore), declaring private/protected
        property names, 46
{ } (curly braces), 5
    associative arrays and, 134
    for statements and, 27
{n,} regular expression metasequence, 331
{n,}? expression, 342
{n,m} regular expression
        metasequence, 331, 341
{n,m}? expression, 342
{n} regular expression metasequence, 331
| (bar)
    bitwise OR, 75, 124
    regular expression metacharacter, 330
|| logical OR, 24–26
£ (British pound), 85
€ (Euro), 85
¥ (Yen), 85
’ (apostrophe), 302
› character, 234

Numbers

32-bit color values, 201

A

<a> HTML tag, 236
    hyperlinks, adding to text, 258
\A regular expression metasequence, 331
ab parameter (drawTriangle( ) method), 191
About Adobe Flash Player 9 menu item, 68
ac parameter (drawTriangle( ) method), 191
acceleration of display objects, 287–289
    springs, 289–291
access modifiers, 33
actions (statements), 7
ActionScript interpreter, 8
ActionScript Project Wizard, 2
ActionScript Virtual Machine (AVM), 141
Active Message Format (AMF), 416, 487
ActiveX, 61, 496
ADCP sounds, 69
addCallback( ) method, 496
addChild( ) method, 153
    adding item to display lists, 141–145
    text fields, making visible, 229
addChildAt( ) method, 153
    adding item to display lists, 141
addEventListener( ) method, 10, 57, 170
    repeating tasks and, 30
addTo( ) method, 360
adjacent sides, 99
Adobe Flash Player Detection Kit, 58
advanced text layout, 261–263
alert( ) function (JavaScript), 495
alignment of movies, changing, 66
allowDomain( ) method, 432
alpha channel, creating bitmats, 201
alpha parameter, 195
    lineStyle( ) method, 182
    MovieClip.beginFill( ) method, 194
ALPHA property (BitmapDataChannel
        class), 211
    noise( ) method, 213
    perlinNoise( ) method, 216
alphaMultiplier property, 268
alphaOffset property (ColorTransform
        class), 267
AMF (Active Message Format), 416, 487
ampersand (&)
    concatenating strings and, 301
    escape sequence for, 436
amplitude, 381

AND (&&) logical, 24–26
angle measurements, converting, 96
angle parameter (drawTriangle( )
        method), 191
animation (programmatic), 281–297
    applying techniques to other
            properties, 294
    moving objects, 282
        specific directions, 283, 285–287
anti-aliasing, 264
antiAliasType property, 264
apostrophe ('), 302
appendChild( ) method, 461
appendText( ) method, 235
applications
    properties, customizing, 3
applyFilter( ) method (BitmapData
            class), 221
arc parameter (drawArc( ) method), 187
arcs, drawing, 187
ArgumentError, 146, 501
arguments
    command-line, 3
    methods, 35
Array class, 103
array of objects, 120
Array.CASEINSENSITIVE constant, 123
Array.DESCENDING constant, 123
Array.NUMERIC constant, 124
Array.pop( ), 105
Array.push( ) method, 105
Array.RETURNINDEXEDARRAY
            constant, 124
Array.UNIQUESORT constant, 124
arrays, 103–136
    associative
        creating, 133
        reading elements of, 135
    comparing, 131
    copies, creating, 116–120
    custom sorts, implementing, 127–129
    date and times, retrieving, 352
    elements, adding to start/end of, 104–105
    inserting elements in the middle of, 113
    looping through, 106
    matching elements, searching for,
            107–111
    minimum/maximum elements,
            getting, 131
    multidimensional, storing, 120–123
    randomizing, 129

removing elements, 111–113
    reversing/sorting, 123–127
    strings, converting, 114
ArrayUtilities.duplicate( ) method, 116
ArrayUtilities.equals( ) method, 132
ArrayUtilities.findLastMatchIndex( )
            method, 107
ArrayUtilities.findMatchIndex( )
            method, 107
ArrayUtilities.findMatchIndices( )
            method, 107
ArrayUtilities.max( ), 131
ArrayUtilities.min( ), 131
.as files, 2
    custom classes, creating, 43
    detecting Flash Players with, 59
    placing code, 4
AS3CBLibrary, 181
/ascb, 419
ascb.drawing.Pen class, 181
ascb.filters.ColorMatrixArrays.getSaturation
            Array( ) method, 278
ascb.play package, 93
ascb.util package, 79
    NumberFormat class, using, 80
    NumberUtilities class and, 86
ascb.util.DateFormat class, 363
ascb.util.DateFormat.formatMilliseconds( )
            method, 355
ascb.util.DateFormat.formatSeconds( )
            method, 355
ascb.util.DisplayObjectUtilities class, 148
ascb.util.StringUtilities.trim( ) method, 320
ASCII
    converting to Unicode, 323
    Socket objects and, 517
assignment operators, 6, 14
    equality operators, differences and, 17
associative arrays, 103
    creating, 133
asterisks (*)
    in password input fields, 232
    loading data from external sources
            and, 452
    regular expression metacharacters, 330
        nongreedy patterns, 341
    URL-encoded escape sequence for, 436
at sign (@)
    adding attributes to XML elements, 463
    reading XML attributes, 470
attachMovie( ) method, 137, 153

attachNetStream( ) method, 393
attributes (XML), 454
    adding to XML elements, 463
    nested nodes and, 455
    reading, 470–472
    removing, 473
attributes( ) method, 470
audio capabilities, detecting, 68
autoSize property, 237
AVM (ActionScript Virtual Machine), 141

B

\b (backspace character), 303
<b> HTML tag, 236
\B (non-word boundary) metasequence, 331
\b (word boundary) regular expression
        metasequence, 331
backgroundColor property, 230
backslash (\)
    escaping quotes and apostrophes, 302
    pattern matching, 234
    regular expressions, 329
backspace (\b) character, 303
bandwidth, 405–408
bar (|) as a regular expression
        metacharacter, 330
bases, representing different, 74
baseX parameter (perlinNoise( )
        method), 214
baseY parameter (perlinNoise( )
        method), 214
basics, 1–42
beginBitmapFill( ) method, 191
    solid/translucent colors, filling
        shapes, 194
beginFill( ) method, 191, 194
beginGradientFill( ) method, 195
    lines styles, setting, 183
    solid/translucent colors, filling
        shapes, 194
    triangles, drawing, 191
BevelFilter class, 270
bevels, 269
Bezier curves, 186, 189
bin folder, creating projects and, 2
binary bases, 74
Bitmap class, 140
bitmap parameter for
        Graphics.beginBitmapFill( )
        method, 197
BitmapData class, 197, 200–228

bitmapData property, 205
BitmapDataChannel class, 211, 213
bitmaps, 200–228
    channels, copying, 211
    copying pixels, 209–211
    dissolving between two, 224–227
    external images, loading, 204
    filling shapes with, 197
    filters, applying to, 221–224
    flood fills, creating, 208
    noise patterns, creating, 212
    objects, drawing to, 203
    Perlin noise, creating, 214–218
    pixels, manipulating, 205–207
    scrolling, 227
bitwise operators, 75
bitwise OR (|), 75, 124
blockindent attribute (<textformat>
        tag), 236
BLUE property (BitmapDataChannel
        class), 211, 213
    perlinNoise( ) method, 216
blueMultiplier property, 268
blueOffset property (ColorTransform
        class), 267
BlurFilter class, 270
blurs, 269
Booleans
    arrays, comparing, 132
    coin toss, simulating and, 88
    conditional operators and, 25
    dragging/dropping objects and, 177
    equality expressions returning, 16
border property, 230
borderColor property, 230
bottomScrollV property (text fields), 238
bounds parameter (startDrag() method), 173

 HTML tag, 236
break statements, 22
    matching elements in arrays and, 107
brightness, changing on display objects, 278
British pound (£), 85
browse( ) method, 503
    filtering files for display, 504
    uploading files and, 507
browsers, filtering files for display, 504
buffers
    setting for sound, 368
    video, managing/monitoring, 399
bufferTime property, 399
Button class, 181
button instances, 158

buttons, creating, 156–161
ByteArray class, 383
bytesLoaded property
    ProgressEvent class, 444
    Sound object, 371
bytesTotal property (Sound object), 371

C

call( ) method, 491
    Flash remoting responses, handling, 492
    JavaScript functions, calling, 494
cancel event, 502, 506
caps parameter (lineStyle method), 183
CardHand objects, 93
Cards class, 93
cards, simulating playing, 93–95
caret (^)
    bitwise operator, 75
    pattern matching, 233, 330
caretIndex property, 255
carriage return character (\r), 303, 331
Cascading Style Sheets (CSS), 242
    embedding fonts with, 250
    hyperlinks, adding to text, 260
    setting fonts in text fields, 250
case keyword, 22
case, converting, 319
case-sensitivity
    converting, 319
    filtering text input, 233
    replace( ) and split( ) methods and, 316
    sorting arrays and, 123
    substrings, searching and, 308
catch blocks, 38–42
    download method, working with, 500
    handling socket error, 524
category property (Unit objects), 96
CDATA tags, 485
cellphone screens, 64
Celsius, converting between Fahrenheit, 101
CGI scripts, 440
    getting current date and time, 348
channel parameter
    noise( ) method, 213
    perlinNoise( ) method, 216
channels, copying, 211
character codes (Unicode), 323
charAt( ) method, 317
charCodeAt( ) method, 324
chmod, 350
circles
    determining points along, 98–101

drawing, 189
classes, 7
    custom, 43–57
        creating, 43–47
    naming, 46
    placing code, 4
    properties, customizing, 3
    saving, 48
    SharedObject, persistent information
        and, 410
    variables, 6
clear( ) method, 183, 405, 415
click event (InteractiveObject), 156, 169
close( ) method, 367, 379, 402
    disconnecting from socket servers, 523
code
    placing, 4–8
    reusable, 32, 34–36
coin toss, simulating, 88–91
ColdFusion, 84, 440, 480, 487
color
    applying changes, 266
    filling shapes, 194
    grayscale, applying, 277
    resetting, 268
    tints, applying, 267
color attribute (<font> tag), 236
color CSS property, 244
color parameter
    beginGradientFill( ) method, 195
    lineStyle method, 182
color property (TextFormat object), 259
color transform objects, 296
ColorMatrixFilter class, 276
    brightness, changing, 278
    contrast, changing, 279
    grayscale, applying, 277
    saturation, changing, 278
ColorTransform object, 76, 203, 266, 268
comma (,), 80
    URL-encoded escape sequence for, 436
comma-delimited
    keys (associative arrays), 134
    strings, 114
command-line compilers, 3
    classpaths, setting, 48
commands, 7
communicating between movies
    local connections, 422
        receipt validation, 430
        sending data and, 427
    same computer, 423
    sending data, 427–430

compare functions, 127
compilers, 3
  saving class files, 48
complete event (LoaderInfo class), 163
complex data, storing, 120–123
composite datatypes, 19, 116
composition of classes, 52
compound assignment operators, 14
concat( ) method, 116, 299, 301
  multidimensional arrays and, 118
concatenate (strings), 298–301
concatenation-assignment operator
    (+=), 299
condenseWhite property, 236
conditional statements, 20–24
connect( ) method, 393, 424, 510–513
connectToSocketServer( ) method, 525
Console view, using trace, 9
const keyword, 56
constants, 56
constructors, 6
  placing code, 4
content property (Loader class), 167, 204
contentLoaderInfo property, 163
ContextMenu class, 58
contrast, changing on display objects, 279
control points, drawing curves, 186
convert( ) method, 102
Converter class, 96
  measurement, converting between
    units, 101
convertWithLabel( ) method, 97
convolution filters, embossing display
    objects, 274
ConvolutionFilter class, 272, 278
cookies, 409
Coordinated Universal Time (UTC), 348
coordinates, making up vector graphics, 200
coping by value (primitive data), 117
copyChannel( ) method, 211
copyPixels( ) method, 209, 211
copySource parameter (threshold( )
    method), 220
country codes (variants), 82
Courier, 250
Courier New, 250
createCircle( ) method, 157
createEmptyMovieClip( ) method, 137
CSS (Cascading Style Sheets), 242
  embedding fonts with, 250
  hyperlinks, adding to text, 260

setting fonts in text fields, 250
cue points, 400
curly braces ({ }), 5
  associative arrays and, 134
  for statements and, 27
currency, formatting amounts, 84
currencyFormat( ) method, 84
curves, drawing, 186
curveTo( ) method
  arcs, drawing, 187
  curves, drawing, 186
  lines, drawing, 184
custom classes, 43–57
  creating, 43–47
  serializing, 416–418

D

\D regular expression metasequence, 331
\d regular expression metasequence, 331
dash (-)
  pattern matching, 233
  URL-encoded escape sequence for, 436
data, sending/loading, 435–451
dataFormat property (URLLoader.load( )
    method), 474
datatypes, 19
Date class, 348
date property (Date object), 351
DateFormat class, 352
  parsing dates from strings, 363
dates, 348–364
  calculating elapsed time/intervals
    between, 358–363
  date values, retrieving, 351
  day/month names, retrieving, 352
  finding current, 348–351
  formatting, 353–355
  parsing from strings, 363
DateUtilities class, 358
DateUtilities.addTo( ) method, 360
day property (Date object), 351
DAYS constant (DateFormat class), 352
days parameter (addTo( ) method), 361
DAYS_ABBREVIATED constant
    (DateFormat class), 352
deal( ) method, 93
Debugger menu item, 68
declarations (XML), 454
declaring methods, 47
default keyword, 22

defaultTextFormat property, 248

Delegate class, 11

delete keyword, 473

deleteCount parameter (splice( ) method), 114

delimiter parameter (split( ) method), 115

dependencies of classes, 45

deselected text, responding to, 256

destBitmap object (threshold( ) method), 218

destPoint parameter
  applyFilter( ) method, 221
  pixelDissolve( ) method, 225
  threshold( ) method, 219

dice, simulating, 91–93

digital negatives, 276

direction (acceleration), 288

directories
  holding classes, 5
  saving class files, 48
  sharing data between Flash applications, 419

discard( ) method, simulating playing cards, 94

dispatchEvent( ), 57

display ActionScript property, 244

display lists, 137–180
  adding items to, 141–145
  objects, moving forward/backward, 149–153
  removing items from, 146–149

display object containers, 137

display settings, detecting, 63

DisplayObectContainer class, 141
  moving objects forward/backward, 149
  removing items from display lists, 146

DisplayObject class, 140
  adding items to display list, 141
  custom visual classes, creating, 153–155
  external movies and, 168
  mouse interactions, creating, 168
  simple buttons, creating, 157

DisplayObject.mask, 198

DisplayObjectUtilities.removeAllChildren( ) method, 149

DMYHMSM format (days, months, years, hours, minutes, seconds, milliseconds), 356

documents (XML), 453

dollar sign ($)
  escape sequence for, 436
  regular expression metacharacter, 330

domains, loading .swfs from different, 72

dot (.), 80
  regular expression metacharacter, 330
  XML objects, adding elements, 458, 463

"dot down"
  finding elements, 465
  text nodes, reading, 468

dotall (s) flag, 332

dots (.)
  saving class files, 44

double quotes ("), escape sequence for, 436

doubleClick event (InteractiveObject), 169

download( ) method, 499
  uploading files, detecting selections, 502

downloading files, 499–502

downState property (SimpleButton class), 156

drag( ) method, 177

DraggableSprite custom visual class, 177

dragging objects with the mouse, 173–180

draw( ) method
  BitmapData class, 203
  simulating playing cards, 94

drawArc( ) method, 187

drawCircle( ) method, 189

drawing, 181–199
  arcs, 187
  circles, 189
  curves, 186
  ellipses, 190
  lines, 184
  polygons, 192
  rectangles, 187
  stars, 193
  triangles, 191

Drawing API, 155

drawRectangle( ) method, 40

drawRegularPolygon( ) method, 192

drawRoundRect( ) method, 188

drawTriangle( ) method, 191

drop shadows, 269

drop( ) method, 177

dropping objects with the mouse, 173–180

DropShadowFilter class, 270

dropTarget property (Sprite class), 173

duplicate arrays, 116

duplicate( ) method, 116
  multidimensional arrays and, 119

duplicateMovieClip( ) method, 137

duration metadata value, 395

dynamic classes, 425

dynamic text fields, 231

E

E4X syntax, 458
  finding elements by name, 465
  searching XML, 482
  text nodes, adding, 461
  text nodes, reading, 468
easing, moving display objects, 285
Eclipse IDE, 1
  parameters, keeping track of, 3
  trace, using, 9
edge detection matrixes, 275
edges (display object), detecting, 275
elapsed( ) method, 362
elements (arrays)
  adding to start/end of, 104–105
  associative
    creating, 133
    reading, 135
  copies of, 116–120
  inserting in middle of, 113
  looping through, 106
  minimum/maximum, getting, 131
  multidimensional/complex data,
    storing, 120–123
  randomizing, 129
  removing, 111–113
  reversing/sorting, 123–127
  searching for matching, 107
elements (XML), 453
  extracting, 464
  finding by name, 465–467
  removing, 473
elements( ) method, 464
ellipses, drawing, 190
else statements, 20
else...if statements, 21
  coin toss, simulating with, 89
[Embed] metadata tag, 162
  embedding fonts and, 250
emboss matrixes, 274
embossing, 274
encrypting passwords, 232
endFill( ) method, 194
  gradients, filling shapes with, 195
endIndex parameter
  setSelection( ) method, 255
  setTextFormat( ) method, 249
  substring( ) and slice( ) methods, 309
enterFrame event, 10, 29, 281, 295
  dissolving between two bitmaps, 224
  repeating tasks over time, 30–32

  responding to mouse/key events, 12
  sound files and, 372
Epoch milliseconds, 356
equal sign (=)
  assignment statements and, 14
    differences with == and, 17
  variables, assigning, 6
equality operators, 17
equality, checking, 16–19
equals( ) method, 132
error handling, 38–42
ErrorReportingEnable variable (mm.cfg), 9
escape sequences, 436
  Unicode for Latin 1 characters, 527–531
escaping characters, 234
Euro (€), 85
event object, 11
event protocol, 260
EventDispatcher class, 57, 374
EventDispatcher class, handling events, 10
events, 7
  dispatching, 57
  handling, 10
exactFit mode, 65
exclamation point (!), escape sequence
    for, 436
exec( ) (RegExp class), 333–336
Express Install (Flash Player Detection
    Kit), 59
extended (x) flag, 332
extends keyword, 52
external images
  bitmaps, loading into, 204
  runtime, loading, 161–165
external movies, loading/interacting
    with, 165–168
ExternalInterface class, 494
ExternalInterface.addCallback( )
    method, 496
ExternalInterface.call( ) method, 494

F

\f (form feed character), 303
face attribute (<font> tag), 236
Fahrenheit, converting between Celsius, 101
fault events, listening for, 490
file management, 499–508
  browsing for files and, 503
  detecting when users select files for
    uploading, 506
  downloading files, 499–502

filtering files for display, 504
monitoring download progress, 503
monitoring file upload progress, 507
uploading files, 502, 506
FileFilter objects, 504
FileReference object, 503, 506
fillColor parameter, 201
MovieClip.beginFill( ) method, 194
fillColor parameter (pixelDissolve( )
method), 225
fillRect( ) method, 207
filters, 212, 266–280
advanced effects, applying, 272–274
applying basic, 269–272
applying to bitmaps, 221–224
detecting edges, 275
digital negatives, making, 276
sharpening display objects, 276
filters property, 270
finally blocks, 41
findLastMatchIndex( ) method, 109
findMatchIndex( ) method, 109
findMatchIndices( ) method, 109
Firefox, 61
.fla files, 3, 44
class files, saving, 48
.flas files, detecting Flash Players with, 59
Flash cookies, 410
Flash Player
detecting, 58–60
menu items, hiding, 67
prompting users to change settings, 70
type, checking, 61
Flash Player Detection Kit, 58–60
Flash Player Settings Manager, 420
Flash remoting, 487–493
methods, calling, 490
responses, handling, 492
Flash Remoting gateway, 491
Flash Video Exporter, 400
flash.display package, 5, 137, 201
TextField class, 229
flash.display.CapsStyle class, 183
flash.display.Graphics class, 181
flash.display.JointStyle class, 183
flash.display.LineScaleMode class, 182
flash.display.Loader class, 162, 204
flash.display.SpreadMethod constants, 196
flash.display.Stage class, 58
flash.display.TexfieldType class, 231
flash.errors package, 39
flash.events, 57

flash.events.DataEvent.DATA constant, 518
flash.events.Event class, 241
flash.events.FocusEvent objects, 256
flash.events.TextEvent type, 260
flash.events.TextEvent.TEXT_INPUT
constant, 257
flash.filters package, 270
flash.filters.ColorMatrixFilter class, 276
flash.filters.ConvolutionFilter class, 272
flash.geom.ColorTransform class, 266
flash.geom.Matrix class, 203, 269
flash.geom.Matrix object, 196
flash.geom.Rectangle class, 207, 219
copying pixels, 210
flash.geom.Rectangle object, 261
flash.media.ID3Info class, 374
flash.media.Video class, 393
flash.net.FileReference class, 499
flash.net.navigateToURL( ) method, 476
flash.net.NetConnection class, 491
flash.net.registerClassAlias( ) method, 416
flash.net.Responder object, 492
flash.net.sendToURL( ) method, 476
flash.net.URLLoader class, 162, 245, 349,
443
flash.net.URLStream instance, 446
flash.net.XMLSocket class, 509
flash.system.Capabilities class, 58
video capabilities, detecting, 69
flash.system.Capabilities object, 64
flash.system.Capabilities.hasAudio
property, 68
flash.system.Capabilities.language
property, 62
flash.system.Capabilities.os property, 60
flash.system.Capabilities.version
property, 59
flash.system.IME class, 62, 63
flash.system.IME.enabled property, 63
flash.system.Security class, 58
flash.system.Security.allowDomain( ), 72
flash.system.Security.allowInsecure-
Domain( ), 72
flash.system.Security.showSettings( )
method, 70
flash.text.AntiAliasType.ADVANCED, 264
flash.text.GridFitType class, 264
flash.text.TextField class, 229
flash.text.TextFieldAutoSize class, 237
flash.util.getTimer( ) function, 359
flash.util.Timer class, 357
flash.utils package, 31

FlashVars, 497
Flex Builder, 1, 44, 488
    class files, saving, 48
    trimming whitespace and, 322
floating-point numbers
    random, generating, 86
    rounding, 78
flood fills, creating, 208
floodFill( ) method, 208
flush( ) method, 412, 513, 524
.flv files, 392
focalPointRatio parameter
        (beginGradientFill( ) method), 196
FocusEvent.preventDefault( ) method, 256
focusIn event, 256
focusOut event, 256
font groups, 250
<font> HTML tag, 236
    embedding fonts, 250
    setting fonts in text fields, 249
font property (TextFormat object), 249
fontFamily ActionScript property, 244
font-family CSS property, 244
fonts
    embedding, 250–252
    rotating, 252
    text fields, setting in, 249
fontSize ActionScript property, 244
font-size CSS property, 244
fontStyle ActionScript property, 244
font-style CSS property, 244
fontWeight ActionScript property, 244
font-weight CSS property, 244
for keyword, 26
for statement, 24
    array, looping through, 106
    associative arrays, reading, 135
    matching elements in arrays with, 107
    removing elements from arrays, 113
    repeating operations many times, 26
for...each loops, reading XML elements, 471
form feed character (\f), 303
format( ) method, 79
    dates and time, 353
    formatting numbers for displaying
        without masks, 83
FormatSeconds( ) method, 355
forward slash (/), storing data and, 419
fps (frames per second), 3
fractal parameter (perlinNoise( )
        method), 216
frames per second (fps), 3

Friedl, Jeffrey E.F., 333
fromCharCode( ) method, 51, 324
fscommand( ) function, 422
fullYear property (Date object), 351
function keyword, 47
functions, 7, 495
    fscommand( ), 422

G

g (global) flag, 332, 335
    replace( ) method and, 339
    search( ) method and, 337
gamescore.cfm, 480
getCategories( ) method, 102
getCharBoundaries( ) method, 261
getCharIndexAtPoint( ) method, 261
getChildAt( ) method, 149–153
getChildIndex( ) method, 149–153
getColor( ) method, 168
getConverterFrom( ) method, 102
getConverterTo( ) method, 96, 102
getFirstCharInParagraph( ) method, 261
getLineIndexAtPoint( ) method, 261
getLineIndexOfChar( ) method, 261
getLineLength( ) method, 261
getLineMetrics( ) method, 261
getLineOffset( ) method, 261
getLineText( ) method, 261
getLocal( ) method, 410, 418
getNextHighestDepth( ) method, 139
getObjectsUnderPoint( ) method, 178
getParagraphLength( ) method, 261
getPixel( ) method, 205
getPixel32( ) method, 205
getTimer( ), 358
getTimer( ) function, 31
.gif files, 161
global (g) flag, 332, 335
    replace( ) method and, 339
    search( ) method and, 337
GlowFilter class, 270
glows, 269
GMT (Greenwich Mean Time), 348
GradientBevelFilter class, 270
GradientGlowFilter class, 270
gradientType parameter (beginGradientFill( )
        method), 195
Graphics class, 181–199
Graphics object
    line styles, setting, 182
Graphics.beginBitmapFill( ) method, 197

Graphics.beginFill( ) method, 194
Graphics.curveTo( ) method, 186
Graphics.drawRect( ) method, 188
Graphics.drawRoundRect( ) method, 188
Graphics.drawRoundRectComplex( )
        method, 188
Graphics.endFill( ) method, 194
Graphics.lineGradientStyle( ) method, 183
Graphics.lineTo( ) method, 184
grayscale, 277
grayscale parameter
    noise( ) method, 213
    perlinNoise( ) method, 216
greater than (>)
    equality operators and, 19
    threshold( ) method, as a parameter, 220
greedy patterns, 341
GREEN property (BitmapDataChannel
        class), 211
    noise( ) method, 213
    perlinNoise( ) method, 216
greenMultiplier property, 268
greenOffset property (ColorTransform
        class), 267
Greenwich Mean Time (GMT), 348
gridTypeFit property, 264

H

handheld devices, supporting Flash
        Players, 64
handleClick( ) method, 158
handleComplete( ) method, 164
handleOpen( ) method, 164
handleProgress( ) method, 164
handlers, 7
handling errors, 38–42
handshaking, 519–523
hasAudio property, detecting audio
        capabilities, 68
hasEmbeddedVideo property, 69
hash tables, 133
hasMP3 property, detecting audio
        capabilities, 68
hasStreamingVideo property, 69
hasVideoEncoder property, 69
hexadecimal numbers, 74
hierarchy tree (display lists), 138
high parameter (noise( ) method), 213
hitTestPoint( ) method, 177
hitTestState property (SimpleButton
        class), 156, 158

Hooke's Law, 289
host parameter (connect( ) method), 510
hours parameter (addTo( ) method), 361
hours property (Date object), 351
HTML (Hypertext Markup Language)
    <a> tag, 236, 258
    <b> tag, 236

 tag, 236
    displaying, 235
    <font> tag, 236, 249, 250
    fonts, setting in text fields, 249
    formatting text, 242
    <i> tag, 236
    <img> tag, 236
    <li> tag, 236
    loading a block of text, 442
    <p> tag, 236
    passing parameters from, 497
    removing tags with regular
            expressions, 341
    <textformat> tag, 236
    <u> tag, 236
    XML, special characters and, 485
.html files, 2
htmlText property, 235
    hyperlinks, adding to text, 258
http protocol, 259
https protocol, 259
httpStatus event (LoaderInfo class), 163
httpStatus failure event, 438
hyperlinks, 235
    adding to text, 258–260
    calling ActionScript from, 260
HyperText Markup Language (see HTML)
hypotenuse, 97
    circles, determining points along, 99

I

i (ignoreCase) flag, 332, 337
<i> HTML tag, 236
id3 property (Sound object), 373
ID3 tag, reading, 373–375
if statements, 20–24
    complex conditional testing, using, 24
ignoreCase (i) flag, 332, 337
IllegalOperationError, 38, 501
images
    bitmaps, loading into, 204
    runtime, loading, 161–165
IMAP, 510
IME (Input Method Editor), 63

<img> HTML tag, 236
import statements, 5
#include directives, 5
indent attribute (<textformat> tag), 236
index parameter (setTextFormat( )
    method), 248
index variables (loop counters), 26
indexes (arrays), 103
    associative arrays and, 133
    looping through, 105
    multidimensional data and, 120
    removing elements with, 113
indexOf( ) method, 304–308
inequality, checking, 16–19
inheritance, defining, 52
init event (LoaderInfo class), 163
    external movies and, 167
initialization expressions, 26
innerRadius parameter (Pen.drawStar( )
    method), 193
input fields, 231
    filtering input, 233
    maximum length, setting, 234
    password, 232
    user-input
        formatting, 247
Input Method Editor (IME), 63
insertChildAfter( ) method, 458, 461
insertChildBefore( ) method, 458, 461
insertion points, setting, 255
instances (object), 7
int keyword, 29
int type, 74
integer-indexed arrays, 103
InteractiveObject class, 168
InteractiveObject display object, 169
internal keyword, 6, 46
    reusing code and, 33
internal variables, 7
Internet Explorer, 61
interpolationMethod parameter
    (beginGradientFill( ) method), 196
interpreter (ActionScript), 8
ioError event (LoaderInfo class), 163
ioError failure event, 438
IOErrorEvent event listener, 501
isNaN( ), 16
ISO-639-1 language codes, 62

J

Java, 487
JavaScript
    ActionScript functions, calling, 496
    Flash Players, detecting, 59
    functions, calling, 494
    passing parameters from HTML, 498
join( ) method, 315
    converting arrays to stings, 115
    reversing strings, 322
    trimming whitespace, 321
joints parameter (lineStyle method), 183
.jpg files, 161

K

kerning ActionScript property, 244
kerning CSS property, 244
key events, responding tp, 12
KeyboardEvent class, 13
keyDown event, 13
keyFocusChange events, 256
keyframes, 281
keys, 103, 134
kilograms, converting between pounds, 101

L

label property (Unit objects), 96
labelPlural property (Unit objects), 96
language codes, 82
languages (system), checking, 61–63
last in, first out (LIFO), 105
lastIndexOf( ) method, 304–308
Latin 1 characters, 527–531
lazy expressions, 342
leading attribute (<textformat> tag), 236
leftmargin attribute (<textformat> tag), 236
length parameter
    drawRegularPolygon( ) method, 192
    substr( ) method, 309
less than (<)
    equality operators and >, 19
letterSpacing ActionScript property, 244
letter-spacing CSS property, 244
<li> HTML tag, 236
LIFO (last in, first out), 105
limit (split( ) method), 115
line styles
    gradient, 183
    setting, 182

lineGradientStyle( ) method, 183
lines, drawing, 184
lineStyle( ) method, 182
lineTo( ) method, 184
    rectangles, drawing, 188
literal notation (arrays), 104
literals (regular expressions), 329
load( ) method, 162, 165, 379, 437, 474
Loader class, 140, 161
    external images, loading as bitmaps, 204
    external movies, loading/interacting
        with, 165–168
    mouse interactions and, 169
LoadVars class, 439
LoadVars.load( ) method, 440, 442
    loading variables from text file, 437
LoadVars.sendAndLoad( ) method, 450
loadWSDL( ) method, 488
local connections
    communication and, 422
    communication between movies
        sending data and, 427
local shared objects (LSO), 409
    controlling size of, 420
    creating/opening, 409
    reading data from, 414
    removing data from, 415
    saving, 411–414
    sharing data between Flash
        applications, 418–420
    writing data to, 411
LocalConnection class, 168, 423
LocalConnection.connect( ) method, 423
LocalConnection.send( ) method, 426
Locale class, 81
Locale.slanguage property, 82
Locale.svariant property, 82
localToGlobal( ) method, 171
localX property (MouseEvent class), 171
localY property (MouseEvent class), 171
lockCenter parameter (startDrag()
        method), 173
logical AND (&&), 24–26
logical inequality operator (!=), 17, 25
logical NOT (!), 24–26
logical OR (||), 24–26
loop counters, 26
loop statements, 26
    arrays, 106
looping sounds, 370
low parameter (noise( ) method), 213
LSO (see local shared objects)

M

m (multiline) flag, 332
Mac OS X mm.cfg file, locating, 9
Macromedia XML (MXML), 1, 44
    class files, saving, 48
magnitude (acceleration), 288
mailto links, 260
major radii, 190
marginLeft ActionScript property, 244
margin-left CSS property, 244
marginRight ActionScript property, 244
margin-right CSS property, 244
markup languages, 441
mask parameter (threshold( ) method), 219
masks, 181–199
    formatting numbers for display
        without, 83
    scripting, 198
Mastering Regular Expressions (Friedl,
        Jeffrey), 333
math, 74–102
Math class, 34, 51
Math.atan2( ) function, 291–294
Math.ceil( ) method, 78, 395
Math.cos( ) function, 98, 291–294
Math.floor( ) method, 78, 395
Math.PI, 56
Math.pow( ), 97
Math.random( ), 86
    randomizing elements in arrays, 130
Math.round( ) method, 78, 395
Math.sin( ) function, 98, 291–294
Math.sqrt( ), 97
mathematical operators, 14–16
Matrix class
    drawing objects to bitmaps, 203
    shearing display objects, 269
matrix parameter
    beginGradientFill( ) method, 196
    Graphics.beginBitmapFill( ) method, 197
maxChars property, 234
maximum parameter
        (NumberUtilities.random( )
        method), 86
maxScrollH property (text fields), 238
maxScrollV property (text fields), 238
MaxWarnings variable (mm.cfg), 10
measurements, converting between units
        of, 101
Media Players, 372
MemoryError, 38, 501

menu items (Flash Player), hiding, 67
messages, tracing, 8–10
metacharacters, 328
metadata, specifying properties, 3
metasequences, 328
methods, 7
  allowDomain( ), 432
  exiting, 36
  generating to enhance reusability, 34–36
  LoadVars.load( ), 437
  LoadVars.sendAndLoad( ), 450
  obtaining results, 37
  placing code, 4
  reusing code, 32
  String.split( ), 452
  web services, calling, 488
Microsoft Windows, 410
milliseconds parameter (addTo( )
     method), 361
milliseconds property (Date object), 351
milliseconds, formatting, 355
minimum parameter
     (NumberUtilities.random( )
     method), 86
minor radii, 190
minutes parameter (addTo( ) method), 361
minutes property (Date object), 351
minutes, formatting, 355
miterLimit parameter (lineStyle
     method), 183
mm.cfg file, 9, 10
month property (Date object), 351
MONTHS constant (DateFormat class), 352
months parameter (addTo( ) method), 361
MONTHS_ABBREVIATED constant
     (DateFormat class), 352
mouse events
  dragging/dropping objects with, 173–180
  interactions, creating, 168–172
  responding to, 12
mouseDown event (InteractiveObject), 169
MouseEvent class, 12, 168–172
  dragging dropping objects, 177
MouseEvent.CLICK, 158
MouseEvent.MOUSE_UP, 56
mouseFocusChange event, 256
mouseMove event (InteractiveObject), 169
mouseOut event (InteractiveObject), 170
mouseUp event (InteractiveObject), 169
mouseWheel event (InteractiveObject), 170
mouseWheelEnabled property, 241

mouseX property (DisplayObject class), 168,
     171
mouseY property (DisplayObject class), 168,
     171
moveTo( ) method, 184
MovieClip class, 137, 140, 181
  adding items to display list, 141
  custom visual classes and, 153
  mouse interactions and, 169
movies
  alignment of, changing, 66
  communication, 422, 432–434
  communication between
    local connections and, 427
    same computer, 423
  external, loading/interacting, 165–168
  scaling, 65
Mozilla, 61
MP3s, detecting audio capabilities and, 69
multidimensional arrays, 118–123
multiline (m) flag, 332
multiplier properties, 267
mx.rpc.events.FaultEvent, 490
mx.rpc.soap.WebService object, 488
mx.utils.StringUtil.trim( ) static method, 320
MXML (Macromedia XML), 1, 44
  class files, saving, 48
mxmlc, 48
  viewing command-line arguments, 4

N

\n (newline character), 303, 331
name property (Unit objects), 96
names of packages, 45
NaN (not a number) constant, 18
navigateToURL( ) method, 495
Navigator view (Flex Builder 2), 2
nested for statements, 28
nested nodes, XML, 455
  attributes and, 455
.NET, 487
NetConnection class, 491
NetStream class, 392
New ActionScript Project Wizard, 2
new operator, 141
newline character (\n), 303
NNTP, 510
noBorder mode, 65
nodes (XML), 453, 455
noise patterns, creating, 212
  Perlin, 214–218

noise( ) method, 212
  BitmapData class, 206
  perlinNoise method and, 214
nongreedy patterns, 341–343
non-word boundary (\B) metasequence, 331
non-word character (\W) metasequence, 331
noScale mode, 65
NOT (!) logical, 24–26
not (false), creating bitmaps, 201
not a number (NaN) constant, 18
Number keyword, 29
number parameter (NumberUtilities.round( )
    method), 79
number systems, converting between, 75–77
number type, 74
NumberFormat class, 79
  currency amounts, formatting, 84
  formatting numbers for displaying
      without masks, 83
NumberFormat.currencyFormat( )
    method, 84
numbers, 74–102
  angle measurements, converting, 96
  bases, representing different, 74
  calculating distance between two
      points, 97
  circles, determining points along, 98–101
  converting between different systems,
      75–77
  currency, formatting amounts, 84
  masks, formatting for display without, 83
  measurement, converting between
      units, 101
  random, generating, 86
  rounding, 77–79
  simulating
      coin tosses, 88–91
      playing cards, 93–95
  unique, generating, 95
NumberUtilities.getUnique( ) method, 95
NumberUtilities.random( ) method, 86
  coin toss, simulating, 88
  dice, simulating, 91
NumberUtilities.round( ) method, 78
numChildren property, 148
numLines property, 261
numPixels parameter (pixelDissolve( )
    method), 225
  setting, 227

O
Object class, 133
Object.registerClass( ) method, 416
objects, 7
  acceleration of, 287–289
  dragging/dropping with the mouse,
      173–180
  drawing to bitmaps, 203
  easing, 285
  moving, 282
  moving forward and backward, 149–153
  sound, creating/loading, 365–367
  springs, 289–291
  XML
      creating, 456
      populated, 456
octal bases, 74
octal literals, 74
octaves parameter (perlinNoise( )
    method), 214
offsets parameter (perlinNoise( )
    method), 217
On2 Flix, 400
onCuePoint( ) callback, 400
onLoad( ) method, 442
onMetaData( ) method, 395, 400
onMouseDown method, 12
onMouseUp method, 12
onTextScroll( ) method, 242
onvertWithLabel( ) method, 102
open event (LoaderInfo class), 163
operating systems, detecting, 60
operation parameter (threshold ( )
    method), 219
opposite sides, 99
OR (|) bitwise, 75, 124
OR (||) logical, 24–26
outerRadius parameter (Pen.drawStar( )
    method), 193
Outline view (Flex Builder 2), 3
outlines, creating around text fields, 230
override attribute, 55
overState property (SimpleButton class), 156

P
<p> HTML tag, 236
package keyword, 5
packages, 44–47
packet (XML), 453
parallel arrays, 120

parameters (method), generalizing for
    enhancing reusability, 34
parentheses (( ))
    conditional operators and, 25
    regular expression metacharacters, 330
    URL-encoded escape sequence for, 436
parse( ) method, 363
parseCSS( ) method, 245
parseInt( ) function, 74
    converting between number systems
        and, 76
password input fields, 232
password property, 232
pattern parameter
    regular( ) method, 338
    String.replace( ) method, 315
patterns (see regular expressions)
pause( ) method, 402
pausing sound, 379–381
Pen class, 181
    ellipses, drawing, 190
    polygons, drawing, 192
    triangles, drawing, 191
pen locations
    curves, drawing, 186
    lines, drawing, 184
Pen.drawArc( ) method, 187
Pen.drawEllipse( ) method, 190
Pen.drawLine( ) method, 185
Pen.drawRegularPolygon( ) method, 192
Pen.drawStar( ) method, 193
Pen.drawTriangle( ) method, 191
percent sign (%), escape sequence for, 436
Perl, 440, 487
Perlin noise, 214–218, 228
Perlin, Ken, 214
perlinNoise( ) method, 214–218
permissions for .cgi scripts, 350
persistent data, 409–421
PHP, getting current date and time, 349
pixelDissolve( ) method (BitmapData
        class), 224–227
pixelHinting parameter (lineStyle
        method), 182
pixels (bitmaps), 200
    copying, 209–211
    manipulating, 205–207
place( ) method, 177
play( ) method, 367, 379
    finding out when a sound finishes, 375
    ID3 tag and, 374

looping sounds, 370
offsetting the start of a sound, 369
playback time
    controlling, 397
    reading, 394
player versions, detecting, 58–60
playing cards, simulating, 93–95
plus sign (+)
    as a regular expression
        metacharacter, 330
        nongreedy patterns and, 341
    URL-encoded escape sequence for, 436
.png files, 161
points parameter (Pen.drawStar( )
        method), 193
policy files, 72
polygons, drawing, 192
pop( ) method, 111
POP3, 510
port parameter (connect( ) method), 511
position property (SoundChannel class), 379
postfix operators, 15
pound sign (#), 80
    escape sequence for, 436
pound sign (British) (£), 85
pounds, converting between kilograms, 101
predicate filtering, 482
prefix operators, 15
prependChild( ) method, 461
primitive data, 116
primitive datatypes, 19
Print menu item, 68
private keyword, 6, 46
    reusing code, 33
programmatic animation, 281–297
progress event, 503, 507
    LoaderInfo class, 163
    URLLoader class, 444
ProgressEvent, 503
progressive .jpg, 161
Project Wizard, 2
projects (Flex), 1
    creating, 2
properties, 6
    applications, customizing, 3
    associative arrays, 134
protected keyword, 6, 46
    reusing code, 33
    subclasses, creating, 52
    superclass methods and, 55
protected variables, 6

public keyword, 5, 46
    reusing code and, 33
    subclasses, creating, 52
    superclass methods and, 55
push( ) method, 104
Pythagorean Theorem, 97

Q

Quality menu item, 68
question mark (?), as a regular expression
      metacharacter, 330
QuickTime Players, 372
quotes ('), 302
    URL-encoded escape sequence for, 436

R

\r (carriage return character), 331, 303
radialLines parameter (drawArc( )
      method), 187
radii, 190
radius parameter
    drawArc( ) method, 187
    drawCircle( ) method, 189
radix parameter (parseInt( ) function), 76
random numbers, 86
random( ) method
    coin toss, simulating, 88
    dice, simulating, 91
RangeErrors, 143, 147, 152
ratios parameter (beginGradientFill( )
      method), 195
readBoolean( ) method, 516
readByte( ) method, 515, 516
readChallenge( ) method, 521
readDouble( ) method, 516
readFloat( ) method, 516
readInt( ) method, 515, 516
readNormalProtocol( ) method, 521
readObject( ) method, 516
readShort( ) method, 516
readUnsignedByte( ) method, 516
readUnsignedInt( ) method, 516
readUnsignedShort( ) method, 516
readUTF( ) method, 516
readVersion( ) method, 521
Rectangle region, 173
rectangles, drawing, 187–189
rectangular fills, creating, 207
recursion, 119
RED property (BitmapDataChannel
      class), 211

noise( ) method, 213
perlinNoise( ) method, 216
redMultiplier property, 268
redOffset property (ColorTransform
      class), 267
regexes (see regular expressions)
RegExp class, 328
RegExp.test( ) method, 333
regexps (see regular expressions)
registerClassAlias( ) method, 416
regular expressions, 233, 327–347
    literals, 329
    nongreedy patterns, 341–343
    pattern matches
      looking for, 336–338
      removing and replacing
        characters/words, 338–341
    splitting strings, 314
    testing, 333–336
    understanding patterns, 328–333
    user input, validating, 343–347
Regular Expressions Pocket Reference
      (Stubblebine, Tony), 333
relatedObject property, 256
remote procedure calls (RPC), 476, 487
remote shared objects (RSO), 409
removeChild( ) method, 146–149
removeChildAt( ) method, 146–149
Rendering Engine, 141
reparenting, 144
repeat parameter, for
      Graphics.beginBitmapFill( ), 197
replace parameter
    replace( ) method, 338
    String.replace( ) method, 315
replace( ) method, 315
replacement codes, 339
replaceSelectedText( ) method, 265
replaceText( ) method, 265
reserved words, 6
Responder class, 492
restarting sound, 379–381
restrict property, filtering text input
      with, 233
result event listener, 489
ResultEvent parameter, 489
results
    variables, server-side processing, 449
return character (see carriage return
      character)
return statements, 36
reusable code, 32, 34–36

reverse( ) method, 125
   reversing strings, 322
RexExp.exec( ) method, 333
RGB color values, 74
rgb property, 267
right triangles, calculating distance of, 98
rightmargin attribute (<textformat>
      tag), 236
root nodes (XML), 454
root.loaderInfo.parameters property, 498
rotation parameter
   createGradientBox( ) method, 196
   drawRegularPolygon( ) method, 192
   drawTriangle( ) method, 191
   Pen.drawStar( ) method, 193
_rotation property, 96
round( ) method, 51
   random numbers, generating, 86
rounding numbers, 77–79
roundToInterval parameter
   NumberUtilities.random( ) method, 86
   NumberUtilities.round( ) method, 79
RPC (remote procedure calls), 476, 487
RSO (see remote shared objects)
runtime environment, 58–73

S

s (dotall) flag, 332
S (single non-whitespace) metasequence, 331
\s (single white space) metasequence
      character, 331
_sans font group (sans font group), 250
saturation, changing on display objects, 278
save dialog boxes, 500
scale modes (movies), 65
scaleMode parameter (lineStyle
      method), 182
scaleX parameter (createGradientBox( )
      method), 196
scaleY parameter (createGradientBox( )
      method), 196
scope, 7
screenResolutionX property, 64
screenResolutionY property, 64
scripts, server-side
   variable results, 449
ScriptTimeoutError, 38
scroll events, responding to, 241
scroll( ) method (BitmapData class), 227
scrollH property (text fields), 238
scrollV property (text fields), 238

scrubbing video, 403
search( ) method, 336
seconds parameter (addTo( ) method), 361
seconds property (Date object), 351
seconds, formatting, 355
Secure Socket Layer (SSL), 232
security (system), dealing with, 71–73
Security.showSettings( ) method, 420
securityError event (LoaderInfo class), 163
securityError failure event, 438
SecurityErrorEvent event listener, 501
SecurityPanel.CAMERA value
      (flash.system.SecurityPanel
      class), 71
SecurityPanel.DEFAULT value
      (flash.system.SecurityPanel
      class), 71
SecurityPanel.LOCAL_STORAGE value
      (flash.system.SecurityPanel
      class), 71
SecurityPanel.MICROPHONE value
      (flash.system.SecurityPanel
      class), 71
SecurityPanel.PRIVACY value
      (flash.system.SecurityPanel
      class), 71
SecurityPanel.SETTINGS_MANAGER value
      (flash.system.SecurityPanel
      class), 71
seed parameter
   noise( ) method, 212
   perlinNoise( ) method, 216
   pixelDissolve( ) method, 225
seek( ) method, 403
   NetStream class, 397
select events, 502, 506
selected text, responding to, 256
semicolon (;), 7
   concatenating strings and, 301
send( ) method, 524
sending data to server-side script, 447
_serif font group, 250
servers, loading .swfs from different, 72
setChildIndex( ) method, 149–153
   dragging/dropping objects, 176
setColor( ) method, 168
setInterval( ) function, 30
setPixel( ) method, 205
   noise patterns, creating with, 212
setPixel32( ) method, 205
setSelection( ) method, 255
setStyle( ) method, 244

setTextFormat( ) method, 243
    formatting portions of text, 248
setTimeout( ) function, 30
setting (display), detecting, 63
Settings dialog box, 70
Settings menu item, 68
Shape class, 138, 140, 181
    custom visual classes, 154
shapes
    bitmaps, filling with, 197
    gradient, filling with, 195–197
    solid/translucent colors, filling, 194
shared objects, 409
    reading data from, 414
    removing data from, 415
SharedObject class, 409
SharedObject classes
    persistent information and, 410
SharedObject.clear( ) method, 412
SharedObject.flush( ) method, 412
sharpening, 276
sharpness property, 264
shearing, 269
shift( ) method, 111
Show All menu item, 68
Show Redraw Regions menu item, 68
showAll mode, 65
showSettings( ) method, 71
sides parameter (drawRegularPolygon( )
        method), 192
simple buttons, creating, interactive buttons,
        creating, 156–161
Simple Object Access Protocol (see SOAP)
SimpleButton class, 156
    mouse interactions and, 169
single non-whitespace (\s)
        metasequence, 331
single whitespace (\s) metasequence, 331
size attribute (<font> tag), 236
skewing, 269
slice( ) method, 116, 308–311
    multidimensional arrays and, 118
smooth parameter
        (Graphics.beginBitmapFill( )
        method), 197
SMTP, 510
SOAP (Simple Object Access Protocol), 487
Socket objects, 511
    handling socket errors, 524
    receiving data, 515
    sending data, 513
socket programming, 509–525

connecting to, 510–513
disconnecting from servers, 523
handling socket errors, 524
handshaking, 519–523
receiving data, 515
sending data, 513–515
Socket.close( ) method, 523
Socket.connect( ) method, 510
socketData event handler, 520
solid colors, filling shapes, 194
sort( ) method, 123–127
    custom sorts, implementing, 127
    randomizing elements in arrays, 130
sorter function, 127
sorting arrays, 123–127
    custom, implementing, 127–129
sortOn( ) method, 123–127
sound, 365–386
    applications, creating, 386
    buffers, setting for, 368
    creating/loading objects, 365–367
    finding out when finishes, 375–377
    getting the size of, 371–373
    ID3 tag, reading, 373–375
    looping, 370
    offsetting the start of, 369
    pausing/restarting, 379–381
    reading the level of, 381
    spectrums, reading, 383–385
    starting/stopping, 367
    stopping, 382
    tracking the progress of, 377–379
    video, 394
    volume and pan of, 385
Sound object, 365–386
Sound.length, 377
SoundChannel class, 375, 381
    pausing/restarting sounds, 379
    tracking the progress of sounds, 377
SoundChannel.leftPeak property, 381
SoundChannel.position, 377
SoundChannel.rightPeak property, 381
soundComplete event, 375
SoundLoaderContext class, 368
SoundMixer class, 382, 383
SoundMixer.computeSpectrum( )
        method, 383
SoundTransform class, 381, 385
soundTransform property, 394
sourceBitmap object (threshold( )
        method), 218
-source-path option (mxmlc), 49

sourceRect parameter (pixelDissolve( ) method), 225
spaces inserting leading/trailing, 79–83
special whitespace characters, 303
spectrums (sound), 383–385
speed of display objects, 282
splice( ) method, 111
    inserting elements in the middle of arrays, 113
split( ) method, 311–315
    converting strings to arrays, 114
    randomizing elements in arrays, 130
    removing and replacing characters/words, 315–317
    retrieving one character at a time, 318
    reversing strings, 322
spreadMethod parameter for beginGradientFill( ) method, 196
springs, 289–291
Sprite class, 5, 138, 140, 181
    adding items to display list, 141
    custom visual classes, 154
    dragging/dropping objects with the mouse, 173
    mouse interactions and, 169
Sprite.rotation property, 75
square brackets ([ ]), 104
    regular expression metacharacters, 330
SSL (Secure Socket Layer), 232
stage, 137
stage.align property, 66
Stage.focus property, 253
stage.scaleMode property, 65
stage.showDefaultContextMenu property, 67
standalone players, 61
stars, drawing, 193
start( ) method (addEventListener), 30
startDrag( ) method, 177, 404
startDrop( ) method, 173
startIndex parameter
    indexOf( ) method, 304
    lastIndexOf( ) method, 306
    setSelection( ) method, 255
    setTextFormat( ) method, 249
    substr( ), substring( ), and slice( ) methods, 309
startingAngle parameter (drawArc( ) method), 187
statement body, 27
statements, 7
static attribute, 51

static methods, 34
    creating, 51
static properties, 51
stitch parameter (perlinNoise( ) method), 216
stop( ) (addEventListener), 30
stopAll( ) method, 382
stopDrag( ) method, 173
strict equality/inequality, 16
strict flag, 16
String class, 298–325
String data type, 298
String( ) conversion function, 300
String.charAt( ) method, 317
String.charCodeAt( ) method, 324
String.concat( ) method, 299, 301
String.fromCharCode( ) method, 324
String.match( ) method, 336
String.replace( ) method, 315, 338
String.search( ) method, 336
String.split( ) method, 114, 317, 452
strings, 298–325
    arrays, converting, 114
    dates, parsing, 363
    joining, 298–301
    parsing into words, 311–315
    quotes and apostrophes in, 302
    removing and replacing characters/word, 315–317
    retrieving one character at a time, 317–319
    reversing by words/characters, 322
    special whitespace characters, 303
    substrings
        extracting, 308–311
        searching for, 304–308
    Unicode, converting between, 323–326
    whitespace, trimming, 320–322
StringUtils class, 5
structure (XML), 454–456
Stubblebine, Tony, 333
StyleSheet object, 242
StyleSheet property, 242
subclasses
    creating, 52–54
    superclass methods, implementing, 54
subdirectories, saving class files, 44
substr( ) method, 308–311
substring parameter
    indexOf( ) method, 304
    lastIndexOf( ) method, 306
substring( ) method, 308–311

substrings
   extracting, 308–311
   searching for, 304–308
super cookies, 410
super keyword, 56
superclasses, 52
   implementing subclass versions of, 54
swapDepths( ), 139
.swf files, 2
   detecting Flash Players with, 59
switch statements, 20–24
system languages, checking, 61–63
system security, dealing with, 71–73
systemFont attribute, 251

T

\t (tab character), 303, 331
tabstops attribute (<textformat> tag), 236
tags, XML, 455
ternary conditional operator (? :), 20
test expressions, 26
test( ) (RegExp class), 333–336
TexField.setTextFormat( ) method, 242
text, 229–265
   advanced layout, working with, 261–263
   anti-aliasing, applying advanced, 264
   backgrounds, creating, 230
   displaying, 235
   fonts, 249
      embedding, 250–252
   formatting, 242–247
      portions of, 248
   HTML, displaying, 235
   hyperlinks, 258–260
      calling ActionScript from, 260
   input fields, 231
      filtering, 233
      maximum length, setting, 234
      password, 232
   insertion points, setting, 255
   outlines around, 230
   replacing, 265
   responding to user entries, 257
   rotating, 252
   scroll events, responding, 241
   scrolling programmatically, 238–241
   selected/deselected, responding to, 256
   selecting with ActionScript, 254
   sizing fields, 237
   Unicode, displaying, 252
   user-input, formatting, 247
   whitespace, condensing, 236

text files, loading variables from, 436
text nodes, 454
   adding, 461–462
   reading, 468–470
   removing, 473
   trees, 464
textAlign ActionScript property, 244
text-align CSS property, 244
textDecoration ActionScript property, 244
text-decoration CSS property, 244
TextField class, 138, 140, 229
   adding items to display list, 141
   loading external content and, 164
   mouse interactions and, 169
   removing items from display lists, 147
TextField.password property, 232
TextField.restrict property, 233
TextField.setSelection( ) method, 254, 255
<textformat> HTML tag, 236
TextFormat object, 242
textFormat parameter (setTextFormat( )
      method), 248, 249
TextFormat.align property, 85
textIndent ActionScript property, 244
text-indent CSS property, 244
textInput event, 257
thickness parameter (lineStyle method), 182
threshold, 218–221
threshold parameter (threshold( )
      method), 219
threshold( ) method (BitmapData class), 218
time, 348–364
   calculating intervals between dates,
      358–363
   DMYHMSM and Epoch milliseconds,
      converting between, 356
   finding current, 348–351
   formatting, 353–355
   formatting seconds/milliseconds as
      minutes and seconds, 355
   timers, using, 357
time property (NetStream class), 395
Timer class, 30–32
Timer( ) method, 357
TimerEvent.TIMER constant, 357
timers, 357
Times, 250
Times New Roman, 250
tints (colors), 267
toLowerCase( ) method, 308, 319
   converting case, 319
toString( ) method, 55, 76, 116, 300, 468

toUpperCase( ) method, 308
  converting case, 319
trace( ), 8
  loading external images and, 165
TraceOutputFileEnable variable (mm.cfg), 9
TraceOutputFileName variable (mm.cfg), 9
transform.colorTransform property, 266, 267, 268
transforms, 266–280
translucent colors, filling shapes, 194
traversing XML trees, 464
trees (XML), 454
triangles
  calculating distance of, 98
  drawing, 191
trigonometry, 291–294
try blocks, 38–42
  download method, working with, 500
  handling socket errors, 524
tweens, 281
two-dimensional arrays, 119
tx parameter (createGradientBox( ) method), 196
ty parameter (createGradientBox( ) method), 196
type parameter of addEventListener( ), 10
type property, 231
_typewriter font group, 250

U

<u> HTML tag, 236
uint type, 74
uint values, setting values for rgb property, 267
undefined elements (arrays), 112
underline property (TextFormat object), 259
underscore (_), declaring private/protected property names, 46
Unicode, 252
  converting between strings and, 323–326
  escape sequences for Latin 1 characters, 527–531
unique numbers, 95
Unit class, 96
  measurement, converting between units, 101
Unit.DEGREE constant (Unit class), 96
Unit.getUnits( ) method, 102
Unit.GRADIAN constant (Unit class), 96
Unit.RADIAN constant (Unit class), 96
unload event (LoaderInfo class), 163

\unnnn regular expression metasequence, 331
unshift( ) method, 104
update expressions, 27
updateAfterEvent( ) method, 177
upload( ) method, 507
UpperCase( ) method, 319
upState property (SimpleButton class), 156
URL-encoded escape sequences, 436
URLLoader class, 437–451
URLLoader object, 115
  external content, loading, 162
URLLoader.load( ) method, 474, 476
URLRequest class, 366
  downloading files, 501
URLRequest instances, 476
URLs (Uniform Resource Locators)
  variables, loading from text files, 437
user input
  fields, 231
  formatting, 247
  regular expressions, validating with, 343–347
  responding to, 257
UTC (Coordinated Universal Time), 348

V

values, 103, 134
var keyword, 6
  constants, creating, 56
variables, 6
  loading
    from server-side script, 440
variants (country codes), 82
VBScript, Flash Player detecting, 59
vector graphics, 200
velocities for display objects, 282
video, 392–408
  bandwidth, determining, 405–408
  controlling playback time, 397
  cue points, listening for, 400
  display, 405
  duration, reading, 395–397
  loading/playing back, 392–394
  managing/monitoring buffering, 399
  pausing/resuming, 402
  playback time, reading, 394
  scaling, 398
  scrubbing, 403–405
  sound, controlling, 394
  stopping, 402
video capabilities, detecting, 69

Video class, 140, 398
visual class, creating custom, 153–155
void, declaring methods, 37
volume (sound), 385

W

\W (non-word character) metasequence, 331
w (word character) metasequence, 331
Web Service Description Language
         (WSDL), 488
web services, 487–493
    errors, handling, 490
    handling responses, 489
    methods, calling, 488
WebService object, 488
while statement, 24
    indexOf( ) method and, 306
whitespace (text)
    condensing, 236
    inserting special characters, 303
    trimming, 320–322
wildcards, 327
Windows 2000
    mm.cfg file, locating, 9
Windows XP
    mm.cfg file, locating, 9
Wizard (Project), 2
word boundary (\d) metasequence, 331
w (word character) metasequence, 331
writeBoolean( ) method, 513
writeByte( ) method, 513
writeDouble( ) method, 513
writeFloat( ) method, 513
writeInt( ) method, 513
writeMultiByte( ) method, 513
writeObject( ) method, 513
writeShort( ) method, 513
writeUnsignedInt( ) method, 513
writeUTF( ) method, 513
writeUTFBytes( ) method, 513
WSDL (Web Service Description
         Language), 488

X

x (extended) flag, 332
X coordinates, 98
    flood fills, creating, 208
    Perlin noise and, 217
    rectangles, drawing, 188
    scrolling bitmaps, 227

x parameter
    drawArc( ) method, 187
    drawCircle( ) method, 189
    drawEllipse( ) method, 190
    drawRegularPolygon( ) method, 192
    drawTriangle( ) method, 191
    Pen.drawStar( ) method, 193
x-axis, moving objects, 282
XML, 452–486
    advantages, 453
    attributes, 455
        nested nodes and, 455
    elements
        adding to objects, 458
    HTML, using, 485
    loading, 474
        block of text, 442
        from different domains, 475
    nodes, 455
        nested, 455
    objects
        creating, 456
        populated, 456
    policy files, 73
    root node, 454
    searching, 482–485
    sending, 476–481
    socket objects, 518, 523
        sending data, 513
    tags, 455
    text nodes, 454
        adding to objects, 461–462
XMLList, 468
    reading attributes, 470
XML-RPC, 476
XMLSocket objects, 509, 511
    handling socket errors, 524
    receiving data, 515
XMLSocket.close( ) method, 523
XMLSocket.connect( ) method, 510
xnn ASCII character metasequence, 331
XPath, 482
xRadius parameter (drawEllipse( )
         method), 190

Y

Y coordinates, 98
    flood fills, creating, 208
    Perlin noise and, 217
    rectangles, drawing, 188
    scrolling bitmaps, 227

y parameter
    drawArc( ) method, 187
    drawCircle( ) method, 189
    drawEllipse( ) method, 190
    drawRegularPolygon( ) method, 192
    drawTriangle( ) method, 191
    Pen.drawStar( ) method, 193
y-axis, moving objects, 282
years parameter (addTo( ) method), 361
Yen (¥), 85
yRadius parameter (drawEllipse( )
        method), 190

Z

Z regular expression metasequence, 331
z regular expression metasequence, 331
zero-indexed arrays, 105
zeros, inserting leading/trailing, 79–83
Zoom In menu item, 68
Zoom Out menu item, 68

About the Authors

Joey Lott is the author of several O'Reilly books on Macromedia technology, including *Flash 8 Cookbook*, *Programming Flash Communication Server*, and the *ActionScript Cookbook*. He is also the author of *Flash 8 ActionScript Bible* (Wiley) and *Advanced ActionScript with Design Patterns* (Adobe Press, October 2006). Joey has been teaching Flash and ActionScript since 1999. His professional experience in the Internet industry includes co-founding RightSpring, Inc., as well as consulting for YourMobile/Premium Wireless Services (J2EE B2C application) and Ads.com (leading the development of a J2EE B2B application).

Darron Schall is an independent consultant specializing in the Flash platform, with a Bachelor's Degree in Computer Science from Lehigh University. He has been using ActionScript since the early days and is a prominent voice in the Flash and Flex communities. He is actively involved in the Open Source Flash movement with projects ranging from software development tools to a Commodore 64 emulator. Darron has spoken at various conferences about ActionScript and has contributed to books and magazines. You can find his Flash platform-related blog at *http://www.darronschall.com*.

Keith Peters is a Flash developer in the Boston area. He has been working with Flash since 1999 and is currently a Senior Flash Developer at Brightcove (*http://www.brightcove.com*). Keith has been a contributing author to nine other Flash and ActionScript books. His personal web site, *http://www.bit-101.com*, features an active blog, more than 700 open source Flash experiments, and lots of other random Flash-related stuff.

Colophon

The animal on the cover of *ActionScript 3.0 Cookbook* is a crab-eating opossum (*Philander opossum*). It can be found throughout Mexico, Central America, and South America. The length of the animal varies, though it is usually between 250 and 350 millimeters. Its prehensile tail often grows to about the same length.

P. opossum is an omnivore. It eats insects, lizards, eggs, worms, frogs, small mammals, and birds, along with seeds, bananas, and leaves. It reproduces all year round, although the number of offspring varies. During the dry summer months when food is scarce, the litters can be as few as one or two young, while as many as seven can be born during the more plentiful rainy season.

Most opossum nests are built in the low branches of trees, though they can also be found on the ground or in burrows. *P. opossum* spends most of its time on the forest floor, where it forages for food, though it will occasionally take to the trees. It was once thought that *P. opossum* was nocturnal, but it has often been observed scampering and foraging during the day. When it senses danger, *P. opossum* will hiss or yelp, and it can be a capable fighter.

The cover image is from *Cuvier's Animals*. The cover font is Adobe ITC Garamond. The text font is Linotype Birka; the heading font is Adobe Myriad Condensed; and the code font is LucasFont's TheSans Mono Condensed.

Better than e-books

Buy *ActionScript 3.0 Cookbook* and access
the digital edition FREE on Safari for 45 days.

Go to www.oreilly.com/go/safarienabled
and type in coupon code V9NU-BAGL-XJ5Y-FGL5-25YP

Search
thousands of
top tech books

Download
whole chapters

Cut and Paste
code examples

Find
answers fast

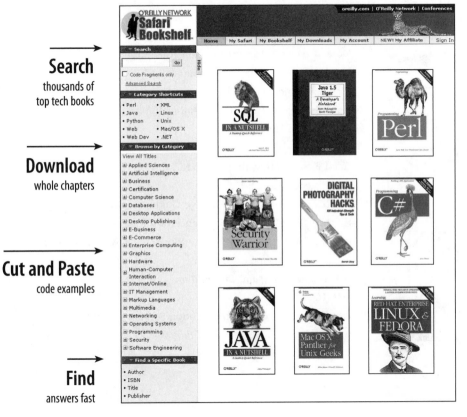

Search Safari! The premier electronic reference
library for programmers and IT professionals.

Related Titles from O'Reilly

Web Authoring and Design

ActionScript 3 Cookbook

Ajax Hacks

Ambient Findability

Cascading Style Sheets: The Definitive Guide, *2nd Edition*

Creating Web Sites: The Missing Manual

CSS Cookbook

CSS Pocket Reference, *2nd Edition*

CSS: The Missing Manual

Dreamweaver 8: Design and Construction

Dreamweaver 8: The Missing Manual

Essential ActionScript 2.0

Flash 8: Projects for Learning Animation and Interactivity

Flash 8: The Missing Manual

Flash Hacks

Head First HTML with CSS & XHTML

Head Rush Ajax

HTML & XHTML: The Definitive Guide, *5th Edition*

HTML & XHTML Pocket Reference, *3rd Edition*

Information Architecture for the World Wide Web, *2nd Edition*

Information Dashboard Design

Learning Web Design, *2nd Edition*

PHP Hacks

Programming Flash Communication Server

Web Design in a Nutshell, *3rd Edition*

Web Site Measurement Hacks

Our books are available at most retail and online bookstores.

To order direct: 1-800-998-9938 • *order@oreilly.com* • *www.oreilly.com*

Online editions of most O'Reilly titles are available by subscription at *safari.oreilly.com*

The O'Reilly Advantage

Stay Current and Save Money